www.wadsworth.com

wadsworth.com is the World Wide Web site for Wadsworth Publishing Company and is your direct source to dozens of online resources.

At *wadsworth.com* you can find out about supplements, demonstration software, and student resources. You can also send e-mail to many of our authors and preview new publications and exciting new technologies.

wadsworth.com
Changing the way the world learns®

Criminal Law

SIXTH EDITION

Joel Samaha
University of Minnesota

West/Wadsworth
I(T)P® An International Thomson Publishing Company

Belmont, CA • Albany, NY • Boston • Cincinnati • Johannesburg • London
Madrid • Melbourne • Mexico City • New York • Pacific Grove, CA • Scottsdale, AZ
Singapore • Tokyo • Toronto

Criminal Justice Editor: Sabra Horne
Development Editor: Dan Alpert
Project Development Editor: Claire Masson
Editorial Assistant: Cherie Hackelberg
Marketing Manager: Mike Dew
Production Services Manager: Debby Kramer
Print Buyer: Karen Hunt
Permissions Editor: Susan Walters

Production: Ruth Cottrell Books
Designer: Andrew Ogus
Copy Editor: Kevin Gleason
Illustrator: Judith Ogus, Random Arts
Cover Design: Cassandra Chu
Compositor: R&S Book Composition
Printer: R.R. Donnelley/Crawfordsville
Cover Printer: Phoenix Color Corp.

Printed in the United States of America
1 2 3 4 5 6 7 8 9 10

For more information, contact Wadsworth Publishing Company, 10 Davis Drive, Belmont, CA 94002, or electronically at http://www.wadsworth.com

International Thomson Publishing Europe
Berkshire House
168-173 High Holborn
London, WC1V 7AA, United Kingdom

Nelson ITP, Australia
102 Dodds Street
South Melbourne
Victoria 3205 Australia

Nelson Canada
1120 Birchmount Road
Scarborough, Ontario
Canada M1K 5G4

International Thomson Publishing Southern Africa
Building 18, Constantia Square
138 Sixteenth Road, P.O. Box 2459
Halfway House, 1685 South Africa

International Thomson Editores
Seneca, 53
Colonia Polanco
11560 México D.F. México

International Thomson Publishing Asia
60 Albert Street
#15-01 Albert Complex
Singapore 189969

International Thomson Publishing Japan
Hirakawa-cho Kyowa Building, 3F
2-2-1 Hirakawa-cho, Chiyoda-ku
Tokyo 102 Japan

Library of Congress Cataloging-in-Publication Data
Samaha, Joel.
    Criminal law/Joel Samaha.—6th ed.
    p.   cm.
    Includes index.
    ISBN 0-534-54720-6
    1. Criminal law—United States—Cases.   I. Title.
KF9218.S26   1998
345.73—dc21   98-11857

 This book is printed on acid-free recycled paper.

About the Author

Professor Joel Samaha teaches Criminal Law, Criminal Procedure, Introduction to Criminal Justice, and the History of Criminal Justice at the University of Minnesota. He is both a lawyer and a historian whose primary research interest is the history of criminal justice. He received his B.A., J.D., and Ph.D. from Northwestern University. Professor Samaha also studied at Cambridge University, England, while doing research for his first book, *Law and Order in Historical Perspective*, a quantitative and qualitative analysis of law enforcement in pre-industrial society.

Professor Samaha was admitted to the Illinois Bar. He taught at UCLA before coming to the University of Minnesota. At the University of Minnesota, he served as Chairman of the Department of Criminal Justice Studies from 1974 to 1978. Since then he has returned to teaching, research, and writing full-time. He has taught both television and radio courses in criminal justice, and has co-taught a National Endowment for the Humanities seminar in legal and constitutional history. He was named Distinguished Teacher at the University of Minnesota in 1974, a coveted award.

Professor Samaha is an active scholar. In addition to his monograph on pre-industrial law enforcement and a transcription with scholarly introduction of English criminal justice records during the reign of Elizabeth I, he has written numerous articles on the history of criminal justice, published in such scholarly journals as *Historical Journal*, *American Journal of Legal History*, *Minnesota Law Review*, *William Mitchell Law Review*, and *Journal of Social History*. In addition to his best-seller, *Criminal Law*, he has written two other successful textbooks, *Criminal Procedure*, now in its fourth edition, and *Criminal Justice*, now being revised for its fifth edition.

For Doug and my students

Contents

Table of Cases

Note: Principle cases are in italic type. Non-principal cases are in roman type.

Table of Cases

Note: Principle cases are in italic type. Non-principal cases are in roman type.

Preface

I have loved the study and teaching of criminal law since I took Criminal Law and Procedure at Northwestern University Law School in 1958. I am proud to have the privilege to write this sixth edition of my *Criminal Law*. To have my modest innovation to the study of criminal law — the text/casebook — meet with such success is (to borrow a word from my students' lexicon) "awesome."

Criminal Law, sixth edition, like its predecessors, stresses the general principles that affect the whole of criminal law rather than the specific rules that define the crimes of particular states and localities. Knowledge of the principles of criminal law is not a mere intellectual exercise, although examining them has proven stimulating to hundreds of thousands of students through five previous editions of *Criminal Law*. This knowledge also provides the tools necessary to apply the general principles to the varied and changing definitions of specific crimes. These general principles have remained remarkably constant over time and space. Definitions of specific crimes, on the other hand, differ among states and change over time. The continuing relevance of the general principles of criminal law to new developments and jurisdictional differences testifies both to the durability and to the utility of understanding the general part of the criminal law. This is also practical knowledge, since the general principles form the bases for both the elements of the specific crimes that prosecutors must prove beyond a reasonable doubt and the defenses with which defendants can justify or excuse their guilt.

Criminal Law, sixth edition, rests on this solid foundation, but it cannot remain static any more than the subject of criminal law can remain frozen in time. Studying and teaching criminal law is a process of constant discovery. There is so much that I still haven't learned; so much of what I know that requires rethinking; so many existing cases that I didn't know about; and so many new cases that were decided since the last edition. I feel deeply obligated to incorporate some of this discovery for the benefit of both the teachers who use and the students who buy *Criminal Law*, sixth edition. But obligation is hardly a word that can describe the thrill, the fascination — the sheer plea-sure — that this work of preparing new editions of *Criminal Law* gives me. Finding ex-isting or new cases that not only elaborate on a principle in clear terms but also stimulate students to think is one of the most exciting things I do. Searching for cases with facts that will get the attention of students and give them pleasure at the same time is one of my favorite pastimes.

Criminal Law, sixth edition, also continues the interactive approach to learning rep-resented by the text/casebook method. The use of text to explain general principles and their application to specific crimes, followed by cases that apply the general principles to the facts of specific cases, proved to be a great success in previous editions. The text/case approach invites students to participate actively in learning. They can agree or dis-agree with the application made by the court in its opinion, but they must *understand* the principles and definitions in order to apply them. The text/case approach has demonstrated that students not only understand what they have learned, not only that they actually *enjoy* what they have learned, but also that they *remember* what they have learned. Perhaps the most gratifying part of teaching criminal law by the text/case method is having students tell me many years after they have had the course that they remember the cases and the principles they stood for.

The case excerpts portray the criminal law in action, applying the general principles to the facts of individual cases. They show that courts can arrive at different conclusions according to the interpretation of the principles that the court adopts. Seeing criminal law in action stimulates students to think about, to formulate their own interpretations of, and to apply the principles of criminal law. In my own course, I require students to act as legislators, prosecutors, defense attorneys, judges, and juries in order to see the principles and rules of criminal law from all perspectives. They must demonstrate that they understand the principles and rules first by stating them as they are presented in the text and then by applying them to the facts and reasoning as presented in the case excerpts. This close relationship between the principles and rules appearing in the text and the case excerpts remains central to *Criminal Law*, sixth edition.

New to This Edition

Criminal Law, sixth edition, contains thirty-two new cases and many re-edited existing cases. The selection of new cases and the revision of existing ones is based on a number of factors. First is the need to keep the cases current. Second is the discovery of cases that explain the general principles better and apply the facts in clearer and more inter-esting ways than cases in previous editions. Third, cases from previous editions some-times require re-editing after use in the classroom.

Case excerpts in *Criminal Law*, sixth edition, remain tailored to teach students the principles, doctrines, and rules of criminal law, but with more of an eye toward policy than the technical knowledge needed by lawyers. They remain distinct from the text, as they have in previous editions. The text, therefore, can stand alone as an analysis of the criminal law. Instructors can, if they wish, omit the cases altogether from assignments; they can use them simply as illustrations of the points made in the text; they can use them as a means to test whether students understand the text; or they can integrate them fully in the course. The text covers all of the main points completely and coherently.

However, the cases elaborate on, enrich, and test the students' understanding of the concepts presented and analyzed in the text.

Case questions introduce each case, focusing students' attention on the point of the case excerpt. Introductions to the case excerpts briefly state the case history, including the outcome of the case, and the sentence imposed if it is known. The excerpts present—in the words of the court—the facts and the opinion of the case. **Case discussions** follow the excerpts. The case discussions test the students' understanding of the principle, doctrine, and rule of the case excerpt. They also test the students' mastery of the facts. Finally, the **case discussion questions** provoke students to evaluate, criticize, and propose alternatives to the arguments and the decisions of the court as presented in the case excerpt.

Note cases elaborate on and often present a different application of the principle, doctrine, or rule covered in the main case excerpt. Instructors and students have convinced me that the note cases are a valuable tool both in understanding and applying the topics covered in the text.

A special section, **"How to Read, Analyze, and Find Cases,"** appears in chapter 2. This section explains in detail the major parts of an appellate court opinion and tells students how they can look for an opinion in the printed reports. A new feature in this edition is an annotated case, *State v. Knight*, that walks students through an unedited reported case and explains in detail every part of the case as it appears in the published reports.

Organization of Chapters

The chapters in the text follow a traditional and widely accepted arrangement. The first seven chapters cover the general part of the criminal law. The general part includes the following topics: the nature, origins, structure, and purposes of criminal law; the constitutional limits on the criminal law; the general principles of criminal liability; the doctrines of complicity and inchoate crimes and the defenses of justification and excuse to criminal liability. The remaining five chapters cover the special part of the criminal law. The special part of the criminal law deals with the major crimes against persons, habitation, property, public order, and public morals. The logic of the arrangement is to treat first the principles and doctrines common to all crimes and then to apply the general principles and doctrines to the crimes against persons, habitation, property, public order, and public morals. For example, chapter 3 examines the general principles of criminal liability—*actus reus, mens rea*, concurrent, causation, and resulting harm. Chapter 8 applies these general principles to the rules governing criminal homicide. In other words, chapter 8 examines the *actus reus, mens rea*, concurrent, causation, and resulting harm required to satisfy the requirements of the law of homicide. Similarly, chapter 9 applies the general principles to the law of criminal sexual conduct, assault, and kidnapping. Chapter 10 applies the principles to the law of burglary and arson. Chapter 11 applies them to the major property crimes. Chapter 12 is entirely rewritten. It addresses some of the traditional public order and morals crimes in the context of the new "quality of life" crimes. It invites debate about the use of criminal law to regulate conduct that not only physically injures people, their homes, and their property, but that also creates community disorder by "offending respectable people."

Criminal Law, sixth edition, is the product not only of my own efforts but those of many others. I gratefully acknowledge the contributions of the following reviewers: William Calathes, Jersey City State College; George Dery, California State University at Fullerton; Daniel Doyle, University of Montana; Leroy Maxwell, Missouri Western State College; Mickey McDermott, Alabama State University; Anne Miller, Vincennes University; and Gene Straughan, Lewis-Clark State College. The warm welcome, generous support, and regular assurances of Criminal Justice Editor Sabra Horne and Senior Development Editor Dan Alpert made the transition from West to Wadsworth easy and comfortable. But they did more. They also provided excellent suggestions that surely improved the text. These included the chapter openers and the increased number of Elements boxes, to mention but two of many. Ruth Cottrell's calm efficiency, warm kindness, careful editing, and strong support were more important and welcome than she can know. Kevin Gleason's superb copyediting definitely improved the text; his keen wit and sense of humor were big bonuses. What would I do without Sally who keeps on praising my work and me, even when I don't deserve it. Or Doug who is always there, helping me with my work, providing constructive criticisms and sharp insights, all the while putting up with my mercurial temperament. Friends and associates like these have made *Criminal Law,* sixth edition a better book. Whatever the book's failings, they are mine.

Joel Samaha
Minnetonka, Minnesota
April 6, 1998

CHAPTER ONE

The Nature, Origins, and Purposes of Criminal Law

CHAPTER OUTLINE

CHAPTER MAIN POINTS

1. Criminal law is the study of the ordinary phenomena of life under extraordinary circumstances.

2. Criminal law consists of the power and limits of government authority to define, prohibit, grade, and punish socially harmful behavior.

Define, prohibit, punish

3. Criminal law is distinguished from all other law because it carries with it the moral condemnation of the whole community.

4. Rational criminal law is criminal law based on general principles applicable to all crimes, graded according to the seriousness of the crime and the culpability of the offender, and carrying penalties no greater than punishment and prevention require.

Prevention

5. Rational criminal law emphasizes that law is a last resort as a method of social control.

6. Every state has its own criminal code, as does the federal government.

7. The general part of the criminal law consists of the constitutional provisions; the general principles of liability, justification, and excuse; and the doctrines of criminal law that apply to all crimes.

8. The special part of criminal law consists of the definitions of specific crimes.

9. Criminal law prohibits and punishes a wide range of conduct.

10. Criminal law distinguishes between criminal conduct, illegal but not criminal conduct, and reprehensible but not illegal conduct.

11. Criminal law grades criminal behavior according to several schemes.

12. Criminal punishment requires the infliction of pain, prescribed by law, administered intentionally by the state.

intent

13. The general purposes of criminal punishment are retribution and prevention.

14. Prevention comprises general deterrence, incapacitation, and rehabilitation.

15. The predominant justification for punishment shifts from one time and place to another, but all justifications are more or less present at all times.

16. The ideological, irrational, historical, and ethical core perspectives enrich our understanding of how and why the principles, doctrines, and rules of criminal law originated.

Police Officer: "There ought to be a big billboard at our city limits that reads:

'Welcome to Bloomington, you're under arrest.'"

Professor: "Why?"

Police Officer: "Because everything in Bloomington is a crime."

Professor: "But Bloomington is a city in the freest country in the history of the world."

INTRODUCTION

The police officer in the opener is jokingly referring to the vast range of behavior that is technically against the law in the United States. The professor is referring to the idea that people in a free society should have the maximum freedom to do as they please. The study of criminal law in the United States is the study of both the extent and the limits of criminal law in a constitutional democracy. Throughout our history we have relied heavily on criminal law to control a broad range of conduct, encompassing everything from murder to spitting on the street. In Palo Alto, California, for example, "harboring overdue library books" is punishable by thirty days in jail! In Minnesota, it is a crime to fornicate with a bird. In some places, it is a crime to park your own car on your own lawn, to hang laundry out on a clothesline in your own back yard, to eat on a bus (see chapter 12 on public order and morals offenses).

Why do we have criminal law? What is criminal law good for? Two purposes of criminal law are obvious:

1. Prevent wrongdoing.
2. Punish wrongdoers.

Three other purposes are equally important, if not so obvious:

3. Defining criminal behavior.
4. Classifying criminal behavior.
5. Grading criminal behavior.

As an introduction to all five of these purposes of criminal law, consider the following hypothetical scenarios. Which of them would you define as crimes? Rank the scenarios from most to least serious misdeed. What punishments would you prescribe in the scenarios you believe describe crimes? In those scenarios that you believe do not

3

describe crimes, do you think the state should take some action? If so, what kind? Should the law regulate the behavior by taxing it, or by requiring a license to engage in it? Should the law allow the "victims" to sue the person who injured them? What should be the outcome of such lawsuits? Do some actors deserve condemnation by families and friends but not the label of "criminal" and its accompanying criminal punishment? Do any behaviors deserve no sanction at all? Do any deserve praise or other reward?

1. Sheila hates Rosemary because Rosemary is rich, charming, and beautiful, but most of all because she is more intelligent, aggressive, and successful than Sheila. Sheila reaches the breaking point when a prestigious medical school accepts Rosemary, while the law school at the same university rejects Sheila. Enraged, Sheila decides to murder Rosemary. Sheila waits patiently for the appropriate time and gets her chance when Rosemary invites Sheila to a celebration party. Sheila takes a deadly drug from the medical center where she works, conceals it in her pocket, and puts it in Rosemary's drink. Then she watches with immense pleasure as Rosemary writhes in pain and dies a slow, agonizing death.

2. Tom's wife suffers excruciating pain from what the doctors say is terminal bone cancer. The family has exhausted its insurance coverage and savings in order to keep her alive. For the past few weeks now, every time Tom sees his wife, she pleads, "Tom, please put me out of my misery. I can't take this anymore." Tom loves his wife dearly and cannot bear her pain. An avid hunter, he takes one of his guns and shoots her in the head, killing her instantly.

3. Driving down an icy city street, David accelerates rapidly as he approaches a particularly slick spot, hoping for the thrill of feeling the car spin out. As it does, David sees a pedestrian, a frail ninety-year-old man, crossing the street in front of him. He tries to swerve away but cannot. He hits the old man, seriously injuring him. "Oh, my God!" cries David. "This is the last thing I wanted to happen." Two days later, while still in the hospital for treatment of his injuries, the man dies of a heart attack.

4. Kim is drowning in a lake. Steve, his lifelong enemy, sees Kim struggling but walks on, laughing at the thought of getting Kim out of the way. Kim drowns.

5. Every night when he gets home from work, Doug watches child pornography videos. He finds them highly erotic, especially when they involve sex between teenage boys. After getting his "release," Doug falls asleep until it's time to get up for work the next morning.

6. Michael is a demonstrative person who really likes women. He goes into a singles' bar, where he is immediately drawn to Theresa. Michael puts his arm around her waist and introduces himself. Theresa, offended by a stranger touching her, says firmly, "Stop that!" Michael does not remove his arm, saying, "Don't be such a prude, I'm just trying to be friendly."

7. Adam sees a radio in a department store that he wants. When the clerk walks away, Adam takes the radio. His friend Steve watches Adam take the radio. Outside the store, Steve says, "Good work, Adam. I really like a good rip-off."

8. Bill is addicted to cocaine.

9. Jessica, a highly successful attorney in a major law firm, smokes marijuana on weekends.

10. Kristen hates men. She loves breaking their hearts. Her latest victim is Lucas, who is vulnerable because he has just broken up with Allison. As soon as Kristen succeeds in getting Luke to fall in love with her, she dumps him. She tells him he was just a foil, laughing at his pain. Brokenhearted and thoroughly distraught, Luke loses his highly successful video business, goes bankrupt, acquires enormous medical bills for treatment of a nervous breakdown, and ends up an alcoholic.

11. Michelle has two boyfriends, Dan and Tony. Dan and Tony think they are Michelle's only boyfriend.

12. Monty tells his boyfriend Brad that he is HIV negative. It's a lie. Monty is HIV positive.

13. A major pharmaceutical corporation introduced to the U.S. market a drug used to treat hypertension. Although knowing that the drug had been reported to cause death and liver damage in French patients, the corporation labeled the product saying that no cause-and-effect relationship existed between the drug and liver damage. After the drug was linked to thirty-six deaths and more than five hundred cases of liver and kidney damage, the corporation withdrew the drug from the U.S. market.

14. Hilary, a gynecologist, recommends a hysterectomy for Jane, who suffers from back pain. After the surgery, the pain continues. Another doctor discovers that the source of Jane's pain is the difference in length between her left and right leg. He recommends platform shoes, and Jane's pain disappears.

15. John, a respected surgeon in a major hospital, refuses to take an AIDS test.

16. Sonya burns the American flag while chanting, "I hate America."

17. Jane, a respected African-American professor at a private college, allows only African-American women to enroll in her class. She believes whites are inferior and will corrupt African-American students. In addition, she maintains that African-American men have had too many advantages over African-American women and that it's now time to let African-American women have some.

18. Matt dances nude in a local tavern. A sign outside the bar reads: "All male strippers. Adults welcome."

Can you state specifically why you defined, classified, and graded the examples the way you did? Can you explain why you believe some examples deserve criminal prohibition and punishment? Write down your answers. Reconsider these hypotheticals and your preliminary answers to them as you study this and the remaining chapters.

THE NATURE OF CRIMINAL LAW

CL to prevent & punish harmful behavior socially

Criminal law represents the power of government to prevent and punish socially harmful behavior. In a constitutional democracy such as that in the United States, the interests of economy, effectiveness, individual autonomy, and the **rule of law** (the supremacy of established rules and procedures over individual whim or caprice) limit that power. The study of criminal law therefore examines both the extent and the limits of government power. Criminal law consists of six fundamental characteristics:

limits of govt power

Six fundamental characteristics of C.L. →

1. *It is a list of commands, of dos and don'ts telling people what they must do or refrain from doing.* Common don'ts include "Do not murder, rape, rob, steal, panhandle, fornicate outside marriage, or urinate in public." Common dos include "Pay your taxes, support your children, report child abuse."   *Dos & Don'ts*

2. *These commands are formally enacted into law.* Only commands enacted by legislatures or established in the common law (discussed later in this chapter) qualify as criminal laws.   *Law*

3. *The law prescribes a punishment to accompany the crime.* Criminal laws are not bare commands; failure to obey them carries legally defined painful consequences.   *punishments*

4. *The dos and don'ts apply to everyone under the authority of the body that created the criminal law.* The commands, therefore, "speak to [all] members of the community . . . in the community's behalf, with all the power and prestige of the community behind them."   *Application*

5. *Crimes injure both individual victims and society.* A mugging not only results in injury to its immediate victim but also puts the whole community in fear; forgery not only cheats the object of the forgery but also undermines public confidence in a variety of transactions necessary to life in modern society.[1]   *Injury*

6. *Conviction of crime carries with it the community's formal moral condemnation.*   *conviction*

Civil law →

The first five characteristics are not peculiar to criminal law. They also describe civil law, or the law concerned with private rights and remedies, especially the law of contracts, property, and torts. Civil law operates by commands enacted and established. Complex laws govern contracts, property rights, and torts. Unpleasant consequences befall losers in private lawsuits: they have to pay money, perform duties, or give up employment. Society also has an interest in seeing contracts performed, in protecting the rights of property, and in preventing personal injuries covered by tort law.

Moral condemnation →

The sixth characteristic, moral condemnation, is unique to criminal law. In his classic "The Aims of the Criminal Law," the legal philosopher Henry M. Hart, Jr. writes of this unique characteristic of criminal law:

> The essence . . . lies in the criminal conviction itself. One may lose more money on the stock market than in a court-room; a prisoner of war camp may well provide a harsher environment than a state prison; death on the field of battle has the same characteristics as death by sentence of law. It is the expression of the community's hatred, fear, or contempt for the convict which alone characterizes physical hardship as punishment.[2]

THE GENERAL AND SPECIAL PARTS OF CRIMINAL LAW

C.L. is ÷ in 2 parts
1. General
2. Special

Criminal law is divided into a general part and a special part. The general part covers the general principles and doctrines that apply to all crimes. The principles relate to legality, punishment, and the requirements for criminal liability (see chapters 2 and 3). The doctrines refer to tenets that may apply to all crimes but are not necessarily present in all cases. The doctrines include liability for complicity, such as that exhibited by accomplices and accessories (chapter 4); liability for uncompleted crimes, such as at-   *General part of principles & doctrines*

actus reus / mens rea

tempt and conspiracy (chapter 5); and the defenses to criminal liability, such as self-defense and insanity (chapters 6 and 7).[3]

The special part of criminal law defines the specific crimes—murder, rape, robbery, theft, and disturbing the peace, for example (see chapters 8 through 12). These definitions must agree with the principles and, where relevant, the doctrines in the general part. For example, the general principle actus reus bases criminal liability on action—on what people do, not on what they think or who they are. The acts defined in specific crimes embody this general principle, such as the act of killing in the crime of murder, breaking and entering in burglary, taking another's property in theft. Similarly, criminal liability, at least for serious crimes, requires a mens rea, or a mental element. Particular crimes have individual mental element requirements, such as the intent to kill in the crime of murder, to permanently deprive another of property in theft, and to take property by fear or force in robbery.

CLASSIFYING CRIMES

Fair and effective social control calls both for grading social harms as well as establishing a measured response to them. Not all immoral, reprehensible, and indecent conduct is criminal, nor should it be. A "creep" is not necessarily a criminal! The law does no more than reflect social reality in drawing lines between mere immoralities, torts, and crimes.

Crime, Tort, and Nonlegal
Responses to Social Harms

A measured response calls for leaving some wrongs entirely to the conscience of the wrongdoer. Some conduct, while reprehensible, does not demand a criminal law response; private sanctions suffice. Appropriate private sanctions include suspending students who cheat on exams, exacting a penance for churchgoers who lie to their friends, and censuring peers who maliciously reject their lovers.

Some harms may call for legal redress but not a criminal law response. Law is divided into two basic parts: civil law and criminal law. **Civil law** provides private and individual redress, by means of which injured persons sue those who have injured them. The formal title to a civil action reflects these individual and private qualities—for example, Marconi (**plaintiff,** that is, the injured person who brings the suit) v. (versus or against) Yu (**defendant,** or the person sued). **Torts,** the technical term for personal injuries for which the injured party can sue the injuring party, are common civil actions that complement criminal law. The primary object of a civil action is to recover money, known legally as **damages.** Damages are not fines; damages compensate injured individuals, whereas **fines** are penalties paid to the state as criminal punishment. Although tort actions can include **punitive damages** (damages intended to punish the wrongdoer) the primary purpose of damages is to restore injured persons to their position before injury, not to punish defendants for hurting plaintiffs. Damages cover medical expenses, lost wages, disability, and sometimes pain and suffering.

Criminal law treats society as a whole as the injured party, because harms to individuals and their property undermine social security, harmony, and well-being. The government prosecutes criminal defendants to protect the social interest in harmony, order, and security. The titles of criminal cases—*State v. Wenz, People v. Twohy, Commonwealth v. McDonald,* or *United States v. Storlie*—denote the societal nature of criminal prosecution. The stigma attached to criminal conviction and incarceration is far greater than that associated with losses in private lawsuits, even though the financial cost may be lower.

Civil actions and criminal prosecution are not mutually exclusive responses to social harms. States may prosecute, injured parties may sue, friends may censure, and conscience may pang the same person, all for a single event. Most crimes are also torts: Burglary is the tort of trespass, theft is the tort of conversion, and assault is both civil and criminal. Burglary victims can sue burglars for trespass, and states can prosecute burglars for burglary. The double jeopardy clause in the United States Constitution—"no person shall . . . be subject for the same offence to be twice put in jeopardy of life or limb"—does not prohibit tort and criminal actions for the same conduct. Defendants in tort actions do not lose "life or limb"; they can only lose money.

As you study criminal law, keep this range of alternative responses—personal and private sanctions, tort, and criminal prosecution—in mind. The most serious harms are designated as crimes. Murder, rape, robbery, and burglary are obvious examples; they call for society's strongest response. Imprisonment and sometimes death, the consequences for committing serious crimes, evidence the gravity of criminal law. Criminal law is society's last resort in dealing with social harms. Where something less will do, common sense requires that something less be done. Thus, if friends' disapproval makes avaricious people less greedy, then making avarice a crime does not make sense.[4]

Felony, Misdemeanor, and Violation

Criminal law grades offenses according to several schemes. One scheme focuses on the penalties imposed. From most severe to least severe, the penalty categories are capital felonies, felonies, gross misdemeanors, petty misdemeanors, and violations. In some states, capital felonies are punishable by death; in states without the death penalty, committing a capital offense can result in life imprisonment without parole. In the United States, aggravated murder is currently the only capital felony punishable by death. However, some states have recently enacted life-without-parole statutes for some drug law violations. Michigan, for example, punishes the possession of more than 650 grams of cocaine with life imprisonment without parole.[5]

The broad distinction between felonies and misdemeanors is that felony convictions are punishable by incarceration in state prisons, whereas misdemeanors are punishable by incarceration in local jails or by fines. Noncapital **felonies** in most jurisdictions are punishable by imprisonment for between one year and life. **Misdemeanors** are punishable by jail sentences, fines, or both. Although disparity exists among **jurisdictions,** gross misdemeanors typically carry maximum penalties of close to one year in jail, ordinary misdemeanors are usually punishable in the ninety-day range, and petty misdemeanors result in a jail sentence of up to thirty days. **Violations,** consisting mainly of traffic offenses punishable by fines, are not designated criminal convictions in most jurisdictions.[6]

One problem with grading is the large number of offenses and penalties that exist in the criminal codes of most jurisdictions. At one time, Oregon, for instance, had 1,413 separate offenses and 466 different sentencing levels. Some maintain that this multitude of crimes and penalties creates "anarchy in sentencing."[7]

Furthermore, chaotic sentencing patterns undermine public confidence in, and respect for, the criminal law and its administration. According to the distinguished criminal law professor, Herbert Wechsler, these sentencing patterns are "nonsense":

> The human mind cannot draw an infinite number of distinctions about crime. You can see the most serious crimes and the less serious ones, and you can see some gradations in between. And there may be some difference of opinion whether you can see three or four or six or seven categories. But there is a finite number that it is prudent to attempt to perceive.[8]

Wrongs *Mala in Se* and *Mala Prohibita*

[handwritten: evil v. prohibited conduct]

Another classification scheme divides crimes between inherently evil conduct, *malum in se*, and merely prohibited conduct, *malum prohibitum*. The serious felonies — murder, rape, robbery, burglary, arson, larceny — are classified as evil by their very nature. Killing another without justification or excuse, raping, robbing, burglarizing, and stealing are bad even if they were not crimes under the law. On the other hand, the long list of violations that attend regulating modern urban industrial society, such as traffic codes, building codes, and health regulations, are illegal, but most do not consider them inherently bad. Society does not label drivers who make illegal left turns or park in no-parking zones bad, even though they have broken the law.

Classifications According to Subject

[handwritten: Crimes according to subject matter.]

At least as early as the sixteenth century, some criminal law commentators classified crimes according to their subject matter. This scheme still influences the classification of crimes in most jurisdictions. This scheme divides the special part of criminal law into the following subject classifications:

[handwritten margin: Subject Classifications]

- Crimes against the state, including treason and sedition.
- Crimes against persons, including murder, manslaughter, rape, kidnapping, assault, and battery.
- Crimes against habitation, including burglary and arson.
- Crimes against property, including larceny, embezzlement, false pretenses, malicious mischief, and robbery (really a combination of a crime against a person and property).
- Crimes against public order, including disorderly conduct and public drunkenness.
- Crimes against the administration of justice, including obstruction of justice and bribery.
- Crimes against public morals, including prostitution, fornication, and profanity.

Professors Andrew von Hirsch and Nils Jareborg have worked out a precise subject matter grading system called a living standard analysis of criminal harm. Living standard means the quality of life, including both economic well-being and other noneconomic capabilities that affect the quality of a person's life. According to von Hirsch and Jareborg, crimes invade four general interests that affect the quality of life:

Crimes invade :

1. Physical integrity.
2. Material support and amenity.
3. Freedom from humiliation.
4. Privacy and autonomy.

They rank the seriousness of crimes according to the degree to which they invade these interests.[9]

PUNISHMENT
criminal punishment to attach to socially harmful behavior.

The aims of criminal law do not end with the definition, classification, grading, and prohibition of criminal behavior. Some would say that these aims are only preliminary to the main purpose of criminal law—criminal punishment. In other words, the purpose of defining, classifying, grading, and prohibiting crime is to determine what, if any, criminal punishment to attach to socially harmful behavior. Punishment, in the general sense, takes many forms. A parent who grounds a teenager, a club that expels a member, a church that excommunicates a parishioner, a friend who rejects a companion— all punish because they intentionally inflict pain or other unpleasant consequences on the recipient. None of these examples involves criminal punishment, however. To qualify as criminal punishment, penalties must satisfy four criteria: A penalty must

Penalty must :

1. impose pain or other unpleasant consequences,
2. be prescribed by the law,
3. be administered intentionally,
4. be administered by the state.

Of the four, only the first criterion requires elaboration.

The phrase "pain or other unpleasant consequences" is both broad and vague. It does not define the kind and amount of pain. A violent mental patient confined indefinitely to a padded cell in a state security hospital suffers more pain than a person incarcerated for five days in the county jail for disorderly conduct. Nevertheless, only the jail sentence is criminal punishment. The difference lies in the purpose. Hospitalization, at least formally, aims to treat and cure; the pain accompanying treatment is incidental to, not a reason for, the hospitalization. On the other hand, punishment—the intentional infliction of pain—is the reason for the jail inmate's incarceration. (See Table 1.1.)

Criminal punishment + treatment

This distinction between criminal punishment and treatment is rarely clear-cut. For example, the government may sentence certain convicted criminals to be confined to maximum-security hospitals while sentencing other convicted criminals to prison for "treatment" and "cure." Furthermore, pain and pleasure do not always distinguish punishment from treatment. Shock treatment and padded cells inflict more pain than confinement in some minimum-security federal prisons with their "country club" atmospheres. When measured by pain, punishment may often be preferable to treatment. Indeed, some critics maintain that the major shortcoming of treatment is that "helping" a patient justifies extreme measures: massive surgery, castration, and lobotomy.[10]

TABLE 1.1 TYPICAL SENTENCES

**"What Types of Sentences
Usually Are Given to Offenders?"**

Death Penalty

For the most serious crimes such as murder, the courts in most states may sentence an offender to death by lethal injection, electrocution, exposure to lethal gas, hanging, or other method specified by state law.

■ As of 1985, 37 states had laws providing for the death penalty.
■ Virtually all death penalty sentences are for murder.
■ As of year-end 1985, 50 persons had been executed since 1976, and 1,591 inmates in 32 states were under a sentence of death.

Incarceration

Incarceration is the confinement of a convicted criminal in a federal or state prison or a local jail to serve a court-imposed sentence. Confinement is usually in a jail, administered locally; or in a prison, operated by the state or federal government. In many states offenders sentenced to 1 year or less are held in a jail; those sentenced to longer terms are committed to a state prison. More than 4,200 correctional facilities are maintained by federal, state, and local governments. They include 47 federal facilities, 922 state-operated adult confinement and community-based correctional facilities, and 3,300 local jails, which usually are county operated.

On any given day in 1985, about 503,000 persons were confined in state and federal prisons. About 254,000 were confined in local jails on June 30, 1985.

Probation

Probation is the sentencing of an offender to community supervision by a probation agency, often as a result of suspending a sentence to confinement. Such supervision normally entails specific rules of conduct while in the community. If the rules are violated, a sentence to confinement may be imposed. Probation is the most widely used correctional disposition in the United States.

■ State or local governments operate more than 2,000 probation agencies. At year-end 1985, nearly 1.9 million adults were on probation, or about 1 of every 95 adults in the nation.

Split Sentences, Shock Probation, and Intermittent Confinement

These are penalties that explicitly require the convicted person to serve a brief period of confinement in a local, state, or federal facility (the "shock") followed by a period of probation. This penalty attempts to combine the use of community supervision with a short incarceration experience. Some sentences are periodic rather than continuous; for example, an offender may be required to spend a certain number of weekends in jail.

In 1984 nearly a third of those receiving probation sentences in Idaho, New Jersey, Tennessee, Utah, and Vermont also were sentenced to brief periods of confinement.

Restitution and Victim Compensation

In these dispositions, the offender is required to provide financial repayment—or, in some jurisdictions, services in lieu of monetary restitution—for the losses incurred by the victim.

Nearly all states have statutory provisions for the collection and disbursement of restitution funds. A restitution law was enacted at the federal level in 1982.

Community Service

The offender is required to perform a specified amount of public service work, such as collecting trash in parks or other public facilities.

(continues)

TABLE 1.1 *(continued)*

Community Service *(continued)*

Many states authorize community service work orders. Community service often is imposed as a specific condition of probation.

Fines

A fine is an economic penalty that requires the offender to pay a specified sum of money within limits set by law. Fines often are imposed in addition to probation or as alternatives to incarceration.

- The Victims of Crime Act of 1984 authorizes the distribution of fines and forfeited criminal profits to support state victim-assistance programs, with priority given to programs that aid victims of sexual assault, spouse abuse, and child abuse. These programs, in turn, provide assistance and compensation to crime victims.
- Many laws that govern the imposition of fines are being revised. The revisions often provide for more flexible means of ensuring equity in the imposition of fines, flexible fine schedules, "day fines" geared to the offender's daily wage, installment payment of fines, and the imposition of confinement only when there is an intentional refusal to pay.
- [According to one study,] . . . more than three-fourths of criminal courts use fines extensively, and that fines levied each year exceed $1 billion.

Source: *Report to the Nation on Crime and Justice: The Data,* Bureau of Justice Statistics, United States Justice Department, Washington, D.C., 1988, page 96.

Professor Herbert Packer resolved the dilemma of treatment and punishment by adding a fifth element to criminal punishment, suggesting that its dominant purpose is not to make offenders better but to inflict "deserved pain" and prevent crimes. Although criminal punishment aims primarily to hurt and not help offenders, treatment can also deter crime. **Rehabilitation** assumes deterrence as a utilitarian aim. New York clearly asserted this aim in its 1967 Revised Penal law:[11]

> The general purposes of this chapter are to insure public safety by preventing the commission of offenses through the deterrent influence of the sentences authorized, [and] the rehabilitation of those convicted.[12]

Two basic justifications underlie all criminal punishment: retribution and prevention. **Retribution** looks back to the crime committed, punishing it because it is right to do so. **Prevention** looks forward, punishing offenders in order to prevent crimes in the future. Prevention takes four forms: general deterrence, special deterrence, incapacitation, and rehabilitation.

Retribution

Striking out to hurt what hurts us is a basic human impulse. In one commentator's words, "It is what makes us kick the table leg on which we stub our toe." This impulse captures the idea of retribution, which appears in the Old Testament: "When one man strikes another and kills him, he shall be put to death. When one man injures and disfigures his fellow-countryman, it shall be done to him as he had done; fracture for fracture, eye for eye, tooth for tooth."[13]

Retribution rests on the assumption that hurting the wicked is right. As forcefully stated by Englishman Sir James F. Stephen, a nineteenth-century judge and historian of the criminal law, the wicked deserve to suffer for their evil deeds.

[T]he infliction of punishment by law gives definite expression and a solemn ratification and justification to the hatred which is excited by the commission of the
offense. The criminal law thus proceeds upon the principle that it is morally right
to hate criminals, and it confirms and justifies that sentiment by inflicting on
criminals punishments which express it. I think it highly desirable that criminals
should be hated, that the punishments inflicted upon them should be so con-
trived as to give expression to that hatred, and to justify it so far as the public provision of means for expressing and gratifying a healthy natural sentiment can
justify and encourage it. The forms in which deliberate anger and righteous dis-
approbation are expressed, and the execution of criminal justice is the most emphatic of such forms, stand to the one set of passions in the same relation in
which marriage stands to sexual passion.[14]

Proponents of retribution contend that it benefits not only society, as Stephen emphasized, but also criminals. Just as society feels satisfied in retaliating against, or paying
back, criminals, offenders themselves benefit through expiating their evil, or paying their
debt to society. Retaliation, by which society pays back criminals, and expiation, through
which criminals pay back society, are both central to retribution. Retribution assumes
that offenders are free to choose between committing and not committing crimes. Because offenders have this choice, society can blame them for making the wrong choice.
This blameworthiness is called **culpability.** Culpability means that offenders are responsible for their actions and must suffer the consequences if they act irresponsibly.

Retribution has several appealing qualities. First, it assumes free will, or human autonomy. This assumption upholds a basic value—that individuals have the power to
determine their own destinies and are not at the mercy of uncontrollable forces. Retribution also makes sense because it seems to accord with human nature. Hurting that
which hurts and hating wrongdoers—especially murderers, rapists, robbers, and other
violent criminals—appear to be natural impulses.[15]

From the Old Testament's philosophy of taking an eye for an eye, to the nineteenth-
century Englishman's claim that it is right to hate and hurt criminals, to the modern
idea of "lock 'em up and throw away the key," the desire for retribution has run strong
and deep in both religion and criminal justice. This long tradition endorses retribution,
especially in the average person's mind. The sheer tenacity of the principle seems to val-
idate its use in modern criminal justice. Retributionists, however, maintain that retribution rests not only on long use but also on a firm jurisprudential (legal philosophical)
foundation. Two reasons support this claim: the first centering on culpability, the second on justice.

According to its proponents, retribution requires culpability; it requires that criminals choose and intend to harm their victims. Accidents do not qualify for retribution.
Hence, people who load, aim, and fire guns into their enemies' chests deserve punishment; hunters who lie down and leave loaded guns that fire and kill companions who
bump them do not deserve punishment. Civil law can deal with careless people; the
criminal law ought to punish only people who purposely perpetrate harm. Retribution
focuses the criminal law on culpable behavior.

Retributionists also claim that justice is the only proper measure of punishment. **Justice** is a philosophical concept whose application depends on culpability. Only those
who deserve punishment can receive it, or it is unjust. Similarly, justice is the only

criterion by which to determine the quality and quantity of punishment—the culpable defendant's just deserts.

It is difficult to translate abstract justice into concrete penalties. What are a rapist's just deserts? Is castration justice? How many years in prison is robbery worth? How much offender suffering will repay the pain of a maimed aggravated assault victim? The pain of punishment cannot be equivalent to the suffering caused by the crime. Furthermore, critics, such as Henry Wiehofen, contend that retribution is the last holdout of barbarism.

> All of this abstract philosophizing about punishment as requital for crime has a musty smell about it, a smell of the professor's study. The people who have the responsibility for fighting crime and dealing with criminals have learned that it is pointless to talk about "how much punishment" is deserved. In the nineteenth century [it] had its appeal. [But] the modern behavioral sciences have shown that armchair abstractions about the "justice" of retribution by philosophers who reject human experience are sadly defective in human understanding, not to say human sympathy. The retributive approach is too subjective and too emotional to solve problems that have their roots in social conditions and the consequent impact on individual personality.[16]

Wiehofen denies that the urge to retaliate inheres in human nature. Therefore, the law ought to reject any demand for vengeance. Furthermore, he argues that retributionists merely assume, but do not have proof, that a bloodthirsty human nature craves vengeance.

The determinists reject the free-will assumption that underlies retribution. They suggest that forces beyond human control determine individual behavior. Social scientists have shown the relationship between social conditions and crime. Psychiatrists point to subconscious forces, beyond the conscious will's control, that determine criminal conduct. A few biologists link violent crime to an extra Y chromosome. Determinism undermines the theory of retribution because it forecloses blame, and punishment without blame is unjust.[17]

Probably the strongest argument against retribution is that so much of criminal law is not based on moral blameworthiness. A vast number of crimes do not require intentional wrongdoing to qualify for criminal punishment. To cite but two of many examples: Statutory rape is not excused by the consent of the victim or an honest and reasonable mistake about the victim's age. Pulling the trigger of a gun believed to be unloaded does not justify or excuse a death resulting from the shots. As you study the rest of this book, you will find many examples of these crimes in which the actors did not intend to do wrong.[18]

Prevention

Retribution justifies punishment on the ground that it is right to inflict pain on criminals. Prevention inflicts pain not for its own sake but to prevent future crimes. General prevention, also called **general deterrence,** aims by threat of punishment to prevent the general population who have not committed crimes from doing so. **Special deterrence** aims at individual offenders, hoping to deter their future conduct by the threat of punishment. Incapacitation prevents convicted criminals from committing future crimes by confining them or, more rarely, by altering them surgically or executing them. Rehabilitation aims to prevent crime by changing individuals so that they will obey the law. These purposes all have in common the aim of preventing future crime; inflicting pain for its own sake is not the aim of prevention.

Jeremy Bentham, an eighteenth-century English law reformer, promoted deterrence. Bentham was part of, and was heavily influenced by, the intellectual movement called the Enlightenment. At the core of the movement was the notion that natural laws govern the universe and, by analogy, human society. One of these laws, hedonism, posits that human beings seek pleasure and avoid pain. A related law, rationalism, states that individuals can, and ordinarily do, act to maximize pleasure and minimize pain. Rationalism also permits human beings to apply natural laws mechanistically (that is, according to rules, rather than by **discretion,** that is, the individual judgment of the decision makers).

These ideas, which are much oversimplified here, led Bentham to formulate classical deterrence theory. It states that rational human beings will not commit crimes if they know that the pain of punishment outweighs the pleasure gained from committing crimes. Prospective criminals weigh the pleasure derived from present crime against the pain from the threat of future punishment. According to the natural law of hedonism, if prospective criminals fear future punishment more than they derive pleasure from present crime, they will not commit crimes.

Deterrence is considerably more complex than Bentham's useful but oversimplified crime prevention model suggests. Threatened punishment does not always deter—it goads some to do the very thing it aims to prevent. During the Vietnam War, for example, Congress made burning draft cards a crime. Instead of avoiding such conduct, protesters turned out in scores to flout the law. Deterrence, then, has two dimensions.[19]

Deterrence proponents argue that the principle of utility—permitting only the minimum amount of pain necessary to prevent the crime—better limits criminal punishment than retribution does. English playwright George Bernard Shaw, a strong deterrence supporter, put it this way: "Vengeance is *mine* saith the Lord; which means it is *not* the Lord Chief Justice's." According to this argument, divinity enables only God, the angels, or some other divine being to measure just deserts, while social scientists can determine how much pain, or threat of pain, deters crime. With this knowledge, the state can scientifically inflict the minimum pain needed to produce the maximum crime reduction.

Deterrence proponents concede that impediments to implementing deterrence exist. The emotionalism surrounding punishment impairs objectivity. Often, prescribed penalties rest more on faith than on evidence. For example, one economist's study shows that every execution under capital punishment laws saves about eight lives by deterring potential murderers. This finding sparked a controversy having little to do with the study's empirical validity. Instead, the arguments turn to ethics—whether killing anyone is right, no matter what social benefits it produces.[20]

Deterrence proponents do not argue against the need for an inquiry into the ethics, wisdom, and humaneness of punishment, but they do maintain that empirical research necessarily precedes answers to those questions. The problem of punishment involves a division of labor. Researchers answer the empirical question, "What works?" Policymakers answer the questions, "Is it wise? Is it humane? Is it legal?" For instance, research might demonstrate that the death penalty for rape prevents rape, but the United

States Supreme Court has declared that capital punishment for rape violates the Eighth Amendment of the Constitution.[21]

Even if particular punishments are constitutional, they may still be unwise public policy. For example, suppose it is found that a statute authorizing surgery to prevent erections deters male sex offenders. Even if the statute were constitutional (an issue about which there are grave doubts), the inhumaneness of this draconian measure should be considered. Amputating thieves' hands, an effective deterrent in some countries, is rejected on humanitarian grounds in the United States.

Critics find several faults with deterrence theory and its application to criminal punishment. The wholly rational, free-will individual that deterrence theory assumes exists is as far from reality as the eighteenth-century world that spawned the idea. Complex forces within the human organism and in the external environment, both of which are beyond individual control, strongly influence behavior.[22]

Human beings and their behavior are too unpredictable to reduce to a mechanistic formula. For some people, the existence of criminal law suffices to deter them from committing crimes; others require more. Information about just who these others are and of what the "more" consists has not been determined sufficiently so that policy can rest upon it. Furthermore, severity is not the only influence on the effectiveness of punishment. Tentative conclusions are that certainty and celerity (speed) have a greater deterrent effect than severity.[23]

Moreover, threats do not affect all crimes or potential criminals equally. Crimes of passion, such as murder and rape, are probably little affected by threats; whereas speeding, drunken driving, and corporate crime are probably greatly affected by threats. The leading deterrence theorist, Johannes Andenaes, sums up the state of our knowledge about deterrence:

> There is a long way to go before research can give quantitative forecasts. The long-term moral effects of the criminal law and law enforcement are especially hard to isolate and quantify. Some categories of crime are so intimately related to specific social situations that generalizations of a quantitative kind are impossible. An inescapable fact is that research will always lag behind actual developments. When new forms of crime come into existence, such as hijacking of aircraft or terrorist acts against officers of the law, there cannot possibly be a body of research ready as a basis for the decisions that have to be taken. Common sense and trial by error have to give the answers.[24]

Finally, critics maintain that even if obtaining empirical support for criminal punishment is possible, deterrence is unjust because it punishes for example's sake. Supreme Court Justice Oliver Wendell Holmes described the example dimension to deterrence:

> If I were having a philosophical talk with a man I was going to have hanged (or electrocuted) I should say, "I don't doubt that your act was inevitable for you but to make it more avoidable by others we propose to sacrifice you to the common good. You may regard yourself as a soldier dying for your country if you like. But the law must keep its promises."[25]

Punishment should not be a sacrifice to the common good, according to retributionists; it is just only if administered for the redemption of particular individuals. According to critics, punishment is personal and individual, not general and societal. Deterrence proponents respond that so long as offenders are in fact guilty, punishing them is personal; hence, it is just to use individual punishment for society's benefit.

Incapacitation restrains offenders from committing further crimes. At the extreme, incapacitation includes mutilation—castration, amputation, and lobotomy—or even death in capital punishment. Incapacitation in most cases means imprisonment. Incapacitation works: Dead people cannot commit crimes, and prisoners do not commit them, at least not outside prison walls. Incapacitation, then, offers much to a society determined to repress crime. According to criminologist James Q. Wilson,

> The chances of a persistent robber or burglar living out his life, or even going a year with no arrest are quite small. Yet a large proportion of repeat offenders suffer little or no loss of freedom. Whether or not one believes that such penalties, if inflicted, would act as a deterrent, it is obvious that they could serve to incapacitate these offenders and, thus, for the period of the incapacitation, prevent them from committing additional crimes.[26]

Like deterrence and retribution, incapacitation has its share of critics. Some stress the distant relationship between offense and punishment. The basic problem with incapacitation is predicting behavior, particularly violent criminal conduct. Kleptomaniacs will almost surely steal again, exhibitionists will expose themselves, and addicts will continue to use chemicals. But when will murderers, rapists, or bank robbers strike again? Nobody really knows. Therefore, punishment is based, empirically, on a poor guess concerning future danger.[27]

Furthermore, critics argue, incapacitation merely shifts criminality from outside prisons to inside prisons. Sex offenders and other violent criminals can and do still find victims among other inmates; property offenders abound in trading contraband and other smuggled items. Incarceration is also expensive. According to current estimates, it costs approximately $100,000 to construct a prison cell and as much as $22,000 a year to feed, house, and clothe every prisoner. Finally, critics maintain that several incapacitative measures—death, psychosurgery, mutilation, and long-term incarceration—violate the Eighth Amendment.[28]

In a widely acclaimed essay, *The Limits of the Criminal Sanction*, Herbert Packer succinctly summarized the aims of rehabilitation: "The most immediately appealing justification for punishment is the claim that it may be used to prevent crimes by so changing the personality of the offender that he will conform to the dictates of law; in a word, by reforming him."[29]

Rehabilitation borrows much from medicine. Indeed, it is based on what has been called the medical model. In this model, crime is a "disease" that criminals have contracted. The major purpose in punishment is to "cure" criminal patients through "treatment." The length of imprisonment depends upon how long it takes to effect this cure. On its face, rehabilitation is the most humane form of criminal punishment. Its proponents contend that treating offenders is much more civilized than other forms of punishment.

Two assumptions underlie rehabilitation theory. First, external and internal forces beyond offenders' control determine criminality. Rehabilitationists are determinists when it comes to crime causation. Because offenders do not freely choose to commit crimes, they cannot be blamed for doing so. The second assumption is that experts can modify subjects' behavior to prevent further crimes. After treatment or rehabilitation, former criminals will control their own destinies, at least enough so that they will not commit crimes. In this respect, rehabilitationists subscribe to free will: Criminals can choose to change their life habits and often do, after which society can hold them responsible for their actions.

The view that criminals are sick has profoundly affected criminal law and has generated acrimonious debate. The reason is not that reform and rehabilitation are new ideas; quite the contrary. Victorian Sir Francis Palgrave summed up a seven-hundred-year-old attitude when he stated the medieval church's position on punishment: It was not to be "thundered in vengeance for the satisfaction of the state, but imposed for the good of the offender; in order to afford the means of amendment and to lead the transgressor to repentance, and to mercy." Sixteenth-century Elizabethan pardon statutes were laced with the language of repentance and reform; the queen hoped to achieve a reduction in crime by mercy rather than by vengeance. Even Jeremy Bentham, most closely associated with deterrence, claimed that punishment would "contribute to the reformation of the offender, not only through fear of being punished again, but by a change in his character and habits."[30]

Despite its long history, rehabilitation has suffered serious attacks. The most fundamental criticism is that rehabilitation is based on false, or at least unproven, assumptions. The causes of crime are so complex, and the wellsprings of human behavior as yet so undetermined, that sound policy cannot rest on treatment. A second criticism is that it makes no sense to brand everyone who violates the criminal law as sick and needing treatment.[31]

Some critics call rehabilitation inhumane because cure justifies administering large doses of pain. British literary critic C. S. Lewis argued as follows:

> My contention is that good men (not bad men) consistently acting upon that position would act as cruelly and unjustly as the greatest tyrants. They might in some respects act even worse. Of all tyrannies a tyranny sincerely exercised for the good of its victims may be the most oppressive. It may be better to live under robber barons than under omnipotent moral busybodies. The robber baron's cruelty may sometimes sleep, his cupidity may at some point be satiated; but those who torment us for our own good will torment us without end for they do so with the approval of their own conscience. They may be more likely to go to Heaven yet at the same time likelier to make a Hell of earth. Their very kindness stings with intolerable insult. To be "cured" against one's will and cured of states which we may not regard as disease is to be put on a level with those who have not yet reached the age of reason or those who never will; to be classed with infants, imbeciles, and domestic animals. But to be punished, however severely, because we have deserved it, because we "ought to have known better," is to be treated as a human person made in God's image.[32]

Deciding what mixture of retribution and prevention ought to determine the sentence and what specific punishment to impose in particular cases is not easy. Consider the following excerpt from the California Sentencing Institute for trial court judges. It is a rare opportunity to consider the thinking of practioners who must apply the purposes of punishment to specific cases.

C A S E

1971 Sentencing Institute
for California Superior Court Judges

Case #1

The Sentencing Institute was a conference of state criminal court trial judges. The case was drawn from the file of an actual case. It provided judges who sentence offenders an opportunity to discuss and compare what they would have done, had they had the case before them for sentencing. The excerpt below contains part of the case file, the comments of the judges who participated in the discussions at the conference, and their votes for disposition of the case.

OFFENSE: POSSESSION OF NARCOTICS Defendant WDS arrested for assault with a deadly weapon and possession of heroin. He was found guilty by a jury for possession of heroin. The victim, who lived next door, stated that defendant entered his residence, pointed a gun at him and his family, fired it once and fled. The defendant claimed that the victim had stolen one of his guns and that he threatened the victim in order to have it returned. The defendant told the arresting officers that he kept his guns in a small overnight case in his bedroom and led the officers to it. It was open and inside was a blank starter pistol and 12 balloons containing 51 grams of heroin. The officers also found a plastic box containing syringes, needles, spoons and razor blades. Defendant was observed to have numerous fresh puncture wounds on his right arm.

PRIOR CRIMINAL HISTORY:

2/53	burglary	juvenile, 3 mos. camp, probation
6/56	suspicion of robbery	Released
12/56	petty theft	2 mos. jail, 1 year probation, fined
1959–65	Several drunk arrests	Fined
3/66	Assault	30 days, county jail
4/67	Possession of dangerous drugs	2 years probation
2/71	PRESENT OFFENSE	

CASE HISTORY INFORMATION: Defendant, now age 35, is the youngest of seven children born to a Caucasian laboring class, urban family whose parents separated shortly after his birth. His mother never remarried and the family largely was supported by public welfare. He says he had a very close relationship with his mother, being the youngest child. He dropped out of school in the tenth grade to go to work as an unskilled factory worker.

He was married at the age of 20 and now has two children. The marriage was dissolved five years later in 1961. In recent years he has drifted into a mode of life, and his mannerisms, gestures and speech are now feminine. He has supported himself during the past four years working steadily as a female impersonator in night clubs. He has not maintained close contact with his mother or with his siblings, one of whom served a prison term, and reveals that there has been open conflict with them because of his homosexuality. He says that he occasionally hears from his former wife on the progress of his children, and that when he is able he sends money for their support, but that his contact has been irregular. He doesn't visit them because he feels it might be adverse for them to see him in his present homosexual status.

He has had a series of arrests and short sentences over the years beginning at the age of 17. He was made a juvenile court ward in 1953 for stealing, and placed in a boys' camp for three months. Later, as an adult, he was arrested for a variety of offenses, including assault (a fight with a homosexual in which the victim was knifed), suspicion of robbery, petty theft, and for furnishing dangerous drugs (amphetamine) to a minor. The latter offense was subsequently reduced to possession of dangerous drugs. He completed his probation successfully on the latter charge and for the past 3½ years he has had no arrest or known law violations.

He denies that he uses or is addicted to heroin and asserts that the drugs belonged to his friend. He maintains the needle marks are from the injection of vitamin supplements to give him additional energy for his performances as a female impersonator.

CASE EVALUATION: Defendant is an admitted homosexual with a long history of social maladjustment, intermixed with periods of superficial social conformity, and abstinence from crime. By embracing homosexuality, he has come to grips with his underlying problem of sexual identification, and that source of conflict seems to have been reduced in part. Coming from a broken family, the youngest of seven children, his delinquent behavior began at age 17, following partly in the footsteps of an older brother. Since then he has had several arrests and brief periods of confinement and intermittent periods of abstinence from criminal behavior. It should be noted, however, that during the past 3½ years he has had no arrests and, in fact, successfully completed probation.

Defendant obviously needs help, and the question is in [sic] what form it should take. Since he seems to do well under probationary supervision, several of those who participated in his P.C. § 1203.03 study suggested that he be placed in a specialized probationary caseload, including a testing program to determine whether he is reverting to narcotics use. [Note: §1203.03 allows the court to order offenders to be sent to a diagnostic center for up to 90 days for evaluation. The diagnostic center can recommend various sentencing options to the court.] Others feel that his pattern of aggressive behavior is potentially dangerous and believe that commitment to the California Rehabilitation Program would be inappropriate. [The California Rehabilitation Program is a treatment program.] They favor confinement either in the Department of Corrections or in a county penal institution.

JUDGE LELAND C. NIELSEN: It seems to me whoever prepared this case summary certainly did the first thing that I would have done, and that is, send this man up on a 90-day study under Penal Code Section 1203.03. As far as I'm concerned, the Department of Corrections has no chance to get this man from me at this time. I don't think that he is a candidate for state prison. CRC [California Rehabilitation Center] is out for two reasons: One, he denies his addiction or being in imminent danger

of addiction; and second, it's obvious that even if he were sentenced to CRC, he wouldn't cooperate in the program. So he'd be back in front of you just as fast as they could process him and get him back to you.

So my sentence would be to give him some honor camp time, perhaps. I'm not sure that I'd give him any more time since he's been in custody now a minimum of 110 days. First, he was at the Reception Center for 90 days on the 1203.03 study. He has also been in custody the time necessary to find out if he was in imminent danger of becoming a drug addict, and, in all likelihood, he has been confined from the time of his conviction until now. So he's been in custody probably at least four months.

I'd probably put him on the streets on a three-year probationary sentence and suspend his prison sentence. I would require him to have narcotics testing. We use nalline and/or urine testing, as a standard thing in San Diego County. We take away their Fourth Amendment rights, and they have to agree to submit their person, residence, and personal effects to search and seizure at any hour of the day or night without a search warrant upon the request of any peace officer. That would be one condition. Second, I would order him to cooperate in and carry out any program of psychotherapy as recommended by the probation officer.

I don't consider this man to be violent. I must assume from the statement of the offense that what he actually fired in this house was this starter pistol. To me he is not a threat to the community. His crime is against himself; that's the use of the heroin. And I don't know if Mr. Burdman from the Department of Corrections will agree with me, but if he is sent to prison, the chances are he's going to be warehoused there for the rest of his life, which may be a short one under prison circumstances because he is a homosexual.

. . .

JUDGE WILLIAM J. HAYES: I have a hard time buying that altogether. He got himself committed previously and did use force, if you take a look at the history. I also notice there is more than one gun. He kept his guns in a small overnight bag. So I'm not sure whether or not he's just using a starter pistol. He did use a weapon in the section mentioned a littler earlier.

. . .

JUDGE KONGSGAARD: Anybody here want to send this man to prison? (All members indicate in the negative.) . . .

JUDGE KONGSGAARD: Well, how about jail time? Is anybody opposed to jail time for this fellow? In some of the small counties, they don't have space; they have only a miserable county jail.

JUDGE ROBERT R. ROSSON: I'd put him in jail. However, in my county, I would use jail to prove that he is a narcotic addict. . . .

JUDGE KONGSGAARD: What about psychotherapy with an admitted homosexual? Are these people amenable to this psychotherapy?

. . .

JUDGE HENRY J. BRODERICK (Marie County): I have a question about his having come to grips with homosexuality as a female impersonator. I guess that sounds like it's a solution to this fellow's problem, but is it your suggestion that a homosexual who has come to grips with it by embracing it and has no record of violence just shouldn't be committed to the state prison?

. . .

JUDGE NIELSEN: That's mine.

JUDGE BRODERICK: Do you think that embracing homosexuality insulates them from terms of prison?

JUDGE NIELSEN: I don't send many people to prison unless they were violent offenders.

JUDGE BRODERICK: I expect that the husband who found this man pointing a gun wouldn't really count him as being nonviolent. Maybe we could agree in the abstract, but the victim would probably disagree with this as being characterized as nonviolent.

. . .

JUDGE MCDERMOTT: . . .I'm impressed with the fact that every time he goes to jail for thirty or sixty days, he's done all right for two or three years.

MR. MILTON BURDMAN (Deputy Director, Department of Corrections): Six months, I think somebody here said, and I think the shock would help him for two or three years.

JUDGE KONGSGAARD: Judge Dell, what do you think? You were the presiding judge in the Los Angeles criminal department last year.

JUDGE GEORGE M. DELL (Los Angeles County): I don't see any particular purpose in putting the guy in prison excepting for punitive purposes, primarily because he frightened his neighbor in this particular matter. Obviously he can't go to CRC with his homosexual background.

JUDGE KONGSGAARD: Would you put him in the street right away?

JUDGE DELL: After doing four or five months, what's the purpose of more time in jail? I would sentence him, and give him probation.

JUDGE WILLIAM M. GALLAGHER (Sacramento County): I would give probation and time in the county jail. I'd give him a longer period of time in jail, though, as a deterrent to other people in addition to punishing him, if it does deter.

JUDGE KONGSGAARD: Let's hear from Milt Burdman, Deputy Director of the Department of Corrections. Do you want these types in your establishment?

MR. BURDMAN: Not necessarily. What you're dealing with are the kinds of questions to which we have less than perfect answers. We don't have a perfect solution. The points that were brought out are true. If this chap wound up in prison, the chances are that he would get worse during the time he is in prison because of the homosexuality. All that it would mean is that for the time he is there, you're protecting the community. But looking downstream the problems that he has are going to get worse in a prison. I think that's true.

JUDGE WILLIAM T. LOW (San Diego County): I think in any big institution of men only, his problems are going to get worse, because he has had some other problems in the past in which the victim was knifed. It means that he's not adjusting completely to his homosexuality. The thing that stood out to me in this case is that each time he has had an arrest and some confinement, the time spent confined would make him a danger. The more time he's in, I think the greater his chances of reacting violently.

JUDGE JOHN A. ERTOLA (San Francisco County): If he only puts in a few months in jail and gets probation, what kind of an impression does it make on him? I would let him know that when the time for judgment came, that he was wrong and was going to be punished. He might as well learn that alone.

JUDGE LOW: From the point of view of most offenders, the arrest, the trial, the conviction, the placement in the institution, being in jail for even two or three months, is where I think the major impact takes place. Beyond that there is not much impact except in some rape cases. So that in terms of the effect of punishment, I don't think that if he stepped out today, he'd feel he had a break.

. . .

JUDGE ROSSON: If he is going to do some time, he might as well do it in prison as opposed to giving him jail time as a condition of probation. I think you would get as much out of a probation report as you would out of a 1203.03 in this case.

JUDGE KONGSGAARD: Climbing on prison doors for ninety days can be very useful.

. . .

JUDGE JOHN RACANELLI (Santa Clara County): I'm having trouble assessing this fellow's potential. It's true he has been without difficulty for almost four years. He's obviously a hard drug user. This fellow, in my judgment, is fairly close to the borderline, because his violence potential hasn't been adequately assessed. I'd feel much more comfortable with him if I could put him under very close supervision so we could move in if he steps out of line again.

JUDGE KONGSGAARD: Is there anybody now that wants to send this fellow to prison? None.

How about straight probation with no jail time? Six.

How about some additional jail time? How about six months? Ten.

QUESTIONS FOR DISCUSSION

1. Identify the purposes of punishment adopted by each of the judges.

2. Are they appropriate?

3. Do the judges adopt a mixture of the purposes discussed in the text? If so, explain the mixture.

4. Do you find that the judges include purposes that are not discussed in the text? If so, what are they?

5. What sentence would you impose in this case?

6. What purposes would your sentence serve? Defend your answer with specific facts of the case relevant to serving the purposes of punishment that you favor.

Trends in Punishment

Historically, societies have justified punishment on the grounds of retribution, deterrence, incapacitation, and rehabilitation. But the weight given to each has shifted over the centuries. Retribution and rehabilitation, for example, run deep in English criminal law from at least the year 1200. The church's emphasis on atoning for sins and rehabilitating sinners affected criminal law variously. Sometimes the aims of punishment and reformation conflict in practice.

In Elizabethan England, for example, the letter of the law was retributionist: the penalty for all major crimes was death. Estimates show that in practice, however, most accused persons never suffered this extreme penalty. Although some escaped death because they were innocent, many were set free on the basis of their chances for rehabilitation. The law's technicalities, for example, made death a virtually impossible penalty for first-time property offenders. In addition, the queen's general pardon, issued almost annually, gave blanket clemency in the hope that criminals, by this act of mercy, would reform their erring ways.[33]

Gradually, retribution came to dominate penal policy, until the eighteenth century, when deterrence and incapacitation were introduced to replace what contemporary humanitarian reformers considered ineffective, brutal, and barbaric punishment in the name of retribution. By the turn of the twentieth century, humanitarian reformers concluded that deterrence was neither effective nor humane. Rehabilitation replaced deterrence as the aim of criminal sanctions and remained the dominant form of criminal punishment until the 1960s. Most states enacted indeterminate sentencing laws that made prison release dependent on rehabilitation. Most prisons created treatment programs intended to reform criminals so they could become law-abiding citizens. Nevertheless, considerable evidence indicates that rehabilitation never really won the hearts of most criminal justice professionals despite their strong public rhetoric to the contrary.[34]

In the early 1970s, little evidence existed to show that rehabilitation programs reformed offenders. The "nothing works" theme dominated reform discussions, prompted by a highly touted, widely publicized, and largely negative study evaluating the effectiveness of treatment programs. At the same time that academics and policymakers were becoming disillusioned with rehabilitation, public opinion was hardening into demands for severe penalties in the face of steeply rising crime rates. The time was clearly ripe for retribution to return to the fore as a dominant aim of punishment.[35]

California, a rehabilitation pioneer in the early twentieth century, reflected this shift in attitude in 1976. In its Uniform Determinate Sentencing Law, the state legislature abolished the indeterminate sentence, stating boldly that "the purpose of imprisonment is punishment," not treatment or rehabilitation. Called just deserts or even simply deserts, retribution was touted as "right" by conservatives who believed in punishment's morality and as "humane" by liberals convinced that rehabilitation was cruel and excessive. Public opinion supported it, largely on the ground that criminals deserve to be punished.[36]

Since the middle of the 1980s, reformers have heralded retribution and incapacitation as the primary criminal punishments. There are, to be sure, some powerful holdouts. One was the *Model Penal Code*, first written in 1961, when rehabilitation dominated penal policy. After thoroughly reviewing current research and debate, its reporters decided to retain rehabilitation as the primary form of punishment.[37]

CRIMINAL LAW IN A FEDERAL SYSTEM

Throughout this book, you will frequently see the term criminal law used in the singular. This use is not strictly accurate because our federal system of government allows for the creation of a federal criminal code, fifty state criminal codes, and innumerable city ordinances containing myriad violations. The result of this system is that the United States has federal crimes, state crimes, and local crimes. In practice, the use of the term criminal law in the singular refers to the similarities in most state codes. For example, all state codes include the most serious crimes—murder, rape, robbery, burglary, arson, theft, and assault; all allow the most common defenses—self-defense and insanity; and all punish serious crimes by imprisonment. However, they define differently the conduct crimes encompass. For example, in some jurisdictions, burglary requires actual unlawful breaking and entering; in others, it requires only entering without breaking; and in still others, it requires merely unlawfully remaining in a building entered lawfully, such as hiding until after closing time in a department store rest room lawfully entered during business hours (see chapter 10 on burglary).

The defenses to crime also vary across state lines. In some states, insanity may require proof *both* that defendants did not know what they were doing *and* that they did not know that it was wrong to do it. In other states, it suffices to prove *either* that defendants did not know what they were doing *or* that they did not know that it was wrong. (See chapter 7 on insanity.) Some states permit individuals to use deadly force to protect homes from intruders; others require proof that the occupants in the home were in danger of serious bodily harm or death before they can shoot intruders (see chapter 6 on deadly force).

Criminal penalties also differ widely among jurisdictions. Several states prescribe death for some convicted murderers; others, life imprisonment. Hence, where murderers kill determines whether those murderers will live or die. It also determines how they will die: by electrocution, lethal injection, the gas chamber, hanging, or even the firing squad.

The death penalty is only the most dramatic example of disparate penalties, and it affects only a few individuals. Other, less dramatic examples affect far more people. Some states subject those who engage in "open and notorious" sexual intercourse to fines; others make the mere fact of cohabitation outside marriage punishable by three to five years' imprisonment. Some states imprison individuals who possess small quantities of marijuana; others have protected private marijuana use as a constitutional right.[38]

These disparities in crime and punishment among jurisdictions stem from several sources related to the type of community, the period in time, and the social problems of particular localities. In Texas, for example, stealing property valued between $750 and $20,000 is a third-degree felony. It is also a third-degree felony theft to steal crude petroleum oil "regardless of the value" (see chapter 11 on crimes against property).[39]

SOURCES OF CRIMINAL LAW

The complicated system of defining, classifying, grading, prohibiting, and punishing criminal behavior has several sources. They include

- U.S. Constitution
- State constitutions
- U.S. Criminal Code
- State criminal codes
- Municipal ordinances
- Common law of England and the United States
- Judicial decisions interpreting codes and the common law

Treason is the only specific crime defined in constitutions. The U.S. Criminal Code, enacted by the United States Congress, includes all the offenses against the United States government. Municipal ordinances include long lists of minor violations, such as traffic offenses, and a wide range of misbehavior in parks, on public transportation, and other public places. Despite a growing federal criminal code, particularly relating to drugs and violence, the bulk of criminal law originates in the separate criminal codes of the fifty states. Most of the law you will read about in this book appears in the judicial decisions that interpret and apply the crimes defined in these state codes.

The Common-Law Origins of Criminal Law

State criminal codes did not spring full grown from state legislatures. They evolved from a long history of offenses called the **common-law crimes,** crimes that originated in the ancient customs transformed by the English common-law courts in their judicial decisions into written law. We are used to legislatures defining crimes, but this was not always so. Before legislatures existed, social order depended on obedience to unwritten rules—the *lex non scripta*—based on local community customs and mores. These traditions were passed on from generation to generation and altered from time to time in order to meet changed conditions. In England, from which American law descended, these unwritten rules were eventually incorporated into court decisions. These incorporated traditions became the **common law.**

The eighteenth-century English jurist Sir William Blackstone, whose *Commentaries on the Laws and Customs of England* was the only law book most American lawyers read until well into the nineteenth century, described the common law as follows:

> As to general customs, or the common law, properly so called, this is that law, by which proceedings and determinations in the king's ordinary courts of justice are guided and directed. This, for the most part, settles . . . the several species of temporal offenses, with the manner and degree of punishment . . . ; all these are doctrines that are not set down in any written statute or ordinance, but depend merely upon immemorial usage, that is, upon the common law, for their support.[40]

By the seventeenth century, the courts had created a substantial list of common-law felonies and misdemeanors. Most have familiar names today, and many have retained the core of their original meaning, although most have been adapted to meet modern conditions. The common-law felonies included murder, suicide, manslaughter, burglary, arson, robbery, larceny, rape, sodomy, and mayhem. The common-law misdemeanors included (and in some jurisdictions still include) assault, battery, false imprisonment, libel, perjury, corrupting morals, and disturbing the peace.[41]

Exactly how the common law began lies shrouded in obscurity, but like the traditions it incorporated, the common law grew and changed to meet new conditions. At first, its growth depended mainly on judicial decisions. The courts formulated basic principles, rules, and standards based on the common law. They considered these the law of the land. Judges felt bound to follow these common-law principles, standards, and rules, and interpreted new cases according to them. As judges decided more cases according to them, common law became more elaborate and complete. The prior decisions upon which judges interpreted new cases came to be called **precedent.** Common-law judges devised the principle of *stare decisis* that bound them to follow these precedents. Supreme Court Justice Benjamin Cardozo, in a lecture about precedent and *stare decisis,* explained why he relied on prior scholars' work in preparing his lecture. In doing so, he also explained precedent itself:

> It is easier to follow the beaten track than it is to clear another. In doing this, I shall be treading in the footsteps of my predecessors, and illustrating the process that I am seeking to describe, since the power of precedent, when analyzed, is the power of the beaten path.[42]

You will realize the importance of precedent and *stare decisis* in the cases excerpted throughout this book. Court opinions contain many references to prior cases, relying on them to decide the case under review. Sometimes, an opinion expresses regret concerning an undesirable decision reached but explains that prior decisions—precedent and *stare decisis*—bind the court to follow the prior cases even if they do not produce the best result. *Stare decisis* does not prevent courts from ever changing precedent. One way courts avoid following prior decisions is to **distinguish cases.** That is, they decide or "find" that the prior case is not similar enough to bind the present court to the decision in the prior case. Precedent binds courts only in cases with similar facts. For example, a court may have decided in a prior case that the battered woman syndrome applied to the facts in which a battered wife kills her husband following his threats to kill her while he is lying on his bed awake. But the court might decide that the battered woman syndrome does not apply to a later case in which a battered wife kills her husband while he is asleep. This is called distinguishing the case "on its facts." (See chapter 6 on self-defense for a discussion of the battered woman syndrome.)

Courts can also set a precedent directly, although they do it rarely and reluctantly. If a court finds that a prior court decided a case wrongly, it can overrule the prior decision. In one case, a court had earlier ruled that a defendant who obtained money by false pretenses had a defense if the victim was also engaged in crime. Later, it reconsidered its decision. Because most jurisdictions did not allow the defense of criminality of the victim, and in any event because it is a bad rule to allow one wrongdoer to escape punishment simply because the victim was also engaged in wrongdoing, the court overruled its precedent and abolished the defense.[43]

As legislatures became more established, **statutes,** that is, the laws enacted by legislatures, were added to the common law, partly to clarify existing common law, partly to fill in blanks left by the common law, and partly to adjust the common law to new conditions. Court decisions interpreted these statutes according to common-law principles and past decisions. These judicial decisions interpreting the statutes became part of the growing body of precedent making up the common law.

The English colonists brought this common law with them to the New World and incorporated the common-law crimes into their legal systems. Following the American Revolution, the thirteen original states, in turn, incorporated the common law into their new state legal systems. Virtually every new state after that enacted "reception statutes," adopting or receiving the English common law. The Florida reception statute, for example, reads: "The Common Law of England in relation to crimes . . . shall be of full force in this state where there is no existing provision by statute on the subject."[44]

Criminal Codes

Periodically, reformers have called for abolishing the common law in America. The first such effort appeared in 1648, the work of the first generation of English Puritans to arrive in New England. The *Laws and Liberties of Massachusetts* codified the criminal law, defining crimes and prescribing punishments. The authors state their case for a code: "So soon as God had set up political government among his people Israel he gave them a body of laws for judgment in civil and criminal causes. . . . For a commonwealth without laws is like a ship without rigging and steerage."[45]

Although the code included offenses, some capital, that sound odd in today's world (witchcraft, cursing parents, blasphemy, idolatry, and adultery), others, such as rape—

> If any man shall ravish any maid or single woman, committing carnal copulation with her by force, against her own will, that is above ten years of age he shall be punished either with death or some other grievous punishment—

and murder—

> If any man shall commit any wilful murder, which is manslaughter, committed upon premeditate malice, hatred, or cruelty not in a man's necessary and just defense, nor by mere casualty against his will, he shall be put to death—

do not strike us as all that strange or out of place.[46]

Hostility to English institutions following the American Revolution led reformers to call again for codes to replace the English common law. The eighteenth-century Enlightenment, with its emphasis on natural law and order, inspired reformers to put aside the piecemeal common law scattered throughout judicial decisions and to replace it with criminal codes that implemented the natural law of crimes. Despite anti-British feeling, Blackstone's *Commentaries* remained popular with reformers who hoped to transform Blackstone's complete and orderly outline of criminal law into criminal codes.

Reformers contended that judge-made law was not only disorderly and incomplete but also antidemocratic. They maintained that legislatures, which they believed reflected the popular will, should make laws, not aloof judges out of touch with public opinion. Thomas Jefferson proposed a reformation of Virginia's penal code that reflected these influences. The proposed Virginia code never passed the Virginia legislature, not because it codified the law but because it recommended too many drastic reductions in criminal punishments.[47]

Reformers' fears of judicial oppression seemed realized when a federal court in Connecticut attempted to create a new common law of libel early in the nineteenth century. The defendants were indicted for "a libel against the President and Congress of the United States, contained in the *Connecticut Courant* of 7th May, 1806, charging them with having in secret voted $2,000,000 as a present to Bonaparte, for leave to make a treaty with Spain." No statute made such conduct an offense. In *United States v. Hudson and Goodwin*, the United States Supreme Court only partially alleviated reformers' fear of judge-made law. The Court denied the federal courts the power to create common-law crimes. The Supreme Court held that federal courts were not

> vested with jurisdiction over any particular act done by an individual in supposed violation of the peace and dignity of the sovereign power. The legislative authority

of the Union must first make an act a crime, affix a punishment to it, and declare the court that shall have jurisdiction over the offense.

Hudson and Goodwin, however, did not prohibit state courts from creating common-law crimes.[48]

The codification movement had an uneven history, but the concept of common-law crimes retreated throughout the nineteenth century. During the twentieth century, the codification movement strengthened. The American Law Institute supported codification, and the earliest drafts of the *Model Penal Code* abolished common-law crimes:

§ 1.05 All Offenses Defined by Statute. (1) No conduct constitutes an offense unless it is a crime or violation under this Code or another statute of this State.

Common-Law Crimes
and Modern Criminal Law

Since the American Law Institute adopted § 1.05, twenty-five states have abolished the common-law crimes and ten others have proposed to do so. Several states, however, still recognize the common law of crimes: Florida, Idaho, Mississippi, New Mexico, North Carolina, Rhode Island, and Washington. Others do so at least in part: Connecticut, Nevada, Virginia, and Oregon.[49]

Abolishing the common-law crimes does not render the common law irrelevant. Most states that have abolished common-law offenses (these states are called code jurisdictions) retain the common-law defenses, such as self-defense and insanity. Furthermore, statutes frequently contain the terms murder, manslaughter, robbery, burglary, rape, and assault without defining them, and courts turn to the common law to determine the meanings of those terms. For example, the 1975 Alabama Criminal Code provides as follows: "Any person who commits . . . voluntary manslaughter, shall be guilty of a felony. Voluntary manslaughter is punishable as a Class 5 felony."[50]

California, a code jurisdiction, included the common-law felonies in its criminal code. The California Supreme Court reviewed the common law to determine the meaning of its murder statute in *Keeler v. Superior Court*. Keeler's wife was pregnant with another man's child. Keeler kicked his pregnant wife in the stomach, causing her to abort the fetus. The California court had to decide whether fetuses were included in the murder statute. The court, in the following passage, reveals the importance of the common law in interpreting present statutes:

Penal code § 187 provides: "Murder is the unlawful killing of a human being, with malice aforethought." The dispositive question is whether the fetus which petitioner is accused of killing was, on February 23, 1969, a "human being" within the meaning of this statute. . . . We therefore undertake a brief review of the origins and development of the common law of abortional homicide. . . . From that inquiry it appears that by the year 1850 — the date with which we are concerned — an infant could not be the subject of homicide at common law unless it had been born alive. . . . Perhaps the most influential statement of the "born alive" rule is that of Coke, in mid-17th century: "If a woman be quick with childe and by a potion or otherwise killeth it in her wombe, or if a man beat her, whereby the childe dyeth in her body, and she is delivered of a dead childe, this is a great misprision (i.e., misdemeanor), and no murder; but if the childe be born alive and dyeth of the potion, battery, or other cause, this is murder; for in law it is accounted a reasonable creature . . . when it is born alive." (3 Coke, Institutes 58 (1648)) . . .

We hold that in adopting the definition of murder in Penal Code § 187 the Legislature intended to exclude from its reach the act of killing an unborn fetus.[51]

As a result of the court's decision, the California legislature changed the criminal homicide statute to include fetuses.[52]

Jurisdictions that still recognize the common-law crimes (these are called common-law jurisdictions) have created many offenses, particularly misdemeanors, that extend far beyond the common-law felonies. All of the following are crimes without statutes in some states: committing conspiracy, attempt, and solicitation; uttering grossly obscene language in public; burning a body in a furnace; keeping a house of prostitution; maliciously killing a horse; being a common scold; negligently permitting a prisoner to escape; discharging a gun near a sick person; being drunk in public; using libel; committing an indecent assault; and eavesdropping.[53]

Three problems arise in common-law jurisdictions. First, what if statutes do not prescribe penalties for individual common-law crimes? Statutes prescribing general penalties for felonies and misdemeanors alleviate this problem in some states. The problem remains when the common law does not designate an offense a felony or misdemeanor. Some states solve this problem by enacting statutes that define all common-law offenses as misdemeanors.

Second, if both statutes and common law cover the same conduct, which takes precedence? Some states construe statutes narrowly, that is, the words of the statute must either specifically repeal the common law or preempt the entire field of law covered by the common-law crimes. So, where a state conspiracy statute listed five criminal conspiracies while the common law listed many more, the court held that the statute was not meant to take over the whole field of conspiracy; hence, the conspiracies not listed in the statute remained common-law crimes.[54]

Third, what conduct constitutes a common-law crime? Courts approach this subject from two perspectives. Some courts eagerly define new crimes without precedent; others do so only reluctantly. The perspective that courts adopt depends on their view of the common law. If they believe that decided cases merely illustrate broad principles of the unwritten common law, then defining new offenses requires no precedent. According to this view, the common law can expand to meet new conditions. Courts do not invent new crimes; they only apply existing common-law principles to new problems. Courts following this view of the common law are likely to define new crimes without precedent. Other courts view the decisions themselves as embodying the whole of common law. These courts maintain that U.S. courts cannot define new crimes. Therefore, they depend on specific precedent to justify expanding the scope of common-law crimes.

"RATIONAL CRIMINAL LAW"

During the nineteenth century, discontent with the disorganized and illogical state of criminal law and the complex scheme of punishments led to calls for a more rational organization of criminal law and punishments. The phrase "rational criminal law" applies to criminal law limited by four criteria:

1. It is based on general principles, not on the discretion and personal philosophies of legislators and judges.
2. The general principles of criminal law apply to all crimes.
3. Criminal law grades punishment according to both the seriousness of the harm and the blameworthiness of the conduct.
4. Criminal law prescribes no greater penalty than punishment and prevention require.

A rational criminal law emphasizes that criminal law is a limited method of social control, that is to say, a method of last resort. According to this limited method, if informal private sanctions secure compliance, criminal law has no role to play. If informal sanctions fail and civil actions can secure compliance, then criminal law should not apply. If civil actions fail and criminal law becomes necessary, and if a lesser penalty is as effective as a greater penalty, then a rational criminal law relies on the lesser penalty. Rational criminal law rests on values of individual autonomy and social economy. In a rational criminal law, government should intervene in human actions only when absolutely necessary and should expend no more money and power than are required to prevent and punish antisocial conduct.[55]

The American Law Institute's **Model Penal Code** has substantially advanced the pursuit of a rational criminal code. The American Law Institute (ALI) is a private association whose membership includes eminent lawyers, judges, and professors. Founded in 1923, it works to clarify and improve the law. In 1950, with Rockefeller Foundation aid, it undertook a major effort to establish a rational criminal law. The ALI created a large advisory committee drawn from all disciplines concerned with criminal justice and charged it with drafting a model penal code. For ten years, these specialists met and drafted, redrafted, and finally in 1961 completed the *Model Penal Code and Commentaries*, a learned and influential document.[56]

As its title indicates, the code is a model to guide actual legislation. Jurisdictions vary in which specific provisions meet their needs. By 1985, when the ALI published an updated code and commentary, thirty-four states had enacted widespread criminal law revision and codification based on its provisions; fifteen hundred courts had cited its provisions and referred to its commentary. The *Model Penal Code* fulfills the criteria outlined at the beginning of this section for a rational criminal code, but it is not the final word on the subject. Much of the criminal law is not "rational" as the term is defined here. Moreover, rational does not necessarily mean "best." Finally, some jurisdictions, such as the state of California, have not followed much of what the model code proposes.

NONLEGAL INFLUENCES
ON CRIMINAL LAW

Prosecutors, defense attorneys, and judges view criminal law from the perspective of practitioners. They accept the existing definitions of crime in the criminal law and proceed from there to argue and decide cases. But practicing lawyers are not the only people who study and think about criminal law. Historians, philosophers, doctors, and social scientists to name but a few, have studied criminal law too. However, instead of focusing on what criminal law *is* and how to apply it to specific cases, they have tried to find out how and why criminal law *came to be* what it is. They have demonstrated for us the importance of morality, history, social forces and processes, and ideology in the creation, development, and operation of our criminal law. You should keep these influences in mind as you study the topics in the remainder of this book. These influences do not necessarily contradict the legal definition of crime. Rather, they enrich our understanding of when, how, and why the principles, doctrines, and definitions of specific crimes developed.

The Influence of Ideology

Political scientists and sociologists study the political and social influences on the formation and administration of criminal law. All crimes are political in the sense that the legislatures that enact criminal codes are not neutral bodies. Also, community standards informally and, perhaps, imperceptibly influence judges when they interpret the law. Statutes outline broad categories of conduct, permitting judges room in which to fit particular cases. In applying broad categories to individual cases, judges' own ideas and community standards influence their decisions; applying criminal law to individual cases is never a value-neutral exercise.[57]

Two opposing theories inform the ideological perspective. The democratic-consensus theory, originating in the insights of the great sociologist Emile Durkheim, holds that elected representatives define crime. The criminal law expresses the will of the people through their elected representatives. Criminal law represents society's stand against conduct that violates its values and describes what punishments society inflicts on those who flout its values. This reading of the legislative process rests on two assumptions: First, politics and laws reflect consensus; people work together and compromise their individual interests so the state can work efficiently and effectively to satisfy the majority's collective needs. Second, criminal statutes embody the people's will. In fact, recent research suggests that criminal codes express neither the will of the people nor the will of their legislators; instead, criminal justice professionals write most criminal laws.[58]

The conflict-elitist theory assumes that society operates according to conflict, not consensus. Interest groups, each ensconced in a bailiwick, come out fighting for their selfish interests — interests promoted only at the expense of other groups' interests. The most powerful interest group wins every major contest and then imposes its values on the rest of society. The rich and powerful use the legal system to protect their wealth and secure their dominant position of power. The ruling elite brandish the criminal laws as weapons to coerce weaker elements of society into submission.[59]

The conflict-elitist theory is considerably more complicated than this brief summary suggests. First, the criminal process is rarely so personal and purposely exploitative. Second, the ruling elite often disagree over which criminal laws best serve their interests. Third, not all laws promote the dominant class's interests, at least not in the short term.[60]

Both theories reflect part of the social reality of criminal law. Without question, much criminal law exhibits consensus. Most people, for example, agree that murder, rape, and robbery should be crimes; in fact, widespread agreement exists about the seriousness of more than one hundred crimes. Legislatures represent most people when they enact these statutes, as do judges when they apply them. Much criminal law, however, does not represent consensus. Historically, the powerful have used vagrancy laws to keep in their place certain elements of society — the poor, the unattached, and others on the fringes of "respectable" society. Vagrancy legislation therefore supports the claim of the conflict-elitist theory that criminal law results from the ruling class's effort to keep the "lower orders" in line. Similarly, recent ordinances against "aggressive panhandling," sleeping on park benches, and camping within city limits represent efforts of the middle class to control the public behavior of "street people."[61]

Both theories also display considerable naiveté. The democratic-consensus theory fails to account for the powerful effects that money, class, race, and other social factors have on both the political and the legal processes. Decisions throughout every stage of the criminal process — reporting crimes; arresting suspects; prosecuting, trying, and convicting defendants; and sentencing or releasing offenders — require judgments, or discretion, the amount of freedom that victims, police officers, prosecutors, judges, or juries have in making these decisions.[62]

A debate as old as law itself exists concerning how much leeway law officers and the public should have in enforcing criminal law. Good reasons support tempering the letter of the law with flexibility to do justice in individual cases. In his advice to new judges, Sir Nicholas Bacon, a sixteenth-century English lord chancellor, stressed that legislators could not possibly write statutes clear enough or complete enough to cover all cases. Because of this, "the judge is not always so narrowly to weigh the words of the law, but sometimes in respect of the person, place, time and occasion or other circumstance to qualify and moderate such extremities as the particular words of the law written may offer."

Sir Nicholas was no fool. Realizing that discretion was equally a means to evil as well as good, he warned his new judges accordingly:

> For albeit his knowledge be never so great and his discretion equal to it, if he will suffer them to be subject and governed by fear, by love, by malice or gain, then shall all his judgments be such as his affections be and not such as knowledge and discretion doth require.[63]

Class, wealth, power, and prejudice influence the operation of the law, perhaps even more than they influence its formulation. Selective enforcement has characterized the administration of criminal law from as early as the sixteenth century. For example, in one English town in the 1570s, poor, wandering people without family or other community ties were arrested more often, prosecuted more vigorously, and punished more harshly than were "respectable," established residents.[64]

Discretion creates a gap between what law books say and what law officers do because class, race, economics, and politics influence discretionary action. Victims who never report crimes, suspects whom police could arrest but do not, arrested suspects whom prosecutors could charge but do not, and offenders who could be punished but are not — they, as much as any statute or universal moral code, shape the criminal law. Commenting on social forces and their current impact on the administration of justice, the late criminologist Donald R. Cressey concluded that

> [t]here is a great deal of evidence that current statutes calling for punishment of lawbreakers are not administered uniformly, or with celerity or certainty. This suggests that the actual reactions to crime are not really reflected in the laws governing the administration of justice. Statutes are so severe they must be mitigated

in the interests of justice, and in order to maintain the consent of the governed. The following conclusions have been drawn by so many investigators that they may be accepted as factual:

1. Blacks are more likely to be arrested than whites.
2. Blacks are more likely to be indicted than whites.
3. Blacks have a higher conviction rate than whites.
4. Blacks are usually punished more severely than whites, but this is not true for all crimes, especially those in which a black person victimizes a black person.
5. Blacks are less likely to receive probation and suspended sentences.
6. Blacks receive pardons less often than do whites.
7. Blacks have less chance of having a death sentence commuted than do whites.[65]

The conflict-elitist theory, no more than the democratic-consensus theory, fully explains the origins and nature of criminal laws. Just as the democratic-consensus theory minimizes the pluralistic conflict of interests in society, the conflict-elitist theory ignores the very real core of values about which wide agreement exists. The same sixteenth-century English town that favored established members of the community over poor, wandering strangers also exhibited wide consensus on some values. Town officials adhered to the principle of legality in the administration of justice, enforcing procedural safeguards such as rules of proof requiring reliable witnesses to bring charges and testify in court against the accused. They also firmly recognized that despite the letter of the law prescribing death as a punishment for all felonies—from murder to the theft of a chicken—only murderers and some other violent criminals should hang for their crimes. This consensus persists today.

The Influence of the Irrational

Both the conflict-elitist and the democratic-consensus theories possess one major flaw in common. Neither takes into account the influence of chance and the irrational on criminal law. Human institutions, of which criminal law and its administration are two, rarely develop and operate strictly according to democratic-consensus and conflict-elitist theories. Police officers on patrol, for example, may arrest citizens as much because they are tired, irritable, or bored as because they revere law and order. A question endlessly repeated to my generation of law students in explaining why a court made a particular decision was, "What did the judge have for dinner the night before the court decided the case?"

Irrational forces give rise to more than erratic individual decisions. They affect criminal codes as well, as sex psychopath laws illustrate. Shortly after World War II, a small spate of brutal sex crimes generated public fear. One ghoulish man dismembered and killed several young girls after sexually assaulting them. In response, most states hastily passed sex psychopath statutes, enabling states to confine potential sex offenders indefinitely without a trial. Some experts questioned the effectiveness, propriety, and constitutionality of these statutes. Critics argued that the statutes were unconstitutional because they denied procedural safeguards to those affected by them. Furthermore, they rested on the erroneous assumption that society could predict who would commit sex offenses.[66]

Considerable empirical evidence since the passage of sex psychopath legislation has demonstrated the shortcomings of the laws. Yet, despite this knowledge, the laws remain largely in force today. Fear and panic explain their enactment. Any complete explanation of the nature and origins of criminal law must account for the unpredictable, irrational, and chance elements in human behavior.[67]

The Influence of History

The great jurist and United States Supreme Court justice, Oliver Wendell Holmes, maintained that in understanding the law, "a page of history is worth a volume of logic." He meant that real-life experience, not abstract reasoning, creates law. Most crimes originate in the circumstances of time and place. In addition to law's response to time and place, lawyers' reverence for precedent enhances history's strength. Imbued with the importance of precedent, lawyers approach change in the law cautiously. As a result, the current body of criminal law retains laws that were once believed necessary but are no longer relevant. The great English legal historian, William Maitland, noted that the past rules us from the grave. The ghosts of the past stalk silently through our courts and legislatures, ruling our modern law by means of outdated and irrelevant but venerated ancient principles and doctrines. Thus, history plays a powerful part in maintaining, in today's criminal law, that which yesterday's social, economic, political, and philosophical considerations created.[68]

The development of the modern law of theft illustrates the historical perspective on criminal law. In early times, larceny—forcibly taking and carrying away another's cattle—was the only theft. The original crime resembles the modern law of robbery—taking another's property by force or by threat of force (see chapter 11). Later, larceny came to include taking another's property by stealth (from which our word stealing descends). Getting another's property by trickery was not a crime; it was shrewd or clever. Neither was taking property left for safekeeping (examples would be taking a car left in an attended parking lot, or clothes left at a dry cleaner's); it was the owner's folly. Hence, only stealing or forcibly taking another's property constituted larceny; cheating was not a crime.[69]

Such was the law of theft in medieval England before commerce and industry had advanced beyond the most rudimentary stages. Most people lived in small communities, rarely dealt with strangers, and had few personal property items available to misappropriate. Furthermore, larceny was a felony, punishable by death. Judges were reluctant to expand the definition of larceny if doing so meant hanging more property offenders.

The complexities of modern life changed all this. More people, personal property, and strangers; a greater need to leave property and money with strangers; and less bloody punishments for larceny all led to alterations in theft law. Larceny came to include the theft of most movable personal property, such as jewelry, furniture, clothing, and utensils. Then it was expanded to include the stealing of paper instruments representing ownership, such as checks, bank notes, and deeds. Finally, new crimes were created to embrace more misappropriations than the taking of property by force or stealth. Misappropriating money entrusted to another became embezzlement, tricking another out of money became false pretenses; both became felonies.

Theft law developed to meet the needs of a complex society and to ameliorate a harsh criminal law; these historical facts explain theft law. In the past twenty years, thirty states have overcome this history by consolidating larceny, embezzlement, false pretenses, and other theft offenses into one crime. The remaining twenty states cling to a host of theft offenses, of which the arcane larceny, embezzlement, fraud, and false pretenses are only the most common.

To cite one more example, the criminal law enacted in seventeenth-century New England to secure Puritan religious values, despite its clear irrelevance to modern behavior, remains surprisingly intact. For example, until their recent demise in the face of a constitutional assault on their validity, vagrancy statutes were based on the needs of sixteenth-century England. Yet, until the 1970s, American vagrancy statutes copied their sixteenth-century English legal forebears verbatim. Fornication, profanity, and curfews still remain on the books, although they are rarely enforced. The retention of these "morals" offenses demonstrates that the past rules the present in criminal law.[70]

The Influence of an "Ethical Core"

The political, legal, historical, and irrational theories discussed thus far all rest on the assumption that environment determines criminal law: Crime does not reflect permanent values; it is relative to time and place. In other words, irrational outbursts, ideology, social conditions, and other circumstances shape what society condemns in its criminal law. What one age considers evil, another may tolerate, even promote as good.

Philosophers take a fundamentally different approach, assuming that crime represents universal, permanent, inherent evil in codified form. According to this theory, lawmaking, politics, history, and emotional outbursts do not affect this ethical core of criminal law.

The ethical core theory stems in part from religion. For example, some proponents maintain that criminal law reflects the Ten Commandments: "Thou shalt not kill" and "Thou shalt not steal" illustrate this view. Other commandments, however, do not comport with modern criminal law. "Thou shalt not covet thy neighbor's wife" violates the basic principle that the state cannot punish thoughts unaccompanied by action. Moreover, consensus supports only some commandments; deep controversy surrounds others (see chapter 3).

The ethical core theory is not always articulated in strictly religious form; sometimes it is cast in general moral terms. For instance, criminal law manifests the universally high value placed on the rights to life, liberty, and property. The English common law first enshrined these rights; then Americans entrenched them in constitutions, statutes, and court decisions. The ethical core theory strikes a responsive chord in those who accept that life, liberty, and property are widely valued, uniformly defined, and universally protected by law. But the theory does not fully match reality. Take, for example, the enormous body of regulatory traffic offenses. Although driving seventy-five miles per hour in a sixty-five-mile-an-hour zone may violate the law, few would call it an inherently evil act, violating some ethical core of values. On the other hand, even though many might believe that Kristen is violating an ethical core of values in breaking Lucas's heart (recall the hypothetical cases early in the chapter), the law does not make her action a crime.

Some critics argue that equating values or notions of good and bad with crime, as the ethical core theory does, is both dangerous and improper. Professor Louis B. Schwartz criticized the statement of purpose in the Federal Criminal Justice Reform Act of 1973 on the ground that

> the bill injects a new, false, and dangerous notion that the criminal code "aims at the articulation of the nation's public values" and its vindication through punishment. A criminal code necessarily falls far short of expressing the nation's morality. Many things are evil or undesirable without being at all appropriate for imprisonment: lying, overcharging for goods and services, marital infidelity, lack of charity or patriotism. Nothing has been more widely recognized in modern criminal law scholarship than the danger of creating more evil by ill-considered use of the criminal law than is caused by the target misconduct. Accordingly, the failure to put something under the ban of the penal code is not an expression of a favorable "value" of the non-penalized behavior. It is a fatal confusion of values to see the Criminal Code as anything but a list of those most egregious misbehaviors, which according to a broad community consensus, can be usefully dealt with by social force.[71]

Several of the hypothetical cases presented earlier in this chapter illustrate other weaknesses in the ethical core theory. They demonstrate that the meaning of life, liberty, and property is by no means settled. Controversy surrounds issues such as whether looking at pornography, smoking marijuana, or even using heroin should be considered crimes. What constitutes life and property, not to mention liberty? Should these be protected by the criminal law, and if so, to what extent? The answers vary from place to place and over time.

One major theme in criminal law is the need to reconcile stability with change. Changed conditions, new knowledge, and shifts in ideals all require that the law advance beyond what it was in the eighteenth or nineteenth centuries. Stealing a chicken was once a capital offense. Wives who scolded their husbands were considered criminals in the not-too-distant past. Most of the adult population in India can remember a time when a widow's burning herself to death after her husband died was considered the highest form of love. Recent cases involving people whose hearts are beating and who are still breathing but whose brains have stopped functioning have raised new questions about the meanings of life and death. A term has even been created to describe this new dilemma: brain death. Equally controversial is the heated debate over whether a fetus is property subject to contract law and whether it is a life for purposes of criminal law (see chapter 8).

SUMMARY

Criminal law is a method, or way of doing things, that aims to reduce crime and punish criminals. It is a list of commands, or dos and don'ts, written into law, with penalties attached that apply to everyone in the jurisdiction or under the authority of the government making the law. Criminal law shares these qualities with other forms of law, but it has another distinctive feature: Criminal conviction carries with it the formal moral condemnation of the community.

Criminal law has two parts. The general part establishes the general principles of criminal law that apply to all crimes. It also sets forth the doctrines that may apply to all crimes, such as accomplice liability, attempts, justifications, and excuses. The special part includes the rules, or definitions, or specific crimes.

Crimes are classified according to several schemes. One scheme, the felony, misdemeanor, violation scheme, organizes crimes according to the penalty. Capital felonies are punishable by death or life imprisonment without parole. Felonies are punishable by incarceration in prisons for one year or more. Misdemeanors are punishable by fine or incarceration in local jails for up to one year. Violations, often not designated crimes at all, are punishable by fine only. Another classification scheme ranks crimes according to their degree of "badness" or "evil." Crimes *mala in se*, like rape and murder, are inherently evil. Crimes *mala prohibita*, such as parking violations, are illegal but not evil. Another scheme classifies crimes according to their subject matter, including crimes against the state, crimes against the person, crimes against habitation, crimes against property, crimes against the administration of justice, crimes against public order, and crimes against public morals.

Criminal punishment rests on two basic purposes: retribution and prevention. Retribution is meant to inflict pain on the person who harmed another in order to give offenders their just deserts. The major types of prevention are (1) deterrence, or using the threat of punishment to deter people generally from future crime; (2) incapacitation, or preventing specific offenders from committing future crimes; and (3) rehabilitation, or changing individual offenders' behavior so that they will not commit crimes in the future.

Throughout history, criminal law has reflected these purposes, but the emphasis has shifted among them over time. During most of early history, retribution predominated; during the first sixty years of the twentieth century, rehabilitation held sway; during the last two decades, retribution and incapacitation have returned to prominence.

The United States does not have a unified criminal law. Each of the fifty states has its own criminal law, and the federal government has a separate criminal code. The states and federal criminal codes share similarities in general terms, but the specific definitions of crimes—and the penalties attached—differ widely across jurisdictions.

American criminal law stems from several sources. The United States Constitution and the state constitutions define the crimes against the nation and state, specifically treason. Statutes define crimes; in fact, most criminal law today originates in statutes, primarily state criminal codes. Definitions of crimes in statutes, and defenses to crimes, require reference to the common law, another major source of criminal law. Some states have retained the common-law crimes; others have abolished the common-law crimes but retained the common-law defenses. All, however, require reference to the common law for definition of terms. A final source of criminal law is judicial opinions interpreting constitutions, statutes, and the common law.

The common-law origins of criminal law eventually produced a disorganized illogical arrangement of crimes and punishments. By contrast, a rational criminal law rests on fundamental principles, universally applied, that grade and punish crimes according to their seriousness and blameworthiness. Criminal law acts economically to use only that punishment needed to reduce crime and punish criminals. Criminal law, therefore, is a limited instrument of social control. It consists of both government power and limits on that power.

Studying the principles, doctrines, and rules of criminal law reveals the body of criminal law. However, it does not tell us how or why the criminal law established the principles, doctrines, and rules. Sociology, political science, psychology, history, and philosophy shed light on the rationale, policies, and values of the criminal law and how they developed in the context of specific times and places; we find that criminal law did not spring full-grown from rational minds. Social forces, political power, emotions, past traditions and practices, and philosophy have shaped the criminal law as we know it today.

REVIEW QUESTIONS

1. Why can we say criminal law is the study of ordinary phenomena under extraordinary circumstances?

2. Why do we say criminal law is a method, or way, of doing things?

3. Describe the major characteristics of criminal law. How do they compare and contrast with other branches of law? What one characteristic most distinguishes criminal law from other branches of law?

4. Why is the term criminal law used in the singular incorrect?

5. Explain the major characteristics of a "rational criminal law."

6. Describe the general and special parts of the criminal law.

7. Identify the four main characteristics of criminal punishment.

8. What distinguishes retribution from prevention?

9. Explain general deterrence, special deterrence, incapacitation, and rehabilitation. What do they all have in common?

10. Describe the major classification schemes for organizing and grading crimes.

KEY TERMS

civil law The law that deals with private rights and remedies.

common law The body of law consisting of all the statutes and case law background of England and the colonies before the American Revolution, based on principles and rules that derive from usages and customs of antiquity.

common-law crimes Crimes originating in the English common law.

culpability Deserving of punishment because of individual responsibility for actions.

damages Money awarded in civil lawsuits for injuries.

defendant The person against whom a civil or criminal action is brought.

discretion The freedom of individuals to base decisions on factors other than written rules.

distinguish cases To find that facts differ enough from those in a prior case to release judges from the precedent of the decision in that case.

felonies Serious crimes generally punishable by one year or more in prison.

fines Money penalties paid to the state as criminal punishment.

general deterrence or prevention Preventing crime by threatening potential lawbreakers.

incapacitation Punishment by imprisonment, mutilation, and even death.

jurisdiction Territory or subject matter under the control of a government body.

justice The philosophical position of rendering to offenders their just deserts.

malum in se A crime inherently bad, or evil.

malum prohibitum A crime not inherently bad, or evil, but merely prohibited.

misdemeanor A minor crime for which the penalty is usually less than one year in jail or a fine.

Model Penal Code The code developed by the American Law Institute to guide reform in criminal law.

plaintiff The person who sues another party in a civil action.

prevention The punishing of offenders in order to prevent crimes in the future.

punitive damages Payments to injured parties intended to punish the wrongdoer.

precedent Prior court decision that guides judges in deciding future cases.

rehabilitation Prevention of crime by treatment.

retribution Punishment based on just deserts.

rule of law Decisions made on the basis of principles, not individual discretion.

special deterrence The threat of punishment aimed at individual offenders in the hope of deterring future criminal conduct.

stare decisis The principle that binds courts to stand by prior decisions and to leave undisturbed settled points of law.

statutes Rules or doctrines enacted by legislatures.

tort A legal wrong for which the injured party may sue the injuring party.

violation A minor legal infraction subject to a small fine.

Suggested Readings

1. Wayne R. LaFave and Austin W. Scott, Jr., *Criminal Law*, 2d ed. (St. Paul, Minn.: West Publishing Company, 1986). This updated version of a classic law school textbook is a good place for the undergraduate to research further the problems of criminal law.

2. Rollin M. Perkins and Ronald N. Boyce, *Criminal Law*, 3d ed. (Mineola, N.Y.: Foundation Press, 1982). This is a law school hornbook (textbook) covering the general and special parts of criminal law. It is an excellent reference book for anyone who wishes to pursue in further detail topics suggested here.

3. George P. Fletcher, *Rethinking Criminal Law* (Boston: Little, Brown, 1978). Fletcher's provocative effort to write a comprehensive theory of criminal law is challenging and difficult but well worth the serious student's efforts.

4. Lawrence M. Friedman, *A History of American Law* (New York: Simon and Schuster, 1973). Friedman has written an interesting history of American law for the general public. Although it covers all law, sections on criminal law are clearly set apart and can be read separately without difficulty.

5. American Law Institute, *Model Penal Code* (Philadelphia: American Law Institute, 1954–61); and American Law Institute, *Model Penal Code and Commentaries* (Philadelphia: American Law Institute, 1980, 1985). These are excellent works full of the latest scholarship, thoughtful analyses, and commentary by some of the leading judges, lawyers, and academics in American law. The works present, in imposing fashion, the democratic-consensus approach to criminal law; but

their value stretches well beyond. They contain the most comprehensive coverage of American criminal law in existence.

6. Lawrence M. Friedman, *American Law* (New York: Norton, 1984). This is a general introduction to American law, filled with anecdotes and discussion intended to explain the nature and processes of American law to the general reader. It is a vivid picture of American law and its role in American life. Well worth the time spent reading it.

7. Jerome Hall, *General Principles of Criminal Law*, 2d ed. (Indianapolis, Ind.: Bobbs-Merrill, 1960). Hall covers the general principles and doctrines of criminal law, arranging them into a theory of criminal law. This text is a classic in the literature of criminal law.

8. Leo Katz, *Bad Acts and Guilty Minds* (Chicago: University of Chicago, 1987). The author presents an interesting, thought-provoking look at the philosophy of criminal law. He focuses on the basic problems of criminal law, using real cases from several countries, many challenging hypothetical cases, and critical suggestions. Difficult to read, but well worth the effort.

9. Henry M. Hart, Jr., "The Aims of the Criminal Law," *Law and Contemporary Problems* 23 (1958): 104–441. This essay is the best brief statement about the nature of criminal law and its characteristics.

10. Jeffrey H. Reiman, *The Rich Get Richer and the Poor Get Prison*, 2d ed. (New York: Wiley, 1984). In this book, Reiman forcefully presents the conflict-elitist theory.

Notes

1. These characteristics modify and expand on those listed in Henry M. Hart, Jr.'s classic, "The Aims of the Criminal Law," *Law and Contemporary Problems* 23 (1958):403–405.

2. Ibid., p. 405.

3. See Jerome Hall, *The General Principles of Criminal Law*, 2d ed. (Indianapolis: Bobbs-Merrill, 1960), pp. 16–26, for a detailed discussion of the differences among principles, doctrines, and rules.

4. American Law Institute, *Model Penal Code and Commentaries*, vol. 1 (Philadelphia: American Law Institute, 1985), pp. 1–30; Norval Morris and Gordon Hawkins, *The Honest Politician's Guide to Crime Control* (Chicago: University of Chicago Press, 1969), chapter 1.

5. See *Harmelin v. Michigan*, excerpted in chapter 2, for a discussion of the Michigan statute. For an excellent discussion of capital crimes and punishment, see Hugo Adam Bedau, ed., *The Death Penalty in America*, 3d ed. (New York: Oxford University Press, 1982).

6. For a thorough summary of the wide disparity in existing misdemeanor classification, see American Law Institute, *Model Penal Code and Commentaries*, vol. 1, pp. 1–30.

7. American Law Institute, *Model Penal Code and Commentaries*, vol. 3, part I, pp. 34–38.

8. Ibid., p. 34.

9. Andrew von Hirsch and Nils Jareborg, "Gauging Criminal Harm: A Living-Standard Analysis," *Oxford Journal of Legal Studies* 11 (1991):1–38.

10. Thomas Szasz, M.D., *Law, Liberty, and Psychiatry* (New York: Collier Books, 1963).

11. Herbert Packer, *The Limits of the Criminal Sanction* (Palo Alto, Calif.: Stanford University Press, 1968), pp. 33–34.

12. *McKinney's New York Criminal Law Pamphlet* (St. Paul: West Publishing Co., 1988); New York Penal Code, § 1.05(6).

13. *Leviticus*, 24:20.

14. *A History of the Criminal Law of England*, vol. 3 (London: Macmillan, 1883), pp. 81–82.

15. James Q. Wilson and Richard Herrnstein thoroughly discuss free will in *Crime and Human Nature*, chap. 19 (New York: Simon and Schuster, 1985); see also psychiatrist Willard Gaylin's fascinating *The Killing of Bonnie Garland* (New York: Simon and Schuster, 1982).

16. Henry E. Wiehofen, "Retribution Is Obsolete," in *Responsibility*, ed. C. Friedrich, Nomos series, no. 3 (New York: Lieber-Atherton, 1960), pp. 116, 119–120.

17. These theories are discussed at length in James Q. Wilson and Richard Herrnstein, *Crime and Human Nature*. An intriguing case study applying the theories to one criminal homicide is Andre Mayer and Michael Wheeler, *The Crocodile Man: A Case of Brain Chemistry and Criminal Violence* (Boston: Houghton Mifflin, 1982).

18. John L. Diamond, "The Myth of Morality and Fault in Criminal Law," *American Criminal Law*, 34 (1996): 111–131 discusses this problem with a criminal law system based on morality and fault.

19. Joseph Goldstein, "Psychoanalysis and Jurisprudence," *Yale Law Journal* 77 (1968):1071–1072.

20. This topic is explored fully in Bedau, ed., *The Death Penalty in America*, chap. 4.

21. *Coker v. Georgia*, 433 U.S. 584, 97 S.Ct. 2861, 53 L.Ed.2d 982 (1977).

22. See Wilson and Herrnstein, *Crime and Human Nature*, for a full discussion.

23. Johannes Andenaes, "Deterrence," *Encyclopedia of Crime and Justice*, ed. Sanford H. Kadish (New York: Free Press, 1983), pp. 2, 593.

24. Ibid., p. 596.

25. Mark DeWolfe Howe, ed., *Holmes-Laski Letters* (Cambridge, Mass.: Harvard University Press, 1953), p. 806.

26. James Q. Wilson, *Thinking About Crime* (New York: Basic Books, 1975).

27. See Mark H. Moore et al., *Dangerous Offenders: The Elusive Target of Justice* (Cambridge, Mass.: Cambridge University Press, 1984).

28. Sandra Gleason, "Hustling: The 'Single' Economy of a Prison," *Federal Probation* (June 1978), pp. 32–39; Samuel Walker, *Sense and Nonsense about Crime: A Policy Guide* (Monterey, Calif.: Brooks/Cole, 1985), pp. 59–61; Steven R. Donziger, ed., *The Real War on Crime* (New York: Harper Perennial, 1996).

29. *The Limits of the Criminal Sanction*, p. 50.

30. For these early reformation ideas, see Joel Samaha, "Hanging for Felony," *Historical Journal* 21 (1979); and "Some Reflections on the Anglo-Saxon Heritage of Discretionary Justice," in Lawrence E. Abt and Irving R. Stuart, eds., *Social Psychology and Discretionary Law* (New York: Van Nostrand, 1979), pp. 4–16.

31. See Richard D. Schwartz, "Rehabilitation," in *Encyclopedia of Crime and Justice*, pp. 1364–1373.

32. "The Humanitarian Theory of Punishment," *Res Judicatae* 6 (1953):224.

33. Joel Samaha, *Law and Order in Historical Perspective* (New York: Academic Press, 1974); Samaha, "Hanging for Felony."

34. See David J. Rothman, *Conscience and Convenience* (Boston: Little, Brown, 1980), for the history of rehabilitation during the early twentieth century.

35. Robert Martinson, "What Works? Questions and Answers about Prison Reform," *The Public Interest* 35 (Spring 1974):22–54.

36. Quoted in Malcom M. Feeley, *Court Reform on Trial* (New York: Basic Books, 1983), 139; Walker, *Sense and Nonsense about Crime*, chapters 1, 5, 6, and 11.

37. See the excellent review of these issues in American Law Institute, *Model Penal Code and Commentaries*, 3, 11–30.

38. *Ravin v. State*, 537 P.2d 494 (Alaska 1975), excerpted in chapter 2.

39. Texas Penal Code, § 31.03(5)(a)(1) (St. Paul, Minn.: West Publishing Co., 1988).

40. Sir William Blackstone, *Commentaries*, book IV.

41. LaFave and Scott, *Criminal Law*, p. 59.

42. *The Growth of the Law* (New Haven, Conn.: Yale University Press, 1924), p. 62.

43. *State v. Mellenberger*, 163 Or. 233, 95 P.2d 709 (1939) overruling *State v. Alexander*, 76 Or. 329, 148 P. 1136 (1915).

44. *West's Florida Statutes Annotated* (1991), Title XLVI, § 775.01.

45. Max Farrand, ed., *The Laws and Liberties of Massachusetts* (Cambridge, Mass.: Harvard University Press, 1929), A2.

46. Ibid., pp. 5, 6.

47. Julian P. Bond, ed., *The Papers of Thomas Jefferson*, vol. 2 (Princeton, N.J.: Princeton University Press, 1950) reprints this proposed code and Jefferson's fascinating notes about it. Also, Kathryn Preyer's "Crime, the Criminal Law and Reform in Post-Revolutionary Virginia," *Law and History Review* 1 (1983):53–85, contains an informative discussion about Jefferson's code.

48. 11 U.S. (7 Cranch) 32, 3 L.Ed. 259 (1812).

49. American Law Institute, *Model Penal Code and Commentaries*, part I, § 1.01 to 2.13 (Philadelphia: American Law Institute, 1985), 75–80.

50. § 13A-1-4, Code of Alabama 1975.

51. 2 Cal. 3d 619, 87 Cal.Rptr. 481, 470 P.2d 617 (Cal. 1970).

52. *West's California Penal Code* (St. Paul, Minn.: West Publishing Company, 1988) § 187(a).

53. LaFave and Scott, *Criminal Law*, pp. 68–69.

54. *State v. McFeely*, 25 N.J. Misc. 303, 52 A.2d 823 (Quar.Sess. 1947).

55. Herbert Packer, "The Aims of the Criminal Law Revisited: A Plea for a New Look at 'Substantive Due Process,'" *Southern California Law Review* 44 (1970–71):490–498.

56. A useful survey of the *Model Penal Code* written by its leading light can be found in Herbert Wechsler, "The Model Penal Code and the Codification of American Criminal Law," Roger Hood, ed., *Crime, Criminology, and Public Policy* (London: Heineman, 1974), pp. 419–468; American Law Institute, tentative drafts 1–13 (Philadelphia: American Law Institute, 1954–61).

57. An excellent discussion of some of these matters appears in David W. Neubauer, *Criminal Justice in Middle America* (Morristown, N.J.: General Learning Press, 1974), pp. 86–105. For an earlier but provocative analysis, see Jerome Frank, *Courts on Trial: Myth and Reality in American Justice* (Princeton, N.J.: Princeton University Press, 1949), chap. 14.

58. Emile Durkheim, *The Division of Labor in Society* (New York: Free Press, 1933), pp. 73–80; the insight concerning policy formulation stems from the research of Timothy Lenz, Department of Political Science, University of Minnesota.

59. George B. Vold and Thomas J. Bernard, *Theoretical Criminology*, 3d ed. (New York: Oxford University Press, 1986); chapters 14 through 16 develop these points fully.

60. For good introductions to this theory, see Richard Quinney, *Criminology*, 2d ed. (Boston: Little, Brown, 1979), pp. 120–125; and William Chambliss and Robert Seidman, *Law, Order, and Power*, 2d ed. (Reading, Mass.: Addison-Wesley, 1982), pp. 171–207.

61. Peter Rossi et al., "The Seriousness of Crimes: Normative Structure and Individual Differences," *American Sociological Review* 39 (1974): 224–237; William J. Chambliss, "The Law of Vagrancy," in *Criminal Law in Action*, 2d ed., edited by William J. Chambliss (New York: Macmillan, 1984), pp. 33–42.

62. An excellent introduction to discretion is Kenneth Culp Davis, *Discretionary Justice* (Baton Rouge, La.: Louisiana State University Press, 1969).

63. Sir Nicholas Bacon, quoted in Joel Samaha, "Hanging for Felony," *Historical Journal* (1979):75.

64. Ibid., pp. 769–771.

65. Edwin H. Sutherland and Donald R. Cressey, *Criminology*, 10th ed., rev. (Philadelphia: Lippincott, 1978), pp. 333–334.

66. Edwin Sutherland, "The Sexual Psychopath Laws," *Journal of Criminal Law, Criminology, and Police Science* 40 (1950):543–554.

67. Francis A. Allen, *The Borderland of Criminal Justice* (Chicago: University of Chicago Press, 1964), p. 15.

68. Holmes's famous aphorism appears in *New York Trust Company v. Eisner*, 256 U.S. 345, 41 S.Ct. 506, 65 L.Ed. 963 (1921), 349.

69. See Rollin M. Perkins and Ronald N. Boyce, *Criminal Law*, 3d ed. (Mineola, N.Y.: Foundation Press, 1982), pp. 289–292; and American Law Institute, *Model Penal Code and Commentaries*, vol. 2, pp. 128–130. For a full and interesting treatment of the relationship of history and society to theft, see Jerome Hall, *Theft, Law, and Society* (Indianapolis, Ind.: Bobbs-Merrill, 1952).

70. Joel Samaha, "John Winthrop and the Criminal Law," *William Mitchell Law Review* (1989):217.

71. Quoted in Sanford Kadish and Manfred Paulson, *Criminal Law and Its Processes*, 3d ed., rev. (Boston and Toronto: Little, Brown, 1975), p. 40.

CHAPTER TWO

Constitutional Limits on Criminal Law

CHAPTER OUTLINE

CHAPTER MAIN POINTS

1. The United States Constitution creates a balance between the need for government power to control crime and criminals and the need to control excesses of government power.

2. The Constitution requires that the law define crimes and prescribe penalties before prosecution and punishment.

3. The Constitution requires that criminal statutes define crimes with enough clarity to both notify individuals as to what the law prohibits and prevent law enforcement officers from abusing their discretion.

4. The Constitution allows classifications in criminal law that treat one group of citizens differently from other groups, but such classifications must have a rational basis.

5. The right of privacy, implicit in the U.S. Constitution, and specifically provided for in some state constitutions, prohibits making crimes out of behavior protected by the right of privacy.

6. The Constitution prohibits making a crime out of speech protected by the First Amendment.

7. The Constitution prohibits the infliction of "cruel and unusual punishments," that is, both "barbaric" punishments and punishments disproportionate to the seriousness of the crime.

Was Metzger's Behavior Indecent, Immodest, or Filthy?

Metzger lived in Lincoln, Nebraska, in a garden-level apartment with a large window facing a parking lot. At about 7:45 A.M., on April 30, 1981, another resident of the building was parking his automobile in a space directly in front of Metzger's apartment window. While doing so, he observed, for a period of 5 seconds, Metzger standing naked in the window with his arms at his sides. The resident testified that he saw Metzger's body from the thighs up.

The resident called the police, and two officers arrived at the apartment at about 8 A.M. The officers testified that they observed Metzger standing in front of the window, within a foot of it, eating a bowl of cereal, and that his naked body was visible from the mid-thigh up.

INTRODUCTION

The authors of the United States Constitution created a complex structure in order to balance the need for government power to control crime and criminals with the need to control excesses of government power. According to James Madison, president of the United States and eighteenth-century American political theorist:

> If men were angels, no government would be necessary. If angels were to govern men, neither external nor internal controls on government would be necessary. In framing a government which is to be administered by men over men, the great difficulty is this: You must first enable the government to control the governed; and in the next place, oblige it to control itself.[1]

As we saw in chapter 1, criminal law consists of the power of the state to define, prohibit, and punish behavior as criminal—the power to "control the governed" in Madison's famous passage. But criminal law in a constitutional democracy requires limits on that state power—limits that "oblige the government to control itself," according to Madison. Chapter 1 touched on the effects of the common-law tradition and the federal system on the power of the state to define, prohibit, and punish crimes. Chapters 3 through 7 examine in some detail the boundaries placed on the criminal law by the general principles of criminal liability, justification, and excuse, and the doctrines of attempt, conspiracy, solicitation, complicity, and vicarious liability. Chapters 8 through 12 analyze how the definitions of specific crimes limit the reach of the criminal law. This chapter focuses on the U.S. Constitution and parallel provisions in state constitutions that "oblige the government to control itself." These constitutional limits include:

1. Legality
2. "Void for vagueness"
3. Equal protection of the law
4. Prohibition against *ex post facto* laws
5. Freedom of speech
6. Right to privacy
7. Right against "cruel and unusual punishment."

THE PRINCIPLE OF LEGALITY

The U.S. Constitution rests on the popular eighteenth-century idea of the rule of law. The rule of law, stated here as the principle of legality, requires that rules not whim govern both the creation of crimes and the punishments for committing them. The principle of legality is deeply embedded in the U.S. Constitution, the state constitutions, and in the statutes and judicial decisions of federal and state courts. The **principle of legality** states that the government can punish people only if specific laws have defined the crime clearly and prescribed the punishment specifically.

VOID-FOR-VAGUENESS DOCTRINE

The **due process clauses** of the Fifth and Fourteenth Amendments to the U.S. Constitution prohibit the federal and state governments from depriving any person of "life, liberty, or property without due process of law." Criminal punishment involves the deprivation of life, liberty, or property. Some criminal statutes define criminal behavior so vaguely that neither private persons nor law enforcement officers know what the law prohibits. Punishing behavior defined that vaguely deprives persons of life, liberty, or property without due process of law. According to the **void-for-vagueness doctrine,** statutes that do not adequately warn both private individuals and law enforcement officers what the law prohibits violate the due process clauses of the Fifth and Fourteenth Amendments.

The Constitution does not specifically prohibit vague laws. Nevertheless, the refusal of courts to enforce vague and uncertain laws has a long history. Under the common law of England and colonial America, judges refused to enforce vague statutes. The United States Supreme Court from early in its history refused to enforce uncertain laws. First, according to the Court, they violated the separation of powers. The Court likened clarifying vague statutes to making new ones. Only legislatures can make laws, not courts. In addition, the Court ruled that vague laws denied defendants in criminal cases their Sixth Amendment right to know "the nature and cause of the accusation" against them.

In the twentieth century, the Court formulated a two-pronged test to determine whether laws are void-for-vagueness. One prong is aimed at private individuals, the other at criminal justice officials:

1. Provide fair warning to individuals as to what the law prohibits.

2. Prevent arbitrary and discriminatory criminal justice administration.

At first, the Supreme Court focused on the aim of fair warning to citizens. In *Lanzetta v. New Jersey*, for example, the Supreme Court struck down a statute that made it a crime to be a member of a "gang." After holding that the word *gang* was too vague to give fair warning, the Court commented:

> No one may be required at peril of life, liberty, or property to speculate as to the meaning of penal statutes. All are entitled to be informed as to what the State commands or forbids. . . . [A] statute which either forbids or requires the doing of an act in terms so vague that men of common intelligence must necessarily guess at its meaning and differ as to its application, violates the first essential of due process of law.[2]

The Court has also ruled that in addition to defining a statute "with sufficient definiteness that ordinary people can understand what conduct is prohibited," it must do so in a manner that does not encourage arbitrary and discriminatory law enforcement; hence, the two prongs of the doctrine. The first points to ordinary people, requiring that they receive fair warning about the possible criminality of their conduct; the second points to criminal justice officials, requiring that they refrain from abusing their discretionary power. On occasion, the Court has even gone so far as to hold that the "more important aspect of the vagueness doctrine is not actual notice, but the other principal element of the vagueness doctrine—the requirement that a legislature establish minimal guidelines to govern law enforcement."[3]

 HOW TO READ, ANALYZE, AND FIND CASES

In *State v. Metzger*, which appears just after this section, you will encounter your first case. In the case, the Nebraska Supreme Court was faced with the question of whether a Lincoln, Nebraska, indecent exposure ordinance was void for vagueness. Cases are an integral part of this book; they are essential to understanding the principles, doctrines, and rules of criminal law. Cases bring criminal law to life. In the cases, courts apply the abstract general principles, doctrines,

and rules presented in the text to events involving real people in real life. Therefore, it is important that you know how to read and analyze these cases. It is also useful for you to know how to find cases. You may want to look up other cases that are referred to in the cases presented here, that are mentioned in the text, and that your instructor brings up in class.

Notice that the cases in this book are excerpts, that is, shortened, edited versions of the complete reports

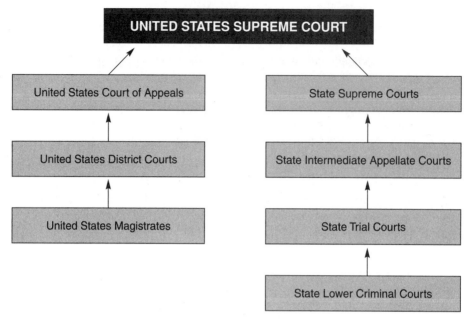

FIGURE 2.1 CRIMINAL COURT STRUCTURE

of the cases. Ellipses (. . .) represent deletions; added material appears inside brackets ([ ]).

In most of the case excerpts, a jury (or in cases without juries, the trial court judge) has already convicted the accused, and the convicted defendant is now asking a higher court to review the trial court's decision and/or the jury's *guilty* verdict (see Figure 2.1). Notice that you will never read a review of a jury's "*not* guilty" verdict. In the criminal law of the United States, a jury's acquittal is final and not subject to review.

The review of criminal convictions takes several forms. Convicted defendants may ask the trial court for a new trial. If this request fails, they may appeal a trial court's decision directly to an **appellate court** (in most cases, a state supreme court, but sometimes to an intermediate appellate court). These appeals are called appellate cases, those who appeal them are called **appellants,** and the parties appealed against are called **appellees.** Convicted defendants are most often appellants in criminal cases. Most case excerpts in this book are appellate cases in which convicted defendants are

appellants and states are appellees. These defendants are appealing their convictions, asking appellate courts to overturn, or reverse, them.

Convicted defendants may also challenge the trial court's jurisdiction by another procedure called **collateral attack.** Collateral attacks are not appeals; they are actions that challenge the authority of a court to hear a case, or that challenge the legality of a detention in a prison or jail. The most widely known collateral attack (although not the only one) is **habeas corpus.** The proceeding begins by the habeas corpus petition. In this petition, a prisoner asks for a court order demanding that the agency detaining the prisoner demonstrate that the agency has the legal authority to incarcerate the prisoner. Defendants who proceed by collateral attack are called **petitioners.**

The case excerpts focus on the principles, doctrines, and rules of criminal law. You should read them with that in mind. Ask yourself what principle, doctrine, or rule does this case elucidate, and to what specific relevant facts does the principle, doctrine, or rule apply.

The case excerpts begin with the title of the case and its **citation,** that is, the reference to the published report where it appears in full. The name of the judge who wrote the court's opinion follows. Then appear the facts of the case. Facts are always the critical starting point for understanding the principles, doctrines, and rules at issue. The court's opinion follows. It is in the opinion that the court applies the law to the facts of the case. The opinion contains two essential ingredients:

1. The court's **holding**—the legal rule that the court has decided applies to the facts of the cases.

2. The court's **reasoning**—the reasons it gives to support its holding.

Occasionally, such as in *State v. Metzger,* the first case excerpt in this book, both a **majority opinion** and a **dissent,** or minority opinion, appear. A majority opinion, as its name indicates, represents the majority of the justices on the court. For an opinion to become the binding interpretation of the law, a majority of justices must vote for it. Although the majority opinion represents the established law of the case, the dissent usually presents a plausible alternative resolution to the question of the case.

Dissents of former times frequently become the law of later times. In criminal procedure law, for example, many dissents of the 1960s have become the law of the 1990s, and before that many dissents of the 1930s became the law of the 1960s. Occasionally, **concurring opinions** appear. In concurring opinions, justices agree with the judgment of the court but not the reasons. This can lead to a **plurality opinion,** an opinion in which a majority stands behind the result in the case but cannot agree on the reasons for the result.

To get the most from the cases, concentrate on answering the following questions about each case excerpt:

1. *What are the facts?* Be prepared to state the facts in simple narrative form in chronological order. As one law professor said, "Tell me the story as if you were telling it to your grandmother." Then, select, sort, and arrange the facts into the following categories:
   a. Actions of the defendant.

   b. Intent of the defendant, or if not relevant, say none.
   c. Harm, or if not relevant, say none.
   d. Cause of the harm, or if not relevant, say none.
   e. Justification or excuse, or defense(s), if relevant. If not, say none.

2. *What is the legal issue in the case?* That is, what question or problem regarding the principles, doctrines, and rules of criminal law does the case raise?

3. *What is the court's holding?* In other words, what answer does the court give to the problem raised in the case?

4. *What is the court's opinion?* That is, what reasons does the court give for its decision and holdings? How did it arrive at the conclusions it reached? The court's reasoning, or opinion, applies the general principle, doctrine, and rule to the facts of the case.

5. *How did the court dispose of the case?* Did the court **affirm** (agree with and uphold) the trial court's decision, **reverse** it (set it aside and substitute its own decision), reverse it in part (partially reverse and partially affirm it), or **remand** it (send the case back to the trial court for further proceedings in accord with the appellate opinion)?

You cannot answer all these questions in every case, especially at this point. The answers depend on knowledge that you will accumulate as this text and your instructor introduce more principles, doctrines, and rules. Furthermore, courts do not necessarily follow the same procedure in reviewing an appeal as that outlined above. Finally, not all of the issues raised in item 1 ("What are the facts?") arise in every case.

Developing the skills needed to sort out the elements of the case excerpts requires practice but is worth the effort. Answering the questions given here can challenge you to think not only about the basic principles, doctrines, and rules of criminal law but also about your personal values concerning life, property, privacy, and morals.

For those who wish to go further and read the full cases excerpted here, or who wish to read cases referred to in either the text or the cases, I have included the case citation. You will notice that numbers, letters, and punctuation follow the title of a case in the excerpts, or in the endnote referencing cases in the text. These symbols tell you where to locate the full case report.

For example, in the first excerpt that follows this section, just after the title of the case, *State v. Metzger*, you read "211 Neb. 593, 319 N.W.2d 459 (1982)." This citation indicates that you can find this case reported in two places: the *Nebraska Reports*, designated by the abbreviation "Neb." and the *Northwestern Reports*, second series, designated by the abbreviation "N.W.2d". These are multivolume sets that report the appellate cases in Nebraska and several other states in the central region of the United States. The number preceding the title indicates the volume of the reports in which the case appears. Hence, *State v. Metzger* appears in volume 211 of the Nebraska Reports and in volume 319 of the *Northwestern Reports*, second series. The number following the title of the reports indicates on which page of the volume the case appears. Thus, *State v. Metzger* appears on page 593, volume 211 of the Nebraska Reports and on page 459 of volume 319 of the Northwestern Reports, second series. The symbols inside the parentheses include the state court opinion reported and the year the court decided the case. Hence, the Nebraska Supreme Court decided *State v. Metzger* in 1982. You can tell if the court was the highest or an intermediate appellate court by the abbreviation. For example, if this were an intermediate appellate court decision, the abbreviation would read "Neb.App." If only the name of the state appears, such as in *State v. Metzger*, then you know that it is the report of a decision of the highest appellate court in the state. These highest appellate state courts are usually known as supreme courts.

Study the unedited case of *State v. Knight* reproduced here. I have annotated it both to help you to learn how to analyze the case excerpts throughout the book and to help you to read other cases that you may want to look up or that your instructor may require or recommend that you go to the library and read. The regular text represents the court's writing; the texts in brackets are my annotations.

STATE of Delaware v. William KNIGHT, Defendant

[This is the full title of the case. When citing the case in other opinions, in books such as this textbook, and

other publications, you will only see the short title, or the words in capital letters, that is, *State v. Knight*.]

Superior Court of Delaware, New Castle County

[This is the name of the court that decided the case reported here.]

Submitted: Dec. 15, 1993.

[This is the date the court heard arguments on the motions submitted to the court.]

Decided: Jan. 19, 1994.

[This is the date the Superior Court of Delaware, New Castle County, ruled on the motions.]

(1994 WL 19938 (Del.Super.)

[This is the citation to West Publishing Company's electronic online database of reported cases. You would enter it to retrieve the report of the case. The "1994 WL" means the case was decided in 1994 and WL refers to Westlaw. The "19938" is the rest of the citation required to retrieve the case. "Del. Sup" refers to the Superior Court of the state of Delaware.]

Ferris W. Wharton, Deputy Atty. Gen., Dept. of Justice, Wilmington, for State.

[This is the name of the attorney representing the state who argued against the motions submitted by the defendant.]

Michael P. Maguire, Wilmington, for defendant.

[This is the name of the attorney for the defendant who argued in favor of the motions.]

OPINION

CARPENTER, JUDGE.

On December 7, 1992, the defendant was indicted [the formal criminal charge that begins criminal prosecution] for stalking, in violation of 11 Del.C. Section 1312A. [This is the citation of the Delaware anti-stalking statute.] After a two day trial, the defendant was found guilty. On November 4, 1993, the defendant filed a "Motion for Judgment N.O.V. ["non obstante veredicto," or a motion asking that the court enter a judgment of not guilty even though the jury found the defendant guilty] and For a New Trial." The motion alleges that (a) the state failed to prove that the activities of the defendant caused the victim substantial emotional distress, (b) the evidence failed to demonstrate that the actions of the defendant were performed maliciously, and (c) the state failed to show that the defendant's conduct served no legitimate purpose. The Court will treat the defendant's request as a Motion for Judgment of Acquittal under Rule 29 of the Rules of Criminal Procedure for the Superior Court. [The court is treating the two motions for a judgment of acquittal.]

I.

In considering a Motion for Judgment of Acquittal under Rule 29 of the Rules of Criminal Procedure for the Superior Court, the Court is required to review the evidence and all legitimately drawn inferences in the light most favorable to the state. Only when the prosecution has presented insufficient evidence to support the guilty verdict [Enough evidence to support a guilty verdict means proof beyond a reasonable doubt.] can the motion be granted. [The court is explaining the requirement for granting a motion for acquittal following a guilty verdict.] *Vouras v. State*, Del.Supr., 452 A.2d 1165 (1982); *Conyers v. State*, Del.Supr., 396 A.2d 157 (1978). [In most cases excerpted in this book, you will not see most of these citations. They are the names and references to cases that support the court's interpretation of the requirement for granting a motion of acquittal. If you looked these cases up, they should say that only when the prosecution has not presented enough evidence to prove the defendant guilty beyond a reasonable doubt can the court grant a motion for acquittal.] Under this standard, there was clearly sufficient evidence to support the verdict, and the defendant's motion is denied. [This is a holding or ruling of the court and the reason for it.]

II.

While the Indictment charged that the defendant's stalking activity occurred between July and September 1992, to appreciate the trauma experienced by the victim in this case it is necessary to begin in the fall of 1990.[4] [The following are called "the facts of the case." Legal reasoning, sometimes called reasoning by example, requires that courts fit the facts of the case within the appropriate principle, doctrine, or rule. The facts concern the elements of the crime, or the ordi-nary phenomena of action, intention, causation, result, justification, excuse, and circumstances elaborated in the remaining chapters of this book.] At that time, the defendant entered a short term job training program offered at the Delaware Technical and Community College, Wilmington campus, specifically designed to assist the homeless. The victim was the lead counselor in the program and, as such, she provided counseling services to the twelve male participants in the program. Her responsibilities, in addition to assisting with classroom studies, included the referral and follow up to community agencies for participants to obtain housing, clothing and other specialized needs relating to their homeless status. It was in relation to this program that the defendant and the victim first met in September 1990.

Approximately a month and a half into the program, the defendant began to exhibit an infatuation with the victim, leaving love notes on her car and in her office. In the early stages of this obsession, the defendant was counseled concerning the professional relationship between the defendant and the victim and of the inappropriateness of his behavior. Unfortunately, his activities continued and the college administration advised the defendant that he could no longer have any contact with the victim, restricted him from the wing of the campus in which the victim's office was located, and assigned him a new counselor. The defendant refused to comply with the restrictions imposed by the college and was eventually banned completely from the Delaware Technical and Community College campus. [These facts relate to both the actions and the intentions of the defendant.]

Instead of curtailing the activity, the reasonable actions of the college appeared only to increase the defendant's fixation toward the victim. He began to call her at home and to leave notes on her car reflecting a desire to make love to her and insisting that it was "God's will" that they be together. As a result of the defendant's persistent behavior, the victim believed that her safety and that of her roommates was in jeopardy and decided to move from their townhouse in April 1991 in the hope of "starting over." Within weeks of the move, the defendant located the victim's new residence and again attempted to contact her. On one occasion, the defendant came to the victim's home and became belligerent when she refused to open the door. The victim contacted police and the defendant was arrested on harassment charges. The Court imposed a no contact order but the defendant continued to send her letters and, within months, appeared again at her apartment. [This paragraph states more facts relating to the actions and the intentions of the defendant.]

After learning that additional criminal charges were outstanding because of his continued harassment of the victim, the defendant left the area and moved to North Carolina. Unfortunately, the move failed to change the defendant's behavior. Over a period of months, the defendant sent thousands of love letters, poems, a subscription to Bride Magazine and mail order catalogs that specialized in wedding invitations to the victim. The defendant was eventually arrested in North Carolina and extradited back to Delaware to answer to these charges. [This paragraph contains yet more facts relating to the actions and the intentions of the defendant.]

III.

The relevant part of 11 Del.C. Section 1312A requires that the defendant "wilfully, maliciously and repeatedly follow or harass another person" to be guilty of the crime of stalking. Subsection (b)(1) of the statute defines "harasses" as: ". . . a knowing and wilful course of conduct directed at a specific person which seriously alarms, annoys or harasses the person, and which serves no legitimate purpose. The course of conduct must be such as to cause a reasonable person to suffer substantial emotional distress, and must actually cause substantial emotional distress to the person." [This part of the opinion identifies the major issue or legal question of the case: Did the defendant's actions and intentions fit within the definition of the stalking statute? In other words, did the ordinary phenomena of action and intention become the *actus reus* and *mens rea* of stalking under the Delaware statute?] The defendant first argues that the state has failed to establish that the victim suffered substantial emotional distress because of his activity. The Court finds this assertion to be totally without merit. [These sentences and the following paragraphs consist of the arguments and reasoning of the court that led to its

conclusion or decision that the defendant's actions and intentions did amount to stalking and therefore did violate the Delaware statute.]

It is unrefuted that the defendant's course of conduct created a sense of hopelessness in the victim, since all reasonable means to stop the defendant's behavior had proven fruitless. The victim testified that she feared for her safety; had developed a feeling of losing control over her life; had difficulty sleeping and eating; had nightmares over the events; twice changed residence in an attempt to prevent his contact; and finally left her chosen field of employment, counseling, as a result of the trauma she experienced from the defendant's activity. Under these facts, the Court finds that there was sufficient evidence to establish that the defendant's behavior not only caused substantial emotional distress to the victim, but that the victim's reactions were reasonable under the circumstances.

The Court is not persuaded by the defendant's argument that, to demonstrate substantial emotional distress, the state is required to present independent medical testimony on this issue. There is no requirement to present such testimony under the statute and to do so would only traumatize the victim further. The credibility of the victim was an issue for the jury to decide, and their decision to believe her version of the events and the effect it had on her personal and professional life is clearly supported by the evidence.

The defendant's second argument in support of his motion is that, since his actions were initiated to only express his love and affection for the victim, the state has failed to establish that his actions were performed maliciously. In its instructions to the jury, the Court indicated that the jury was required to find that the defendant's actions were performed "wilfully, maliciously and repeatedly." In defining for the jury the term "maliciously," the Court stated: "The word 'maliciously' means it imports a wish to vex, annoy, or injure another or an intent to do a wrongful act without just cause or in reckless disregard of another's rights." Regardless of the inferences one draws from the testimony provided in this case, there is no doubt that the defendant continued his actions in reckless disregard for the victim's fundamental right of privacy in spite of numerous attempts by the victim to stop his behavior. From having the defendant banned from the college campus to having him arrested for harassment, the victim did everything reasonable under the law to stop the defendant's behavior. For the defendant to now argue as a defense to this charge that he merely performed this outrageous conduct out of love for the victim is merely a reflection of the defendant's refusal to separate fantasy from reality. The defendant was repeatedly told by officials at Delaware Technical and Community College, by police, by the Court, and by the victim that his activity was unwelcome and annoying. In spite of these warnings, the defendant chose to continue to perform these acts in violation of a Court order and in obvious reckless disregard for the rights of the victim. The jury could easily find sufficient evidence to believe the acts of the defendant were performed maliciously.

Finally, the defendant argues that the state has failed to show that the course of conduct of the defendant served no legitimate purpose as required under the statute. In support of his argument, the defendant asserts his desire for "closure" in his alleged relationship with the victim as a legitimate purpose. The court finds this argument to be totally without merit. There was no personal relationship between the defendant and the victim except for what may have existed in the fantasy world of the defendant. To attempt to legitimatize his actions by arguing the need to seek some sort of psychological "closure" for himself of a non-existent relationship is outrageous. A defendant cannot attempt to justify his illegal actions by arguing that "closure" of a relationship is a legitimate purpose of harassment activity. The Court strongly rejects this argument.

IV.

Based upon the foregoing, it is ordered that the defendant's motion for acquittal is DENIED. [This is the court's decision or judgment, in this case the denial of the defendant's motion for acquittal.]

The void-for-vagueness doctrine cannot cure, although it might reduce, the ambiguity that inheres in all laws. Words can never match the precision of numbers. Besides, lawmakers cannot foresee all the variations that might arise under statutes. As a result, no litmus test can mark a law "vague." *State v. Metzger* is a good example of a court having to deal with the ambiguity inherent in statutes.

C A S E

Was the Ordinance Void for Vagueness?

State v. Metzger,
211 Neb. 593, 319 N.W.2d 459 (1982)

Douglas E. Metzger was convicted in the Municipal Court of Lincoln, Nebraska, of violating § 9.52.100 of the Lincoln Municipal Code. The judgment was affirmed by the District Court for Lancaster County, Nebraska, and Metzger appealed. Reversed and dismissed. Chief Justice Krivosha wrote the opinion of the court.

FACTS

Metzger lived in a garden-level apartment located in Lincoln, Nebraska. A large window in the apartment faces a parking lot which is situated on the north side of the apartment building. At about 7:45 A.M., on April 30, 1981, another resident of the apartment, while parking his automobile in a space directly in front of Metzger's apartment window, observed Metzger standing naked with his arms at his sides in his apartment window for a period of 5 seconds. The resident testified that he saw Metzger's body from the thighs on up.

The resident called the police department and two officers arrived at the apartment at about 8 A.M. The officers testified that they observed Metzger standing in front of the window eating a bowl of cereal. They testified that Metzger was standing within a foot of the window and his nude body, from the mid-thigh on up, was visible.

OPINION

... The pertinent portion of § 9.52.100 ... under which Metzger was charged, provides as follows:

"It shall be unlawful for any person within the City of Lincoln ... to commit any indecent, immodest or filthy act in the presence of any person, or in such a situation that persons passing might ordinarily see the same." ...

The ... basic issue presented to us by this appeal is whether the ordinance, as drafted, is so vague as to be unconstitutional. We believe that it is. There is no argument that a violation of the municipal ordinance in question is a criminal act. Since the ordinance in question is criminal in nature, it is a fundamental requirement of due process of law that such criminal ordinance be reasonably clear and definite. Moreover, a crime must be defined with sufficient definiteness and there must be ascertainable standards of guilt to inform those subject thereto as to what conduct will render them liable to punishment thereunder.

The dividing line between what is lawful and unlawful cannot be left to conjecture. A citizen cannot be held to answer charges based upon penal statutes whose mandates are so uncertain that they will reasonably admit of different constructions. A criminal statute cannot rest upon an uncertain foundation. The crime and the elements constituting it must be so clearly expressed that the ordinary person can intelligently choose in advance what course it is lawful for him to pursue. Penal statutes prohibiting the doing of certain things and providing a punishment for their violation should not admit of such a double meaning that the citizen may act upon one conception of its requirements and the courts upon another.

A statute which forbids the doing of an act in terms so vague that men of common intelligence must necessarily guess as to its meaning and differ as to its application violates the first essential elements of due process of law. It is not permissible to enact a law which in effect spreads an all-inclusive net for the feet of everybody upon the chance that, while the innocent will surely be entangled in its meshes, some wrongdoers may also be caught. *State v. Adkins*, 196 Neb. 76, 241 N.W.2d 655 (1976).

In *State ex rel. English v. Ruback*, 135 Neb. 335, 281 N.W. 607 (1938), this court laid down guidelines to assist in determining whether a statute defining an offense is void for uncertainty. In *Ruback*, we said: "The test to determine whether a statute defining an offense is void for uncertainty (1) is whether the language may apply not only to a particular act about which there can be little or no difference of opinion, but equally to other acts about which there may be radical differences, thereby devolving on the court the exercise of arbitrary power of discriminating between the several classes of acts. (2) The dividing line between what is lawful and what is unlawful cannot be left to conjecture."

In the case of *Papachristou v. City of Jacksonville*, 405 U.S. 156, 162, 92 S.Ct. 839, 31 L.Ed.2d 110 (1972), the U.S. Supreme Court said: "Living under a rule of law entails various suppositions, one of which is that '[all persons] are entitled to be informed as to what the State commands or forbids.'" In *Papachristou*, the U.S. Supreme Court declared a vagrancy statute of the city of Jacksonville, Florida, invalid for vagueness, saying: "This aspect of the vagrancy ordinance before us is suggested by what this Court said in 1876 about a broad criminal statute enacted by Congress: 'It would certainly be dangerous if the legislature could set a net large enough to catch all possible offenders, and leave it to the courts to step inside and say who could be rightfully detained, and who should be set at large.'"

Several other jurisdictions which have viewed ordinances with the same general intent in mind have reached similar conclusions. In the case of *State v. Sanders*, 37 N.C.App. 53, 245 S.E.2d 397 (1978), the North Carolina Court of Appeals was presented with a statute making it a misdemeanor for members of the opposite sex to occupy the same bedroom at a hotel for "any immoral purpose." In finding the ordinance too vague and indefinite to comply with constitutional due process standards, the court said: "A criminal statute or ordinance must be sufficiently definite to inform citizens of common intelligence of the particular acts which are forbidden. G.S. 14–186 [the statute] fails to define with sufficient precision exactly what the term 'any immoral purpose' may encompass."

The word "immoral" is not equivalent to the word "illegal"; hence, enforcement of G.S. 14–186 may involve legal acts which, nevertheless, are immoral in the view of many citizens. One must necessarily speculate, therefore, as to what acts are immoral. If the legislative intent of G.S. 14–186 is to proscribe illicit sexual intercourse the statute could have specifically so provided."

And in the case of *City of Detroit v. Sanchez*, 18 Mich.App. 399, 171 N.W.2d 452 (1969), the Michigan Court of Appeals was asked to determine whether an ordinance prohibiting ogling, insulting, annoying, following, or pursuing any person in any public street in the city was overbroad. In holding the ordinance void, the Michigan court said: "We are compelled to decide this because this provision of the ordinance is unconstitutionally vague.

By 'vague' we do not mean here that sort of vagueness . . . [in which] the ordinance is put in terms which require men of common intelligence to guess as to its meaning and differ as to its application. The vagueness which invalidates this ordinance is its overbreadth of coverage rather than imprecise terminology or phraseology. The conviction cannot be sustained, because the ordinance makes criminal innocent as well as culpable conduct."

The ordinance in question makes it unlawful for anyone to commit any "indecent, immodest or filthy act." We know of no way in which the standards required of a criminal act can be met in those broad, general terms. There may be those few who believe persons of opposite sex holding hands in public are immodest, and certainly who might believe that kissing in public is immodest. Such acts cannot constitute a crime. Certainly one could find many who would conclude that today's swimming attire found on many beaches or beside many pools is immodest. Yet, the fact that it is immodest does not thereby make it illegal, absent some requirement related to the health, safety, or welfare of the community.

The dividing line between what is lawful and what is unlawful in terms of "indecent," "immodest," or "filthy" is simply too broad to satisfy the constitutional requirements of due process. Both lawful and unlawful acts can be embraced within such broad definitions. That cannot be permitted. One is not able to determine in advance what is lawful and what is unlawful. We do not attempt, in this opinion, to determine whether Metzger's actions in a particular case might not be made unlawful, nor do we intend to encourage such behavior. Indeed, it may be possible that a governmental subdivision using sufficiently definite language could make such an act as committed by Metzger unlawful. We simply do not decide that question at this time because of our determination that the ordinance is so vague as to be unconstitutional.

We therefore believe that § 9.52.100 of the Lincoln Municipal Code must be declared invalid. Because the ordinance is therefore declared invalid, the conviction cannot stand. Reversed and Dismissed.

DISSENT

Boslaugh, Justice, dissenting.

The ordinance in question prohibits indecent acts, immodest acts, or filthy acts in the presence of any person. Although the ordinance may be too broad in some respects . . . [t]he exhibition of [Metzger's] genitals under the circumstances of this case was, clearly, an indecent act. Statutes and ordinances prohibiting indecent exposure generally have been held valid. I do not subscribe to the view that it is only "possible" that such conduct may be prohibited by statute or ordinance.

Clinton and Hastings, JJ., join in this dissent.

QUESTIONS FOR DISCUSSION

1. In your understanding of the words, was Metzger standing in front of his window naked: "Immodest"? "Indecent"? "Filthy"?

2. How does the court conclude that these words in the ordinance are vague?

3. Does the dissenting justice have a point when he argues that displaying genitals when others can see them is clearly an indecent act? Or does the ordinance refer to intentionally exposing genitals, or "flashing"?

NOTE CASES

1. Graham struck Suzanne Olson on the face, legs, and arms with "a four-foot metal floor lamp with a large metal base." A Minnesota statute provides: "Whoever assaults another with a deadly weapon . . . may be sentenced to imprisonment for not more than five years or to payment of a fine of not more than $5,000 or both." The statute defines dangerous weapon as "any device or instrumentality which, in the manner it is used or intended to be used, is calculated to produce death or great bodily harm." Did the statute invite arbitrary law enforcement due to its vagueness? No, said the court:

   > Due process does not . . . require impossible standards of clarity. It would be impossible to specify any and all objects capable of producing death or great bodily harm when used to inflict injury on another. . . . Whether the lamp as allegedly used in this case does constitute a dangerous weapon is

for the jury to determine. *State v. Graham*, 366 N.W.2d 335 (Minn. 1985)

2. A statute makes it a felony to possess a "switchblade or gravity knife." Is it void for vagueness? The court ruled that it was not: "The term has a readily ascertainable and consistent definition. As commonly understood, a gravity knife is one in which the blade opens, falls into place, or is ejected into position by the force of gravity or by centrifugal force." *State v. Weaver*, 736 P.2d 781 (Alaska App.1987)

3. A statute provides: "Whoever has in his possession any device, gear, or instrument specially designed to assist in shoplifting . . . may be sentenced to . . . not more than three years of imprisonment and to payment of a fine of not more than $5,000, or both." Danny Skinner wore a long blue trench coat into a discount store. The coat had a hidden pocket beneath the lining. He argued that the statute was void for vagueness because it did not specify what items qualified as "specially designed" shoplifting gear, by whom the device must be specifically designed, whether the item must be purchased from a manufacturer or altered after purchase, and whether common items of everyday use can qualify as shoplifting gear.

   Was the statute void for vagueness? The court ruled that the statute was not void for vagueness: "The statute puts individuals on notice of the prohibited conduct, possession of 'gear specially designed to assist in shoplifting.' The language is clear and can be understood by an ordinary person." Is it as clear as the court says? *State v. Skinner*, 403 N.W.2d 912 (Minn.App.1987)

EQUAL PROTECTION
OF THE LAWS

In addition to the due process guarantee, the Fourteenth Amendment to the United States Constitution also provides that "no state shall deny to any person within its jurisdiction the equal protection of the laws." Equal protection does not require the government to treat everybody exactly alike. Specific statutes can—and frequently do— classify certain people and conduct for special treatment. For example, statutes classify embezzlement by public officials as a more serious crime than embezzlement by private citizens. Virtually every state labels premeditated killings as more heinous than negligent homicides. Several states punish habitual criminals more severely than first-time offenders. None of these classifications based on occupation, state of mind, and type of person violates the equal protection clause. Nor do statutes that exempt particular conduct or groups from criminal liability. For example, Sunday closing laws typically apply to large operations, not "mom and pop stores." In these kinds of classifications, the equal protection challenge to a statute is no more than "the usual last resort of constitutional arguments." With good reason. The courts almost always uphold these kinds of statutory classification schemes, striking down only statutory classifications that wholly lack any "reasonable basis." And it is up to defendants to prove that the scheme lacks a reasonable basis.[5]

Classifications based on race and gender are a different matter. Courts scrutinize race and gender much more carefully. According to the United States Supreme Court, any statute that

> invidiously classifies similarly situated people on the basis of the immutable characteristics with which they were born ... *always* [emphasis added] violates the Constitution, for the simple reason that, so far as the Constitution is concerned, people of different races are always similarly situated.[6]

Gender classifications are scrutinized more carefully than general classifications but less so than race classifications. Unlike race classifications, gender classifications are not always unconstitutional. On the other hand, they receive closer scrutiny than general classifications. The Supreme Court has had difficulty deciding exactly how carefully to scrutinize gender classifications in criminal statutes. The plurality, but not a majority, of the justices in *Michael M. v. Superior Court of Sonoma County* agreed that gender classifications must have a "fair and substantial relationship" to legitimate state ends.

The Alaska Court of Appeals applied the equal protection clauses of both the United States and the Alaska constitution to an age-based possession of marijuana criminal statute in *Allam v. State*.

C A S E

Did the Age Distinction Violate the Equal Protection Clause?

Allam v. State,
830 P.2d 435 (Alaska App. 1992)

Peter Allam pleaded no contest to a charge of possession of marijuana by a person under the age of 19. When he entered his plea, Allam preserved the right to challenge the constitutionality of this statute on appeal. The court imposed a suspended imposition of sentence conditioned on his good behavior for a period of 90 days, his performance of 24 hours of community work, and his being screened by the Alcohol Safety Action Program. The Alaska Court of Appeals

affirmed. Judge Mannheimer wrote the opinion for the court.

FACTS

On May 15, 1990, Allam was 18 years old and a senior at Dimond High School in Anchorage. He and the rest of his high school class were at Kincaid Park, participating in "Senior Fun Day," a school-sponsored event. Allam and three other boys, one of whom was also 18 years old and two of whom were under 18 years of age, left the main group of students and went off by themselves to an area several hundred yards away. A school official found the four of them rolling marijuana cigarettes. The boys were taken back to the high school, where school officials called the police. Allam and the other 18-year-old were arrested.

OPINION

Allam asserts that, under former AS 11.71.060(a), he and all other 18-year-olds were denied the equal protection of the law. He contends that the legislature unreasonably put 18-year-olds in a class by themselves: a person older than 18 who possessed up to four ounces of marijuana committed no crime, an 18-year-old like Allam who possessed the same amount of marijuana would be criminally prosecuted, while persons 17 years old or younger who possessed marijuana would be dealt with under the juvenile justice system. AS 47.10.010(a)(1). We reject Allam's attack on the statute and affirm his conviction.

The Alaska Supreme Court has recognized that the legislature may restrict minors' freedom in ways that would be unconstitutional if applied to adults. In *Hanby v. State*, 479 P.2d 486, 498 (Alaska 1970), the court upheld a criminal statute that prohibited the distribution or showing of certain sexually oriented material to minors, even though the material did not qualify as "obscene" and thus could not be banned for the general population. Similarly, in *Anderson v. State*, 562 P.2d 351, 358–59 (Alaska 1977), the court upheld criminal prohibitions on consensual sexual activity with minors. Lastly, in *Ravin v. State*, 537 P.2d 494, 511 & n. 69 (Alaska 1977), when the court declared that the Alaska Constitution protected marijuana possession and use in the privacy of one's home, the court emphasized that this rule did not apply to minors. . . .

Allam concedes that he has no fundamental or protected right to smoke or possess marijuana. He argues, however, that if the legislature allows people 19 years of age or older to engage in these activities then the equal protection clauses of the federal and state constitutions (United States Constitution, Fourteenth Amendment, Section 1; Alaska Constitution, Article I, Section 1) require the legislature to extend the same freedom of action to 18-year-olds. . . . Under federal equal protection law, when neither a fundamental

right nor a suspect or quasi-suspect classification is involved, a statute will satisfy the requirement of equal protection if it is rationally related to furthering a legitimate state interest. Under this test, a statute will not be invalidated unless its "varying treatment of different groups or persons is so unrelated to the achievement of any combination of legitimate purposes that . . . the legislature's actions were irrational." *Vance v. Bradley*, 440 U.S. 93, 97, 99 S.Ct. 939, 942–43, 59 L.Ed.2d 171 (1979). . . .

Former AS 11.71.060(a)(3) established 19 years as the age of majority for the purpose of regulating the possession of marijuana. This statute was passed in 1982, when the general age of majority was 18 years. Nevertheless, the legislative history of former AS 11.71.060 demonstrates that, for purposes of possessing and using marijuana, the legislature intended to set the age of majority at 19 years. The sectional analysis adopted by the legislature states that "the prohibition in paragraph 3 [of AS 11.71.060(a)] codifies a holding implicit in *Ravin v. State*, [537 P.2d 494, 511 & n. 69 (Alaska 1977)], that the protection afforded to adults in possessing small amounts of marijuana in the home for personal use does not apply to minors." 1982 House Journal, Supplement No. 4 (January 22) at 23.

The legislature's sectional analysis of Title 4 provides further evidence of the legislature's intent to make 19 years the age of majority for purposes of regulating alcohol and controlled substances. The House Journal's analysis of AS 11.71.010 (the statute prohibiting delivery of a scheduled IA controlled substance to a person under nineteen who is at least three years younger than the defendant) explains that "the cut-off age of nineteen has been selected in order to be consistent with laws involving alcohol in Title 04." In the sectional analysis of AS 04.16.050 (the statute prohibiting possession or consumption of alcohol by persons under the age of nineteen), the statute is described as a prohibition on "minors consuming." 1980 Senate Journal, Supplement No. 23 (April 1) at 16. In the analyses of other sections of Title 4, the legislature repeatedly refers to persons under the age of nineteen as "minors."

Thus, while the Alaska legislature has, since 1977, been willing to recognize 18-year-olds as legal adults in most respects, the legislature has consistently affirmed its view that, for purposes of alcohol and drug use, the age of majority should be set higher.

To satisfy the requirement of . . . [equal protection] legislation must be rationally related to a valid legislative purpose. The Alaska Supreme Court has repeatedly recognized the protection of minors as a valid legislative purpose. *Anderson v. State*, 562 P.2d 351; *Ravin v. State*, 537 P.2d 494; *L.A.M. v. State*, 547 P.2d 827; and *Hanby v. State*, 479 P.2d 486. Within our system of government, subject to constitutional limitations, it is the legislature's prerogative to restrict or forbid the use of dangerous intoxicants and, if a restriction is based on age, to establish the age at which persons can presumably be trusted to handle those intoxicants in a mature and socially acceptable manner. Former AS 11.71.060(a)(3) set the age for marijuana use at 19 years. We conclude that this choice was rational.

Allam concedes that the legislature's current decision to establish the drinking age at 21 years is supported by "years of scientific study and years of conscious legislative debate." If a drinking age of either 19 years (Alaska law until 1983) or 21 years (current Alaska law) is constitutional, then we have no difficulty concluding that reasonable people could also conclude that 19 years should be the minimum age for using marijuana, another intoxicant.

The facts of Allam's particular case demonstrate another rationale for establishing the age of marijuana use at 19 years. Allam and another 18-year-old were found sharing marijuana with two other high school students who were under the age of 18 years. Like Allam, many 18-year-olds attend high school and regularly associate with students under the age of 18 years. Establishment of a minimum age of 19 years for marijuana use is justified by the danger that, if 18-year-olds were allowed to possess and use marijuana, they would share the drug with other younger students or would at least frequently expose those younger students to drug use. . . .

The final question is whether former AS 11.71.060(a)(3) violated the Alaska Constitution's equal protection guarantee. In *State v. Enserch Alaska Construction, Inc.*, 787 P.2d at 631–32, the Alaska Supreme Court reviewed the steps of analysis an appellate court must undertake to decide a challenge to a statute under Alaska equal protection law.

This court must first identify the individual interest impaired by the statute and evaluate its importance; we then identify the social purposes underlying the statute and evaluate their importance. The level of justification required for the statute rises in proportion to the importance of the individual interest it affects. Depending upon the importance of that individual interest, the government's interest in enacting the statute must fall somewhere on a continuum between "mere legitimacy" to a "compelling interest."

Second, if the government's interest in enacting the statute is sufficiently strong, this court must examine the connection between the social policies underlying the statute and the means adopted in the statute to further those policies. Again, depending upon the importance of the individual interest affected, this nexus between ends and means must fall somewhere on a continuum between "substantial relationship" and "least restrictive alternative."

Here, Allam concedes that he has no protected interest in possessing or using marijuana. Even if Allam had not conceded this point, we would recognize the legislature's legitimate interest in regulating marijuana. Indeed, the Alaska Supreme Court has already held that, except for personal use of marijuana by adults in their own home, the legislature is justified in regulating the possession and use of this drug.

The second prong of the equal protection test is also satisfied. Because Allam has no interest in possessing or using marijuana, the classification drawn by former AS 11.71.060(a)(3) between people at least 19 years old and people younger than 19 years must bear a "substantial relationship" to the policy interests underlying the regulation of marijuana. We conclude that, given the relationship between age and discretion, the establishment of a minimum age of 19 years for marijuana use bears a substantial relationship to the social interests advanced by marijuana regulation. . . .

For these reasons, we conclude that the Alaska legislature acted constitutionally when they enacted former AS 11.71.060(a)(3), establishing 19 years as the minimum age for possession and use of marijuana guarantee, and when they left the maximum age for juvenile jurisdiction at 18 years, so that 18-year-olds who violated former AS 11.71.060(a)(3) would be prosecuted as adults. . . .

The judgement of the district court is AFFIRMED.

QUESTIONS FOR DISCUSSION

1. What exactly are Allam's arguments as to why the Alaska statute denies him equal protection of the laws?

2. How does the Alaska court answer Allam's arguments?

3. What are the two prongs of the equal protection clause to which the court refers?

4. Do you agree with Allam or the court? Defend your answer.

5. What arguments can you give for making special rules for marijuana use that are different from those governing the drinking age?

NOTE CASES

1. A Florida statute provided: "Any negro man and white woman, or any white man and negro woman, who are not married to each other, who shall habitually live in and occupy in the nighttime the same room shall each be punished by imprisonment not exceeding twelve months, or by fine not exceeding five hundred dollars." Florida convicted McLaughlin under the statute. He challenged the statute on the grounds that it invidiously discriminated on the basis of race.

The U.S. Supreme Court held

Normally, the widest discretion is allowed the legislative judgment in determining whether to attack some, rather than all, of the manifestations of the evil aimed at; and normally that judgment is given the benefit of every conceivable circumstance which might suffice to characterize the classification as reasonable rather than arbitrary and invidious. But we deal here with a classification based upon the race of the participants, which must be viewed in light of the historical fact that the central purpose of the Fourteenth Amendment was to eliminate racial discrimination emanating from official sources in the States. This strong policy renders racial classifications "constitutionally suspect," and subject to the "most rigid scrutiny," and "in most circumstances irrelevant" to any constitutionally acceptable legislative purpose.

We deal here with a racial classification embodied in a criminal statute. In this context, where the power of the State weighs most heavily upon the individual or the group, we must be especially sensitive to the policies of the Equal Protection Clause. . . . Our inquiry, therefore, is whether there clearly appears . . . some overriding statutory purpose requiring the proscription of the specified conduct when engaged in by a white person and a Negro, but not otherwise. Without such justification the racial classification . . . is reduced to an invidious discrimination forbidden by the Equal Protection Clause.

There is involved here an exercise of the state police power which trenches upon the constitutionally protected freedom from invidious official discrimination based on race. Such a law, even though enacted pursuant to a valid state interest, bears a heavy burden of justification, as we have said, and will be upheld only if it is necessary, and not merely rationally related, to the accomplishment of a permissible state policy.

Two justices went further. Justice Stewart wrote for himself and Justice Douglas:

I concur in the judgment and agree with most of what is said in the Court's opinion. But the Court implies that a criminal law of the kind here involved might be constitutionally valid if a State could show "some overriding statutory purpose." This is an implication in which I cannot join, because I cannot conceive of a valid legislative purpose under our Constitution for a state law which makes the color of a person's skin the test of whether his conduct is a criminal offense.

These appellants were convicted, fined, and imprisoned under a statute which made their conduct criminal only because they were of different races. . . . There might be limited room under the Equal Protection Clause for a civil law requiring the keeping of racially segregated public records for statistical or other valid public purposes. But we deal here with a criminal law which imposes criminal punishment. And I think it is simply not possible for a state law to be valid under our Constitution which makes the criminality of an act depend upon the race of the actor. Discrimination of that kind is invidious per se. *McLaughlin v. Florida*, 379 U.S. 184 (1964)

2. Colorado prohibits the possession, use, and sale of "narcotic drugs." It defines narcotic drug as "coca leaves, opium, cannabis [i.e., marijuana], isonipecaine, amidone, isoamidone, ketobemidone, and every other substance neither chemically nor physically distinguishable from them, and any other drug to which the federal narcotic laws may apply."

Stark was convicted of possessing marijuana and argued that the classification of cannabis in the same category as addicting narcotic drugs denied him the equal protection of the law. Was he right? The Colorado Supreme Court said no:

> We recognize that differences of opinion exist as to whether cannabis causes physical or psycho-logical addiction. This fact is not material in determining what drugs may be included within the classification of "narcotic drugs" in an exercise of police powers by a state. The important and pivotal consideration is whether the classification bears a reasonable relation "to the public purpose sought to be achieved by the legislation involved." Clearly, the use of marijuana and other drugs identified in the Colorado statute presents a danger to the public safety and welfare of the community since they are clearly related to each other and to the commission of crime. *People v. Stark*, 400 P.2d 923 (1965)

EX POST FACTO LAWS

Article X, Section 10 of the U.S. Constitution provides that: "No state shall . . . pass any *ex post facto* law. . . ." (a law passed after the occurrence of the conduct). Most state constitutions contain similar provisions. The idea that the law must define the crime and penalty in advance of prosecution and punishment had already enjoyed a long history by the time the provision appeared in Article X of the Constitution. The ancient Greeks prohibited *ex post facto* laws, and the Roman Civil Law read: "[A] penalty is not inflicted unless it is expressly imposed by law, or by some other authority." In the fierce struggle between king and Parliament in seventeenth-century England, the great jurist Lord Edward Coke said: "[I]t is against the law, that men should be committed [to prison] and no cause shewed . . . [I]t is not I, Edward Coke, that speaks it, but the Records that speak it; we have a national appropriate Law to this nation." Hence, the rule *nullum crimen sine lege; nulla poena sine lege* (no crime without law; no punishment without law).[7]

The *ex post facto* prohibition has two major goals:

1. To give fair warning to private individuals.

2. To prevent arbitrary action by government officials.

The framers of the U.S. Constitution considered the *ex post facto* principle so important that they wrote it into the main body of the Constitution before adding the Bill of Rights. (The Bill of Rights includes most of the provisions affecting criminal law.) According to the Supreme Court, which addressed the question as early as 1798, the *ex post facto* clause prohibits criminal laws that

1. Punish actions committed before the laws were enacted.

2. Aggravate the degree of the crime after it was committed.

3. Increase the punishment for a specific crime after the crime was committed.

4. Reduce the amount or alter the kind of evidence required for conviction when the offense was committed.[8]

The *ex post facto* prohibition does not apply to changes in the law that *benefit* defendants, only those that *hurt* them. For example, a statute that changes the definition of grand larceny from the taking of property worth $500 to requiring the worth of the property to be $1,000 does not involve the *ex post facto* principle. Laws that reduce penalties for particular crimes do not violate the *ex post facto* clause either. For example, a defendant who committed a capital murder before a statute retroactively replaced the death penalty with life imprisonment benefits from the statute. Hence, the prohibition against *ex post facto* laws does not apply.[9]

Justice Peckham, in the New York case of *People v. Hayes*, eloquently explained why the *ex post facto* clause does not apply to laws that benefit defendants.

> A statute which permits the infliction of a lesser degree of the same kind of punishment than was permissible when the offense was committed cannot be termed or regarded as an ex post facto law. The leading object in prohibiting the enactment of such a law in this country was to create another barrier between the citizen and the exercise of arbitrary power by a legislative assembly. It was well understood by the framers of our federal constitution that the executive was not the only power, in a government such as they were about to establish, which would require constitutional limitations. The possible tyranny by a majority of a representative assemblage was well understood and appreciated, and there were for that reason many provisions inserted in the constitution limiting the exercise of legislative power by the federal and also by state legislatures. . . .
>
> No act that mollified the rigor of the criminal law was regarded as an ex post facto law, but only a law that created or aggravated the crime, increased the punishment, or changed the rules of evidence in order to secure conviction. . . . Nowhere is it suggested that legislative interference by way of mitigating the punishment of an offense could be regarded as an ex post facto law, if applicable to offenses committed before its passage. There is no reason for any such holding. It was never supposed that constitutional obstacles would be necessary in order to prevent the improper exercise of legislative clemency. There was little to fear from that quarter upon such a subject.
>
> Those who framed the constitution were not engaged in creating obstacles to be placed in the path of those legislators who desired, by legislative enactment, to exercise clemency towards offenders, nor were they anxious lest those who were intrusted with power should be disinclined to exercise it with sufficient sternness. Human experience had furnished them with no examples of danger from that direction, and their anxiety on that account cannot be discerned from a perusal of the federal constitution. . . .
>
> That it materially affects the punishment prescribed for a crime is not the true test of an ex post facto law. In regard to punishment, it must affect the offender unfavorably before it can be thus determined. It seems to us plain that there can be no reason for any other view. I do not think that the mere fact of an alteration in the manner of punishment, without reference to the question of mitigation, necessarily renders an act obnoxious to the constitutional provision.[10]

THE RIGHT TO PRIVACY

One looks in vain for the word "privacy" in the United States Constitution. But this absence has not stopped the United States Supreme Court from reading a right to privacy into the Constitution. According to the Court, the constitutional right to privacy arises out of an amalgam of clauses in four amendments:

1. The First Amendment right to free expression and association.

2. The Third Amendment prohibition against quartering soldiers in private homes.

3. The Fourth Amendment right to be secure in one's person, house, and effects.

4. The Ninth Amendment provision that "The enumeration in the Constitution, of certain rights, shall not be construed to deny or disparage others retained by the people."

According to the Court, these amendments protect "against all governmental invasions of the sanctity of a man's home and the privacies of life." The right to privacy reflects the notion that the essence of a free society is the guarantee that its citizens will be "left alone," particularly by the government. The federal right to privacy has generated much controversy, particularly when applied to abortion and sexual orientation.[11]

Several state constitutions — Alaska, Hawaii, and Florida — contain specific provisions guaranteeing the right to privacy. For example, the Florida Declaration of Rights provides: "Every natural person has the right to be let alone and free from governmental intrusion into his private life."[12]

The Supreme Court has restricted the right to privacy mainly to intimate relationships inside the traditional family and home. Hence, in the leading case on the point, *Griswold v. Connecticut*, the Court struck down a statute making it a crime for married couples to use contraceptives. Justice Douglas, writing for the majority, said that the prohibition against contraceptives

> operates directly on an intimate relation of husband and wife. . . . The present case . . . concerns a relationship lying within the zone of privacy created by several different fundamental constitutional guarantees. And it concerns a law which, in forbidding the use of contraceptives rather than regulating their manufacture or sale, seeks to achieve its goals by means having a maximum destructive impact upon that relationship. Such a law cannot stand.[13]

Four years later, in *Stanley v. Georgia*, the Supreme Court struck down a statute that made it a crime to possess pornography within the privacy of a home. It appeared to some that the Court had permanently locked the criminal law out of private homes, believing that the Court's holding meant that whatever citizens do within their homes is not the law's business. The Court has not, however, ruled that the right to privacy so restricts the criminal law.[14]

In 1986, in *Bowers v. Hardwick*, the Court upheld Georgia's sodomy statute against a challenge that what consenting adult homosexuals do in the privacy of their own homes cannot be made a crime by the state. Hardwick and a friend left a gay bar and went to Hardwick's house. They passed a sleeping guest in the living room. Atlanta police, who had followed Hardwick and his friend from the bar, awoke the guest and entered Hardwick's home with the guest's permission but without Hardwick's knowledge. The police surprised Hardwick in his bedroom, where he was engaged in sodomy with his friend, an adult. The police arrested Hardwick for violating Georgia's sodomy statute. In an ensuing lawsuit, Hardwick argued that "the Georgia statute violated [Hardwick's] fundamental rights because his homosexual activity is a private and intimate association that is beyond the reach of state regulation by reason of the Ninth Amendment." The Court held that the right of privacy does not prevent states from making homosexual conduct criminal, even within the privacy of homes.[15]

In *Ravin v. State*, the Alaska Supreme Court addressed the question of whether Alaska's right to privacy provision—"[t]he right of the people to privacy is recognized and shall not be infringed"—protected Ravin from prosecution for possession of marijuana in the privacy of his home. Alaska makes possession of marijuana a crime.[16]

C A S E

Does He Have a "Right" to Possess Marijuana in His Home?

Ravin v. State, 537 P.2d 494 (Alaska 1975)

Ravin was convicted of possession of marijuana. He appealed on the grounds that if the statute made the possession of small amounts of marijuana for personal use in the privacy of his own home a crime, it violated his right to privacy. The Alaska Supreme Court reversed Ravin's conviction. Chief Justice Rabinowitz wrote the opinion for the court.

FACTS

. . . Ravin was arrested on December 11, 1972 and charged with violating AS [Alaska Statute] 17.12.010, [which] provides: Except as otherwise provided in this chapter, it is unlawful for a person to manufacture, compound, counterfeit, possess, have under his control, sell, prescribe, administer, dispense, give, barter, supply or distribute in any manner, a depressant hallucinogenic or stimulant drug. [AS 17.12.150 defines "depressant, hallucinogenic, or stimulant drug" to include all parts of the plant Cannabis Sativa L.]

Before trial Ravin attacked the constitutionality of AS 17.12.010 by a motion to dismiss in which he asserted that the State had violated his right of privacy under both the federal and Alaska constitutions. . . . Lengthy hearings on the questions were held before District Court Judge Dorothy D. Tyner, at which tes-

timony from several expert witnesses was received. Ravin's motion to dismiss was denied by Judge Tyner. The superior court then granted review and after affirmance by the superior court, we, in turn, granted Ravin's petition for review from the superior court's affirmance.

OPINION

. . . Ravin raises two basic claims: first, that there is no legitimate state interest in prohibiting possession of marijuana by adults for personal use, in view of the right to privacy. . . . Ravin's basic thesis is that there exists under the federal and Alaska constitutions a fundamental right to privacy, the scope of which is sufficiently broad to encompass and protect the possession of marijuana for personal use. . . . Ravin's argument that he has a fundamental right to possess marijuana for personal use rests on both federal and state law, and centers on what may broadly be called the right to privacy . . . [which] was recently made explicit in Alaska by an amendment to the state constitution.

In Ravin's view, the right to privacy involved here is an autonomous right which gains special significance when its situs is found in a specially protected area, such as the home. Ravin begins his privacy argument by citation of and reliance upon *Griswold v. Connecticut*, 381 U.S. 479, 85 S.Ct. 1678, 14 L.Ed.2d 510 (1965), in which the Supreme Court of the United

States struck down as unconstitutional a state statute effectively barring the dispensation of birth control information to married persons. Writing for five members of the Court, Mr. Justice Douglas noted that rights protected by the Constitution are not limited to those specifically enumerated in the Constitution:

> In order to secure the enumerated rights, certain peripheral rights must be recognized. In other words, the 'specific guarantees in the Bill of Rights have penumbras, formed by emanations from those guarantees that help give them life and substance.' Certain of these penumbral rights create 'zones of privacy,' for example, First Amendment rights of association, Third and Fourth Amendment rights pertaining to the security of the home, and the Fifth Amendment right against self-incrimination.

The Supreme Court of the United States then proceeded to find a right to privacy in marriage which antedates the Bill of Rights and yet lies within the zone of privacy created by several fundamental constitutional guarantees.... [The court reviewed other important Supreme Court opinions concerning the right to privacy.] These Supreme Court cases indicate to us that the federal right to privacy arises only in connection with other fundamental rights, such as the grouping of rights which involve the home. And even in connection with the penumbra of home related rights, the right of privacy in the sense of immunity from prosecution is absolute only when the private activity will not endanger or harm the general public.

The view is confirmed by the Supreme Court's abortion decision, *Roe v. Wade*, 410 U.S. 113, 93 S.Ct. 705, 35 L.Ed.2d 147 (1973). There appellant claimed that her right to decide for herself concerning abortion fell within the ambit of a right to privacy flowing from the federal Bill of Rights. The Court's decision in her favor makes clear that only personal rights which can be deemed "fundamental" or "implicit in the concept of ordered liberty" are protected by the right to privacy. The Supreme Court found this right "broad enough to encompass a woman's decision whether or not to terminate her pregnancy," but it rejected the idea that a woman's right to decide is absolute. At some point, the state's interest in safe-

guarding health, maintaining medical standards, and protecting potential life becomes sufficiently compelling to sustain regulations. One does not, the Supreme Court said, have an unlimited right to do with one's body as one pleases.

The right to privacy which the Court found in *Roe* is closely akin to that in *Griswold*; in both cases the zone of privacy involves the area of the family and procreation, more particularly, a right of personal autonomy in relation to choices affecting an individual's personal life....

... Article I, § 22 [Alaska Constitution] reads:

> The right of the people to privacy is recognized and shall not be infringed. The legislature shall implement this section.

The effect of this amendment is to place privacy among the specifically enumerated rights in Alaska's constitution. But this fact alone does not, in and of itself, yield answers concerning what scope should be accorded to this right of privacy.

We have suggested that the right to privacy may afford less than absolute protection to "the ingestion of food, beverages or other substances." *Gray v. State*, 525 P.2d 524, 528 (Alaska 1974).... [I]n our view, the right to privacy amendment to the Alaska Constitution cannot be read so as to make the possession or ingestion of marijuana itself a fundamental right....

Few would believe they have been deprived of something of critical importance if deprived of marijuana, though they would if stripped of control over their personal appearance.... Therefore, if we were employing our former test, we would hold that there is no fundamental right, either under the Alaska or federal constitutions, either to possess or ingest marijuana.

The foregoing does not complete our analysis of the right to privacy issues. For... the right of privacy amendment of the Alaska Constitution "clearly... shields the ingestion of food, beverages, or other substances," but... this right may be held to be subordinate to public health and welfare measures. Thus, Ravin's right to privacy contentions are not susceptible to disposition solely in terms of answering the question whether there is a general fundamental constitutional right to possess or smoke marijuana.

This leads us to a more detailed examination of the right to privacy and the relevancy of where the right is exercised. At one end of the scale of the scope of the right to privacy is possession or ingestion in the individual's home. If there is any area of human activity to which a right to privacy pertains more than any other, it is the home. The importance of the home has been amply demonstrated in constitutional law. . . .

Privacy in the home is a fundamental right, under both the federal and Alaska constitutions. We do not mean by this that a person may do anything at anytime as long as the activity takes place within a person's home. There are two important limitations on this facet of the right to privacy. First, we agree with the Supreme Court of the United States, which has strictly limited the . . . guarantee to possession for purely private, noncommercial use in the home. And secondly, we think this right must yield when it interferes in a serious manner with the health, safety, rights and privileges of others or with the public welfare.

No one has an absolute right to do things in the privacy of his own home which will affect himself or others adversely. Indeed, one aspect of a private matter is that it is private, that is, that it does not adversely affect persons beyond the actor, and hence is none of their business. When a matter does affect the public, directly or indirectly, it loses its wholly private character, and can be made to yield when an appropriate public need is demonstrated.

The privacy amendment to the Alaska Constitution was intended to give recognition and protection to the home. Such a reading is consonant with the character of life in Alaska. Our territory and now state has traditionally been the home of people who prize their individuality and who have chosen to settle or to continue living here in order to achieve a measure of control over their own lifestyles which is now virtually unattainable in many of our sister states.

Thus, we conclude that citizens of the State of Alaska have a basic right to privacy in their homes under Alaska's constitution. This right to privacy would encompass the possession and ingestion of substances such as marijuana in a purely personal, noncommercial context in the home unless the state can meet its substantial burden and show that proscription of possession of marijuana in the home is supportable by achievement of a legitimate state interest.

This leads us to the second facet of our inquiry, namely, whether the State has demonstrated sufficient justification for the prohibition of possession of marijuana in general in the interest of public welfare; and further, whether the State has met the greater burden of showing a close and substantial relationship between the public welfare and control of ingestion or possession of marijuana in the home for personal use. . . .

[Here, the court reviewed voluminous studies on the dangers of marijuana.]

The state is under no obligation to allow otherwise "private" activity which will result in numbers of people becoming public charges or otherwise burdening the public welfare. But we do not find that such a situation exists today regarding marijuana. It appears that effects of marijuana on the individual are not serious enough to justify widespread concern, at least as compared with the far more dangerous effects of alcohol, barbiturates and amphetamines. Moreover, the current patterns of use in the United States are not such as would warrant concern that in the future consumption patterns are likely to change. . . .

Given the relative insignificance of marijuana consumption as a health problem in our society at present, we do not believe that the potential harm generated by drivers under the influence of marijuana, standing alone, creates a close and substantial relationship between the public welfare and control of ingestion of marijuana or possession of it in the home for personal use. Thus we conclude that no adequate justification for the state's intrusion into the citizen's right to privacy by its prohibition of possession of marijuana by an adult for personal consumption in the home has been shown. The privacy of the individual's home cannot be breached absent a persuasive showing of a close and substantial relationship of the intrusion to a legitimate governmental interest. Here, mere scientific doubts will not suffice. The state must demonstrate a need based on proof that the public health or welfare will in fact suffer if the controls are not applied.

The state has a legitimate concern with avoiding the spread of marijuana use to adolescents who may not be equipped with the maturity to handle the experience prudently, as well as a legitimate concern with the problem of driving under the influence of marijuana. Yet these interests are insufficient to justify intrusions into the rights of adults in the privacy of their own homes. Further, neither the federal or Alaska constitution affords protection for the buying or selling of marijuana, nor absolute protection for its use or possession in public. Possession at home of amounts of marijuana indicative of intent to sell rather than possession for personal use is likewise unprotected.

In view of our holding that possession of marijuana by adults at home for personal use is constitutionally protected, we wish to make clear that we do not mean to condone the use of marijuana. The experts who testified below, including petitioner's witnesses, were unanimously opposed to the use of any psychoactive drugs. We agree completely. It is the responsibility of every individual to consider carefully the ramifications for himself and for those around him of using such substances. With the freedom which our society offers to each of us to order our lives as we see fit goes the duty to live responsibly, for our own sakes and for society's. This result can best be achieved, we believe, without the use of psychoactive substances. . . .

The record does not disclose any facts as to the situs of Ravin's arrest and his alleged possession of marijuana. In view of these circumstances, we hold that the matter must be remanded to the district court for the purpose of developing the facts concerning Ravin's arrest and circumstances of his possession of marijuana. Once this is accomplished, the district court is to consider Ravin's motion to dismiss in conformity with this opinion.

Remanded for further proceedings consistent with this opinion.

CONCURRING OPINION

Boochever, Justice (concurring, with whom Connor, Justice, joins).

. . . While we must enforce the minimum constitutional standards imposed upon us by the United States Supreme Court's interpretation of the Fourteenth Amendment, we are free, and we are under a duty, to develop additional constitutional rights and privileges under our Alaska Constitution if we find such fundamental rights and privileges to be within the intention and spirit of our local constitutional language and to be necessary for the kind of civilized life and ordered liberty which is at the core of our constitutional heritage. We need not stand by idly and passively, waiting for constitutional direction from the highest court of the land. Instead, we should be moving concurrently to develop and expound the principles embedded in our constitutional law. . . .

Since the citizens of Alaska, with their strong emphasis on individual liberty, enacted an amendment to the Alaska Constitution expressly providing for a right to privacy not found in the United States Constitution, it can only be concluded that that right is broader in scope than that of the Federal Constitution. As such, it includes not only activities within the home and values associated with the home, but also the right to be left alone and to do as one pleases as long as the activity does not infringe on the rights of others. Thus, the decision whether to ingest food, beverages or other substances comes within the purview of that right to privacy.

QUESTIONS FOR DISCUSSION

1. Do you agree with the court that the home is a special place with a zone of privacy around it that protects citizens in the possession of small amounts of marijuana for personal use? The people of Alaska did not think so. They passed a referendum that effectively overturned the Alaska Supreme Court's decision.

2. Is the right to privacy a "fundamental right"?

3. What harms might justify limiting the right to privacy?

4. Is it true that possessing marijuana at home does not harm anyone?

5. Would the government have to prove the harm to society? Or would defendants have to prove that their conduct did not harm society?

6. If you were compiling a list, what could citizens do in the privacy of their homes that government could not make a crime?

7. What criteria would you establish for determining what falls within the right to privacy, and what does not?

8. Would you extend the privacy right to motor homes? To motel rooms? To cars?

NOTE CASES

1. Florida prosecuted Borras for possession of marijuana in his home. Borras argued that "the primary purpose of smoking marijuana is the 'psychological reaction' it produces in the user and that by smoking marijuana he was 'merely asserting the right to satisfy his intellectual and emotional needs' in the privacy of his own home."

Did the law violate Borras's right to privacy? No, according to the Florida Supreme Court. The court ruled:

> This Court is aware that commission of other types of crime, particularly violent crimes, has an emotional effect on the perpetrator. This, however, does not give a constitutional right to commit the crime. . . . Marijuana is a harmful, mind-altering drug. An individual might restrict his possession of marijuana to the privacy of his home, but the effects of the drug are not so restricted. The interest of the state in preventing harm to the individual and to the public at large amply justifies the outlawing of marijuana, in private and elsewhere. *Borras v. State*, 229 So.2d 244 (Fla. 1969)

FREE SPEECH

The First Amendment provides that "Congress shall make no law . . . abridging the freedom of speech." Although the Amendment directs its prohibition to Congress, the Supreme Court long ago applied the prohibition to the States. In *Gitlow v. New York*, the Court ruled that a state law abridging free speech denied people liberty without due process of law under the Fourteenth Amendment.

The First Amendment does not protect all expression, despite the unqualified language in the Amendment—"no law." Statutes can restrict speech that creates a "clear and present danger" of evils that legislatures have a right to prevent. According to the Supreme Court:

> There are certain well-defined and narrowly limited classes of speech, the prevention and punishment of which has never been thought to raise any Constitutional problem. These include the lewd and obscene, the profane, the libelous, and the insulting or "fighting" words—those which by their very utterance inflict injury or tend to incite an immediate breach of the peace.[17]

United States Supreme Court Justice Oliver Wendell Holmes, in a famous reference to the limits of free speech, wrote: "The most stringent of free speech would not protect a man in falsely shouting fire in a theatre and causing a panic."[18]

Most of the problems in making speech and expressive conduct criminal involve laws that reach so far that they prohibit not only expression that the Constitution does not protect but also expression that it does. They are, according to the United States Supreme Court, void for overbreadth because they deny people freedom of expression without due process of law. For example, in *New York v. Ferber*, Ferber was arrested and prosecuted for distributing films that depicted young boys masturbating. The statute under which New York prosecuted Ferber prohibited all traffic in the depiction of children engaged in sexual conduct. Although the Supreme Court had no difficulty concluding that the First Amendment did not protect Ferber's conduct, the statute was so broadly drawn that it could also include selling medical texts or some issues of National Geographic. Hence, the Court struck down the statute because it was void for overbreadth.[19]

Speech includes more than words alone. The word *speech*, according to the United States Supreme Court, includes "expressive conduct," such as wearing black arm bands to protest war, "sitting in" to protest racial segregation, and picketing to support strikes. The Court grappled with the problem of flag burning as expressive conduct in *Texas v. Johnson.*

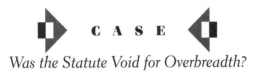

C A S E

Was the Statute Void for Overbreadth?

Texas v. Johnson,
491 U.S. 397, 109 S.Ct. 2533,
105 L.Ed.2d 342 (1989)

Johnson was charged with burning the American flag. After a trial, he was convicted, sentenced to one year in prison, and fined $2,000. The Court of Appeals for the Fifth District of Texas at Dallas affirmed Johnson's conviction. However the Texas Court of Criminal Appeals reversed, holding that the State could not, consistent with the First Amendment, punish Johnson for burning the flag in these circumstances. The Supreme Court granted certiorari and affirmed.

Justice Brennan delivered the opinion of the Court, in which Justices Marshall, Blackmun, Scalia, and Kennedy joined. Justice Kennedy filed a concurring opinion. Chief Justice Rehnquist filed a dissenting opinion, in which Justices White and O'Connor joined. Justice Stevens filed a dissenting opinion.

FACTS

While the Republican National Convention was taking place in Dallas in 1984, respondent Johnson participated in a political demonstration dubbed the "Republican War Chest Tour." As explained in literature distributed by the demonstrators and in speeches made by them, the purpose of this event was to protest the policies of the Reagan administration and of certain Dallas-based corporations. The demonstrators marched through the Dallas streets, chanting political

slogans and stopping at several corporate locations to stage "die-ins" intended to dramatize the consequences of nuclear war. On several occasions they spray-painted the walls of buildings and overturned potted plants, but Johnson himself took no part in such activities. He did, however, accept an American flag handed to him by a fellow protestor who had taken it from a flag pole outside one of the targeted buildings.

The demonstration ended in front of Dallas City Hall, where Johnson unfurled the American flag, doused it with kerosene, and set it on fire. While the flag burned, the protestors chanted, "America, the red, white, and blue, we spit on you." After the demonstrators dispersed, a witness to the flag-burning collected the flag's remains and buried them in his backyard. No one was physically injured or threatened with injury, though several witnesses testified that they had been seriously offended by the flag-burning.

Of the approximately 100 demonstrators, Johnson alone was charged with a crime. The only criminal offense with which he was charged was the desecration of a venerated object in violation of Tex.Penal Code Ann. § 42.09(a)(3) (1989). After a trial, he was convicted, sentenced to one year in prison, and fined $2,000. The Court of Appeals for the Fifth District of Texas at Dallas affirmed Johnson's conviction, but the Texas Court of Criminal Appeals reversed, holding that the State could not, consistent with the First Amendment, punish Johnson for burning the flag in these circumstances. . . . We granted certiorari, and now affirm.

OPINION

. . . The First Amendment literally forbids the abridgment only of "speech," but we have long recognized that its protection does not end at the spoken or written word. While we have rejected "the view that an apparently limitless variety of conduct can be labeled 'speech' whenever the person engaging in the conduct intends thereby to express an idea, we have acknowledged that conduct may be sufficiently imbued with elements of communication to fall within the scope of the First and Fourteenth Amendments." . . .

Especially pertinent to this case are our decisions recognizing the communicative nature of conduct relating to flags. Attaching a peace sign to the flag, *Spence [v. Washington]*, 418 U.S. 405 (1974); saluting the flag, *Barnette*, 319 U.S., at 632, 63 S.Ct., at 1182; and displaying a red flag, *Stromberg v. California*, 283 U.S. 359, 368–369, 51 S.Ct. 532, 535–36, 75 L.Ed. 1117 (1931), we have held, all may find shelter under the First Amendment. That we have had little difficulty identifying an expressive element in conduct relating to flags should not be surprising. The very purpose of a national flag is to serve as a symbol of our country; it is, one might say, "the one visible manifestation of two hundred years of nationhood." . . . Pregnant with expressive content, the flag as readily signifies this Nation as does the combination of letters found in "America."

We have not automatically concluded, however, that any action taken with respect to our flag is expressive. Instead, in characterizing such action for First Amendment purposes, we have considered the context in which it occurred. In Spence, for example, we emphasized that Spence's taping of a peace sign to his flag was "roughly simultaneous with and concededly triggered by the Cambodian incursion and the Kent State tragedy." . . .

Johnson burned an American flag as part — indeed, as the culmination — of a political demonstration that coincided with the convening of the Republican Party and its renomination of Ronald Reagan for President. The expressive, overtly political nature of this conduct was both intentional and overwhelmingly apparent. At his trial, Johnson explained his reasons for burning the flag as follows: "The American Flag was burned as Ronald Reagan was being renominated as President. And a more powerful statement of symbolic speech, whether you agree with it or not, couldn't have been made at that time. It's quite a just position [juxtaposition]. We had new patriotism and no patriotism." In these circumstances, Johnson's burning of the flag was conduct "sufficiently imbued with elements of communication," to implicate the First Amendment. . . .

Texas claims that its interest in preventing breaches of the peace justifies Johnson's conviction for flag desecration. However, no disturbance of the peace actually occurred or threatened to occur because of Johnson's burning of the flag. Although the State stresses the disruptive behavior of the protestors during their march toward City Hall, it admits that "no actual breach of the peace occurred at the time of the flagburning or in response to the flagburning." . . .

The State's position, therefore, amounts to a claim that an audience that takes serious offense at particular expression is necessarily likely to disturb the peace and that the expression may be prohibited on this basis. Our precedents do not countenance such a presumption. On the contrary, they recognize that a principal "function of free speech under our system of government is to invite dispute. It may indeed best serve its high purpose when it induces a condition of unrest, creates dissatisfaction with conditions as they are, or even stirs people to anger." . . .

Nor does Johnson's expressive conduct fall within that small class of "fighting words" that are "likely to provoke the average person to retaliation, and thereby cause a breach of the peace." *Chaplinsky v. New Hampshire*, 315 U.S. 568, 574, 62 S.Ct. 766, 770, 86 L.Ed. 1031 (1942). No reasonable onlooker would have regarded Johnson's generalized expression of dissatisfaction with the policies of the Federal Government as a direct personal insult or an invitation to exchange fisticuffs.

We thus conclude that the State's interest in maintaining order is not implicated on these facts. The State need not worry that our holding will disable it from preserving the peace. We do not suggest that the First Amendment forbids a State to prevent "imminent lawless action." . . .

If there is a bedrock principle underlying the First Amendment, it is that the Government may not prohibit the expression of an idea simply because society finds the idea itself offensive or disagreeable. We have not recognized an exception to this principle even where our flag has been involved. In *Street v. New York*, 394 U.S. 576, 89 S.Ct. 1354, 22 L.Ed.2d 572 (1969), we held that a State may not criminally punish a person for uttering words critical of the flag. . . .

In holding in *Barnette* that the Constitution did not leave this course open to the Government, Justice Jackson described one of our society's defining principles in words deserving of their frequent repetition: "If there is any fixed star in our constitutional constellation, it is that no official, high or petty, can prescribe what shall be orthodox in politics, nationalism, religion, or other matters of opinion or force citizens to confess by word or act their faith therein." . . .

We are fortified in today's conclusion by our conviction that forbidding criminal punishment for conduct such as Johnson's will not endanger the special role played by our flag or the feelings it inspires. To paraphrase Justice Holmes, we submit that nobody can suppose that this one gesture of an unknown man will change our Nation's attitude towards its flag. . . .

We can imagine no more appropriate response to burning a flag than waving one's own, no better way to counter a flag-burner's message than by saluting the flag that burns, no surer means of preserving the dignity even of the flag that burned than by—as one witness here did—according its remains a respectful burial. We do not consecrate the flag by punishing its desecration, for in doing so we dilute the freedom that this cherished emblem represents.

Johnson was convicted for engaging in expressive conduct. The State's interest in preventing breaches of the peace does not support his conviction because Johnson's conduct did not threaten to disturb the peace. Nor does the State's interest in preserving the flag as a symbol of nationhood and national unity justify his criminal conviction for engaging in political expression. The judgment of the Texas Court of Criminal Appeals is therefore Affirmed.

CONCURRING OPINION

Justice Kennedy, concurring.

. . . The hard fact is that sometimes we must make decisions we do not like. We make them because they are right, right in the sense that the law and the Constitution, as we see them, compel the result. And so great is our commitment to the process that, except in the rare case, we do not pause to express distaste for the result, perhaps for fear of undermining a valued principle that dictates the decision. This is one of those rare cases. Our colleagues in dissent advance powerful arguments why respondent may be convicted for his expression, reminding us that among those who will be dismayed by our holding will be some who have had the singular honor of carrying the flag in battle. And I agree that the flag holds a lonely place of honor in an age when absolutes are distrusted and simple truths are burdened by unneeded apologetics. . . .

The case here today forces recognition of the costs to which [our] . . . beliefs commit us. It is poignant but fundamental that the flag protects those who hold it in contempt. . . . So I agree with the court that he must go free.

DISSENT

Chief Justice Rehnquist, with whom Justice White and Justice O'Connor join, dissenting.

. . . The flag symbolizes the Nation in peace as well as in war. It signifies our national presence on battleships, airplanes, military installations, and public buildings from the United States Capitol to the thousands of county courthouses and city halls throughout the country. Two flags are prominently placed in our courtroom. Countless flags are placed by the graves of loved ones each year on what was first called Decoration Day, and is now called Memorial Day. The flag is traditionally placed on the casket of deceased members of the Armed Forces, and it is later given to the deceased's family. . . .

With the exception of Alaska and Wyoming, all of the States now have statutes prohibiting the burning of the flag. Most of the state statutes are patterned after the Uniform Flag Act of 1917, which in § 3 provides: "No person shall publicly mutilate, deface, defile, defy, trample upon, or by word or act cast contempt upon any such flag, standard, color, ensign or shield."

The American flag . . . throughout more than 200 years of our history, has come to be the visible symbol embodying our Nation. It does not represent the views of any particular political party, and it does not represent any particular political philosophy. The flag is not simply another "idea" or "point of view" competing for recognition in the marketplace of ideas. Millions and millions of Americans regard it with an almost mystical reverence regardless of what sort of social, political, or philosophical beliefs they may have. I cannot agree that the First Amendment invalidates the Act of Congress, and the laws of 48 of the 50 States, which make criminal the public burning of the flag. . . .

[T]he public burning of the American flag by Johnson was no essential part of any exposition of ideas, and at the same time it had a tendency to incite a breach of the peace. Johnson was free to make any verbal denunciation of the flag that he wished; indeed, he was free to burn the flag in private. He could publicly burn other symbols of the Government or effigies of political leaders. He did lead a march through the streets of Dallas, and conducted a rally in front of the Dallas City Hall. He engaged in a "die-in" to protest nuclear weapons. He shouted out various slogans during the march, including: "Reagan, Mondale which will it be? Either one means World War III;" "Ronald Reagan, killer of the hour, perfect example of U.S. power;" and "red, white and blue, we spit on you, you stand for plunder, you will go under." For none of these acts was he arrested or prosecuted; it was only when he proceeded to burn publicly an American flag stolen from its rightful owner that he violated the Texas statute. . . .

The Texas statute deprived Johnson of only one rather inarticulate symbolic form of protest—a form of protest that was profoundly offensive to many—and left him with a full panoply of other symbols and every conceivable form of verbal expression to express his deep disapproval of national policy. . . .

But the Court today will have none of this. The uniquely deep awe and respect for our flag felt by virtually all of us are bundled off under the rubric of "designated symbols," that the First Amendment prohibits the government from "establishing." But the government has not "established" this feeling; 200 years of history have done that. The government is simply recognizing as a fact the profound regard for the American flag created by that history when it enacts statutes prohibiting the disrespectful public burning of the flag. . . .

Surely one of the high purposes of a democratic society is to legislate against conduct that is regarded as evil and profoundly offensive to the majority of people—whether it be murder, embezzlement, pollution, or flag burning. . . . Uncritical extension of constitutional protection to the burning of the flag risks the frustration of the very purpose for which organized governments are instituted. The Court decides that the American flag is just another symbol, about which not only must opinions pro and con be tolerated, but for which the most minimal public respect may not be enjoined. The government may conscript men into the Armed Forces where they must fight and perhaps die for the flag, but the government may not prohibit the public burning of the banner under which they fight. I would uphold the Texas statute as applied in this case.

Justice Stevens, dissenting.

. . . The ideas of liberty and equality have been an irresistible force in motivating leaders like Patrick Henry, Susan B. Anthony, and Abraham Lincoln, schoolteachers like Nathan Hale and Booker T. Washington, the Philippine Scouts who fought at Bataan, and the soldiers who scaled the bluff at Omaha Beach. If those ideas are worth fighting for—and our history demonstrates that they are—it cannot be true that the flag that uniquely symbolizes their power is not itself worthy of protection from unnecessary desecration. I respectfully dissent.

QUESTIONS FOR DISCUSSION

1. What distinguishes speech from expressive conduct?

2. Can conduct actually say more than words?

3. Were Johnson's actions speech? Expressive conduct? Conduct?

4. How does the Court distinguish them? How would you?

5. Does the emotion created over flag burning prove that it is expression?

6. If so, should the government have the power to control the passions it arouses?

7. What role, if any, does criminal law have to play in flag burning?

8. What does Justice Kennedy mean by saying that the painful decision in the case must rest with the judiciary?

9. Does Chief Justice Rehnquist have a point that this decision flouts the will of the majority of Americans who want flag burners punished?

10. What is your position on the matter?

11. If you think Johnson committed a crime, how serious was the crime?

NOTE CASES

1. The New York Transit Authority, which has the authority to make rules equivalent to laws, made it unlawful to panhandle or beg in the New York subways. Several homeless people argued that the rule violated their right to free speech. The United States Second Circuit Court of Appeals ruled: "Common sense tells us that begging is much more 'conduct' than it is 'speech.'" The court acknowledged that the conduct had an element of expression in it, but said: "The only message that we are able to espy as common to all acts of begging is that beggars want to exact money from those whom they accost. Such conduct, therefore, is subject to regulation." Research and other experts indicated that panhandlers and beggars frighten passengers; this provides adequate grounds to regulate them. *Young v. New York City Transit Authority*, 903 F.2d 146 (2d Cir.1990)

See Chapter 12 for a deeper discussion of panhandling and the criminal law.

2. An Indiana statute prohibits nude dancing in public. Glen Theatre, a bar that featured nude dancing, sought an injunction against enforcing the law, arguing that it violated the First Amendment. The law permitted erotic dancing, so long as the dancers wore "G-strings" and "pasties." It prohibited only totally nude dancing. Dancers can express themselves erotically without total nudity. The United States Supreme Court ruled that it did not unduly restrict expressive conduct. *Barnes v. Glen Theatre, Inc., et al.*, 501 U.S. 560, 111 S.Ct. 2456, 115 L.Ed.2d 504 (1991)

3. Raymond Hill, a "gay activist troublemaker," witnessed a friend intentionally stop traffic on a busy Houston, Texas, street so that a car could enter traffic. Two officers approached Hill's friend to talk to him. Hill began shouting at the officers to divert their attention. First he shouted, "Why don't you pick on somebody your own size?" After Officer Kelley responded, "Are you interrupting me in my official capacity as a Houston police officer?" Hill shouted, "Yes, why don't you pick on somebody my size?" The police arrested Hill for "wilfully or intentionally interrupting an officer by verbal challenge during an investigation." A Houston ordinance makes it unlawful to "in any manner oppose, molest, abuse or interrupt any policeman in the execution of his duty." Hill argued that the ordinance violated his right to free speech. The United States Supreme Court agreed. *City of Houston v. Hill*, 482 U.S. 451, 107 S.Ct. 2562, 96 L.Ed.2d 398 (1987)

CRUEL AND
UNUSUAL PUNISHMENTS

The Eighth Amendment declares that "[e]xcessive bail shall not be required, nor excessive fines imposed, nor cruel and unusual punishments inflicted." The Supreme Court has ruled that the phrase "cruel and unusual punishments" means "not only barbaric punishments, but in some cases also sentences that are disproportionate to the crime committed."[20]

The principle of proportionality of punishment originated long before the Eighth Amendment. In 1215, three articles in the Magna Carta prohibited "excessive" fines. The principle was repeated and extended in the First Statute of Westminster in 1275.

The royal courts relied on these provisions to enforce the principle in actual cases. When imprisonment became a common-law sanction, the courts extended the principle to prison terms. The English Bill of Rights in 1689 repeated the principle of proportionality in the language that later appeared in the Eighth Amendment. Three months later, the House of Lords, the highest court in England, declared that a fine of 30,000 pounds was excessive and exorbitant, against Magna Carta, the common right of the subject, and the law of the land.[21]

The Supreme Court first applied the constitutional principle of proportionality in *Weems v. United States*, in 1910. Weems was convicted of falsifying a public document. The trial court sentenced him to fifteen years in prison at hard labor in chains and permanently deprived him of his civil rights. The Supreme Court ruled that the punishment violated the proportionality requirement of the Eighth Amendment. In the 1960s, the Court reaffirmed its commitment to the principle in *Robinson v. California*, ruling that a ninety-day sentence for drug addiction was disproportionate because addiction is an illness, and it is cruel and unusual to punish persons for being sick. "Even one day in prison would be a cruel and unusual punishment for the 'crime' of having a common cold."[22] (See the discussion of status in chapter 3.)

During the 1970s, the Court considered proportionality mainly in capital cases. For example, it held that the death penalty is disproportionate for raping an adult woman. In 1991, the Supreme Court extended the principle of proportionality to sentences of imprisonment.

C A S E

Was the Punishment "Cruel and Unusual"?

Harmelin v. Michigan,
501 U.S. 957, 111 S.Ct. 2680,
115 L.Ed.2d 836 (1991).

Justice Stevens filed a dissenting opinion, in which Justice Blackmun joined.

Harmelin was convicted of possessing cocaine and sentenced to life in prison without parole. The Michigan Court of Appeals affirmed the conviction. The U.S. Supreme Court granted certiorari and affirmed.

Justice Scalia announced the judgment of the Court in which Chief Justice Rehnquist and Justices O'Connor, Kennedy, and Souter joined. Justice Kennedy filed an opinion concurring in part and concurring in the judgment, in which Justices O'Connor and Souter joined. Justice White filed a dissenting opinion, in which Justices Blackmun and Stevens joined. Justice Marshall filed a dissenting opinion.

FACTS

Petitioner was convicted of possessing 672 grams of cocaine and sentenced to a mandatory term of life in prison without possibility of parole. [Note: Mich. Comp. Laws Ann. § 333.7403(2)(a)(i) (Supp. 1990–1991) provides a mandatory sentence of life in prison for possession of 650 grams or more of "any mixture containing [a schedule 2] controlled substance;" § 333.7214(a)(iv) defines cocaine as a schedule 2 controlled substance. § 791.234(4) provides eligibility for parole after 10 years in prison, except for those convicted of either first-degree murder or "a major controlled substance offense;" § 791.233b[1](b) defines "major controlled substance offense" as, inter alia, a violation of § 333.7403.] . . . [T]he Michigan Court of Appeals . . . affirmed petitioner's sentence, rejecting his argument that the sentence was "cruel and unusual" within the meaning of the Eighth Amendment. [Harmelin petitioned the United States Supreme Court for a writ of certiorari, a court order used by the Supreme Court as a discretionary device to decide which cases from lower courts, in this case the Michigan Court of Appeals, it wishes to review.] Petitioner claims that his sentence is unconstitutionally "cruel and unusual" . . . because it is "significantly disproportionate" to the crime he committed. . . .

OPINION

. . . In *Rummel v. Estelle*, 445 U.S. 263, 100 S.Ct. 1133, 63 L.Ed.2d 382 (1980), we held that it did not constitute "cruel and unusual punishment" to impose a life sentence, under a recidivist statute, upon a defendant who had been convicted, successively, of fraudulent use of a credit card to obtain $80 worth of goods or services, passing a forged check in the amount of $28.36, and obtaining $120.75 by false pretenses. We said that . . . "the length of the sentence actually imposed is purely a matter of legislative prerogative." . . . A footnote in the opinion, however, said: "This is not to say that a proportionality principle would not come into play in the extreme example . . . if a legislature made overtime parking a felony punishable by life imprisonment."

Two years later, in *Hutto v. Davis*, 454 U.S. 370, 102 S.Ct. 703, 70 L.Ed.2d 556 (1982), we similarly rejected an Eighth Amendment challenge to a prison term of 40 years and fine of $20,000 for possession and distribution of approximately nine ounces of marijuana. . . .

A year and a half after *Davis* we uttered what has been our last word on this subject to date. *Solem v. Helm*, 463 U.S. 277, 103 S.Ct. 3001, 77 L.Ed.2d 637 (1983), set aside under the Eighth Amendment, because it was disproportionate, a sentence of life imprisonment without possibility of parole, imposed under a South Dakota recidivist statute for successive offenses that included three convictions of third-

degree burglary, one of obtaining money by false pretenses, one of grand larceny, one of third-offense driving while intoxicated, and one of writing a "no account" check with intent to defraud. . . .

[The court here discussed inconsistencies in *Solem v. Helm* and *Hutto v. Davis* concerning the holdings and precedents regarding proportionality outside death penalty cases.]

It should be apparent from the above discussion that our 5-to-4 decision eight years ago in *Solem* was scarcely the expression of clear and well accepted constitutional law. We have long recognized, of course, that the doctrine of stare decisis is less rigid in its application to constitutional precedents, and we think that to be especially true of a constitutional precedent that is both recent and in apparent tension with other decisions. Accordingly, we have addressed anew, and in greater detail, the question whether the Eighth Amendment contains a proportionality guarantee . . . and to the understanding of the Eighth Amendment before the end of the 19th century. . . . We conclude from this examination that *Solem* was simply wrong; the Eighth Amendment contains no proportionality guarantee.

Solem based its conclusion principally upon the proposition that a right to be free from disproportionate punishments was embodied within the "cruell and unusuall Punishments" provision of the English Declaration of Rights of 1689, and was incorporated, with that language, in the Eighth Amendment. There is no doubt that the Declaration of Rights is the antecedent of our constitutional text. . . . As *Solem* observed, the principle of proportionality was familiar to English law at the time the Declaration of Rights was drafted. . . . When imprisonment supplemented fines as a method of punishment, courts apparently applied the proportionality principle while sentencing. . . . Despite this familiarity, the drafters of the Declaration of Rights did not explicitly prohibit "disproportionate" or "excessive" punishment. Instead, they prohibited punishments that were "cruell and unusuall." The *Solem* court simply assumed, with no analysis, that the one included the other. As a textual matter, of course, it does not: a disproportionate punishment can perhaps always be considered "cruel," but it will not always be (as the text also requires) "unusual." . . .

The language bears the construction, however—and here we come to the point crucial to resolution of the present case—that "cruelty and unusualness" are to be determined not solely with reference to the punishment at issue ("Is life imprisonment a cruel and unusual punishment?") but with reference to the crime for which it is imposed as well ("Is life imprisonment cruel and unusual punishment for possession of unlawful drugs?"). The latter interpretation would make the provision a form of proportionality guarantee. The arguments against it, however, seem to us conclusive. . . .

Throughout the 19th century, state courts interpreting state constitutional provisions with identical or more expansive wording (i.e., "cruel or unusual") concluded that these provisions did not proscribe disproportionality but only certain modes of punishment. For example, in *Aldridge v. Commonwealth*, 4 Va. 447 (1824), the General Court of Virginia had occasion to interpret the cruel and unusual punishments clause that was the direct ancestor of our federal provision. In rejecting the defendant's claim that a sentence of so many as 39 stripes violated the Virginia Constitution, the court said: "As to the ninth section of the Bill of Rights, denouncing cruel and unusual punishments, we have no notion that it has any bearing on this case. That provision was never designed to control the Legislative right to determine ad libitum upon the adequacy of punishment, but is merely applicable to the modes of punishment." . . .

We think it enough that those who framed and approved the Federal Constitution chose, for whatever reason, not to include within it the guarantee against disproportionate sentences that some State Constitutions contained. It is worth noting, however, that there was good reason for that choice—a reason that reinforces the necessity of overruling *Solem*. While there are relatively clear historical guidelines and accepted practices that enable judges to determine which modes of punishment are "cruel and unusual," proportionality does not lend itself to such analysis. Neither Congress nor any state legislature has ever set out with the objective of crafting a penalty that is "disproportionate," yet as some of the examples mentioned above indicate, many enacted dispositions seem to be so—because they were made for other times or other places, with different social attitudes, different criminal epidemics, different public fears, and different prevailing theories of penology. This is not to say that there are no absolutes; one can imagine extreme examples that no rational person, in no time or place, could accept. But for the same reason these examples are easy to decide, they are certain never to occur. The real function of a constitutional proportionality principle, if it exists, is to enable judges to evaluate a penalty that some assemblage of men and women has considered proportionate—and to say that it is not. For that real-world enterprise, the standards seem so inadequate that the proportionality principle becomes an invitation to imposition of subjective values.

This becomes clear, we think, from a consideration of the three factors that *Solem* found relevant to the proportionality determination: (1) the inherent gravity of the offense, (2) the sentences imposed for similarly grave offenses in the same jurisdiction, and (3) sentences imposed for the same crime in other jurisdictions. As to the first factor: Of course some offenses, involving violent harm to human beings, will always and everywhere be regarded as serious, but that is only half the equation.

The issue is what else should be regarded to be as serious as these offenses, or even to be more serious than some of them. On that point, judging by the statutes that Americans have enacted, there is enormous variation—even within a given age, not to mention across the many generations ruled by the Bill of Rights. . . . In Louisiana [for example], one who assaults another with a dangerous weapon faces the same maximum prison term as one who removes a shopping basket "from the parking area or grounds of any store . . . without authorization." La.Rev. Stat.Ann. §§ 14:37; 14:68.1 (West 1986). . . .

The difficulty of assessing gravity is demonstrated in the very context of the present case: Petitioner acknowledges that a mandatory life sentence might not be "grossly excessive" for possession of cocaine with intent to distribute. But surely whether it is a "grave" offense merely to possess a significant quantity of drugs—thereby facilitating distribution, subjecting the holder to the temptation of distribution, and raising the possibility of theft by others who might distribute—depends entirely upon how odious and socially threatening one believes drug use to be.

Would it be "grossly excessive" to provide life imprisonment for "mere possession" of a certain quantity of heavy weaponry? If not, then the only issue is whether the possible dissemination of drugs can be as "grave" as the possible dissemination of heavy weapons. Who are we to say no? The Members of the Michigan Legislature, and not we, know the situation on the streets of Detroit. . . . [Discussion of the other two factors in *Solem v. Helm* is omitted.]

Our 20th-century jurisprudence has not remained entirely in accord with the proposition that there is no proportionality requirement in the Eighth Amendment, but neither has it departed to the extent that *Solem* suggests. In *Weems v. United States*, 217 U.S. 349, 30 S.Ct. 544, 54 L.Ed. 793 (1910), a government disbursing officer convicted of making false entries of small sums in his account book was sentenced by Philippine courts to 15 years . . . at "hard and painful labor" with chains fastened to the wrists and ankles at all times. Several "accessor[ies]" were superadded, including permanent disqualification from holding any position of public trust, subjection to "[government] surveillance" for life, and "civil interdiction," which consisted of deprivation of " 'the rights of parental authority, guardianship of person or property, participation in the family council, [etc.]' "

Justice McKenna, writing for himself and three others, held that the [sentence] . . . was "Cruel and Unusual Punishment. . . . The punishment was both (1) severe and (2) unknown to Anglo-American tradition." [The plurality concluded that some portions of the opinion seemed to support proportionality and some did not.] . . .

The first holding of this Court unqualifiedly applying a requirement of proportionality to criminal penalties was issued 185 years after the Eighth Amendment was adopted. In *Coker v. Georgia* the Court held that, because of the disproportionality, it was a violation of the Cruel and Unusual Punishments Clause to impose capital punishment for rape of an adult woman. Four years later, in *Enmund v. Florida*, 458 U.S. 782, 102 S.Ct. 3368, 73 L.Ed.2d 1140 (1982), we held that it violates the Eighth Amendment, because of disproportionality, to impose the death penalty upon a participant in a felony that results in murder, without any inquiry into the participant's intent to kill.

Rummel v. Estelle treated this line of authority as an aspect of our death penalty jurisprudence, rather than a generalizable aspect of Eighth Amendment law. We think that is an accurate explanation, and we reassert it. Proportionality review is one of several respects in which we have held that "death is different," and have imposed protections that the Constitution nowhere else provides. We would leave it there, but will not extend it further. . . .

The judgment of the Michigan Court of Appeals is AFFIRMED.

CONCURRING OPINION

Justice Kennedy, with whom Justice O'Connor and Justice Souter join, concurring in part and concurring in the judgment.

. . . I write this separate opinion because my approach to the Eighth Amendment proportionality analysis differs from Justice Scalia's. Regardless of whether Justice Scalia or the dissent has the best of the historical argument . . . stare decisis counsels our adherence to the narrow proportionality principle that has existed in our Eighth Amendment jurisprudence for 80 years. Although our proportionality decisions have not been clear or consistent in all respects, they can be reconciled, and they require us to uphold petitioner's sentence.

Our decisions recognize that the Cruel and Unusual Punishments Clause encompasses a narrow proportionality principle. . . . Its most extensive application has been in death penalty cases. . . . [However,] the Eighth Amendment proportionality principle also applies to noncapital sentences. . . . [Justice Kennedy discusses *Solem v. Helm* and *Rummell v. Estelle* here.] . . . Petitioner's life sentence without parole is the second most severe penalty permitted by law. It is the same sentence received by the petitioner in *Solem*. Petitioner's crime, however, was far more grave than the crime at issue in *Solem*. The crime of uttering a no account check at issue in *Solem* was " 'one of the most passive felonies a person could commit.' "

Petitioner was convicted of possession of more than 650 grams (over 1.5 pounds) of cocaine. This amount of pure cocaine has a potential yield between 32,500 and 65,000 doses. From any standpoint, this crime falls in a different category from the relatively minor, nonviolent crime at issue in *Solem*. Possession, use, and distribution of illegal drugs represents "one of the greatest problems affecting the health and welfare of our population." *Treasury Employees v. Von Raab*, 489 U.S. 656, 668, 109 S.Ct. 1384, 1392, 103 L.Ed.2d 685 (1989). Petitioner's suggestion that his crime was nonviolent and victimless, echoed by the dissent, is false to the point of absurdity. To the contrary, petitioner's crime threatened to cause grave harm to society.

Quite apart from the pernicious effects on the individual who consumes illegal drugs, such drugs relate to crime in at least three ways: (1) A drug user may commit crime because of drug-induced changes in physiological functions, cognitive ability, and mood; (2) A drug user may commit crime in order to obtain money to buy drugs; and (3) A violent crime may occur as part of the drug business or culture. Studies bear out these possibilities, and demonstrate a direct nexus between illegal drugs and crimes of violence. . . .

A penalty as severe and unforgiving as the one imposed here would make this a most difficult and troubling case for any judicial officer. Reasonable minds may differ about the efficacy of Michigan's sentencing scheme, and it is far from certain that Michigan's bold experiment will succeed. The accounts of pickpockets at Tyburn hangings are a reminder of the limits of the law's deterrent force, but we cannot say the law before us has no chance of success and is on that account so disproportionate as to be cruel and unusual punishment. . . .

For the foregoing reasons, I conclude that petitioner's sentence of life imprisonment without parole for his crime of possession of more than 650 grams of cocaine does not violate the Eighth Amendment.

DISSENT

Justice White, with whom Justice Blackmun and Justice Stevens join, dissenting. [The portion of Justice White's dissent refuting Justice Scalia's reading of the history of proportionality as part of the meaning of cruel and unusual is omitted.]

. . . [T]he Amendment as ratified contained the words "cruel and unusual," and there can be no doubt that prior decisions of this Court have construed these words to include a proportionality principle. In 1910, in the course of holding unconstitutional a sentence imposed by the Philippine courts, the Court stated: "Such penalties for such offenses amaze those who . . . believe that it is a precept of justice that punishment for crime should be graduated and proportioned to [the] offense. . . . *Robinson v. California*, 370 U.S. 660, 82 S.Ct. 1417, 8 L.Ed.2d 758 (1962), held . . . it to be cruel and unusual to impose even one day of imprisonment for the status of drug addiction."

The plurality opinion in *Gregg*, 428 U.S., at 173, 96 S.Ct., at 2925, observed that the Eighth Amendment's proscription of cruel and unusual punishment is an evolving concept and announced that punishment would violate the Amendment if it "involve[d] the unnecessary and wanton infliction of pain" or if it was "grossly out of proportion to the severity of the crime." . . .

If Justice Scalia really means what he says — "the Eighth Amendment contains no proportionality guarantee," it is difficult to see how any of the above holdings and declarations about the proportionality requirement of the Amendment could survive. . . .

What is more, the court's jurisprudence concerning the scope of the prohibition against cruel and unusual punishments has long understood the limitations of a purely historical analysis. . . . The Court therefore has recognized that a punishment may violate the Eighth Amendment if it is contrary to the "evolving standards of decency that mark the progress of a maturing society." . . .

In evaluating a punishment under this test, "we have looked not to our own conceptions of decency, but to those of modern American society as a whole" in determining what standards have "evolved," and thus have focused not on "the subjective views of individual Justices," but on "objective factors to the maximum possible extent." . . . [Justice White then proceeded to examine the sentence compared to other crimes.]

[T]here is no death penalty in Michigan; consequently, life without parole, the punishment mandated here, is the harshest penalty available. It is reserved for three crimes: first-degree murder; manufacture, distribution, or possession with intent to manufacture or distribute 650 grams or more of narcotics; and possession of 650 grams or more of narcotics. Crimes directed against the persons and property of others—such as second-degree murder, and armed robbery, do not carry such a harsh mandatory sentence, although they do provide for the possibility of a life sentence in the exercise of judicial discretion. It is clear that petitioner "has been treated in the same manner as, or more severely than, criminals who have committed far more serious crimes."

. . . [Furthermore,] [n]o other jurisdiction imposes a punishment nearly as severe as Michigan's for possession of the amount of drugs at issue here. Of the remaining 49 States, only Alabama provides for a mandatory sentence of life imprisonment without possibility of parole for a first-time drug offender, and then only when a defendant possesses ten kilograms or more of cocaine. Ala.Code § 13A-12-231(2)(d) (Supp.1990). Possession of the amount of cocaine at issue here would subject an Alabama defendant to a mandatory minimum sentence of only five years in prison. § 13A-12-231(2)(b). Even under the Federal Sentencing Guidelines, with all relevant enhancements, petitioner's sentence would barely exceed ten years. . . .

Application of *Solem*'s proportionality analysis leaves no doubt that the Michigan statute at issue fails constitutional muster. The statutorily mandated penalty of life without possibility of parole for possession of narcotics is unconstitutionally disproportionate in that it violates the Eighth Amendment's prohibition against cruel and unusual punishment. Consequently, I would reverse the decision of the Michigan Court of Appeals.

[Justice Marshall's dissent, Justice White's dissent, joined by Justices Blackmun and Stevens, and Justice Stevens's dissent, are omitted.]

QUESTIONS FOR DISCUSSION

1. Why does Justice Scalia argue that the Eighth Amendment does not require proportionality in a mandatory life sentence without parole?

2. Do you agree with Justice Scalia that proportionality applies only to death penalty cases?

3. Overruling a prior decision rarely occurs. Why did Justice Scalia argue that the Court should overrule *Solem v. Helm*?

4. How did Justice Kennedy arrive at the judgment but not agree with Justice Scalia?

5. Do you agree with Justice Kennedy that proportionality applies to imprisonment but that this sentence was not cruel and unusual? Or do you agree with the dissent that proportionality applies to imprisonment and that this sentence is cruel and unusual? Notice that the majority of the Court agreed that disproportionate sentences are cruel and unusual punishments. Only Justice Scalia and Chief Justice Rehnquist agree that proportionality applies only to death penalty cases.

NOTE CASES

1. McDougherty sold two pieces of cocaine base to an undercover police officer in a park approximately 690 feet from an elementary school. A statute provides for enhanced penalties for drug offenses taking place in the vicinity of schools. McDougherty was convicted and sentenced to twenty-two years in prison followed by six years of supervised release. Was the sentence cruel and unusual? The Ninth Circuit Court of Appeals said no. Because the sentence did not exceed the statutory maximum (forty years), it was not cruel and unusual. The court said: "Congress has determined that selling cocaine near a school is a very serious offense." *United States v. McDougherty*, 920 F.2d 569 (9th Cir. 1990)

2. Kraft, age twenty-one, killed another person in a drunk-driving incident. The court sentenced him to five years of probation, the first six months of which he had to serve in jail. Kraft is suffering from terminal leukemia and requires chemotherapy. Chemotherapy increases the risk of fatal infections. Kraft's doctor testified that the risk of these infections would increase if Kraft was in jail. Kraft maintained that the sentence subjected him to cruel and unusual punishments. The court held: "It might be cruel and unusual punishment to sentence a person with defendant's condition to jail if the court knew the defendant would thereby be deprived of adequate medical treatment for his condition." Because the treatment was adequate, the punishment was not cruel and unusual. *State v. Kraft*, 326 N.W.2d 840 (Minn.1982)

3. Kevin Sanford committed murder on January 7, 1981, when he was approximately seventeen years and four months of age. Sanford and his accomplice repeatedly raped and sodomized Poore during and after their commission of a robbery at a gas station where she worked as an attendant. They then drove her to a secluded area near the station, where Sanford shot her point-blank in the face and then in the back of her head. The proceeds from the robbery were roughly 300 cartons of cigarettes, two gallons of fuel, and a small amount of cash. A corrections officer testified that petitioner explained the murder as follows: " '[H]e said, I had to shoot her, [she] lived next door to me and she would recognize me. . . . I guess we could have tied her up or something or beat [her up] . . . and tell her if she tells, we would kill her. . . . Then after he said that he started laughing.' " Is it cruel and unusual punishment to execute a person who commits murder while a juvenile? The Supreme Court ruled that it is not.

Of the 37 States that permit capital punishment, 15 decline to impose it on 16-year-olds and 12 on 17-year-olds. This does not establish the degree of national agreement this Court has previously thought sufficient to label a punishment cruel and unusual." *Sanford v. Kentucky*, 492 U.S. 361, 109 S.Ct. 2969, 106 L.Ed.2d 306 (1989)

4. Johnny Paul Penry, who had the mental age of six, raped, beat, and then stabbed Pamela Carpenter to death. Is it cruel and unusual punishment to execute a mentally retarded person? The Supreme Court ruled that it is not. The Court held that there was insufficient "objective evidence today of a national consensus against executing mentally retarded capital murderers, since petitioner has cited only one state statute that explicitly bans that practice and has offered no evidence of the general behavior of juries in this regard. Opinion surveys indicating strong public opposition to such executions do not establish a societal consensus." *Penry v. Lynaugh*, 492 U.S. 302, 109 S.Ct. 2934, 106 L.Ed.2d 256 (1989)

SUMMARY

The constitutional limits overarch the entire criminal law. They differ from the general principles of criminal liability, justification, and excuse; from the doctrines of complicity and incomplete crimes; and from the rules defining specific crimes. The principles of criminal liability govern the elements of crimes—the requirement of criminal conduct (the combination of act and intent), and where relevant, the element of causing a particular result. The doctrines of complicity and incomplete crimes, and the principles of justification and excuses, may or may not apply to a particular case or crime. The rules refer to individual crimes. The constitutional limits, on the other hand, affect all the elements, doctrines, excuses, justifications, rules, and penalties.

The Constitution prescribes limits to the criminal law in a number of provisions and interpretations of those provisions. It requires that the law specifically define the crime and prescribe a penalty. It also includes at least three other limits: (1) the *ex post facto* prohibition against making conduct criminal after it occurs; (2) the void-for-vagueness doctrine, which requires the law to state with precision what conduct it prohibits; and (3) equal protection of the laws. The purposes underlying the principle of legality include (1) forewarning citizens about the conduct the law proscribes, (2) protecting against abuse of state power, and (3) ensuring equal treatment by government.

The Constitution protects a number of specific individual rights of privacy and liberty from criminal prohibition. For example, the right to privacy, although not mentioned in the U.S. Constitution, protects some conduct. The right to free speech protects the freedom to express ideas and feelings consistent with a free society. The underlying purpose of the right to privacy and other civil rights is that the government should not interfere with conduct that either affects only the individuals who engage in it or promotes the free expression and exchange of ideas. Limits on making crimes out of conduct that is included in civil rights reflect the positive side of criminal law — that it ought to promote behavior that it does not prohibit. However, the Bill of Rights permits neither complete privacy nor unrestricted freedom of expression.

Nor does the Bill of Rights permit cruel and unusual punishments. The Supreme Court has interpreted the cruel and unusual punishments clause of the Eighth Amendment to mean that the punishment must be proportionate to the seriousness of the crime. A majority of the Court has agreed that the principle of proportionality applies to all criminal punishments. Some members of the Court, however, have argued that the principle of proportionality applies only to capital punishment.

REVIEW QUESTIONS

1. Describe the "great difficulty" James Madison identified in the quote on government that appears at the beginning of this chapter.

2. Define the rule of law.

3. What are *ex post facto* laws? What are the two goals of the *ex post facto* clause in the U.S. Constitution? What are the four types of laws that the *ex post facto* clause prohibits, according to the Supreme Court?

4. Explain the void-for-vagueness doctrine. What are the two "prongs" of the void-for-vagueness test?

5. What kinds of classifications does the equal protection clause prohibit?

6. According to the Supreme Court, what kinds of privacy does the Constitution protect?

7. According to the Supreme Court, what does the First Amendment protect from criminal law?

8. Define cruel and unusual punishment, as the Supreme Court has interpreted it.

9. Explain the principle of proportionality as it relates to the cruel and unusual punishments clause.

KEY TERMS

affirm To uphold a trial court's decision.

appellant A party who appeals a lower court decision.

appellate court A court that reviews decisions of trial courts.

appellee The party against whom an appeal is filed.

citation A reference to the published report of a case.

collateral attack A proceeding asking an appellate court to rule against the trial court's jurisdiction to decide a question or case.

concurring opinion An opinion that supports the court's result but not its reasoning.

dissent The opinion of the minority of justices.

due process clauses Clauses within the U.S. Constitution stating that government cannot deny citizens life, liberty, or property without notice, hearing, and other established procedures.

ex post facto **laws** Laws passed after the occurrence of the conduct constituting the crime.

habeas corpus **petition** A request for a court to review an individual's detention by the government.

holding The legal principle or rule that a case enunciates.

majority opinion The opinion of the majority of justices.

nullum crimen sine lege; nulla poena sine lege No crime without law; no punishment without law

plurality opinion An opinion that announces the result of the case but whose reasoning does not command a majority of the court.

principle of legality A principle stating that there can be no crime or punishment if there are no specific laws forewarning citizens that certain specific conduct will result in a particular punishment.

principle of proportionality A principle of law stating that the punishment must be proportionate to the crime committed.

procedural due process An expression of the rule of law requiring the government to follow established practices in criminal law enforcement, trial, and punishment.

reasoning The reasons a court gives to support its holding.

remand To send a case back to a trial court for further proceedings consistent with the reviewing court's decision.

reverse To set aside the decision of the trial court and substitute a different decision.

rule of law The principles that require that established written rules and procedures define, prohibit, and prescribe punishments for crimes.

void for overbreadth A description of a statute that is unconstitutional because it includes in its definition of undesirable behavior conduct protected under the U.S. Constitution.

void-for-vagueness doctrine The principle that statutes violate due process if they do not clearly define crime and punishment in advance.

writ of *certiorari* Discretionary Supreme Court order to review lower court decisions.

Suggested Readings

1. Herbert L. Packer, *The Limits of the Criminal Sanction* (Palo Alto, Calif.: Stanford University Press, 1968). Packer's book is a necessary starting point for anyone seriously interested in the aims and purposes of criminal law in general and in criminal punishment in particular. Packer takes the approach that he is writing for the generalists, not the criminal justice specialist. He especially addresses what he calls the rational lawmaker, one who "stops, looks, and listens" before passing laws. The book is written in a thoughtful, clear, easy-to-read style.

2. Lois G. Forer, *Criminals and Victims* (New York: Norton, 1980). Written by a judge with many years of experience in sentencing criminal defendants, this book explores the difficulties in applying general purposes to concrete cases. Forer analyzes the few alternatives judges have in sentencing, particularly the heavy emphasis on imprisonment, which she believes satisfies neither victims nor society. Well documented with interesting, challenging cases from her courtroom, the book is lively, easy to read, and provocative.

3. Andrew von Hirsch, *Doing Justice* (New York: Hill and Wang, 1976). This book is a brief, clear, and concise argument for just deserts. Based on deliberations by the Committee for the Study of Incarceration, it resulted from serious consideration of returning to retribution as the proper aim of punishment.

4. Norval Morris, *The Future of Imprisonment* (Chicago: University of Chicago Press, 1974). Morris, a criminal justice expert, has written an influential book in which he recommends a set of principles upon which punishment should rest. His principles are aimed at preserving what is the best of the rehabilitative ideal in the realities of twentieth-century prisons. These ideas are argued convincingly and written clearly, so that general readers can profit from reading the book.

5. David J. Rothman, *Conscience and Convenience* (Boston: Little, Brown, 1980). Rothman, a professor of history, surveys the origins and historical development of rehabilitation in the early years of the twentieth century. This book is excellent for anyone interested in the history of the rehabilitative ideal.

6. Johannes Andenaes, "Deterrence," in *Encyclopedia of Crime and Justice*, vol. 2, ed. Sanford H. Kadish (New York: Free Press, 1983). This is a brief, excellent summary of deterrence theory and research and of the problems of applying deterrence theory in practice, written by the world's leading deterrence theorist. The article includes a valuable bibliography on deterrence, which can lead to fruitful examination of this basic justification for criminal punishment.

7. Jerome Hall, *General Principles of Criminal Law*, 2d ed. (Indianapolis, Ind.: Bobbs-Merrill, 1960). This book gives the most comprehensive treatment of the general principles of legality and proportionality. Hall, a law professor, writes for the specialist, but his challenging arguments and his knowledge of history, law, and philosophy make the book well worth the effort for the layperson.

Notes

1. James Madison, "The Federalist No. 51," Jacob E. Cooke, ed., *The Federalist* (Middletown, Conn.: Wesleyan University Press, 1961), p. 349.

2. *Lanzetta v. New Jersey*, 306 U.S. 451, 453, 59 S.Ct. 618, 619, 83 L.Ed. 888 (1939).

3. *Kolender v. Lawson*, 461 U.S. 352, 357, 358, 103 S.Ct. 1855, 1858, 1859, 75 L.Ed.2d 903 (1983).

4. 11 Del.C. § 1312A became effective on May 20, 1992.

5. *Buck v. Bell*, 274 U.S. 200, 208, 47 S.Ct. 584, 585, 71 L.Ed. 1000 (1927) (equal protection argument the last resort).

6. *Michael M. v. Superior Court of Sonoma County*, 450 U.S. 464, 477, 101 S.Ct. 1200, 1208, 67 L.Ed.2d 437 (1981).

7. Quotes from Roman Civil Law and Lord Coke appear in Jerome Hall, *General Principles of Criminal Law*, 2d ed. (Indianapolis, Ind.: Bobbs-Merrill, 1960), pp. 31–32.

8. United States Constitution, Art. 1, § 9, cl. 3 prohibits the federal government from passing *ex post facto* laws; Art. 10 § 10, cl. 1 prohibits the states from doing so; *Calder v. Bull*, 3 U.S. (3 Dall.) 386, 390, 1 L.Ed. 648 (1798) defined *ex post facto*.

9. *People ex rel. Lonschein v. Warden*, 43 Misc. 2d 109, 250 N.Y.S.2d 15 (1964) (change from death penalty to life imprisonment effective retroactively).

10. *People v. Hayes*, 140 N.Y. 484 (1894), 490–491.

11. *Roe v. Wade*, 410 U.S. 113, 93 S.Ct. 705, 35 L.Ed.2d 147 (1973) (abortion); *Bowers v. Hardwick*, 478 U.S. 186, 106 S.Ct. 2841, 92 L.Ed.2d 140 (1986) (sexual preference).

12. Florida Constitution, Article I, § 23.

13. *Griswold v. Connecticut*, 381 U.S. 479, 85 S.Ct. 1678, 14 L.Ed.2d 510 (1965).

14. Jed Rubenfeld, "The Right to Privacy," *Harvard Law Review* 102 (1989):737–807. This article includes a detailed, extended discussion of the concept and development in constitutional law of privacy.

15. *Bowers v. Hardwick*, 478 U.S. 186, 106 S.Ct. 2841, 92 L.Ed.2d 140 (1986).

16. Art. I, § 22. See note, "Alaska's Right to Privacy Ten Years After *Ravin v. State*: Developing a Jurisprudence of Privacy," *Alaska Law Review* 2 (1985):159–183, for recent developments in the right to privacy in Alaska.

17. *Dennis v. United States*, 341 U.S. 494, 71 S.Ct. 857, 95 L.Ed. 1137 (1951).

18. *Gitlow v. New York*, 268 U.S. 652, 45 S.Ct. 625, 69 L.Ed 1138 (1925); *Chaplinsky v. New Hampshire*, 315 U.S. 568, 62 S.Ct. 766, 86 L.Ed. 1031 (1942); *Schenck v. United States*, 249 U.S. 47, 39 S.Ct. 247, 63 L.Ed. 470 (1919).

19. 458 U.S. 747, 102 S.Ct. 3348, 73 L.Ed.2d 1113 (1982).

20. *Solem v. Helm*, 463 U.S. 277, 284, 103 S.Ct. 3001, 3006, 77 L.Ed.2d 637 (1983).

21. Ibid., 285 103 S.Ct. at 3007.

22. *Weems v. United States*, 217 U.S. 349, 30 S.Ct. 544, 54 L.Ed. 793 (1910); *Robinson v. California*, 370 U.S. 660, 82 S.Ct. 1417, 8 L.Ed.2d 758 (1962).

CHAPTER THREE

The General Principles
of Criminal Liability

CHAPTER OUTLINE

CHAPTER MAIN POINTS

1. Every crime consists of separate elements, each of which the prosecution must prove beyond a reasonable doubt.

2. There are two categories of crimes, crimes of criminal conduct and crimes requiring the causation of a particular result.

3. Crimes of criminal conduct consist of the elements of *actus reus* and *mens rea*.

4. Crimes requiring the causation of a particular result consist of the elements of *actus reus*, *mens rea*, concurrence, causation, and resulting harm.

5. Each element of a specific crime forms the basis of a general principle of criminal liability.

6. The first principle of criminal liability is *actus reus*.

7. *Actus reus* allows for the inference of intention; it reserves criminal liability for manifest criminality; and it prevents the punishment of status or condition.

8. *Actus reus* includes not only voluntary bodily movements but also omissions, possession, and some involuntary actions and conditions.

9. The second principle of criminal liability is *mens rea*.

10. *Mens rea* includes four mental states — purpose, knowledge, recklessness, and negligence.

11. The requirement of *mens rea* ensures that only the blameworthy receive criminal punishment.

12. Strict liability crimes do not require proof of *mens rea* because they impose lesser penalties than other crimes and because they endanger large numbers of persons.

13. The principle of concurrence requires that *mens rea* prompt action in crimes of criminal conduct and that criminal conduct cause a particular result in crimes requiring the causation of a particular result.

14. The principle of causation requires proof of both factual and legal causation.

15. Purposeful wrongdoing is the most culpable mental state, followed by knowing, recklessness, negligence, and liability without fault.

16. *Mens rea* is the principal means of grading the seriousness of an offense.

Did Mrs. Cogdon Murder Pat?

Mrs. Cogdon went to sleep. She dreamt that "the war was all around the house," that soldiers were in her daughter Pat's room, and that one soldier was on the bed attacking Pat. Mrs. Cogdon, still asleep, got up, left her bed, got an axe from a woodpile outside the house, entered Pat's room, and struck her two accurate forceful blows on the head with the blade of the axe, thus killing her.

INTRODUCTION

Crooking a finger ordinarily attracts no attention; it is a perfectly unremarkable act under ordinary circumstances. But if you crook your finger around the trigger of a gun with the intent to kill someone, squeeze the trigger, and that someone dies from the bullet fired from the gun, then the ordinary act of crooking a finger becomes part of the *actus reus* of murder. Stripping naked in order to take a shower is not an act worthy of comment. However, stripping naked in a classroom transforms the act into the misdemeanor of indecent exposure.[1]

Under the extraordinary circumstances of criminal law, the ordinary phenomena of action, intention, concurrence, and causation translate into specific and distinct **elements of crime.** The prosecution must prove separately each of the elements beyond a reasonable doubt in order to convict defendants of the crimes they are charged with having committed. Crimes fall into two general categories, depending on the elements required to prove them:

1. Crimes of criminal conduct.
2. Crimes in which criminal conduct causes a particular result beyond the harm inherent in the conduct itself.

Crimes of criminal conduct consist of three elements:

1. **Actus reus**, or the physical element, sometimes called the objective element because it can be determined without the intent of the actor;

2. **Mens rea**, or the mental element, sometimes called the subjective element because intent resides inside the person who has it; and

3. **Concurrence,** that is, the union of act and intent.

ELEMENTS OF CRIMES OF CRIMINAL CONDUCT

Actus reus	Concurrence	Mens Rea
1. Voluntary actions **or**		1. Purposes **or**
2. Voluntarily induced involuntary actions **or**		2. Knowledge **or**
3. Voluntarily induced conditions **or**		3. Recklessness **or**
4. Voluntary omissions **or**		4. Negligence **or**
5. Possession		5. Strict liability

Burglary is an example of a crime of criminal conduct. Residential burglary, for example, consists of the *actus reus* of breaking and entering concurring with the *mens rea* of intent to commit a crime once inside the house. The crime of burglary is complete whether or not the intended crime to be committed inside the house is completed. The crime of burglary, therefore, is criminal conduct whether or not it causes any harm beyond the conduct itself.

Some crimes require that criminal conduct cause a specific result in addition to the conduct itself. In these crimes, causing the harmful result adds two elements to *actus reus* and *mens rea*. Hence, crimes requiring a particular harmful result consist of five elements:

1. *Actus reus*
2. *Mens rea*
3. Concurrence
4. Causation
5. Resulting harm.

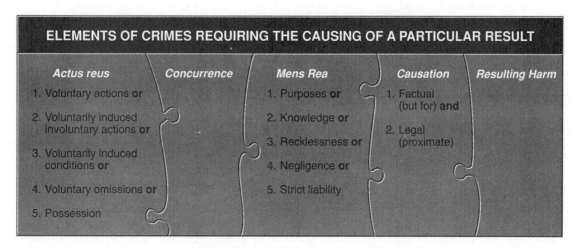

ELEMENTS OF CRIMES REQUIRING THE CAUSING OF A PARTICULAR RESULT

Actus reus	Concurrence	Mens Rea	Causation	Resulting Harm
1. Voluntary actions **or**		1. Purposes **or**	1. Factual (but for) **and**	
2. Voluntarily induced involuntary actions **or**		2. Knowledge **or**	2. Legal (proximate)	
3. Voluntarily induced conditions **or**		3. Recklessness **or**		
4. Voluntary omissions **or**		4. Negligence **or**		
5. Possession		5. Strict liability		

Crimes of this type include all crimes that require some kind of injury to persons or their property, such as battery (chapter 9) and arson (chapter 10). The best example of crimes that consist of conduct causing a particular result is criminal homicide. In criminal homicide, the actions and the intention of the murderer must combine to cause the death of another person (chapter 8). In all crimes consisting of conduct that causes a particular result, the requirement of concurrence applies not only to the union of action and intention but also to the union of criminal conduct and the cause of the particular result, such as the conduct of one who intentionally shoots another, causing the other's death.[2]

Each of the five elements of specific crimes forms the basis for a **general principle of criminal liability.** The act provides the basis for the principle of criminal liability called the *actus reus*, literally the "evil act." The intent provides the basis for the principle of *mens rea*, the "evil mind." The union of act and intent gives rise to the principle of concurrence. The element of **causation**—that criminal conduct causes a particular result—gives rise to the principle of causation. The principle of harm arises from the element of particular result. These general principles allow us to organize the content of the special part of the criminal law, the part that defines the specific crimes in chapters 8 through 12, into a logical, orderly, theoretical framework. For example, every crime (from murder and rape to disorderly conduct and making an illegal left turn) includes a union of *actus reus* and *mens rea*. In murder, the intent to kill unites with the act of killing; in illegal left turn violations, the intent to turn unites with the act of turning. Therefore, applying the general principles of criminal liability to the special part of the criminal law requires that the definitions of individual crimes fit within the parameters set by the general principles of *actus reus* and *mens rea* and, where relevant, causation and result.

ACTUS REUS

The first principle of criminal liability is the requirement of action. Criminal law does not punish evil thoughts alone. In 1562, an English court ruled that "men were not to be tried for their thoughts." Criminal law punishes only thoughts expressed through evil deeds, that is, only through what is called **manifest criminality.** Manifest criminality leaves no doubt about the criminal nature of the action. The modern phrase "caught red-handed" stems from the ancient concept of manifest criminality. Then, it meant catching murderers with the blood still on their hands; now, it means catching someone in the act of wrongdoing. For example, if bank customers see several people enter the bank, draw guns, threaten to shoot if the tellers do not hand over money, take the money the tellers give them, and leave the bank with the money, their criminality—the *actus reus* and *mens rea* of robbery—is clear-cut.[3]

Actus reus, however, requires more, and sometimes less, than bodily movements. A spasm is not *actus reus*; a failure to act can be.

The *actus reus* requirement serves several purposes. For one, it helps to prove the *mens rea*. We cannot observe intentions; we can only infer them from actions. Furthermore, the *actus reus* reserves the harsh sanction of the criminal law for cases of actual danger, and protects the privacy of individuals. The law need not pry into the thoughts of individuals unless the thinker crosses "the threshold of manifest criminality."[4]

Many axioms illustrate the *actus reus* principle: "Thoughts are free"; "We are punished for what we do, not for who we are"; "Criminal punishment depends on conduct, not status"; "We are punished for what we have done, not for what we might do." Although simple to state as a general rule, much in the full statement of the principle of *actus reus* complicates its apparent simplicity.

Status or Condition as Action

"An act . . . is a muscular contraction, and something more. . . . The contraction of muscles must be willed," wrote the great justice and legal philosopher Oliver Wendell Holmes in his usual pithy manner.[5]

Mere bodily movement does not qualify as *actus reus*; *actus reus* requires the freedom to choose action and the exercise of that freedom by acting. *Actus reus*, therefore, comprises two ideas: bodily movements and will. This excludes from criminal liability action resulting from involuntary bodily movements, such as reflexes, spasms, and other involuntary acts discussed later in the chapter. It also excludes most conditions or statuses. Status contrasts with action in that action refers to willed bodily movements while status refers to an ongoing passive condition. Put another way, action refers to what we do, status to who we are. Status can arise in two different ways. Sometimes it results from prior voluntary acts—most cocaine addicts voluntarily used cocaine the first time and alcoholics voluntarily took their first drink. Other conditions result from no act at all. These include gender, age, race, and ethnicity.

In his novel about the imaginary land called Erewhon, Samuel Butler deals with the criminal code of the Erewhonians, which makes it a crime to have tuberculosis. Following conviction for pulmonary consumption (tuberculosis), the judge pronounced sentence on one defendant in these words:

> [I]t only remains for me to pass such a sentence on you, as shall satisfy the ends of the law. That sentence must be a very severe one. It pains me much to see one who is yet so young, and whose prospects in life were otherwise so excellent, brought to this distressing condition by a constitution which I can only regard as radically vicious; but yours is no case for compassion: this is not your first offense: you have led a career of crime, and have only profited by the leniency shown you upon past occasions, to offend yet more seriously against the laws and institutions of your country. You were convicted of aggravated bronchitis last year: and I find that though you are but twenty-three years old, you have been imprisoned on no less than fourteen occasions for illnesses of a more or less hateful character; in fact, it is not too much to say that you have spent the greater part of your life in jail.
>
> It is all very well for you to say that you came of unhealthy parents, and had a severe accident in your childhood which permanently undermined your constitution; excuses such as these are the ordinary refuge of the criminal; but they cannot for one moment be listened to by the ear of justice. I am not here to enter upon curious metaphysical questions as to the origins of this or that—questions to which there would be no end were their introduction once tolerated, and which would result in throwing the only guilt on the tissues of the primordial cell, or on the elementary gasses. There is no question of how you came to be wicked, but only this—namely, are you wicked or not? This has been decided in

the affirmative, neither can I hesitate for a single moment to say that it has been decided justly. You are a bad and dangerous person. . . .

I do not hesitate to sentence you to imprisonment, with hard labor, for the rest of your miserable existence.[6]

Why do we object to the sentencing of someone to life imprisonment for having tuberculosis? Because the defendant did not voluntarily cause the tuberculosis. In *Robinson v. California*, the United States Supreme Court ruled that punishing someone for addiction to heroin violates the Eighth Amendment to the United States Constitution (the cruel and unusual punishments clause — see chapter 2). California had made it a crime not only to manufacture, sell, buy, and use narcotics but also to "be addicted" to them. According to the Court, it would be cruel and unusual punishment to sentence someone to "even one day" for an illness. Why? Because a disease is not an act. If addiction results from no act at all, as in the cocaine addiction of a baby born to an addicted mother, the baby was not responsible for the addiction. We cannot hold individuals responsible for conditions beyond their control. Therefore, if they are not responsible, we cannot blame them, and hence it is unjust to punish them. Of course, Robinson differs from the fictional defendant with tuberculosis in that Robinson's addiction resulted from a prior voluntary act.

What about acts that result from conditions? In *Powell v. Texas*, the United States Supreme Court had to decide whether to extend the prohibition against punishing the status of drug addiction resulting from a prior voluntary act of drug use to an alcoholic's act of public drunkenness resulting from alcoholism.

C A S E

Is Public Drunkenness an Act?

Powell v. Texas,
392 U.S. 514, 88 S.Ct. 2145,
20 L.Ed.2d 1254 (1968)

Powell was found guilty of public drunkenness. He appealed on the ground that punishing his drunkenness was cruel and unusual punishment because it punished a status. The Supreme Court affirmed the conviction. Justice Marshall announced the judgment of the Court and delivered an opinion in which Chief Justice Warren and Justices Black and Harlan joined. Justice Fortas, whom Justices Douglas, Brennan, and Stewart joined, dissented.

FACTS

In late December 1966, appellant was arrested and charged with being found in a state of intoxication in a public place, in violation of Vernon's Ann.Texas Penal Code, Art. 477 (1952), which reads as follows: "Whoever shall get drunk or be found in a state of intoxication in any public place, or at any private house except his own, shall be fined not exceeding one hundred dollars."

Appellant was tried in the Corporation Court of Austin, Texas, found guilty, and fined $20. He appealed to the County Court at Law No. 1 of Travis County, Texas, where a trial *de novo* [a new trial as if the first had not occurred and no decision rendered] was held. His counsel urged that appellant was "afflicted with the disease of chronic alcoholism," that "his appearance in public (while drunk was) . . . not of his own volition," and therefore that to punish him criminally for that conduct would be cruel and unusual, in violation of the Eighth and Fourteenth Amendments to the United States Constitution.

The trial judge in the county court, sitting without a jury ... found appellant guilty, and fined him $50. There being no further right to appeal within the Texas judicial system, appellant appealed to this Court.

The principal testimony was that of Dr. David Wade, a Fellow of the American Medical Association, duly certificated in psychiatry. ... Dr. Wade sketched the outlines of the "disease" concept of alcoholism; noted that there is no generally accepted definition of "alcoholism"; alluded to the ongoing debate within the medical profession over whether alcohol is actually physically "addicting" or merely psychologically "habituating"; and concluded that in either case a "chronic alcoholic" is an "involuntary drinker," who is "powerless not to drink" and who "loses his self-control over his drinking." He testified that he had examined appellant, and that appellant is a "chronic alcoholic," who "by the time he has reached (the state of intoxication) ... is not able to control his behavior, and (who) ... has reached this point because he has an uncontrollable compulsion to drink."

Dr. Wade also responded in the negative to the question whether appellant has "the willpower to resist the constant excessive consumption of alcohol." He added that in his opinion jailing appellant without medical attention would operate neither to rehabilitate him nor to lessen his desire for alcohol. ...

Appellant testified concerning the history of his drinking problem. He reviewed his many arrests for drunkenness; testified that he was unable to stop drinking; stated that when he was intoxicated he had no control over his actions and could not remember them later, but that he did not become violent; and admitted that he did not remember his arrest on the occasion for which he was being tried. ...

OPINION

... Appellant seeks to come within the application of the Cruel and Unusual Punishment Clause announced in *Robinson v. California*, 370 U.S. 660, 82 S.Ct. 1417, 8 L.Ed.2d 758 (1962), which involved a state statute making it a crime to "be addicted to the use of narcotics." This Court held there that "a state law which imprisons a person thus afflicted (with narcotic addiction) as a criminal, even though he has never touched any narcotic drug within the State or been guilty of any irregular behavior there, inflicts a cruel and unusual punishment. ..."

On its face the present case does not fall within that holding, since appellant was convicted, not for being a chronic alcoholic, but for being in public while drunk on a particular occasion. The State of Texas thus has not sought to punish a mere status, as California did in *Robinson*; nor has it attempted to regulate appellant's behavior in the privacy of his own home. Rather, it has imposed upon appellant a criminal sanction for public behavior which may create substantial health and safety hazards, both for appellant and for members of the general public, and which offends the moral and esthetic sensibilities of a large segment of the community. This seems a far cry from convicting one for being an addict, being a chronic alcoholic, being "mentally ill, or a leper. ..."

Robinson so viewed brings this Court but a very small way into the substantive criminal law. ... The entire thrust of *Robinson's* interpretation of the Cruel and Unusual Punishment Clause is that criminal penalties may be inflicted only if the accused has committed some act, has engaged in some behavior, which society has an interest in preventing, or perhaps in historical common-law terms, has committed some *actus reus*. ...

Traditional common-law concepts of personal accountability and essential considerations of federalism lead us to disagree with appellant. We are unable to conclude, on the state of this record or on the current state of medical knowledge, that chronic alcoholics in general, and Leroy Powell in particular, suffer from such an irresistible compulsion to drink and to get drunk in public that they are utterly unable to control their performance of either or both of these acts and thus cannot be deterred at all from public intoxication. And in any event this Court has never articulated a general constitutional doctrine of *mens rea*.

We cannot cast aside the centuries-long evolution of the collection of interlocking and overlapping concepts which the common law has utilized to assess the moral accountability of an individual for his antisocial deeds. The doctrines of *actus reus, mens rea,* insanity, mistake, justification, and duress have historically provided the tools for a constantly shifting adjustment of the tension between the evolving aims of the criminal law and changing religious, moral, philosophical, and medical views of the nature of man. This process of adjustment has always been thought to be the province of the States. . . .

But formulating a constitutional rule would reduce, if not eliminate . . . fruitful experimentation, and freeze the developing productive dialogue between law and psychiatry into a rigid constitutional mold. It is simply not yet the time to write the Constitutional formulas cast in terms whose meaning, let alone relevance, is not yet clear either to doctors or to lawyers.

Affirmed.

CONCURRING OPINION

Mr. Justice Black, whom Mr. Justice Harlan joins, concurring.

. . . Punishment for a status is particularly obnoxious, and in many instances can reasonably be called cruel and unusual, because it involves punishment for a mere propensity, a desire to commit an offense; the mental element is not simply one part of the crime but may constitute all of it. This is a situation universally sought to be avoided in our criminal law; the fundamental requirement that some action be proved is solidly established even for offenses most heavily based on propensity, such as attempt, conspiracy, and recidivist crimes. In fact, one eminent authority has found only one isolated instance, in all of Anglo-American jurisprudence, in which criminal responsibility was imposed in the absence of any act at all.

The reasons for this refusal to permit conviction without proof of an act are difficult to spell out, but they are nonetheless perceived and universally expressed in our criminal law. Evidence of propensity can be considered relatively unreliable and more difficult for a defendant to rebut; the requirement of a specific act thus provides some protection against false charges. Perhaps more fundamental is the difficulty of distinguishing, in the absence of any conduct, between desires of the daydream variety and fixed intentions that may pose a real threat to society; extending the criminal law to cover both types of desire would be unthinkable, since "(t)here can hardly be

anyone who has never thought evil. When a desire is inhibited it may find expression in fantasy; but it would be absurd to condemn this natural psychological mechanism as illegal."

In contrast, crimes that require the State to prove that the defendant actually committed some proscribed act involve none of these special problems. In addition, the question whether an act is "involuntary" is . . . an inherently elusive question, and one which the State may, for good reasons, wish to regard as irrelevant. In light of all these considerations, our limitation of our *Robinson* holding to pure status crimes seems to me entirely proper. . . .

. . . I would hold that *Robinson v. California* establishes a firm and impenetrable barrier to the punishment of persons who, whatever their bare desires and propensities, have committed no proscribed wrongful act. But I would refuse to plunge from the concrete and almost universally recognized premises of *Robinson* into the murky problems raised by the insistence that chronic alcoholics cannot be punished for public drunkenness, problems that no person, whether layman or expert, can claim to understand, and with consequences that no one can safely predict. I join in affirmance of this conviction.

[Justice White's concurring opinion is omitted.]

DISSENT

Mr. Justice Fortas, with whom Mr. Justice Douglas, Mr. Justice Brennan, and Mr. Justice Stewart join, dissenting.

. . . It is settled that the Federal Constitution places some substantive limitation upon the power of state legislatures to define crimes for which the imposition of punishment is ordered. . . . *Robinson v. California* . . . stands upon a principle which, despite its subtlety, must be simply stated and respectfully applied because it is the foundation of individual liberty and the cornerstone of the relations between a civilized state and its citizens: Criminal penalties may not be inflicted upon a person for being in a condition he is powerless to change.

In all probability, Robinson at some time before his conviction elected to take narcotics. But the crime as defined did not punish this conduct. The statute imposed a penalty for the offense of "addiction"—a condition which Robinson could not control. Once Robinson had become an addict, he was utterly powerless to avoid criminal guilt. He was powerless to choose not to violate the law.

In the present case, appellant is charged with a crime composed of two elements—being intoxicated and being found in a public place while in that condition. The crime, so defined, differs from that in *Robinson*. The statute covers more than a mere status. But the essential constitutional defect here is the same as in *Robinson*, for in both cases the particular defendant was accused of being in a condition which he had no capacity to change or avoid.

The trial judge sitting as trier of fact found upon the medical and other relevant testimony, that Powell is a "chronic alcoholic." He defined appellant's "chronic alcoholism" as "a disease which destroys the afflicted person's willpower to resist the constant, excessive consumption of alcohol." . . . I would reverse the judgment below.

QUESTIONS FOR DISCUSSION

1. According to *Powell v. Texas*, is *actus reus* not only a general principle of criminal liability but also a constitutional requirement? Explain.

2. Does it make sense to punish Powell if he was drunk in public because of his alcoholism? Why or why not?

3. Was his alcoholism a condition?

4. If so, did it result from a voluntary act?

5. Was his alcoholism a "disease"?

6. Does the public drunkenness statute punish Powell for being "sick"?

7. Which opinion do you agree with, the plurality or the dissent? Why?

NOTE CASE

In *State v. Perry*, 249 Or. 76, 436 P.2d 252 (1968), Perry was convicted under an Oregon statute making it a crime to be a "common prostitute." The court noted that the statute "does not purport to proscribe and make punishable a specific act of prostitution; it defines the crime in terms of the defendant's status or condition. . . . [E]ven if the defendant had reformed at the time of her arrest, she could still be charged with the violation of the statute on the ground that a crime once committed is not obliterated by reformation." Was the statute valid? The court upheld the conviction, but noted: "The complexities created by the enactment of [common prostitution] . . . as a crime of personal condition as distinguished from a crime of action present serious questions of their constitutionality as well as difficult problems of procedure and evidence and should prompt the legislature to [repeal the law.]" In 1971, the Oregon legislature repealed the statute.

Thoughts and Action

Consider a statute that makes it a crime to intend to kill another person. Why does such a statute strike us as absurd? One reason is because it is almost impossible to prove: "The thought of man is not triable, for the devil himself knoweth not the thought of man," said one medieval English judge. Furthermore, intentions do no harm. Although the moral law may condemn those who have immoral thoughts, the criminal law requires conduct—intention turned into action. Hence, punishing the intent to kill, even if possible to prove, fails to punish the harm the statute contemplates—another's death.[7]

In addition, it is difficult to distinguish mere daydreaming or fantasy from intention. The angry thought, "I'll kill you for that!" rarely turns into actual killing, or even an attempt to kill; it merely expresses anger. Punishment must await action sufficient to prove that the angry thoughts express the resolution and will to commit a crime (see chapter 5). Finally, punishing thoughts expands the meaning of crime to encompass a "mental state that the accused might be too irresolute even to begin to translate into action." Punishing thoughts is impractical, inequitable, and unjust; hence, the exclusion of thoughts from the principle of *actus reus*.[8]

Voluntariness

The principle of *actus reus* excludes not only thoughts and statuses but also some physical movements as well. The criminal law imposes liability on those who act voluntarily of their own free will, not on those who acted upon forces beyond their control. The bizarre case of *The King v. Cogdon* deals with sleepwalking as a criminal act.

C A S E

Is Killing While Asleep a Voluntary Act?

The King v. Cogdon[9]

FACTS

Mrs. Cogdon was charged with the murder of her only child, a daughter called Pat, aged nineteen. Pat had for some time been receiving psychiatric treatment for a relatively minor neurotic condition of which, in her psychiatrist's opinion, she was now cured. Despite this, Mrs. Cogdon continued to worry unduly about her. Describing the relationship between Pat and her mother, Mr. Cogdon testified: "I don't think a mother could have thought any more of her daughter. I think she absolutely adored her." On the conscious level, at least, there was no reason to doubt Mrs. Cogdon's deep attachment to her daughter.

To the charge of murdering Pat, Mrs. Cogdon pleaded not guilty. Her story, though somewhat bizarre, was not seriously challenged by the Crown, and led to her acquittal. She told how, on the night before her daughter's death, she had dreamt that their house was full of spiders and that these spiders were crawling all over Pat. In her sleep, Mrs. Cogdon left the bed she shared with her husband, went into Pat's room, and awakened to find herself violently brushing at Pat's face, presumably to remove the spiders. This woke Pat. Mrs. Cogdon told her she was just tucking

her in. At the trial, she testified that she still believed, as she had been told, that the occupants of a nearby house bred spiders as a hobby, preparing nests for them behind the pictures on their walls. It was these spiders which in her dreams had invaded their home and attacked Pat. There had also been a previous dream in which ghosts had sat at the end of Mrs. Cogdon's bed and she had said to them, "Well, you have come to take Pattie." It does not seem fanciful to accept the psychological explanation of these spiders and ghosts as the projections of Mrs. Cogdon's subconscious hostility towards her daughter; a hostility which was itself rooted in Mrs. Cogdon's own early life and marital relationship.

The morning after the spider dream she told her doctor of it. He gave her a sedative and, because of the dream and certain previous difficulties she had reported, discussed the possibility of psychiatric treatment. That evening Mrs. Cogdon suggested to her husband that he attend his lodge meeting, and asked Pat to come with her to the cinema. After he had gone Pat looked through the paper, not unusually found no tolerable programme, and said that as she was going out the next evening she thought she would rather go to bed early. Later, while Pat was having a bath preparatory to retiring, Mrs. Cogdon went into her room, put a hot water bottle in the bed, turned back the bedclothes, and placed a glass of hot milk beside the bed ready for Pat. She then went to bed herself. There was some desultory conversation between them about the war in Korea, and just before she put out her light Pat called out to her mother, "Mum, don't be so silly worrying there about the war, it's not on our front door step yet."

Mrs. Cogdon went to sleep. She dreamt that "the war was all around the house," that soldiers were in Pat's room, and that one soldier was on the bed attacking Pat. This was all of the dream she could later recapture. Her first "waking" memory was of running from Pat's room, out of the house to the home of her sister who lived next door. When her sister opened the front door Mrs. Cogdon fell into her arms, crying "I think I've hurt Pattie."

In fact Mrs. Cogdon had, in her somnambulistic state, left her bed, fetched an axe from the woodheap, entered Pat's room, and struck her two accurate forceful blows on the head with the blade of the axe, thus killing her.

OPINION

Mrs. Cogdon's story was supported by the evidence of her physician, a psychiatrist, and a psychologist. The jury believed Mrs. Cogdon. The jury concluded that Mrs. Cogdon's account of her mental state at the time of the killing, and by the unanimous support given to it by the medical and psychological evidence completely rebutted the presumption that Mrs. Cogdon intended the natural consequences of her acts. It must be stressed that insanity was not pleaded as a defence because the experts agreed that Mrs. Cogdon was not psychotic. [See chapter 7.] The jury acquitted her because the act of killing itself was not, in law, regarded as her act at all.

QUESTIONS FOR DISCUSSION

1. Was Mrs. Cogdon's act of killing Pat involuntary?

2. Could she have done anything to prevent it?

3. It is widely held that it is wrong to punish those who cannot be blamed. Would it be "right" to punish Mrs. Cogdon? Why or why not?[10]

NOTE CASES

1. *People v. Decina*, 138 N.E.2d 799 (N.Y.1956), Decina suffered an epileptic seizure while driving his car. During the seizure, he struck and killed four children. Was the killing an "involuntary act" because it occurred during the seizure? The court said no:

   This defendant knew he was subject to epileptic attacks at any time. He also knew that a moving vehicle uncontrolled on a public highway is a highly dangerous instrumentality capable of unrestrained destruction. With this knowledge, and without anyone accompanying him, he deliberately took a chance by making a conscious choice of a course of action, in disregard of the consequences which he knew might follow from his conscious act, which in this case did ensue.

2. In *George v. State*, 681 S.W.2d 43 (Tex.Crim.App. 1984), George was convicted of aggravated assault. George put a gun to a friend's head and demanded a dollar. After he cocked the hammer, it "slipped off [his] thumb" and the "gun went off." George did not mean for the gun to go off. He did not intend to hurt his friend; it was an accident. In its opinion, the Texas Court of Criminal Appeals said:

   "[T]here is no law and defense of accident in the present penal code," but . . . the Legislature had not jettisoned the notion. "The function of the former defense of accident is performed now by the requirement of . . . § 6.01(a), that, A person commits an offense if he voluntarily engages in conduct . . ." If the issue is raised by the evidence, a jury may be charged that a defendant should be acquitted if there is a reasonable doubt as to whether he voluntarily engaged in the conduct of which he is accused." . . .

   If the hammer "slipped off [his] thumb," it had to be that the thumb holding the hammer partially back released just enough pressure for the hammer to "slip" forward. However slight, that is "bodily movement" within the meaning of § 1.07(a)(1), and there is no evidence that it was involuntary.

3. In a Danish case, Bjorn Nielson masterminded a robbery by hypnotizing his friend Palle Hardrup. While in the hypnotic trance, Hardrup held up a Copenhagen bank, shooting and killing a teller and director. Nielson was sentenced to life imprisonment because

he masterminded the holdup, even though he was nowhere near the bank when the robbery took place. Hardrup was sent to a mental hospital. He was not tried for robbery because his acts during the holdup were not considered voluntary.[11]

4. Fulcher got into a fight in a bar, passed out, and was picked up by the police. He was taken to jail, where he brutally stomped on another jail inmate and shouted ethnic slurs at him. Fulcher testified that he remembers nothing after passing out in the bar. At the trial, Doctor LeBegue testified that Fulcher suffered from a concussion incurred during the bar fight, and that it caused a brain injury that put Fulcher "in a state of traumatic automatism at the time of his attack on Hernandez . . . the state of mind in which a person does not have conscious and willful control over his actions. . . ." Was Fulcher liable? No, said the court. Unconscious automatism is an af-

firmative defense because "[T]he rehabilitative value of imprisonment for the automatistic offender who has committed the offense unconsciously is nonexistent. The cause of the act was an uncontrollable physical disorder that may never recur and is not a moral deficiency." *Fulcher v. State*, 633 P.2d 142 (Wyo.1981)

5. Jerrett terrorized Dallas and Edith Parsons—he robbed them, killed Dallas, and kidnapped Edith. At trial, Jerrett testified that he could remember nothing of what happened until he was arrested, and that he had suffered previous blackouts following exposure to Agent Orange during military service in Vietnam. The trial judge refused to instruct the jury on the defense of automatism. The North Carolina Supreme Court reversed, and ordered a new trial. *State v. Jerrett*, 309 N.C. 239, 307 S.E.2d 339 (1983)

Voluntarily induced involuntary acts and conditions include many less bizarre cases than hypnosis and sleepwalking. Voluntarily induced involuntary acts arise frequently during the driving of vehicles: Drowsy drivers continue to drive until they fall asleep; intoxicated persons continue to drive; persons with dangerously high blood pressure suffer strokes while driving; epileptics have seizures while driving. For all of these cases, the criminal sanction arguably might deter those whose prior voluntary acts create risks of future involuntary acts and conditions, acts and conditions that threaten harm to others.

Words as Acts

In common usage, act means bodily movement; however, in *actus reus*, the term can also refer to words, or **verbal acts.** Crimes consisting of verbal acts include conspiracy, solicitation, terroristic threats, some kinds of assault, and inciting to riot. These crimes are discussed specifically in other chapters of this book; here it is enough to note that they can be criminal acts under the general principle of *actus reus*. For example, courts can try office supervisors who use sexually explicit language with employees under their supervision, or even comment on the attractiveness of the employee, for the misdemeanor of sexual harassment.

Omission

Voluntary bodily movements, voluntarily induced involuntary conduct, and words are not the only possible criminal acts that fall within the general principle of *actus reus*. Under some circumstances, *omissions*—or failures to act—are also criminal. But the law imposes liability on omissions reluctantly, preferring to punish those who act affirmatively rather than those who merely allow something to happen, as is the case in omissions. However, some commentators, like Professor George Fletcher, do not accept the distinction between affirmative action and failure to act. According to Fletcher,

> It is as much an act of will for the guards at Buckingham Palace to stand motionless as it is for tourists to stroll back and forth in front of them. Conscious non-motion is a greater assertion of personality than casual acting. One can only be puzzled by the widespread belief that the distinction between motion and non-motion is of importance to the law.[12]

Liability for omissions takes two forms. One is the mere *failure to act*, usually the failure to file some kind of report required by law, such as reporting an accident or child abuse, filing an income tax return, registering a firearm, or notifying sexual partners of HIV status. The other form of omission is the *failure to intervene* in order to prevent a serious harm, such as to prevent death and injuries to persons or the destruction and damage of property.

Only the failure to perform legal duties is a criminal omission. Legal duties can arise in three ways:

1. Statutes
2. Contracts
3. Special relationships.

Statutes creating legal duties mainly include failures to report, such as the requirements to file income tax returns, to report accidents and child abuse, and to register firearms. Contracts can also create legal duties. Police officers, for example, agree to perform certain public duties, such as protecting the rights of citizens; failure to perform those duties creates both civil and criminal liability. Special relationships that impose legal duties include the parent-child relationship, the doctor-patient relationship, the employer-employee relationship, the carrier-passenger relationship, and, in some states, the husband-wife relationship.

Failure to perform moral duties does not qualify as a criminal omission. According to Professors Wayne LaFave and Austin Scott:

> Generally one has no legal duty to aid another person in peril, even when that aid can be rendered without danger or inconvenience to himself. He need not shout a warning to a blind man headed for a precipice or to an absent-minded one walking into a gunpowder room with a lighted candle in hand. He need not pull a neighbor's baby out of a pool of water or rescue an unconscious person stretched across the railroad tracks, though the baby is drowning or the whistle of the approaching train is heard in the distance. A doctor is not legally bound to answer a desperate call from the frantic parents of a sick child, at least if it is not one of his regular patients. A moral duty to take affirmative action is not enough to impose a legal duty to do so. But there are situations which do give rise to legal duties.[13]

Limiting criminal omissions to the failure to perform legal duties assumes that individual conscience, peer pressure, and other informal mechanisms condemn and prevent behavior more effectively than criminal prosecution. Furthermore, it assumes that prosecuting omissions unduly burdens an already overburdened criminal justice system. Finally, it assumes that the criminal law cannot compel "Good Samaritans" to help those in need.[14] The court dealt with legal duties and failure to act in *State v. Miranda.*

C A S E

Was There a "Special Relationship"?

State v. Miranda,
675 A.2d 925 (Conn. 1996)

Miranda was convicted in the Superior Court, Judicial District of New Haven, Fracasse, J., of risk of injury to a child and assault in the first degree. The trial court sentenced Miranda to a total effective sentence of forty years, consisting of ten years on the risk of injury count, consecutive two fifteen year sentences on each of two counts of assault in the first degree. As to the four other counts of assault in the first degree, the defendant received sentences of fifteen years concurrent to all other sentences. As part of a plea agreement, Dianek Rodriguez, the mother of the child, will receive a sentence of twelve years suspended after she serves seven years. Miranda appealed, and the Appellate Court affirmed in part, reversed in part, and remanded the case.

Judge Foti wrote the opinion for the Appellate Court.

FACTS

General Statutes § 53a59(a) provides in pertinent part:

A person is guilty of assault in the first degree when . . . (3) under circumstances evincing an extreme indifference to human life he recklessly engages in conduct which creates a risk of death to another person, and thereby causes serious physical injury to another person. . . .

General Statutes § 5321 provides:

Any person who wilfully or unlawfully causes or permits any child under the age of sixteen years to be placed in such a situation that its life or limb is endangered, or its health is likely to be injured, or its morals likely to be impaired, or does any act likely to impair the health or morals of any such child, shall be fined not more than five hundred dollars or imprisoned not more than ten years or both.

. . . On January 27, 1993, the defendant, age twenty-one, lived with his sixteen year old girlfriend, Dianek Rodriguez, and her two children in Meriden, having moved there in September, 1992. The defendant is not the father of either child, a boy, two years old, and a girl, the victim, four months old. He assumed responsibility for the welfare of both children and took care of them as if he were their father. He established a familylike relationship with the children and their mother.

On the evening of January 27, 1993, the defendant was in the shower when Rodriguez screamed that the baby was turning blue and could not breathe. The defendant went to help, saw the baby had turned purple, and the defendant began crying. He then picked up the baby, put her on her back, breathed into her mouth and pushed on her chest. Milk came from the baby's mouth and she began to breathe normally. The defendant went out of the apartment to place a 911 emergency call and returned to the apartment immediately afterward.

At approximately 8:05 P.M., Steven Cushing, a trained paramedic, arrived in response to the call. After observing and examining the child, he placed her in an ambulance, and rushed to Meriden Veterans Memorial Hospital. Because of the serious and extensive injuries to the child, she was transported by Life Star Helicopter to Hartford Hospital, where she remained in intensive care for two and one-half days. She was discharged on February 5, 1993. The department of children and families took custody of the child and her brother.

Upon examination at Hartford Hospital, the child was found to be a textbook example of battered child syndrome. She was found to have multiple rib fractures in the posterior area, multiple skull fractures, bruises to soft tissue areas, a brachial plexus injury, a rectal tear, and bilateral subconjunctival nasal hemorrhages. These injuries were sustained during three or more occasions of wilful and deliberate abuse. [The baby's mother pleaded guilty to charges related to having caused the injuries] Some of the injuries were fresh and some were five to ten days old. The rectal tear was a serious physical injury that created a risk of death because the child's intestine could have been perforated, resulting in an overwhelming infection.

As to the one count of risk of injury, the trial court concluded that, through his failure to act, the defendant, "unlawfully caused and permitted the child to be placed in such a situation that her life and limb were endangered and her health was likely to be injured; in fact her life was endangered and her health was injured and impaired."

The defendant claims that the evidence presented at trial was insufficient to convict him of either assault in the first degree or risk of injury to a child.

OPINION

The central issue in this appeal is whether a person, who is not the biological or legal parent of a child and does not owe a legal duty to that child, can be convicted of assault in the first degree of that child absent evidence of either an overt act causing the injuries, or of aiding and abetting another in the commission of the crime. We conclude that under the circumstances of this case, absent an overt act or an omission to act where there is a legal duty to do so, the defendant, a nonparent, could not be convicted under § 53a59(a)(3). We, therefore, reverse the judgment of the trial court in part.

In reviewing claims of insufficiency, we first review the evidence presented at trial and construe it in the light most favorable to sustaining the trial court's finding of guilt. We then look at the facts established at trial and the reasonable inferences drawn from those facts and decide whether the court could have reasonably concluded that the cumulative effect of the evidence established the defendant's guilt beyond a reasonable doubt. Our standard in reviewing the conclusions of the trier of fact is limited. We will construe the evidence in the light most favorable to sustaining the trial court's judgment and will affirm the court's conclusions if reasonably supported by the evidence and logical inferences drawn therefrom.

The question on appeal is not whether we believe that the evidence established guilt beyond a reasonable doubt, but rather whether, after viewing the evidence in the light most favorable to sustaining the

judgment, any rational trier of fact could have found the essential elements of the crime beyond a reasonable doubt. We give deference to the unique opportunity of the trier of fact to observe the conduct, demeanor and attitude of the trial witnesses and to assess their credibility. The trial court's findings of fact are entitled to great weight; but those findings are not conclusive.

The defendant's claim of insufficiency of the evidence as to the charge of risk of injury to a child under § 53a21 is inadequately briefed. He has neither cited authority nor provided any legal analysis. We are, therefore, precluded from reviewing this claim.

While § 5321 proscribes criminal omissions, such as a person's deliberate indifference to or acquiescence in creating a situation inimical to a child's physical welfare; the same is not true of General Statutes § 53a59(a)(3). A failure to act when one is under no legal duty to do so, thereby permitting a dangerous condition to exist, is not sufficient to support a conviction for assault in the first degree pursuant to § 53a59(a)(3).

Assault in the first degree under § 53a59(a)(3) requires that a defendant recklessly engage in conduct that creates a risk of death to another person and thereby causes serious physical injury to another person. A person acts recklessly with respect to a particular result or a circumstance described by statute "when he is aware of and consciously disregards a substantial and unjustifiable risk that such result will occur or that such circumstance exists. . . ." General Statutes § 53a3(13). The state of mind constituting recklessness may be inferred from conduct.

Generally, if the injury caused by the defendant's conduct is a foreseeable and natural result of that conduct, the defendant is criminally responsible. That conduct, creating criminal liability, may be by an act or an omission to act if within the intendment of the statute. Criminal liability may also arise not only by overt acts but by an omission to act where there is a legal duty to do so.

The defendant's convictions under § 53a59(a)(3) were not based on facts found from the evidence presented that he either inflicted or aided and abetted another in inflicting the injuries suffered by the victim. The basis of the court's convictions is that the defendant knew or should have known of the child's injuries and did nothing, although he had a duty to do something. The court's determination that the defendant "had a duty to act to protect the health and wellbeing of the baby girl" is based on the undisputed evidence that the "defendant took on the responsibility for the care and welfare of . . . [both] children with the mother of these children."

Central to the factfinding process is the drawing of inferences from the evidence or from the facts established by the evidence that the court deems to be reasonable and logical. The trial court could not reasonably and logically have found by direct evidence, or inferred from the evidence or facts established, that the defendant had a legal duty to the victim. Where a single fact is essential to proof of an element, such evidence must support the inference of that fact beyond a reasonable doubt. The facts that the defendant was a member of the household, that he considered himself the stepfather of the baby girl, and that he took on the responsibility of the care and welfare of that child do not establish a legal duty.

The existence of a duty is a question of law. Only if such a duty is found to exist does the court then determine whether the defendant violated that duty in a particular situation. While evidence may have been sufficient to establish that the defendant had a moral duty to act, it was not sufficient to establish that he had a legal duty to act. A legal duty is defined as "[a]n obligation arising from . . . the operation of the law. . . ." Black's Law Dictionary (6th Ed.1990). A duty has been defined as an obligation, "whether imposed by the common law, statute, or contract. . . ." As a matter of law, no legal duty can be found to have existed under the particular circumstances of this case and, therefore, no conviction could be had pursuant to § 53a59(a)(3).

We have reviewed the defendant's remaining claims. After a thorough review of the record, transcripts and briefs and, after affording these claims the appropriate scope of review, we find the defendant's assertions to be without merit.

The judgment of conviction on the six counts of assault in the first degree in violation of General Statutes § 53a59(a)(3) is reversed and the matter is remanded with direction to render judgment of not guilty on those charges; the judgment of conviction of risk of injury to a child in violation of General Statutes § 53a21 is affirmed.

QUESTIONS FOR DISCUSSION

1. What did Miranda do, and what did he fail to do?
2. What was Miranda's relationship to the baby?
3. Why did the court decide that that relationship did not have a legal duty of Miranda to the baby?
4. Do you agree? Defend your answer.

NOTE CASES

1. Michael was convicted of second-degree assault for failing to intervene to prevent his wife from beating their two-month-old baby, who suffered multiple fractures of all four lower leg bones. Was Michael's failure to act a criminal omission? According to the trial court, it was:

   > Mr. Michael had a legal duty to aid and assist his child if she was under the threat or risk of physical damage or assault—from any person, including his wife. . . . Mr. Michael did not aid and did not help his daughter when she was in fact physically mistreated and abused by his wife. . . . Mr. Michael's failure was knowing. In other words . . . I find that Mr. Michael was capable of rescuing and assisting his daughter. And . . . he knew that he was capable and—could have rescued her. And . . . he failed to act in the face of . . . that awareness. As a result . . . of his failure to act . . . his daughter suffered serious physical injury.

   The Alaska Court of Appeals affirmed in *Michael v. State*, 767 P.2d 193 (Alaska App.1988)

2. In *Commonwealth v. Konz*, 498 Pa. 639, 450 A.2d 638 (1982), Mrs. Konz was convicted of involuntary manslaughter in the death of her husband. Reverend Konz, a thirty-four-year-old diabetic, had administered daily doses of insulin to himself for seventeen years. After hearing an evangelist, Reverend Konz decided to give up insulin and rely on God to treat his diabetes. Without the insulin, his condition deteriorated. Within a few days, he died from diabetic ketoacidosis. During the entire time of his last illness, Mrs. Konz was with Reverend Konz, except that she was sleeping at the moment of his death. She was charged with involuntary manslaughter for failure to intervene and prevent Reverend Konz's death. Did

the marital relationship give rise to a legal duty to intervene? On appeal from her conviction, the appellate court held that the marital relationship did not give rise to a legal duty to seek medical attention.

The court reasoned that

Recognition of such a duty would place lay persons in peril of criminal prosecution while compelling them to medically diagnose the seriousness of their spouses' illnesses and injuries. In addition, it would impose an obligation for a spouse to take action at a time when the stricken individual competently chooses not to receive assistance. The marital relationship gives rise to an expectation of reliance between spouses, and to a belief that one's spouse should be trusted to respect, rather than ignore, one's expressed preferences. That expectation would be frustrated by imposition of a broad duty to seek aid, since one's spouse would then be forced to ignore the expectation that the preference to forego [sic] assistance will be honored.

3. Oliver met Cornejo in the afternoon when she was with her boyfriend at a bar. She and her boyfriend purchased jewelry from Cornejo. In the late afternoon, when Oliver was leaving the bar to return home, Cornejo got into the car with her, and she drove home with him. At the time, he appeared to be extremely drunk. At her house, he asked her for a spoon and went into the bathroom. She went to the kitchen, got a spoon and brought it to him. She knew he wanted the spoon to take drugs. She remained in the living room while Cornejo "shot up" in the bathroom. He then came out and collapsed onto the floor in the living room. She tried but was unable to rouse him. Oliver then called the bartender at the bar where she had met Cornejo. The bartender advised her to leave him and come back to the bar, which appellant did.

Oliver's daughter returned home at about 5 P.M. that day with two girlfriends. They found Cornejo unconscious on the living room floor. When the girls were unable to wake him, they searched his pockets and found eight dollars. They did not find any wallet or identification. The daughter then called Oliver on the telephone. Oliver told her to drag Cornejo outside in case he woke up and became violent. The girls dragged Cornejo outside and put him behind a shed so that he would not be in the view of the neighbors. He was snoring when the girls left him

there. About a half hour later, appellant returned home with her boyfriend. She, the boyfriend, and the girls went outside to look at Cornejo. Oliver told the girls that she had watched him "shoot up" with drugs and then pass out.

The girls went out to eat and then returned to check on Cornejo later that evening. He had a pulse and was snoring. In the morning, one of the girls heard appellant tell her daughter that Cornejo might be dead. Cornejo was purple and had flies around him. Oliver called the bartender at about 6 A.M. and told her she thought Cornejo had died in her backyard. Oliver then told the girls to call the police and she left for work. The police were called.

Oliver was convicted of involuntary manslaughter and appealed. Did Oliver have a "special relationship" with Cornejo that created a legal duty? Yes, according to the appeals court:

We conclude that the evidence of the combination of events which occurred between the time appellant left the bar with Cornejo through the time he fell to the floor unconscious, established as a matter of law a relationship which imposed upon appellant a duty to seek medical aid. At the time appellant left the bar with Cornejo, she observed that he was extremely drunk, and drove him to her home. In so doing, she took him from a public place where others might have taken care to prevent him from injuring himself, to a private place—her home—where she alone could provide care. To a certain, if limited, extent, therefore, she took charge of a person unable to prevent harm to himself. She then allowed Cornejo to use her bathroom, without any objection on her part, to inject himself with narcotics, an act involving the definite potential for fatal consequences.

When Cornejo collapsed to the floor, appellant should have known that her conduct had contributed to creating an unreasonable risk of harm for Cornejo—death. At that point, she owed Cornejo a duty to prevent that risk from occurring by summoning aid, even if she had not previously realized that her actions would lead to such risk. Her failure to summon any medical assistance whatsoever and to leave him abandoned outside her house warranted the jury finding a breach of that duty. . . . The judgment is affirmed. *People v. Oliver*, 258 Cal.Rptr. 138 (1989)

Not all failures to perform legal duties are criminal omissions. Only *unreasonable* failures to act in the performance of legal duties are criminal omissions. For example, in one case, a sea captain allowed a crew member who had fallen overboard to drown in order to save other crew members and passengers from a dangerous storm. The court held that failure to try and save the one crew member was not a criminal omission because it was reasonable to allow one crew member to die in order to save many others. Neither is it a criminal omission for a baby-sitter who could not swim to fail to dive into deep water to save the child he was watching.

A famous incident occurring in New York City, the failure of residents to take action to save Kitty Genovese from a brutal murder, raises both the questions of when a legal duty arises and what acts amount to a reasonable fulfillment of a legal duty, once the duty arises.

C A S E

Was Their Omission Criminal?
37 Who Saw Murder Didn't Call the Police
New York Times *(March 17, 1964)*

This news story reported in the *New York Times* generated an enormous debate at the time, and discussions of the incident appear periodically. None of the persons involved was ever arrested, charged, or convicted of any crime.

FACTS

For more than half an hour 37 respectable, law-abiding citizens in Queens watched a killer stalk and stab a woman in three separate attacks in Kew Gardens.

Twice the sound of their voices and the sudden glow of their bedroom lights interrupted him and frightened him off. Each time he returned, sought her out and stabbed her again. Not one person telephoned the police during the assault; one witness called after the woman was dead. But Assistant Chief Inspector Frederick M. Lussen, in charge of the borough's detectives and a veteran of 25 years of homicide investigations, is still shocked. He can give a matter of fact recitation of many murders. But the Kew Gardens slaying baffles him—not because it is a murder, but because the "good people" failed to call the police. "As we have reconstructed the crime," he said, "the assailant had three chances to kill this woman during a 35-minute period. He returned twice to complete the job. If we had been called when he first attacked, the woman might not be dead now."

This is what the police say happened beginning at 3:20 A.M. in the staid, middle-class, tree lined Austin Street area:

Twenty-eight-year-old Catherine Genovese, who was called Kitty by almost everyone in the neighborhood, was returning home from her job as manager of a bar in Hollis. She parked her red Fiat in a lot adjacent to the Kew Gardens Long Island Rail Road Station, facing Mowbray Place. Like many residents of the neighborhood, she had parked there day after day since her arrival from Connecticut a year ago, although the railroad frowns on the practice. She turned off the lights of her car, locked the door and started to walk the 100 feet to the entrance of her apartment at 82-70 Austin Street, which is in a Tudor building, with stores on the first floor and apartments on the second.

The entrance to the apartment is in the rear of the building because the front is rented to retail stores. At night the quiet neighborhood is shrouded in the slumbering darkness that marks most residential areas. Miss Genovese noticed a man at the far end of the lot, near a seven-story apartment house at 82-40 Austin Street. She halted. Then, nervously, she headed up Austin Street toward Lefferts Boulevard, where there is a call box to the 102d Police Precinct in nearby Richmond Hill.

She got as far as a street light in front of a bookstore before the man grabbed her. She screamed. Lights went on in the 10-story apartment house at 82-67 Austin Street, which faces the bookstore. Windows slid open and voices punctured the early morning stillness. Miss Genovese screamed: "Oh, my God, he stabbed me! Please help me! Please help me!" From one of the upper windows in the apartment house, a man called down: "Let that girl alone!"

The assailant looked up at him, shrugged and walked down Austin Street toward a white sedan parked a short distance away. Miss Genovese struggled to her feet. Lights went out. The killer returned to Miss Genovese, now trying to make her way around the side of the building by the parking lot to get to her apartment. The assailant stabbed her again. "I'm dying!" she shrieked. "I'm dying!"

Windows were opened again, and lights went on in many apartments. The assailant got into his car and drove away. Miss Genovese staggered to her feet. A city bus, Q i 10, the Lefferts Boulevard line to Kennedy International Airport, passed. It was 3:35 A.M.

The assailant returned. By then, Miss Genovese had crawled to the back of the building, where the freshly painted brown doors to the apartment house held out hope of safety. The killer tried the first door; she wasn't there. At the second door, 82-62 Austin Street, he saw her slumped on the floor at the foot of the stairs. He stabbed her a third time—fatally.

It was 3:50 by the time the police received their first call, from a man who was a neighbor of Miss Genovese. In two minutes they were at the scene. The neighbor, a 70-year-old woman, and another woman were the only persons on the street. Nobody else came forward.

The man explained that he had called the police after much deliberation. He had phoned a friend in Nassau County for advice and then he had crossed the roof of the building to the apartment of the elderly woman to get her to make the call. "I didn't want to get involved," he sheepishly told the police.

The police stressed how simple it would have been to have gotten in touch with them. "A phone call," said one of the detectives, "would have done it." The police may be reached by dialing "0" for operator or SPring 7-3100. Today, witnesses from the neighborhood, which is made up of one-family homes in the $35,000 to $60,000 range with the exception of the two apartment houses near the railroad station, find it difficult to explain why they didn't call the police.

Lieut. Bernard Jacobs, who handled the investigation by the detectives, said: "It is one of the better neighborhoods. There are few reports of crimes." . . .

The police said most persons had told them they had been afraid to call, but had given meaningless answers when asked what they had feared. "We can understand the reticence of people to become involved in an area of violence," Lieutenant Jacobs said, "but where they are in their homes, near phones, why should they be afraid to call the police?"

Witnesses—some of them unable to believe what they had allowed to happen—told a reporter why. A housewife, knowingly if quite casual, said, "We thought it was a lover's quarrel." A husband and wife both said, "Frankly, we were afraid." They seemed aware of the fact that events might have been different. A distraught woman, wiping her hands in her apron, said, "I didn't want my husband to get involved." . . . A man peeked out from a slight opening in the doorway to his apartment and rattled off an account of the killer's second attack. Why hadn't he called the police at the time? "I was tired," he said without emotion. "I went back to bed." It was 4:25 A.M. when the ambulance arrived for the body of Miss Genovese. It drove off. "Then," a solemn police detective said, "the people came out."

QUESTIONS FOR DISCUSSION

1. Did the residents have a legal duty to intervene?

2. A moral duty?

3. On what basis?

4. Should the "neighborly" relationship give rise to a duty? Why?

5. Should a statute impose a duty of citizens to intervene? Why or why not?

6. Assuming a duty, of what does it consist?

7. What should be the penalty for failing to intervene?

8. Consider two other incidents. In the first, an assailant raped and beat an eighteen-year-old switchboard operator. The victim ran naked and bleeding from the building onto the street, screaming for help. A crowd of forty people gathered and watched, in broad daylight, while the rapist tried to drag her back into the building. No onlooker intervened; two police officers happened on the scene and arrested the assailant. In the second incident, eleven people watched while an assailant stabbed seventeen-year-old Andrew Melmille in the stomach on a subway. The assailant left the subway at the next stop. Not one of the eleven people on the train helped Melmille. He bled to death. Is there a legal duty to act in either of these incidents?

9. What is the duty?

10. How, if at all, do these incidents differ from the Genovese incident?[15]

Possession

In addition to voluntary acts and the failure to reasonably perform legal duties, the passive state of possessing some items and substances sometimes qualifies as a criminal act. Although possession of contraband items and substances itself is passive, action is required to obtain possession. For example, if I put illegal drugs in my pocket, I have acted to obtain possession of them. If, on the other hand, my enemy plants drugs on me without my knowledge, I have taken no action to gain possession of them. If I keep the drugs after discovering them in my pocket, retaining possession of them becomes an act of omission—hence a possible criminal act.

Possession can be either actual or constructive. **Actual possession** means physical possession; that is, the substance or item is on the person of the possessor. I actually possess a gun, for example, if it is in my pocket. **Constructive possession** means that the substance or item is under the control of the possessor. Constructive possession requires that possessors are aware of the contraband and that they are in a "position to exercise dominion or control" over it, "either personally or through others." For example, owners are in a "position to exercise dominion or control" over their homes, even though they do not physically possess the cocaine that a weekend guest keeps in the closet of the guest room.[16]

In addition to being actual or constructive, possession can be either knowing possession or mere possession. **Knowing possession** means that possessors are aware that what they possess is contraband. Hence, those who buy cocaine, conscious that it is cocaine, have knowing possession of the cocaine. They need not know that the possession of cocaine is illegal; it is enough that they know that it is cocaine. **Mere possession** means that possessors do not know that that they possess contraband. One who does a friend a favor by carrying a brown paper bag without knowing that the bag contains stolen money has mere possession of the money.

All states except Washington and North Dakota require knowing possession in order to satisfy the *actus reus* of possession. In Washington, however, the court has created a defense of unwitting possession in order to protect against punishing people who do not know that they possess illegal substances or objects. In *State v. Staley,* unbeknownst to Staley, someone had rolled up cocaine in a dollar bill and put it in Staley's tip jar at a night club where Staley played guitar. The Washington Supreme Court ruled that Staley was entitled to the defense of unwitting possession.

The U.S. District Court for the District of Columbia fully examined the problem of constructive possession in *United States v. Byfield.*[17]

C A S E

Did He Possess the "Crack"?

United States v. Byfield, 928 F.2d 1163 (D.C. Cir. 1991)

After a jury found Byfield guilty on one count of possession with intent to distribute crack cocaine, the United States District Court for the District of Columbia granted Byfield's motion for judgment of acquittal notwithstanding verdict. The government appealed. The Court of Appeals reversed and remanded the case.

Before Mikva, Chief Judge, D. H. Ginsburg and Sentelle, Circuit Judges. Mikva, Chief Judge, delivered the opinion of the court.

FACTS

On August 18, 1989, Wayne Byfield and a young girl took Amtrak's "Night Owl" train from New York to Washington, D.C. Thomas Maher, an Amtrak detective, testified that Byfield and the young girl sat together and talked quietly during the trip. Maher followed them off the train and into Union Station. He testified that they looked "very nervous." Byfield had no luggage, but the young girl carried a tote bag. They stood next to each other and talked as they rode an escalator from the train platform. Byfield then moved ahead of the girl in the station, but she approached him again and had a brief conversation while they walked "very swiftly." Byfield went ahead, looking back at the girl and pushing downward with both hands, evidently motioning her to stay back away from him.

Maher observed Byfield repeat these furtive hand gestures at least two more times. Detective Maher alerted two Metropolitan Police Department ("MPD") detectives on duty at Union Station. Maher and Detective Zattau approached the girl, who was approximately 20–30 feet behind Byfield at this time. Zattau described her as "very hesitant and very nervous" when they talked with her, and testified that "[s]he would look in front of her and . . . up ahead of her towards Mr. Byfield." When asked if she had a ticket, the girl apparently pointed to Byfield. During a consensual search of her tote bag, the detectives found a shoe box for Etonics Transam trainers (size 8-1/2 men's, white and light grey) containing an old pair of New Balance shoes and six plastic bags holding over 600 grams of crack cocaine. The tote bag also contained men's clothing (all size extra-large), but no women's clothing.

William Buss, the other MPD detective, approached Byfield outside the station near the taxicab waiting area. When questioned, Byfield said that he lived in New York and was planning to stay in Washington, D.C. for a couple of days. Byfield added that he had traveled alone and carried no luggage because he had clothing at the place he was going to visit. Byfield consented to a pat-down search and left after Buss found nothing on him. About 15 minutes later, Detective Maher saw Byfield sitting on a wall across the street and proceeded to arrest him. Byfield was wearing a "muscle shirt" (like those found in the tote bag), shorts, and new Etonic running shoes matching the model, size and color of those identified on the shoe box found in the tote bag. (Byfield insists that the government never tried to definitively link the shoes he was wearing with the shoe box in the tote bag.)

Wayne Byfield was charged . . . with one count of possession with intent to distribute more than 50 grams of cocaine base, in violation of 21 U.S.C. § 841(a)(1) & (b)(1)(A)(iii). At a jury trial commencing on December 6, 1989, the government presented testimony from the detectives involved in the case, along with expert testimony to the effect that it is "a very common practice" for adults to use young people as drug couriers because of the lesser penalties faced by juveniles. . . .

The defense then presented several witnesses in an attempt to support its theory that appellee knew nothing about the drugs in the tote bag. Shawn Chambers testified that Byfield had spent part of the previous day in New York City with a friend known only as "Larry," at the home of Rhonda Williams. Ms. Williams had a couple of girls with her, one of whom (called "Shirley") was identified as the girl who accompanied Byfield on the train. Chambers testified that he saw Larry talk to Shirley and that he saw Byfield talk with Rhonda Williams (though not with Shirley). Byfield's brother testified that he saw Larry inside the family's home late that night, "looking for something" in Byfield's closet a few hours before the train left. Byfield's brother and girlfriend both testified that they did not recognize the men's clothing found in the tote bag.

. . . [T]he jury . . . found Byfield guilty. However, the district court then issued an order and opinion granting Byfield's motion for acquittal notwithstanding the verdict. In granting Byfield's motion, the district court expressly stated that it would look only to "the evidence presented as part of the government's case-in-chief." Noting that proof of constructive possession requires some action or conduct that "links the individual to the narcotics and indicates that he had a stake in them, some power over them," the court ruled that "none of the officers testified as to any gesture, action, or word demonstrating that Byfield owned, possessed, or had an ability to control the tote bag or its contents." The court dismissed the fact that the Etonics shoes worn by Byfield at the time of arrest matched the shoe box in which the narcotics were found ("at best" this created "a pos-

sible connection" between Byfield and the girl, according to the trial judge), and also noted that Byfield was "fully cooperative" with the police and "did not act in any manner consistent with knowledge of guilt."

OPINION

A judgment of acquittal notwithstanding the verdict is appropriate "only when there is no evidence upon which a reasonable mind might find guilt beyond a reasonable doubt." The evidence must be viewed "in the light most favorable to the Government." Although a motion for judgment of acquittal made at the close of the government's case-in-chief is decided on the basis of only that evidence so far introduced at trial, this court recently revised the law of the circuit to hold that a court must look at the entire record when ruling on the same motion made after trial. . . . On review, "we do not defer to the district court, because we must make our own independent judgment regarding the sufficiency of evidence." The government contends that the district court erred by failing to apply th[is] standard . . . for review of post-trial motions for acquittal and that a proper review of the record would disclose evidence from which a reasonable jury could find guilt beyond a reasonable doubt. . . .

. . . [O]ur review of the evidence presented by both sides convinces us that a reasonable jury could find Mr. Byfield guilty of constructive possession. Constructive possession requires that the defendant knew of, and was in a position to exercise dominion and control over, the contraband, "either personally or through others." The essential question is whether there is "some action, some word, or some conduct that links the individual to the narcotics and indicates that he had some stake in them, some power over them." Mere proximity to the drugs or association with others possessing drugs will not suffice.

Byfield claims that the evidence in this case showed nothing other than a casual encounter between himself and a female drug courier, distinguishing other constructive possession decisions and arguing that the government's case depended upon impermissible inferences from the evidence. . . .

[T]he government points to [evidence] . . . in the record that would allow a reasonable jury to find guilt beyond a reasonable doubt. One of the crucial links in their chain of proof is evidence that Byfield and the young girl were travelling together.

Although this fact is not undisputed, there is ample evidence from which a jury could infer that they were in fact traveling together, including evidence presented by the defense about Byfield's meeting with Rhonda Williams and Larry's conversation with the girl prior to their departure. In defense counsel's opening statement, Byfield's attorney argued that Byfield was planning to travel with Larry and the girl, but that Larry backed out at the last moment. This is consistent with the behavior observed by the detectives on the train and in the station. There is also evidence that Byfield exercised some control over the girl as they walked through the station, especially by signaling her to stay behind him. Although such conduct may not be as strong as prior cases where the defendant had exercised control over the drugs themselves, it suffices to prove control over the person carrying the drugs. Cf. *United States v. Garcia*, 866 F.2d 147, 152 (6th Cir.1989) (defendant's hand signals to drug courier in airline terminal coupled with association between defendant and courier provided "more than enough" evidence to convict under aiding and abetting theory). Here, we do not have a case where the defendant merely sat beside or was acquainted with a person carrying contraband.

The government also points to the shoes, which it contends strongly tied Byfield to the tote bag and the cocaine. They add that other circumstantial evidence also linked Byfield to the contents of the tote bag (e.g., the men's clothing generally consistent with his size). Finally, the government points to expert testimony describing the modus operandi of using juveniles as couriers. All of this circumstantial evidence removes any potential doubts raised by the direct evidence concerning a controlling connection between Byfield and the girl. As defense counsel points out, however, Byfield's general cooperativeness distinguishes this from previous constructive possession cases where there was clearer evasion of the police, but that alone would not make constructive possession unavailable

on these facts. Although hardly conclusive, the evidence introduced by both the government and the defense in this case would allow a reasonable jury to convict the defendant on a theory of constructive possession.

Because the district court failed to consider evidence presented by the defense which buttressed the government's constructive possession theory and provided an adequate basis for the jury's guilty verdict, its decision to grant Byfield's JNOV [judgment notwithstanding the verdict] motion is reversed and the case is remanded with instructions to enter judgment on the verdict.

It is so ordered.

QUESTIONS FOR DISCUSSION

1. List all of the relevant facts in determining whether Byfield "criminally possessed" crack cocaine.

2. How does the court define constructive possession?

3. Using the court's criteria, if you were on the jury would you convict Byfield?

4. How would you define criminal possession?

5. According to your definition, did Byfield possess the "crack"? Explain.

NOTE CASES

1. The Omaha Police Department was engaged in a reverse sting operation. Kevan Barbour, a narcotics officer, sold crack cocaine to parties who approached him. After the purchase, Barbour signaled fellow officers, who arrested the purchasers. Earl Clark approached Officer Barbour, asking for a "twenty" ($20 worth of crack cocaine). Barbour handed Clark a sack. After examining it, Clark handed it back, saying it was "too small." Barbour then handed Clark a larger sack. According to Barbour, Clark then handed him $20. Barbour signaled for the arrest. While being arrested, Clark dropped the crack. In a trial without a jury for possessing crack cocaine, the court believed Barbour's testimony and convicted Clark.

According to Clark's testimony, he handed back the first package because it was too small. But, when given the larger package, he held it for about a minute and a half while trying to decide whether to buy it. Officer Barbour snatched the $20 from him and signaled for the arrest. Did Clark criminally possess the smaller package? If his story is true, did Clark possess the larger package of crack? *State v. Clark*, 236 Neb. 475, 461 N.W.2d 576 (1990)

2. Leonard Dawkins was convicted of possession of heroin and "controlled paraphernalia." The police testified that when they entered a Baltimore, Maryland, hotel room, Dawkins held a tote bag in his hand. The police searched the bag, finding in it narcotics paraphernalia and a bottle cap containing heroin residue. Dawkins testified that the tote bag belonged to his girlfriend, who had asked him to carry the bag to her hotel room. He testified further that he had arrived only a few minutes before the police and that he did not know what was in the bag. Dawkins's girlfriend produced a receipt for the purchase of the bag and testified that she owned the bag. The trial court refused Dawkins's request for an instruction to the effect that knowledge was a requirement of criminal possession. The Maryland statute prohibits "possession of controlled substances." It is silent on intent, but it defines possession as "the exercise of actual or constructive dominion or control over a thing by one or more persons."

Did Dawkins criminally possess heroin and controlled substance paraphernalia, even if he did not know the bag contained them? The Maryland Supreme Court decided that he did not. It said in part: "[A]n individual ordinarily would not be deemed to exercise 'dominion or control' over an object about which he is unaware. Knowledge of the presence of an object is normally a prerequisite to exercising dominion or control." *Dawkins v. State*, 313 Md. 638, 547 A.2d 1041 (1988)

3. Seattle police armed with a search warrant entered Velma Sykes's boyfriend's apartment and found her sleeping in a bedroom with her two children. Sykes's boyfriend was not present. In a second bedroom police found marijuana in matchboxes stacked on a nightstand. In the closet were both men's and women's clothes and more matchboxes with marijuana. Did Sykes possess the marijuana? The trial court found her guilty of possession of marijuana. On appeal, Sykes argued that she did not know the marijuana was in the apartment. The Supreme Court of Washington held that mere constructive possession is sufficient to impose liability for possession of controlled substances. Washington and North Dakota are the only two states that do not require knowledge as an element of possession. *State v. Cleppe*, 96 Wash. 2d 373, 635 P.2d 435 (1981)

Criminal possession punishes potential harm. It aims to prevent possessors from putting prohibited items and substances to use, such as, for example, taking drugs, shooting guns, and using burglary tools. The law of criminal possession adopts the belief that preventive justice is the best justice. It parallels the medical belief that prevention is better than cure. Nevertheless, the crime of possession runs against the basic premise that our criminal law punishes people only for what they do, not for what they might do or for who they are. Those who possess drugs, weapons, or other prohibited substances and objects have not acted. The punishment of possession also increases the risk that criminal law will punish status and condition — the status or condition of dangerous persons. People who possess drugs, burglary tools, and the like are considered dangerous. The law of criminal possession punishes them for being burglars or drug addicts, but not because they have committed the crimes of burglary or illegal drug use. In times like these, at the end of the twentieth century, when fears of violence, illegal drug use, and disorder increase, preventive justice plays a larger part in the making of criminal law.[18]

The objections that criminal possession punishes future actions and status have led to the recommendation that possession should qualify as *actus reus* only when it amounts to an intentional or conscious possession of substances and objects that unambiguously threaten serious bodily harm. According to this view, the criminal law appropriately includes the prohibition against the possession of guns, explosives, and, increasingly, a number of illegal drugs. The possession of obscene materials, on the other hand, does not threaten serious bodily harm; therefore, the criminal law should not include it. In addition, proponents of a limited definition of criminal possession as *actus reus* maintain that the criminal law ought to exclude substances or items that possessors may use for either harmless or harmful purposes. These include burglary tools, such as lock picks, and drug paraphernalia, such as hypodermic needles and pipes.

Summary of *Actus Reus*

The *actus reus*, that is, the criminal act, includes voluntary bodily movements; omissions, or failures to perform legal duties; and possession. This definition is cumbersome, but it is necessary to include the essential characteristics of the *actus reus*. The meanings of these aspects of *actus reus* vary from jurisdiction to jurisdiction. Whether sleepwalking and hypnosis are voluntary movements, whether harms resulting from failures to act on moral duties are crimes, and whether criminal possession requires knowledge of the thing possessed—these questions appreciably alter the scope of criminal law. In times of public fear of crime, these definitions work to expand the scope of criminal law. In times of public calm, the criminal law confines these definitions more narrowly. It is important to see criminal law in this larger sense of balancing individual autonomy and public safety. Therefore, the definitions of *actus reus*, like the definitions of all of the principles of criminal law, bear heavily on criminal policy, reflecting the basic values that a community hopes its criminal law will uphold and protect.

The prestigious American Law Institute, in its widely cited *Model Penal Code*, succinctly summarizes the main aspects of the general principle of *actus reus* in the following provision:

Section 2.01 Requirement of Voluntary Act; Omission as Basis of Liability; Possession as an Act.
(1) A person is not guilty of an offense unless his liability is based on conduct that includes a voluntary act or the omission to perform an act of which he is physically capable.
(2) The following are not voluntary acts within the meaning of this section:
    (a) a reflex of convulsion;
    (b) a bodily movement during unconsciousness or sleep;
    (c) conduct during hypnosis or resulting from hypnotic suggestion;
    (d) a bodily movement that otherwise is not a product of the effort or determination of the actor, either conscious or habitual.
(3) Liability for the commission of an offense may not be based on an omission unaccompanied by action unless
    (a) the omission is expressly made sufficient by the law defining the offense; or
    (b) a duty to perform the omitted act is otherwise imposed by law. . . .

(4) Possession is an act, within the meaning of this Section, if the possessor knowingly procured or received the thing possessed or was aware of his control thereof for a sufficient period to have been able to terminate his possession.

MENS REA

The idea that some kind of blameworthy state of mind must accompany *actus reus* is fundamental to criminal law. The child's "I didn't mean to" captures this idea, as does Justice Holmes's pithy "Even a dog distinguishes between being stumbled over and being kicked." Since at least 1600, common-law judges required that a "bad state of mind," or "evil intent," accompany criminal acts; the Latin maxim *"actus not facit ream nisi mens sit rea"* ("An act is not bad without an evil mind") expresses this idea.

Mens rea is complex, perhaps the most complex concept in criminal law. Almost seventy years ago, in summing up the history of *mens rea*, the distinguished scholar of criminal law, Professor Francis Sayre, wrote what is still true:

> No problem of criminal law is of more fundamental importance or has proved more baffling through the centuries than the determination of the precise mental element or *mens rea*.[19]

Several things contribute to the complexity of *mens rea*. First, courts and legislatures express *mens rea* in widely varying terminology. Second, *mens rea* consists of several mental states, some more blameworthy than others. Third, *mens rea* may relate to one or more elements of particular crimes. It is possible, for example, that one state of mind is required for *actus reus*, another for causation, and still another for circumstance elements. Fourth, proving *mens rea* can create difficult practical problems for prosecutors in criminal cases.[20]

Determining *Mens Rea*

Intention is invisible. The finest instruments of modern technology cannot detect it. Electroencephalograms can record brain waves, and X-rays can photograph brain tissue, but the medieval judge's words still speak the whole truth: "The thought of man is not triable, for the devil himself knoweth not the thought of man." St. Thomas Aquinas put it even more pointedly:

> Man, the framer of human law, is competent to judge only of outward acts, because man seeth those things that appear . . . while God alone, the framer of the Divine law, is competent to judge of the inward movement of wills.[21]

Confessions are the only direct evidence of *mens rea*. Since defendants rarely confess their intentions, the criminal law determines *mens rea* by circumstantial—that is, indirect—evidence. Action most often supplies the indirect evidence of intent. Our everyday experience permits us to infer intentions from actions. For example, most people do not break into the houses of strangers at night unless they intend to commit crimes. Thus, the acts of breaking into and entering the house of another person permit us reasonably to infer that the intruder intends to commit a crime while inside. Hence, we can know indirectly what actors intend by observing directly what they do.

Do not confuse questions of how to discover intent with questions about what specific mental states justify the imposition and the grading of criminal liability. The principle of *mens rea*, when stated properly, defines the mental states required for criminal liability.

Defining *Mens Rea*

Courts and legislatures do not define *mens rea* precisely or consistently. Instead, they use a host of vague terms to identify the mental element. For example, one count found that the United States Criminal Code used seventy-nine separate words and phrases to define *mens rea*.[22]

The cases, statutes, and commentators accept four mental states that qualify as *mens rea*: general, specific, transferred, and constructive intent. **General intent** has various meanings. Sometimes it means all of the mental states encompassed by *mens rea*. It can also mean an intent to do something at an undetermined time or directed at an unspecified object, such as firing a gun into a crowd, intending to kill whomever the bullet strikes, or setting a bomb to explode in a plane without regard to whom it kills. Most commonly, general intent refers to the *actus reus*—that is, to the intent to commit the act required in the definition of the crime. For example, the required act in burglary is breaking and entering, in larceny the taking and carrying away of another's property, and in rape sexual penetration. General intent refers to the intent to commit those acts.

Specific intent designates an intent to do something beyond the *actus reus*. For example, burglary requires an intent to commit a crime after breaking and entering, and larceny requires the intent to steal in addition to the taking and carrying away. Rape is sometimes called a general intent crime because its *mens rea* requires no more than the intent to penetrate. Usually, however, specific intent refers to crimes requiring an intent to cause a particular result, such as homicide, which requires the intent to cause death.[23]

Transferred intent refers to cases in which actors intend to harm one victim but instead harm another. For example, if David shoots at his enemy Doug but kills Doug's friend Michelle when she steps in front of Doug to block the shot, the law transfers David's intent to kill Doug to an intent to kill Michelle. Transferred intent is sometimes called "bad aim intent" because the cases frequently involve misfired guns; however, the law also transfers intent in other situations. If Matt intends to burn down Michael's house but mistakenly burns down Paul's house instead, Matt has committed arson. Only the intent to cause similar harms transfers. The intent to assault a man by throwing a rock at him does not transfer to intending to break a window when the rock intended to hit the man hits the window instead.

Constructive intent refers to cases in which actors do not intend any harm but should have known that their behavior created a high risk of injury. For example, if one drives above the speed limit on an icy street and the car veers out of control, killing a pedestrian, one has the constructive intent to kill.

The *Model Penal Code* has refined these four types of intent in its *mens rea* provision. After enormous effort and sometimes heated debate, the drafters sorted out, identified, and defined four criminal mental states: purpose, knowledge, recklessness, and negligence. These are roughly equivalent to but more elaborate and precise than general, specific, transferred, and constructive intent. The model Code specifies that all crimes requiring a mental element (some do not) must include one of these mental states.

§ 2.02.

General Requirements of Culpability.

1. *Minimum Requirements of Culpability.* Except as provided in § 2.05, a person is not guilty of an offense unless he acted purposely, knowingly, recklessly or negligently, as the law may require, with respect to each material element of the offense.

2. *Kinds of Culpability Defined*

   a. *Purposely.* A person acts purposely with respect to a material element of an offense when:
      i. if the element involves the nature of his conduct or a result thereof, it is his conscious object to engage in conduct of that nature or to cause such a result; and
      ii. if the element involves the attendant circumstances, he is aware of the existence of such circumstances or he believes or hopes that they exist.

   b. *Knowingly.* A person acts knowingly with respect to a material element of an offense when:
      i. if the element involves the nature of his conduct or the attendant circumstances, he is aware that his conduct is of that nature or that such circumstances exist; and
      ii. if the element involves a result of his conduct, he is aware that it is practically certain that his conduct will cause such a result.

   c. *Recklessly.* A person acts recklessly with respect to a material element of an offense when he consciously disregards a substantial and unjustifiable risk that the material element exists or will result from his conduct. The risk must be of such a nature and degree that, considering the nature and purpose of the actor's conduct and the circumstances known to him, its disregard involves a gross deviation from the standard of conduct that a law-abiding person would observe in the actor's situation.

   d. *Negligently.* A person acts negligently with respect to a material element of an offense when he should be aware of a substantial and unjustifiable risk that the material element exists or will result from his conduct. The risk must be of such a nature and degree that the actor's failure to perceive it, considering the nature and purpose of his conduct and the circumstances known to him, involves a gross deviation from the standard of care that a reasonable person would observe in the actor's situation.

3. *Culpability Required Unless Otherwise Provided.* When the culpability sufficient to establish a material element of an offense is not prescribed by law, such element is established if a person acts purposely, knowingly, negligently, or recklessly with respect thereto.

4. *Prescribed Culpability Requirement Applies to All Material Elements.* When the law defining an offense prescribes the kind of culpability that is sufficient for the commission of an offense, without distinguishing among the material elements thereof, such provision shall apply to all the material elements of the offense, unless a contrary purpose plainly appears.

The facts in real cases often blur the distinctions among these four mental states, particularly between recklessness and negligence. Furthermore, the *Model Penal Code* requires that the state prove **culpability,** or *mens rea*, with respect to all three of the following:

1. The act, or the nature of the forbidden conduct.

2. The attendant circumstances.

3. The result of the conduct.

Hence, according to the *Model Penal Code*, a single offense may require purpose for the nature of the conduct, recklessness with respect to the attendant circumstances, and **negligence** with respect to the result.[24]

Purpose. The mental state of purpose means the specific intent either to engage in criminal conduct or to act for the purpose of—with the conscious object of—causing a particular result. For example, common-law burglary requires that the burglar purposely break into and enter a house, and larceny requires that the thief purposely take and carry away another's property. In murder, the murderer's "conscious object" is the victim's death.

C A S E

Did He Expose His Victims to HIV on Purpose?

State v. Stark,
66 Wash.App. 423, 832 P.2d 109 (1992)

This is a consolidated appeal from a jury trial on one count and a bench trial on two counts of second degree assault. At both trials, Calvin Stark was found guilty of intentionally exposing his sexual partners to the human immunodeficiency virus (HIV). After the jury trial for which he was found guilty of one count, referred to as count one, the trial court imposed an exceptional sentence. After the bench trial for which he was found guilty of two additional counts, referred to as counts two and three, the trial court imposed concurrent standard range sentences. Stark contends that in both trials, the State presented insufficient evidence of intent to expose his sexual partners to HIV. He also contends that the exceptional sentence the court imposed for count one was unjustified. The appeals court affirmed the convictions, but remanded

the case for re-sentencing on count one. Chief Judge Petrich delivered the opinion of the court.

FACTS

On March 25, 1988, Calvin Stark tested positive for HIV, which was confirmed by further tests on June 25 and on June 30, 1988. From June 30, 1988, to October 3, 1989, the staff of the Clallam County Health Department had five meetings with Stark during which Stark went through extensive counseling about his infection. He was taught about "safe sex," the risk of spreading the infection, and the necessity of informing his partners before engaging in sexual activity with them. On October 3, 1989, Dr. Locke, the Clallam County Health Officer, after learning that Stark had disregarded this advice and was engaging in unprotected sexual activity, issued a cease and desist order as authorized by RCW 70.24.024(3)(b).

Stark did not cease and desist, and, consequently, on March 1, 1990, Dr. Locke went to the County prosecutor's office intending to seek the prosecutor's assistance, pursuant to RCW 70.24.030, in obtaining judicial enforcement of the cease and desist order. The prosecutor instead had Dr. Locke complete a police report. The State then charged Stark with three counts of assault in the second degree under RCW 9A.36.021(1)(e).

[RCW 9A.36.021(1)(e) provides:

"(1) A person is guilty of assault in the second degree if he or she, under circumstances not amounting to assault in the first degree: . . . (e) With intent to inflict bodily harm, exposes or transmits human immunodeficiency virus as defined in chapter 70.24 RCW."]

Each count involved a different victim:

Count One: The victim and Stark engaged in sexual intercourse on October 27 and October 29, 1989. On both occasions, Stark withdrew his penis from the victim prior to ejaculation. The victim, who could not become pregnant because she had previously had her fallopian tubes tied, asked Stark on the second occasion why he withdrew. He then told her that he was HIV positive.

Count Two: The victim and Stark had sexual relations on at least six occasions between October, 1989, and February, 1990. Stark wore a condom on two or three occasions, but on the others, he ejaculated outside of her body. On each occasion, they had vaginal intercourse. On one occasion Stark tried to force her to have anal intercourse. They also engaged in oral sex. When she told Stark that she had heard rumors that he was HIV positive, he admitted that he was and then gave the victim an AZT pill "to slow down the process of the AIDS."

Count Three: The victim and Stark had sexual relations throughout their brief relationship. It was "almost nonstop with him," "almost every night" during August 1989. Stark never wore a condom and never informed the victim he was HIV positive. When pressed, Stark denied rumors about his HIV status. The victim broke off the relationship because of Stark's drinking, after which Stark told her that he carried HIV and explained that if he had told her, she would not have had anything to do with him.

. . . At the jury trial, the victim in count one testified to her contacts with Stark and the jury received Dr. Locke's deposition testimony regarding the Health Department's contacts with Stark. Stark did not testify. In the bench trial, Dr. Locke testified. There the State also presented the testimony of one of Stark's neighborhood friends. She testified that one night Stark came to her apartment after drinking and told her and her daughter that he was HIV positive. When she asked him if he knew that he had to protect himself and everybody else, he replied, "I don't care. If I'm going to die, everybody's going to die."

The jury found Stark guilty on count one. A second trial judge found Stark guilty of the second and third counts at a bench trial. On count one, Stark was given an exceptional sentence of 120 months based on his future danger to the community. The standard range for that offense was 13 to 17 months. On counts two and three, Stark was given the low end of the standard range, 43 months each, to be served concurrently, but consecutively to count one. . . .

OPINION

Sufficiency of the Evidence

Stark . . . contends that his convictions should be dismissed because the State failed to present sufficient evidence of an intent to inflict bodily harm. In determining whether sufficient evidence supports a conviction, "[t]he standard of review is whether, after viewing the evidence in a light most favorable to the State, any rational trier of fact could have found the essential elements of the charged crime beyond a reasonable doubt." Under this standard, we resolve all inferences in favor of the State.

Stark contends that there is insufficient evidence to prove that he "exposed" anyone to HIV or that he acted with intent to inflict bodily harm. Since Stark is undisputedly HIV positive, he necessarily exposed his sexual partners to the virus by engaging in unprotected sexual intercourse. The testimony of the three victims supports this conclusion.

The testimony supporting the element of intent to inflict bodily harm includes Dr. Locke's statements detailing his counseling sessions with Stark. With regard to the first victim, we know that Stark knew he was HIV positive, that he had been counseled to use "safe sex" methods, and that it had been explained to Stark that coitus interruptus will not prevent the spread of the virus. While there is evidence to support Stark's position, all the evidence viewed in a light most favorable to the State supports a finding of intent beyond a reasonable doubt. The existence of noncriminal explanations does not preclude a finding that a defendant intended to harm his sexual partners. With regard to the later victims, we have, in addition to this same evidence, Stark's neighbor's testimony that Stark, when confronted about his sexual practices, said, "I don't care. If I'm going to die, everybody's going to die." We also have the testimony of the victim in count two that Stark attempted to have anal intercourse with her and did have oral sex, both methods the counselors told Stark he needed to avoid. See also *Commonwealth v. Brown*, ——Pa. Super.——, 605 A.2d 429 (1992) (Defendant threw his feces into face of prison guard. Court found that there was sufficient evidence to support finding of intent to inflict bodily harm when defendant had been counseled by both a physician and a nurse about being tested HIV positive and that he could transmit the virus through his bodily fluids.); *State v. Haines*, 545 N.E.2d 834 (Ind.App.1989) (sufficient evidence to convict of attempted murder when defendant, knowing he was HIV positive, spit, bit, scratched, and threw blood at officer); *Scroggins v. State*, 198 Ga.App. 29, 401 S.E.2d 13 (1990) (sufficient evidence to convict of aggravated assault with intent to murder when defendant, knowing he was HIV positive, sucked up excess sputum, bit an officer, and laughed about it later); *Zule v. State*, 802 S.W.2d 28 (Tex.App.1990) (sufficient evidence that defendant transmitted virus to victim). . . .

Exceptional Sentence

Stark also contends that the trial court erred in imposing an exceptional sentence. . . . [T]he trial court abused its discretion in imposing a 10-year sentence. In order to commit this crime, a person has to know he or she is HIV positive, know how the virus is transmitted, and engage in activity with intent to cause harm. Although such conduct is by nature very serious and reprehensible, the Legislature fixed the same relatively light standard range term that applies in all other second-degree assault cases. Significantly, since "transmitting" the virus is an alternative means of committing the offense, the standard range remains the same even if the victim acquires the virus.

Here, there was no evidence that as of the date of the trial that any of the victims had contracted the virus, and Stark's conduct does not seem to be the "worst possible" example of this offense. The trial court, therefore, abused its discretion in imposing a 10-year term. Cf. *State v. Farmer*, 116 Wash.2d 414, 431–32, 805 P.2d 200, 812 P.2d 858 (1991) (upholding exceptional 7½-year sentence based on finding of deliberate cruelty where defendant knowingly exposed his two minor victims to HIV). . . .

We affirm the convictions, but remand for resentencing on count one.

ALEXANDER and SEINFELD, JJ., concur.

QUESTIONS FOR DISCUSSION

1. Identify all of the facts relevant to determining Stark's *mens rea*.
2. Using the common-law definition of specific intent and the *Model Penal Code* definitions of purposely, knowingly, recklessly, and negligently, and relying on the relevant facts, identify Stark's intention with respect to his acts.
3. Is motive important in this case?
4. Do you agree that the sentence should fall within the standard range, or was it proper to make it more severe, as the trial court did? Defend your answer.

NOTE CASE

Marks was convicted following a jury trial of the felony of escape from custody. After finishing work outside the prison picking potatoes, a group of prisoners were loaded into a truck to return to prison. One of the prisoners fell out. Marks jumped out to see if the other prisoner was injured. The officer in charge did not realize Marks was gone. Marks and the other prisoner waited alongside the road for authorities to pick them up. Marks "stated that he never had any intent to escape, or to avoid recapture."

Was he guilty of escape? Yes, said the court.

"Appellant . . . does not contend that he fell out of the truck so that there would have been no intent at all on his part to perform the act. Appellant admits that he jumped out of the truck and further admitted that he was at a place where he was not supposed to be. The statute does not spell out a requirement for any specific intent to be formed by the prisoner to commit the crime of escape. It is our conclusion that no specific intent 'to evade the due course of justice' need be proven in order to establish the commission of the crime of escape. . . . The judgment is affirmed." *State v. Marks*, 92 Idaho 368, 442 P.2d 778 (1968)

Knowledge. It is impossible to intend a wrong without knowing it, but it is possible to knowingly cause a harm without that action being one's conscious object. Awareness of conduct or knowledge that a result is practically certain to follow from conduct is not the same as having the conduct or result as a conscious object. For example, the owner of a telephone answering service provided service to women he knew were prostitutes; hence, he knowingly provided the service. However, his purpose, or conscious object, was not to promote prostitution, it was to make a profit; hence, he did not conspire to promote prostitution.

A surgeon who removes a cancerous uterus to save a pregnant woman's life knowingly kills the fetus in her womb. But killing the fetus is not the conscious object of the action. The death of the fetus is an unwelcome, if necessary, side effect to removing the cancerous uterus. Similarly, in treason, defendants may knowingly provide aid and comfort to enemies of the United States without intending to overthrow the government. Such defendants are not guilty of treason, even though they know their conduct is practically certain to contribute to overthrowing the government. Hence, the need for the separate crime of providing secrets to the enemy, an offense that requires only that defendants purposely provide such secrets. The need to distinguish between knowledge and purpose arises most frequently in attempt, conspiracy, and treason.[25] However, as *State v. Jantzi* demonstrates, it can arise in other crimes as well.

C A S E

Did He Knowingly Stab the Victim?

State v. Jantzi, 56 Or.App. 57, 641 P.2d 62 (1982)

Jantzi was found guilty of assault. He appealed on the ground that he did not knowingly stab his victim. The supreme court modified the conviction. Gillette, P. J., Joseph, C. J., and Roberts, J. Pro Tem. Gillette, Presiding Judge.

FACTS

. . . Defendant testified that he was asked to accompany Diane Anderson, who shared a house with defendant and several other people, to the home of her estranged husband, Rex. While Diane was in the house talking with Rex, defendant was using the blade of his knife to let the air out of the tires on Rex's van. Another person put sugar in the gas tank of the van. While the Andersons were arguing, Diane apparently threatened damage to Rex's van and indicated that someone might be tampering with the van at that moment. Rex's roommate ran out of the house and saw two men beside the van. He shouted and began to run toward the men. Rex ran from the house and began to chase defendant, who ran down a bicycle path. Defendant, still holding his open knife, jumped into the bushes beside the path and landed in the weeds. He crouched there, hoping that Rex would not see him and would pass by. Rex, however, jumped on top of defendant and grabbed his shirt. They rolled over and Rex was stabbed in the abdomen by defendant's knife. Defendant could not remember making a thrusting or swinging motion with the knife; he did not intend to stab Rex.

OPINION

The indictment charged that defendant "did unlawfully and knowingly cause physical injury to Rex Anderson by means of a deadly weapon, knife, to wit: by stabbing the said Rex Anderson with said knife." ORS 163.175 provides that: (1) A person commits the crime of assault in the second degree if he: (b) Intentionally or knowingly causes physical injury to another by means of a deadly or dangerous weapon. . . . "Knowingly is defined in ORS 161.085(8): 'Knowingly' or 'with knowledge' when used with respect to conduct or to a circumstance described by a statute defining an offense, means that a person acts with an awareness that his conduct is of a nature so described or that a circumstance so described exists."

The trial court stated: "Basically, the facts of this case are: that Defendant was letting air out of the tires and he has an open knife. He was aware of what his knife is like. He is aware that it is a dangerous weapon. He runs up the bicycle path. He has a very firm grip on the knife, by his own admission, and he knows the knife is dangerous. It is not necessary for the state to prove that he thrust it or anything else. Quite frankly, this could have all been avoided if he had gotten rid of the knife, so he 'knowingly caused physical injury to Rex Anderson.' And, therefore, I find him guilty of that particular charge."

Although the trial judge found defendant guilty of "knowingly" causing physical injury to Anderson, what he described in his findings is recklessness. The court found that defendant knew he had a dangerous weapon and that a confrontation was going to occur. The court believed that defendant did not intend to stab Anderson. The court's conclusion seems to be based on the reasoning that because defendant knew it was possible that an injury would occur, he acted "knowingly." However, a person who "is aware of and consciously disregards a substantial and unjustifiable

risk" that an injury will occur acts "recklessly," not "knowingly." See ORS 161.085(9). Recklessly causing physical injury to another is assault in the third degree. ORS 163.165.

This is a slightly different situation from that presented in *State v. Jackson*, 40 Or.App. 759, 596 P.2d 600 (1979), in which there was insufficient evidence to support the charge for which the defendant was convicted, but the facts necessarily found supported conviction of a lesser offense. Here there was evidence that would have supported a finding of assault in the second degree, but the trial court specifically found the facts to be such that they only support a charge of reckless, rather than knowing, assault.

We have authority, pursuant to Article VII (Amended), § 3 of the Oregon Constitution, to enter the judgment that should have been entered in the court below. Assault in the third degree is a lesser included offense of the crime of assault in the second degree charged in the accusatory instrument in this case. See ORS 136.460. We modify defendant's conviction to a conviction for the crime of assault in the third degree.

QUESTIONS FOR DISCUSSION

1. What are the facts relevant to determining Jantzi's *mens rea* in this case?

2. On what facts did the trial court rely to conclude that Jantzi acted knowingly?

3. How did the appellate court conclude that Jantzi acted recklessly?

4. Relying on the facts, how would you characterize Jantzi's *mens rea*?

5. Did he intend to stab Anderson?

6. Did he stab Anderson knowingly, or did he stab him recklessly? Defend your answer.

NOTE CASE

Jackson was charged with robbery. While the victim was sitting in a bar, he noticed the light in his car go on. He ran outside to investigate. Defendant, using a tire iron, had broken open the glove box, containing more than $500 in currency, but had not taken it. The victim pulled the defendant from the car, and the defendant hit him with a tire iron a number of times. The victim wrested the tire iron from the defendant, and the defendant fled. The trial court found that the blows were struck to effect escape rather than to complete theft.

Therefore, according to the court, Jackson did not have the requisite intent to commit robbery. *State v. Jackson*, 40 Or.App. 759, 596 P.2d 600 (1979)

Standards for Determining Purpose and Knowledge. Most jurisdictions apply a subjective standard to determine whether defendants intended or knowingly engaged in conduct or caused harmful results. In these jurisdictions, purpose and knowledge depend on what specific defendants intended or in fact knew, not on the objective standard that depends on what defendants should have known or on what "most people would have intended." The rationale for the subjective standard is that culpability for serious criminal conduct ought to rest on what defendants actually intend, not on what reasonable people would have intended. Some jurisdictions adopt an objective standard for determining purpose and knowledge. For example, the Washington state criminal code provides:

> A person acts knowingly or with knowledge when:
> (i) he is aware of a fact, facts, circumstances or result . . . ; or
> (ii) he has information which would lead a reasonable man in the same situation to believe that facts exist.[26]

And the Michigan code also permits objective criteria in determining *mens rea* but only for the purpose of inferring the actual intent of defendants. According to the statute, a person acts

> intentionally with respect to a result or conduct . . . when his conscious objective is to cause that result or engage in that conduct. In finding that a person acted intentionally with respect to a result the finding of fact may rely upon proof that such result was the natural and probable consequence of the person's act.[27]

Recklessness and Negligence. Reckless people do not purposely or knowingly cause harm; they consciously create *risks* of harm. Recklessness resembles purpose and knowledge in that both require consciousness. However, consciously creating a risk of harm is less culpable than having the purpose or conscious object to cause harm, or knowing that a result is practically certain to follow from the actions of the defendant. Recklessness deals in probabilities; purpose and knowledge in certainties. Furthermore, conscious risk creation—like purpose and knowledge—may refer to the nature of the actor's conduct, to material attendant circumstances, or to the result.

Recklessness requires more than a consciousness of *ordinary* risks; it requires awareness of *substantial* and *unjustifiable* risks. To reduce the unavoidable imprecision in the terms substantial and unjustifiable, the American Law Institute's *Model Penal Code* proposes that fact finders determine recklessness according to the following two-pronged test:

1. To what extent were defendants actually aware of how substantial and unjustifiable the risks were?

2. Does the disregard constitute so "gross [a] deviation from the standard" that a law-abiding person would observe that it deserves criminal condemnation in that situation?

This standard has both a subjective and an objective component. The first prong of the test focuses on a defendant's actual awareness; the second prong measures conduct according to how it deviates from what most people do.

Harm is not the conscious object of reckless wrongdoers. Indeed, they may hope that no harm befalls anyone. Yet, they are aware that they are creating risks that *might* harm someone. For example, in one case, a large drug company knew that a medication it sold to control high blood pressure could cause liver damage and even death; it sold the drug anyway. The company's officers, who made the decision to sell the drug, did not want to hurt anyone (indeed, they hoped no one would die or suffer liver damage). They sought only profit for the company. But they were prepared to risk the deaths of their customers in order to make a profit.[28]

Like reckless wrongdoers, negligent wrongdoers create risks of harm. Unlike reckless wrongdoers, however, negligent wrongdoers are not aware or conscious that they are creating risks. Hence, negligent wrongdoers *should* know that they are creating substantial and unjustifiable risks, but they do not *actually* know that they are doing so. Therefore, recklessness is conscious risk creation; negligence is unconscious risk creation. The standard for negligence is wholly objective—actors should have known, even though in fact they did not know, that they were creating risks. For example, a reasonable person should know that driving fifty miles an hour down a crowded street can cause harm, even though in fact the driver does not know it. The driver who should know this but does not is negligent. The driver who knows it but drives too fast anyway is reckless. Negligence, like recklessness, requires substantial and unjustifiable creation of risk.

C A S E

Did He Consciously Create a Risk of Death?

People v. Strong,
37 N.Y.2d 568, 376 N.Y.S.2d 87,
338 N.E.2d 602 (1975)

Strong was convicted of manslaughter in the second degree, which carries a penalty of between four and fifteen years. The actual sentence does not appear in the report of the appeal. Strong appealed, and the supreme court reversed his conviction and ordered a new trial. Judge Jasen wrote the opinion for the court. Judge Gabrielli dissented.

FACTS

Defendant was charged ... with manslaughter in the second degree (Penal Law, § 125.15) for causing the death of Kenneth Goings. At the trial, the defense requested that the court submit to the jury, in addition to the crime charged, the crime of criminally negligent homicide (Penal Law, § 125.10). The court refused, and the jury found defendant guilty as charged.

The record discloses that the defendant, 57 years old at the time of trial, had left his native Arabia at the age of 19, emigrating first to China and then coming to the United States three years later. He had lived in Rochester only a short time before committing the acts which formed the basis for this homicide charge. He testified that he had been of the Sudan Muslim religious faith since birth, and had become one of the sect's leaders, claiming a sizable following.

Defendant articulated the three central beliefs of this religion as "cosmic consciousness, mind over matter and physiomatic psychomatic consciousness." He stated that the second of these beliefs, "mind over matter," empowered a "master," or leader, to lie on a bed of nails without bleeding, to walk through fire or on hot coals, to perform surgical operations without anesthesia, to raise people up off the ground, and to suspend a person's heartbeat, pulse, and breathing while that person remained conscious. In one particular type of ceremony, defendant, purportedly exercising his powers of "mind over matter," claimed he could stop a follower's heartbeat and breathing and plunge knives into his chest without any injury to the person. There was testimony from at least one of defendant's followers that he had successfully performed this ceremony on previous occasions. Defendant himself claimed to have performed this ceremony countless times over the previous 40 years without once causing an injury.

Unfortunately, on January 28, 1972, when defendant performed this ceremony on Kenneth Goings, a recent recruit, the wounds from the hatchet and three knives which defendant had inserted into him proved fatal.

OPINION

The sole issue upon this appeal is whether the trial court erred in refusing to submit to the jury the lesser crime of criminally negligent homicide. Recently, in *People v. Stanfield*, [see Note Case 3 following this excerpt] 36 N.Y.2d 467, 369 N.Y.S.2d 118, 330 N.E.2d 75, the same issue was before us and we held that where a reasonable view of the evidence supports a finding that a defendant committed this lesser degree of homicide, but not the greater, the lesser crime should be submitted to the jury. . . .

"The essential distinction between the crimes of manslaughter, second degree, and criminally negligent homicide . . . is the mental state of the defendant at the time the crime was committed. In one, the actor perceives the risk, but consciously disregards it. In the other, he negligently fails to perceive the risk. The result and the underlying conduct, exclusive of the mental element, are the same." Although in *Stanfield* we pointed out that "criminal recklessness and criminal negligence . . . may . . . be but shades apart on the scale of criminal culpability," it would be incorrect to infer from *Stanfield* that in every case in

which manslaughter, second degree, is charged, a defendant is entitled also to an instruction as to criminally negligent homicide. In determining whether the defendant in this case was entitled to the charge of the lesser crime, the focus must be on the evidence in the record relating to the mental state of the defendant at the time of the crime.

We view the record as warranting the submission of the lesser charge of criminally negligent homicide since there is a reasonable basis upon which the jury could have found that the defendant failed to perceive the risk inherent in his actions. The defendant's conduct and claimed lack of perception, together with the belief of the victim and defendant's followers, if accepted by the jury, would justify a verdict of guilty of criminally negligent homicide. There was testimony, both from defendant and from one of his followers, that the victim himself perceived no danger, but in fact volunteered to participate. Additionally, at least one of the defendant's followers testified that the defendant had previously performed this ritual without causing injury.

Assuming that a jury would not believe that the defendant was capable of performing the acts in question without harm to the victim, it still could determine that this belief held by the defendant and his followers were [sic] indeed sincere and that defendant did not in fact perceive any risk of harm to the victim.

That is not to say that the court should in every case where there is some subjective evidence of lack of perception of danger submit the lesser crime of criminally negligent homicide. Rather, the court should look to other objective indications of a defendant's state of mind to corroborate, in a sense, the defendant's own subjective articulation. Thus, in *Stanfield*, there was evidence from which the jury could have reasonably concluded that the victim herself did not view Stanfield's actions as creating any risk of harm. Here, the evidence supporting defendant's claimed state of mind is, if anything, stronger. Therefore, on the particular facts of this case, we conclude that there is a reasonable view of the evidence which, if believed by the jury, would support a finding that the defendant was guilty only of the crime of criminally negligent homicide, and that the trial court erred in not submitting, as requested, this lesser offense to the jury. Accordingly, we would reverse and order a new trial.

DISSENT

Gabrielli, Judge (dissenting).

I dissent and conclude that there is no justification in the record for the majority's holding that "defendant's conduct or claimed lack of perception, together with the belief of the victim and defendant's followers, if accepted by the jury, would justify a verdict of criminally negligent homicide." The Appellate Division was correct in holding that "Defendant's belief in his superhuman powers, whether real or simulated, did not result in his failure to perceive the risk but, rather, led him consciously to disregard the risk of which he was aware."

At trial, it was shown, primarily from defendant's own statements to the police and testimony before the Grand Jury, that during the course of a "religious ordeal," defendant, the self-proclaimed leader of the Sudan Muslim sect of Rochester, New York, stabbed one of his followers, Kenneth Goings, a number of times in the heart and chest causing his death. Additionally, the evidence established defendant's awareness and conscious disregard of the risk his ceremony created and is entirely inconsistent with a negligent failure to perceive that risk. Testimony was adduced that just prior to being stabbed, Goings, a voluntary participant up to that point, objected to continuance of the ceremony saying "No, father" and that defendant, obviously evincing an awareness of the possible result of his actions, answered, "It will be all right, son." Defendant testified that after the ceremony, he noticed blood seeping from the victim's wounds and that he attempted to stop the flow by bandaging the mortally wounded Goings.

Defendant further stated that when he later learned that Goings had been removed to another location and had been given something to ease the pain, he became "uptight," indicating, of course, that defendant appreciated the risks involved and the possible consequences of his acts. . . .

Can it be reasonably claimed or argued that, when the defendant inflicted the several stab wounds, one of which penetrated the victim's heart and was four and three-quarter inches deep, the defendant failed to perceive the risk?

The only and obvious answer is simply "no." Moreover, the record is devoid of evidence pointing toward a negligent lack of perception on defendant's part. The majority concludes otherwise by apparently crediting the testimony of defendant, and one of his followers, that at the time defendant was plunging knives into the victim, the defendant thought "there was no danger to it." However, it is readily apparent that the quoted statement does not mean, as the majority assert, that defendant saw no risk of harm in the ceremony, but, rather, that he thought his powers so extraordinary that resultant injury was impossible. Thus, the testimony does not establish defendant's negligent perception for even a grossly negligent individual would perceive the patent risk of injury that would result from plunging a knife into a human being; instead, the testimony demonstrates defendant's conscious disregard of the possible consequences that would naturally flow from his acts.

This case might profitably be analogized to one where an individual believing himself to be possessed of extraordinary skill as an archer attempts to duplicate William Tell's feat and split an apple on the head of another individual from some distance. However, assume that rather than hitting the apple, the archer kills the victim. Certainly, his obtuse subjective belief in his extraordinary skill would not render his actions criminally negligent. Both in the context of ordinary understanding and the Penal Law definition (§ 15.05, subd. 3), the archer was unquestionably reckless and would, therefore, be guilty of manslaughter in the second degree. The present case is indistinguishable. . . .

Breitel, C. J., and Jones, Wachtler, Fuchsberg and Cooke, J. J., concur with Jasen, J., Gabrielli, J., dissents and votes to affirm in a separate opinion. Order reversed.

QUESTIONS FOR DISCUSSION

1. What precise facts bear on the question of *mens rea* in the case?

2. What mental state did Strong have with respect to stabbing Goings?

3. What was his mental state with respect to Goings's death?

4. If you were deciding this case, would you call the death negligent or reckless? Why?

5. What is the major disagreement between the majority and the dissent?

6. Do you agree with the dissent or the majority? Why?

NOTE CASES

1. Cordell asked his friend Ingle if he could still do his "fast draw" trick. The trick was that a person, "while sitting or standing, would hold his hands extended forward several inches apart; defendant, with a pistol in a holster strapped to his body, would attempt to draw his pistol and place it between the hands of the other person before that person could clap his hands together." Ingle said yes, and tried it with a .22 caliber pistol. The pistol discharged, a bullet struck Cordell in the front of his head and killed him almost instantly. Ingle forgot he had loaded the pistol. Did Ingle recklessly kill Cordell? The court held yes:

> It seems that, with few exceptions, it may be said that every unintentional killing of a human being proximately caused by a reckless use of firearms, in the absence of intent to discharge the weapon, or in the belief that it is not loaded, and under circumstances not evidencing a heart devoid of a sense of social duty, is involuntary manslaughter. *People v. Ingle*

2. Warner-Lambert Co., manufacturer of Freshen-Up chewing gum, was indicted on six counts of manslaughter in the second degree and six counts of criminally negligent homicide. Six employees died in a "massive explosion and fire." Evidence was submitted that "an inspection of the plant by Warner-Lambert's insurance carrier on February 26, 1976 had resulted in advice to the insured that an explosive dust at concentrations above the lowest explosion level presented an explosion hazard." Evidence showed that the company, although beginning to reduce the hazard, continued to operate the plant above the lowest explosion level. Was Warner-Lambert negligent? The court said yes:

> There can be no doubt that there was competent evidence . . . to establish the existence of a broad, undifferentiated risk of explosion from ambient MS dust which had been brought to the attention of defendants. It may be assumed that, if it be so categorized, the risk was both substantial and unjustifiable. *People v. Warner-Lambert Co.,* 51 N.Y.2d 295, 434 N.Y.S.2d 159, 414 N.E.2d 660 (1980)

3. Stanfield and his common-law wife, Thomasina, were not living together. After a date, they returned to Thomasina's house. Stanfield asked Thomasina if she was going out with his friend. She said no. Intending to frighten her, he took out a gun, cocked it, put it near her head, and said he was going to shoot her. Thomasina responded, "Bob, don't mess with the gun like that," and then "slapped his hand or arm." The gun discharged, killing Thomasina. Stanfield tried to revive her. When he failed, he called the police, and made a frantic call to his mother. He then ran outside and summoned a police officer on patrol. Was he reckless or negligent? The trial court refused an instruction on negligent manslaughter, and Stanfield was convicted of reckless manslaughter. The appellate court reversed:

> [C]riminal recklessness and criminal negligence with respect to a particular result—here homicide—may in a particular case, if not hypothetically or definitionally, be but shades apart on the scale of criminal culpability. And the distinction between the two mental states is less clear practically than theoretically. Indeed, the definitional cleavage the People would draw, while theoretically appealing, may be illusory in practical application. Hence it seems manifest that in a practical, if not a literal definitional sense, if one acts with criminal recklessness he is at least criminally negligent. Moreover, negligence may, in a particular case, quickly, even imperceptibly, aggravate on the scale of culpability to recklessness. . . . Whether when the derringer was cocked . . . unawareness escalated or should have escalated to awareness of the ultimate risk created—criminal recklessness—was a factual question for the jury, considering all the circumstances. *People v. Stanfield,* 330 N.E.2d 75 (N.Y.1975)

4. Cameron, a four-year veteran of the Marine Corps, has had extensive training and experience with a vari-

ety of weapons. He owns at least five weapons. At the time of the alleged crime, he and his wife had been married for eleven years. Three days before the incident, he discovered that she had been seeing another man. He planned to divorce her, but after some discussion they decided to remain together. In the late afternoon of March 13, 1979, they were in their bedroom discussing which one of them would pick up the children at the sitter's house. Cameron picked up a revolver from the nightstand and was passing it from hand to hand when it discharged and killed his wife.

The defendant was charged with second-degree murder for knowingly causing his wife's death by "shooting her in the head with a .44 Magnum revolver." Cameron testified that he forgot he had loaded the gun and denied that he killed his wife intentionally. The state argued that because Cameron

knew so much about guns, he knew of the risk of killing his wife and could not be simply negligent. The risk depended on whether the gun was loaded. The appellate court disagreed:

> Under all the circumstances, including the mental distress resulting from finding out that his wife had been unfaithful to him and the emotional strain of deciding whether or not to divorce her, we cannot say that the jury would not be justified in believing that the defendant had forgotten that he had loaded the gun. Thus, the evidence would justify a finding of guilt of negligent homicide rather than manslaughter, and it was error not to submit the issue to the jury. *State v. Cameron*, 121 N.H. 348, 430 A.2d 138 (1981)

Strict Liability. Strict liability offenses are a major exception to the principle that every crime consists of both a physical and a mental element. **Strict liability** crimes require no *mens rea*; they impose liability without fault. Hence, whether a defendant's conduct was purposeful, knowing, reckless, or negligent is neither relevant nor material to criminal liability.

Two main arguments support strict liability. First, a strong public interest sometimes justifies eliminating *mens rea*. Strict liability arose during the industrial revolution when manufacturing, mining, and commerce exposed large numbers of the public to death, disability, and disease in the form of noxious gases, unsafe railroads and other workplaces, and adulterated foods and other products. Second, strict liability offenses carry minimum penalties, usually fines. The combined strong public interest and moderate penalty justify extending criminal liability to cases where there is no *mens rea*, according to supporters.[29]

Despite these arguments, opponents of strict liability criticize it on the grounds that it is too easy to expand it beyond public welfare offenses that seriously endanger the public. They also contend that strict liability weakens the force of criminal law because too many people acting innocently are caught within its net. This, in turn, reduces respect for criminal law, which properly should punish only the blameworthy. It does no good, and probably considerable harm, to punish those who have not purposely, knowingly, recklessly, or negligently harmed others. In the end, critics maintain, strict liability does not fit well into the criminal law because it is inconsistent with the basic nature of criminal law: to serve as a stern moral code. To punish those who accidentally injure others violates that moral code.

C A S E

Did he "Hit and Run"?

People v. Hager,
124 Misc.2d 123, 476 N.Y.S.2d 442 (1984)

A grand jury indicted Hager for leaving the scene of an accident. Hager moved to dismiss the indictment because, among other reasons, the prosecutor did not properly instruct the grand jury on the requirement of intent under the New York "hit and run" statute. The court dismissed the indictment and granted leave to the prosecutor to call another grand jury again within 45 days to consider another indictment in which the prosecutor instructs the grand jury regarding the requirement of intent

RAYMOND HARRINGTON, Judge.

FACTS

"I don't remember anything . . ."

"My mind went blank . . ."

"I blacked out . . ."

"I panicked and don't remember what I did or anything that happened . . ."

So often those of us who habituate the criminal courts have heard such statements or testimony from the accused in a criminal case. A variation on this theme in the Grand Jury testimony of this defendant has raised legal issues concerning that proceeding. This defendant was indicted for leaving the scene of an accident as a felony and driving while impaired (Sections 600(2)(a) and (b) and 1192(1) of the VTL.)

In fact, Douglas Hager told the Grand Jury the following concerning a collision between his car and a young female pedestrian Katherine Kuehhas, who was in a coma at the time of the Grand Jury presentation.

[Excerpt from] Grand Jury testimony of Hager . . . "I tried to step on my brakes, but probably by the time I could respond to it, I hit her. She came rolling over the front of my car, hit my windshield and shattered it and rolled into the street to my left. I immediately pulled over to the right side by the curb and then I looked out my window and saw her lying there and I noticed several people were hurrying over to see if, I assume, to help the girl.

At that point in time I don't know what came over me, but I felt—I was horrified. I couldn't believe this girl walked out in front of my car like this. I couldn't believe this was happening to me. I just kept seeing this girl come up over the front of my car and I guess I saw—I kept picturing all the horrible things that ever happened in my life including the death of my grandparents, the break up of my marriage, my divorce and the next thing I remember I found myself driving down Hempstead Turnpike. I don't even know why. I don't remember ever doing it, but I think what sort of snapped me out of that was the flashing yellow lights of the emergency vehicle right behind me. I must have gotten probably a half mile from the accident and I pulled over to the side. . . . I don't know why I did it. I did not intend to leave that scene of the accident. I have no other explanation as to why I left other than I guess the horror of the situation that I had just been through did something to me."

More particularly, upon inspection of the Grand Jury minutes, the defendant through his attorney seeks dismissal of this indictment on . . . [inter alia] the grounds that the proceedings were defective in that the prosecutor did not instruct the Grand Jury on the proper principles of law. . . . In the alternative to dismissal, the defendant asks for a bill of particulars.

OPINION

. . . [T]he defendant's attack on the legal instructions to the Grand Jury raises fundamental questions concerning the mental state needed to establish the crime of leaving the scene of an accident. Relying upon the presumption against strict liability offenses, the defendant petitions this Court to require that the People prove that the defendant intentionally left the scene of the accident before criminal liability will exist. This the defendant submits should be so, even though the language of the statute omits any such word or phrase expressing a culpable state of mind with respect to the element of leaving the scene.

The People . . . assert that they have instructed the Grand Jury on the statutory language and no more is required. In any event, the People assert that Section 600 of the VTL is a strict liability offense and the People need not establish any culpable state of mind by the defendant as to his leaving the scene.

Section 600 of the Vehicle and Traffic Law provides in pertinent part that:

2(a). Any person operating a motor vehicle who, knowing or having cause to know that personal injury has been caused to another person, due to the culpability of the person operating such motor vehicle, or due to accident, shall, before leaving the place where the said personal injury occurred, stop, exhibit his license and insurance identification card for such vehicle . . . and give his name, residence, . . . insurance carrier and insurance identification information and license number, to the injured party, if practical, and also to a police officer, or in the event no police officer is in the vicinity of the place of said injury, then, he shall report said incident as soon as physically able to the nearest police station or judicial officer. . . . Any violation of the provisions of this subdivision, other than mere failure of an operator to exhibit his license and insurance identification card for such vehicle, where the personal injury involved results in death or serious physical injury as defined in section 10.00 of the penal law, shall constitute a Class E felony.

Section 600 of the VTL is also known, in the vernacular, as the New York "hit and run" statute. Section 600 VTL and its predecessor statutes have been in existence since the advent of the industrial revolution and the general prohibition against "hit and run" is a concept commonly understood by modern man.

The People have asserted that Section 600 of VTL is a "strict liability offense." Often, such offenses are called mala prohibita, i.e. no *mens rea*, or culpable state of mind being required. Such offenses are not in harmony with the common law concept that a wrongful act be accompanied by a guilty state of mind. Wharton's *Criminal Law* § 23.

Our legislature has conveyed the message consistently that "strict liability" crimes are to be frowned upon.

Although no culpable mental state is expressly designated in a statute defining an offense, a culpable mental state may nevertheless be required for the commission of such an offense, or with respect to some or all of the material elements thereof, if the proscribed conduct necessarily involves such culpable mental state. A statute defining a crime, unless clearly indicating a legislative intent to impose strict liability, should be construed as defining a crime of mental culpability. McKinney's, *Penal Law*, § 15.15(2), 1975.

Also,

Generally, it is reasonable to assume that it is the design of the Legislature to punish as criminal offenses only those acts which are intentionally committed. Accordingly, if it is practical to avoid a construction of a statute which eliminates intent as an element of a crime, the courts will do so. McKinney's *Statutes* § 274, 1971.

Section 600 VTL has the apparent indicia of a crime of strict liability in that it is not in the nature of an act of positive aggression and the accused, if he does not will the violation, usually is in a position to prevent it with no more than reasonable care. Furthermore, the penalties have up until recently been relatively small. On the other hand, as it presently exists and is charged in this indictment, the crime is now a felony. Under these circumstances, the Courts should be even more resolute in avoiding a strict liability construction.

Both parties overlook a significant fact in Section 600 of the VTL. The statute requires that the defendant ". . . knowing or having cause to know that personal injury has been caused . . . due to (his) culpability . . . or . . . accident," leave the scene of the incident. This is indeed a culpable state of mind.

". . . When one and only one of such (culpable mental state) terms appears in a statute defining an offense, it is presumed to apply to every element of the offense unless an intent to limit its application clearly appears." Penal Law, Section 15.15(1).

The present charge would appear to require only one mental state, i.e., knowledge by the defendant as the operator of a motor vehicle that he has caused personal injury by his culpability or by accident. . . .

There is then in the first instance a question of statutory construction. . . . The issue is whether the mental state of mind contained in the statute is presumed to apply to every element of the offense (including whether the accused left the scene knowingly or intentionally) or whether a statutory construction limiting the culpable mental state to mere knowledge by defendant of causation of a personal injury by an auto accident is the only state of mind the People need prove. The characterization of the issue presented here as whether this crime is a strict liability offense does not properly frame the issue. . . .

How clearly it appears that the legislature intended to limit scienter in Section 600 of the VTL or indeed in the commentator's examples is a perplexing question. What is certain is that the principle of statutory construction is one that requires, emphasizes and insists that intent be engrafted upon every element of the offense unless the intent to limit is patently clear. The criminal law requires historically a culpable state of mind for every crime. The common law demanded that for any crime that there be a "vicious will". "The existence of a *mens rea* is the rule of, rather than the exception to, the principles of Anglo-American criminal jurisprudence" *Dennis v. US*, 341 US 494, 71 S.Ct. 857, 95 L.Ed. 1137. This Court therefore concludes that not unlike the presumption against strict liability offenses, this principle of statutory construction should be viewed presumptively in favor of the general applicability of intent to every element of the offense. . . .

Therefore, giving great weight to the presumption against limited scienter, and considering the consequences of guilt of a felony with limited intent the Court concludes that "knowingly" applies to the element of leaving the scene of an accident as well as to knowledge of the accident. Fundamentally the crime is "hit and run". The Court believes that before the defendant should be held feloniously responsible for this crime, the People should be required to show knowledge by the defendant of the "hit" and that the "run" or leaving was knowing. . . .

Under all the circumstances, this Court holds that the failure of the prosecutor to instruct the Grand Jury on the applicability of the concepts of knowledge to the leaving the scene of the incident and also related concepts of intoxication and voluntariness of the acts alleged went to the essence of defendant's criminal responsibility and the most salient factual issue before the Grand Jury.

Without commenting on the credibility or incredibility of Mr. Hager's testimony, the Grand Jury is entitled to be guided by the essential principles of law. The failure to so instruct the Grand Jury made it impossible in these circumstances for that body to decide intelligently whether the defendant committed the crime and that failure impaired the integrity of the entire proceeding. . . . [T]he indictment is therefore dismissed. . . . The People are granted leave to represent this entire matter to another Grand Jury within (45) forty-five days. The defendant shall remain at liberty on his present bail status pending the action of the Grand Jury. . . .

QUESTIONS FOR DISCUSSION

1. What reasons did the court give for the strong prejudice against strict liability in general?

2. What reasons did the court give for deciding that the New York "hit and run" statute in particular required intent to "run"?

3. What arguments could you give against his decision?

4. Is strict liability a good idea in general? Why or why not?

5. Is it a good idea in offenses such as "hit and run?" Why or why not?

NOTE CASES

1. Two Fargo police officers found Vogel asleep in his car in a parking lot at about 1:20 A.M. The car engine was running, the headlights were on, and the doors were unlocked. Vogel was slumped over in the front seat. After knocking on the window, an officer opened the driver's door, turned off the engine and lights, and, with difficulty, roused Vogel. Vogel

smelled of alcohol, appeared confused, and responded unintelligibly to questions.

The officer asked Vogel to leave his car and to be seated in the police car. Helped by an officer, Vogel unsteadily walked to the police car. Vogel was not asked to perform any field sobriety tests but was arrested for actual physical control.

A jury convicted Vogel of the offense of actual physical control of a motor vehicle while under the influence of intoxicating liquor. The court held:

> The legislature has the authority to define and punish crimes by enacting statutes. . . . The legislature also has the authority to enact strict liability offenses which require no intent. See § 39–08–07, N.D.C.C. (hit and run); § 39–08–20, N.D.C.C. (driving without liability insurance); § 6–08–16, N.D.C.C. (insufficient funds). "Strict liability statutes in criminal law do not invariably violate constitutional requirements." . . .
>
> The legislature has defined one variation of the crime of actual physical control while under the influence of intoxicating liquor as the accused having an "alcohol concentration of at least ten one-hundredths of one percent by weight at the time of the performance of a chemical test." . . . We conclude that the legislature has constitutionally defined the crime. *State v. Vogel*, 467 N.W.2d 86 (N.D. 1991)

2. Dorothy Lucero's boyfriend Eddie repeatedly beat Dorothy and her five-year-old son Arthur. Lucero's mother finally took Arthur to the hospital emergency room to evaluate marks on Arthur's body. Dr. Sidney Schnidman, who examined Arthur, found:

(1) a partial thickness burn on the left ear, and the hair around the burn singed (he surmised that a flame or fire had caused the burn to his ear); (2) multiple bruises on both cheeks; (3) laceration/cut of the lower lip that was partially healed; (4) scratches in the middle of the neck under the jaw; (5) three small round bruises on the left upper arm; (6) bruises on the right shoulder; (7) bruises on the thigh and knee cap; (8) multiple reddened areas on and between his buttocks; (9) circumferential marks/abrasions on both ankles; and (10) peeled and cracked skin on both feet (the doctor testified that he had seen this injury before in relation to immersion into a hot liquid).

Lucero did not intervene when Eddie attacked her son Arthur because Eddie threatened to beat her more if she did. Lucero was charged with abusing her son, Arthur, by failing to do anything about Eddie's beating him. The court rejected her claim that she did not intend to hurt Arthur. The court held:

> The rationale for a strict liability statute is that the public interest in the matter is so compelling or that the potential for harm is so great, that public interests override individual interests. . . . [T]he child abuse statute . . . [is] a strict liability statute because of the obvious public interest of prevention of cruelty to children. Therefore, in the strict liability crime of child abuse it makes no difference whether a defendant acted intentionally or negligently in committing the act. *State v. Lucero*, 98 N.M. 204, 647 P.2d 406 (1982)

CONCURRENCE

The principle of concurrence requires that *actus reus* join with *mens rea* to produce either criminal conduct or that criminal conduct cause a particular result. The California criminal code, for example, provides that "in every crime or public offense there must exist a union, or joint operation of act and intent, or criminal negligence." Therefore, if I plan to kill my enemy during a hunting expedition and carry out my plans, I have committed murder—the intent to kill (*mens rea*) set my act of shooting her (*actus reus*) into motion. However, it is not murder to shoot my enemy accidentally and rejoice afterwards because, in this example, *mens rea* follows the *actus reus*. The *mens rea* did not set the fatal shot in motion.[30]

Even if *mens rea* precedes action, the combination does not necessarily amount to concurrence. For example, suppose you and your friend agree to meet at her house. She is late and tells you to break the lock on her front door so you can wait inside. Once inside, however, you decide to steal her new VCR. You have not committed common-law burglary because you decided to steal *after* breaking and entering her house. Burglary requires that the intent to steal motivate the breaking (see chapter 10).[31]

In cases where causing a particular result is an element in the crime, concurrence requires a fusion not only of intention and action but also of *mens rea* and resulting harm. This dimension to concurrence requires that the harm flowing from a defendant's conduct concur with the defendant's intent. Throwing a rock at another person is not malicious damage to property if that rock breaks a window instead of hurting the person. Setting fire to the hold of a ship with a match is not arson if the match was intended to illuminate an area of the ship from which the defendant intended to steal liquor.[32]

Actual harm that differs from intended harm only in degree satisfies the concurrence requirement. For example, if I intend to beat my enemy within an inch of his life, and he dies, then *mens rea* and harm concur. Furthermore, harm intended for one victim that falls upon another (transferred intent) also fits within the principle of concurrence. Hence, shooting with the intent to kill Eli but striking and killing Doug instead satisfies the requirement of concurrence.[33]

CAUSATION

The principle of causation applies only to crimes requiring that criminal conduct cause a particular result. The main examples include the various kinds and degrees of criminal homicide, which requires causing the death of another person. Determining whether an *actus reus* causes a particular result is a two-step process:

1. Deciding whether the *actus reus* was the cause in fact, also called the actual cause of the harmful result, and, if so,

2. Deciding whether the *actus reus* was the proximate or legal cause of the harmful result.

What is the actual cause of a result is an empirical question. As the term implies, *actual cause* means the cause in fact of the resulting harm. Also known as **"but for" or sine qua non causation,** it means that an actor's conduct sets in motion a chain of events that, sooner or later, leads to the harmful result; hence the expression: "but for" the actor's conduct, the result would not have occurred. You might think of actual cause this way: "If it hadn't been for the defendant's act, would the harm have happened when it did?" If you answer no, then the defendant's actions are the actual cause of the harm. Actual cause is necessary to impose criminal liability. Suppose Sven asks Steve to meet him in a dark park, where Sven intends to assault Steve. On the way, Michael, who knows nothing of Sven's plan, attacks Steve before Sven arrives on the scene. Sven has not, in fact, caused the injury he wished to inflict. Therefore, Sven is not criminally liable, even though he intended to cause such injury. In other words, criminal liability depends on what actually happened as a result of action, not on what *would* have or *might* have happened, or what the actor *wanted* to happen.

Actual cause is necessary but not sufficient to impose criminal liability. The prosecution must also prove **proximate cause.** What is the proximate cause of a result is a policy question. It asks, "Who is it fair to hold accountable for the result?" Proximate cause is decided case by case. To satisfy the requirement of proximate cause, the prosecution must demonstrate in each case that it is fair to hold the particular defendant accountable for a chain of events set in motion by the acts of the defendant. Most cases satisfy both the actual and proximate cause requirements. For example, if a driver strikes and kills a pedestrian while driving recklessly, the pedestrian would be alive if it had not been for the driver's reckless driving, and it is fair to hold the driver accountable for the pedestrian's death. Proximate cause problems arise, however, when something in addition to the conduct of the actor contributes to the result, something that the actor cannot control, did not foresee, or could not reasonably have foreseen. For example, suppose that Laila intentionally stabs Ari, and Ari dies during the negligent surgery to save his life. If it had not been for the stab wounds inflicted by Laila, Ari would not be in surgery. However, the negligent surgery also contributed substantially to Ari's death. In cases such as this, the question becomes: Who is it "fair" to blame? In the reckless driving case, it seems fair to blame the driver for the harmful consequences of the reckless driving. In the stabbing case, on the other hand, it may appear less fair to blame the assailant because the negligent surgery substantially contributed to the death. Chief Justice Schwab of the Oregon Supreme Court expressed this idea in an excellent statement in *State v. Peterson:*

> The problem . . . is not 'causation in fact,' it is 'legal causation.' . . . [W]hether certain conduct is deemed to be the legal cause of a certain result is ultimately a policy question. The question of legal causation thus blends into the question of whether we are willing to hold a defendant responsible for a prohibited result. Or, stated differently, the issue is not causation, it is responsibility.[34]

Proximate cause means literally the next or closest cause. Perhaps a more practical definition would be the main cause—not main in the factual sense, but in the policy sense of who it is fair to hold criminally accountable for the harm. Courts use commonsense guidelines in determining whether it is fair to blame the defendant for causing harm in particular cases. One guideline is the legal maxim *"de minimus non curat lex"* ("The law does not care for trifles"). For example, if two assailants stab a victim simultaneously in the chest, the law does not inquire out of which wound spilled the blood that actually killed the victim. The differences are too trivial. At the opposite extreme, suppose one assailant stabbed the victim in the jugular vein and blood gushed forth, while the other stabbed the victim in the hand and only a tiny amount of blood oozed out. Both wounds have hastened death, but the law ignores the wound in the hand as a minimal contribution to the death, relying rather on the substantial cause of the stab to the jugular.[35]

Another guideline is that it is not fair to hold defendants accountable for—and proximate cause does not extend to—consequences set in motion by an act beyond the point where the consequences have "come to rest in a position of apparent safety." Suppose, for example, someone rolled a boulder down a hill where a crowd of people gathered below. Halfway down the hill, the boulder caught on a tree trunk that stopped its rolling toward the crowd. Several months later, a vibration dislodged the boulder and it rolled the rest of the way down the hill, striking and killing an unlucky person standing in its path. The person who initially set the boulder in motion is not the legal cause of the death; the boulder had literally come safely to rest on the tree, where an outside force later set in motion the chain of events that killed the ultimate victim.

Several other common-sense considerations help to determine proximate cause. The search for the proximate cause might uncover an intervening cause (sometimes called a supervening cause). **Intervening causes** either significantly interrupt the chain of events set in motion by the actions of defendant or at least substantially contribute to results. Suppose a driver injures a pedestrian while negligently driving her car. While the pedestrian is in the hospital seeking treatment, an inexperienced intern injects her with a fatal dose of a painkiller, given to the intern by a drunken nurse. The intern's inexperience and the drunken nurse's action contributed to the death at least as much as the negligent driving; arguably, they intervened and became themselves the main, dominant, or proximate cause. It is unjust to impose criminal liability in cases where the harmful results of actions are far remote from the initial actions that set a chain of events in motion. Therefore, we are led to conclude that the drunken nurse is an intervening, or supervening, cause of the death of the pedestrian in the hypothetical example.

Intervening causes may be either external forces or responses to the actions of defendants. Courts rarely impose liability when the proximate cause is an outside force. Suppose a robber leaves the victim of the robbery on a country road and the victim climbs over a fence into a field and falls asleep. A horse kicks the victim in the head and the victim dies. The kick is an outside force too remote from the robbery to impose liability for criminal homicide. Where, instead, the defendants' actions generate a direct human response from victims, courts are more likely to impose liability. In one case, Wilson threatened to castrate Armstrong if he didn't hand over two $100 bills. In escaping, Armstrong ran into the Missouri River, where he drowned. The Nebraska Supreme Court affirmed Wilson's conviction for murder because Armstrong's attempt to escape was a direct response to Wilson's threat to castrate him. One type of **legal causation** case involves medical personnel who treat wounded crime victims. The court dealt with actual, proximate, and intervening cause in *People v. Armitage*.

C A S E

Did He Cause the Drowning?

People v. Armitage,
239 Cal.Rptr. 515, (1987)

On a drunken escapade on the Sacramento River in the middle of a spring night, David James Armitage flipped his boat over and caused his companion to drown. As a result of this accident, defendant was convicted of the felony of drunk boating causing death in

violation of former Harbors and Navigation Code. The Court of Appeal affirmed the judgment.

SPARKS, Associate Justice.

FACTS

On the evening of May 18, 1985, defendant and his friend, Peter Maskovich, were drinking in a bar in the riverside community of Freeport. They were observed leaving the bar around midnight. In the early morning hours defendant and Maskovich wound up racing defendant's boat on the Sacramento River while both of them were intoxicated. The boat did not contain any personal flotation devices. At about 3 A.M. Gary Bingham, who lived in a house boat in a speed zone (five miles per hour, no wake), was disturbed by a large wake. He went out to yell at the boaters and observed a small aluminum boat with two persons in it at the bend in the river. The boaters had the motor wide open, were zigzagging, and had no running lights on at the time. About the same time, Rodney and Susan Logan were fishing on the river near the Freeport Bridge when they observed an aluminum boat with two men in it coming up the river without running lights. The occupants were using loud and vulgar language, and were operating the boat very fast and erratically.

James Snook lives near the Sacramento River in Clarksburg. Some time around 3 A.M. defendant came to his door. Defendant was soaking wet and appeared quite intoxicated. He reported that he had flipped his boat over in the river and had lost his buddy. He said that at first he and his buddy had been hanging on to the overturned boat, but that his buddy swam for shore and he did not know whether he had made it. As it turned out, Maskovich did not make it; he drowned in the river.

Mr. Snook notified the authorities of the accident. Deputy Beddingfield arrived and spent some time with defendant in attempting to locate the scene of the accident or the victim. Eventually Deputy Beddingfield took defendant to the sheriff's boat shed to meet with officers who normally work on the river. At the shed they were met by Deputy Snyder. Deputy Snyder attempted to question defendant about the accident and defendant stated that he had been operating the boat at a high rate of speed and zigzagging until it capsized. Defendant also stated that he told the victim to hang on to the boat but his friend ignored his warning and started swimming for the shore. As he talked to defendant, the officer formed the opinion that he was intoxicated. Deputy Snyder then arrested defendant and informed him of his

rights. Defendant waived his right to remain silent and repeated his statement.

OPINION

. . .

Defendant . . . contends his actions were not the proximate cause of the death of the victim. In order to be guilty of felony drunk boating the defendant's act or omission must be the proximate cause of the ensuing injury or death. (Harb. & Nav.Code, § 655, subd. (a).) Defendant asserts that after his boat flipped over he and the victim were holding on to it and the victim, against his advice, decided to abandon the boat and try to swim to shore. According to defendant the victim's fatally reckless decision should exonerate him from criminal responsibility for his death.

We reject defendant's contention. The question whether defendant's acts or omissions criminally caused the victim's death is to be determined according to the ordinary principles governing proximate causation. (1 Witkin, Cal.Crimes (1963) § 78, p. 79.) Proximate cause of a death has traditionally been defined in criminal cases as "a cause which, in natural and continuous sequence, produces the death, and without which the death would not have occurred." (CALJIC Nos. 8.55 (1987 Revision)), 8.93 (1987 Revision); Thus, as Witkin notes, "[p]roximate cause is clearly established where the act is directly connected with the resulting injury, with no intervening force operating." (1 Witkin, Cal. Crimes, supra, § 79, p. 79.)

Defendant claims that the victim's attempt to swim ashore, whether characterized as an intervening or a superseding cause, constituted a break in the natural and continuous sequence arising from the unlawful operation of the boat. The claim cannot hold water. It has long been the rule in criminal prosecutions that the contributory negligence of the victim is not a defense. In order to exonerate a defendant the victim's conduct must not only be a cause of his injury, it must be a superseding cause. "A defendant may be criminally liable for a result directly caused by his act even if there is another contributing cause. If an intervening cause is a normal and reasonably foreseeable result of defendant's original act the intervening act is 'dependent' and not a superseding cause, and will not relieve defendant of liability." As Witkin further notes, "[a]n obvious illustration of a dependent cause is the victim's attempt to escape from a deadly attack or other danger in which he is placed by the defendant's wrongful act." (1 Witkin, Cal. Crimes, supra, § 82, p. 81.) Thus, it is only an unforeseeable intervening cause, an extraordinary and abnormal occurrence, which rises to the level of an exonerating, superseding cause. Consequently, in criminal law a victim's predictable effort to escape a peril created by the defendant is not considered a superseding cause of the ensuing injury or death. As leading commentators have explained it, an unreflective act in response to a peril created by defendant will not break a causal connection. In such a case, the actor has a choice, but his act is nonetheless unconsidered. "When defendant's conduct causes panic an act done under the influence of panic or extreme fear will not negate causal connection unless the reaction is wholly abnormal." (Hart & Honore, Causation in the Law (2d ed. 1985) p. 149.)

Here defendant, through his misconduct, placed the intoxicated victim in the middle of a dangerous river in the early morning hours clinging to an overturned boat. The fact that the panic stricken victim recklessly abandoned the boat and tried to swim ashore was not a wholly abnormal reaction to the perceived peril of drowning. Just as "[d]etached reflection cannot be demanded in the presence of an uplifted knife" (*Brown v. United States* (1921) 256 U.S. 335, 343, 41 S.Ct. 501, 502, 65 L.Ed. 961, 963, Holmes, J.), neither can caution be required of a drowning man. Having placed the inebriated victim in peril, defendant cannot obtain exoneration by claiming the victim should have reacted differently or more prudently. In sum, the evidence establishes that defendant's acts and omissions were the proximate cause of the victim's death.

The judgment is affirmed.

QUESTIONS FOR DISCUSSION

1. State all of the facts relevant to determining whether Armitage caused his friend's death.

2. According to these facts, do you agree that Armitage is both the actual and the proximate cause of his friend's death?

3. Do you agree with the court that his friend's actions were not an intervening cause of his death? Defend your answer.

NOTE CASES

1. At about 2:30 A.M., Velazquez met the deceased Adalberto Alvarez at a Hardee's restaurant in Hialeah, Florida. The two had never previously met, but in the course of their conversation agreed to race each other in a "drag race" with their automobiles. They accordingly left the restaurant and proceeded to set up a quarter-mile drag race course on a nearby public road that ran perpendicular to a canal alongside the Palmetto Expressway in Hialeah; a guardrail and a visible stop sign stood between the end of this road and the canal. The two men began their drag race at the end of this road and proceeded away from the canal in a westerly direction for one quarter mile. Upon completing the course without incident, the deceased Alvarez suddenly turned his automobile 180 degrees around and proceeded east toward the starting line and the canal; Velazquez did the same and followed behind Alvarez. Alvarez proceeded in the lead and attained an estimated speed of 123 m.p.h.; he was not wearing a seat belt and subsequent investigation revealed that he had a blood alcohol level between .11 and .12. Velazquez, who had not been drinking, trailed Alvarez the entire distance back to the starting line and attained an estimated speed of 98 m.p.h. As both drivers approached the end of the road, they applied their brakes, but neither could stop. Alvarez, who was about a car length ahead of Velazquez, crashed through the guardrail first and was propelled over the entire canal, landing on its far bank; he was thrown from his car upon impact, was pinned under his vehicle when it landed on him, and died instantly from the resulting injuries. Velazquez also crashed through the guardrail, but landed in the canal where he was able to escape from his vehicle and swim to safety uninjured.

Velazquez was charged with vehicular homicide. Were his actions in participating in the drag race the legal or proximate cause of Alvarez's death? No, according to the appeals court:

The "proximate cause" element of vehicular homicide in Florida embraces more . . . than . . . "but for" causation-in-fact. . . . Even where a defendant's conduct is a cause-in-fact of a prohibited result, as where a defendant's reckless operation of a motor vehicle is a cause-in-fact of the death of a human being, Florida and other courts throughout the country have for good reason declined to impose criminal liability (1) where the prohibited result of the defendant's conduct is beyond the scope of any fair assessment of the danger created by the defendant's conduct, or (b) where it would otherwise be unjust, based on fairness and policy considerations, to hold the defendant criminally responsible for the prohibited result.

. . . [A] driver-participant in an illegal "drag race" on a public road cannot be held criminally responsible for the death of another driver participant when (a) the deceased, in effect, kills himself by his own reckless driving during the race, and (b) the sole basis for attaching criminal liability for his death is the defendant's participation in the "drag race." The policy reasons for reaching this result are best expressed in *State v. Petersen*, 270 Or. 166, 526 P.2d 1008 (1974)):

> "[T]he question is whether defendant's reckless conduct 'caused' the death of the victim. The problem here is not 'causation in fact,' it is 'legal causation.' In unusual cases like this one, whether certain conduct is deemed to be the legal cause of a certain result is ultimately a policy question. The question of legal causation thus blends into the question of whether we are willing to hold a defendant responsible for a prohibited result. Or, stated differently, the issue is not causation, it is responsibility. In my opinion, policy considerations are against imposing responsibility for the death of a participant in a race on the surviving racer when his sole contribution to the death is the participation in the activity mutually agreed upon. . . .

. . . [I]t is clear that the defendant's reckless operation of a motor vehicle in participating in the "drag race" with the deceased was, technically speaking, a cause-in-fact of the deceased's death under the "but for" test. But for the defendant's participation in the subject race, the deceased would not have recklessly raced his vehicle at all and thus would not have been killed. How-

ever, . . . the defendant's participation in the subject "drag race" was not a proximate cause of the deceased's death because, simply put, the deceased, in effect, killed himself by his own volitional reckless driving—and, consequently, it would be unjust to hold the defendant criminally responsible for this death. Reversed and remanded. *Velazquez v. State*, 561 So.2d 347 (Fla.App. 1990)

2. Kibbe and a companion, Krall, met Stafford in a bar. They noticed Stafford had a lot of money and was drunk. When Stafford asked them for a ride, they agreed, having already decided to rob him. "The three men entered Kibbe's automobile and began the trip toward Canandaigua. Krall drove the car while Kibbe demanded that Stafford turn over any money he had. In the course of an exchange, Kibbe slapped Stafford several times, took his money, then compelled him to lower his trousers and to take off his shoes to be certain that Stafford had given up all his money; and when they were satisfied that Stafford had no more money on his person, the defendants forced Stafford to exit the Kibbe vehicle.

"As he was thrust from the car, Stafford fell onto the shoulder of the rural two-lane highway on which they had been traveling. His trousers were still down around his ankles, his shirt was rolled up towards his chest, he was shoeless and he had also been stripped of any outer clothing. Before the defendants pulled away, Kibbe placed Stafford's shoes and jacket on the shoulder of the highway. Although Stafford's eyeglasses were in Kibbe's vehicle, the defendants, either through inadvertence or perhaps by specific design, did not give them to Stafford before they drove away."

Michael W. Blake, a college student, was driving at a reasonable speed when he saw Stafford in the middle of the road with his hands in the air. Blake could not stop in time to avoid striking Stafford and killing him.

Who legally caused Stafford's death? The court said Kibbe and his companion.

> The defendants do not dispute the fact that their conduct evinced a depraved indifference to human life which created a grave risk of death, but rather they argue that it was just as likely that Stafford would be miraculously rescued by a good samaritan. We cannot accept such an

argument. There can be little doubt but that Stafford would have frozen to death in his state of undress had he remained on the shoulder of the road. The only alternative left to him was the highway, which in his condition, for one reason or another, clearly foreboded the probability of resulting death.

People v. Kibbe, 35 N.Y.2d 407, 362 N.Y.S.2d 848, 321 N.E.2d 773 (1974)

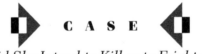

A final causation problem arises when the result differs from what actors intend in purposeful and knowing conduct, expect in reckless conduct, and should expect in negligent conduct. Chapter 5 discusses crimes in which the result is less than actors intend, such as in attempt, conspiracy, and solicitation. In cases where the actual harm exceeds what actors intend, expect, or should expect, criminal law generally does not hold defendants liable for these greater harms unless the harms are close in degree and kind to those intended. For example, a defendant who intends to beat a victim within an inch of her life but does not want to kill her has committed criminal homicide if the victim dies (see chapter 8). More difficult are cases where actual harm greatly exceeds intended harm. *Hyam v. Director of Public Prosecutions* addresses this problem.

CASE

Did She Intend to Kill or to Frighten?

Hyam v. Director of Public Prosecutions, 2 All E.R. 43 (1974)

Mrs. Hyam was convicted of murder. She appealed.

FACTS

The facts are simple, and not in dispute. In the early hours of Saturday, 15th July 1972, the appellant set fire to a dwelling-house in Coventry by deliberately pouring about a half gallon of petrol through the letterbox and igniting it by means of a newspaper and a match. The house contained four persons, presumably asleep. They were a Mrs. Booth and her three children, a boy and the two young girls who were the subjects of the charges. Mrs. Booth and the boy escaped alive through a window. The two girls died as the result of asphyxia by the fumes generated by the fire. The appellant's motive (in the sense in which I shall use the word "motive") was jealousy of Mrs. Booth whom the appellant believed was likely to marry a Mr. Jones of whom the appellant herself was the discarded, or partly discarded, mistress. Her account of her actions, and her defence, was that she had started the fire only with the intention of frightening Mrs. Booth into leaving the neighbourhood, and that she did not intend to cause death or grievous bodily harm. The judge directed the jury:

> The prosecution must prove, beyond all reasonable doubt, that the accused intended to do serious bodily harm to Mrs. Booth, the mother of the deceased girls. If you are satisfied that when the accused set fire to the house she knew that it was highly probable that this would cause serious bodily harm then the prosecution will have established the necessary intent. It matters not if her motive was, as she says, to frighten Mrs. Booth.

OPINION

The [trial] judge explained that he had put brackets round the words "kill or" and "death or" in which it seems to be said that a rational man must be taken to intend the consequences of his acts. It is not a revival of the doctrine of constructive malice or the substitution of an objective for a subjective test of knowledge or intention. It is the man's actual state of knowledge and intent which, as in all other cases, determines his criminal responsibility.

It simply proclaims the moral truth that if a man, in full knowledge of the danger involved, and without lawful excuse, deliberately does that which exposes a victim to the risk of the probable grievous bodily harm (in the sense explained) or death, and the victim dies, the perpetrator of the crime is guilty of murder and not manslaughter to the same extent as if he had actually intended the consequence to follow, and irrespective of whether he wishes it. That is because the two types of intention are morally indistinguishable, although factually and logically distinct, and because it is therefore just that they should bear the same consequences to the perpetrator as they have the same consequences for the victim if death ensues.

This is not very far from the situation in this case. The jury appear to have taken this as a carefully premeditated case and that this was so can hardly be disputed, and, though it was disputed, the jury clearly rejected this view. The appellant had made her way to the house in a van in the early hours of the morning. She took with her a jerry can containing at least half a gallon of petrol. As she passed Mr. Jones's house she carefully made sure that he was in his own home and not with Mrs. Booth, because, as she said, she did not want to do Mr. Jones any harm.

She parked the van at a distance from Mrs. Booth's house, and when she got to the front door she carefully removed a milk bottle from the step in case she might knock it over and arouse somebody by the noise. And when she had started the fire she crept back to her van and made off home without arousing anyone or giving the alarm. Once it is conceded that she was actually and subjectively aware of the danger to the sleeping occupants of the house in what she did, and that was the point which the judge brought to the jury's attention, it must surely follow naturally that she did what she did with the intention of exposing them to the danger of death or really serious injury regardless of whether such consequences actually ensued or not.

QUESTIONS FOR DISCUSSION

1. Do you feel comfortable with making Mrs. Hyam a murderer when she meant only to frighten?

2. Would you give her a punishment as severe as that given to a man who killed his wife, said he had wanted to do it for eight years, and would do it again if he had the chance?

The established law in most jurisdictions is that conscious risk creators are accountable for the "natural and probable consequences" of their actions. Natural and probable consequences include killing a person other than the intended victim—as, for example, if I shoot at Jim, intending to kill him, but instead hit his friend Moira. Natural and probable consequences do not include consequences that are accidental—as, for example, if I shoot at my wife, intending to kill her, but miss, and she is so distraught that she runs off to California, goes horseback riding to forget the horrible incident, is thrown off her horse, and dies when her head strikes a rock. In such cases, the harms are too remote to fairly impose criminal liability. Note that the proximate cause standard also applies to the last example—striking the rock was the main cause of death.

GRADING OFFENSES

The seriousness of an offense depends on several considerations. First, and perhaps most important, is the harm done. Harms to persons are generally considered most serious, followed by harms to habitation, property, public order, and public morals. Chapters 8 through 12 follow this order. Incomplete harms are less serious than completed ones (see chapter 5). Sometimes seriousness depends on *actus reus*, such as in torture murder. *Mens rea* also affects the determination of seriousness. Purpose or specific intent is the most blameworthy, or "evil," mental state. Knowledge is next, followed in order by recklessness, negligence, and strict liability. Purposeful wrongdoing deserves more punishment than reckless harm, because reckless wrongdoers do not intend to harm their victims. Still less blameworthy are negligent wrongdoers, who do not consciously create risks that expose others to serious harm. Least blameworthy of all are those who harm others accidentally—that is, without regard to fault. Penalties account for these degrees of blameworthiness. *Mens rea* also influences the determination of seriousness by suggesting circumstances that justify, excuse, and mitigate. For example, if I kill in self-defense, my intention to kill is justified; if I kill upon adequate provocation, I am guilty of manslaughter, a less serious criminal homicide than murder (see chapter 8).

SUMMARY

Crimes are of two general types: crimes of conduct and crimes that require that criminal conduct cause a particular harmful result. Crimes of conduct comprise three elements: *actus reus, mens rea,* and concurrence. Crimes requiring the causing of a particular result have two elements in addition to the three just named: causation and resulting harm. As a practical matter, the prosecution must prove each element beyond a reasonable doubt in order to convict defendants. Each element is also the basis for a general principle of criminal liability. So, the element of *actus reus* of a particular crime, such as shooting or stabbing in murder, also reflects the general principle of *actus reus*. The *mens rea* of the intent to kill also reflects the general principle of *mens rea*, and so on, for each of the elements in particular crimes.

The general principle of *actus reus* expresses the idea that not only voluntary physical acts but also omissions and possession can satisfy the requirement of action. The general principle of *mens rea* includes four principal mental states: purpose, knowledge, recklessness, and negligence. Some crimes impose liability without fault. These strict liability offenses require no proof of *mens rea*. The general principle of concurrence expresses the idea that there is no criminal conduct without the union of *actus reus* and *mens rea*.

Criminal conduct requires that the *mens rea* prompted the *actus reus* and, in crimes requiring a particular result, that the *actus reus* caused the result. The principle of causation expresses the idea of a relationship between criminal conduct and a harmful result—that the conduct caused the particular result. This causal relation is expressed both as **factual causation,** that is, "but for" or *sine qua non* cause, and as legal or proximate cause, the cause the law looks to in justifying criminal liability. Problems arise when the resulting harm exceeds what actors intended, expected, or should have expected. Actors are criminally liable for those harms, and punishment seems "fair." However, actors are not criminally liable for harms so distinct both in kind and degree from those intended or expected, or that occur too remote from the acts that led to the conduct or result that punishment seems "unfair."

REVIEW QUESTIONS

1. Identify the two types of crime and the elements of each that give rise to the general principles of criminal liability.

2. Identify, and fully explain, all of the general principles of criminal liability.

3. What are the purposes of the requirement of *actus reus* as an element in criminal liability?

4. Under what circumstances might a status satisfy the *actus reus* requirement?

5. What are the reasons for excluding thoughts from *actus reus*?

6. Under what circumstances might an involuntary act satisfy the *actus reus* requirement?

7. When can words amount to *actus reus*?

8. Explain when and why omissions can qualify as *actus reus*. What are the two forms criminal omissions can take?

9. When can possession qualify as *actus reus*?

10. How can we determine *mens rea*?

11. Identify and define the four types of common-law *mens rea*.

12. Identify and define the four levels of culpability under the *Model Penal Code*. Distinguish accurately and completely the differences among the levels of culpability. According to the code, to what three elements can *mens rea* refer?

13. Explain strict liability, how it originated, and under what circumstances it usually applies.

14. Explain the principle of concurrence.

15. Define factual causation and legal causation. Specifically identify the differences between them.

16. What are the main grounds for grading offenses in terms of the general principles of criminal liability?

KEY TERMS

actual possession Physical possession; on the possessor's person.

actus reus The criminal act or the physical element in criminal liability.

"but for" or *sine qua non* causation The actor's conduct sets in motion a chain of events that, sooner or later, leads to a result.

causation The requirement that criminal conduct cause a particular result.

concurrence The requirement that *actus reus* must join with *mens rea* to produce criminal conduct or that conduct cause a harmful result.

constructive intent Intent in which the actors do not intend any harm but should have known that their behavior created a high risk of injury.

constructive possession Legal possession or custody of an item or substance.

culpability Blameworthiness based on *mens rea*.

elements of crime The parts of a crime that the prosecution must prove beyond a reasonable doubt, such as *actus reus*, *mens rea*, causation, and harmful result.

factual causation Conduct that in fact leads to a harmful result.

general intent Intent to commit the *actus reus*—the act required in the definition of the crime.

general principles of criminal liability The theoretical foundation for the elements of *actus reus*, *mens rea*, causation, and harm.

intervening or **supervening cause** The cause that either interrupts a chain of events or substantially contributes to a result.

knowing possession Awareness of physical possession.

legal causation Cause recognized by law to impose criminal liability.

mens rea The mental element in crime, including purpose, knowledge, recklessness, and negligence.

mere possession Physical possession.

negligence The unconscious creation of substantial and unjustifiable risks.

proximate cause The main cause of the result of criminal conduct.

recklessness The conscious creation of substantial and unjustifiable risk.

specific intent The intent to do something beyond the *actus reus*.

strict liability Liability without fault, or in the absence of *mens rea*.

transferred intent Actor intends to harm one victim but instead harms another.

verbal acts Words.

Suggested Readings

1. George Fletcher, *Rethinking Criminal Law* (Boston: Little, Brown, 1978), pt. II. A thorough and thought-provoking discussion of the principles of criminal liability. Difficult in places but worth the effort.

2. Jerome Hall, *General Principles of Criminal Law*, 2d ed. (Indianapolis, Ind.: Bobbs-Merrill, 1960). Difficult but rewarding reading.

3. Hyman Gross, *A Theory of Criminal Justice* (New York: Oxford University Press, 1979), chap. 2. Untangles knotty questions surrounding *actus reus*.

4. American Law Institute, *Model Penal Code and Commentaries* (Philadelphia: American Law Institute, 1985), pt. I. The fullest treatment of the general principles of criminal liability.

5. Rollin M. Perkins and Ronald N. Boyce, *Criminal Law*, 3d ed. (Mineola, N.Y.: Foundation Press, 1982), chaps. 6 and 7. A straightforward analysis of *actus reus*, *mens rea*, and causation.

Notes

1. Oliver Wendell Holmes, *The Common Law* (Boston: Little, Brown and Company, 1963), pp. 45–47.

2. Paul H. Robinson and Jane A. Grall, "Element Analysis in Defining Criminal Liability: The Model Criminal Code and Beyond," *Stanford Law Review* 35 (1983):681–762, esp. 691–705.

3. *Hales v. Petit*, 1 Plowd. 253, 259; 75 Eng. Rep. 387, 397 (cannot punish thoughts); George Fletcher, *Rethinking Criminal Law* (Boston: Little, Brown and Company, 1978), pp. 115–116 (manifest criminality).

4. Fletcher, *Rethinking Criminal Law*, p. 117.

5. Holmes, *The Common Law*, pp. 46–47.

6. Samuel Butler, *Erewhon* (New York: Modern Library, 1927), pp. 104–111.

7. See Herbert Morris, *On Guilt and Innocence* (Los Angeles: University of California Press, 1976), chap. 1, "Punishing Thoughts."

8. Glanville Williams, *Criminal Law*, 2d ed. rev. (London: Stevens and Sons, 1961), pp. 1–2.

9. Narrated in Norval Morris, "Somnambulistic Homicide: Ghosts, Spiders, and North Koreans," *Res Judicata* 5 (1951):29.

10. See Leo Katz, *Bad Acts and Guilty Minds* (Chicago: University of Chicago Press, 1987), chap. 2, for a provocative discussion of this and other cases like it.

11. Joseph Goldstein et al., *Criminal Law: Theory and Process* (New York: Free Press, 1974), p. 766.

12. Fletcher, *Rethinking Criminal Law*, pp. 421–22; *National Law Journal* (October 14, 1991), pp. 3, 38.

13. Wayne R. LaFave, *Criminal Law*, 2d ed. (St. Paul, Minn.: West Publishing Co., 1986), p. 203.

14. Ibid., pp. 581–633.

15. Bibb Latane and John Darley, *The Unresponsive Bystander: Why Doesn't He Help?* (New York: Appleton-Crofts, 1970), pp. 1–2.

16. American Law Institute, *Model Penal Code and Commentaries*, vol. 1 (Philadelphia: American Law Institute, 1985), p. 24; See also *Jenkins v. State*, 215 Md. 70, 137 A.2d 115 (1957) for a case that adopts the mere possession rule.

17. *State v. Staley*, 123 Wash.2d 794, 872 P.2d 502 (1994).

18. *Robinson v. California*, 370 U.S. 660 82 S.Ct. 1417, 8 L.Ed.2d 758 (1962); Fletcher, *Rethinking Criminal Law*, pp. 202–205.

19. Francis Bowes Sayre, *"Mens Rea," Harvard Law Review* 45 (1931–32):974.

20. Holmes, *The Common Law*, p. 7; American Law Institute, *Model Penal Code*, tentative draft no. 11 (1955).

21. Glanville Williams, *Criminal Law*, 1; quoted in Jerome Hall, *General Principles of Criminal Law*, 2d ed. (Indianapolis, Ind.: Bobbs-Merrill, 1960), p. 153.

22. Quoted in Joseph Goldstein et al., *Criminal Law: Theory and Process*.

23. Wayne R. LaFave and Austin W. Scott, Jr., *Handbook on Criminal Law*, 2d ed. (St. Paul, Minn.: West Publishing Co., 1972), pp. 201–202; Jerome Hall, *General Principles of Criminal Law*, pp. 142–144.

24. American Law Institute, *Model Penal Code and Commentaries*, pt. I, p. 229.

25. *Haupt v. United States*, 330 U.S. 631, 67 S.Ct. 874, 91 L.Ed. 1145 (1947) (treason).

26. West's Revised Code Wash. Ann. 9A.08010(1)(b).

27. Michigan Statutes 82; § 305(a) and (b).

28. *New York Times* (September 14, 1985).

29. Rollin M. Perkins and Ronald N. Boyce, *Criminal Law*, 3d ed. (Mineola, N.Y.: Foundation Press, 1982), pp. 896–907.

30. *The Penal Code of California*, § 20, West's California Penal Codes, 1988 compact ed. (St. Paul, Minn.: West Publishing Company, 1988), p. 7.

31. Hall, *General Principles of Criminal Law*, pp. 185–190.

32. *Regina v. Pembleton*, 12 Cox Crim.Cas. 607 (1874) (throwing a rock); *Regina v. Faulkner*, 13 Cox Crim.Cas. 550 (lighting match) (1877).

33. LaFave and Scott, *Handbook on Criminal Law*, pp. 243–246.

34. Katz, *Bad Acts and Guilty Minds*, chap. 4; *State v. Peterson*, 522 P.2d 912, 920 (1974).

35. Perkins and Boyce, *Criminal Law*, pp. 776–777.

CHAPTER FOUR

Parties to Crime: Complicity and Vicarious Liability

CHAPTER MAIN POINTS

1. The doctrines involving parties to crime deal with the ordinary phenomenon of teamwork under the extraordinary circumstance of groups participating in or related to criminal activity.

2. Accomplice liability attributes the *actus reus* and *mens rea* of one or more persons to other participants in the crime.

3. Liability as an accessory depends on the actual commission of a felony, the knowledge of the accessory about the felony, and aid of the accessory given to the principal with the intention of aiding the principal to avoid arrest, prosecution, conviction, and punishment.

4. Vicarious liability replaces the *actus reus* and the *mens rea* with a relationship between parties.

5. Parties before and during crime are liable for the principal crime; parties following crime are liable for separate, lesser offenses.

6. Vicarious liability usually arises out of business relationships.

7. Vicarious liability may be either strict (without fault) or based on culpable conduct.

8. Attributing responsibility to corporate officers is often difficult and sometimes impossible.

9. Businesses can be criminally responsible for harms their officers condoned or recklessly tolerated.

Was David's Mother a Party to the Crime?

When David Hoffman's wife, Carol, refused to make love with him, he lost his temper and choked her to death. He called down to the basement to wake his mother, asking her to come upstairs to sit on the living room couch. From there she would be able to see the kitchen, bathroom, and bedroom doors and could stop his daughter if she awoke and tried to use the bathroom. His mother came upstairs to lie on the couch. In the meantime David had moved the body to the bathtub. His mother was aware that while she was in the living room her son was dismembering the body, but she turned her head away so that she could not see. After dismembering the body and putting it in bags, Hoffman cleaned the bathroom, took the body to a lake and disposed of it. On returning home he told his mother to wash the cloth covers from the bathroom toilet and tank, which she did. David fabricated a story about Carol leaving the house the previous night after an argument, and his mother agreed to corroborate it. David phoned the police with a missing person report and during the ensuing searches and interviews with the police, he and his mother continued to tell the fabricated story.

INTRODUCTION

"Two heads are better than one." "The whole is greater than the sum of its parts." These well-known sayings express the positive side of teamwork, an ordinary phenomenon under ordinary circumstances. When, under extraordinary circumstances, teamwork turns malicious, then teamwork becomes complicity in criminal law. A group of young men playing football generates no criminal liability; a gang rape—teamwork turned malicious—is worse than each individual rape. The **doctrine of complicity**—also called the doctrine of parties to crime—establishes the conditions under which two or more persons incur liability for the conduct of another before, during, and after the commission of crimes. Complicity attributes the *actus reus* and the *mens rea* of one person to the actions and intentions of someone else. It is immaterial whether the defendant, someone else, or both together establish the elements of the crime charged. Those who join with others to commit crimes are all liable as if they had committed the crime alone.

Vicarious liability bases criminal liability on the *relationship* between the party who commits the crime and another party. Vicarious liability requires proof of neither action nor intention; the relationship itself creates the liability. In the main, it is business and employment relationships that give rise to vicarious liability: employer-employee, manager-corporation, buyer-seller, producer-consumer, service provider-recipient. But vicarious liability can also arise in other situations, such as making the owner of a car liable for the driver's traffic violations and holding parents liable for their minor children's crimes.

PARTIES TO CRIME

The common law recognized four parties to crime:

1. Principals in the first degree—those who actually commit the crime.
2. Principals in the second degree—aiders and abettors present when crimes are committed, such as lookouts, getaway drivers, and co-conspirators.
3. Accessories before the fact—aiders and abettors not present when crimes are committed, such as those who provide the weapons that others use in murders.
4. Accessories after the fact—individuals who give aid and comfort to persons known to have committed crimes, such as those who harbor fugitives.

The significance of these distinctions lay largely in the rule that only after principals were convicted could the government try accomplices. If principals were not convicted before the government brought accomplices to trial, common-law complicity shielded accomplices even in the face of certain proof of their guilt. The doctrine arose during a period in history when all felonies were capital offenses; it provided a way to avoid the application of the death penalty. As the number of capital crimes diminished (and thus

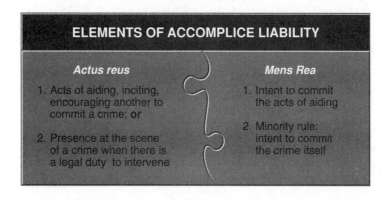

ELEMENTS OF ACCOMPLICE LIABILITY

Actus reus

1. Acts of aiding, inciting, encouraging another to commit a crime; **or**

2. Presence at the scene of a crime when there is a legal duty to intervene

Mens Rea

1. Intent to commit the acts of aiding

2. Minority rule: intent to commit the crime itself

the severity of punishment), the need to distinguish between principals and accessories dissipated.

Modern statutes have abolished the common-law distinction by making both accessories before and during crime principals. These principals are called **accomplices.** In most states, complicity following the commission of crimes — the common-law **accessory** after the fact — remains a separate but lesser offense.

Judge Learned Hand, a distinguished federal judge, summed up the doctrine of complicity as requiring that defendants "in some sort associate [themselves] with the venture, that [t]he[y] participate in it as in something that [t]he[y] wish . . . to bring about, that [t]he[y] seek by . . . their action to make it succeed."[1]

Accomplice liability is often confused with conspiracy. They are related only in the sense that they both involve more than one party. However, they are two distinct crimes. Conspiracy, discussed in Chapter 5, is an agreement to commit some other crime. A conspiracy to commit murder is not murder, it is an agreement to commit murder. Participating in a murder makes the participants parties to the crime of murder. For example, two people agree to commit a murder. They go and buy a gun and drive together to the victim's house. One acts as a look out while the other kills the victim. They drive away together. They have committed both conspiracy to commit murder and murder itself. The rule that conspiracy and the underlying crime are separate offenses is called the *Pinkerton* rule. The name derives from the leading U.S. Supreme Court case involving both offenses, *Pinkerton v. United States.* In the case, two brothers conspired to evade taxes. Both were found guilty of both conspiracy to evade taxes and of tax evasion itself. According to Justice Douglas, who wrote the opinion for the Court,

> It has been long and consistently recognized by the Court that the commission of the substantive offense and a conspiracy to commit it are separate and distinct offenses.[2]

Actus Reus of Accomplice Liability

Statutes have substantially altered the common-law categories of complicity. Nevertheless, the words describing the common-law acts required to establish accomplice *actus reus* remain in the modern statutes. Those who act to "aid," "abet," "assist," "counsel," "procure," "hire," or "induce" others to commit crime are themselves liable for committing the crime. A widely accepted rule is that "aiding and abetting contemplates some positive act in aid of the commission of the offense." Determining just how much action qualifies as accomplice *actus reus* is difficult. Courts have ruled that all of the following acts satisfy the requirements of accomplice *actus reus*:

- Providing guns, supplies, or other instruments of crime
- Serving as a lookout
- Driving a getaway car
- Sending the victim to the principal
- Preventing warnings from reaching the victim.[3]

One rule of complicity liability is certain: Mere presence at the scene of a crime by itself does not satisfy the requirements of accomplice *actus reus*. Even presence at the scene of a crime followed by flight is not enough action to satisfy the *actus reus* requirement of accomplice liability. In *Bailey v. United States*, Bailey spent most of the afternoon shooting craps with another man. Then, when a man carrying cash walked by, Bailey's craps partner pulled a gun and robbed the man with the cash. Both Bailey and the other man fled the scene. Bailey was caught; the other man never was. The court held that although flight from the scene of a crime can be taken into account, it is not enough to prove accomplice *actus reus*. According to the court,

> We no longer hold tenable the notion that "the wicked flee when no man pursueth, but the righteous are as bold as a lion." The proposition that "one flees shortly after a criminal act is committed or when he is accused of something does so because he feels some guilt concerning the act" is not absolute as a legal doctrine "since it is a matter of common knowledge that men who are entirely innocent do sometimes fly from the scene of a crime through fear of being apprehended as guilty parties or from an unwillingness to appear as witnesses."[4]

An exception to the mere presence rule occurs when defendants have a legal duty to act; their presence then suffices as *actus reus*. In *State v. Walden*, Walden stood by and did nothing while her boyfriend beat her young son. A jury found Walden guilty as an accomplice to assault. On appeal, the court said that

> the trial court properly allowed the jury . . . to consider a verdict of guilty of assault . . . upon a theory of aiding and abetting, solely on the ground that the defendant was present when her child was brutally beaten. . . . A person who so aids or abets under another in the commission of a crime is equally guilty with that other person as a principal.[5]

Words can amount to accomplice *actus reus* if they encourage and show approval of the crime. Furthermore, although actions following the crime are not themselves accomplice *actus reus*, they are circumstances from which finders of fact can infer participation. In *State v. Ulvinen*, the court dealt with the problem of words as accomplice *actus reus*, and also grappled with two additional problems in accomplice liability:

1. Imposing liability if defendants are not present when crimes are committed.
2. Inferring participation in crimes from actions taken after the commission of crimes.

C A S E

Was She an Accomplice to Murder?

State v. Ulvinen,
313 N.W.2d 425 (Minn. 1981)

Ulvinen was convicted of first degree murder pursuant to Minn.Stat. § 609.05, subd. 1 (1980), imposing criminal liability on one who "intentionally aids, advises, hires, counsels, or conspires with or otherwise procures" another to commit a crime. The Minnesota

supreme court reversed. Justice Otis wrote the opinion for the court.

FACTS

Carol Hoffman, appellant's daughter-in-law, was murdered late on the evening of August 10th or the very early morning of August 11th by her husband, David

Hoffman. She and David had spent an amicable evening together playing with their children, and when they went to bed David wanted to make love to his wife. However, when she refused him he lost his temper and began choking her. While he was choking her he began to believe he was "doing the right thing" and that to get "the evil out of her" he had to dismember her body.

After his wife was dead, David called down to the basement to wake his mother, asking her to come upstairs to sit on the living room couch. From there she would be able to see the kitchen, bathroom, and bedroom doors and could stop the older child if she awoke and tried to use the bathroom. Appellant didn't respond at first but after being called once, possibly twice more, she came upstairs to lie on the couch. In the meantime David had moved the body to the bathtub. Appellant was aware that while she was in the living room her son was dismembering the body but she turned her head away so that she could not see.

After dismembering the body and putting it in bags, Hoffman cleaned the bathroom, took the body to Weaver Lake and disposed of it. On returning home he told his mother to wash the cloth covers from the bathroom toilet and tank, which she did. David fabricated a story about Carol leaving the house the previous night after an argument, and Helen agreed to corroborate it. David phoned the police with a missing person report and during the ensuing searches and interviews with the police, he and his mother continued to tell the fabricated story.

On August 19, 1980, David confessed to the police that he had murdered his wife. In his statement he indicated that not only had his mother helped him cover up the crime but she had known of his intent to kill his wife that night. After hearing Hoffman's statement the police arrested appellant and questioned her with respect to her part in the cover up. Police typed up a two-page statement which she read and signed. The following day a detective questioned her further regarding events surrounding the crime, including her knowledge that it was planned.

Appellant's relationship with her daughter-in-law had been a strained one. She moved in with the Hoffmans on July 26, two weeks earlier to act as a live-in babysitter for their two children. Carol was unhappy about having her move in and told friends that she hated Helen, but she told both David and his mother that they could try the arrangement to see how it worked. On the morning of the murder Helen told her son that she was going to move out of the Hoffman residence because "Carol had been so nasty to me." In his statement to the police David reported the conversation that morning as follows:

. . . Sunday morning I went downstairs and my mom was in the bedroom reading the newspaper and she had tears in her eyes, and she said in a very frustrated voice, "I've got to find another house." She said, "Carol don't want me here," and she said, "I probably shouldn't have moved in here." And I said then, "Don't let what Carol said hurt you. It's going to take a little more period of readjustment for her." Then I told mom that I've got to do it tonight so that there can be peace in this house.

Q. What did you tell your mom that you were going to have to do that night?

A. I told my mom I was going to have to put her to sleep.

Q. Dave, will you tell us exactly what you told your mother that morning, to the best of your recollection?

A. I said I'm going to have to choke her tonight and I'll have to dispose of her body so that it will never be found. That's the best of my knowledge.

Q. What did your mother say when you told her that?

A. She just—she looked at me with very sad eyes and just started to weep. I think she said something like "it will be for the best."

David spent the day fishing with a friend of his. When he got home that afternoon he had another conversation with his mother. She told him at that time about a phone conversation Carol had had in which she discussed taking the children and leaving home. David told the police that during the conversation with his mother that afternoon he told her "Mom, tonight's got to be the night."

Q. When you told your mother, "Tonight's got to be the night," did your mother understand that you were going to kill Carol later that evening?

A. She thought I was just kidding her about doing it. She didn't think I could. . . .

Q. Why didn't your mother think that you could do it?

A. . . . Because for some time I had been telling

her I was going to take Carol scuba diving and make it look like an accident.

Q. And she said?

A. And she always said, "Oh, you're just kidding me." . . .

Q. But your mother knew you were going to do it that night?

A. I think my mother sensed that I was really going to do it that night.

Q. Why do you think your mother sensed you were really going to do it that night?

A. Because when I came home and she told me what had happened at the house, and I told her, "Tonight's got to be the night," I think she said, again I'm not certain, that ["]it would be the best for the kids."

OPINION

. . . It is well-settled in this state that presence, companionship, and conduct before and after the offense are circumstances from which a person's participation in the criminal intent may be inferred. The evidence is undisputed that appellant was asleep when her son choked his wife. She took no active part in the dismembering of the body but came upstairs to intercept the children, should they awake, and prevent them from going into the bathroom.

She cooperated with her son by cleaning some items from the bathroom and corroborating David's story to prevent anyone from finding out about the murder. She is insulated by statute from guilt as an accomplice after-the-fact for such conduct because of her relation as a parent of the offender. See Minn. Stat. § 609.495, subd. 2 (1980). The jury might well have considered appellant's conduct in sitting by while her son dismembered his wife so shocking that it deserved punishment. Nonetheless, these subsequent actions do not succeed in transforming her behavior prior to the crime to active instigation and encouragement. Minn.Stat. § 609.05, subd. 1 (1980) implies a high level of activity on the part of an aider and abettor in the form of conduct that encourages another to act. Use of terms such as "aids," "advises," and "conspires" requires something more of a person than mere inaction to impose liability as a principal.

The evidence presented to the jury at best supports a finding that appellant passively acquiesced in her son's plan to kill his wife. The jury might have believed that David told his mother of his intent to kill his wife that night and that she neither actively discouraged him nor told anyone in time to prevent the murder. Her response that "it would be the best for the kids" or "it will be the best" was not, however, active encouragement or instigation. There is no evidence that her remark had any influence on her son's decision to kill his wife. Minn.Stat. § 609.05, subd. 1 (1980), imposes liability for actions which affect the principal, encouraging him to take a course of action which he might not otherwise have taken.

The state has not proved beyond a reasonable doubt that appellant was guilty of anything but passive approval. However morally reprehensible it may be to fail to warn someone of their impending death, our statutes do not make such an omission a criminal offense. We note that mere knowledge of a contemplated crime or failure to disclose such information without evidence of any further involvement in the crime does not make that person liable as a party to the crime under any state's statutes. . . .

David told many people besides appellant of his intent to kill his wife but no one took him seriously. He told a co-worker, approximately three times a week that he was going to murder his wife, and confided two different plans for doing so. Another co-worker heard him tell his plan to cut Carol's air hose while she was scuba diving, making her death look accidental, but did not believe him. Two or three weeks before the murder, David told a friend of his that he and Carol were having problems and he expected Carol "to have an accident sometime." None of these people has a duty imposed by law, to warn the victim of impending danger, whatever their moral obligation may be. . . .

[H]er conviction must be reversed.

QUESTIONS FOR DISCUSSION

1. What were Mrs. Ulvinen's specific actions relevant to her liability?

2. Did she participate in the murder?

3. Are Mrs. Ulvinen's actions *after* the killing relevant to determining her complicity, if any, before and during the crime? Why or why not?

4. If she is not an accomplice, should she nevertheless be guilty of some crime?

5. Do you agree with the court that however morally reprehensible her behavior, she nonetheless did not commit a crime?

6. Why should she not be guilty of accessory after the fact?

7. Why isn't her remark that "it would be for the best" sufficient to amount to the *actus reus*? Should it be? Explain.

NOTE CASES

1. Pace, his wife, and one child were in the front seat of their car driving from South Bend to LaPorte, Indiana. Rootes and another of the Pace children sat in the back seat. Pace, after receiving his wife's permission, picked up Reppert, a hitchhiker. Later, Rootes pulled a knife on Reppert and took his wallet. Just before Reppert got out of the car, Rootes took Reppert's watch. Pace said nothing during the entire episode. Was he an accomplice to robbery? He was convicted, but on appeal, the supreme court said:

> [W]e have found no evidence . . . which might demonstrate that the appellant aided and abetted in the alleged crime. While he was driving his car, nothing was said nor did he act in any manner to indicate his approval or countenance of the robbery. While there is evidence from which a jury might reasonably infer that he knew the crime was being committed, his situation was not one which would demonstrate a duty to oppose it.

State v. Pace, 224 N.E.2d 312 (Ind.1967)

2. Mobley's boyfriend Fagan beat Mobley's young child, threw her in the air and let her drop on the concrete floor, burned her with cigarettes, and told her to run and pushed her over. These, and a series of other violent actions over a period of weeks, eventually led to the child's death. Mobley did not intervene in any of the actions Fagan took because, according to her, she was afraid Fagan would leave her. Was Mobley an accomplice to murder? The court said yes:

It is true that mere presence of a person at the scene of a crime is insufficient to constitute him a principal therein. In the absence of anything in his conduct showing a design to encourage, incite, aid, abet or assist in the crime, the trier of the facts may consider failure of such person to oppose the commission of the crime in connection with other circumstances and conclude therefrom that he assented to the commission of the crime, lent his countenance and approval thereto and thereby aided and abetted it. This, it seems to us, is particularly true when the person who fails to interfere owes a duty to protect as a parent owes to a child.

Mobley v. State, 85 N.E.2d 489 (Ind.1949)

3. Roberts's wife suffered from multiple sclerosis, which according to her doctor was incurable. She asked Roberts to get her some poison so she could kill herself. She could not do it herself because the disease had disabled her so she could no longer walk. Roberts complied with the request, placing the poison in a glass by her bed. She took the poison and died. Was Roberts an accomplice to murder? The court said yes.

Where one person advises, aids, or abets another to commit suicide, and the other by reason thereof kills himself, and the adviser is present when he does so, he is guilty of murder as a principal. . . . It is said by counsel that suicide is no crime . . . and that therefore there can be no accessories or principals . . . in suicide. This is true. But the real criminal act charged here is not suicide, but the administering of poison. . . . We are of the opinion that, when defendant mixed the paris green with water and placed it within reach of his wife to enable her to put an end to her suffering by putting an end to her life, he was guilty of murder by means of poison within the meaning of the statute, even though she requested him to do so. By this act he deliberately placed within her reach the means of taking her own life, which she could have obtained in no other way by reason of her helpless condition.

People v. Roberts, 178 N.W. 690 (Mich.1920)

Mens Rea of Accomplice Liability

Confusion surrounds the *mens rea* required to convict accomplices because criminal intent can refer to both the acts of aiding and abetting and to the crime defendants aid and abet. Most courts hold that accomplice liability requires both of the following:

1. The specific intent or purpose to commit the acts that amount to aiding another to commit a crime.

2. The specific intent or the purpose to commit the crime itself.

A minority of courts, however, hold that the *mens rea* of accomplice liability requires

1. purpose to commit the acts of aiding and abetting; and

2. knowledge of the perpetrator's criminal purpose.

Further confusion arises because both recklessness and negligence can sometimes satisfy the *mens rea* requirement. For example, if participants can foresee that the consequences of their aiding and abetting one crime can reasonably lead to the commission of another crime, they are also criminally liable for the other crime. This was the holding of the court in *People v. Poplar*. Poplar acted as a lookout for his companions in the burglary of a recreation center. When the manager discovered Poplar's companions, one of them shot the manager in the face with a shotgun. Poplar was convicted as an accomplice to the crime of assault with intent to murder. The court held that the shooting was reasonably foreseeable because Poplar knew a gun was in the car he and his companions drove prior to the burglary. Hence, the purpose to aid and abet as a lookout and either his recklessness or negligence with respect to the shooting were enough to convict Poplar of assault with intent to commit murder, the latter a crime that requires *mens rea* of purpose. The court dealt with the *mens rea* required for accomplice liability in *People v. Nguyen*.[6]

C A S E

Were They Parties to Criminal Sexual Conduct?

People v. Nguyen et al.,
21 Cal.App.4th 518, 26 Cal.Rptr.2d 323
(1993)

Thiep Van Nguyen, Ahn Van Tran, and Dung Van Nguyen were sentenced to state prison after juries convicted them of multiple counts of robbery, one count of genital penetration with a foreign object in concert, and one count of being accessories to genital penetration with a foreign object in concert based upon two separate incidents. They appealed. The California Court of Appeal for the Third District af-

firmed in part, reversed in part, and modified in part the judgments of the trial court.

SPARKS, Acting Presiding Justice.

FACTS

. . .

Nancy B. is the owner of a tanning salon in Sacramento. In the late afternoon of December 4, 1990, three young Vietnamese men knocked on the door of the salon and sought admittance, saying they wanted massages. Through an opening in the door Nancy told them that she did not provide massages and that at any rate they were too young for her services. After the men left the front door Nancy noticed a number of young men prying open the back door. The door was forced open and eight young men, seven of whom had guns, burst in. The one intruder who did not have a gun appeared to be of mixed ancestry, part Black and part Asian.

The intruders demanded money. Nancy was threatened, struck with guns, pushed onto the floor, and then tied up with a telephone cord. A jacket was placed over her head. Three men held her down, then three other perpetrators exchanged places and held her down. While she was held down someone pulled her pants down, pushed a gun into her vagina, and threatened to fire it if she did not give up her valuables. The gun was kept in her vagina for 10 to 15 minutes. Eventually the intruders removed the gun, put a breath-spray canister into Nancy's vagina, and left. During the incident the intruders had ransacked the business and stolen money and jewelry.

Shortly after the incident at the tanning salon, a group of young Asian men forced their way into a relaxation spa in Sacramento. The modus operandi was similar to that employed in the tanning salon incident. Two men sought admittance purportedly to partake of the services offered and then forced the door open when the proprietor, Chung, C., sought to examine their identification. Up to nine young men then entered, forced the occupants to lie on the floor, bound them with tape, and put covers over their heads. Since the occupants were caught by surprise and their eyes were covered, they did not get a complete view of all of the perpetrators, but they were able to see that at least three of the perpetrators had guns. The perpetrators ransacked the business and stole money, jewelry and other personalty from the occupants. During the incident one occupant, Kyuok W., was fondled and sexually violated with a finger. [One of the robbers said, "Stop it, quit doing that to her."]
. . .

Based upon these incidents . . . [the defendants were convicted of multiple counts of armed robbery, genital penetration by a foreign object in concert, and accessory to genital penetration by a foreign object in

concert. The part of the opinion dealing with the accessory charge is not included in this excerpt.]

OPINION

Each of the defendants contends that the trial court erred in instructing the jury on the liability of an aider and abettor with respect to the sexual offenses. Specifically, they assert that the court erred by [instructing the jury concerning] . . . the liability of an aider and abettor for the natural and probable consequences of the act originally contemplated pursuant to [California's standard jury instructions. The instructions provide:]

CALJIC No. 3.00 "The persons concerned in the commission of a crime who are regarded by law as principals in the crime thus committed and equally guilty thereof include: One, those who directly and actively commit the act constituting the crime, or; two, those who aid and abet the commission of the crime."

CALJIC No. 3.01: "A person aids and abets the commission of a crime when he or she: One, with knowledge of the unlawful purpose of the perpetrator and; two, with the intent or purpose of committing, encouraging, or facilitating the commission of the crime, by act or advice aids, promotes, encourages or instigates the commission of the crime. A person who aids and abets the commission of a crime need not be personally present at the scene of the crime. Mere presence at the scene of a crime which does not itself assist the commission of the crime does not amount to aiding and abetting. Mere knowledge that a crime is being committed and the failure to prevent it does not amount to aiding and abetting."

CALJIC No. 3.02: "One who aids and abets is not only guilty of the particular crime that to his knowledge his confederates are contemplating committing, but he is also liable for the natural and probable consequences of any criminal act that he knowingly and intentionally aided and abetted. You must determine

whether the defendant is guilty of the crime originally contemplated, and, if so, whether the crime charged in Counts two and five was a natural and probable consequence of such originally contemplated crime."

CALJIC No. 3.03: "One who has aided and abetted the commission of a crime may end his responsibility for the crime by notifying the other party or parties of whom he has knowledge of his intention to withdraw from the commission of the crime and by doing everything in his power to prevent its commission."

Defendants argue that forcible sexual penetration with a foreign object cannot be considered a reasonably foreseeable or natural and probable consequence of robbery and that the court erred by instructing that it was for the jury to determine whether the charged sexual offenses were natural and probable consequences of the robberies. . . .

The aider and abettor in a proper case is not only guilty of the particular crime that to his knowledge his confederates are contemplating committing, but he is also liable for the natural and reasonable consequences of any act that he knowingly aided or encouraged. Whether the act committed was the natural and probable consequence of the act encouraged and the extent of defendant's knowledge are questions of fact for the jury. "It follows that a defendant whose liability is predicated on his status as an aider and abettor need not have intended to encourage or facilitate the particular offense ultimately committed by the perpetrator. His knowledge that an act which is criminal was intended, and his action taken with the intent that the act be encouraged or facilitated, are sufficient to impose liability on him for any reasonably foreseeable offense committed as a consequence by the perpetrator. It is the intent to encourage and bring about conduct that is criminal, not the specific intent of the target offense, which must be found by the jury."

For a criminal act to be a "reasonably foreseeable" or a "natural and probable" consequence of another criminal design it is not necessary that the collateral act be specifically planned or agreed upon, nor even that it be substantially certain to result from the com-

mission of the planned act. For example, murder is generally found to be a reasonably foreseeable result of a plan to commit robbery and/or burglary despite its contingent and less than certain potential. . . . The Supreme Court [has] formulated the question as whether the collateral criminal act was the ordinary and probable effect of the common design or was a fresh and independent product of the mind of one of the participants, outside of, or foreign to, the common design.

The determination whether a particular criminal act was a natural and probable consequence of another criminal act aided and abetted by a defendant requires application of an objective rather than subjective test. This does not mean that the issue is to be considered in the abstract as a question of law. Rather, the issue is a factual question to be resolved by the jury in light of all of the circumstances surrounding the incident. Consequently, the issue does not turn on the defendant's subjective state of mind, but depends upon whether, under all of the circumstances presented, a reasonable person in the defendant's position would have or should have known that the charged offense was a reasonably foreseeable consequence of the act aided and abetted by the defendant.

. . .

A person may aid and abet a criminal offense without having agreed to do so prior to the act. In fact, it is not necessary that the primary actor expressly communicate his criminal purpose to the defendant since that purpose may be apparent from the circumstances. Aiding and abetting may be committed "on the spur of the moment," that is, as instantaneously as the criminal act itself. Since, as we have noted, any person concerned in the commission of a crime, however slight that concern may be, is liable as a principal in the crime, it follows that an aider and abettor will be responsible for a collateral offense if at any time that he does something that directly or indirectly aids or encourages the primary actor in the commission of a crime, it is reasonably foreseeable that a collateral offense may result. . . .

Robbery is a crime that can be committed in widely varying circumstances. It can be committed in a public place, such as on a street or in a market, or it can be committed in a place of isolation, such as in the victim's home. It can be committed in an instant, such as in a forcible purse snatching, or it can be committed over a prolonged period of time in which the victim is held hostage. During hostage-type robberies in isolated locations, sexual abuse of victims is all too common. . . . Robbery victims are sexually assaulted far too often for this court to conclude, as a matter of law, that sexual offenses cannot be a reasonably foreseeable consequence of a robbery.

In turning to the facts of this case we find ample evidence to support a theory that the sexual offenses were a reasonably foreseeable result of the defendants' participation in the group criminal endeavor. The defendants and their cohorts chose to commit robberies in businesses with a sexual aura, both from the types of services they held themselves out as providing and from the strong suspicion, repeatedly expressed by the participants at the trial, that they were actually engaged in prostitution. The businesses were arranged much like a residence, with separate rooms furnished as bedrooms might be. The businesses operated behind locked doors, which both added to their sexual aura and gave the robbers security against intrusion or discovery by outsiders. The robbers went to the businesses in sufficient numbers to easily overcome any potential resistance and to maintain control over the victims for as long as they desired.

When the robbers entered the tanning salon they took control of the premises and took hostage the proprietor and her employee. They maintained their control over the premises and the victims for a significant period of time. At least some of the robbers sexually assaulted the proprietor with a pistol as a means of adding to her fear and forcing her to give up her valuables. While the proprietor was sexually assaulted all of the robbers continued to carry out their criminal endeavor. Assuming the defendants were not actual perpetrators of the sexual offense, their continuing participation in the criminal endeavor aided the perpetrators by providing the control and security they needed to tarry long enough to commit the sexual offense, by helping to convince the victim that resistance would be useless, and by dissuading the victim's employee from any notion she may have formed of going to the victim's assistance. While the defendants participated in the criminal endeavor the foreseeability of sexual assault

went from possible or likely to certain, yet defendants continued to lend their aid and assistance to the endeavor. Under these circumstances it will not do for defendants to assert that they were concerned only with robbery and bear no responsibility for the sexual assault. . . .

. . . First, an aider and abettor need not share the intent of the principal actor, although that is one example of the intent required for aiding and abetting. What is required is that the aider and abettor either share the actor's intent or intend to commit, encourage, or facilitate the commission of a crime. The defendant might act out of friendship for the perpetrator, dislike for the victim, general meanness, or just for the thrill of it, but so long as he intentionally encourages or facilitates the commission of the offense he is guilty as an aider and abettor. Second, the rejected instruction ignores the rule we have applied above, that an aider and abettor "need not have intended to encourage or facilitate the particular offense ultimately committed by the perpetrator" but is responsible for any reasonably foreseeable consequence of the criminal conduct he intentionally encouraged or facilitated. . . .

The test for an aider and abettor's liability for collateral criminal offenses is neither legally abstract nor personally subjective. It is case specific, that is, it depends upon all of the facts and circumstances surrounding the particular defendant's conduct. Within that context it is objective; it is measured by whether a reasonable person in the defendant's position would have or should have known that the charged offense was a reasonably foreseeable consequence of the act aided and abetted. The test is not, as defendant asserts, subjective in nature.

[The part of the court's opinion that found the defendants guilty as accessories after the fact is omitted.]

In this instance the basic criminal endeavor at the relaxation spa (robbery) was quite similar to the criminal endeavor at the tanning salon. However, the sexual assault at the relaxation spa differed from the sexual assault at the tanning salon. At the tanning salon the sexual assault was a component of the robbery, that is, it was committed as a means of threatening the victim to force her to give up her valuables. The victim was assaulted sexually with two foreign objects, a gun and a breath-spray canister. The sexual assault occurred over a protracted period of time during which all of the robbers continued in their criminal enterprise. In contrast, the sexual assault at the relaxation spa was not utilized as a means of threatening the victim for her valuables, was accompanied by sexual rather than larcenous comments, and was committed with a finger. When one or more of the robbers were sexually assaulting the victim, another robber said, "Stop it, quit doing that to her." Under these circumstances the jury found defendants to be principals in the robbery and sexual assault at the tanning salon and in the robberies at the relaxation spa, but had at least a reasonable doubt that the sexual assault at the relaxation spa was a natural and probable consequence of the criminal endeavor in which they participated. That doubt entitled defendants to outright acquittal on charges arising out of the commission of the sexual assault. Defendants cannot be convicted as accessories based upon some notion of responsibility for the commission of the offense less than that which is sufficient for conviction as principals. . . .

[The Court of Appeal affirmed the convictions of armed robbery of both the tanning salon and the spa, and affirmed the convictions of sexual penetration by a foreign object in concert at the tanning salon.]

QUESTIONS FOR DISCUSSION

1. Exactly how does the court define the *mens rea* of complicity?
2. What facts in the two robberies are relevant to determining whether the individual defendants were guilty of the sex offenses that occurred at the time of the robberies at the tanning salon and the relaxation spa?
3. Why did the court decide that the defendants were accomplices in the sex offense at the tanning salon but not accomplices in the sex offense at the relaxation spa?
4. Assume you are a prosecutor and argue the case for conviction of the sex offense in the relaxation spa.
5. Assume you are a defense attorney and argue the case against conviction for the sex offense at the relaxation spa.

NOTE CASES

1. In *Lewis et al. v. State*, 220 Ark. 914, 251 S.W.2d 490 (1952), Wren was driving his friend Lewis's car. En route from Atkins to Morrilton, they purchased twelve cans of beer and drank a considerable amount of beer and gin from 7 P.M. until immediately before colliding head on with another car. Occupants of both automobiles were seriously injured, and Mrs. Pounds, driver of the other car, died from her injuries three days later. Was Lewis guilty of criminal homicide? The court said yes:

   > If the owner of a dangerous instrumentality like an automobile knowingly puts that instrumentality in the immediate control of a careless and reckless driver, sits by his side, and permits him without protest so recklessly and negligently to operate the car as to cause the death of another, he is as much responsible as the man at the wheel.

2. Foster believed Bill had raped Foster's girlfriend. Foster beat Bill up. He handed his friend Otha a knife, telling him to keep Bill from leaving until Foster returned from getting his girlfriend to verify the rape. After Foster left, Otha got nervous and stabbed Bill, who died from the stab wounds. Was Foster an accomplice to negligent homicide? The courts said yes, because even though Foster did not intend to kill Bill, he was negligent with respect to the death: He should have foreseen the consequences of leaving Otha, armed with the knife, to guard Bill. *State v. Foster*, 202 Conn. 520, 522 A.2d 277 (1987)

Complicity Following Crime

The common law included accessories after the fact—complicity following the commission of crimes—within the scope of liability for the main offense. For example, one who gave a burglar a place to hide was an accessory after the fact and as such was also guilty of burglary. Modern statutes impose liability for complicity following commission

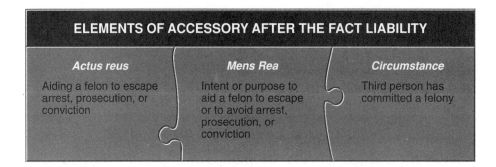

ELEMENTS OF ACCESSORY AFTER THE FACT LIABILITY

Actus reus	Mens Rea	Circumstance
Aiding a felon to escape arrest, prosecution, or conviction	Intent or purpose to aid a felon to escape or to avoid arrest, prosecution, or conviction	Third person has committed a felony

of the main crime, but the liability is for separate, less serious offenses, such as obstructing justice, interfering with prosecution, and aiding in escape.

Most statutes retain the following common-law requirements for accessories after the fact:

1. A third person has actually committed a felony.

2. The accessory knew of the commission of the felony.

3. The accessory personally aided the third person with the intent to hinder the prosecution of the third person.

The Supreme Court of Louisiana dealt with that state's accessory-after-the-fact statute in *State v. Chism.*

C A S E

Was He an Accessory After the Fact?

State v. Chism,
436 So.2d 464 (La.1983)

Brian Chism was convicted by a judge of being an accessory after the fact, and sentenced to three years in prison, with two and one-half years suspended. He was placed on supervised probation for two years. The supreme court affirmed. Justice Dennis wrote the opinion for the court. Chief Justice Dixon dissented.

FACTS

On the evening of August 26, 1981 in Shreveport, Tony Duke gave the defendant Brian Chism a ride in his automobile. Brian Chism was impersonating a female, and Duke was apparently unaware of Chism's disguise. After a brief visit at a friend's house the two stopped to pick up some beer at the residence of

Chism's grandmother. Chism's one-legged uncle, Ira Lloyd, joined them, and the three continued on their way, drinking as Duke drove the automobile. When Duke expressed a desire to have sexual relations with Chism, Lloyd announced that he wanted to find his ex-wife Gloria for the same purpose. Shortly after midnight, the trio arrived at the St. Vincent Avenue Church of Christ and persuaded Gloria Lloyd to come outside. As Ira Lloyd stood outside the car attempting to persuade Gloria to come with them, Chism and Duke hugged and kissed on the front seat as Duke sat behind the steering wheel.

Gloria and Ira Lloyd got into an argument, and Ira stabbed Gloria with a knife several times in the stomach and once in the neck. Gloria's shouts attracted the attention of two neighbors, who unsuccessfully tried to prevent Ira from pushing Gloria into the front seat of the car alongside Chism and Duke. Ira Lloyd climbed into the front seat also, and Duke drove off. One of the bystanders testified that she could not be sure but she thought she saw Brian's foot on the accelerator as the car left.

Lloyd ordered Duke to drive to Willow Point, near Cross Lake. When they arrived, Chism and Duke, under Lloyd's direction, removed Gloria from the vehicle and placed her in some high grass on the roadway, near a wood line. Ira was unable to help the two because his wooden leg had come off. Afterwards, as Lloyd requested, the two drove off, leaving Gloria with him. There was no evidence that Chism or Duke protested, resisted or attempted to avoid the actions which Lloyd ordered them to take. Although Lloyd was armed with a knife, there was no evidence that he threatened either of his companions with harm.

Duke proceeded to drop Chism off at a friend's house, where he changed to male clothing. He placed the blood-stained women's clothes in a trash bin. Afterward, Chism went with his mother to the police station at 1:15 A.M. He gave the police a complete statement, and took the officers to the place where Gloria had been left with Ira Lloyd. The police found Gloria's body in some tall grass several feet from the spot. An autopsy indicated that stab wounds had caused her death. Chism's discarded clothing disappeared before the police arrived at the trash bin.

OPINION

An accessory after the fact is any person, who, after the commission of a felony, shall harbor, conceal, or aid the offender, knowing or having reasonable ground to believe that he has committed the felony, and with the intent that he may avoid or escape from arrest, trial, conviction, or punishment. La. R.S. 14:25

[A] person may be punished as an accessory after the fact if he aids an offender personally, knowing or having reasonable ground to believe that he has committed the felony, and has a specific or general intent that the offender will avoid or escape from arrest, trial, conviction, or punishment . . .

An accessory after the fact may be tried and convicted, notwithstanding the fact that the principal felon may not have been arrested, tried, convicted, or

amenable to justice. . . . [I]t is essential to prove that a felony was committed and completed prior to the time the assistance was rendered the felon, although it is not also necessary that the felon already have been charged with the crime. . . .

We must determine whether, after viewing the evidence in the light most favorable to the prosecution, any rational trier of fact could have found beyond a reasonable doubt that

(a) a completed felony had been committed by Ira Lloyd before Brian Chism rendered him the assistance described below;

(b) Chism knew or had reasonable grounds to know of the commission of the felony by Lloyd; and

(c) Chism gave aid to Lloyd personally under circumstances that indicate either that he actively desired that the felon avoid or escape arrest, trial, conviction, or punishment or that he believed that one of these consequences was substantially certain to result from his assistance.

There was clearly enough evidence to justify the finding that a felony had been completed before any assistance was rendered to Lloyd by the defendant. The record vividly demonstrates that Lloyd fatally stabbed his ex-wife before she was transported to Willow Point and left in the high grass near the wood line. Thus, Lloyd committed the felonies of attempted murder, aggravated battery, and simple kidnapping, before Chism aided him in any way. . . .

The evidence overwhelmingly indicates that Chism had reasonable grounds to believe that Lloyd had committed a felony before any assistance was rendered. In his confessions and his testimony Chism indicates that the victim was bleeding profusely when Lloyd pushed her into the vehicle, that she was limp and moaned as they drove to Willow Point, and that he knew Lloyd had inflicted her wounds with a knife. . . .

The closest question presented is whether any reasonable trier of fact could have found beyond a reasonable doubt that Chism assisted Lloyd under circumstances that indicate that either Chism actively desired that Lloyd would avoid or escape arrest, trial, conviction, or punishment, or that Chism believed that one of these consequences was substantially certain to result from his assistance. After carefully reviewing the record, we conclude that the prosecution satisfied its burden of producing the required quantity of evidence. . . .

(1) Chism did not protest or attempt to leave the car when his uncle, Lloyd, shoved the mortally wounded victim inside;

(2) he did not attempt to persuade Duke, his would-be lover, exit [sic] out the driver's side of the car and flee from his uncle, whom he knew to be one-legged and armed only with a knife;

(3) he did not take any of these actions at any point during the considerable ride to Willow Point;

(4) at their destination, he docilely complied with Lloyd's direction to remove the victim from the car and leave Lloyd with her, despite the fact that Lloyd made no threats and that his wooden leg had become detached;

(5) after leaving Lloyd with the dying victim, he made no immediate effort to report the victim's whereabouts or to obtain emergency medical treatment for her;

(6) before going home or reporting the victim's dire condition he went to a friend's house, changed clothing and discarded his own in a trash bin from which the police were unable to recover them as evidence;

(7) he went home without reporting the victim's condition or location;

(8) and he went to the police station to report the crime only after arriving home and discussing the matter with his mother. . . .

Therefore, we affirm the defendant's conviction. We note, however, that the sentence imposed by the trial judge was illegal. The judge imposed a sentence of three years. He suspended two and one half of years [sic] of the term. The trial judge has no authority to suspend part of a sentence in a felony case. The correct sentence would have been a suspension of all three years of the term, with a six-month term as a condition of two years of probation. . . .

DISSENT

I respectfully dissent from what appears to be a finding of guilt by association. The majority lists five instances of inaction, or failure to act, by defendant:

(1) did not protest or leave the car;

(2) did not attempt to persuade Duke to leave the car;

(3) did neither (1) nor (2) on ride to Willow Point;

(5) made no immediate effort to report crime or get aid for the victim;

(7) failed to report victim's condition or location after changing clothes.

The three instances of defendant's actions relied on by the majority for conviction were stated to be:

(4) complying with Lloyd's direction to remove the victim from the car and leave the victim and Lloyd at Willow Point;

(6) changing clothes and discarding bloody garments; and

(8) discussing the matter with the defendant's mother before going to the police station to report the crime.

None of these actions or failures to act tended to prove defendant's intent, specifically or generally, to aid defendant avoid arrest, trial, conviction or punishment.

QUESTIONS FOR DISCUSSION

1. Was the crime completed at the time Chism aided Lloyd? What facts show this?

2. Do you agree that Chism intended to help Lloyd avoid arrest, trial, conviction, or punishment?

3. What does the dissent mean in saying that the ruling makes a person guilty of crime by association?

4. Do you agree?

5. In Louisiana, according to this ruling, is the *mens rea* for accessory after the fact purpose, knowledge, recklessness, or negligence? Explain.

NOTE CASE

On two separate occasions, Charles Lee Dunn was a passenger in a car when two grand larcenies occurred. He contends that he did not know that the others planned to break into cars, and did not participate in the thefts of stereo equipment and CDs. He admitted that, after the first theft on September 4th, he voluntarily went with the others when they sold the equipment and he received a small piece of crack cocaine from the proceeds. Regarding one of the offenses, he testified that he took no active part in the theft and was taken home immediately thereafter.

The Commonwealth's evidence included testimony from the investigating officer, Detective Ramsey, that appellant told him that he knew the purpose of going to the location of the first offense was "[t]o take equipment belonging to Mr. Roberts. It was known there was equipment in his car." As to the September 7, 1995 offense, Ramsey testified that appellant stated as follows:

> [T]he three of them went to a location near Mr. Jackson's house. Mr. Dunn waited in the car, and Mr. Walker and Mr. Kraegers approached Mr. Jackson's vehicle. They entered the vehicle through an unlocked door and took stereo equipment from the vehicle, brought it back to the car. [Appellant] states that they put the speaker box in the trunk, put the amp and a CD player in the car, and he says, I think they got some CD's. That equipment was also taken to the city and traded for crack cocaine which they all used, and that property has not been recovered.

Ramsey stated that appellant admitted to participating and taking the property to the city in exchange for crack cocaine.

Was Dunn an accessory after the fact? Yes, according to the Virginia Court of Appeals:

> In order to convict as an accessory after the fact, the felony must be completed, appellant must know that the felon is guilty and he must receive, relieve, comfort, or assist him. Mere presence and consent will not suffice to make one an accomplice. It must be shown that the alleged accomplice intended to encourage or help the person committing the crime to commit it. Whether a person aids or abets another in the commission of a crime is a question which may be determined by circumstantial as well as direct evidence.

While appellant contends that the evidence failed to establish that he did anything other than ride in a car with friends, the trial court was not required to accept his explanation. Appellant admitted to Ramsey that he knew that the others intended to steal on both occasions; he smoked crack cocaine purchased with the money received from disposing of the goods; and he went out with the codefendants three days after the first larceny occurred. Under the facts of this case, the Commonwealth's evidence was sufficient to prove beyond a reasonable doubt that appellant was an accessory after the fact to the two grand larcenies. Affirmed. *Dunn v. Commonwealth*, 1997 WL 147448 (1997)

VICARIOUS LIABILITY

The doctrine of complicity applies to accomplices and accessories because they *participate* in crime. The doctrine of vicarious liability bases criminal liability on the *relationship* between the party who commits the crime and another party. Vicarious liability applies mainly to business relationships: employer-employee, manager-corporation, buyer-seller, producer-consumer, service provider-recipient. But it can also apply to other situations, such as making the owner of a car liable for the driver's traffic violations and holding parents liable for their minor children's crimes.

Conviction and punishment for crimes on the basis of vicarious liability, particularly when the defendants are large businesses, are difficult to obtain. Pinpointing responsibility for corporate crime is especially difficult. Often, not one person but many participate in decisions that violate the law. This problem increases as corporate structures become more complex. The larger and more dispersed the corporation or business, the harder it is to attribute responsibility. Furthermore, it is difficult to prove *mens rea* in corporate crimes. A corporation cannot have a *mens rea* because it cannot think. Prosecutors rely on two doctrines to prove corporate criminal liability:

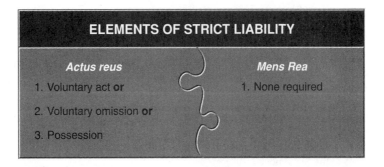

1. **Strict liability** eliminates the element of *mens rea.*
2. **Vicarious liability** attributes the intent of managers and agents to the corporation.

Although vicarious and strict liability work together to impose criminal liability, they are distinct doctrines: strict liability *eliminates* the *mens rea*; vicarious liability *transfers* the *actus reus* and *mens rea*.[7]

Criminal punishment based on the actions of others and in the absence of criminal intent raises constitutional questions. Some courts have ruled that imprisonment based on vicarious liability violates the due process clause. Even imposing fines based on vicarious liability violates the due process clause if noncriminal measures can regulate improper business practices. In addition to questionable constitutionality, fairness is also a problem. Ultimately, stockholders, "most of whom ordinarily had nothing to do with the offense and were powerless to prevent it," pay the fines. Fines probably do not deter officers or other agents who do not have to pay them. Moreover, the deterrent effect is also weakened when businesses treat fines simply as a business expense. Officers suffer no stigma if their organizations violate "mere regulations," and not "real criminal laws." Quite the contrary. Some authorities maintain that officers enhance their reputations for "shrewd business" by risking prosecution and conviction for violating "mere regulations" in order to increase profits.[8]

Business crime deserves special note for two reasons. First, some crimes are peculiar to business. Unlike the gains from most other crimes, the gains sought through corporate crime are neither individual nor personal. For example, corporate executives usually do not fix prices for their personal profit but rather to enhance the company's business position. Second, corporations do not ordinarily injure or cause disease or death because of personal vendettas and anger. They do so while their officers pursue company interests. For example, corporate executives may cut corners in areas such as safety, not to injure workers or customers, but to make the company competitive. Of course, most bank robbers do not want to injure their victims either, but they are prepared to risk doing so in order to get the money they seek.[9]

According to a report of the House Subcommittee of the Judiciary of the U.S. Congress:

> [W]e are talking about . . . economic crime. We have tended in the past to call it property crime as distinguished from violent crime. And even there it is not easy to draw the line. If a surgeon knowingly commits unneeded surgery on a human being because he wants money, is that a less violent physical assault on an individual than to be mugged in the streets? I have to tell you that at a purely moral level I find it far more reprehensible.[10]

The Wisconsin Supreme Court dealt with vicarious corporate liability in *State v. Beaudry.*

C A S E

Did She Unlawfully Remain Open for Business?

State v. Beaudry,
123 Wis.2d 40, 365 N.W.2d 593 (1985)

Janet Beaudry, as the agent of a corporation licensed to sell alcoholic beverages, was convicted and fined $200 for violating the closing hours law. She appealed. The Wisconsin Court of Appeals affirmed the conviction, and the Wisconsin supreme court affirmed the decision of the court of appeals. Justice Abrahamson wrote the opinion of the court. Justice Ceci dissented.

FACTS

. . . Janet Beaudry's conviction grew out of events occurring during the early morning hours of February 9, 1983. At approximately 3:45 A.M., a deputy sheriff for the Sheboygan County Sheriff's Department drove past the Village Green Tavern. He stopped to investigate after noticing more lights than usual inside the building and also seeing two individuals seated inside. As he approached the tavern, he heard music, saw an individual standing behind the bar, and saw glasses on the bar. Upon finding the tavern door locked, the

deputy sheriff knocked and was admitted by Mark Witkowski, the tavern manager.

The tavern manager and two men were the only persons inside the bar. All three were drinking. The deputy sheriff reported the incident to the Sheboygan County district attorney's office for a formal complaint. At about noon on February 9, the tavern manager reported to Wallace Beaudry about the deputy's stop earlier that morning. After further investigation Wallace Beaudry discharged the tavern manager on February 11.

On March 2, 1983, the Sheboygan County Sheriff's Department served the defendant with a summons and a complaint charging her with the crime of keeping the tavern open after hours contrary to § 125.68(4)(c), Stats. and § 125.11(1), Stats. The tavern manager was not arrested or charged with an offense arising out of this incident.

The case was tried before a jury on May 20, 1983. At trial Janet Beaudry testified that she was not present at the tavern the morning of February 9. Wallace Beaudry testified that Janet Beaudry had delegated to him, as president of Sohn Manufacturing, the responsibilities of business administration associated with the

Village Green Tavern; that he had hired Mark Witkowski as manager; that he had informed Witkowski that it was his duty to abide by the liquor laws; and that he never authorized Witkowski to remain open after 1:00 A.M., to throw a private party for his friends, or to give away liquor to friends.

Witkowski testified that he had served drinks after hours to two men. During cross-examination Witkowski confirmed that Wallace Beaudry had never authorized him to stay open after hours; that he had been instructed to close the tavern promptly at the legal closing time; that he knew it was illegal to serve liquor after 1:00 A.M. to anyone, including friends; that his two friends drank at the bar before 1:00 A.M. and had paid for those drinks; that he was having a good time with his friends before closing hours and wanted to continue partying and conversing with them after 1 A.M.; that after closing hours he was simply using the tavern to have a private party for two friends; that he did not charge his friends for any of the liquor they drank after 1:00 A.M.; and that by staying open he was trying to benefit not Wallace Beaudry but himself.

At the close of evidence, the jury was instructed that the law required the premises to be closed for all purposes between 1:00 A.M. and 8:00 A.M. and that if the jury found that there were patrons or customers on the premises after 1:00 A.M., it must find the premises open contrary to statute.

The jury was also instructed regarding Janet Beaudry's liability for the conduct of the tavern manager: As designated agent of the corporation, the defendant had full authority over the business and would be liable for the tavern manager's violation of the closing hour statute if he was acting within the scope of his employment. The instructions describe what activities are within the scope of employment and what are outside the scope of employment. Specifically, the jury was instructed as follows regarding the defendant's liability for the conduct of the tavern manager:

> It is also the law of the State of Wisconsin that violations of statutes regulating the sale of liquor do not require a showing of a willful or intentional act.
>
> It is a law that when a corporation is a li-

censee, the corporation vests in its agent, in this case Janet Beaudry, full control and authority over the premises and of the conduct of all business on the premises relative to alcohol beverages that the licensee could have exercised if it were a natural person.

Under Wisconsin law if a person employs another to act for him in the conduct of his business, and such servant or agent violates the law, as in this case relating to open after hours, then the employer is guilty of that violation as if he had been present or had done the act himself, if such act was within the scope of the employment of the servant or agent.

It is no defense to prosecution under the statute that the employer was not upon the premises, did not know of the acts of his servant or agent, had not consented thereto, or even had expressly forbidden such act.

A servant or agent is within the scope of his employment when he is performing work or rendering services he was hired to perform and render within the time and space limits of his authority and is actuated by a purpose in serving his employer in doing what he is doing. He is within the scope of his employment when he is performing work or rendering services in obedience to the express orders or directions of his master of doing that which is warranted within the terms of his express or implied authority, considering the nature of the services required, the instructions which he has received, and the circumstances under which his work is being done or the services are being rendered.

A servant or agent is outside the scope of his employment when he deviates or steps aside from the prosecution of his master's business for the purpose of doing an act or rendering a service intended to accomplish an independent purpose of his own, or for some other reason or purpose not related to the business of his employer.

Such deviation or stepping aside from his employer's business may be momentary and slight, measured in terms of time and space, but if it involves a change of mental attitude in serving his personal interests, or the interests of another instead of his employer's, then his conduct falls outside the scope of his employment.

If you are satisfied beyond a reasonable doubt from the evidence in this case that Mark Witkowski, the employee of the registered agent, committed the acts charged in the complaint, that Mark Witkowski was the servant or agent of the defendant, and that the acts charged in the complaint were committed by him in the scope of his employment, then you should find the defendant guilty.

If, however, you are not so satisfied, then you must find the defendant not guilty.

Having been so instructed, the jury returned a verdict of guilty.

OPINION

. . . The state's prosecution of the defendant under the criminal laws rests on a theory of vicarious liability, that is *respondeat superior*. Under this theory of liability, the master (here the designated agent) is liable for the illegal conduct of the servant (here the tavern manager). Vicarious liability should be contrasted with liability for one's own acts as a party to a crime: that is, for directly committing the crime, for aiding and abetting the commission of a crime, or for being a party to a conspiracy to commit the crime. § 939.05, Stats. 1981–82. It is apparently undisputed that the tavern manager violated the closing hour statute and could have been prosecuted as a party to the crime. . . .

While the focus in this case is on the defendant's vicarious criminal liability, it is helpful to an understanding of vicarious liability to compare it with the doctrine of strict liability. Strict liability allows for criminal liability absent the element of *mens rea* found in the definition of most crimes.

Thus under strict liability the accused has engaged in the act or omission; the requirement of mental fault, *mens rea*, is eliminated. This court has construed violations of several statutes regulating the sale of alcoholic beverages which command that an act be done or omitted and which do not include words sig-

nifying scienter as imposing strict liability on the actor. . . .

Vicarious liability, in contrast to strict liability, dispenses with the requirement of the *actus reus* and imputes the criminal act of one person to another. . . .

[T]he defendant . . . [argues] that due process requires blameworthy conduct on the part of the defendant as a prerequisite to criminal liability. Although the imposition of criminal liability for faultless conduct does not comport with the generally accepted premise of Anglo-American criminal justice that criminal liability is based on personal fault, this court and the United States Supreme Court have upheld statutes imposing criminal liability for some types of offenses without proof that the conduct was knowing or wilful or negligent.

The defendant's chief challenge to the constitutionality of the statute in issue in this case appears to be that the defendant could have received a jail sentence of up to 90 days for the violation. As the state points out, the defendant was fined $200, and the due process issue the defendant raises, whatever its validity, is not presented by the facts in this case. A decision by this court on the constitutionality of a jail term where the statute imposes vicarious liability would not affect the judgment of conviction in this case or the sentence imposed on this defendant. We therefore do not consider this issue.

We turn now to the question of whether the evidence supports the verdict that the tavern manager was acting within the scope of his employment. As we stated previously, the jury was instructed that the defendant is liable only for the acts of the tavern manager that were within the scope of his employment. Thus the defendant is not liable for all the acts of the tavern manager, only for those acts within the scope of employment. Neither the state nor the defense challenges this statement of the law limiting the designated agent's vicarious criminal liability. The scope of employment doctrine does not represent the only means of limiting the circumstances under which the acts of an employee may be imputed to the corporation or to a corporate officer for purposes of criminal liability. . . .

The application of the standard of scope of employment limits liability to illegal conduct which occurred while the offending employee was engaged in some job-related activity and thus limits the accused's vicarious liability to conduct with which the accused has a factual connection and with which the accused has some responsible relation to the public danger envisaged by the legislature.

The defendant argues that . . . in this case the tavern manager went outside his scope of authority.

We agree with the conclusion reached by the court of appeals. The credibility of the bar manager's testimony was a matter for the jury. The bar manager's testimony which supports the defendant's position that the manager was acting outside the scope of employment was based on a statement the bar manager gave defendant's counsel the night before trial. The jury may not have believed this testimony which was favorable to the defendant. Considering that the conduct occurred on the employer's premises and began immediately after "closing time"; that the employee had access to the tavern after hours only by virtue of his role as an employee of the corporate licensee, which role vested him with the means to keep the tavern open; and that the defendant may anticipate that employees may be tempted to engage in such conduct; the jury could conclude that the tavern manager's conduct was sufficiently similar to the conduct authorized as to be within the scope of employment. The jury could view the tavern manager's conduct as more similar to that of an employee to whom the operation of the business had been entrusted and for whose conduct the defendant should be held criminally liable than to that of an interloper for whose conduct the defendant should not be held liable.

For the reasons set forth, we affirm the decision of the court of appeals affirming the conviction.

Decision of the court of appeals is affirmed.

DISSENT

Ceci, Justice

I respectfully dissent from the majority's conclusion that there is sufficient evidence to support the verdict in this case finding that Mark Witkowski, the tavern manager, was acting within the scope of his employment. In reviewing the evidence in the light most favorable to sustaining Janet Beaudry's conviction, I believe that the record is devoid of evidence to sustain the verdict. I would reverse the decision of the court of appeals which affirmed the defendant's conviction because I am convinced that, as a matter of law, no trier of fact, acting reasonably, could conclude beyond a reasonable doubt that Mark Witkowski was acting within the scope of his employment when he kept the Village Green tavern open after 1:00 A.M. in violation of § 125.68(4)(c), Stats.

We have previously held that a servant is not within the scope of his employment if (a) his acts were different in kind than those authorized by the master, (b) his acts were far beyond the authorized time or space limits, or (c) his acts were too little actuated by a purpose to serve the master. It is important to note that this test is set out in the disjunctive and not the conjunctive, and, thus, not all three elements must be satisfied before there can be a finding that the servant was outside the scope of his authority.

In conformance with this test, the jury was instructed that, "[a] servant or agent is within the scope of his employment when he is performing work or rendering services he was hired to perform and render within the time and space limits of his authority and is actuated by a purpose in serving his employer in doing what he is doing. . . ."

"A servant or agent is outside the scope of his employment when he deviates or steps aside from the prosecution of his master's business for the purpose of doing an act or rendering a service intended to accomplish an independent purpose of his own, or for some other reason or purpose not related to the business of his employer." . . .

I conclude that Mark Witkowski was not within the scope of employment when he kept the tavern open after 1:00 A.M. The first element of the test asks whether Witkowski's acts were different in kind than those authorized by the defendant. Witkowski stated that one of his duties as a manager included closing the tavern at one o'clock. He testified that Wallace Beaudry never authorized him to stay open after the legal closing time. In fact, he was specifically instructed to close promptly at the legal closing time. Additionally, Witkowski testified, "I knew that Wally would not want me to stay open after hours but I decided to do it anyway." Wally Beaudry also testified at the trial. He confirmed Witkowski's testimony by stating that one of Witkowski's duties was to follow all the liquor laws of this state and that he never authorized Witkowski to remain open after 1:00 A.M., throw a private party for his friends, or give away liquor.

A thorough review of the trial transcript reveals that this testimony of Witkowski and Wally Beaudry was in no way impeached by the state. The majority admits that this evidence is undisputed. This testimony was wrongly ignored by the majority. I conclude that Witkowski was not within his scope of employment, because his act of keeping the tavern open until 3:45 A.M. was not authorized by Mr. or Mrs. Beaudry.

The second element of the test . . . asks whether Witkowski's acts were far beyond the authorized time or space limits. I conclude that Witkowski's acts were beyond the authorized time limit because, as stated above, there was testimony that Witkowski was not hired to stay open after hours, and, at the time the police arrived at the tavern, it was 3:45 A.M. Witkowski testified that he usually was done with his normal cleanup between 1:15 A.M. and 1:30 A.M. Over two hours passed between the time he should have locked up and left the tavern and the time the police arrived. Although there is no testimony to this fact, it can reasonably be inferred that Witkowski did not expect to get paid for these two hours when he was sitting at the bar and drinking with his friends. It is clear that Witkowski was no longer working at 3:45 A.M. and that his acts were far beyond the time limit authorized by Janet or Wally Beaudry.

The third and final factor to be considered is whether Witkowski's acts were too little actuated by a purpose to serve the defendant. Not only the direct testimony of Witkowski, but also the circumstantial evidence, provide support for the finding that Witkowski's acts were in no way intended to further the defendant's business, but were motivated solely for his own enjoyment and convenience.

Witkowski testified that after the other patrons left the Village Green tavern, he was not performing any work duties, but was entertaining his "real good friends." Witkowski stated, "I was not trying to benefit Wallace Beaudry by staying open after hours. I was simply using Wally's tavern to have a private party for my two friends. By staying open for my two friends I was not trying to benefit Wallace Beaudry in any way, rather I was trying to benefit myself by continuing the conversation I had started with my friends."

The undisputed circumstantial evidence also bears out the fact that Witkowski's acts were not serving the purpose of the defendant. Deputy Sheriff Kenneth Van Ess testified that he arrived at the tavern at 3:45 A.M. Loud music was coming from within the tavern. The door was locked to outside patrons. Witkowski and Pethan were sitting at the bar, and Dickman, a nonemployee, was standing behind the bar. Dickman later testified that he went behind the bar to get another bottle of liquor. There were glasses and a bottle of liquor sitting on the bar. Van Ess testified that it was quite apparent that all three men had been drinking. Witkowski was not performing any cleanup or maintenance duties. Finally, Witkowski, Dickman, and Pethan all testified that Witkowski had been charging Dickman and Pethan for drinks before 1:00 A.M. Witkowski testified that he did not charge his friends for drinks after 1:00 A.M. This statement is also confirmed by the testimony of Dickman. Ken Pethan testified that he does not remember if he had anything to drink after 1:00 A.M.

Based on this testimony, I conclude that Witkowski was not acting within the scope of his authority, because his acts were in no way intended to serve the defendant. The fact that Witkowski gave his employer's liquor to his friends without charge after 1:00 A.M., when he knew it was illegal and contrary to his authority as a manager of the tavern to stay open after closing hours, strongly supports the conclusion that Witkowski did not intend to further the defendant's business, but was acting solely for his own enjoyment and convenience. Unfortunately, the majority fails to consider these factors in making its determination. . . .

For the above-stated reasons, I dissent.

QUESTIONS FOR DISCUSSION

1. What circumstances does the court conclude justify imposing vicarious liability on Janet Beaudry?

2. How do you justify criminal liability when there is neither *actus reus* nor *mens rea*?

3. Do you believe that punishing Janet Beaudry violates the due process clause?

4. If she were put in jail, would you answer differently?

5. Was the majority or dissent correct in its conclusion regarding Witkowski's acting within the scope of his employment? Explain.

NOTE CASE

The City of Chicago brought three actions against Hertz Commercial Leasing Corporation, Avis Rent-A-Car System, Inc., and Chrysler Leasing Corporation (defendants). The City sought to recover payment of fines from the defendants as the registered owners of vehicles allegedly parked in violation of municipal ordinances. The City prayed for judgments of $88,185 against Hertz, charging 5,879 violations; $73,425 against Avis, charging 4,895 violations; and $37,395 against Chrysler, charging 2,493 violations. The City sought to have the applicable parking ordinance interpreted to preclude the defendants from raising the defense that the owner was not in possession of the vehicle at the time of the violation.

The ordinance provides:

Whenever any vehicle shall have been parked in violation of any of the provisions of any ordinance prohibiting or restricting parking, the person in whose name such vehicle is registered shall be prima facie responsible for such violation and subject to the penalty therefor.

Were the rental companies vicariously liable for their customers' parking tickets? Yes, according to the Illinois appeals court:

... There is no indication in the ordinance that the owner, to be presumed responsible for the violation, must be presumed to have been the person who parked the vehicle. In practice, the defendant, to absolve himself of responsibility, may show that the vehicle was not parked illegally or that he was not the registered owner of the vehicle at the time of the alleged violation. The defenses are limited, but the plain meaning of the ordinance admits of no more. . . . [The ordinance] imposes both strict and vicarious liability on the owner whenever his vehicle is illegally parked, irrespective of whether the owner was the person who parked the vehicle.

We believe that the City intended, under . . . [the] ordinance, to subject the owner of an illegally parked vehicle to the penalty for such parking violation. . . . Accordingly, we hold that the Chicago parking ordinance imposes vicarious liability on the registered owner and that proof that the vehicle was in the possession of another at the time of the violation is irrelevant to the substantive offense.

A question then arises as to whether the imposition of vicarious liability on an owner who rents a vehicle for hire, thereby voluntarily relinquishing the possession and control of the vehicle for the term of the lease agreement, is a constitutional denial of due process. . . . As to owners who rent vehicles for hire, contractual provisions such as an express acknowledgment of personal liability to pay the lessor on demand for all parking fines and court costs or the requirement of security deposits would also serve to deter the irresponsible commission of parking violations. Therefore, the imposition of vicarious liability on an owner who voluntarily relinquishes control of his vehicle to another is constitutionally permissible. Affirmed . . . *City of Chicago v. Hertz et al.*, 375 N.E.2d 1285, (Ill. 1978)

Vicarious Individual
Liability for Corporate Crime

Under most modern statutes, individuals who act for the corporation's benefit are as liable for that conduct as they would be if they were acting in their own behalf for their own private gain. In *United States v. Park*, the court analyzed the criminal liability of a corporate officer for the crimes of the corporation.

◗ C A S E ◖

Did the Corporation President Commit the Crime?

United States v. Park,
421 U.S. 658, 95 S.Ct. 1903,
44 L.Ed.2d 489 (1975)

The president of Acme Markets, Inc., was charged with and convicted of five counts of violating the Federal Food, Drug, and Cosmetic Act because food in the corporation's warehouses was exposed to rodent contamination. The act provides for up to a $1,000 fine or not more than one year of imprisonment or both. Park was fined $250, $50 on each count. He appealed. Chief Justice Burger delivered the opinion, in which justices Douglas, Brennan, White, Blackmun, and Rehnquist joined. Justice Stewart filed a dissenting opinion in which justices Marshall and Powell joined.

FACTS

§ 402 of the act, 21 U.S.C.; § 342, provides in pertinent part: "A food shall be deemed to be adulterated (a) (3) if it consists in whole or in part of any filthy, putrid, or decomposed substance, or if it is otherwise unfit for food; or (4) if it has been prepared, packed or held under insanitary conditions whereby it may have become contaminated with filth, or whereby it may have been rendered injurious to health." § 301 of the act, 21 U.S.C. § 331, provides in pertinent part: "The following acts and the causing thereof are prohibited: (k) The alteration, mutilation, destruction, obliteration, or removal of the whole or any part of the labeling of, or the doing of any other act with respect to, a food, drug, device, or cosmetic, if such act is done while such article is held for sale (whether or not the first sale) after shipment in interstate commerce and results in such article being adulterated or misbranded."

In April 1970 the Food and Drug Administration (FDA) advised respondent by letter of insanitary conditions in Acme's Philadelphia warehouse. In 1971 the FDA found that similar conditions existed in the firm's Baltimore warehouse. An FDA consumer safety officer testified concerning evidence of rodent infestation and other insanitary conditions discovered during a 12-day inspection of the Baltimore warehouse in November and December 1971. The witness testified with respect to the inspection of the basement of the "old building" in the warehouse complex:

> We found extensive evidence of rodent infestation in the form of rat and mouse pellets throughout the entire perimeter area and along the wall. We also found that the doors leading to the basement area from the rail siding had openings at the bottom or openings beneath part of the door that came down at the bottom large enough to admit rodent entry. There were also roden[t] pellets found on a number of different packages of boxes of various items stored in the basement, and looking at this document, I see there were also broken windows along the rail siding.

On the first floor of the "old building," the inspectors found:

> Thirty mouse pellets on the floor along walls and on the ledge in the hanging meat room. There were at least twenty mouse pellets beside bales of lime Jello and one of the bales had a chewed rodent hole in the product. He also related that a second inspection of the warehouse had been conducted in March 1972. On that occasion the inspectors found that there had been improvement in the sanitary conditions, but that "there was still evidence of rodent activity in the building and in the warehouses and we found some rodent-contaminated lots of food items."

The Government also presented testimony by the Chief of Compliance of the FDA's Baltimore office, who informed respondent by letter of the conditions at the Baltimore warehouse after the first inspection. The letter, dated January 27, 1972, included the following:

We note with much concern that the old and new warehouse areas used for food storage were actively and extensively inhabited by live rodents. Of even more concern was the observation that such reprehensible conditions obviously existed for a prolonged period of time without any detection, or were completely ignored. We trust this letter will serve to direct your attention to the seriousness of the problem and formally advise you of the urgent need to initiate whatever measures are necessary to prevent recurrence and ensure compliance with the law.

There was testimony by Acme's Baltimore division vice president, who had responded to the letter on behalf of Acme and respondent and who described the steps taken to remedy the insanitary conditions discovered by both inspections. The Government's final witness, Acme's vice president for legal affairs and assistant secretary, identified respondent as the president and chief executive officer of the company and read a bylaw prescribing the duties of the chief executive officer. The bylaw provided in pertinent part:

> The Chairman of the board of directors or the president shall be the chief executive officer of the company as the board of directors may from time to time determine. He shall, subject to the board of directors, have general and active supervision of the affairs, business, offices and employees of the company.
>
> He shall, from time to time, in his discretion or at the order of the board, report the operations and affairs of the company. He shall also perform such other duties and have such other powers as may be assigned to him from time to time by the board of directors.

He testified that respondent functioned by delegating "normal operating duties," including sanitation, but that he retained "certain things, which are the big, broad, principles of the operation of the company," and had "the responsibility of seeing that they all work together."

At the close of the Government's case in chief, respondent moved for a judgment of acquittal on the ground that "the evidence in chief has shown that Mr. Park is not personally concerned in this Food and Drug violation." The trial judge denied the motion. Respondent was the only defense witness. He testified that, although all of Acme's employees were in a sense under his general direction, the company had an "organizational structure for responsibilities for certain functions" according to which different phases of its operation were "assigned to individuals who, in turn, have staff and departments under them." He identified those individuals responsible for sanitation, and related that upon receipt of the January 1972 FDA letter, he had conferred with the vice president for legal affairs, who informed him that the Baltimore division vice president "was investigating the situation immediately and would be taking corrective action and would be preparing a summary of the corrective action to reply to the letter." Respondent stated that he did not "believe there was anything [he] could have done more constructively than what [he] found was being done."

On cross-examination, respondent conceded that providing sanitary conditions for food offered for sale to the public was something that he was "responsible for in the entire operation of the company," and he stated that it was one of many phases of the company that he assigned to "dependable subordinates." Respondent was asked about and, over the objections of his counsel, admitted receiving, the April 1970 letter addressed to him from the FDA regarding insanitary conditions at Acme's Philadelphia warehouse. The April 1970 letter informed respondent of the following "objectionable conditions" in Acme's Philadelphia warehouse:

1. Potential rodent entry ways were noted via ill fitting doors and door in irrepair at Southwest corner of warehouse; at dock at old salvage room and at receiving and shipping doors which were observed to be open most of the time.

2. Rodent nesting, rodent excreta pellets, rodent stained bale bagging and rodent gnawed holes were noted among bales of flour stored in warehouse.

3. Potential rodent harborage was noted in discarded paper, rope, sawdust and other debris piled in cor-

ner of shipping and receiving dock near bakery and warehouse doors. Rodent excreta pellets were observed among bags of sawdust (or wood shavings).

He acknowledged that, with the exception of the division vice president, the same individuals had responsibility for sanitation in both Baltimore and Philadelphia. Finally, in response to questions concerning the Philadelphia and Baltimore incidents, respondent admitted that the Baltimore problem indicated the system for handling sanitation "wasn't working perfectly" and that as Acme's chief executive officer he was responsible for "any result which occurs in our company."

At the close of the evidence, respondent's renewed motion for a judgment of acquittal was denied. The relevant portion of the trial judge's instructions to the jury challenged by respondent . . . [include]:

In order to find the Defendant guilty on any count of the Information, you must find beyond a reasonable doubt on each count. . . . Thirdly, that John R. Park held a position of authority in the operation of the business of Acme Markets, Incorporated.

However, you need not concern yourselves with the first two elements of the case. The main issue for your determination is only with the third element, whether the Defendant held a position of authority and responsibility in the business of Acme Markets.

The statute makes individuals, as well as corporations, liable for violations. An individual is liable if it is clear, beyond a reasonable doubt, that the elements of the adulteration of the food as to travel in interstate commerce are present. As I have instructed you in this case, they are, and that the individual had a responsible relation to the situation, even though he may not have participated personally.

The individual is or could be liable under the statute, even if he did not consciously do wrong. However, the fact that the Defendant is pres[id]ent and is a chief executive officer of the Acme Markets does not require a finding of guilt. Though, he need not have personally participated in the situation, he must have had a responsible relationship to the issue. The issue is, in this case, whether the Defendant, John R. Park, by virtue of his position in the company, had a position of authority and responsibility in the situation out of which these charges arose.

Respondent's counsel objected to the instructions on the ground that they failed . . . to define "responsible relationship." The trial judge overruled the objection. The jury found respondent guilty on all counts of the information, and he was subsequently sentenced to pay a fine of $50 on each count. § 303(a) and (b) of the act, 21 U.S.C. §§ 333(a) and (b), provide:

(a) Any person who violates a provision of § 331 of this title shall be imprisoned for not more than one year or fined not more than $1,000, or both.

(b) Notwithstanding the provisions of subsection (a) of this section, if any person commits such a violation after a conviction of him under this section has become final, or commits such a violation with the intent to defraud or mislead, such person shall be imprisoned for not more than three years or fined not more than $10,000, or both.

The Court of Appeals reversed the conviction and remanded for a new trial. That court viewed the Government as arguing "that the conviction may be predicated solely upon a showing that [respondent] was the President of the offending corporation," and it stated that as "a general proposition, some act of commission or omission is an essential element of every crime." . . . The Court of Appeals concluded that the trial judge's instructions "might well have left the jury with the erroneous impression that Park could be found guilty in the absence of 'wrongful action' on his part," and that proof to his element was required by due process.

OPINION

. . . [T]hose corporate agents vested with the responsibility, and power commensurate with that responsibility, to devise whatever measures are necessary to ensure compliance with the [Federal Food, Drug, and Cosmetic] Act [of 1938] bear a "responsible relationship" to, or have a "responsible share" in, violations.

[I]n providing sanctions which reach and touch the individuals who execute the corporate mission the Act imposes not only a positive duty to seek out and remedy violations when they occur but also, and primarily, a duty to implement measures that will insure that violations will not occur. The requirements of foresight and vigilance imposed on responsible corporate agents are beyond question demanding, and perhaps onerous, but they are no more stringent than the public has a right to expect of those who voluntarily assume positions of authority in business enterprises whose services and products affect the health and well-being of the public that supports them.

Cases under the Federal Food and Drug Act reflected the view both that knowledge or intent were not required to be proved in prosecutions under its criminal provisions, and that responsible corporate agents could be subjected to the liability thereby imposed. Moreover, the principle had been recognized that a corporate agent, through whose act, default, or omission the corporation committed a crime, was himself guilty individually of that crime. The principle had been applied whether or not the crime required "consciousness of wrongdoing," and it had been applied not only to those corporate agents who themselves committed the criminal act, but also to those who by virtue of their managerial positions or other similar relation to the actor could be deemed responsible for its commission.

In the latter class of cases, the liability of managerial officers did not depend on their knowledge of, or personal participation in, the act made criminal by the statute. Rather, where the statute under which they were prosecuted dispensed with "consciousness of wrongdoing," all omission or failure to act was deemed a sufficient basis for a responsible corporate agent's liability. It was enough in such cases that, by virtue of the relationship he bore to the corporation, the agent had the power to prevent the act complained of.

Thus, the Court has reaffirmed the proposition that "the public interest in the purity of its food is so great as to warrant the imposition of the highest standard of care on distributors." In order to make "distributors of food the strictest censors of their merchandise," the Act punishes "neglect where the law requires care, or inaction where it imposes a duty." "The accused, if he does not will the violation, usually is in a position to prevent it with no more care than society might reasonably expect and no more exertion than it might reasonably exact from one who assumed his responsibilities."

Turning to the jury charge in this case, it is of course arguable that isolated parts can be read as intimating that a finding of guilt could be predicated solely on respondent's corporate position. But this is not the way we review jury instructions, because "a single instruction to a jury may not be judged in artificial isolation, but must be viewed in the context of the overall charge."

Reading the entire charge satisfies us that the jury's attention was adequately focused on the issue of respondent's authority with respect to the conditions that formed the basis of the alleged violations. Viewed as a whole, the charge did not permit the jury to find guilt solely on the basis of respondent's position in the corporation; rather, it fairly advised the jury that to find guilt it must find respondent "had a responsible relation to the situation," and "by virtue of his position had authority and responsibility" to deal with the situation. The situation referred to could only be "food held in unsanitary conditions in a warehouse with the result that it consisted, in part, of filth or may have been contaminated with filth."

[The evidence showed that] respondent was on notice that he could not rely on his system of delegation to subordinates to prevent or correct insanitary conditions at Acme's warehouses, and that he must have been aware of the deficiencies of this system before the Baltimore violations were discovered. The evidence was therefore relevant since it served to rebut respondent's defense that he had justifiably relied upon subordinates to handle sanitation matters.

Affirmed.

QUESTIONS FOR DISCUSSION

1. The Park case tries to resolve the very difficult issue of just how far individual vicarious liability for corpo-

rate crime extends, particularly when the officer does not intend to commit crimes and did not act directly to violate the law. Park was the corporation president and was generally responsible for the corporation's operation, but was he responsible for keeping rats out of the corporation's warehouses?

2. Did the court base Park's individual liability merely on his position in the company or on something he did or failed to do? In other words, is this a status offense, or is it liability based on conduct?

3. If liability is based on conduct and not on status, was Park reckless or negligent with respect to the rats in the warehouse?

4. Or was he strictly liable for the contamination?

5. If keeping foods pure is so important, why did the trial court fine Park only $250?

6. And why did he appeal his case all the way to the United States Supreme Court? Why was so much made of a $250 fine?

Noncorporate Vicarious Liability

It used to be that vicarious liability was limited to business crimes. However, the doctrine of vicarious liability has occasionally also been used when relationships other than business relationships cause problems under extraordinary circumstances. One of those problems is the criminal activities of street gangs, a topic we take up in Chapter 12. However, here we look at one aspect of the use of vicarious liability to control gang activity—making parents responsible for the delinquent acts of their minor children. California passed a statute that did just that. The California court of appeals dealt with this controversial statute in *Williams and others v. Reiner*.

C A S E

Is the Mother Liable for her Minor Son's Crimes?

Williams and others v. Reiner, 2 Cal.Reptr. 2d (1992)

Plaintiffs were taxpayers who claim the enforcement of Penal Code section 272 is void for vagueness. The defendants were Ira Reiner, in his capacity as District Attorney for the County of Los Angeles (district attorney), and James K. Hahn, in his capacity as City Attorney for the City of Los Angeles (city attorney). Upon the parties' cross-motions for summary judgment, the trial court entered summary judgment for the defendants. The plaintiffs appealed. The amendment provides that the parents' or guardians' failure to exercise "reasonable care, supervision, and control over their minor child" is a crime if the failure causes or tends to cause or encourage either dependency or delinquency. The appeals court reversed the summary

judgment for the defendants and directed the trial court to enter summary judgment for the plaintiffs.

ORTEGA, Associate Justice.

FACTS

The Legislature recently enacted Senate Bill No. 1555, 1987–1988 Regular Session (the bill), in an effort to control violent criminal street gang activity. A major portion of the bill consisted of the Street Terrorism Enforcement and Prevention Act (§ 186.20 et seq., the STEP Act) which among other things made the knowing, willful and active participation in a criminal street gang and its criminal activities punishable as either a misdemeanor or a felony. (§ 186.22, subd. (a.).) . . .

Our focus here, however, is upon the bill's amendment of section 272, which prohibits the causing, encouraging, or contributing to the delinquency of a minor. Unlike the STEP Act, section 272 is not specifically targeted at controlling juvenile criminal street gang activity. We quote section 272 in relevant part and delineate the final sentence which was added by the 1988 amendment: "Every person who commits any act or omits the performance of any duty, which act or omission causes or tends to cause or encourage any person under the age of 18 years to come within the provisions of Section 300, 601, or 602 of the Welfare and Institutions Code or which act or omission contributes thereto, . . . is guilty of a misdemeanor and upon conviction thereof shall be punished by a fine not exceeding two thousand five hundred dollars ($2,500), or by imprisonment in the county jail for not more than one year, or by both such fine and imprisonment in a county jail, or may be released on probation for a period not exceeding five years. For purposes of this section, a parent or legal guardian to any person under the age of 18 years shall have the duty to exercise reasonable care, supervision, and control over their [sic] minor child."

In addition to amending section 272, the bill also added chapter 2.9B to the Penal Code, entitled "Parental Diversion" (§ 1001.70 et seq.). Under the parental diversion program, parents or legal guardians who are accused of violating section 272 with respect to their own minor children may seek education, treatment or rehabilitation services and also obtain the eventual dismissal of the section 272 charges upon fulfilling the program's requirements.

The plaintiffs filed their original complaint for injunctive and declaratory relief to halt the enforcement of the amendment to section 272 on July 20, 1989. The complaint's introductory paragraph alleged that the final sentence of section 272 (hereafter the amendment) created a new but vague standard of parental conduct which subjects parents or legal guardians "to criminal prosecution for failing 'to exercise reasonable care, supervision, protection, and control over their minor child.'"

In their statement of facts, the plaintiffs alleged that this new standard of parental conduct was "recently enforced . . . against Ms. Gloria Williams, the mother of a 15 year old boy suspected of being a gang member. Although Ms. Williams was arrested and jailed for an alleged violation of . . . [s]ection 272, the defendants subsequently dismissed the charge against her. Defendants' enforcement of this provision against Ms. Williams indicates that [p]laintiffs and parents o[f] minor children are similarly at risk of prosecution."

In their first cause of action, the plaintiffs maintained that the amendment to section 272 is impermissibly vague because it fails to provide fair and adequate notice of the parental conduct which it prohibits, and it also fails to establish a standard for police enforcement and ascertainment of guilt. The plaintiffs asserted the amendment violates both federal and state due process requirements.

In their second cause of action, the plaintiffs claimed the amendment is "overbroad in violation of [their] fundamental liberty interests in directing the rearing of their children and their freedom of association [under both federal and state constitutions]. The vague and general terms, 'reasonable care, supervision, protection, and control,' which delineate the new standard of parental conduct embrace a wide area of innocent and legal parental conduct."

. . .

With respect to the vagueness challenge to the amendment, the trial court stated in part: . . . The [amendment] gives parents and legal guardians fair notice of what they must do to avoid criminal prosecution, and simply makes explicit a duty which society has long understood to be incumbent upon parents and legal guardians and which has been elaborated upon by an abundance of statutory authority and case law. . . ."

The trial court concluded that the amendment "is not unconstitutionally vague or overbroad. . . ."

. . .

OPINION

. . . We conclude, for the following reasons, that the Section 272 amendment is unconstitutionally vague.

The issues we must decide are whether the amendment is unconstitutionally uncertain, and if so, whether a reasonable and commonsense interpretation may be provided to eliminate the uncertainty.

Preliminarily, we note that our discussion of the amendment is limited to the context of delinquent behavior. . . .

Because this case involves a purely facial challenge based on the amendment's lack of specificity, our discussion will not focus on any specific factual setting including the Gloria Williams case. . . .

. . .

Amendment 272 is impermissibly vague, however, because it criminalizes the parents' failure to exercise reasonable care, supervision, and control over their child without establishing a standard for determining what constitutes reasonable care, supervision, and control. The amendment leaves much room for abuse and mischief in its enforcement because any law enforcement agency is free to decide, based on purely subjective factors, whether the parents exercised reasonable control and supervision over their child.

For example, suppose some parents in Los Angeles regularly permitted their minor children to play outdoors without adult supervision in a housing project where it was commonly known that criminal street gang members were openly selling narcotics. Based on this evidence alone, a law enforcement officer might conclude that the children were at risk of being exposed to delinquent behavior and charge the parents with violation of the amendment. But in the absence of a common standard for objectively evaluating the parents' conduct, while the officer might believe there was sufficient evidence to support the charge, another officer might believe otherwise.

The defendants point out that parents who were intentionally and criminally negligent in supervising their children should have known by their morally reprehensible behavior "that [their] continued wrongful acts might, in the individual judgment of the jurors, be deemed unlawful, a result which [they] can readily avoid by righteous living." The defendants failed to mention, however, that the *Daniel* case was later disapproved by the California Supreme Court. (In re *Newbern* (1960) 53 Cal.2d 786, 797, 3 Cal.Rptr. 364, 350 P.2d 116.) In *Newbern*, the California Supreme Court considered the same statute which was upheld in *Daniel*, and voided it for being impermissibly vague. The *Newbern* court also stated that the statute, which punished "common drunk[s]," was incapable of uniform enforcement because "a person drunk, for example, once a week for four months could be found guilty of a violation of [the statute] in one jurisdiction but not in another." (Id. at p. 797, 3 Cal.Rptr. 364, 350 P.2d 116.)

Similarly here, the amendment fails to provide fair notice to the parents that their behavior may be deemed criminal, and fails to provide an objective standard of enforcement. The amendment creates the hazard that some law enforcement agency might seek to criminalize parental behavior in one neighborhood, but not in another, based on purely subjective standards.

We are not persuaded by the defendants' assertion that the amendment is not vague because the ordinary negligence standard has been applied in other contexts such as vehicular manslaughter (§ 192, subds. (c)(2), (c)(3)). Whereas objective rules of driving are regularly taught in public and private schools, there is no universal guide for teaching parents how to prevent delinquent behavior.

Contrary to the defendants, we do not believe the amendment can be reasonably compared to drunk driving statutes. Defendants' reliance on *Burg v. Municipal Court* (1983) 35 Cal.3d 257, 198 Cal.Rptr. 145, 673 P.2d 732, which involved the constitutionality of a drunk driving statute, is misplaced. Intoxication, unlike the duty to supervise minors to prevent delinquency, is capable of being measured by objective standards. Accordingly, standards of negligence and criminal negligence can be meaningfully applied to drunk driving statutes. But as we will discuss in section C, infra, the vague phrase, "reasonable care, supervision and control," is not made clearer by applying a criminal negligence standard.

" '[A] statute which either forbids or requires the doing of an act in terms so vague that men of common intelligence must necessarily guess at its meaning and differ as to its application, violates the first essential of due process of law.' (*Connally v. General Const. Co.* [(1926)] 269 U.S. 385, 391 [46 S.Ct. 126, 127, 70 L.Ed. 322]. . . .) A statute must be definite enough to provide a standard of conduct for those whose activities are proscribed as well as a standard for the ascertainment of guilt by the courts called upon to apply it. [Citations.]" (*People v. McCaughan*, supra, 49 Cal.2d at p. 414, 317 P.2d 974.)

. . .

Parental rights are fundamentally protected rights. They include " 'the right to direct [the child's] activities and make decisions regarding [the child's] care and control, education, health, and religion.' [Citation.]

The United States Supreme Court has termed this constellation of parental interests 'essential,' among the 'basic civil rights of man', and '[r]ights far more precious . . . than property rights.'

We believe the Legislature must give careful consideration to penal statutes which affect the fundamental and sensitive area of the family. (See Note, "Constitutional Limitations on State Power to Hold Parents Criminally Liable for the Delinquent Acts of Their Children" (1991) 44 Vanderbilt L.Rev. 441, 459472.) "The unique role in our society of the family, the institution by which 'we inculcate and pass down many of our most cherished values, moral and cultural,' [citation] requires that constitutional principles be applied with sensitivity and flexibility to the special needs of parents and children."

The legislative branch, with its ability to hold factfinding hearings and to debate issues, is better equipped than the judicial branch to establish parental standards of conduct. This undoubtedly is one of the most sensitive areas of governmental regulation. As Justice Powell stated: " 'It is cardinal with us that the custody, care and nurture of the child reside first in the parents, whose primary function and freedom include preparation for obligations the state can neither supply nor hinder.'

Unquestionably, there are many competing theories about the most effective way for parents to fulfill their central role in assisting their children on the way to responsible adulthood. While we do not pretend any special wisdom on this subject, we cannot ignore that central to many of these theories, and deeply rooted in our Nation's history and tradition, is the belief that the parental role implies a substantial measure of authority over one's children. Indeed, 'constitutional interpretation has consistently recognized that the parents' claim to authority in their own household to direct the rearing of their children is basic in the structure of our society.'

Properly understood, then, the tradition of parental authority is not inconsistent with our tradition of individual liberty; rather, the former is one of the basic presuppositions of the latter." (*Bellotti v. Baird,* supra, 443 U.S. at p. 638, 99 S.Ct. at p. 3045 (lead opn. of Powell, J.).)

. . .

We conclude that the amendment to section 272 is impermissibly vague and incapable of being uniformly enforced or applied by law enforcement agencies and courts.

. . .

We reverse the judgment and remand the matter to the trial court, which is ordered to enter summary judgment for the plaintiffs. The plaintiffs are entitled to recover their costs on appeal.

SPENCER, P.J., and VOGEL, J., concur.

QUESTIONS FOR DISCUSSION

1. Summarize the arguments of both the plaintiff Ms. Williams and the defendants, the County and City attorneys of the city of Los Angeles.

2. Who has the stronger argument?

3. Should vicarious liability only apply to business relationships? Why? Why not?

4. Do you favor its extension to parent-child relationships? Defend your answer.

5. To what other relationships might you extend vicarious liability?

6. Should vicarious liability apply only to business relationships? Consider the two note cases that follow.

NOTE CASES

1. New Hampshire makes parents vicariously liable for offenses committed by their minor children. Two fathers were convicted because their minor sons drove snowmobiles on a public road in violation of a New Hampshire statute. According to the New Hampshire Supreme Court:

> [W]e have no hesitancy in holding that any attempt to impose . . . [vicarious] liability on parents simply because they occupy the status of parents, without more, offends the due process clause of our State constitution. Parenthood lies at the very foundation of our civilization. The continuance of the human race is entirely dependent upon it. . . . Considering the nature of parenthood, we are convinced that the status of parenthood cannot be made a crime. . . . Even if the parent has been as careful as anyone could be, even if the parent has forbidden the conduct, and

even if the parent is justifiably unaware of the activities of the child, criminal liability is still imposed under the wording of the present statute. *State v. Akers*, 400 A.2d 38 (N.H.1979)

2. Nolan was convicted of more than a dozen parking violations and fined $20. Would Nolan have to pay the fine even if the violations occurred when someone else was driving his car? The court said yes. "Not only may public welfare legislation dispense with a *mens rea* or *scienter* requirement, it may, and frequently does, impose a vicarious 'criminal' liability for the acts of another." *Iowa City v. Nolan*, 239 N.W.2d 102 (Iowa 1976)

SUMMARY

Several persons may participate before, during, and after committing crimes. The doctrine of complicity defines the extent to which criminal liability attaches to these parties to crime. The common-law doctrine of complicity recognized four categories of participants: (1) principals in the first degree, (2) principals in the second degree, (3) accessories before the fact, and (4) accessories after the fact. Modern statutes have merged complicity before and during crime into one category—accomplices—while retaining the category of accessory after the fact. Accomplices are equally liable for the principal crime; accessories after the fact are liable for separate, lesser offenses.

Accomplice and accessory liability depend upon *participation*. Relationships substitute for participation in vicarious liability. Business relationships—employer-employee, principal-agent, and corporation-management—most commonly give rise to vicarious criminal liability. However, states have occasionally imposed vicarious liability on parents for minor children and on owners of cars for those who drive them. Vicarious liability may be strict, in which case the vicariously liable party lacks both *actus reus* and *mens rea*. Penalties for vicarious strict liability are limited to fines.

REVIEW QUESTIONS

1. What is the ordinary phenomenon that the doctrine of complicity examines under extraordinary circumstances?

2. Distinguish between common-law and statutory accomplice liability.

3. Distinguish accomplices from accessories under modern law.

4. How do accomplices, accessories, and vicariously liable parties differ from each other?

5. Identify the two conditions for liability before and during the commission of crimes.

6. State the *actus reus* and the *mens rea* of accomplice liability.

7. Identify and explain the main conditions of accessory liability, that is, liability following the commission of crimes.

8. State the *actus reus* and the *mens rea* of accessory liability.

9. Define and explain the differences between vicarious and strict liability. Give the arguments in favor of and against each of the two types of liability.

10. What does it mean to say that corporate officers are a corporation's brain?

11. Who in the corporate structure should be punished for corporate crimes?

12. Summarize the arguments for and against extending vicarious liability to the parent-child relationship.

KEY TERMS

accessory The party liable for separate, lesser offenses following a crime.

accomplices The parties liable as principals before and during a crime.

doctrine of complicity The principle regarding parties to crime that establishes the conditions under which more than one person incurs liability before, during, and after committing crimes.

Pinkerton **rule** The rule that conspiracy and the underlying crime are separate offenses.

respondeat superior The doctrine that employers are responsible for their employees' actions.

strict liability Liability without fault, or in the absence of *mens rea*.

vicarious liability The principle regarding liability for another based on relationship.

Suggested Readings

1. George P. Fletcher, *Rethinking Criminal Law* (Boston: Little, Brown, 1978), pp. 131–205, 218–232. This work contains provocative discussions about complicity, which Fletcher clearly defines in considerable detail. He also assesses participation in crime in ways that provoke considerable thought about the role of those terms in criminal law.

2. American Law Institute, *Model Penal Code and Commentaries*, vol. 1 (Philadelphia: American Law Institute, 1985), pt. 1, pp. 295–348. A detailed analysis of all elements in complicity and vicarious liability, especially of corporations, as well as arguments why these should be included in criminal law and to what extent participants should be criminally liable. This is an advanced discussion written for experts in the field but is well worth the effort to read and consider its points.

3. Rollin M. Perkins and Ronald N. Boyce, *Criminal Law*, 3d ed. (Mineola, N.Y.: Foundation Press, 1982), pp. 718–720, 911–922. The authors discuss vicarious liability and corporate crime in some detail. They also provide a brief history of how these arose.

4. John Monahan, Raymond W. Novaco, and Gilbert Geis, "Corporate Violence: Research Strategies for Community Psychology," in *Challenges to the Criminal Justice System*, ed. Theodore R. Sarbin and Daniel Adelson (New York: Human Sciences Press, 1979), pp. 117–141. An excellent, clearly written, and easy-to-understand discussion of corporate violence. It defines and describes corporate violence, and includes a thorough bibliography for those who wish to read further.

Notes

1. *United States v. Peoni*, 100 F.2d 401 (2d. Cir. 1938).
2. *Pinkerton v. U.S.*, 328 U.S. 640 (1946), 643.
3. *Model Penal Code*, tentative draft no. 1, p. 43 (1953); *State v. Spillman*, 105 Ariz. 523, 468 P.2d 376 (1970); Wayne LaFave and Arthur Scott, *Criminal Law* (St. Paul, Minn.: West Publishing Co., 1972), 504.
4. 416 F.2d 1110 (D.C.Cir. 1969).
5. 306 N.C. 466, 293 S.E.2d 780 (1982).
6. 20 Mich. App. 132, 173 N.W.2d 732 (1969).
7. Brian Fisse, "Sanctions against Corporations: Economic Efficiency or Legal Efficacy?" in W. Byron Groves and Graeme Newman, eds., *Punishment and Privilege* (Albany: Harrow and Heston, 1986), pp. 23–54.
8. *Commonwealth v. Koczwara*, 397 Pa. 575, 155 A.2d 825 (1959); *Davis v. Peachtree*, 251 Ga. 219, 304 S.E.2d 701 (1983).
9. Marshall B. Clinard and Richard Quinney, *Criminal Behavior Systems*, 2d ed. (Cincinnati, Ohio: Anderson, 1986), chap. 7–8.
10. U.S. Congress, House Subcommittee on the Judiciary, Hearings before the Subcommittee on White Collar Crime, 95th Cong., 2d sess., June 21, July 12, and December 1, 1978 (Washington, D.C.: U.S. Government Printing Office, 1979).

CHAPTER FIVE

Uncompleted Crimes:
Attempt, Conspiracy, and Solicitation

CHAPTER OUTLINE

CHAPTER MAIN POINTS

1. The doctrine of inchoate offenses imposes criminal liability on those who intend to commit crimes and take some steps toward completing crimes.

2. Attempts to commit crimes stand closest to completed crimes, conspiracies are further removed, and solicitations are furthest removed.

3. The elements of attempt include the purpose, or specific intent, to commit a crime (*mens rea*); steps to carry out the criminal purpose (*actus reus*); and failure to complete the crime.

4. According to attempt doctrine, those bent on committing crimes should not benefit from a stroke of luck that interrupts their purpose.

5. A voluntary abandonment of a planned crime that has gone some way toward completion sometimes removes criminal liability and sometimes mitigates the punishment for attempt.

6. Legal impossibility is a defense to attempt; factual impossibility is not.

7. The elements of conspiracy include an agreement or combination (*actus reus*) entered into for the specific purpose of committing an unlawful act or committing a lawful act by unlawful means (*mens rea*).

8. The elements of solicitation include the specific intent to induce another to commit a crime (*mens rea*) accompanied by action, usually words, urging the other person to commit the crime (*actus reus*).

Did He Attempt to Rob
the Convenience Store?

James Kimball went into a convenience store and began talking to and whistling at the Doberman Pinscher guard dog on duty at the time. Susan Stanchfield, the clerk, gave Kimball a "dirty look," because she didn't want him playing with the dog. Kimball then approached the cash register, where Stanchfield was stationed, and demanded money. Stanchfield then began fumbling with the one dollar bills until Kimball directed her to the "big bills." According to Kimball, he then said, "Hey, I'm just kidding," and something to the effect that "you're too good looking to take your money." As Kimball was leaving, Stanchfield called after him, saying that she would not call the police if he would "swear never to show your face around here again." Kimball replied, "You could only get me on attempted anyway."

INTRODUCTION

Criminal law punishes not only completed crimes but also conduct that falls short of completion. Reckless driving or driving while intoxicated are crimes even if the driver injures no one; possessing a bomb may be a crime even though no harm occurs unless the bomb explodes; and burglary consists of breaking and entering with the intent to commit a crime, even if the crime intended is never committed. The doctrine of **inchoate crimes,** the subject of this chapter, applies specifically to three types of incomplete crimes: attempt, conspiracy, and solicitation. According to the doctrine, attempting to commit a crime, conspiring with another or others to commit a crime, and soliciting another or others to commit a crime are three distinct offenses. Each inchoate offense has its own elements, but they all share the *mens rea* of purpose, that is, the specific intent to commit the crime and the *actus reus* of acts taken to fulfill the criminal purpose but which fall short of completing the crime.

Incomplete criminal conduct poses a dilemma: whether to punish someone who has harmed no one or to set free someone determined to commit a crime. The doctrine of inchoate crimes asks to what extent criminal law ought to serve as an instrument of crime prevention by punishing action that does not accomplish its criminal purpose. The doctrine of inchoate crimes conflicts with the notion that free societies punish people for what they have done, not for what they might do. On the other hand, the doctrine of inchoate crimes accords with the widely held belief that "an ounce of prevention is worth a pound of cure." The law of inchoate crimes resolves the dilemma between restricting criminal law to what people have done and setting people determined to commit crimes free by:

1. Requiring some action toward the completion of the crime.
2. Requiring a specific intent to commit the crime.
3. Imposing lesser penalties than for completed crimes.[1]

ATTEMPT

Failure is an unwelcome but nonetheless ordinary phenomenon of everyday life. Criminal attempt is about failure under extraordinary circumstances: shooting at someone and missing the target; holding up a convenience store and discovering no money in the cash register; reaching to steal a CD off a department store shelf and getting caught by the store detective.

History of the Law of Attempt

The place of attempt in criminal law has plagued lawmakers, judges, and philosophers for centuries. In *Laws*, Plato wrote that one who "has a purpose and intention to slay another and he [merely] wounds him should be regarded as a murderer." But, he added, the law should punish such wounding less than it would murder. In the thirteenth century, the great English jurist Bracton disagreed: "For what harm did the attempt cause, since the injury took no effect?" By the next century, English judges were applying what became a famous common-law maxim: "The will shall be taken for the deed." Justice Shardlowe held that "one who is taken in the act of robbery or burglary, even though he does not carry it out, will be hanged."[2]

According to the common law, the crime of attempt required more than the mere intention to harm: "The thoughts of man shall not be tried, for the devil himself knoweth not the thought of man." The early cases required that both substantial acts and some kind of harm accompany the intent. The two leading cases involved a servant who, after cutting his master's throat, fled with the latter's goods, and a wife's lover who attacked and seriously injured her husband, leaving him for dead. The servant and the lover were punished for attempted murder because they had not only taken substantial steps toward completing the crime, but they had also seriously injured their victims.[3]

During the sixteenth century, English criminal attempt law began to resemble its modern counterpart. Criminal attempt law was a response to the threats to peace and safety in a society known for hot, short tempers and violent, quarrelsome tendencies.

The English Court of Star Chamber punished a wide range of potential harms, hoping to nip violence in the bud. Typical cases included lying in wait, threats, challenges, and even words that "tended to challenge." Surviving records are replete with efforts to punish incipient violence that too often erupted into serious injury and death.[4]

By the early seventeenth century, an attempt doctrine in English law was emerging. Stressing a need to prevent the serious harms spawned by dueling, Francis Bacon maintained that "all the acts of preparation should be punished." He then went on to argue for adopting the following criminal attempt principle:

> I take it to be a ground infallible: that wheresoever an offense is capital, or matter of felony, though it be not acted, there the combination or acting tending to the offense is punishable. . . . Nay, inceptions and preparations in inferior crimes, that are not capital have likewise been condemned.[5]

As this brief historical sketch shows, Anglo-American criminal law has punished incomplete crimes since at least the sixteenth century, albeit at first without a clear attempt doctrine. Since the seventeenth century, a formal attempt doctrine has governed the law of criminal attempt. Not until the late eighteenth century, however, did the English courts adopt a doctrine that applied to all of the inchoate offenses. In *Rex v. Scofield*, a servant put a lighted candle in his master's house, intending to burn the house down. The house did not burn, but the servant suffered punishment for attempt nevertheless. The court held that "the intent may make an act, innocent in itself, criminal; nor is the completion of an act, criminal in itself, necessary to constitute criminality."[6]

By the nineteenth century, common-law attempt was well defined:

> [A]ll attempts whatever to commit indictable offenses, whether felonies or misdemeanors, and whether, if misdemeanors[,] they are so by statute or at common law, are misdemeanors, unless by some special statutory enactment they are subjected to special punishment.[7]

Some jurisdictions have retained the common law of attempt. In 1979, the Maryland Supreme Court held that "the common law is still alive and well in Maryland," and that the common law of attempt, "still prospers on these shores."[8]

Theories of Criminal Attempt

Two theories underlie criminal attempt doctrine. One focuses on *actus reus*, the objective dimension to criminal liability, justifying the punishment of attempts because it controls dangerous conduct. The other focuses on *mens rea*, the subjective element, justifying punishment because it controls dangerous persons. Jurisdictions adopting the dangerous conduct rationale focus on how close the actor came to completing the crime. The dangerous person rationale aims at curbing persons determined to commit crimes; it concentrates not on how close actors came to completing their plans but on how fully they have developed their criminal designs. Both rationales measure dangerousness according to actions: The dangerous conduct rationale does so in order to determine proximity to completion; the dangerous person rationale in order to gauge developed design.[9]

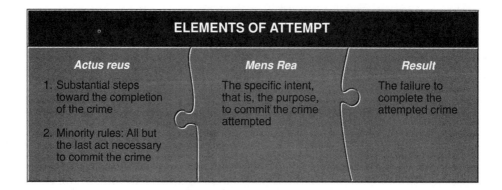

ELEMENTS OF ATTEMPT		
Actus reus	**Mens Rea**	**Result**
1. Substantial steps toward the completion of the crime 2. Minority rules: All but the last act necessary to commit the crime	The specific intent, that is, the purpose, to commit the crime attempted	The failure to complete the attempted crime

The Elements of Criminal Attempt

Common-law attempt consisted of an intent either to carry out an act or to bring about certain consequences that amounted to a crime, coupled with an act beyond mere preparation, in furtherance of that intent.[10]

The elements of attempt include

1. Intent, that is, the purpose to commit a crime;

2. Act or acts in pursuance of the intention; and, in most jurisdictions,

3. Failure to consummate the crime.

Most states do not define attempts individually; that is, they do not define attempted murder, attempted robbery, attempted rape, and so on in separate statutes. They usually define attempt in a general attempt statute. A typical general attempt statute might read something like "Any person who shall attempt to commit any offense prohibited by law shall be punished."[11]

Attempt *Mens Rea*. Attempt is a crime of purpose, that is, it requires specific intent. There are no reckless, negligent, or strict liability attempts. According to one authority, "To attempt something . . . necessarily means to seek to do it, to make a deliberate effort in that direction. Intent is inherent in the notion of attempt; it is the essence of the crime. An attempt without intent is unthinkable; it cannot be."[12]

Supreme Court Justice and legal philosopher Oliver Wendell Holmes, in his classic *The Common Law*, criticized the view that there can be no attempt without specific intent:

> Acts should be judged by their tendency, under the known circumstances, not by the actual intent which accompanies them. It may be true that in the region of attempts, as elsewhere, the law began with cases of actual intent, as these cases were the most obvious ones. But it cannot stop with them, unless it attaches more importance to the etymological meaning of the word attempt than to the general principles of punishment.[13]

Despite the weight that the views of Holmes deserve, specific intent remains central to the *mens rea* element of the modern crime of attempt.

▶ C A S E ◀

Did He Intend to Rob the Convenience Store?

People v. Kimball,
109 Mich.App. 273, 311 N.W.2d 343
(1981)

MAHER, JUDGE

James Kimball was charged with and convicted of attempted unarmed robbery at a bench trial. He was sentenced to a prison term of from 3 to 5 years. He appealed and the Michigan appeals court reversed the conviction. Although the appeals court found that the evidence proved that Kimball had the requisite intent, it reversed the conviction and ordered a new trial because the trial court rejected defendant's claim that voluntary abandonment was a defense to a prosecution for criminal attempt; in so doing, it never determined whether defendant's abandonment was voluntary or involuntary. Defendant was entitled to a new trial at which defendant could present such defense. (Voluntary abandonment is discussed later in this chapter.)

FACTS

It appears that on the day in question the defendant went to the home of a friend, Sandra Storey, where he proceeded to consume a large amount of vodka mixed with orange juice. Defendant was still suffering from insect stings acquired the previous day so he also took a pill called "Eskaleth 300," containing 300 milligrams of Lithium, which Storey had given him. After about an hour, the pair each mixed a half-gallon container of their favorite drinks (vodka and orange juice, in the defendant's case), and set off down the road in Storey's '74 MGB roadster.

At approximately 8:15 or 8:30 in the evening, defendant (who was driving) pulled into the parking lot of the Alpine Party Store. Although he apparently did not tell Storey why he pulled in, defendant testified that the reason for the stop was to buy a pack of cigarettes. Concerning events inside the store, testimony was presented by Susan Stanchfield, the clerk and sole employee present at the time. She testified that

defendant came in and began talking to and whistling at the Doberman Pinscher guard dog on duty at the time. She gave him a "dirty look," because she didn't want him playing with the dog. Defendant then approached the cash register, where Stanchfield was stationed, and demanded money.

Stanchfield testified that she thought the defendant was joking, and told him so, until he demanded money again in a "firmer tone."

STANCHFIELD: "By his tone I knew he meant business; that he wanted the money."

PROSECUTION: "You felt he was serious?"

STANCHFIELD: "I knew he was serious."

Stanchfield then began fumbling with the one dollar bills until defendant directed her to the "big bills." Stanchfield testified that as she was separating the checks from the twenty dollar bills defendant said "I won't do it to you; you're good looking and I won't do it to you this time, but if you're here next time, it won't matter."

A woman then came in (Storey) who put a hand on defendant's shoulder and another on his stomach and directed him out of the store. Stanchfield testified that she called after the defendant, saying that she would not call the police if he would "swear never to show your face around here again." To this defendant is alleged to have responded: "You could only get me on attempted anyway." Stanchfield then directed a customer to get the license plate number on defendant's car while she phoned the owner of the store.

Defendant also testified concerning events inside the store. He stated that the first thing he noticed when he walked in the door was the Doberman Pinscher. When he whistled the dog came to him and started licking his hand. Defendant testified that while he was petting the dog Stanchfield said "[w]atch out for the dog; he's trained to protect the premises."

DEFENDANT: "Well, as soon as she told me that the dog was a watchdog and a guarddog [sic], I just walked up in front of the cash register and said to Sue (Stanchfield) I said, 'I want your money.'"

"I was really loaded and it just seemed to me like it was kind of a cliché because of the fact that they've got this big bad watchdog there that's supposed to watch the place and there I was just petting it, and it was kind of an open door to carry it a little further and say hey, I want all your money because this dog isn't going to protect you. It just kind of happened all at once."

"She said I can't quote it, but something to the effect that if this is just a joke, it's a bad joke, and I said, 'Just give me your big bills.'

"Then she started fumbling in the drawer, and before she pulled any money out of the drawer I don't know whether she went to the ones or the twenties I said as soon as she went toward the drawer to actually give me the money, I said, 'Hey, I'm just kidding,' and something to the effect that you're too good-looking to take your money.

And she said, 'Well, if you leave right now and don't ever come back, I won't call the police,' and I said, 'Okay, okay,' and I started to back up.

"And Sandy (Storey) I mean I don't know if I was stumbling back or stepping back, but I know she grabbed me, my arm, and said, 'Let's go,' and we turned around and left, and that was it."

Both Stanchfield and the defendant testified that there were other people in the store during the time that defendant was in the store, but the testimony of these people revealed that they did not hear what was said between Stanchfield and the defendant.

Storey testified that she remained in the car while defendant went into the store but that after waiting a reasonable time she went inside to see what was happening. As she approached the defendant she heard Stanchfield say "just promise you will never do that again and I won't take your license number." She then took defendant's arm, turned around, gave Stanchfield an "apologetic smile," and took defendant back to the car. Once in the car, defendant told Storey what had happened in the store, saying "but I told her (Stanchfield) I was only kidding." Defendant and Storey then drove to a shopping center where defendant was subsequently arrested.

OPINION

The general attempt statute, under which defendant was prosecuted, provides in part as follows: "Any person who shall attempt to commit an offense prohibited by law, and in such attempt shall do any act towards the commission of such offense, but shall fail in the perpetration, or shall be intercepted or prevented in the execution of the same, when no express provision is made by law for the punishment of such attempt, shall be punished. . . ."

The elements of an attempt are (1) the specific intent to commit the crime attempted and (2) an overt act going beyond mere preparation towards the commission of the crime. Considering the second element first, it is clear that in the instant case defendant committed sufficient overt acts. As the trial court noted, there was evidence on every element of an unarmed robbery except for the actual taking of money. From the evidence presented, including the evidence of defendant's intoxication, the question of whether defendant undertook these acts with the specific intent to commit an unarmed robbery is a much closer question. After hearing all the evidence, however, the trial court found that defendant possessed the requisite intent and we do not believe that finding was clearly erroneous. Reversed on other grounds.

QUESTIONS FOR DISCUSSION

1. If you were a juror and heard the testimony of Kimball and Stanchfield, who would you believe?

2. Has the prosecution proved the *mens rea* beyond a reasonable doubt?

3. What in the testimony of each specifically bears on Kimball's *mens rea*?

4. Did he have the specific intent to rob the store?

5. Is the answer as clear as the court believes? Why or why not?

NOTE CASES

1. Thacker shot a gun through a tent, intending to "shoot the light out." The shot passed through the tent. People were inside the tent at the time Thacker fired the shot. A bullet hit the bed, barely missing the heads of a woman and her baby who were lying on the bed. Did Thacker attempt to murder them? The Virginia Supreme Court said no, because Thacker lacked the specific intent to kill. He intended to put the light out, not to kill the woman and her baby. *Thacker v. Commonwealth*, 134 Va. 767, 114 S.E. 504 (1922)

2. Robert and his mother were visiting Johnnie Shields's apartment. Robert got drunk and fell, breaking a table. Some time after Robert and his mother returned to their apartment (which was next door to Johnnie Shields's), Johnnie appeared at Robert's door with a gun, threatening to kill him. Robert and his mother fled the apartment; Johnnie chased them. Outside, Robert's mother stood in front of Robert to shield him. Johnnie told her to step aside or he "would blow her brains out." After a scuffle over possession of the gun, Johnnie fired, wounding her. Did he attempt to murder her? The trial court instructed the jury that they could find Johnnie guilty of attempted murder if they believed that he intended to kill or cause great bodily harm. The jury found him guilty. The Illinois Supreme Court reversed, holding that attempted murder required the specific intent to kill and did not include the alternative intent to cause great bodily harm. *People v. Shields*, 72 Ill.2d 16, 17 Ill.Dec. 838, 377 N.E.2d 28 (1978)

3. On January 15, 1994, a Platte County sheriff's deputy attempted to stop Hemmer for a speeding violation. When Hemmer would not stop, a high-speed chase ensued. The chase continued from Platte County through Madison County and into Pierce County, at which time there were 8 to 10 law enforcement officers from four different law enforcement agencies involved in the chase. During the chase, Hemmer ran two roadblocks set up by police. One roadblock had been set up by the Pierce County sheriff in the town of Osmond. As Hemmer's vehicle was being chased through Osmond by a State Patrol trooper, the sheriff parked his vehicle in the middle of a street in the path of the pursuit and exited the vehicle. The sheriff then attempted to "flag the Hemmer vehicle down" as it approached, but when Hemmer's vehicle did not stop, the sheriff was forced to "dive into a snowbank" to avoid being struck. Hemmer was later apprehended in a rural area after his vehicle ran out of gas.

Hemmer was charged with several crimes relating to the incident, including attempted assault on an officer in the second degree. The charge in the form of an information alleged that Hemmer attempted to "intentionally or recklessly cause bodily injury with a dangerous instrument to a peace officer." Hemmer filed a motion to quash the attempted assault charge, alleging that it is "legally impossible to commit the crime of attempting to recklessly cause bodily injury with a dangerous instrument to a peace officer."

Hemmer claims that it is legally impossible to commit a crime of attempt to recklessly cause bodily injury because the attempt statute requires that the actor intentionally attempt to commit the underlying crime. Before addressing this argument, we find it necessary to clarify the levels of culpability that are involved in the two statutes at issue in this case. Was Hemmer guilty of attempting to recklessly assault a police officer? No, said the Nebraska Supreme Court:

> The attempt statute mentions two levels of culpability, "intentional" and "knowing." See § 28201(1) and (2). The crime of assault on a peace officer in the second degree has three potential levels of culpability: intentional, § 28930(1)(a); knowing, § 28930(1)(a); and reckless, § 28930(1)(b). However, the information only charged Hemmer with attempted "reckless" assault on an officer in the second degree.
>
> . . .
>
> In *State v. Sodders*, 208 Neb. 504, 304 N.W.2d 62 (1981), the Nebraska Supreme Court discussed the attempt statute and the requisite mental states that accompany § 28201(1)(a), (1)(b), and (2). In its discussion, the court indicated that where a particular result is an element of the underlying crime, subsections (1)(a) and (b) of the attempt statute require that the actor intended the result, i.e., an intentional *mens rea*. . . .
>
> The underlying crime, as charged in this case, does not contain an intentional or a knowing state of mind as an element, as is required by § 28201. As charged in the amended information, the crime is not an intentional or knowing one, but, rather, a reckless one. As the Supreme Court stated in *Sodders*, the attempt statute only applies to crimes committed knowingly or intentionally. The attempt statute thus does not apply to a crime such as an attempt to recklessly cause bodily injury to a peace officer because the *mens rea* of "reckless" does not rise to the level of "knowing" or "intentional" as required by the attempt statute. See § 28201. . . .
>
> . . . [W]e conclude that there is no crime in the State of Nebraska for attempted reckless assault on a peace officer in the second degree. We note, however, that our decision in no way affects the validity of the crimes of attempted intentional or knowing assault on a peace officer in the second degree. The crime of attempted reckless assault on a peace officer in the second degree is

not a crime under the statutes and case law of Nebraska. Hemmer, therefore, correctly asserts that the amended information was insufficient to charge a crime, and accordingly, we reverse his conviction. Reversed. *State v. Hemmer*, 531 N.W.2d 559 (Neb. 1995)

4. Thames and his friends, David Bost and Sean Rhodes, met at Rhodes's home to smoke marijuana and drink gin. Thereafter, Thames and Bost began "playing" with guns and Thames accidently shot Bost. Instead of taking Bost to a hospital, out of fear that they would be caught by the police, Thames and Rhodes put Bost in the trunk of Rhodes's car and drove around, looking for an open garage to dump the body. After Thames and Rhodes left Bost in a vacant garage, they left in the car. They returned to the garage when their car ran out of gas. When Thames and Rhodes returned, Rhodes instructed Thames to "put him [Bost] to rest." Thames shot Bost again. Thames then burned the body.

Thames was charged with attempted intentional homicide while armed with a dangerous weapon for the second shot. Thames filed a motion to dismiss, arguing that there was no probable cause to charge him with attempted intentional homicide. The trial court denied the motion. Did Thames attempt to kill Bost? Yes, according to the appeals court:

> The first issue involves application of the attempt and intentional homicide statutes. See §§ 939.32(3) and 940.01(1), Stats. Section 940.01(1) states, in relevant part, that "whoever causes the death of another human being with intent to kill that person . . . is guilty of a Class A felony." Section 939.32(3) defines attempt. It provides:
>
> An attempt to commit a crime requires that the actor have an intent to perform acts and attain a result which, if accomplished, would constitute such crime and that the actor does acts toward the commission of the crime which demonstrate unequivocally, under all the circumstances, that the actor formed that intent and would commit the crime except for the intervention of another person or some other extraneous factor.
>
> Thames accidently shot Bost while the two were intoxicated and had been "playing" with

loaded guns. After shooting Bost, Thames saw Bost on the floor moving, with blood seeping out of his head. Afraid that Bost would inform the police about what had happened, Thames and Rhodes decided not to take Bost to a hospital. Instead, Thames and Rhodes put Bost in the trunk of a car and drove around, looking for an open garage to dump the body. After Thames and Rhodes dumped Bost in a garage, Rhodes told Thames to "put him to rest," and Thames then shot Bost again. Thames then set fire to Bost, after dousing him with gasoline. The complaint further alleges that an autopsy concluded that Bost died as a result of the bullet that entered behind his ear and lodged in his brain, the first shot, and that the second shot, the one which entered the left side of his jaw and lodged in the right side, was "nonfatal."

> Thames argues that the complaint does not show that he intended to kill Bost when he shot him the second time because Bost died as a result of the first shot. We disagree. Although the complaint alleges that the first shot was the fatal shot and that the second shot was nonfatal, the complaint does not allege that Bost was already dead when Thames shot him the second time. The complaint merely alleges that Bost died from the wound he received as a result of the first shot. Further, the allegations in the complaint give every indication that Thames believed that Bost was still alive immediately before he shot Bost the second time and that he fired the second shot with every intention of making sure Bost was dead. As noted, Rhodes instructed Thames to "put him to rest." Thames then shot Bost at close range. Notwithstanding Thames's argument, we find that the circumstances of the crime allow the clear inference of an intent to kill. Further, the attempt element is satisfied because the complaint establishes probable cause that Thames would have killed Bost except for the extraneous factor that the second shot was nonfatal. The allegations of Count 2 of the complaint establish probable cause to believe that Thames committed the crime of attempted first-degree intentional homicide. . . . Judgment affirmed. *State v. Thames*, Unpublished Opinion, Court of Appeals, Wisconsin, No. 95-3313-CR, 1996

Attempt *Actus Reus*. Criminal attempt does not require a completed crime, but mere preparation to commit a crime is not a criminal attempt. If you sit in your room plotting to kill someone, then get up and walk out to your car in order to buy a gun and then say to yourself, "What am I thinking? I can't kill him," and do no more, you have not committed a crime. Attempt law determines at which point on the spectrum between mere intention and completed crime an attempt to commit a crime has taken place.[14]

Criminal attempt requires action or steps beyond plotting and preparation. However, jurisdictions vary in distinguishing between preparation and attempt. Some states require "some steps." At the other extreme, a few states demand "all but the last act." Most states, along with the *Model Penal Code*, require "substantial steps" toward completing the crime. Under all three tests, if you stand over your enemy on the verge of pulling the trigger, you have committed attempted murder. Most jurisdictions require considerably less. But how much less? If you leave your house only to buy a handgun to do the job, you are merely preparing to murder. Courts distinguish mere preparation from criminal attempt according to four tests:

1. Physical proximity doctrine

2. Probable desistance approach

3. Equivocality approach

4. Substantial steps or the *Model Penal Code* standard.

The **physical proximity doctrine** focuses on time, space, and the number of necessary acts remaining to complete the crime. The easiest point at which to justify criminal liability is when the attempter has taken all but the last act necessary to commit the crime. This was the test applied in the old and famous case, *Commonwealth v. Peaslee*. (See Note Case 3 following *Young v. State*.) The court reversed Peaslee's conviction for attempted arson because Peaslee, "the would-be criminal," had not "done his last act." According to the New York Supreme Court, the conduct must come "dangerously near completion of the criminal endeavor before the boundary is reached where preparation ripens into punishable conduct." This rule insulates some dangerous conduct from criminal liability. Physical proximity looks to dangerous conduct, not dangerous actors. According to the physical proximity doctrine, the criminal law punishes conduct when it reaches a "dangerous proximity to success." Great importance, therefore, attaches to how close the actor's conduct has come to completing the intended crime. The physical proximity doctrine does not answer the question "how close is close enough to attempt liability?"[15]

The **probable desistance approach** considers whether an act in the ordinary course of events would lead to the commission of the crime but for some timely interference. Acts must pass the point where ordinary law-abiding citizens would think better of what they are about to do and desist from going further. The **equivocality approach** distinguishes preparation from attempt *actus reus* when the act can have no other purpose than committing the crime intended.

The ***Model Penal Code* standard** requires "substantial steps" to corroborate intent. In contrast to the proximity doctrines, the *Model Penal Code* focuses on neutralizing dangerous persons. To satisfy the *actus reus* of attempt, the code requires "substantial steps in a course of conduct planned to culminate in his [the actor's] commission of the crime" and that are "strongly corroborative of the actor's criminal purpose." These substantial steps corroborate the *mens rea*. In other words, the code requires enough action toward completing the crime, not so much in order to demonstrate that crimes are about to occur but in order to prove that attempters are determined to commit crimes.

According to the authors of the code, lying in wait for, and searching for and following, potential victims also satisfy the *actus reus* of criminal attempt. Many jurisdictions, however, consider these actions mere preparation. In the often cited old case of *People v. Rizzo*, for example, the court ruled that searching for a victim to rob was merely preparing, not attempting, to commit robbery. Some states, such as Louisiana, consider lying in wait and searching for and following, to be attempts but only when those who are lying in wait or searching for and following are armed.

Borrowing from indecent liberties statutes, which make it a crime to lure minors into cars or houses for sex, the *Model Penal Code* provides that enticement satisfies the *actus reus* of criminal attempt. In defending their position, the drafters of the code note that enticement demonstrates a firm purpose to commit a crime; hence, enticers are sufficiently dangerous to deserve punishment.[16]

The code provides that reconnoitering — popularly called "casing a joint" — satisfies the *actus reus* of attempt because "scouting the scene of a contemplated crime" sufficiently demonstrates a firm criminal purpose. By their unlawful entries, intruders also demonstrate their criminal purpose under the code. The unlawful entry provision particularly helps in two types of cases: entries to commit sexual abuse and entries to commit larceny. In one case, for example, two defendants entered a car intending to steal it, but they got out when the owner returned. The court ruled that the defendants had not attempted to steal the car. Under the *Model Penal Code* provision, however, they would have committed unlawful entry for a criminal purpose.[17]

In most states, collecting, possessing, or preparing materials used to commit crimes is preparation, not attempt. Hence, courts have found that buying a gun to murder someone, making a bomb to blow up a house, and collecting tools for a burglary are preparations, not attempts. Although these activities are not criminal attempts, many criminal codes include provisions making crimes of the possession of designated items and substances such as burglary tools, illegal drugs, drug paraphernalia, and concealed weapons. Under the *Model Penal Code*, these possessions are criminal only if they strongly corroborate a purpose to commit a crime. The authors of the code concluded that people who carry weapons and burglary tools with the clear intent to commit crimes are dangerous enough to punish.[18]

The *Model Penal Code* also provides that bringing weapons, equipment, and other materials to the scene of a crime satisfies the *actus reus* of criminal attempts. Examples include bringing guns to a robbery, explosives to an arson, a ladder to a burglary. Only the bringing of materials that are plainly the instrumentalities of crime qualify as taking a substantial step toward completing the crime. A potential robber who takes a gun to a bank clearly falls within the scope of this provision; a would-be forger who takes a fountain pen into a bank does not.[19]

Preparation is not criminal attempt. However, some states have created a few separate, less serious offenses involving the act of preparation. In Nevada, for example, preparing to commit arson is a crime. Preparing to manufacture illegal substances is an offense in other states. These statutes are aimed at balancing the degree of threatening behavior and the dangerousness of persons against the remoteness in time and place of the intended harm. *Young v. State* deals with the problem of distinguishing preparation from attempt and what standard to apply in the determination of attempt *actus reus*.[20]

C A S E

Did He Take Substantial Steps Toward Robbing the Bank?

Young v. State,
303 Md. 298, 493 A.2d 352 (1985)

Orth, Judge

Young was tried and convicted of attempted armed robbery and transporting a handgun. He appealed. Both the intermediate court of appeal and Maryland's highest court, the Court of Appeals, affirmed the conviction.

FACTS

Several banks in the Oxon Hill-Fort Washington section of Prince George's County had been held up. The Special Operations Division of the Prince George's Police Department set up a surveillance of banks in the area. In the early afternoon of 26 November 1982 the police . . . observed Young driving an automobile in such a manner as to give rise to a reasonable belief that he was casing several banks. They followed him in his reconnoitering. At one point when he left his car to enter a store, he was seen to clip a scanner onto his belt. The scanner later proved to contain an operable crystal number frequency that would receive Prince George's County uniform patrol transmissions. At that time Young was dressed in a brown waist-length jacket and wore sunglasses.

Around 2:00 P.M. Young came to rest at the rear of the Fort Washington branch of the First National Bank of Southern Maryland. Shortly before, he had driven past the front of the Bank and had parked in the rear of it for a brief time. He got out of his car and walked hurriedly beside the Bank toward the front door. He was still wearing the brown waist-length jacket and sunglasses, but he had added a blue knit stocking cap pulled down to the top of the sunglasses, white gloves and a black eye-patch. His jacket collar was turned up. His right hand was in his jacket pocket and his left hand was in front of his face. As one of the police officers observing him put it, he was sort of "duck[ing] his head."

It was shortly after 2:00 P.M. and the Bank had just closed. Through the windows of his office the Bank Manager saw Young walking on the "landscape" by the side of the Bank toward the front door. Young had his right hand in his jacket pocket and tried to open the front door with his left hand. When he realized that the door was locked and the Bank was closed, he retraced his steps, running past the windows with his left hand covering his face. The Bank Manager had an employee call the police.

Young ran back to his car, yanked open the door, got in, and put the car in drive "all in one movement almost," and drove away. The police stopped the car and ordered Young to get out. Young was in the process of removing his jacket. . . . The butt of what proved to be a loaded .22 caliber revolver was sticking out of the right pocket of his jacket. On the front seat of the car were a pair of white surgical gloves, a black eye-patch, a blue knit stocking cap, and a pair of sunglasses. Young told the police that his name was Morris P. Cunningham. As Young was being taken from the scene, he asked "how much time you could get for attempted robbery."

OPINION

. . . The determination of the overt act which is beyond mere preparation in furtherance of the commission of the intended crime is a most significant aspect of criminal attempts. If an attempt is to be a culpable offense serving as the basis for the furtherance of the important societal interests of crime prevention and the correction of those persons who have sufficiently manifested their dangerousness, the police must be able to ascertain with reasonable assurance when it is proper for them to intervene. It is not enough to say merely that there must be "some overt act beyond mere preparation in furtherance of the crime" as the general definition puts it.

It is true that this definition is in line with the observation of Justice Holmes that

[i]ntent to commit a crime is not itself criminal. There is no law against a man's intending to

commit a murder the day after tomorrow. The law deals only with conduct. An attempt is an overt act. O. Holmes, *The Common Law* 65 (1923). . . .

What act will suffice to show that an attempt itself has reached the stage of a completed crime has persistently troubled the courts. They have applied a number of approaches in order to determine when preparation for the commission of a crime has ceased and the actual attempt to commit it has begun. It is at the point when preparation has been completed and perpetration of the intended crime has started that a criminal attempt has been committed and culpability for that misdemeanor attaches. . . .

[Here the court defines the proximity, probable desistance, the equivocality, and *Model Penal Code* approaches.]

We believe that the preferable approach is one bottomed on the "substantial step" test as is that of *Model Penal Code* [sic]. We think that using a "substantial step" as the criterion in determining whether an overt act is more than mere preparation to commit a crime is clearer, sounder, more practical and easier to apply to the multitude of differing fact situations which may occur. . . .

We are by no means alone in the belief that an approach based on the substantial step is superior. This belief was shared by the Commission which drafted a proposed criminal code for this State following the *Model Penal Code* approach with respect to criminal attempts. Courts in eight of the federal circuits and courts or legislatures in 23 states also share this belief. . . .

When the facts and circumstances of [this] . . . case are considered in the light of the overt act standard which we have adopted, it is perfectly clear that the evidence was sufficient to prove that Young attempted the crime of armed robbery as charged. As we have seen, the police did not arrive on the scene after the fact. They had the advantage of having Young under observation for some time before his apprehension. They watched his preparations. They were with him when he reconnoitered or cased the banks. His observations of the banks were in a manner not usual for law-abiding individuals and were under circumstances that warranted alarm for the safety of persons or property.

Young manifestly endeavored to conceal his presence by parking behind the Bank which he had apparently selected to rob. He distinguished himself with an eyepatch and made an identification of him difficult by turning up his jacket collar and by donning sunglasses and a knit cap which he pulled down over his forehead. He put on rubber surgical gloves. Clipped on his belt was a scanner with a police band frequency. Except for the scanner, which he had placed on his belt while casing the Bank, all this was done immediately before he left his car and approached the door of the Bank.

As he walked towards the Bank he partially hid his face behind his left hand and ducked his head. He kept his right hand in the pocket of his jacket in which, as subsequent events established, he was carrying, concealed, a loaded handgun, for which he had no lawful use or right to transport. He walked to the front door of the Bank and tried to enter the premises.

When he discovered that the door was locked, he ran back to his car, again partially concealing his face with his left hand. He got in his car and immediately drove away. He removed the knit hat, sunglasses, eyepatch and gloves, and placed the scanner over the sun visor of the car. When apprehended, he was trying to take off his jacket. His question as to how much time he could get for attempted bank robbery was not without significance.

It is clear that the evidence which showed Young's conduct leading to his apprehension established that he performed the necessary overt act towards the commission of armed robbery, which was more than mere preparation. Even if we assume that all of Young's conduct before he approached the door of the Bank was mere preparation, on the evidence, the jury could properly find as a fact that when Young tried to open the bank door to enter the premises, that act constituted a "substantial step" toward the commission of the intended crime. It was strongly corroborative of his criminal intention.

One of the reasons why the substantial step approach has received such widespread favor is because it usually enables the police to intervene at an earlier stage than do the other approaches. In this case, however, the requisite overt act came near the end of the line. Indeed, it would qualify as the necessary act under any of the approaches — the proximity approach, the probable desistance approach or the equivocality approach. It clearly met the requirements of the substantial step approach.

Since Young, as a matter of fact, could be found by the jury to have performed an overt act which was more than mere preparation, and was a substantial step towards the commission of the intended crime of armed robbery, it follows as a matter of law that he committed the offense of criminal attempt.

We think that the evidence adduced showed directly, or circumstantially, or supported a rational inference of, the facts to be proved from which the jury could fairly be convinced, beyond a reasonable doubt, of Young's guilt of attempted armed robbery as charged. Therefore, the evidence was sufficient in law to sustain the conviction. We so hold. Judgments of the Court of Special Appeals affirmed; costs to be paid by appellant.

QUESTIONS FOR DISCUSSION

1. Identify the relevant facts in the case to determine *actus reus*.

2. What four tests does the court outline to determine whether the actions of the defendant amount to the *actus reus* of attempted armed robbery?

3. What reasons does the court give for adopting the *Model Penal Code* standard?

4. Do you agree that it is the best test of attempt *actus reus*?

5. If you were deciding this case, what test would you adopt?

6. According to your test, did Young attempt an armed robbery?

7. At what point, if any, in the chronology of events did preparation become attempt? Defend your position.

NOTE CASES

1. On September 21, 1976, at Dallas State Correctional Institution, a guard discovered that the bars of the window in Gilliam's cell had been cut and were being held in place by sticks and paper. The condition of the bars was such that they could be removed manually at will. The same guard observed that a shelf hook was missing from its place in the cell. A subsequent search revealed visegrips concealed in-

side appellant's mattress, and two knotted extention cords attached to a hook were found in a box of clothing. At trial, evidence showed that the hook had been fashioned from the missing shelf hook. The visegrips were capable of cutting barbed wire of the type located along the top of the fence that was the sole barrier between appellant's cell window and the perimeter of the prison compound. Inspection of the cell immediately before it was assigned to Gilliam as its sole occupant had disclosed bars intact and the shelf hooks in place.

Did Gilliam commit the crime of attempted escape? The court said yes, because Gilliam had taken substantial steps by not only gathering the tools for his escape but also sawing through the bars. According to the court, the substantial step test "broadens the scope of attempt liability by concentrating on the acts the defendant has done and does not . . . focus on the acts remaining to be done before actual commission of the crime." *Commonwealth v. Gilliam,* 273 Pa.Super. 586, 417 A.2d 1203 (1980)

2. In *People v. Rizzo,* Rizzo and his cohorts were driving through New York City looking for a payroll clerk they intended to rob. While Rizzo and his cohorts were still looking for their victim, the police apprehended and arrested them. They were tried for attempted robbery but were acquitted because "they had not found or reached the presence of the person they intended to rob." The New York Court of Appeals held:

> [M]any acts in the way of preparation are too remote to constitute the crime of attempt. The line has been drawn between those acts which are remote and those which are proximate and near to the consummation. The law must be practical, and therefore considers those acts only as tending to the commission of the crime which are so near to its accomplishment that in all reasonable probability the crime itself would have been committed but for timely interference. The cases which have been before the courts express this idea in different language, but the idea remains the same. The act or acts must come or advance very near to the accomplishment of the intended crime. *People v. Rizzo,* 158 N.E. 888 (N.Y.App.1927)

3. Peaslee had constructed and arranged combustibles in a building he owned in such a way that they were ready to be lighted and, if lighted, would have set fire to the building and its contents. He got within a quarter of a mile of the building, but his would-be

accomplice refused to light the fire. Did Peaslee attempt to commit arson? According to the court, he did not:

> A mere collection and preparation of materials in a room, for the purpose of setting fire to them, unaccompanied by any present intent to set the fire, would be too remote and not all but "the last act" necessary to complete the crime. *Commonwealth v. Peaslee,* 59 N.E. 55 (Mass.1901)

Legal and Factual Impossibility

In order to avoid paying the tax, a man sneaks an antique book past customs. In fact, however, the law exempts antique books from custom duty. Has he committed a crime by attempting to evade customs? A woman stabs her sleeping victim. In fact, her victim died of a heart attack two hours before she stabbed him. Has she committed attempted murder? The man in the first hypothetical case represents an example of legal impossibility. **Legal impossibility** means that actors intended to commit crimes and they have done everything that they could do in order to commit them. However, the law does not prohibit what they did. The man intended to evade customs, and he did everything he could do to commit what he believed was a crime. But it was legally impossible to commit the crime because antiques are not subject to the customs laws.

Stabbing an already dead victim is an example of factual impossibility. **Factual impossibility** exists when the actor intends to commit a crime but some fact or circumstance — extraneous factor — prevents its completion. The woman intended to commit murder. She did all that she could in order to commit it; if the facts were different, that is if her victim had been alive, she would have committed murder.

Legal impossibility requires a different *law* in order to make the conduct criminal; factual impossibility requires different *facts* or *circumstances* in order to complete the crime. In most jurisdictions, legal impossibility is a defense to criminal attempt; factual impossibility is not. The principal reason for the difference is that to convict someone for conduct that the law does not prohibit, no matter what the actor's intentions, violates the principle of legality — no crime without a law, no punishment without a law (see chapter 2). Factual impossibility, on the other hand, would allow chance to determine criminal liability. A person who is determined to commit a crime, and who acts sufficiently to succeed in that determination, should not escape liability and punishment because of a stroke of good luck.[21]

C A S E

Was the Unloaded Gun a "Stroke of Luck"?

State v. Damms,
9 Wis.2d 183, 100 N.W.2d 592 (1960)

A jury convicted Ralph Damms of attempt to commit murder in the first degree. Damms was sentenced to imprisonment for not more than ten years. Damms appealed. The supreme court of Wisconson affirmed the conviction. Justice Currie wrote the opinion for the court. Justice Dietrich dissented.

FACTS

. . . Marjory Damms, wife of the defendant, had instituted an action for divorce against him and the parties lived apart. She was thirty-nine years and he thirty-three years of age. Marjory Damms was also estranged from her mother, Mrs. Laura Grant. That morning, a little before eight o'clock, Damms drove his automobile to the vicinity in Milwaukee where he knew Mrs. Damms would take the bus to go to work. He saw her walking along the sidewalk, stopped, and induced her to enter the car by falsely stating that Mrs. Grant was ill and dying. They drove to Mrs. Grant's home. Mrs. Damms then discovered that her mother was up and about and not seriously ill. Nevertheless, the two Damms remained there nearly two hours conversing and drinking coffee. Apparently it was the intention of Damms to induce a reconciliation between mother and daughter, hoping it would result in one between himself and his wife, but not much progress was achieved in such direction.

At the conclusion of the conversation Mrs. Damms expressed the wish to phone for a taxi-cab to take her to work. Damms insisted on her getting into his car, and said he would drive her to work. They again entered his car but instead of driving south towards her place of employment, he drove in the opposite direction. Some conversation was had in which he stated that it was possible for a person to die quickly and not be able to make amends for anything done in the past, and referred to the possibility of "judgment day" occurring suddenly. Mrs. Damms' testimony as to what then took place is as follows:

> When he was telling me about this being judgment day, he pulled a cardboard box from under the seat of the car and brought it up to the seat and opened it up and took a gun out of a paper bag. [He] aimed it at my side and he said, 'This is to show you I'm not kidding.' I tried to quiet him down. He said he wasn't fooling. I said if it was just a matter of my saying to my mother that everything was all right, we could go back and I would tell her that.

They did return to Mrs. Grant's home and Mrs. Damms went inside and Damms stayed outside. In a few minutes he went inside and asked Mrs. Damms to leave with him. Mrs. Grant requested that they leave quietly so as not to attract the attention of the neighbors. They again got into the car and this time drove out on Highway 41 towards Menomonee Falls. Damms stated to Mrs. Damms that he was taking her "up North" for a few days, the apparent purpose of which was to effect a reconciliation between them. As they approached a roadside restaurant, he asked her if she would like something to eat. She replied that she wasn't hungry but would drink some coffee. Damms then drove the car off the highway beside the restaurant and parked it with the front facing, and in close proximity to, the restaurant wall.

Damms then asked Mrs. Damms how much money she had with her and she said "a couple of dollars." He then requested to see her checkbook and she refused to give it to him. A quarrel ensued between them. Mrs. Damms opened the car door and started to run around the restaurant building screaming, "Help!"

Damms pursued her with the pistol in his hand. Mrs. Damms' cries for help attracted the attention of the persons inside the restaurant, including two officers of the State Traffic Patrol who were eating their lunch. One officer rushed out of the front door and the other the rear door. In the meantime, Mrs. Damms had run nearly around three sides of the building.

In seeking to avoid colliding with a child, who was in her path, she turned, slipped and fell. Damms crouched down, held the pistol at her head, and pulled the trigger, but nothing happened. He then exclaimed, "It won't fire. It won't fire." Damms testified that at the time he pulled the trigger the gun was pointing down at the ground and not at Mrs. Damms' head. However, the two traffic patrol officers both testified that Damms had the gun pointed directly at her head when he pulled the trigger.

The officers placed Damms under arrest. They found that the pistol was unloaded. The clip holding the cartridges, which clip is inserted in the butt of the gun to load it, they found in the cardboard box in Damms' car together with a box of cartridges.

That afternoon, Damms was questioned by a deputy sheriff at the Waukesha county jail, and a clerk in the sheriff's office typed out the questions and Damms' answers as they were given. Damms later read over such typed statement of questions and answers, but refused to sign it. In such statement Damms stated that he thought the gun was loaded at the time of the alleged attempt to murder. Both the deputy sheriff and the undersheriff testified that Damms had stated to them that he thought the gun was loaded. On the other hand, Damms testified at the trial that he knew at the time of the alleged attempt that the pistol was not loaded.

OPINION

The two questions raised on this appeal are:

1. Did the fact, that it was impossible for the accused to have committed the act of murder because the gun was unloaded, preclude his conviction of the offense of attempt to commit murder?

2. Assuming that the foregoing question is answered in the negative, does the evidence establish the guilt of the accused beyond a reasonable doubt?

§ 939.32(2), Stats., provides as follows:

An attempt to commit a crime requires that the actor have an intent to perform acts and attain a result which, if accomplished, would constitute such crime and that he does acts toward the commission of the crime which demonstrate unequivocally, under all the circumstances, that he formed that intent and would commit the crime except for the intervention of another person or some other extraneous factor.

The issue with respect to the first . . . question boils down to whether the impossibility of accomplishment due to the gun being unloaded falls within the statutory words, "except for the intervention of . . . some other extraneous factor." We conclude that it does.

Prior to the adoption of the new criminal code by the 1955 legislature the criminal statutes of this state had separate sections making it an offense to assault with the intent to do great bodily harm, to murder, to rob, and to rape, etc. The new code did away with these separate sections by creating § 939.32, Stats., covering all attempts to commit a battery or felony, and making the maximum penalty not to exceed one-half the penalty imposed for the completed crime, except that, if the penalty for a completed crime is life imprisonment, the maximum penalty for the attempt is thirty years imprisonment.

In an article in 1956 *Wisconsin Law Review*, 350, 364, by assistant attorney general Platz, who was one of the authors of the new criminal code, explaining such code, he points out that "attempt" is defined therein in a more intelligible fashion than by using such tests as "beyond mere preparation," "locus poenitentiae" (the place at which the actor may repent and withdraw), or "dangerous proximity to success." Quoting the author

Emphasis upon the dangerous propensities of the actor as shown by his conduct, rather than upon how close he came to succeeding, is more appropriate to the purposes of the criminal law to protect society and reform offenders or render them temporarily harmless.

Robert H. Skilton, in an article entitled, "The Requisite Act in a Criminal Attempt (1937)," advances the view, that impossibility to cause death because of the attempt to fire a defective weapon at a person, does not prevent the conviction of the actor of the crime of attempted murder:

[If] the defendant does not know that the gun he fires at B is defective, he is guilty of an attempt to kill B, even though his actions under the circumstances given never come near to killing B. . . . The possibility of the success of the defendant's enterprise need only be an apparent possibility to the defendant, and not an actual possibility.

. . .

Sound public policy would seem to support the majority view that impossibility not apparent to the actor should not absolve him from the offense of attempt to commit the crime he intended. An unequivocal act accompanied by intent should be sufficient to constitute a criminal attempt. Insofar as the actor knows, he has done everything necessary to insure the commission of the crime intended, and he should not escape punishment because of the fortuitous circumstance that by reason of some fact unknown to him it was impossible to effectuate the intended result.

. . .

It is not a defense . . . that, because of a mistake of fact or law . . . which does not negative the actor's intent to commit the crime, it would have been impossible for him to commit the crime attempted. . . . It is our considered judgment that the fact that the gun was unloaded when Damms pointed it at his wife's head and pulled the trigger, did not absolve him of the offense charged, if he actually thought at the time that it was loaded.

We do not believe that the further contention raised in behalf of the accused, that the evidence does not establish his guilt of the crime charged beyond a reasonable doubt, requires extensive consideration on our part. The jury undoubtedly believed the testimony of the deputy sheriff and undersheriff that Damms told them on the day of the act that he thought the gun was loaded. This is also substantiated by the written statement constituting a transcript of his answers given in his interrogation at the county jail on the same day. The gun itself, which is an exhibit in the record, is the strongest piece of evidence in favor of Damms' present contention that he at all times knew the gun was unloaded. Practically the entire bottom end of the butt of the pistol is open. Such opening is caused by the absence of the clip into which the cartridges must be inserted in order to load the pistol. This readily demonstrates to anyone looking at the gun that it could not be loaded.

Because the unloaded gun with this large opening in the butt was an exhibit which went to the jury room, we must assume that the jury examined the gun and duly considered it in arriving at their verdict. We are not prepared to hold that the jury could not come to the reasonable conclusion that, because of Damms' condition of excitement when he grabbed the gun and pursued his wife, he so grasped it as not to see the opening in the end of the butt which would have unmistakably informed him that the gun was unloaded. Having so concluded, they could rightfully disregard Damms' testimony given at the trial that he knew the pistol was unloaded. Judgment affirmed. Martin, C. J., not participating.

DISSENT

Dietrich, Justice (dissenting).

I disagree with the majority opinion in respect to their interpretations and conclusions of § 939.32(2), Stats. The issue raised on this appeal: Could the defendant be convicted of murder, under § 939.32(2), Stats., when it was impossible for the defendant to have caused the death of anyone because the gun or pistol involved was unloaded?

§ 939.32(2), Stats., provides:

> An attempt to commit a crime requires that the actor have an intent to perform acts and attain a result which, if accomplished, would constitute such crime and that he does acts toward the commission of the crime which demonstrate unequivocally, under all the circumstances, that he formed that intent and would commit the crime except for the intervention of another person or some other extraneous factor.

In view of the statute, the question arising under § 939.32(2), is whether the impossibility of accomplishment due to the pistol being unloaded falls with the statutory words "except for the intervention of . . . some other extraneous factor." In interpreting the statute we must look to the ordinary meaning of words. Webster's New International Dictionary defines "extraneous" as not belonging to or dependent upon a thing . . . originated or coming from without.

The plain distinct meaning of the statute is: A person must form an intent to commit a particular crime and this intent must be coupled with sufficient preparation on his part and with overt acts from which it can be determined clearly, surely and absolutely the crime would be committed except for the intervention of some independent thing or something originating or coming from someone or something over which the actor has no control.

As an example — if the defendant actor had formed an intent to kill someone, had in his possession a loaded pistol, pulled the trigger while his intended victim was within range and the pistol did not fire because the bullet or cartridge in the chamber was defective or because someone unknown to the actor had removed the cartridges or bullets or because of any other thing happening which happening or thing was beyond the control of the actor, the actor could be guilty under § 339.32(2), Stats.

But when as in the present case (as disclosed by the testimony) the defendant had never loaded the pistol, although having ample opportunity to do so, then he had never completed performance of the act essential to kill someone, through the means of pulling the trigger of the pistol. This act, of loading the pistol, or using a loaded pistol, was dependent on the defendant himself. It was in no way an extraneous factor since by definition an extraneous factor is one which originates or comes from without.

Under the majority opinion the interpretations of the statute are if a person points an unloaded gun (pistol) at someone, knowing it to be unloaded and pulls the trigger, he can be found guilty of an attempt to commit murder. This type of reasoning I cannot agree with.

He could be guilty of some offense, but not attempt to commit murder. If a person uses a pistol as a bludgeon and had struck someone, but was prevented from killing his victim because he (the actor) suffered a heart attack at that moment, the illness would be an extraneous factor within the statute and the actor could be found guilty of attempt to commit murder, provided the necessary intent was proved.

In this case, there is no doubt that the pistol was not loaded. The defendant testified that it had never been loaded or fired. The following steps must be taken before the weapon would be capable of killing. . . .

Type of Pistol: 32 semiautomatic
Assembly of Pistol
   A. Pistol grip or butt hand grasp
   B. Barrel
   C. Slide
   D. Trigger housing.
Mechanism
   A. To load pistol requires pulling of slide operating around barrel toward holder or operator of pistol.
   B. After pulling slide to rear, safety latch is pushed into place by operator of pistol to hold pistol in position for loading.

   C. A spring lock is located at one side of opening of magazine located at the bottom grip or butt of gun.
   D. This spring is pulled back and the clip is inserted into magazine or bottom of pistol and closes the bottom of the grip or butt of the pistol.
   E. The recoil or release of the safety latch on the slide loads the chamber of the pistol and it is now ready to fire or be used as a pistol.

The law judges intent objectively. It is impossible to peer into a man's mind particularly long after the act has been committed. Viewing objectively the physical salient facts, it was the defendant who put the gun, clip and cartridges under the car seat. It was he, same defendant, who took the pistol out of the box without taking clip or cartridges. It is plain he told the truth, he knew the gun would not fire, nobody else knew that so well. In fact his exclamation was "It won't fire. It won't fire."

The real intent showed up objectively in those calm moments while driving around the county with his wife for two hours, making two visits with her at her mother's home, and drinking coffee at the home. He could have loaded the pistol while staying on the outside at his mother-in-law's home on his second trip, if he intended to use the pistol to kill, but he did not do this required act.

The majority states: "The gun itself, which is an exhibit in the record, is the strongest piece of evidence in favor of Damms' present contention that he at all times knew the gun was unloaded. Practically the entire bottom end of the butt of the pistol is open. . . . This readily demonstrates to anyone looking at the gun that it could not be loaded." They are so correct.

The defendant had the pistol in his hand several times before chasing his wife at the restaurant and it was his pistol. He, no doubt, had examined the pistol at various times during his period of ownership — unless he was devoid of all sense of touch and feeling in his hands and fingers it would be impossible for him not to be aware or know that the pistol was unloaded.

He could feel the hole in the bottom of the butt, and this on at least two separate occasions for he handled the pistol by taking it out of the box and showing it to his wife before he took her back to her mother's home the second time, and prior to chasing her at the restaurant.

Objective evidence here raises reasonable doubt of intent to attempt murder. It negatives intent to kill. The defendant would have loaded the pistol had he intended to kill or murder or used it as a bludgeon. . . .

The Assistant Attorney General contends and states in his brief: "In the instant case, the failure of the attempt was due to lack of bullets in the gun but a loaded magazine was in the car. If defendant had not been prevented by the intervention of the two police officers, or possibly someone else, or conceivably by the flight of his wife from the scene, he could have returned to the car, loaded the gun, and killed her. Under all the circumstances the jury were justified in concluding that that is what he would have done, but for the intervention."

If that conclusion is correct, and juries are allowed to convict persons based on speculation of what might have been done, we will have seriously and maybe permanently, curtailed the basic rights of our citizenry to be tried only on the basis of proven facts. I cannot agree with his contention or conclusion. The total inadequacy of the means (in this case the unloaded gun or pistol) in the manner intended to commit the overt act of murder, precludes a finding of guilty of the crime charged under § 939.32(2), Stats.

QUESTIONS FOR DISCUSSION

1. Does it matter whether or not the gun was loaded?

2. Hasn't Damms done everything possible to commit the crime of murdering his wife?

3. What if Damms subconsciously "forgot" to load the gun because he meant only to frighten his wife?

4. Such speculation depends on a belief in Freudian psychology, but assuming that Damms forgot, was the unloaded gun then an extraneous factor, or within Damms's control?

5. Is the Wisconsin rule punishing attempts at about half the amount for completed crimes a good idea?

6. Some states punish attempts at the same level on the ground that when a person intends to commit a crime and only a fortuity prevents its commission, that person deserves punishment equal to that of the person for whom a fortuity did not prevent commission of the crime. Should criminal law consider only intent in determining the seriousness of an offense?

7. What else should it take into account?

NOTE CASE

Wagner accosted Candace I. on October 24, 1990, in a laundromat at 3910 North 76th Street in Milwaukee. He approached her from behind, put a gun to her right side, and tried to force her into the bathroom a few feet away. She struggled and escaped. On June 11, 1991, Wagner accosted Megan M. in a laundromat at 10440 West Silver Spring Drive in Milwaukee. As with Candace I. eight months earlier, he approached her from behind and put a gun to her right side. This time, however, he was able to force his victim into the laundromat's bathroom. While in the bathroom, Megan M. refused his demand that she remove her clothes. After a struggle, she escaped. Wagner was convicted of attempted kidnapping and sentenced to 72 years in prison. Was the victim's escape an extraneous factor, a stroke of luck that prevented Wagner from completing the crime? Yes, according to the Wisconsin appeals court. *State v. Wagner*, Nos. 94-0978-CR and 94-1980-CR, Court of Appeals, Wisconsin, 1995

Distinguishing between factual and legal impossibility is not always easy. In the two opinions that follow, *Rooks v. State* and *State v. Rooks*, the Georgia trial court and supreme court differed with the intermediate court of appeals on the point of legal impossibility.

C A S E

Is Attempted Stalking a Legal Impossibility?

Rooks v. State, 458 S.E.2d 667 (Ga. App. 1995)

Rooks was convicted in the Barrow Superior Court, of a criminal attempt to commit aggravated stalking, and he appealed. The Court of Appeals reversed.

McMURRAY, Presiding Judge.

FACTS

. . . The victim in each case is defendant's former wife. They have been divorced for ten years. Their daughter is now 20 years old. On September 17, 1993, the victim received a telephone call at work. When she answered, a voice asked her by name: "[I]s [her daughter] pregnant?" The victim said "What?" and the caller repeated the question. The victim then hung up the telephone. She recognized the caller's voice as that of defendant, her former husband. On October 27, 1993, defendant again called his former spouse at work and asked her: " 'Are you the one with the double chin and the pointed nose?' And then he slammed the phone down." That day, defendant "repeated that three times, maybe, and then [he would call but] wouldn't say anything, so [the victim] decided [to] get a warrant." When she returned to her office, defendant was still "calling within every few minutes." Ann Fulcher also recognized defendant's voice when one of these calls was "placed on a speaker phone[.]"

OPINION

"A person commits the offense of criminal attempt when, with intent to commit a specific crime, he performs any act which constitutes a substantial step toward the commission of that crime." OCGA § 1641. . . . [W]e conclude that the crime of attempted stalking . . . is a legal impossibility.

A person commits the offense of "stalking" as proscribed by OCGA § 16590 when he "places under surveillance, or contacts another person . . . for the purpose of harassing and intimidating the other per-

son. . . . [T]he term 'harassing and intimidating' means a knowing and willful course of conduct directed at a specific person which causes emotional distress by placing such person in reasonable fear of death or bodily harm to himself . . . or to a member of his . . . immediate family, and which serves no legitimate purpose." This is in essence a common law assault, which by definition "is nothing more than an attempted battery." We know of no law authorizing the conviction for an attempt to commit a crime which itself is a particular type of attempt to commit a crime. As an assault is itself an attempt to commit a crime, an attempt to make an assault can only be an attempt to attempt to do it, or to state the matter still more definitely, it is to do any act towards doing an act towards the commission of the offense. This is simply absurd. . . . The refinement and metaphysical acumen that can see a tangible idea in the words an attempt to attempt to act is too great for practical use. It is like conceiving of the beginning of eternity or the starting place of infinity. . . . Defendant's conviction for criminal attempt to commit aggravated stalking . . . is reversed.

State v. Rooks, 266 Ga. 528, 468 S.E.2d 354 (1996)

FLETCHER, Presiding Justice.

FACTS

[The facts are reproduced in *Rooks v. State* above.]

OPINION

In reversing Rooks' conviction, the court of appeals reasoned that stalking is in essence an assault. Because there is no such crime as an attempted assault, the court of appeals reasoned that attempted stalking is likewise a legal impossibility. While we agree that there is no such crime as an attempted assault, we disagree that stalking is merely an assault crime. In recent years states have begun to enact stalking laws in response to the increase in stalking behavior and the ineffectiveness of traditional criminal statutes in preventing and curtailing this behavior. Georgia's stalking law, OCGA § 16590, mirrors this trend by proscribing intentional actions not covered by the assault statutes.

Under OCGA § 16590 a person commits stalking when with a specific intent he "follows, places under surveillance, or contacts another person." Aggravated stalking is the same behavior when done in violation of a judicial order prohibiting such conduct. Generally, none of these actions would constitute an assault, which requires a demonstration of violence and a present ability to inflict injury. The intent element of the stalking statute requires proof of intentional conduct that "causes emotional distress by placing such person in reasonable fear of death or bodily harm to himself or herself or to a member of his or her immediate family." This element differs from assault in two significant ways. The assault statute requires proof that the accused induced fear of an immediate violent injury. The stalking law contains no immediacy requirement. Secondly, assault requires proof that the victim perceived the threat of violent injury to himself, whereas stalking may be committed by inducing fear that the victim's family may be harmed. These differences in both the act and intent elements demonstrate that stalking is not "in essence a common law assault."

While assault and stalking may overlap in some circumstances, the rationale for not punishing an attempted assault does not apply to an attempted stalking. In refusing to recognize the crime of attempted assault, this court stated that to attempt an assault is "to do any act towards doing an act towards the commission of the offense" and noted the absurdity and impracticality of criminalizing such behavior. To attempt to stalk, however, is to attempt to follow, place under surveillance or contact another person. It is neither absurd nor impractical to subject to criminal sanction such actions when they are done with the requisite specific intent to cause emotional distress by inducing a reasonable fear of death or bodily injury.

After reviewing the evidence in the light most favorable to the jury's determination of guilt, we conclude that a rational trier of fact could have found Rooks guilty of attempted aggravated stalking. Judgment reversed.

QUESTIONS FOR DISCUSSION

1. Explain specifically the difference between legal and factual impossibility.
2. Why should the law reject the defense of factual but not legal impossibility?
3. Why does the law accept the defense of legal impossibility?
4. Should the law recognize the defense of legal impossibility?
5. If you were deciding this case, would Rooks be guilty of attempted stalking? Defend your answer.

Abandonment

We know from the last section that those bent on committing crimes who have taken steps to carry out their criminal plans cannot escape criminal liability just because an outside force interrupted them. But what about those who with the requisite *mens rea* take enough steps to satisfy the *actus reus* of attempt, then change their mind and voluntarily abandon the scheme? Should the law benefit those who themselves are the force that interrupts their crime, rather than being interrupted by some outside force — the stroke of luck embodied in some extraneous factor? The traditonal view was that voluntary abandonment is no defense once the *actus reus* and *mens rea* of attempt are established. According to *People v. Kimball* (the case excerpted in the earlier section on attempt *mens rea*),

Once a defendant has gone so far as to have committed a punishable attempt, the crime is "complete" and he or she cannot then abandon the crime and avoid liability any more than a thief can abandon a larceny by returning the stolen goods.[22]

Nevertheless, several respected commentators have recommended, and some states have adopted, a defense of voluntary abandonment. For example, the Michigan criminal code provides

It is an affirmative defense . . . that, under circumstances manifesting a voluntary and complete renunciation of his criminal purpose, the actor avoided the commission of the offense attempted by abandoning his criminal effort. . . .

A renunciation is not "voluntary and complete" within the meaning of this chapter if it is motivated in whole or in part by either of the following:
(a) A circumstance which increases the probability of detection or apprehension of the defendant or another participant in the criminal operation or which makes more difficult the consummation of the crime.
(b) A decision to postpone the criminal conduct until another time or to substitute another victim or another but similar objective.[23]

According to the *Model Penal Code*, voluntary abandonment means

a change in the actor's purpose not influenced by outside circumstances, what may be termed repentance or change of heart. Lack of resolution or timidity may suffice. A reappraisal by the actor of the criminal sanctions hanging over his conduct would presumably be a motivation of the voluntary type as long as the actor's fear of the law is not related to a particular threat of apprehension or detection.[24]

Supporters of the defense concede that it may encourage would-be criminals to take initial steps to commit crimes because they know that they can escape punishment. However, they retort, two powerful reasons support the defense. First, those who voluntarily renounce their criminal conduct are not the dangerous people the law of attempt is designed to punish, and indeed were probably not bent on committing crimes in the first place. Second, the defense encourages would-be criminals to give up their criminal designs by the promise of escaping punishment. One of the most cited cases involving the defense of abandonment is *Le Barron v. State*.[25]

C A S E

Did He Voluntarily Renounce His Intent to Rape?

**Le Barron v. State,
32 Wis.2d 294, 145 N.W.2d 79 (1966)**

Le Barron was convicted of attempted rape and sentenced to not more than fifteen years in prison. He appealed. The Wisconsin Supreme Court affirmed. Chief Justice Currie wrote the opinion of the court.

FACTS

On March 3, 1965 at 6:55 P.M., the complaining witness, Jodean Randen, a housewife, was walking home across a fairly well-traveled railroad bridge in Eau Claire. She is a slight woman whose normal weight is 95 to 100 pounds. As she approached the opposite side of the bridge she passed a man who was walking in the opposite direction. The man turned and followed her, grabbed her arm and demanded her purse. She surrendered her purse and at the command of the man began walking away as fast as she could. Upon discovering that the purse was empty, he caught up with her again, grabbed her arm and told her that if she did not scream he would not hurt her. He then led her—willingly, she testified, so as to avoid being hurt by him—to the end of the bridge. While walking he shoved her head down and warned her not to look up or do anything and he would not hurt her.

On the other side of the bridge along the railroad tracks there is a coal shack. As they approached the coal shack he grabbed her, put one hand over her mouth, and an arm around her shoulder and told her not to scream or he would kill her. At this time Mrs. Randen thought he had a knife in his hand. He then forced her into the shack and up against the wall. As she struggled for her breath he said, "You know what else I want," unzipped his pants and started pulling up her skirt. She finally succeeded in removing his hand from her mouth, and after reassuring him that she would not scream, told him she was pregnant and pleaded with him to desist or he would hurt her baby. He then felt her stomach and took her over to the door of the shack, where in the better light he was able to ascertain that, under her coat, she was wearing maternity clothes. He thereafter let her alone and left after warning her not to scream or call the police, or he would kill her.

OPINION

The material portions of the controlling statutes provide: § 944.01(1), Stats. "Any male who has sexual intercourse with a female he knows is not his wife, by force and against her will, may be imprisoned not more than 30 years."

§ 939.32(2), Stats.

An attempt to commit a crime requires that the actor have an intent to perform acts and attain a result which, if accomplished, would constitute such crime and that he does acts toward the commission of the crime which demonstrate unequivocally, under all the circumstances, that

he formed that intent and would commit the crime except for the intervention of another person or some other extraneous factor.

The two statutory requirements of intent and overt acts which must concur in order to have attempt to rape are as follows: (1) The male must have the intent to act so as to have intercourse with the female by overcoming or preventing her utmost resistance by physical violence, or overcoming her will to resist by the use of threats of imminent physical violence likely to cause great bodily harm; (2) the male must act toward the commission of the rape by overt acts which demonstrate unequivocally, under all the circumstances, that he formed the intent to rape and would have committed the rape except for the intervention of another person or some other extraneous factor.

The thrust of defendant's argument, that the evidence was not sufficient to convict him of the crime of attempted rape, is twofold: first, defendant desisted from his endeavor to have sexual intercourse with complainant before he had an opportunity to form an intent to accomplish such intercourse by force and against her will; and, second, the factor which caused him to desist, viz., the pregnancy of complainant, was intrinsic and not an "extraneous factor" within the meaning of § 939.32(2), Stats.

It is difficult to consider the factor of intent apart from that of overt acts since the sole evidence of intent in attempted rape cases is almost always confined to the overt acts of the accused, and intent must be inferred therefrom. In fact, the express wording of § 939.32(2), Stats. recognizes that this is so.

We consider defendant's overt acts, which support a reasonable inference that he intended to have sexual intercourse with complainant by force and against her will, to be these: (1) He threatened complainant that he would kill her if she refused to cooperate with him; (2) he forced complainant into the shack and against the wall; and (3) he stated, "You know what else I want," unzipped his pants, and started pulling up her skirt. The jury had the right to assume that defendant had the requisite physical strength and weapon (the supposed knife) to carry out the threat over any resistance of complainant.

We conclude that a jury could infer beyond a reasonable doubt from these overt acts of defendant that he intended to have sexual intercourse with the victim by force and against her will. The fact, that he desisted from his attempt to have sexual intercourse as a result of the plea of complainant that she was pregnant, would permit of the opposite inference. However, such desistance did not compel the drawing of such inference nor compel, as a matter of law, the raising of a reasonable doubt to a finding that defendant had previously intended to carry through with having intercourse by force and against complainant's will.

Defendant relies strongly on *Oakley v. State* where this court held that defendant Oakley's acts were so equivocal as to prevent a finding of intent beyond a reasonable doubt to have sexual intercourse by force and against the will of the complainant. The evidence in the case disclosed neither physical violence nor threat of physical violence up to the time Oakley desisted from his attempt to have sexual intercourse with the complainant. He did put his arm around her and attempted to kiss her while entreating her to have intercourse, and also attempted to put his hand in her blouse and to lift up her skirt but did not attempt to renew this endeavor when she brushed his hand away. Thus the facts in *Oakley* are readily distinguishable from those of the case at bar.

To argue that the two cases are analogous because, in the one instance the accused desisted because the complainant was menstruating and in the other because of pregnancy, is an oversimplification. Such an argument overlooks the radical difference in the nature of the overt acts relied upon to prove intent.

The argument, that the pregnancy of the instant complainant which caused defendant's desistance does not qualify as an "extraneous factor" within the meaning of § 939.32, Stats., is in conflict with our holding in *State v. Damms*. There we upheld a conviction of attempt to commit murder where the accused pulled the trigger of an unloaded pistol intending to kill his estranged wife thinking the pistol was loaded. It was held that the impossibility of accomplishment due to the gun being unloaded fell within the statutory words, "except for the intervention of some other extraneous factor." Particularly significant is this statement in the opinion:

An unequivocal act accompanied by intent should be sufficient to constitute a criminal at-

tempt. Insofar as the actor knows, he has done everything necessary to insure the commission of the crime intended, and he should not escape punishment because of the fortuitous circumstance that by reason of some fact unknown to him it was impossible to effectuate the intended result.

Affirmed.

QUESTIONS FOR DISCUSSION

1. *Le Barron* demonstrates how difficult it can be to apply the renunciation doctrine. Did Le Barron desist because he believed it was morally wrong to rape a pregnant woman, or did the pregnancy simply repel him sexually?

2. Should his reason make a difference?

3. Is Le Barron equally dangerous, whichever reason led to interrupting the rape?

4. Do you agree that Le Barron's victim's pregnancy was an extraneous factor?

5. The court said a jury could conclude either that it was or that Le Barron voluntarily renounced his intention to rape because the victim was pregnant. If you were a juror, how would you have voted on the pregnancy question?

NOTE CASES

1. Wiley had wedged a large pinch bar between the door and jamb of a real estate office, trying to pry open the door in the early morning hours. A police officer testified that he surprised Wiley in the act of prying open the door. Wiley testified that he intended to break into the office and had actually begun to do so but that "I had only hit the door with [the pinch bar] twice . . . and . . . I just got scared and I abandoned the idea of breaking in the place." Was he guilty of attempting to enter the real estate office? The court said yes, rejecting Wiley's defense of voluntary abandonment:

[I]f one who has intended to attempt to commit a crime freely and voluntarily abandons the idea before it has progressed beyond mere preparation, he has not committed the crime of attempt; but . . . a voluntary abandonment of an attempt which has proceeded beyond mere preparation into an overt act or acts in furtherance of the commission of the attempt does not expiate the guilt of, or forbid punishment for, the crime already committed. *Wiley v. State*, 207 A.2d 478 (Md.1965)

2. [F]ollowing a fight with a friend outside a bar where the two had been drinking. . . . [Johnson] walked a mile to his house, retrieved his .22 rifle and ten cartridges, walked back to the bar, and crawled under a pickup truck across the street to wait for the friend. . . . [Johnson] testified that he, at first, intended to shoot the friend to "pay him back" for the beating he had received in their earlier altercation. When the owner of the pickup arrived, . . . [Johnson] obtained his keys, instructed him to sit in the pickup, and gave him one or more bottles of beer. . . . [Johnson] then crawled back under the pickup to resume his wait for his friend. The police were alerted by a passerby and arrested . . . [Johnson] before his friend emerged from the bar. There was also testimony that while he was lying under the pickup truck, . . . [Johnson] sobered up somewhat and began to think through his predicament. He testified that he changed his mind and removed the shells from the rifle, placing them in his pocket. By that time there were two persons in the pickup truck, and he began a discussion with them, telling them his name and address and inviting them to his residence to have a party. The three of them were still there drinking and conversing when the police arrived, at which time the rifle was found to be unloaded and the shells were still in . . . [Johnson's] pocket.

The trial court refused Johnson's request for an instruction on the question of abandonment. The appellate court reversed, holding that sufficient evidence existed to instruct the jury on the question of voluntary renunciation. *People v. Johnson*, 750 P.2d 72 (Colo.App.1987)

3. [W]hile his wife was away on a trip, . . . [Staples], a mathematician, under an assumed name, rented an office on the second floor of a building in Hollywood which was over the mezzanine of a bank. Directly below the mezzanine was the vault of the bank. . . . [Staples] was aware of the layout of the building, specifically of the relation of the office he rented to the bank vault. . . . [Staples] paid rent for the period from October 23 to November 23. The landlord had 10 days before commencement of the rental period within which to finish some interior repairs and painting. During this prerental period . . . [Staples] brought into the office certain equipment. This included drilling tools, two acetylene gas tanks, a blow torch, a blanket, and a linoleum rug. The landlord observed these items when he came in from time to time to see how the repair work was progressing. . . . [Staples] learned from a custodian that no one was in the building on Saturdays. On Saturday, October 14, . . . [Staples] drilled two groups of holes into the floor of the office above the mezzanine room. He stopped drilling before the holes went through the floor. He came back to the office several times thinking he might slowly drill down, covering the holes with the linoleum rug. At some point in time he installed a hasp lock on a closet, and planned to, or did, place his tools in it. However, he left the closet keys on the premises. Around the end of November, apparently after November 23, the landlord notified the police and turned the tools and equipment over to them. . . . [Staples] did not pay any more rent. It is not clear when he last entered the office, but it could have been after November 23, and even after the landlord had removed the equipment. On February 22, 1968, the police arrested . . . [Staples].

After receiving advice as to his constitutional rights, . . . [Staples] voluntarily made an oral statement: "Saturday, the 14th . . . I drilled some small holes in the floor of the room. Because of tiredness, fear, and the implications of what I was doing, I stopped and went to sleep. At this point I think my motives began to change. The actual (sic) commencement of my plan made me begin to realize that even if I were to succeed, a fugitive life of living off of stolen money would not give the enjoyment of the life of a mathematician however humble a job I might have. I still had not given up my plan however. I felt I had made a certain investment of time, money, effort and a certain psychological (sic) commitment to the concept. I came back several times thinking I might store the tools in the closet and slowly drill down (covering the hole with a rug of linoleum square). As time went on (after two weeks or so), my wife came back and my life as bank robber seemed more and more absurd."

Did Staples voluntarily renounce his attempt to commit burglary? A jury found Staples guilty of attempted burglary and the appellate court affirmed the conviction. It held that although the police did not directly intercept Staples, he knew that the landlord had turned the tools over to the police and had resumed control over the office. This, the court held, was equivalent to a direct interception. In other words, an extraneous factor prevented the burglary, not Staples's change of heart. *People v. Staples*, 6 Cal.App.3d 61, 85 Cal.Rptr. 589 (1970)

Summary of Attempt Law

Attempt requires the *mens rea* of a purpose, that is, the specific intent, to commit a crime combined with the *actus reus* of some steps that go toward commiting the crime but that fall short of completing it. Several difficult issues surround attempt law. First, conflicting rationales support criminal attempt. Attempt is sometimes justified as a means to control dangerous persons. Another rationale is that the law of criminal attempt prevents criminal harm. Second, there is a dispute over how many acts toward completion amount to attempt. Jurisdictions vary as to whether any act toward completion, substantial steps toward completion, or all but the last act necessary to complete the crime suffices. Third, difficulties surround legal and factual impossibility. Is it attempt if it was impossible to complete the crime? Most jurisdictions say no to legal impossibility but yes to factual impossibility. Factual impossibilities are generally referred to as extraneous factors. Finally, renunciation creates problems: Should it matter if a person bent on criminal conduct has a change of heart and desists from committing the crime? If the answer is yes, does it matter whether moral or nonmoral considerations prompted the change?

CONSPIRACY

As a general rule, the more remote from completion, the less justifiable is punishment for crimes. In this respect preparation, attempt, conspiracy, and solicitation stand on a continuum, with attempt closest to and solicitation farthest from actual commission of the crime. Conspiracy "strikes against the special danger incident to group activity, facilitating prosecution of the group, and yielding a basis for imposing added penalties when combination is involved."[26]

At common law, conspiracy is a combination between two or more persons formed for the purpose of doing either an unlawful act or a lawful act by an unlawful means. In words famous in conspiracy law, Justice Oliver Wendell Holmes defined conspiracy as "a partnership in criminal purpose." Holmes's broad definition needs some refinement, but it captures the basic idea of conspiracy. Criminal conspiracy consists of two elements:

1. *Actus reus*—an agreement or combination (Holmes's "partnership")
2. *Mens rea*—the purpose of attaining either
   a. an unlawful (Holmes's "criminal") objective, or
   b. a lawful objective by an unlawful means.

ELEMENTS OF CONSPIRACY

Actus reus	*Mens Rea*
1. Agreement	1. Specific intent or purpose to commit an illegal act, **or**
2. Minority Rule: Agreement plus some act in furtherance of the agreement	2. Specific intent or purpose to commit an illegal act by illegal means

Conspiracy *Actus Reus*

Conspiracy *actus reus* is an agreement. The agreement need not be a formal signed contract; unwritten understandings suffice. This provision makes sense because conspirators rarely put their agreements in writing. Some courts hold that agreement includes "aid," even when given without another party's consent. In one case, a judge learned that someone planned to kill one of the judge's enemies. The judge wanted the plan to succeed, so he intercepted a letter warning the intended victim of the plan. The court held that the judge committed conspiracy to commit murder because he aided the other conspirators, even though he had nothing to do with them.

Defining agreement imprecisely can lead to abuses. In one famous trial, the government tried Dr. Benjamin Spock for conspiracy to avoid the draft law. Videotapes showed several hundred spectators clapping while Spock urged young men to resist the draft during the Vietnam War. According to the prosecutor, any person seen clapping on videotape was a coconspirator. By virtue of their encouragement, according to the prosecutor, these people were aiding Spock, hence agreeing to violate the draft law.[27]

In most jurisdictions, the agreement alone amounts to the conspiracy *actus reus*. Some jurisdictions, however, require action beyond the agreement. They differ as to how much action in addition to the agreement the criminal design requires. Some specify "some act"; in others, "any act" suffices. One jurisdiction demands that conspirators "go forth for the purpose of committing" the prohibited act. The federal statute requires an "act to effect the object of the conspiracy."[28]

C A S E

Did They Agree to Distribute Heroin?

United States v. Brown,
776 F.2d 397 (2d Cir. 1985)

A jury convicted Brown and Valentine (a fugitive) of conspiring to distribute heroin. The Circuit Court affirmed. Circuit judge Friendly delivered the opinion.

FACTS

[William Grimball, a New York City undercover police officer, purchased a "joint" of "D" ($40 worth of heroin) in Harlem.] Officer Grimball was the government's principal witness. He testified that in the evening of October 9, 1984, he approached Gregory Valentine on the corner of 115th Street and Eighth Avenue and asked him for a joint of "D." Valentine asked Grimball whom he knew around the street. Grimball asked if Valentine knew Scott. He did not.

Brown "came up" and Valentine said, "He wants to buy a joint, but I don't know him." Brown looked at Grimball and said, "He looks okay to me." Valentine then said, "Okay. But I am going to leave it somewhere and you [Grimball] can pick it up." Brown interjected, "You don't have to do that. Just go and get it for him. He looks all right to me." After looking at Grimball, Brown said, "He looks all right to me" and "I will wait right here."

Valentine then said, "Okay. Come on with me around to the hotel." Grimball followed him to 300 West 116th Street, where Valentine instructed him, "Sit on the black car and give me a few minutes to go up and get it." Valentine requested and received $40, which had been prerecorded, and then said, "You are going to take care of me for doing this for you, throw some dollars my way?" to which Grimball responded, "Yeah."

Valentine then entered the hotel and shortly returned. The two went back to 115th Street and Eighth

Avenue, where Valentine placed a cigarette box on the hood of a blue car. Grimball picked up the cigarette box and found a glassine envelope containing white powder, stipulated to be heroin. Grimball placed $5 of the prerecorded buy money in the cigarette box, which he replaced on the hood. Valentine picked up the box and removed the $5. Grimball returned to his car and made a radio transmission to the backup field team that "the buy had went down" and informed them of the locations of the persons involved. Brown and Valentine were arrested. Valentine was found to possess two glassine envelopes of heroin and the $5 of prerecorded money. Brown was in possession of $31 of his own money; no drugs or contraband were found on him. The $40 of marked buy money was not recovered, and no arrests were made at the hotel.

[At the trial Grimball testified that] the typical drug buy in the Harlem area involved two to five people. As a result of frequent police sweeps, Harlem drug dealers were becoming so cautious that they employed people who act as steerers and the steerer's responsibility is basically to determine whether or not you are actually an addict or a user of heroin and they are also used to screen you to see if there is any possibility of you being a cop looking for a bulge or some indication that would give them that you are not actually an addict. And a lot of the responsibility relies [sic] on them to determine whether or not the drug buy is going to go down or not.

Officer Grimball . . . then . . . testif[ied] that based on his experience as an undercover agent he would describe the role that Ronald Brown played in the transaction as that of a steerer. When asked why, he testified . . . "Because I believe that if it wasn't for his approval, the buy would not have gone down."

OPINION

. . . Since the jury convicted on . . . conspiracy . . . the evidence must permit a reasonable juror to be convinced beyond a reasonable doubt not simply that Brown had aided and abetted the drug sale but that he had agreed to do so. . . .

A review of the evidence convinces us that it was sufficient. . . . Although Brown's mere presence at the scene of the crime and his knowledge that a crime

was being committed would not have been sufficient to establish Brown's knowing participation in the conspiracy, the proof went considerably beyond that. Brown was not simply standing around while the exchanges between Officer Grimball and Valentine occurred. He came on the scene shortly after these began and Valentine immediately explained the situation to him. Brown then conferred his seal of approval on Grimball, a most unlikely event unless there was an established relationship between Brown and Valentine. Finally, Brown took upon himself the serious responsibility of telling Valentine to desist from his plan to reduce the risks by not handing the heroin directly to Grimball. A rational mind could take this as bespeaking the existence of an agreement whereby Brown was to have the authority to command, or at least to persuade. Brown's remark, "Just go ahead and get it for him," permits inferences that Brown knew where the heroin was to be gotten, that he knew that Valentine knew this, and that Brown and Valentine had engaged in such a transaction before. . . .

When we add to the inferences that can be reasonably drawn from the facts to which Grimball testified . . . his testimony about the use of steerers in street sales of narcotics . . . we conclude that the Government offered sufficient evidence . . . for a reasonable juror to be satisfied beyond a reasonable doubt not only that Brown had acted as a steerer but that he had agreed to do so. Affirmed.

DISSENT

While it is true that this is another $40 narcotics case, it is also a conspiracy case. . . . An agreement—a "continuous and conscious union of wills upon a common undertaking"—. . . [was not proved here] unless an inference that Brown agreed to act as a "steerer" can be drawn from the fact that he said to Valentine (three times) that Grimball "looks okay [all right] to me," as well as "[j]ust go and get it for him." . . . It could not be drawn from Brown's possession, constructive or otherwise, of narcotics or narcotics paraphernalia, his sharing in the proceeds of the street sale, his conversations with others, or even some hearsay evidence as to his "prior arrangements" with Valentine or an "established working relationship" with Brown and Valentine. . . . [I]ndeed, Brown was apprehended after leaving the area of the crime with only thirty-one of his own dollars in his pocket, and no drugs or other contraband. He did not even stay around for another Valentine sale. . . .

I cannot believe there is proof of conspiracy, or Brown's membership in it, beyond a reasonable doubt. . . .

This case may be unique. It . . . supports Justice Jackson's reference to the history of the law of conspiracy as exemplifying, in Cardozo's phrase, the "tendency of a principle to expand itself to the limits of its logic." . . . If today we uphold a conspiracy to sell narcotics on the street, on this kind of evidence, what conspiracies might we approve tomorrow? The majority opinion will come back to haunt us, I fear. . . . Accordingly, I dissent.

QUESTIONS FOR DISCUSSION

1. What specific facts point to an agreement in the case?

2. Do they convince you beyond a reasonable doubt that Brown and Valentine had a "continuous and conscious union of wills upon a common undertaking?"

3. Is the dissent right that this case pushes conspiracy law to "the limits of its logic"?

4. Why do you think the prosecution chose to charge Brown with conspiracy instead of with aiding and abetting? (Review relevant sections in chapter 4.)

5. If the police had found evidence of possession (see chapter 3) or the marked money, would they have charged Brown with conspiracy?

6. Should they have done so?

Conspiracy *Mens Rea*

Both legislatures and courts frequently define conspiracy *mens rea* vaguely. Common-law and modern statutes traditionally have not mentioned conspiracy *mens rea*, leaving courts to define it. The courts in turn have taken imprecise, widely divergent, and inconsistent approaches to the *mens rea* problem. According to former Supreme Court Justice Robert Jackson, "The modern crime of conspiracy is so vague that it almost defies definition."[29]

Authorities frequently call conspiracy a specific intent crime. But what does that mean? Does it mean that conspiracy involves intent to enter a criminal agreement or combination? Or must conspiracy also include an intent to attain a particular criminal objective, or at least to use a specific criminal means to attain the objective? For example, if two men agree to burn down a building, they have conspired to commit arson. However, if they do not intend to hurt anyone, do they also conspire to commit murder? Surely not, if the conspiracy *mens rea* requires an intent to attain a particular criminal objective. The example demonstrates the importance of distinguishing between the intent to make agreements or combinations and the intent to attain a particular criminal objective. If the objective is to commit a specific crime, it must satisfy that crime's *mens rea*. Hence, conspiring to take another's property is not conspiring to commit larceny unless the conspirators intended to permanently deprive the owner of possession (see the discussion of larceny in chapter 11).

Courts further complicate conspiracy *mens rea* by not clarifying whether it requires purpose. Consider cases involving suppliers of goods and services, such as doctors who order from drug supply companies drugs that they then use or sell illegally. At what point do suppliers become coconspirators, even though they have not agreed specifically to supply drugs for illegal distribution? Must prosecutors prove that suppliers entered an agreement or combination intending specifically to further buyers' criminal purposes? Most courts require such proof, even though it is difficult to obtain, because conspirators rarely subject their purposes to written contracts. Purpose must therefore be inferred from circumstances surrounding the combination, such as sales quantities, the continuity of the supplier-recipient relationship, the seller's initiative, a failure to keep records, and the relationship's clandestine nature.[30]

Some argue that knowing, or conscious, wrongdoing ought to satisfy the conspiracy *mens rea*. However, in *People v. Lauria*, the court refused to substitute knowledge for purpose.

C A S E

Did He Conspire to Run a "Call Girl" Service?

People v. Lauria,
251 Cal.App.2d 471, 59 Cal.Rptr. 628
(1967)

Lauria was indicted for conspiracy to commit prostitution. The trial court set aside the indictment. The People appealed. The California Supreme Court affirmed. Associate Justice Fleming wrote the opinion of the court.

FACTS

In an investigation of call-girl activity police focused their attention on three prostitutes actively plying their trade on call, each of whom was using Lauria's telephone answering service, presumably for business purposes. On January 8, 1965, Stella Weeks, a policewoman, signed up for telephone service with Lauria's answering service. Mrs. Weeks, in the course of her conversation with Lauria's office manager, hinted broadly that she was a prostitute concerned with the secrecy of her activities and their concealment from the police. She was assured that the operation of the service was discreet and "about as safe as you can get." It was arranged that Mrs. Weeks need not leave her address with the answering service, but could pick up her calls and pay her bills in person.

On February 11, Mrs. Weeks talked to Lauria on the telephone and told him her business was modelling and she had been referred to the answering service by Terry, one of the three prostitutes under investigation. She complained that because of the op-

eration of the service she had lost two valuable customers, referred to as tricks. Lauria defended his service and said that her friends had probably lied to her about having left calls for her. But he did not respond to Mrs. Weeks' hints that she needed customers in order to make money, other than to invite her to his house for a personal visit in order to get better acquainted. In the course of his talk he said "his business was taking messages."

On February 15, Mrs. Weeks talked on the telephone to Lauria's office manager and again complained of two lost calls, which she described as a $50 and a $100 trick. On investigation the office manager could find nothing wrong, but she said she would alert the switchboard operators about slip-ups on calls.

On April 1 Lauria and the three prostitutes were arrested. Lauria complained to the police that this attention was undeserved, stating that Hollywood Call Board had 60 to 70 prostitutes on its board while his own service had only 9 or 10, that he kept separate records for known or suspected prostitutes for the convenience of himself and the police. When asked if his records were available to police who might come to the office to investigate call girls, Lauria replied that they were whenever the police had a specific name.

However, his service didn't "arbitrarily tell the police about prostitutes on our board. As long as they pay their bills we tolerate them." In a subsequent voluntary appearance before the Grand Jury Lauria testified he had always cooperated with the police. But he admitted he knew some of his customers were prostitutes, and he knew Terry was a prostitute because he had personally used her services, and he knew she was paying for 500 calls per month.

Lauria and the three prostitutes were indicted for conspiracy to commit prostitution, and nine overt acts were specified. Subsequently the trial court set aside the indictment as having been brought without reasonable or probable cause. (Pen.Code, § 995.) The People have appealed, claiming that a sufficient showing of an unlawful agreement to further prostitution was made.

OPINION

To establish agreement, the People need show no more than a tacit, mutual understanding between co-conspirators to accomplish an unlawful act. Here the People attempted to establish a conspiracy by showing that Lauria, well aware that his codefendants were prostitutes who received business calls from customers through his telephone answering service, continued to furnish them with such service. This approach attempts to equate knowledge of another's criminal activity with conspiracy to further such criminal activity, and poses the question of the criminal responsibility of a furnisher of goods or services who knows his product is being used to assist the operation of an illegal business. Under what circumstances does a supplier become a part of a conspiracy to further an illegal enterprise by furnishing goods or services which he knows are to be used by the buyer for criminal purposes?

Proof of knowledge is ordinarily a question of fact and requires no extended discussion in the present case. The knowledge of the supplier was sufficiently established when Lauria admitted he knew some of his customers were prostitutes and admitted he knew that Terry, an active subscriber to his service, was a prostitute. In the face of these admissions he could scarcely claim to have relied on the normal assumption an operator of a business or service is entitled to make, that his customers are behaving themselves in the eyes of the law. Because Lauria knew in fact that some of his customers were prostitutes, it is a legitimate inference he knew they were subscribing to his answering service for illegal business purposes and were using his service to make assignations for prostitution. On this record we think the prosecution is entitled to claim positive knowledge by Lauria of the use of his service to facilitate the business of prostitution.

The more perplexing issue in the case is the sufficiency of proof of intent to further the criminal enterprise. The element of intent may be proved either by direct evidence, or by evidence of circumstances from which an intent to further a criminal enterprise by supplying lawful goods or services may be inferred. Direct evidence of participation, such as advice from the supplier of legal goods or services to the user of those goods or services on their use for illegal purposes . . . provides the simplest case. When the intent to further and promote the criminal enterprise comes from the lips of the supplier himself, ambiguities of inference from circumstances need not trouble us. But in cases where direct proof of complicity is lacking, intent to further the conspiracy must be derived from the sale itself and its surrounding circumstances in order to establish the supplier's express or tacit agreement to join the conspiracy.

In the case at bench the prosecution argues that since Lauria knew his customers were using his service for illegal purposes but nevertheless continued to furnish it to them, he must have intended to assist them in carrying out their illegal activities. Thus through a union of knowledge and intent he became a participant in a criminal conspiracy. Essentially, the People argue that knowledge alone of the continuing use of his telephone facilities for criminal purposes provided a sufficient basis from which his intent to participate in those criminal activities could be inferred. In examining precedents in this field we find that sometimes, but not always, the criminal intent of the supplier may be inferred from his knowledge of the unlawful use made of the product he supplies. [Here the court conducted an exhaustive examination of precedents.] . . .

From this analysis of precedent we deduce the following rule: the intent of a supplier who knows of the criminal use to which his supplies are put to participate in the criminal activity connected with the use of his supplies may be established by (1) direct evidence that he intends to participate, or (2) through an inference that he intends to participate based on, (a) his special interest in the activity, or (b) the aggravated nature of the crime itself.

When we review Lauria's activities in the light of this analysis, we find no proof that Lauria took any direct action to further, encourage, or direct the call-girl activities of his codefendants and we find an absence of circumstances from which his special interest in their activities could be inferred. Neither excessive charges for standardized services, nor the furnishing of services without a legitimate use, nor an unusual quantity of business with call girls, are present. The offense which he is charged with furthering is a misdemeanor, a category of crime which has never been made a required subject of positive disclosure to public authority. Under these circumstances, although proof of Lauria's knowledge of the criminal activities of his patrons was sufficient to charge him with that fact, there was insufficient evidence that he intended to further their criminal activities, and hence insufficient proof of his participation in a criminal conspiracy with his codefendants to further prostitution. Since the conspiracy centered around the activities of Lauria's telephone answering service, the charges against his codefendants likewise fail for want of proof.

In absolving Lauria of complicity in a criminal conspiracy we do not wish to imply that the public authorities are without remedies to combat modern manifestations of the world's oldest profession. Licensing of telephone answering services under the police power, together with the revocation of licenses for the toleration of prostitution, is a possible civil remedy. The furnishing of telephone answering service in aid of prostitution could be made a crime. (Cf. Pen.Code, § 316, which makes it a misdemeanor to let an apartment with knowledge of its use for prostitution.) Other solutions will doubtless occur to vigilant public authorities if the problem of call-girl activity needs further suppression. The order is affirmed.

QUESTIONS FOR DISCUSSION

1. Of what exactly did the agreement in this case consist?

2. What is the precise point of the court's distinguishing between knowledge and purpose?

3. In what circumstances can courts infer intent from knowledge in conspiracy cases?

4. Do you agree that the law has better, or at least other, ways to deal with prostitution than convicting Lauria?

5. Which of the alternatives, if any, that the court suggests would you adopt?

The Objective of the Conspiracy

What objectives amount to conspiratorial agreements and combinations? In some states — Texas and Arkansas, for example — only combinations or agreements to commit felonies qualify as conspiracies. Several other states — such as Colorado, Arizona, and Hawaii — include both felonies and misdemeanors. Still other states follow the broad, common-law definition, making it a crime to enter into any conspiracies, agreements, or combinations to "accomplish any unlawful object by lawful means," or "any lawful object by unlawful means," or "any unlawful object by unlawful means." Courts have even extended "unlawful" to embrace civil wrongs. For example, an agreement to interfere unfairly with trade is not a crime in most states, but it may be against the law. An agreement to engage in unfair trade practices has an unlawful, if not criminal, objective and is considered a conspiracy.

Some conspiracy statutes reach still further. In Alabama, for instance, conspiracy not only applies to agreements and combinations to accomplish criminal and other unlawful objectives, it also encompasses "any act injurious to public health, morals, trade, and commerce." Agreements and combinations falling within this sweeping phrase are almost limitless in number. Examples include combinations to commit fornication, to interfere with social intercourse at a picnic, and to use another person's car without permission.[31]

Reformers have urged courts to declare the most sweeping statutes void for vagueness. In *State v. Musser*, the state of Utah prosecuted Mormons for practicing polygamy. The Utah Supreme Court ruled that the "public morals" provision in Utah's conspiracy statute was unconstitutionally vague. Most efforts to limit the reach of conspiracy law have failed, however. Courts have actually expanded the federal conspiracy to defraud provision in the United States Code to encompass "virtually any impairment of the Government's operating efficiency." The United States Supreme Court remarked that these broad statutes "would seem to be warrant for conviction for agreement to do almost any act which a judge and jury might find at the moment contrary to his or its notions of what was good for health, morals, trade, commerce, justice or order."[32]

Another path toward reform is to draft narrower conspiracy statutes. The *Model Penal Code*, for example, includes only agreements or combinations with "criminal objectives." Several states have followed suit. Connecticut, Georgia, Illinois, and others now include only agreements or combinations made to pursue criminal objectives.

Parties to the Conspiracy

At common law and in most jurisdictions today, a conspiracy requires two or more parties to the agreement. The criminal law punishes conspiracies in part because group offenses threaten more danger than offenses committed by individuals. Thus, some have argued that when unlawful combinations do not have an element of added danger, they are not conspiracies unless they involve more than the number of parties required to commit the completed crime. According to **Wharton's rule** (named after a nineteenth-century criminal law commentator), in a crime that requires two or more persons (such as bigamy, bribery, incest, and gambling), the state must prove that three or more persons agreed to commit the offense. For example, a police officer who agreed not to arrest a person in exchange for money did not conspire to obstruct justice because bribery itself requires at least two persons—the offerer and receiver. Had two police officers agreed to take the money, then conspiracy would have occurred because three parties (the two officers and the briber) agreed to commit the crime.[33]

Some jurisdictions have abolished the Wharton rule on the ground that whether or not the completed offense required more than one party, the danger the actor poses to society justifies making the effort criminal. The *Model Penal Code* adopts this unilateral approach to liability for conspiracy. The New Jersey Supreme Court took this approach in *State v. Lavary*.[34]

C A S E

Did She Conspire to Commit Atrocious Assault and Battery?

State v. Lavary,
152 N.J.Super. 413, 377 A.2d 1255 (1977),
163 N.J.Super. 576, 395 A.2d 524 (1978)

After her conviction of conspiracy to commit atrocious assault and battery and to commit mayhem upon a police officer, Lavary sought postconviction relief. The Superior Court, Law Division, Arnone, J. S. C., held that Lavary could be convicted of conspiracy even though the person with whom she allegedly conspired was actually himself an undercover police officer. The motion to dismiss the indictment or grant judgment notwithstanding, the verdict was denied. Judge Arnone wrote the opinion of the court.

FACTS

Defendant brings this motion seeking a number of different postconviction remedies. She seeks (1) the merger of the three counts of the indictment; (2) a new trial pursuant to R. 3:20-1, or (3) dismissal of the indictment. [The excerpt here deals only with the conspiracy.]

Briefly, the evidence indicated that defendant had gone to Maryland at the request of New Jersey law enforcement authorities for whom she had been working as an informant from time to time. The purpose of the trip was to ascertain if defendant could provide evidence against her former husband who was suspected of involvement in a murder.

While there she met a woman named Billie, a prior acquaintance from New Jersey. In the course of renewing their acquaintance defendant represented to Billie that the major irritation in her life was a Lt. Halliday of the Middletown Twp. Police Dept. She indicated to Billie that Lt. Halliday was constantly harassing her and was the source of all her major problems. She also stated to Billie that she was looking for someone who could "get" Lt. Halliday. Billie, who was an informant for the Maryland State Police, told defendant that she might know such a person. Billie subsequently told the Maryland State Police of the conversation.

When the Maryland State Police learned that the intended victim was a New Jersey police officer, they resolved to have one of their undercover agents, Lt. Mazzone, introduced by Billie to defendant as the "hit man" defendant was seeking.

A number of telephone conversations ensued, beginning December 19, 1975. These conversations were taped by Lt. Mazzone. The gist of the conversations was that Lt. Mazzone would be paid a sum of money plus expenses to severely beat Lt. Halliday.

Defendant was subsequently indicted and convicted on three counts of an indictment charging conspiracy with an "undercover agent with the Maryland State Police" (Lt. Mazzone). Two counts charged conspiracy to commit atrocious assault and battery; one charged conspiracy to commit mayhem.

Defendant and the undercover agent of the Maryland State Police were the only individuals named in the indictment.

. . . [T]he jury had available for its consideration the following conversations and statements by defendant:

MAZZONE: Well, how much you got to pay for the present?

LAVARY: Well, you see, that's not too much of a problem, cause what I want done, I waited many years for. I mean if it's a whole lot then I have to wait a little bit, but, I don't know, I need an idea about how much it would cost. I don't know if she explained it, I don't want a permanent Christmas present, did she explain that to you?

MAZZONE: No, why don't you give me a rundown?

LAVARY: Well, I just rather it be put out of commission but around to realize it, you know what I mean, cause to me that's so much more appropriate. The other way it's done, it's over with, and you know, use it up and it's all gone. Once you use something, it's forgotten, but I'd like this one to kind of linger on for years and years, and years, so he'll always remember who gave it to him.

MAZZONE: That ain't bad. Understand the Dude's a cop or wears some kind of uniform.

LAVARY: Yeah.

MAZZONE: That makes it extra special.

LAVARY: Yes. They immediately start right here, but there's been so many other people that, they could bat their head against the wall for the next 20 years with just a list; it's been a long time comin [sic]. I never had it done before because it was always right here, I mean they knew, I came into a lot of money once before, and that's when I planned to give him his last present, but I couldn't because they watched me like a hawk for almost a year, and it was just no good, now things have lightened up for over a year.

LAVARY: I'll meet him on the turnpike, that's not far from my house anyway. You don't know how much I appreciate this Billie, cause, I've been waiting a long time, biting my tongue, biding my time, all fall directly in my head, and I feel the time is quite appropriate now, specially being you know, I got such good backing right now.

MAZZONE: You want him crippled?

LAVARY: I just want him maimed for the rest of his life. Every time he looks at his twisted (expletive) self he'll know somebody who hated him wanted it.

MAZZONE: You want him maimed for the rest of his life. What do you mean, legs, arms, eyes, what?

LAVARY: Just about everything, I just wanted him (expletive) up.

MAZZONE: Who you talking it over with?

LAVARY: My old man.

MAZZONE: He's ok with just the maiming?

LAVARY: I don't want him dead.

MAZZONE: No, I mean the old man.

LAVARY: Well it's me who wanted it, he kind of wanted me to forget it for a while because they picked me up once since then, you know, he's afraid of a little heat coming back on me, but I don't care. . . .

[On other grounds,] defendant's motion for a new trial is denied.

Defendant's final argument which she advances on this motion is for dismissal of the indictment . . . or a judgment of acquittal. . . .

OPINION

The question presented by defendant's argument is whether a defendant may be convicted of conspiracy when the conspiracy is between two persons, one of whom is defendant and the other an undercover agent for a law enforcement agency who only pretends to participate in the conspiracy for the purpose of obtaining evidence against the defendant.

The gist of the offense of conspiracy lies not in the doing of the act, nor in effecting the purpose for which the conspiracy is formed, nor in attempting to accomplish that purpose, but in the forming of the scheme or agreement between the parties. It is the unlawful purpose upon which they agreed which makes a conspiracy punishable once any overt act is committed in furtherance of it. This is so because such unions are vested with a potentiality for evil that renders the plans criminal in themselves and punishable as such if acts are done to effect their object.

The legislative intent underlying the statute is founded upon the plain fact that a conspiracy is an evil apart from the substantive offense, and at times even a greater evil, for the conspiracy may lead to other substantive offenses of a like sort and perhaps to habitual practices. . . .

[D]efendant was found guilty of conspiring with an undercover agent of the Maryland State Police. She now seeks to assert as a complete defense the fact that since her coconspirator could not be guilty of committing the crime, neither could she. She argues that since Lt. Mazzone did not intend to agree, it is irrelevant that she did intend to agree, since a conspiracy requires a common intent in the minds of both conspirators.

Closer examination of defendant's position reveals that its basis is "factual impossibility." She argues that Lt. Mazzone's status as an undercover police officer makes a conspiracy an impossibility since the facts reveal that Lt. Mazzone only pretended to enter the conspiracy and that her mistake as to his actual intent is sufficient to vitiate the conspiracy.

In this case defendant's intent to have bodily harm inflicted upon Lt. Halliday is clear; believing Lt. Mazzone to intend the same result, she did all that was in her power to bring about the criminal result she desired. The fact that Lt. Mazzone was an undercover agent does not diminish the criminal quality of defendant's intent. The consequence which defendant intended was a result which, if successful, would have been a crime. The fact that Lt. Mazzone was an undercover agent should in no way negate defendant's clearly manifested intent to commit a criminal act. It should be immaterial to her guilt that the person with whom she is alleged to have conspired might have a complete defense in that he did not have the prerequisite intent. . . .

This court holds that when the consequences sought by defendant are unlawful, it is no defense to a charge of conspiracy that she could not reach her goal because of circumstances unknown to her, or that the person with whom she conspired has not been or cannot be convicted. . . . To hold otherwise here would mock justice, interfere with the interest of society in repressing crime, and lead to absurd results. The court finds that a unilateral approach to the crime of conspiracy is appropriate and fully justified in New Jersey. . . .

The court finds this interpretation . . . consistent with the increased danger and social harm inherent in the crime of conspiracy. The "intricacies and artificial distinctions" urged by defendant thwart rather than serve substantial justice and are hereby rejected.

For the above reasons, the motion to dismiss the indictment or grant judgment notwithstanding the verdict is denied.

QUESTIONS FOR DISCUSSION

1. What reasons does the court give for rejecting the Wharton rule and adopting the "unilateral" approach?

2. Do you think Lavary is equally blameworthy and dangerous whether or not the undercover police officer only pretended to enter the agreement? Why or why not?

3. Is it fair to punish someone for an agreement that never results in injury to anyone? Why or why not?

The relationship of parties to conspiracies can get intricate, particularly when they involve large operations. Most of these large-scale conspiracies fall into two major patterns: "wheel" and "chain" conspiracies. In wheel conspiracies, one or more defendants participate in every transaction. These participants make up the hub of the wheel conspiracy. Others participate in only one transaction; they are the spokes in the wheel. Chain conspiracies usually involve the distribution of some commodity, such as illegal drugs. In chain conspiracies, participants at one end of the chain may know nothing of each other, but every participant handles the same commodity at different points, such as manufacture, distribution, and sale. In *United States v. Bruno*, for example, smugglers brought narcotics into New York, middlemen purchased the narcotics, and two groups of retailers (one operating in New York and the other in Louisiana) bought narcotics from middlemen.[35]

Failure to convict one party does not prevent conviction of other parties to conspiracies. Typically, statutes similar to the Illinois Criminal Code provide:

It shall not be a defense to conspiracy that the person or persons with whom the accused is alleged to have conspired
1. Has not been prosecuted or convicted, or
2. Has been convicted of a different offense, or
3. Is not amenable to justice, or
4. Has been acquitted, or
5. Lacked the capacity to commit an offense.[36]

The court in *Williams v. State* dealt with whether Carl and Diane Williams were parties.

C A S E

Were They Partners in Crime?

Williams v. State,
274 Ind. 94, 409 N.E.2d 571 (1980)

Carl and Diane Williams were convicted of conspiracy to commit murder. Carl Williams was sentenced to thirty years in prison. Diane Williams was sentenced to twenty years in prison. She appealed. The

Indiana Supreme Court affirmed. Justice Pivarnik delivered the opinion.

FACTS

[The Indiana Criminal Code codifies the offense of conspiracy. That section provides:]

Conspiracy. — (a) A person conspires to commit a felony when, with intent to commit the felony, he agrees with another person to commit the felony. A conspiracy to commit a felony is a felony of the same class as the underlying felony. However, a conspiracy to commit murder is a class A felony. (b) The state must allege and prove that either the person or the person with whom he agreed performed an overt act in furtherance of the agreement.

In early January, 1978, Hammond police officer James Lawson was working as an undercover agent for the Drug Enforcement Administration branch of the United States Department of Justice. During the course of his work for the federal government, he came in contact with Dr. Carl N. Williams and Diane Kendrick Williams, the defendants in this case. On January 5, Lawson was in the Williams' home in Gary, Indiana, discussing certain other matters not related to the present case. Dr. Williams and appellant both engaged in conversation with Lawson. Late in the afternoon, appellant began reading that day's edition of the *Gary Post-Tribune*. The January 5 edition of the *Post-Tribune* carried an article on page one under the by-line of Alan Doyle. This article related how the Williamses had been charged in connection with an automobile theft. Appellant Diane Williams brought the story to the attention of Dr. Williams and Officer Lawson. Dr. and Mrs. Williams became very angry over the contents of the article. Appellant explained the general content of the story to Lawson, and he remarked, "It sounds like they are really trying to get you." Dr. Williams explained that his family had been involved in politics and that Gary was a "dog town."

When Diane Williams asked what they were going to do about the article, Dr. Williams stated that he wanted "something" done about it. Lawson's suggestion that they talk to their attorneys and pursue legal remedies was rejected out of hand by both Dr. Williams and appellant. Diane Williams stated that lawyers were of no help, and Dr. Williams said he was tired of dealing with lawyers. Both remained very angry over the article, and appellant again asked what they were going to do about Doyle and his article. Dr. Williams then stated that he wanted Doyle "shut up."

Dr. Williams then asked Lawson if he could "undertake an extra service." Lawson asked what he was referring to, and Dr. Williams repeated that he wanted Doyle "shut up." When Lawson asked him exactly what he meant by "shutting someone up," the doctor said he wanted to stop what he called "this malicious slander." Lawson remarked that breaking somebody's legs and arms wouldn't necessarily shut them up, and appellant Diane Williams agreed. Dr. Williams asked Lawson again if he would "perform an extra service." He stated that he wanted Alan Doyle killed, and he asked Lawson if he knew someone who would do the job. Lawson said he could put them in touch with someone who would, but that whoever he contacted would want to know "specifics" about the intended victim, such as his appearance, his place of employment, and what kind of car he drove. Dr. Williams said he would go to the newspaper office to learn this information, but appellant Diane Williams counselled against such an idea, saying it would connect Dr. Williams too closely with what was going to happen.

Lawson and Dr. Williams left the room to pick up a two-way police radio Williams possessed, because he thought it would be helpful in their plans. A short time later, they returned to the room where Diane was sitting. Lawson reiterated his feeling that the people he contacted to perform the killing would need to know who Doyle is, where he worked, and the kind of car he drove. Appellant Diane Williams volunteered to obtain this information.

The next day, Lawson returned to the Williams home with Michael Bolin, another undercover police officer. Lawson identified Bolin to Dr. Williams as the person who would perform the killing for them. Bolin demanded one thousand dollars for his services, half to be paid at that time, and the remainder after the job was completed. Dr. Williams then paid five hundred dollars to Bolin. Appellant Diane Williams was not present during this conversation. On January 12, 1978, Lawson and Bolin went back to the Williams residence. After a brief conversation, Lawson, Bolin and Dr. Williams went for a drive in the agents' car. At their request, Dr. Williams directed them to the location of the *Post-Tribune* offices in Gary. During the course of the conversation in the car, Dr. Williams stated on two occasions that appellant Diane Williams knew of and concurred in their plan to kill Alan Doyle.

OPINION

Thus, in this case, the prosecution must have proved that Diane Williams had the intent to commit murder; that she agreed with another person to commit murder; and that some overt act was performed in furtherance of that agreement. The requisite intent, of course, may be inferred from the acts committed and the circumstances surrounding the case.

We think there was substantial evidence from which the jury could have found beyond a reasonable doubt that Diane Williams had the intent to kill Alan Doyle, and that she had an intelligent understanding with Dr. Williams and Lawson that the killing would be done. Clearly, Dr. Williams committed several overt acts in pursuance of this agreement and plan.

Thus, the evidence is sufficient to support the jury's finding that appellant Diane Williams conspired to commit murder.

QUESTIONS FOR DISCUSSION

1. Did Diane Williams conspire to commit murder?

2. What was the agreement?

3. The act in furthering it?

4. The criminal purpose?

5. Do you think the penalty is excessive?

6. Is Diane Williams as guilty as her husband, Dr. Williams?

7. Why is he punished more severely?

Summary of Conspiracy Law

Conspiracy is further removed from completed crimes than are both attempt and preparation. Conspiracy law is based on the rationale that it not only prevents dangerous persons from completing their evil plans but also strikes at a second evil, combinations for wrongful purposes, a serious social problem in itself. Conspiracy's elements are simply stated—conspiracy is an agreement or combination intended to achieve an illegal objective—but are applied according to widely varied interpretation and meaning.

The often vague definitions of the elements in conspiracy offer considerable opportunity for prosecutorial and judicial discretion. At times, this discretion borders on abuse, leading to charges that conspiracy law is unjust. First, a general criticism is that conspiracy law punishes conduct far remote from actual crime. Second, labor organizations, civil liberties groups, and large corporations charge that conspiracy is a weapon against their legitimate interests of collective bargaining and strikes, dissent from accepted points of view and public policies, and profit making. Critics say that when prosecutors do not have enough evidence to convict for the crime itself, they turn as a last hope to conspiracy. Conspiracy's vague definitions greatly enhance the chance for a guilty verdict.

Not often mentioned, but extremely important, is that intense media attention to conspiracy trials can lead to abuse. This happened in the conspiracy trials of Dr. Benjamin Spock and the Chicago Eight, and in other conspiracy trials involving radical politics during the 1960s. It also occurred in the Watergate conspiracy trials involving President Nixon's associates during the 1970s, and in the alleged conspiracies surrounding the sale of arms to Iran for hostages and the subsequent alleged diversion of funds during the 1980s.

Several states have made efforts to overcome these criticisms by defining conspiracy elements more narrowly. The definitions of agreement or combination are no longer as vague as they once were. The *Model Penal Code* requires acts in furtherance of agreement, and several states are following that lead. Those states have refined *mens rea* to include only purposeful conduct, that is, a specific intent to carry out the objective of the agreement or combination. Knowledge, recklessness, and negligence are increasingly attacked as insufficient culpability for an offense as remote from completion as conspiracy. Furthermore, most recent legislation restricts conspiratorial objectives to criminal ends. Phrases like "unlawful objects," "lawful objects by unlawful means," and "objectives harmful to public health, morals, trade, and commerce" are increasingly regarded as too broad and, therefore, unacceptable.

On the other hand, the Racketeer Influenced and Corrupt Organizations Act (RICO) demonstrates the continued vitality of conspiracy law. RICO reflects the need for effective means to meet the threat posed by organized crime. It imposes enhanced penalties for "all types of organized criminal behavior, that is, enterprise criminality — from simple political to sophisticated white collar schemes to traditional Mafia-type endeavors."[37]

Racketeering activity includes any act chargeable under state and federal law, including murder, kidnaping, bribery, drug dealing, gambling, theft, extortion, and securities fraud. Among other things, the statute prohibits using income from a "pattern of racketeering activity" to acquire an interest in or establish an enterprise affecting interstate commerce; conducting an enterprise through a pattern of racketeering; or conspiring to violate these provisions.[38]

RICO's drafters intended the statute to "break the back of organized crime." The racketeers they had in mind were "loansharks, drug kingpins, prostitution overlords, and casino operators who hired murderers and arsonists to enforce and extort — you know, the designated bad guys who presumably did not deserve the rights of due process that should protect all of us." Now, however, aggressive prosecutors use RICO against white-collar crime. Rudolf Giuliani, as a U.S. Attorney, for example, caused Drexel Burnham Lambert to plead guilty to several counts of securities violations in order to avoid RICO prosecution, which would not only result in harsher legal penalties but also attach the label of "racketeer" to white-collar criminals.[39]

SOLICITATION

Most remote from its underlying substantive crime is solicitation. At common law — and under most modern statutes — solicitation is a command, urging, or request to a third person to commit a crime. Suppose I want to murder my wife but am afraid to do it. If I ask a friend and he kills her, then we are both murderers. If he tries to kill her and fails because his gun is defective, then he has committed attempted murder. If he agrees to kill her and buys the gun but gets no further, then we have conspired to commit murder. But simply soliciting or urging another to commit murder is also a crime. Hence, if I ask my friend to commit murder and offer him money to do it, even if he rejects the offer, I have committed the crime called solicitation to commit murder.

Opinion differs as to whether solicitation to commit a crime presents a sufficient social danger to constitute a crime. On one side, it is argued that solicitation is not dangerous because an independent moral agent (the person solicited) stands between solicitors and their criminal objectives. Furthermore, by soliciting others to commit crimes, solicitors demonstrate their reluctance to commit crimes themselves. On the

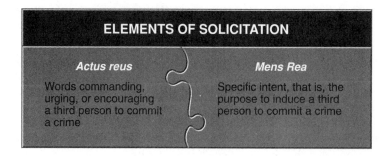

other side, advocates argue that solicitation creates the special danger inherent in group participation in crime; in this sense, solicitation is an attempt to conspire. In addition, solicitors manifest masterful and intelligent manipulation of their underlings. According to the commentary of the *Model Penal Code*, "[t]here should be no doubt on this issue. Purposeful solicitation presents dangers calling for preventive intervention and is sufficiently indicative of a disposition towards criminal activity to call for liability."[40]

Solicitation consists of words, but the law imprecisely prescribes what words qualify as the *actus reus* of solicitation. Courts generally agree that statements simply favoring or approving crime do not constitute solicitation. Hence, someone who merely says, "I think it would be great if someone killed that terrorist," has not solicited murder. Courts demand some sort of inducement. Statutes and judicial decisions have deemed sufficient a statement that does any of the following: advises, commands, counsels, encourages, entices, entreats, importunes, incites, induces, instigates, procures, requests, solicits, or urges. Uttering the proper inducement accompanied by the required *mens rea* constitutes solicitation. In other words, criminal solicitation consists of the effort to engage another in crime, whether or not the inducement ever ripens into a completed crime. The law considers that those who urge others to commit crimes are sufficiently dangerous to punish.[41]

Does the solicitor have to address the words to particular individuals? Some say yes, but courts have ruled that public exhortations to audiences suffice. One speaker who was convicted urged his audience from a public platform to commit murder and robbery. Soliciting is a crime even if the solicitor does not personally communicate the inducement, and despite the inducement's failure to reach its object. Hence, if I send a letter to my hoped-for collaborator, offering her $30,000 to kill my enemy, I have solicited murder even if the letter gets lost in the mail. The danger of a criminal solicitation does not depend on the inducement's reaching its object. Rather, the danger lies in a solicitor bent on engaging another in crime who continue to seek for someone more willing to accept the solicitation.[42]

Some statutes restrict the objective in solicitation to felonies; in some cases to violent felonies. In other jurisdictions, it is a crime to solicit another to commit any crime, whether felony, misdemeanor, or violation. Furthermore, solicitation need not include an inducement to commit a crime. For example, suppose a robber urges a friend to borrow money and lend it to the robber for a plane ticket to escape from the jurisdiction. The robber has solicited escape, or aiding and abetting a robbery. Although borrowing money is not a crime, and lending money to a robber is not by itself a crime, both escape and aiding and abetting robbers are crimes. One who urges another to commit those crimes has committed the crime of solicitation.

Solicitation *mens rea* requires purpose or specific intent. The words in a solicitation must convey the author's intention to induce another to commit the substantive offense. If I urge my friend who works in an expensive jewelry shop to take a gold chain for me, I have solicited larceny. If, on the other hand, I ask another friend who works in a clothing shop to get a coat for me to use for the evening, and I plan to return the coat the next morning before anyone knows it is missing, I have not solicited larceny because I do not intend to steal the coat, only to use it for the night (see the discussion of larceny in chapter 11).

A problem arises when law enforcement officers solicit in order to determine whether someone is disposed to commit a crime. For example, police decoys who try to get suspected prostitutes to offer sex for money have not solicited criminally under current law because the decoys' motive is not dangerous. Proponents of current law maintain (not without objection) that the decoys' motives are nobly addressed to upholding the law, hardly a dangerous propensity. Similarly, narcotics police or street decoys hoping to catch muggers are working to prevent and control crime, not to foster crime, according to supporters. Others argue that decoys encourage innocent people to commit crimes. Although law enforcement officers acting properly in the course of their duties may not be guilty of solicitation, their too-energetic encouragement may constitute entrapment (see chapter 7).

C A S E

Did He Solicit His Wife's Murder?

State v. Furr,
292 N.C. 711, 235 S.E.2d 193 (1977)

Furr was convicted of three counts of soliciting to commit his wife's murder. He was sentenced to three consecutive eight- to ten-year prison terms—one for each solicitation. He appealed and the North Carolina Supreme Court affirmed. Justice Exum wrote the opinion for the court.

FACTS

The defendant and his wife had been married about 21 years and had four children when they separated in 1973. After the separation, Furr moved his real estate office from their home to a nearby location near the square in Locust, North Carolina. His wife, Earlene, continued to live at the house on Willow Drive and

Furr moved into Western Hills Mobile Home Park. The couple's relationship was apparently quite volatile and Furr exhibited increasing hostility towards Earlene after the separation.

In April, 1973, Earlene filed a civil action against defendant resulting in a judgment against him in October, 1973. A year later, on his wife's motion, defendant was adjudged to be in contempt and was committed to jail. While in Stanly County jail, Furr met Raymond Clontz and Donald Owens, and related his marital problems to them, especially his concern over the property dispute. He was released from jail on December 6, 1974, upon payment of $13,623.00. After his release, Furr approached Clontz and Owens, drove them by Earlene's home and explained how to get into the house. He offered Owens $3,000.00 to kill Earlene and offered to give Clontz a lot which the latter wanted to store cars on if Clontz would do the job. Neither man accepted the offer.

In October, 1973, defendant asked "Buck" Baker if he knew a "hit man." At the time Furr was angry because Earlene had disposed of some racing equipment. Furr also approached Donald Eugene Huneycutt on several occasions to ask whether Huneycutt knew a "hit man." In the initial encounters, Furr wanted Johny Jhue Laney killed because Laney had murdered his own wife, Doris, who was defendant's girl friend. By early 1975, however, Furr's plans extended as well to Earlene and her attorney, Charles Brown. Huneycutt told him killing women and lawyers would create "too much heat," but defendant responded that he could stand the heat and had his mother for an alibi.

Defendant also asked George Arnold Black, Jr., to kill Earlene, and drove him by the house in the fall of 1974. Like the others, Black declined the offer.

OPINION

Solicitation of another to commit a felony is a crime in North Carolina, even though the solicitation is of no effect and the crime solicited is never committed. The gravamen of the offense of soliciting lies in counseling, enticing or inducing another to commit a crime.

Defendant argues that the evidence shows only that defendant requested that Huneycutt find someone else to murder each of the three intended victims, and not that Huneycutt himself commit the crime. "Under no authority," says defendant, "is that a criminal offense." Accepting for the moment defendant's argument that defendant solicited Huneycutt only to find another "hit man," we hold that such a request constitutes the crime of solicitation to commit a felony in North Carolina. In W. LaFave and A. Scott, *Criminal Law*, 419 (1972) it is observed that

> [i]n the usual solicitation case, it is the solicitor's intention that the criminal result be directly brought about by the person he has solicited; that is, it is his intention that the crime be committed and that the other commit it as a principal in the first degree, as where A asks B to kill C. However, it would seem sufficient that A requested B to get involved in the scheme to kill C in any way which would es-

tablish B's complicity in the killing of C were that to occur. Thus it would be criminal for one person to solicit another to in turn solicit a third party, to solicit another to join a conspiracy, or to solicit another to aid and abet the commission of a crime.

Defendant further contends that there was no evidence to support three indictments alleging solicitation of Raymond Clontz to murder Earlene Furr. There is no merit to these contentions in two of the counts. Indictment Number 76–CR–700 alleges that Clontz was solicited in January to murder Furr's wife. The evidence is that during that month, shortly after both men were released from jail where defendant had been quite talkative about his marital problems, Clontz and Furr met to discuss a lot which Clontz wished to purchase. Furr said he wanted $3,000.00 for the lot and Clontz agreed to take it. Then, as Clontz related at trial Furr told him not to be so hasty, that "he would make some arrangements about the payment for the lot in another way; that he wanted me to do a job for him." Clontz told Furr that he "knew what he was talking about, but that [he] wasn't interested in it." Defendant then told him he had to go to court with his wife in a few weeks and "that he had to have something done before court time or he was going to be in serious trouble. He said his wife was already getting $250.00 a week from him, and she had possession of the house, and had his property tied up and that he had to have something done." In the context, we find no other reasonable interpretation of defendant's words on this occasion than that he was requesting Clontz to kill his wife.

Affirmed.

QUESTIONS FOR DISCUSSION

1. Can you identify Furr's *mens rea* and *actus reus*?

2. Do you think the prosecution proved them beyond a reasonable doubt?

3. Solicitation is aimed at controlling dangerous persons. Is Furr a dangerous social problem who should be punished whether or not his inducements ever came to fruition?

4. Do you think eight to ten years' imprisonment per solicitation is too little, too much, or just about enough punishment for what he did? Why or why not?

SUMMARY

Criminal laws against attempt, conspiracy, and solicitation aim primarily to prevent crime and control dangerous persons. Clear commitment to crime, measured by intent and conduct, sufficiently indicates a person's dangerousness. Persons who demonstrate their determination to commit crimes deserve punishment and justify making even some incomplete crimes punishable. If extraneous factors interrupt or frustrate completion—such as when police officers or others arrive at the scene—that fortuity should not permit would-be criminals to escape punishment. However, if perpetrators voluntarily renounce their efforts because their consciences compel them, some argue that the law should excuse them because they are no longer dangerous. Because the dangerousness of the actor, not the actuality of harm, justifies making inchoate harms criminal, most agree that it does not matter whether it was impossible to complete the harm intended. It is enough that the crime could have been committed if circumstances were as the perpetrator reasonably believed they would be.

The justification for imposing criminal liability in inchoate crimes rests, therefore, not only on the danger of potential conduct but also on the danger of individuals. When dangerousness (and not harmful result) is the criterion for punishment, it is always possible to erroneously predict who is dangerous. Available research strongly suggests that high risks of error attend any such predictions, especially when those predictions are directed toward violent behavior. This finding has led some to argue that criminal law should never punish potential harm, only past conduct.

REVIEW QUESTIONS

1. Identify and define the three inchoate offenses.

2. What two elements do all of the inchoate offenses share?

3. What is the dilemma posed by the inchoate offenses? How does the criminal law resolve this dilemma?

4. Identify the major steps in the history of the law of attempt.

5. Identify and explain the two theories of the law of criminal attempt.

6. State the *mens rea* of the crime of attempt. What criticisms of this requirement did Justice Holmes make?

7. Identify and explain the four main tests courts have adopted to determine the *actus reus* of criminal attempts.

8. Explain the difference between legal and factual impossibility in the law of criminal attempt.

9. Explain the defense of renunciation in the law of criminal attempt. What are the arguments in favor of allowing the defense?

10. Identify and describe the elements of the crime of conspiracy.

11. Identify the objectives that satisfy the requirements of the crime of conspiracy.

12. Define the Wharton rule in the law of criminal conspiracy and explain the justification for it. Why have some jurisdictions abolished the rule?

13. Identify and describe the elements of the crime of solicitation.

14. Summarize the arguments for and against having a crime of solicitation.

15. Define the *actus reus* and the *mens rea* of solicitation.

KEY TERMS

equivocality approach The theory that attempt *actus reus* requires an act that can have no other purpose than the commission of a crime.

extraneous factor A condition beyond the attempter's control.

factual impossibility The defense that some extraneous factor makes it impossible to complete a crime.

inchoate crimes Offenses based on crimes not yet completed.

legal impossibility The defense that what the actor attempted was not a crime.

Model Penal Code **standard** The precept that attempt *actus reus* requires substantial steps that strongly corroborate the actor's purpose.

physical proximity doctrine The principle that the number of remaining acts in attempt determines attempt *actus reus.*

probable desistance approach An approach that considers whether the act in attempt would naturally lead to the commission of the crime.

Wharton rule The principle that more than two parties must conspire to commit crimes that naturally involve at least two parties.

Suggested Readings

1. Jerome Hall, *General Principles of Criminal Law,* 2d ed. (Indianapolis, Ind.: Bobbs-Merrill, 1960), chap. 15. An excellent survey of attempt law. Hall includes a good history of attempt and the theoretical justifications for it, and discusses some proper limits to be placed on it.

2. George P. Fletcher, *Rethinking Criminal Law* (Boston: Little, Brown, 1978), pp. 131–205, 218–232. Contains provocative discussions about the inchoate offenses. Fletcher clearly defines the terms in considerable detail. He also assesses the inchoate crimes and participation in crime in ways that provoke considerable thought about the roles of those terms in criminal law.

3. Jessica Mitford, *The Trial of Dr. Spock* (New York: Knopf, 1969). An excellent narrative, written for the general public. It reveals much about conspiracy within the context of a real case that attracted enormous publicity.

4. American Law Institute, *Model Penal Code and Commentaries,* vol. 1 (Philadelphia: American Law Institute, 1985), pt. 1, pp. 295–328. A detailed analysis of all elements in complicity, as well as arguments for why complicity should be included in criminal law and to what extent participants should be criminally liable. This is an advanced discussion written for experts in the field but is well worth the effort to read and consider its points. In vol. 2, pt. 1, the inchoate offenses are treated similarly.

Notes

1. Rollin M. Perkins and Ronald N. Boyce, *Criminal Law,* 3d ed. (Mineola, N.Y.: Foundation Press, 1982), pp. 611–658, 700–714; American Law Institute, *Model Penal Code and Commentaries,* vol. 2 (Philadelphia: American Law Institute, 1985), pp. 293–298.

2. George P. Fletcher, *Rethinking Criminal Law* (Boston: Little, Brown, 1978), p. 131; Plato, *Laws,* trans. Trevor J. Saunders (Middlesex, England: Penguin Books, 1975), pp. 397–398; Jerome Hall, *General Principles of Criminal Law,* 2d ed. (Indianapolis, Ind.: Bobbs-Merrill, 1960), pp. 560–564.

3. Ibid., Hall.

4. Geoffrey R. Elton, *The Tudor Constitution* (Cambridge, England: Cambridge University Press, 1972), pp. 170–171.

5. Joel Samaha, *Law and Order in Historical Perspective* (New York: Academic Press, 1974); Joel Samaha, "The Recognizance in Elizabethan Law Enforcement," *American Journal of Legal History* 25 (1981): 189–204.

6. Cald. 397 (1784).

7. Sir James F. Stephen, *A History of the Criminal Law of England,* reprint (New York: Burt Franklin, 1973), p. 224.

8. Justice Moylan in *Gray v. State,* 43 Md.App. 238, 403 A.2d 853 (1979).

9. Arnold N. Enker, "*Mens Rea* and Criminal Attempt," *American Bar Foundation Research Journal* (1977):845.

10. Wayne R. LaFave and Austin W. Scott, Jr., *Criminal Law* (St. Paul, Minn.: West Publishing Co., 1972), 423.

11. *United States. v. Mandujano*, 499 F.2d 370, 374 (5th Cir. 1974); *Young v. State*, 303 Md. 298, 493 A.2d 352 (1985) (failure not an element); see also Perkins and Boyce, *Criminal Law*, pp. 612–617.

12. Enker, "*Mens Rea* and Criminal Attempt," p. 847.

13. Oliver Wendell Holmes, *The Common Law* (Boston: Little, Brown, 1963), pp. 54–55.

14. *United States v. Mandujano*, 499 F.2d 370, 375–376 (5th Cir. 1974) (more than intention required).

15. *Commonwealth v. Peaslee*, 177 Mass. 267, 59 N.E. 55 (1901); Fletcher, *Rethinking Criminal Law*, 139–140; American Law Institute, *Model Penal Code and Commentaries*, vol. 2, pp. 321–322; *People v. Acosta*, 172 A.D.2d 103, 578 N.Y.S.2d 525 (1991).

16. *Commonwealth v. Peaslee*.

17. *Bradley v. Ward*, N.Z.L.R. 471 (1955).

18. American Law Institute, *Model Penal Code and Commentaries*, vol. 2, pp. 337–346.

19. Ibid.

20. Nev.Rev.Stat. 205.055; American Law Institute, *Model Penal Code and Commentaries*, vol. 2, pp. 354–355.

21. Fernand N. Dutile and Harold F. Moore, "Mistake and Impossibility: Arranging a Marriage between Two Difficult Partners," *Northwestern University Law Review* 74 (1979): 166, 181ff.

22. *People v. Kimball*, 311 N.W.2f 343 (Mich. 1981), p. 347.

23. Ibid., pp. 346–348.

24. American Law Institute, *Model Penal Code and Commentaries*, vol. 2, pp. 356–362.

25. Ibid.; Daniel G. Moriarty, "Extending the Defense of Renunciation," *Temple Law Review* 62 (1989):1.

26. *Model Penal Code and Commentaries*, vol. 2, p. 387.

27. Jessica Mitford, *The Trial of Dr. Spock* (New York: Knopf, 1969), pp. 70–71.

28. Fletcher, *Rethinking Criminal Law*, pp. 218, 223, 225; Kentucky Rev. Stat. 427.110 (1958).

29 Concurring in *Krulewitch v. United States*, 336 U.S. 440, 445–446, 69 S.Ct. 716, 719–720, 93 L.Ed. 790 (1949).

30. *Direct Sales Co. v. United States*, 319 U.S. 703, 63 S.Ct. 1265, 87 L.Ed. 1674 (1943).

31. Ala.Gen.tat. 54–197 (1958); *Baker v. Commonwealth*, 204 Ky. 420, 264 S.W. 1069 (1924); *State v. Ameker*, 73 S.C. 330, 53 S.E. 484 (1906); *State v. Davis*, 229 S.E. 811 (1911).

32. 118 Utah 537, 223 P.2d 193 (1950); 18 U.S.C.A.; st 371 (1976); *Musser v. Utah*, 333 U.S. 95, 97, 68 S.Ct. 397, 92 L.Ed. 562 (1948).

33. *People v. Davis*, 408 Mich. 255, 290 N.W.2d 366 (1980).

34. *Model Penal Code*, § 5.03.

35. *United States v. Bruno*, 105 F.2d 921 (2d Cir. 1939).

36. *Illinois Criminal Law and Procedure* (St. Paul, Minn.: West Publishing Co., 1988), chap. 38, § 8–4.

37. Blakely and Gettings, "Racketeer Influenced and Corrupt Organizations (RICO): Basic Concepts—Criminal and Civil Remedies," *Temple Law Quarterly* 53 (1980):1013–1014.

38. 18 U.S.C.A. § 1961 et seq.

39. William Safire, "The End of RICO," *The New York Times* (January 30, 1989), p. 19.

40. American Law Institute, *Model Penal Code and Commentaries*, vol. 2, pp. 365–366.

41. LaFave and Scott, *Criminal Law*, p. 419.

42. *State v. Schleifer*, 99 Conn. 432 121 A. 805 (1923).

CHAPTER SIX

Defenses to Criminal Liability: Justifications

CHAPTER MAIN POINTS

1. In the defense of justification, defendants admit responsibility but maintain that under the circumstances what they did was right.

2. In the defenses of excuse, defendants admit what they did was wrong but maintain that under the circumstances they were not responsible.

3. Self-defense justifies the use of force or threats of force to prevent attacks from individuals who the victim honestly and reasonably believes threaten imminent death or serious bodily harm and when it is reasonable for the victim to believe that force is necessary to prevent the attack.

4. Self-defense does not justify either retaliation for past attacks or preemptive strikes to prevent future, nonimminent attacks.

5. Owners may use reasonable force, sometimes including deadly force, to defend their homes and property.

6. Law enforcement officers may use force, including deadly force, when it is reasonable to use such force in order to uphold the criminal law.

7. In a few jurisdictions, citizens may use force (but not deadly force) to prevent an unlawful arrest.

8. The defense of necessity justifies otherwise criminal conduct (a lesser evil) when the commission of the lesser offense avoids a greater imminent evil.

9. Voluntary, knowing consent of the victim is a defense to minor assaults in some jurisdictions.

Was He Justified in Shooting?

Canty approached Goetz, possibly with Allen beside him, and said to Goetz, "Give me five dollars." Goetz stated that he knew from the smile on Canty's face that they wanted to "play with me." Although he was certain that none of the youths had a gun, he had a fear, based on prior experiences, of being "maimed." Goetz then established "a pattern of fire," deciding specifically to fire from left to right. His stated intention at that point was to "murder [the four youths], to hurt them, to make them suffer as much as possible." When Canty again requested money, Goetz stood up, drew his weapon, and began firing, aiming for the center of the body of each of the four. Goetz recalled that the first two he shot "tried to run through the crowd [but] they had nowhere to run." Goetz then turned to his right to "go after the other two." Cabey "tried pretending that he wasn't with [the others]" by standing still, holding on to one of the subway hand straps, and not looking at Goetz. Goetz nonetheless fired his fourth shot at him. He then ran back to the first two youths to make sure they had been "taken care of." Seeing that they had both been shot, he spun back to check on the other two. Goetz noticed that the youth who had been standing still was now sitting on a bench and seemed unhurt. As Goetz told the police, "I said '[y]ou seem to be all right, here's another,'" and he fired the shot which severed Cabey's spinal cord. Goetz added that "if I was a little more under self-control . . . I would have put the barrel against his forehead and fired." He also admitted that "if I had had more [bullets], I would have shot them again, and again, and again."

INTRODUCTION

In all criminal cases, the government has the **burden of proof**. This means that the prosecution must prove all of the elements of criminal liability—*actus reus, mens rea,* and, where relevant, causing a particular result—beyond a reasonable doubt. The **defenses** allow defendants to avoid criminal liability even when the government has met its burden to prove the elements beyond a reasonable doubt. Defenses are of three types:

1. **Alibi.** Defendants prove that they were in a different place than the scene of the crime at the time the crime was committed, and it was therefore impossible for them to have committed the crime.

2. **Justifications** (the subject of this chapter). Defendants accept responsibility for the crime but claim that what they did was right under the circumstances.

3. **Excuses** (the subject of chapter 7). Defendants admit that what they did was wrong but argue that under the circumstances they were not responsible for what they did.[1]

According to the principle of justification, some circumstances justify otherwise criminal conduct and the causing of criminal harms. Justified conduct does not deserve punishment because such behavior lacks blameworthiness. For example, it is wrong to blame—hence, to punish—one who has killed an attacker in self-defense. The argument of the defense runs something like this: I intended to kill my attacker and as a result he died. But under the circumstances (being forced to choose between his life and mine) it was right to kill him. Similarly, it is not fair to punish those who are insane. For example, it is not right to punish a woman who is so mentally diseased that she thought she was squeezing a lemon when, in fact, she was choking her husband to death. The argument of the defense of insanity runs something like this: I admit that killing my husband was wrong no matter what I was thinking. However, because I am insane I was not responsible for killing him. (See chapter 7.) The distinguished professor of criminal law, George Fletcher, sums up the difference between justification and excuse this way: "A justification speaks to the rightfulness of the act; an excuse, to whether the actor is accountable for a concededly wrongful act."[2]

Most of the justifications and excuses are **affirmative defenses.** Affirmative defenses require that defendants bear some burden in presenting evidence to support it. In effect, an affirmative defense admits the crime charged but, according to the authors of a leading treatise on the criminal law, Professors LaFave and Scott, "seeks to justify, excuse, or mitigate the defendant's conduct." In all jurisdictions, defendants bear the **burden of production,** that is, defendants are "obliged to start matters off by putting in some evidence in support" of the defense. According to LaFave and Scott, "We can assume that those who commit crimes are sane, sober, conscious, and acting freely. It makes sense, therefore, to make defendants responsible for injecting these extraordinary circumstances into the proceedings." The amount of evidence required "is not great; some credible evidence" suffices. Once defendants meet the burden of production by introducing some evidence of justification or excuse, they may or may not have the further **burden of persuasion,** that is, the responsibility to prove justification or excuse. Typically, jurisdictions require defendants to prove their defenses by a preponderance of the evidence, that is, by proving that more evidence than not supports justification or excuse. Occasionally, jurisdictions require that once defendants meet the burden of persuasion, the burden shifts to the prosecution to prove beyond a reasonable doubt that the defendant did not have the defense.[3]

Perfect defenses, such as self-defense successfully pleaded, lead to outright acquittal — the defendant "walks." Sometimes, evidence that does not amount to a perfect defense results in conviction for a lesser charge, such as when provocation reduces murder to manslaughter. **Imperfect defense** can mean the difference between death or life imprisonment for murder and ten to twenty years for manslaughter (see chapter 8). The defense of insanity, even if successfully pleaded, ordinarily does not set defendants free, at least not automatically. Special insanity hearings follow insanity verdicts. The outcome of these hearings is to send most defendants to maximum-security hospitals until they regain their sanity. Often, defendants never regain their sanity; they remain committed for life to maximum-security hospitals (see chapter 7).

Even when defenses do not lead either to acquittal or to conviction for lesser crimes, they may still influence punishment. Evidence that does not amount to a perfect or imperfect defense might still demonstrate that there are **mitigating circumstances,** that is, information that convinces judges or juries that defendants do not deserve the maximum penalty for the crimes they committed. For example, if a state authorized the death penalty for first-degree murder, a murderer who killed without *legal* provocation might still get life imprisonment instead of the death penalty. Although words, however provocative, do not amount to legal provocation that reduces murder to manslaughter, they are a mitigating circumstance that might reduce capital punishment to life imprisonment. Hence, if an African-American person killed someone in an outburst of rage brought about by the victim's relentless taunting with the racist epithet "nigger," the taunting might mitigate the death penalty (see chapter 8).

Motive also influences punishment, or even conviction itself in some cases. **Motive** refers to the reason why individuals commit crimes. Criminal law distinguishes it from *mens rea*, which refers to intention. *Mens rea* reveals whether defendants acted or caused a result purposely, knowingly, recklessly, or negligently. Suppose a burglar purposely breaks into and enters a house with the intent to steal food because he is hungry. Hunger is the motive; breaking and entering with the intent to steal food is the *mens rea*. Mercy killing also illustrates both *mens rea* and motive: The mercy killer kills on purpose in order to ease the victim's suffering. The law does not recognize motive in most instances; *mens rea* suffices. However, motive might aid in proving *mens rea*: Knowing that defendant killed to end the victim's suffering helps prove purpose and knowledge.

The motive of mercy might also affect conviction and punishment. A jury might refuse to convict a mercy killer of first-degree murder even though the *mens rea* clearly exists — the premeditated, purposeful causing of another's death (see chapter 8). The murder conviction of Robert Latimer is a good example of this. Robert Latimer could no longer stand the constant pain from which his twelve-year-old daughter, Tracy Latimer, was suffering because of her incurably severe case of cerebral palsy. She wore diapers, weighed only 38 pounds, and could not walk, talk, or feed herself. So, he put her into the cab of his pickup truck on the family farm and pumped the exhaust into the cab of the truck. He told the police he stood by, ready to stop if Tracy started to cry, but that Tracy simply went quietly "to sleep. My priority was to put her out of her pain." He pleaded not guilty to first-degree murder, but the jury found him guilty of second-degree murder. Despite the verdict of guilty on the lesser charge, many people in the town agreed with an eighteen-year-old high school student who said Latimer "did what he had to do for his daughter's sake. And that's the way a lot of people in town are feeling."[4]

Or, a judge might reduce the sentence to a minimum, and corrections officials might parole the mercy killer at the earliest possible date. For example, seventy-eight-year-old Oscar Carlson, who could no longer endure his wife's suffering from advanced Alzheimer's disease, shot and killed his wife. On his first day in prison, Carlson said, "I know it's better for me to sit here in prison than for Agnes to sit up there in the home like she was." A barrage of negative publicity surrounded his sentence to prison, generating considerable sympathy for the elderly murderer and leading to his early release.[5]

SELF-DEFENSE

Self-defense is the use of force to prevent attacks against individuals, their homes, and their property. It involves self-help, the classic example of "taking the law into your own hands." In allowing individuals to take the law into their own hands, self-defense conflicts with a fundamental part of criminal law in a constitutional democracy — the rule of law. The rule of law requires that the government have a monopoly on the use of force. But that monopoly carries with it the obligation to protect people from illegal attacks. Sometimes, agents of the government are not there when they are needed. Self-defense, and the defense of homes and property, allows individuals to use force to protect themselves, their homes, and their property in those circumstances when the government cannot fulfill its obligation to do it for them.

Self-defense, as the term suggests, is a defensive action. Those who rely on it need to act right *now* because if they do not, they themselves, others, their homes, or their property will be attacked. Self-defense does not extend to preemptive strikes; that is, the law does not justify attacks intended to ward off some *future* attack. Nor does self-defense embrace retaliation, that is, the use of force to "pay back" an assailant for a *past* attack. In short, self-defense is about protective action required and taken right now. Preemptive strikes come too soon and retaliation comes too late. Individuals must rely on other means to prevent future attacks, and only the state can legally punish past attacks.[6]

Elements of Self-Defense

The law of self-defense defines the conditions under which individuals can disregard the monopoly of force held by the government, and "take the law into their own hands." These conditions strictly limit when individuals may engage in violent self-help. At common law, self-defense was defined as follows:

> A man may repel force by force in the defense of his person, habitation, or property, against one or many who manifestly intend and endeavor, by violence or surprise, to commit a known felony on either. In such a case he is not obliged to retreat, but may pursue his adversary until he finds himself out of danger; and if, in a conflict between them, he happens to kill, such killing is justifiable. The right of self-defense in cases of this kind is founded on the law of nature; and is not, nor can be, superseded by any law of society. . . . To make homicide excusable on the ground of self-defense, the danger must be actual and urgent.[7]

ELEMENTS OF SELF DEFENSE

Reasonable Belief of Imminent Danger of	*Reasonable Use of Force to Protect Against*
1. Death **or**	1. Death **or**
2. Serious bodily harm **or**	2. Serious bodily injury **or**
3. Specific felonies, such as rape, sodomy, kidnapping, robbery, in some jurisdictions	3. Specific felonies in some jurisdictions

The modern law of self-defense legally justifies the use of force only under the following conditions:

1. *Reasonable belief in imminent danger.* Defenders reasonably believe that they, others, their homes, or their property are in imminent danger from the use of unlawful force.

2. *Reasonable use of force.* Defenders use only the amount of force that is reasonably necessary to repel the imminent unlawful attack.

We usually think of self-defense as the killing of assailants who threaten to kill defenders. However, self-defense is not simply the justifiable use of deadly force in order to repel a deadly attack. Less-than-deadly attacks justify the resort to less-than-deadly responses. Hence, self-defense can justify the use of force in all crimes against persons, including homicide, rape, other assaults, battery, and kidnapping. The common element in all of these crimes is threats to persons. Self-defense also applies to defending homes and property, but ordinarily the defense of property justifies only the use of nondeadly force.

Defender-Provoked Attacks. Self-defense requires that defenders honestly and reasonably believe that they, others, their homes, or their property are in imminent danger. However, self-defense does not require that defenders face actual danger. For example, if an attacker threatens a victim with an unloaded gun that the potential victim has no way of knowing is not loaded, the belief in danger is reasonable even if it is not real.

In most instances, defenders who provoke attacks cannot later claim that they were defending themselves. However, if attackers completely withdraw from the fights they start, they can forcibly defend themselves against a subsequent attack by their initial victims. Thus, in one case a small man attacked a much larger man with a knife. He soon realized that he had taken on too much, so he retreated in an effort to escape. But to no avail. The larger man, by then thoroughly angered, pursued him relentlessly. Unable to escape, the smaller man finally stood his ground and, in the process, stabbed his attacker to death. He was acquitted on self-defense because the jury was satisfied that he "withdrew in good faith" and had not merely retreated in order to regain enough strength to resume the attack. The court dealt with the issue of self-defense to provoked attacks in *Jackson v. State.*[8]

CASE

Did He Provoke the Attack?

State v. Jackson,
936 P.2d 761 (Kan. 1997)

Defendant Robert L. Jackson was convicted on two counts of first-degree murder, one count of voluntary manslaughter, two counts of aggravated battery, one count of unlawful possession of a firearm, one count of criminal damage to property, and one count of criminal trespass. All but the misdemeanor sentences were imposed to run consecutively. Jackson appealed his convictions and sentences, claiming the trial court erred by, among other things, failing to instruct on self-defense. The supreme court affirmed the murder conviction and the sentence.

LOCKETT, Justice.

FACTS

At approximately 12:45 A.M. on April 8, 1994, Robert Jackson left the home of Jamie Brown for Shanghi Lil's, a nightclub in Topeka, Kansas. As Jackson left, Brown noticed Jackson had a gun.

Tracy Freel and Heidi Childers, dancers at a nightclub called Teezers, went to Shanghi Lil's to meet Childers' boyfriend, Scott Wilson, who worked there as a bouncer. At Shanghi Lil's, Childers and Freel were approached by Jackson, who tried to pick them up. Jackson also made comments of a sexual nature to Childers, Freel, and other women in the club. After an announcement that the club was closing, Jackson lingered at the bar and attempted to persuade Childers and Freel to leave with him. They declined.

When Matt Fabry, a bouncer at the club, told Jackson it was time to leave the club because the club was closing, Jackson refused to leave. Fabry grabbed Jackson by the shoulder to escort him out and again told Jackson to leave. Jackson struck Fabry and knocked him to the floor.

As Jon Stratton, a patron at the club, intervened to assist Fabry, Jackson took a black automatic pistol from his waistband and shot Fabry in the chest and arm. Fabry was unarmed. Jackson then shot Stratton

in the right side. Dan Rutherford, the club's disc jockey, jumped over a brass rail to assist Fabry. Jackson shot Rutherford twice in the face. Jackson backed out of the inner doors of the club, returned, and shot Rutherford two or three more times. Jackson then straddled the fallen Fabry and asked, "You want some more of this, motherfucker?"

When Scott Wilson attempted to push Jackson out the door, Jackson started firing again. Alan Eastman, a customer, attempted to escape out the door. Jackson turned and shot Eastman in the thigh. After Jackson shot Eastman, the club manager, John Iturralde, left his office in the back of the club carrying a .45 caliber handgun. After more shots were fired by Jackson, Iturralde took cover behind the bar. Iturralde testified that he never fired his gun.

Wilson threw Childers to the floor to protect her, and she landed next to Jon Stratton. While on the floor, she felt a burning and stinging on her leg and saw a bruise forming across her right leg going over to her left leg and a tear in her knee.

Brenda Strahm, an acquaintance of Jackson's, heard a loud noise at her front door in the early morning hours of April 8, 1994. She opened the door and saw Jackson standing there. She let Jackson in and returned to her bedroom. Later she heard a gunshot. After Jackson fell asleep in Strahm's kitchen, she took her children, left the house, went to a nearby service station, and called 911. The police found Jackson asleep in Strahm's house, arrested him, and confiscated a 9 mm Taurus handgun found next to Jackson.

The police also found an empty 9 mm Norinco handgun underneath Dan Rutherford's body at the club. Seven cartridges fired from the Norinco were found at the club. A total of 21 shell casings were recovered. Hugh Kizer, a KBI firearms expert who testified at trial regarding the ballistics evidence, stated that at least 15 of the 21 spent cartridges found in the club were fired by a 9 mm Taurus pistol and 7 of the shell casings were fired by a Norinco handgun. The evidence was inconclusive as to whether the bullets and bullet fragments recovered after the incident were fired from the Norinco or the Taurus handgun.

Dr. Eric Mitchell performed post mortem examinations on the three persons killed during the shooting. Jon Stratton died from a single bullet wound. The bullet which killed Stratton came from the Norinco. Matt Fabry sustained bullet wounds to the right arm, chest, and right side. A bullet fragment taken from Fabry's body was fired by the Norinco handgun. Dan Rutherford sustained multiple wounds to his left hand, face, right arm, right armpit, as well as three wounds to right side of chest and wounds to his right hand and left arm. Analysis of bullets taken from Rutherford's body indicated they had not been fired by the Norinco handgun and tests were inconclusive regarding the Taurus handgun.

Prior to trial, Jackson pled to unlawful possession of a firearm. Jackson presented no evidence at trial and did not allege someone else shot the victims. Jackson was convicted of the firstdegree murders of Matt Fabry and Dan Rutherford and voluntary manslaughter of Jon Stratton. He was also convicted of aggravated battery of Alan Eastman, aggravated battery of Heidi Childers, unlawful possession of a firearm, misdemeanor criminal damage to property, and criminal trespass.

OPINION

Jackson argues the district court erred by failing to instruct the jury on self-defense as to the shooting and deaths of Matt Fabry, Dan Rutherford, and Jon Stratton. It is the duty of the trial court to instruct the jury on self-defense so long as there is evidence tending to establish self-defense. In order to rely on self-defense as a defense, a person must have a belief that the force used was necessary to defend himself and, also, show the existence of facts that support such a belief.

Jackson's claim that he was entitled to a self-defense instruction ignores the statutory requirements for giving a self-defense instruction. K.S.A. 213211 provides: "A person is justified in the use of force against an aggressor when and to the extent it appears to him and he reasonably believes that such conduct is necessary to defend himself or another against such aggressor's imminent use of unlawful force." However, K.S.A. 213214(3) states that the justification for using force in self-defense is not available to a person who:

Otherwise initially provokes the use of force against himself or another, unless:

(a) He has reasonable ground to believe that he is in imminent danger of death or great bodily harm, and he has exhausted every reasonable means to escape such danger other than the use of force which is likely to cause death or great bodily harm to the assailant; or

(b) In good faith, he withdraws from physical contact with the assailant and indicates clearly to the assailant that he desires to withdraw and terminate the use of force, but the assailant continues or resumes the use of force.

Here, it was uncontroverted that Jackson was the initial aggressor. The facts indicated that Jackson was told to leave the club more than once. After Fabry placed his hand on Jackson and asked Jackson to leave the club, Jackson struck and then shot the unarmed Fabry. After shooting Fabry, Jackson then shot Rutherford and Stratton as they came to assist Fabry. Fabry and Stratton were unarmed. Although there is evidence that Rutherford had a gun, there was no testimony that Rutherford fired the gun. Jackson, the initial aggressor, made no effort to withdraw, escape, or avoid the killings. Jackson's claim that he was entitled to a self-defense instruction is without merit.

. . .

Jackson's convictions and other sentences are affirmed.

QUESTIONS FOR DISCUSSION

1. List all of the facts relevant to determining whether Jackson provoked the attack.

2. Exactly what is the effect of provoked attacks on self-defense in Kansas?

3. What is the rationale for the rule of provoked attacks?

4. Do you support it? Defend your answer.

NOTE CASE

Townshend and some of his friends were rabbit hunting near the deceased's farm. Their automobiles were parked on the side of a public road near decedent's home. After the day's hunting was over and while the hunters were standing in the road attempting to get their dogs in their respective cars, they were fired upon with a shotgun from the direction of decedent's home. Some of the buckshot struck Townshend but did not injure him. Townshend placed his shotgun inside his motor vehicle without unloading it and started home.

As Townshend approached the decedent's house, which was on the road Townshend was traveling, the decedent was in his front yard talking to another man. Townshend stopped his car and asked why decedent had fired upon him. Decedent denied firing the shotgun whereupon Townshend called him a "god-damned-liar." Decedent then whirled around and started toward Townshend, bending forward in a crouching manner. At some point in time Townshend got out of his car. As the decedent advanced upon him, Townshend repeatedly told him not to come any closer. He backed up to his car, reached inside and obtained his shotgun and told decedent if he came any closer he would have to shoot him. Decedent continued to advance toward Townshend with his hand inside his shirt front and Townshend testified that he thought he saw an object resembling a pistol in decedent's hand. Townshend shot decedent and then struck him in the head with the butt of the shotgun. No weapon was discovered on the body of the decedent.

Did Townshend provoke the attack? Townshend was convicted of voluntary manslaughter. On appeal, the Kentucky Supreme Court affirmed the conviction:

> One who by his words and acts provokes and brings about a fight cannot claim self defense. The law does not allow a man to create a bad or dangerous situation and then fight his way out. The evidence in this case did not conclusively establish that the shooting was done in self defense and that issue was therefore properly submitted to the jury. *Townshend v. Commonwealth*, 474 S.W.2d 352 (Ky.1971)

Defense Against Felonies. Some states have added to the danger of death or serious bodily harm the danger of the commission, or the attempt to commit, certain felonies. These felonies are usually crimes against persons, such as rape, sodomy, kidnapping, and robbery. The court in *People v. Goetz* dealt with the problem of honest and reasonable belief under such a statute.[9]

C A S E

Did He Shoot in Self-Defense?

People v. Goetz,
68 N.Y.2d 96, 506 N.Y.S.2d 18,
497 N.E.2d 41 (1986)

A Grand Jury indicted Goetz on attempted murder, assault, and other charges for having shot and wounded four youths on a New York City subway train after one or two of the youths approached him and asked for $5. The lower courts, concluding that the prosecutor's charge to the Grand Jury on the defense of justification was erroneous, dismissed the attempted murder, assault, and weapons possessions charges. The supreme court reversed and reinstated all counts of the indictment. Chief Justice Watchler delivered the opinion.

FACTS

The precise circumstances of the incident giving rise to the charges against defendant are disputed, and ultimately it will be for a trial jury to determine what occurred. We feel it necessary, however, to provide some factual background to properly frame legal issues before us. . . .

On Saturday afternoon, December 22, 1984, Troy Canty, Darryl Cabey, James Ramseur, and Barry

Allen boarded an IRT express subway train in The Bronx and headed south toward lower Manhattan. The four youths rode together in the rear portion of the seventh car of the train. Two of the four, Ramseur and Cabey, had screw drivers inside their coats, which they said were to be used to break into the coin boxes of video machines.

Defendant Bernhard Goetz boarded this subway train at 14th Street in Manhattan and sat down on a bench towards the rear section of the same car occupied by the four youths. Goetz was carrying an unlicensed .38 caliber pistol loaded with five rounds of ammunition in a waistband holster. The train left the 14th Street station and headed towards Chambers Street.

It appears from the evidence before the Grand Jury that Canty approached Goetz, possibly with Allen beside him, and stated "give me five dollars." Neither Canty nor any of the other youths displayed a weapon. Goetz responded by standing up, pulling out his handgun and firing four shots in rapid succession. The first shot hit Canty in the chest; the second struck Allen in the back; the third went through Ramseur's arm and into his left side; the fourth was fired at Cabey, who apparently was then standing in the corner of the car, but missed, deflecting instead off of a wall of the conductor's cab. After Goetz briefly surveyed the scene around him, he fired another shot at Cabey, who was then sitting on the end bench of the car. The bullet entered the rear of Cabey's side and severed his spinal cord.

All but two of the passengers fled the car when, or immediately after, the shots were fired. The conductor, who had been in the next car, heard the shots and instructed the motorman to radio for emergency assistance. The conductor then went into the car where the shooting occurred and saw Goetz sitting on a bench, the injured youths lying on the floor or slumped against a seat, and two women who had apparently taken cover, also lying on the floor. Goetz told the conductor that the four youths had tried to rob him.

While the conductor was aiding the youths, Goetz headed towards the front of the car. The train had stopped just before the Chambers Street station and Goetz went between two of the cars, jumped onto the tracks, and fled. Police and ambulance crews arrived at the scene shortly thereafter. Ramseur and Canty, initially listed in critical condition, have fully recovered. Cabey remains paralyzed, and has suffered some degree of brain damage.

On December 31, 1984, Goetz surrendered to police in Concord, New Hampshire. . . . Later that day, after receiving Miranda warnings, he made two lengthy statements, both of which were tape recorded with his permission. In his statements, which are substantially similar, Goetz admitted that he had been illegally carrying a handgun in New York City for three years. He stated that he had first purchased a gun in 1981 after he had been injured in a mugging. Goetz also revealed that twice between 1981 and 1984 he had successfully warded off assailants simply by displaying the pistol.

According to Goetz's statement, the first contact he had with the four youths came when Canty, sitting or lying on the bench across from him, asked "how are you," to which he replied "fine." Shortly thereafter, Canty, followed by one of the other youths, walked over to the defendant and stood to his left, while the other two youths remained to his right, in the corner of the subway car. Canty then said "give me five dollars." Goetz stated that he knew from the smile on Canty's face that they wanted to "play with me." Although he was certain that none of the youths had a gun, he had a fear, based on prior experiences, of being "maimed."

Goetz then established "a pattern of fire," deciding specifically to fire from left to right. His stated intention at that point was to "murder [the four youths], to hurt them, to make them suffer as much as possible." When Canty again requested money, Goetz stood up, drew his weapon, and began firing, aiming for the center of the body of each of the four. Goetz recalled that the first two he shot "tried to run through the crowd [but] they had nowhere to run." Goetz then turned to his right to "go after the other two." One of these two "tried to run through the wall of the train, but . . . he had nowhere to go." The other youth (Cabey) "tried pretending that he wasn't with [the others]" by standing still, holding on to one of the subway hand straps, and not looking at Goetz. Goetz nonetheless fired his fourth shot at him. He then ran back to the first two youths to make sure they had been "taken care of." Seeing that they had both been shot, he spun back to check on the other two. Goetz noticed that the youth who had been standing still was now sitting on a bench and seemed unhurt. As Goetz told the police, "I said '[y]ou seem to be all right, here's another,'" and he fired the shot which severed Cabey's spinal cord. Goetz added that "if I was a little more under self-control . . . I would have put the barrel against his forehead and fired." He also admitted that "if I had had more [bullets], I would have shot them again, and again, and again."

After waiving extradition, Goetz was brought back to New York and arraigned on a felony complaint charging him with attempted murder and criminal possession of a weapon. The matter was presented to a Grand Jury in January 1985, with the prosecutor seeking an indictment for attempted murder, assault, reckless endangerment, and criminal possession of a weapon. . . . [T]he Grand Jury indicted defendant on one count of criminal possession of a weapon in the third degree for possessing the gun used in the subway shootings, and two counts of criminal possession of a weapon in the fourth degree. . . . It dismissed, however, the attempted murder and other charges stemming from the shootings themselves.

Several weeks after the Grand Jury's action, the People, asserting that they had newly available evidence, moved for an order authorizing them to resubmit the dismissed charges to a second Grand Jury. . . . [T]he second Grand Jury filed a 10-count indictment, containing four charges of attempted murder, four charges of assault in the first degree, one charge of reckless endangerment in the first degree, and one charge of criminal possession of a weapon in the second degree. . . .

On October 14, 1985, Goetz moved to dismiss the charges contained in the second indictment alleging, among other things, that the evidence before the second Grand Jury was not legally sufficient to establish the offenses charged and that the prosecutor's instructions to that Grand Jury on the defense of justification were erroneous and prejudicial to the defendant so as to render its proceedings defective.

On November 25, 1985, while the motion to dismiss was pending before Criminal Term, a column

appeared in the *New York Daily News* containing an interview which the columnist had conducted with Darryl Cabey the previous day in Cabey's hospital room. The columnist claimed that Cabey had told him in this interview that the other three youths had all approached Goetz with the intention of robbing him. . . .

. . . The court, after inspection of the Grand Jury minutes, . . . held . . . that the prosecutor, in a supplemental charge elaborating upon the justification defense, had erroneously introduced an objective element into this defense by instructing the grand jurors to consider whether Goetz's conduct was that of a "reasonable man in [Goetz's] situation." The court . . . concluded that the statutory test for whether the use of deadly force is justified to protect a person should be wholly subjective, focusing entirely on the defendant's state of mind when he used such force. It concluded that dismissal was required for this error because the justification issue was at the heart of the case. . . .

On appeal by the People, a divided Appellate Division affirmed Criminal Term's dismissal of the charges. . . .

Justice Asch, in a dissenting opinion in which Justice Wallach concurred, disagreed with both bases for dismissal relied upon by Criminal Term. On the justification question, he opined that the statute requires consideration of both the defendant's subjective beliefs and whether a reasonable person in defendant's situation would have had such beliefs. . . . Justice Wallach stressed that the plurality's adoption of a purely subjective test effectively eliminated any reasonableness requirement contained in the statute.

Justice Asch granted the People leave to appeal to this court.

OPINION

Penal Law article 35 recognizes the defense of justification, which "permits the use of force under certain circumstances." . . . Penal Law § 35.15 (1) sets forth the general principles governing all such uses of force:

> [a] person may . . . use physical force upon another person when and to the extent he *reasonably believes* such to be necessary to defend

himself or a third person from what he *reasonably believes* to be the use or imminent use of unlawful physical force by such other person. [emphasis added]

§ 35.15 (2) . . . A person may not use deadly physical force upon another person under circumstances specified in subdivision one unless (a) He *reasonably believes* that such other person is using or about to use deadly physical force . . . or (b) He *reasonably believes* that such other person is committing or attempting to commit a kidnapping, forcible rape, forcible sodomy or robbery. [emphasis added]

Thus, consistent with most justification provisions, Penal Law § 35.15 permits the use of deadly physical force only where requirements as to triggering conditions and the necessity of a particular response are met. As to the triggering of conditions, the statute requires that the actor "reasonably believes" that another person either is using or about to use deadly physical force or is committing or attempting to commit one of certain enumerated felonies, including robbery. As to the need for the use of deadly physical force as a response, the statute requires that the actor "reasonably believes" that such force is necessary to avert the perceived threat.

Because the evidence before the second Grand Jury included statements by Goetz that he acted to protect himself from being maimed or to avert robbery, the prosecutor correctly chose to charge the justification defense. . . . The prosecutor properly instructed the grand jurors to consider whether the use of deadly physical force was justified to prevent, either serious physical injury or a robbery, and, in doing so, to separately analyze the defense with respect to each of the charges. . . .

When the prosecutor had completed his charge, one of the grand jurors asked for clarification of the term "reasonably believes." The prosecutor responded by instructing the grand jurors that they were to consider the circumstances of the incident and determine "whether the defendant's conduct was that of a reasonable man in the defendant's situation." It is this response by the prosecutor—and specifically his use of "a reasonable man"—which is the basis for the dis-

missal of the charges by the lower courts. As expressed repeatedly in the Appellate Division's plurality opinion, because § 35.15 uses the term "he reasonably believes," the appropriate test, according to that court, is whether a defendant's beliefs and reactions were "reasonable to him." Under that reading of the statute, a jury which believed a defendant's testimony that he felt that his own actions were warranted and were reasonable would have to acquit him, regardless of what anyone else in defendant's situation might have concluded. Such an interpretation defies the ordinary meaning and significance of the term "reasonably" in a statute, and misconstrues the clear intent of the Legislature, in enacting § 35.15, to retain an objective element as part of any provision authorizing the use of deadly physical force. . . .

We cannot lightly impute to the Legislature an intent to fundamentally alter the principles of justification to allow the perpetrator of a serious crime to go free simply because the person believed his actions were reasonable and necessary to prevent some perceived harm. To completely exonerate such an individual, no matter how aberrational or bizarre his thought patterns, would allow citizens to set their own standards for the permissible use of force. It would also allow a legally competent defendant suffering from delusions to kill or perform acts of violence with impunity, contrary to fundamental principles of justice and criminal law.

We can only conclude that the Legislature retained a reasonableness requirement to avoid giving a license for such actions. The plurality's interpretation, as the dissenters . . . recognized, excises the impact of the word "reasonably." . . .

Accordingly, the order of the Appellate Division should be reversed, and the dismissed counts of the indictment reinstated.

QUESTIONS FOR DISCUSSION

New York tried Goetz for attempted murder and assault. The jury acquitted him of both charges. The jury said Goetz "was justified in shooting the four men with a silver-plated .38-caliber revolver he purchased in Florida." They did convict him of illegal possession of a firearm, for which the court sentenced Goetz to one year in jail. Following the sentencing, Goetz told the court that

> [t]his case is really more about the deterioration of society than it is about me. . . . I believe society needs to be protected from criminals.[10]

Criminal law professor George Fletcher followed the trial closely. After the acquittal, he commented that

> [t]he facts of the Goetz case were relatively clear, but the primary fight was over the moral interpretation of the facts. . . . I am not in the slightest bit convinced that the four young men were about to mug Goetz. If he had said, "Listen buddy, I wish I had $5, but I don't," and walked to the other side of the car the chances are 60-40 nothing would have happened. Street-wise kids like that are more attuned to the costs of their behavior than Goetz was.[11]

1. If Professor Fletcher is right, was Goetz justified in shooting?

2. Under what circumstances can people use deadly force, according to the New York statutes cited in the opinion?

3. Do you agree with those circumstances?

4. Would you add more? Remove some? Which ones? Why?

5. Were Goetz's shots a preemptive strike? Retaliation? Necessary for self-protection? Explain.

Excessive Force. Self-defense prohibits the use of *excessive* force. That is to say, defenders may use only the amount of force that they reasonably believe is necessary to repel an attack. If someone slaps my face, I cannot shoot my assailant. Defenders may use only nondeadly force to repel a nondeadly attack; they may use deadly force only to prevent death or grievous bodily harm. It is always reasonable to use nondeadly force to repel deadly force. Threatened force is justified to stave off threatened physical injury and is reasonable to stop attacks in progress, whether deadly or not. However ominous, threats by themselves do not justify using physical force. For example, a prisoner threatened another prisoner with sodomy if the prisoner did not immediately pay back a loan. The prisoner stabbed his would-be sodomizer. The court held that mere threats do not justify preventive assaults.[12]

Imminent Attacks. Only the danger of *imminent* attacks, that is attacks that are either in progress or that are going to happen *now,* justify the use of force. So, in one case, after a street gang member threw a brick at a cabdriver from the far side of an intersection, the driver justifiably shot into the gang because, despite their distance, they could have killed the driver at any moment. It is sometimes argued that *present* danger (that is danger that is continuing but not necessarily immediately pending) should suffice and that self-defense should not require immediate or imminent danger. For example, if an assailant leaves the scene to get reinforcements so that she can continue an attack to better advantage, the victim is not in immediate danger because the attack is not on the verge of happening. According to the *Model Penal Code* self-defense ought to permit the use of force to repel present danger. A few states, such as Delaware, Hawaii, New Jersey, Nebraska, and Pennsylvania, have followed the *Model Penal Code*, substituting present for imminent danger. Most states, however, retain the immediate or imminent danger requirement. The court dealt with the problem of imminent and present danger in *State v. Stewart*.[13]

C A S E

Was She in "Imminent" Danger?

State v. Stewart,
243 Kan. 639, 763 P.2d 572 (1988)

Stewart was charged with the first degree murder of her husband. A jury found her not guilty. The prosecution appealed. The Kansas supreme court sustained the appeal. Justice Lockett wrote the opinion of the court. Chief Justice Prager and Justice Herd dissented.

FACTS

. . . Following an annulment from her first husband and two subsequent divorces in which she was the petitioner, Peggy Stewart married Mike Stewart in 1974. Evidence at trial disclosed a long history of abuse by Mike against Peggy and her two daughters from one of her prior marriages. Laura, one of Peggy's daughters, testified that early in the marriage Mike hit and kicked Peggy, and that after the first year of marriage Peggy exhibited signs of severe psychological problems. Subsequently, Peggy was hospitalized and diagnosed as having symptoms of paranoid schizophrenia; she responded to treatment and was soon released. It appeared to Laura, however, that Mike was encouraging Peggy to take more than her prescribed dosage of medication.

In 1977, two social workers informed Peggy that they had received reports that Mike was taking indecent liberties with her daughters. Because the social workers did not want Mike to be left alone with the girls, Peggy quit her job. In 1978, Mike began to taunt Peggy by stating that Carla, her 12-year-old daughter, was "more of a wife" to him than Peggy.

Later, Carla was placed in a detention center, and Mike forbade Peggy and Laura to visit her. When Mike finally allowed Carla to return home in the middle of summer, he forced her to sleep in an un-air-conditioned room with the windows nailed shut, to wear a heavy flannel nightgown, and to cover herself with heavy blankets. Mike would then wake Carla at 5:30 A.M. and force her to do all the housework. Peggy and Laura were not allowed to help Carla or speak to her.

When Peggy confronted Mike and demanded that the situation cease, Mike responded by holding a shotgun to Peggy's head and threatening to kill her. Mike once kicked Peggy so violently in the chest and ribs that she required hospitalization. Finally, when Mike ordered Peggy to kill and bury Carla, she filed for divorce. Peggy's attorney in the divorce action testified in the murder trial that Peggy was afraid for both her and her children's lives.

One night, in a fit of anger, Mike threw Carla out of the house. Carla, who was not yet in her teens, was forced out of the home with no money, no coat, and no place to go. When the family heard that Carla was in Colorado, Mike refused to allow Peggy to contact or even talk about Carla. Mike's intimidation of Peggy continued to escalate. One morning, Laura found her mother hiding on the school bus, terrified and begging the driver to take her to a neighbor's home. That Christmas, Mike threw the turkey dinner to the floor, chased Peggy outside, grabbed her by the hair, rubbed her face in the dirt, and then kicked and beat her.

After Laura moved away, Peggy's life became even more isolated. Once, when Peggy was working at a cafe, Mike came in and ran all the customers off with a gun because he wanted Peggy to go home and have sex with him right that minute. He abused both drugs and alcohol, and amused himself by terrifying Peggy, once waking her from a sound sleep by beating her with a baseball bat. He shot one of Peggy's pet cats, and then held the gun against her head and threatened to pull the trigger. Peggy told friends that Mike would hold a shotgun to her head and threaten to blow it off, and indicated that one day he would probably do it.

In May 1986, Peggy left Mike and ran away to Laura's home in Oklahoma. It was the first time Peggy had left Mike without telling him. Because Peggy was suicidal, Laura had her admitted to a hospital. There, she was diagnosed as having toxic psychosis as a result of an overdose of her medication. On May 30, 1986, Mike called to say he was coming to get her. Peggy agreed to return to Kansas. Peggy told a nurse she felt like she wanted to shoot her husband. At trial, she testified that she decided to return with Mike because she was not able to get the medical help she needed in Oklahoma.

When Mike arrived at the hospital, he told the staff that he "needed his housekeeper." The hospital released Peggy to Mike's care, and he immediately drove her back to Kansas. Mike told Peggy that all her problems were in her head and he would be the one to tell her what was good for her, not the doctors. Peggy testified that Mike threatened to kill her if she ever ran away again. As soon as they arrived at the house, Mike forced Peggy into the house and forced her to have oral sex several times.

The next morning, Peggy discovered a loaded .357 magnum. She testified she was afraid of the gun. She hid the gun under the mattress of the bed in a spare room. Later that morning, as she cleaned house, Mike kept making remarks that she should not bother because she would not be there long, or that she should not bother with her things because she could not take them with her. She testified she was afraid Mike was going to kill her.

Mike's parents visited Mike and Peggy that afternoon. Mike's father testified that Peggy and Mike were affectionate with each other during the visit. Later, after Mike's parents had left, Mike forced Peggy to perform oral sex. After watching television, Mike and Peggy went to bed at 8:00 P.M.

As Mike slept, Peggy thought about suicide and heard voices in her head repeating over and over, "kill or be killed." At this time, there were two vehicles in the driveway and Peggy had access to the car keys. About 10:00 P.M. Peggy went to the spare bedroom and removed the gun from under the mattress, walked back to her bedroom, and killed her husband while he slept. She then ran to the home of a neighbor, who called the police.

When the police questioned Peggy regarding the events leading up to the shooting, Peggy stated that things had not gone quite right that day, and that when she got the chance she hid the gun under the mattress. She stated that she shot Mike to "get this over with, this misery and this torment." When asked why she got the gun out, Peggy stated to the police:

> I'm not sure exactly what . . . led up to it . . . and my head started playing games with me and I got to thinking about things and I said I didn't want to be by myself again. . . . I got the gun out because there had been remarks made about me being out there alone. It was as if Mike was going to do something again like had been done before. He had gotten me down here from McPherson one time and he went and told them that I had done something and he had me put out of the house and was taking everything I had. And it was like he was going to pull the same thing over again.

Two expert witnesses testified during the trial. The expert for the defense, psychologist Marilyn Hutchinson, diagnosed Peggy as suffering from "battered woman syndrome," or post-traumatic stress syndrome. Dr. Hutchinson testified that Mike was preparing to escalate the violence in retaliation for Peggy's running away. She testified that loaded guns, veiled threats, and increased sexual demands are indicators of the escalation of the cycle. Dr. Hutchinson believed Peggy had a repressed knowledge that she was in a "really grave lethal situation."

The State's expert, psychiatrist Herbert Modlin, neither subscribed to a belief in the battered woman syndrome nor to a theory of learned helplessness as an explanation for why women do not leave an abusive relationship. Dr. Modlin testified that abuse such as repeated forced oral sex would not be trauma sufficient to trigger a post-traumatic stress disorder. He also believed Peggy was erroneously diagnosed as suffering from toxic psychosis. He stated that Peggy was unable to escape the abuse because she suffered from schizophrenia, rather than the battered woman syndrome.

At defense counsel's request, the trial judge gave an instruction on self-defense to the jury. The jury found Peggy not guilty [of first-degree murder. Upon a special appeals procedure, the state appealed, arguing that the trial judge erred in his self-defense instruction.]

OPINION

...

K.S.A. 21-3211 provides:

A person is justified in the use of force against an aggressor when and to the extent it appears to him and he reasonably believes that such conduct is necessary to defend himself or another against such aggressor's imminent use of unlawful force.

The traditional concept of self-defense has posited one-time conflicts between persons of somewhat equal size and strength. When the defendant claiming self-defense is a victim of long-term domestic violence, such as a battered spouse, such traditional concepts may not apply. Because of the prior history of abuse, and the difference in strength and size between the abused and the abuser, the accused in such cases may choose to defend during a momentary lull in the abuse, rather than during a conflict. However, in order to warrant the giving of a self-defense instruction, the facts of the case must still show that the spouse was in imminent danger close to the time of killing.

A person is justified in using force against an aggressor when it appears to that person and he or she reasonably believes such force to be necessary. A reasonable belief implies both an honest belief and the existence of facts which would persuade a reasonable person to that belief. A self-defense instruction must be given if there is any evidence to support a claim of self-defense, even if that evidence consists solely of the defendant's testimony.

Where self-defense is asserted, evidence of the deceased's long-term cruelty and violence towards the defendant is admissible. In cases involving battered spouses, expert evidence of the battered woman syndrome is relevant to a determination of the reasonableness of the defendant's perception of danger. . . .

In order to instruct a jury on self-defense, there must be some showing of an imminent threat or a confrontational circumstance involving an overt act by an aggressor. There is no exception to this requirement where the defendant has suffered long-term domestic abuse and the victim is the abuser. In such cases, the issue is not whether the defendant believes homicide is the solution to past or future problems with the batterer, but rather whether circumstances surrounding the killing were sufficient to create a reasonable belief in the defendant that the use of deadly force was necessary. . . . Here . . . there is an absence of imminent danger to defendant.

Peggy told a nurse at the Oklahoma hospital of her desire to kill Mike. She later voluntarily agreed to return home with Mike when he telephoned her. She stated that after leaving the hospital Mike threatened to kill her if she left him again. Peggy showed no inclination to leave. In fact, immediately after the shooting, Peggy told the police that she was upset because she thought Mike would leave her. Prior to the shooting, Peggy hid the loaded gun. The cars were in the driveway and Peggy had access to the car keys. After being abused, Peggy went to bed with Mike at 8 P.M. Peggy lay there for two hours, then retrieved the gun from where she had hidden it and shot Mike while he slept.

Under these facts, the giving of the self-defense instruction was erroneous. Under such circumstances, a battered woman cannot reasonably fear imminent life-threatening danger from her sleeping spouse. We note that other courts have held that the sole fact that the victim was asleep does not preclude a self-defense instruction. In *State v. Norman*, 89 N.C.App. 384, 366 S.E.2d 586 (1988) . . . the defendant's evidence disclosed a long history of abuse. Each time defendant attempted to escape, her husband found and beat her. On the day of the shooting, the husband beat defendant continually throughout the day, and threatened either to cut her throat, kill her, or cut off her breast. In the afternoon, defendant shot her husband while he napped.

The North Carolina Court of Appeals held it was reversible error to fail to instruct on self-defense. The court found that, although decedent was napping at the time defendant shot him, defendant's unlawful act was closely related in time to an assault and threat of death by decedent against defendant and that the decedent's nap was "but a momentary hiatus in a continuous reign of terror."

There is no doubt that the North Carolina court determined that the sleeping husband was an evil man who deserved the justice he received from his battered wife. Here, similar comparable and compelling facts exist. But, as one court has stated: "To permit capital punishment to be imposed upon the subjective conclusion of the [abused] individual that prior acts and conduct of the deceased justified the killing would amount to a leap into the abyss of anarchy." *Jahnke v. State*, 682 P.2d 991, 997 (Wyo.1984).

Finally, our legislature has not provided for capital punishment for even the most heinous crimes. We must, therefore, hold that when a battered woman kills her sleeping spouse when there is no imminent danger, the killing is not reasonably necessary and a self-defense instruction may not be given. To hold otherwise in this case would in effect allow the execution of the abuser for past or future acts and conduct.

One additional issue must be addressed. In its amicus curiae brief, the Kansas County and District Attorney Association contends the instruction given by the trial court improperly modified the law of self-defense to be more generous to one suffering from the battered woman syndrome than to any other defendant relying on self-defense. We agree. . . .

The appeal is sustained.

DISSENT

Herd, Justice, dissenting.

. . .

It is evident . . . appellee met her burden of showing some competent evidence that she acted in self-defense, thus making her defense a jury question. She testified she acted in fear for her life, and Dr. Hutchinson corroborated this testimony. The evidence of Mike's past abuse, the escalation of violence, his threat of killing her should she attempt to leave him, and Dr. Hutchinson's testimony that appellee was indeed in a "lethal situation" more than met the minimal standard of "any evidence" to allow an instruction to be given to the jury.

The evidence showed Mike had a "Dr. Jekyll and Mr. Hyde" personality. He was usually very friendly and ingratiating when non-family persons were around, but was belligerent and domineering to family members. He had a violent temper and would blow up without reason. Mike was cruel to his two stepdaughters, Carla and Laura, as well as to the appellee. He took pride in hurting them or anything they held dear, such as their pets. Mike's violence toward appellee and her daughters caused appellee to

have emotional problems with symptoms of paranoid schizophrenia. He would overdose appellee on her medication and then cut her off it altogether. Mike's cruelty would culminate in an outburst of violence, and then he would suddenly become very loving and considerate. This was very confusing to appellee. She lived in constant dread of the next outburst. . . .

It is a jury question to determine if the battered woman who kills her husband as he sleeps fears he will find and kill her if she leaves, as is usually claimed. Under such circumstances the battered woman is not under actual physical attack when she kills but such attack is imminent, and as a result she believes her life is in imminent danger. She may kill during the tension-building stage when the abuse is apparently not as severe as it sometimes has been, but nevertheless has escalated so that she is afraid the acute stage to come will be fatal to her. She only acts on such fear if she has some survival instinct remaining after the husband-induced "learned helplessness." . . .

The majority claims permitting a jury to consider self-defense under these facts would permit anarchy. This underestimates the jury's ability to recognize an invalid claim of self-defense. Although this is a case of first impression where an appeal by the State has been allowed, there have been several similar cases in which the defendant appealed on other grounds. In each of these cases where a battered woman killed the sleeping batterer, a self-defense instruction has been given when requested by the defendant. . . .

The majority bases its opinion on its conclusion appellee was not in imminent danger, usurping the right of the jury to make that determination of fact. The majority believes a person could not be in imminent danger from an aggressor merely because the aggressor dropped off to sleep. This is a fallacious conclusion. For instance, picture a hostage situation where the armed guard inadvertently drops off to sleep and the hostage grabs his gun and shoots him. The majority opinion would preclude the use of self-defense in such a case. . . . I would deny this appeal.

QUESTIONS FOR DISCUSSION

1. How does the court define imminent?
2. Can battered women ever be in imminent danger when their husbands are sleeping?

3. Should we have a special battered women's defense of justification?

4. Or should we expand the definition of imminent or change the requirement from imminent to present, or continuing, danger?

5. Why does the court talk about putting the power of capital punishment into the hands of battered wives?

6. Consider the following comment:

> [R]etaliation, as opposed to defense, is a common problem in cases arising from wife battering and domestic violence. The injured wife waits for the first possibility of striking against a distracted or unarmed husband. The man may even be asleep when the wife finally reacts. Retaliation is the standard case of "taking the law into your own hands." There is no way, under the law, to justify killing a wife batterer or a rapist in retaliation or revenge, however much sympathy there may be for the wife wreaking retaliation. Private citizens cannot act as judge and jury toward each other. They have no authority to pass judgment and to punish each other for past wrongs.

Do you agree?

7. Was Peggy's act one of self-defense, a preemptive strike, or retaliation?

NOTE CASES

1. Ms. Gallegos suffered a long history of physical and sexual abuse, dating back to oppressive childhood encounters with her father, her brother, and one of her mother's boyfriends. Her father beat her; her brother physically and sexually abused her; and one of her mother's lovers tied defendant to her mother's bed and fondled her while making love to her mother. Out of her turbulent relationship with the victim, George Gallegos, four children were born, but the relationship was marred with violence.

George was a heavy drinker, and she displayed to the jury scars near her eye, on her forehead, and on her nose, resulting from beatings she claimed George administered to her. Ms. Gallegos testified that George threatened to cut off her breasts with the knife if her breasts grew any larger. When she was pregnant with their second child, defendant testified that George picked her up and threw her against a wall, causing the premature birth of the child. George's gun also was put into evidence. Ms. Gallegos claimed that George would place the loaded gun

at her head and threaten to shoot her if she ever left him. On numerous occasions, Gallegos testified, George would tie her hands behind her back and sodomize her to the point of inducing rectal bleeding. He would also force her to engage in fellatio. On one occasion, according to defendant's testimony, the Gallegos' neighbors, aware that George was abusing defendant, summoned the police. The police, however, apparently failed to take action because they had not witnessed the brutality.

On the day Ms. Gallegos killed George, she had taken her older children to school. She testified that when she returned home, George sodomized her against her will, making her cry and bleed. During the course of the day, George apparently drank beer. At one point in the day, defendant said that she told George that she was tired of being hurt and that she threatened to leave him. George pulled out his gun and threatened to kill her if she left. Also, on that day, George had struck one of their sons in the face with a belt buckle.

That evening, after the children went to bed, George asked the victim why she was not a virgin when they married. She answered that she was not a virgin because of her brother. Gallegos testified that George became angry, called her a profane name, and said "you probably liked it." At that moment, when she looked at George, she saw her father, her brother, and George, all coming toward her.

George then called her into the bedroom. He added something to the effect that if she did not come, he would find someone else. Defendant testified that she feared for her life. She did not know whether George intended to kill her, to rape her, or to beat her. Gallegos picked up a loaded rifle which George kept in the living room. While George was lying on the bed, she cocked the rifle and shot him. After shooting him, she stabbed George numerous times.

Was Ms. Gallegos in imminent danger of death or serious bodiy harm? Yes, according to the New Mexico Supreme Court:

> In order to assert a valid self-defense claim . . . there must have been the appearance to the defendant of immediate danger of death or great bodily harm. . . . We believe that defendant presented evidence sufficient to allow reasonable minds to differ as to whether defendant believed that she was in imminent danger of death or great bodily harm. Defendant was a victim of recurrent violence. On the day of George's death, he had

been drinking. Already that day he had sexually abused defendant; he had struck a child in the face with a belt buckle; he had threatened to kill defendant; and, finally, he was angry and calling her into the bedroom. Based upon that evidence, reasonable minds could believe that defendant was afraid. While one inference from George's statement, that if defendant did not come into the bedroom he would find someone else, might be that George only desired sex, another equally permissible inference could be that he was using that as a ploy to catch defendant off guard so he could harm her.

She stated she was put in fear. Dr. Cave, a clinical psychologist who regularly treats battered wife cases, testified at the trial. According to Dr. Cave's opinion, the above facts, coupled with a history of prior physical, sexual and verbal abuse and her testing of defendant, the appearance of immediate danger of "great bodily harm, even death" was present. Dr. Cave testified that the history of abuse in this case, as extensive as any she had ever seen, combined with the events of the day, created "great fear" which was real to defendant.

The fear present in this case also was prompted by more than a history of abuse. Based on the brutality which defendant testified she had experienced that day, George's anger, and her knowledge of what had happened to her in similar circumstances, George's calling her into the bedroom could provide the requisite immediacy of danger.

. . . To deny the defense of self-defense under the facts of this case would ignore reality. We, therefore, hold that the trial court erred in rejecting defendant's tendered self-defense instruction. . . . We reverse and remand this case for a new trial, consistent with this opinion. *State v. Gallegos*, 719 P.2d 1268 (N.M. 1986)

2. On the night of his death the father took the mother out to dinner, apparently to celebrate the anniversary of their meeting. Earlier the son, Richard Jahnke, aged 16, had been involved in a violent altercation with his father, and he had been warned not to be at the home when the father and mother returned. During the absence of his parents Jahnke made elaborate preparation for the final confrontation with his father. He changed into dark clothing and prepared a number of weapons which he positioned at various places throughout the family home that he selected to serve as "backup" positions in case he was not suc-

cessful in his first effort to kill his father. These weapons included two shotguns, three rifles, a .38 caliber pistol and a Marine knife. In addition, he armed his sister, Deborah, with a .30 caliber M1 carbine which he taught her how to operate so that she could protect herself in the event that he failed in his efforts. Richard removed the family pets from the garage to the basement to protect them from injury in a potential exchange of gunfire between him and his father, and he closed the garage door. He then waited inside the darkened garage in a position where he could not be seen but which permitted him to view the lighted driveway on the other side of the garage door. Shortly before 6:30 P.M. the parents returned, and the appellant's father got out of the vehicle and came to the garage door. Jahnke was armed with a 12-gauge shotgun loaded with slugs, and when he could see the head and shoulders of his father through the spacing of the slats of the shade covering the windows of the garage door, he blew his R.O.T.C. command-sergeant-major's whistle for courage, and he opened fire. All six cartridges in the shotgun were expended, and four of them in one way or another struck the father. The most serious wound was caused by a slug which entered the father on the right chest just above and to the inside of the right nipple, followed a trajectory which took it through the right rib cage and the right lobe of the liver, bruising the right lung and tearing the diaphragm along the way, into the middle of the chest cavity where it passed behind the heart nearly severing the aorta, inferior vena cava and the esophagus, then through the lower lobe of the left lung, finally lodging just under the skin in the mid-part of the victim's back. About one hour after the shooting incident the father was pronounced dead from the wounds inflicted by Jahnke.

After the shooting, and while the mother still was screaming in the driveway, Jahnke and his sister exited the family home through a window in the mother's bedroom, which was at the far end of the house from the garage. He and his sister then went separate ways, and Richard was arrested at the home of his girl friend. Prior to the arrival of authorities Richard told his girl friend's father that he had shot his dad for revenge. Subsequently, after being advised of his constitutional rights, he made a statement in which he explained he had shot his father "for past things."

Richard Jahnke was tried as an adult, convicted of voluntary manslaughter, and sentenced to 5 to 15 years in prison. Did Richard Jahnke kill his father in self-defense? Although he was entitled to an instruction on self-defense, according to the Wyoming Supreme Court, there is no special defense for battered persons. According to the court:

> . . . Although many people, and the public media, seem to be prepared to espouse the notion that a victim of abuse is entitled to kill the abuser that special justification defense is antithetical to the mores of modern civilized society. It is difficult enough to justify capital punishment as an appropriate response of society to criminal acts even after the circumstances have been carefully evaluated by a number of people. To permit capital punishment to be imposed upon the subjective conclusion of the individual that prior acts and conduct of the deceased justified the killing would amount to a leap into the abyss of anarchy.

In *People v. White*, and *State v. Thomas*, the courts suggest that the true role of any evidence with respect to family abuse is to assist the jury to determine whether the defendant's belief that he was in danger of his life or serious bodily injury was reasonable under the circumstances. In those cases the courts indicate that expert testimony with respect to such an issue is neither necessary nor relevant and for that reason is best eschewed. It is clear that if such evidence has any role at all it is in assisting the jury to evaluate the reasonableness of the defendant's fear in a case involving the recognized circumstances of self-defense which include a confrontation or conflict with the deceased not of the defendant's instigation.

In a concurring opinion, one of the justices noted:

> At the outset I confess to a philosophical bias against people who take the law into their own hands and execute their supposed tormentors. I am particularly opposed to patricide. After considering the news, particularly letters to the editor, I conclude that I must represent a view contrary to that of the public.
>
> Appellant is handsome, personable, intelligent and ready of tongue. He is an all American boy, except that he has a predilection toward patricide. Appellant and his incredible story caught the imagination of the media and public.
>
> Richard thought about killing his father many times before November 16. On the 16th he made elaborate plans for the execution. He lay in wait for an hour and one half, then blew his ROTC whistle to freeze his victim. He fired repeatedly,

propelling lead into his father's body. His first comment after the slaying was that he did it for revenge. This is a textbook case of first-degree murder.

> The jury convicted appellant of killing his father voluntarily upon a sudden heat of passion. If lying in wait for one and one-half hours is a "sudden heat of passion," then appellant must have been frozen in time. This must have been the longest "sudden" in history.
>
> In his defense appellant employed the oldest, most common and most successful tactic in homicide cases. He put the deceased on trial. His strategy was largely successful as he was convicted of a lesser offense when the uncontradicted evidence and appellant's admission pointed only to murder.
>
> Evidence produced by appellant characterized the deceased father as a cruel, sadistic and abusive man. Experience, common sense and the conduct of Mrs. Jahnke indicated to me that the testimony in support of this characterization was greatly exaggerated. There was no one at trial to speak for the deceased. All defense witnesses were at liberty to say anything they wanted about the deceased, knowing that they could not be contradicted. Defense witnesses had a motive to make the deceased look like a bad man; they wanted to make the jury believe that appellant's father deserved to be executed. By no stretch of the imagination was this a case of self-defense. Arming and barricading himself and lying in wait for one and one-half hours for his father's return is not self-defense under the law.
>
> The trial judge was eminently fair with appellant and resolved any doubt in his favor. Appellant was not entitled to an instruction on self-defense, nor was he entitled to an instruction on the lesser included offense of manslaughter because there was no evidence justifying either instruction. However, the judge being abundantly cautious gave these instructions.
>
> Richard's avowed motives for gunning down his father have changed during this ordeal depending upon his forum. While he was in an excited state he told his girlfriend's father that he did it for revenge. While still exhilarated he told Officer Hildago that he killed for past things. Then his expressed reason briefly changed and he claimed self-defense at the trial. Richard now says he did it for his mother and sister. He said at a

later trial he killed his father to "stop him from further abuse of his family."

Many in our society are fascinated by violence. We make folk heroes out of our criminals. Ballads and odes are written about murders. The more bizarre or unusual the murder, the greater the proliferation of songs, poems and books. The public's thirst for this sort of literature will not be stilled. If a person wants to become famous and even wealthy, he just needs to commit a grotesque crime.

John Herbert Dillinger and Alphonse Capone will live in our history for more than one hundred years. Good men, contemporaries of Dillinger and Capone are already forgotten. "The evil that men do lives after them; the good is oft interred with their bones." Wm. Shakespeare, Julius Caesar (The Tragedy of), Act 3, Scene 2.

Perhaps Richard Jahnke was entitled to compassion because of his age. The jury meted out that compassion when they found him guilty of manslaughter, despite the fact that the evidence pointed to murder. The judge's sentence evidences further compassion. He could have sentenced Richard to not less than nineteen years, eleven months and twenty-nine days. The judge and jury deserve to be commended, rather than harangued by the public. They demonstrated intelligence, good judgment and compassion.

One of the dissenting justices noted:

This case concerns itself with what happens — or can happen — and did happen when a cruel, ill-tempered, insensitive man roams, gun in hand, through his years of family life as a battering bully — a bully who, since his two children were babies, beat both of them and his wife regularly and unmercifully. Particularly, this appeal has to do with a 16-year-old boy who could stand his father's abuse no longer — who could not find solace or friendship in the public services which had been established for the purpose of providing aid, comfort and advice to abused family members — and who had no place to go or friends to help either him or his sister for whose protection he felt responsible and so in fear and fright, and with fragmented emotion, Richard Jahnke shot and killed his father one night in November of 1982. In these courts, Richard pleads self-defense and, since the jury was given a self-defense in-

struction, it must be conceded that the trial judge recognized this as a viable defense theory under the evidence adduced at trial.

It is my conception that Richard Jahnke properly came to the courts of Wyoming asking — not that he be judged as one who, at the time and place in question, was insanely unreasonable — but that his 14 years of beatings and uncivilized emotional abuse be explained by a qualified expert in order that judgment be passed on the question which asks whether or not his behavior was sanely reasonable. One might wonder why — since our courts admit expert testimony with commendable regularity upon the issue of sanity when that is the ultimate fact — and the plea is insanity — it is not acceptable that a psychiatrist testify about whether behavior such as that with which this case is concerned and which is unlike that which lay jurors would understand to be the expected, is, nevertheless, sanely typical of the behavior of a reasonable person acting in the same or similar circumstances. Richard was not, however, permitted to have the impact of 14 years of abuse upon his alleged self defensive behavior explained to the jury through the testimony of a psychiatrist even though this is the only way the fallout from brutality can be communicated.

Denied this opportunity, the appellant was forced to submit his case to the jury with what consequently presents itself as a ridiculous, unbelievable, outrageous defense. Without medical input, what possible sense could it make to a lay juror or any other nonprofessional person for the citizen accused to urge self-defense where the evidence is that, even though the recipient of untold battering and brutalizing by the victim, the defendant nevertheless contemplated the possibility of the use of deadly force as he lay in wait, gun in hand, for his father's return? How could any jury be receptive to such a defense on an informed basis if its members are not to be permitted to hear from those who understand how brutalized people — otherwise "reasonable" in all respects — entertain what, for them, is a belief that they are in imminent danger from which there is no escape and how they, with their embattled psyche, responsively behave? Jahnke v. State, 682 P.2d 991 (Wyo. 1984)

How does the law determine whether an attack is immediate or present? Most jurisdictions adopt an **objective test.** They permit the use of force only if under the circumstances actors reasonably believed that the use of force was necessary. In some states, such as Illinois, Connecticut, and Wisconsin, statutes spell this out specifically. In states where statutes do not prescribe a test—**subjective test** (honest belief), objective test (reasonable belief), or combination (honest and reasonable belief)—courts imply a reasonableness test (what a reasonable person would do under the circumstances). Before Illinois legislated an objective test, for example, the Illinois Supreme Court ruled that a man who turned and immediately shot an unknown attacker who struck him in the head from behind "was not under a reasonable apprehension of death or great bodily harm."[14]

Occasionally, courts adopt a combined objective-subjective test. In *Beard v. United States,* for example, Beard killed an attacker who had threatened to assault him. The court ruled that Beard must have had "reasonable grounds to believe, and in good faith believed" that he had to use force in order to protect himself against great bodily harm. The reasonableness test and the objective-subjective test create *mens rea* problems. Defendants who, like Beard, make honest but unreasonable mistakes about danger—that is, reckless or negligent mistakes—cannot claim that they acted in self-defense.[15]

Glanville Williams, a distinguished British criminal law scholar, strongly objects to the reasonableness test:

> The criminal law of negligence works best when it gives effect to the large number of rules of prudence which are commonly observed though not directly incorporated into the law. Such rules include the rule against pulling out on a blind corner, the rule against carrying a gun in such a way that it is pointing at another person, the rule against deliberately pointing a gun at another person, even in play, and so on. These rules are not part either of enacted or of common law, but as customary standards of behavior they become binding via the law of negligence. Are there any similar rules of behavior applicable when a person acts in self-defense or in making an arrest? It must be recollected that the injury he inflicts on the other is in itself intentional, so that the usual rules of prudence in respect to the handling of weapons are not in question. The only question is whether the defendant was negligent in arriving at the conclusion that the use of the force in question was called for. It is hard to imagine what rules of prudence could normally serve in this situation. Either the defendant is capable of drawing the inferences that a reasonable man would draw or he is not. If he is not, and he is a peace officer, his tendency to make miscalculations would certainly justify his dismissal from the police force. But there is no obvious case for the intervention of the criminal courts.[16]

Despite criticism, few states have removed the reasonableness requirement from the law of self-defense. Tennessee is one that has. In a famous old case, *Frazier v. State,* a hemophiliac assaulted Frazier. Frazier struck a moderate blow to defend himself. The hemophiliac bled to death from Frazier's moderate blow. The court stated the self-defense requirement as follows: "If the defendant honestly fears himself to be in danger of life or great bodily harm from the circumstances as they appear to him, and he acts under that fear to kill his assailant, it is justifiable homicide."[17]

The Retreat Doctrine

What if those who are about to be attacked can avoid it by escaping? Must they retreat? Or can they stand their ground? Different values underlie each of these alternatives. The retreat rule places a premium on human life and discourages inflicting bodily injury and death except as a last resort. A different rule permitting victims to stand their ground against unwarranted attacks rests on the idea that retreat forces innocent people to take a cowardly or humiliating position. This idea is captured by the phrase used to describe the rule: the true man doctrine. Most jurisdictions require retreat if retreat does not unreasonably risk the retreater's life.[18]

Jurisdictions requiring retreat have carved out a major exception to the retreat doctrine, sometimes called the **castle exception.** According to the castle exception to the retreat doctrine, when attacked in their homes, defenders may stand their ground and use deadly force to repel an unprovoked attack, if the unprovoked attack reasonably threatens life or serious bodily injury. A problem arises over just what "home" means. Does it include the entryway? The sidewalk in front of the house? Does it extend to the property line? What if a person lives in a car, a hotel room, or under a bridge? Similarly, does it include businesses? The court, in *State v. Quarles*, dealt with the castle exception when both the attacker and victim live in the same house.

C A S E

Was He Required to Retreat from His Own Home?

State v. Quarles,
504 A.2d 473 (R.I. 1986)

Ronald Quarles (Quarles), indicted for murder in the second degree, was convicted by a Providence County jury of manslaughter in the slaying of Lorraine Pinto (Pinto), his cohabitant. After his post verdict motion for a new trial was denied, a fourteen-year sentence was imposed. On appeal Quarles claims that the trial justice committed prejudicial error in refusing to instruct the jury that he was not obligated to retreat before resorting to the use of deadly force in his own defense. The Rhode Island supreme court affirmed. Kelleher, Justice.

FACTS

[According to Quarles]: . . . After eating dinner at home with Pinto, Quarles went to a union meeting, planning to meet Pinto at a local barroom after the meeting ended. Upon entering the bar, Quarles saw Pinto talking with a man he did not recognize. At first he felt angry because he thought Pinto was "trying to sneak around behind my back" with another man, but his anger quickly subsided.

As the night wore on, Quarles and Pinto drank and shot some pool. Several arguments erupted over Pinto's refusals to go home with Quarles; finally he walked back to their common residence in Newport. About ten minutes later Pinto walked into the house and informed Quarles that he had one week to find another place to live. Quarles agreed to leave in a week and went upstairs to their bedroom and began to undress. Pinto followed him upstairs and started to choke him. He punched her in order to get her to release him. Infuriated, she told him to get out "tonight." Quarles called her a "tramp" and indicated that he would not put up with her antics any longer. Pinto went downstairs into the kitchen.

After Quarles dressed, he followed her downstairs. When he entered the kitchen, Pinto swung a nine-inch kitchen knife at him. He stepped back and wrestled the knife out of her hands. Quarles conceded that at this point he could have left the house with the knife under his control. But Pinto suddenly grabbed his arm and struggled with him in an attempt to regain control over the knife.

During the ensuing affray, in the early morning hours of October 5, Pinto was fatally stabbed by Quarles. Quarles claims that the stabbing occurred when Pinto grabbed his arm and drew the knife toward herself. When he withdrew the knife and saw blood on it, he realized that there had been a stabbing. He insists that Pinto's wound was self-inflicted.

The trial justice instructed the jury on second-degree murder, on manslaughter, and on the defense theories of accident and self-defense. His instruction on the issue of self-defense follows:

> [A] person who reasonably believes that he's in imminent danger of harm at the hands of another may defend himself. He does not have to wait for the first blow to land. However, if such person strikes first, he may only use such force as is reasonably necessary for his own protection. The permissible degree of force used in self-defense depends on that which is necessary under all the circumstances to prevent an impending injury.
>
> In a case such as this it is the burden of the State to prove beyond a reasonable doubt that the defendant was not acting in self-defense. If it is not proved, this element, beyond a reasonable doubt, then you must find the defendant not guilty.
>
> The test of whether or not the defendant acted in self-defense is not whether the fact finder, you, the jury, believe the force used was necessary, but whether the defendant, under the circumstances he experienced at the time in question, reasonably believed that the force used by him was necessary to prevent imminent harm.

The trial justice refused to instruct the jury that Quarles was not obligated to attempt retreat prior to resorting to the use of deadly force. The defendant submitted the following instruction concerning this issue:

REQUEST NO. 31 If the defendant had reasonable grounds to believe and actually did believe that he was in imminent danger of death or serious bodily harm and that deadly force was necessary to repel such danger, he is not required to retreat or to consider whether he can retreat safely. He was entitled to stand his ground and use such force as was reasonably necessary under the circumstances to save his life or protect himself from serious bodily harm. *Beard v. United States,* 158 U.S. 550, 563, 15 S.Ct. 962, 967 [39 L.Ed. 1086] (1895).

OPINION

Quarles objected to the omission of his requested instruction and now contends that the failure to instruct the jury in accordance with his request was reversible error requiring a new trial. We disagree.

The law concerning self-defense in Rhode Island permits persons who believe that they are in imminent peril of bodily harm to use such non deadly force as is reasonably necessary in the circumstances to protect themselves. Before resorting to the use of deadly force, the person attacked must attempt retreat if he or she is consciously aware of an open, safe, and available avenue of escape. The only exception in Rhode Island to the obligation to attempt retreat was created by statute. It exempts an individual from the duty to retreat and permits the use of deadly force by an owner, tenant, or occupier of premises against any person engaged in the commission of an unlawful breaking and entering or burglary.

Quarles attempts to persuade us to create a new exception to the retreat requirement by adopting the common-law castle doctrine. He asserts that this "universally recognized" doctrine exempts the person assailed from the obligation of attempting retreat when the attack occurs in the defendant's dwelling. Quarles contends that the castle doctrine, which embodies the notion that a person's authority is paramount in his own home and need not be compromised in the face of an unlawful attack, should be adhered to even when, as in the instant case, the assailant is a cohabitant.

We have grave doubts that Quarles's reliance on the theory of self-defense was relevant once he had wrested the deadly weapon from his assailant, especially since he insists the wound inflicted was accidental. However, because the issue of retreat that Quarles attempted to raise is one that will undoubtedly be raised again, we believe that we should make our position clear.

We are of the opinion that a person assailed in his or her own residence by a co-occupant is not entitled under the guise of self-defense to employ deadly force and kill his or her assailant. The person attacked is obligated to attempt to retreat if he or she is aware of a safe and available avenue of retreat.

In *State v. Guillemet*, we noted that a majority of jurisdictions have recognized an exception to the requirement of retreat when the attack occurs in the occupant's home. This exception prevails without regard to whether the assailant's status is that of an intruder or a co-occupant.

However, several jurisdictions that have adopted the castle doctrine have held that it has no application to cases between two persons entitled to occupy the same dwelling. . . .

In *Commonwealth v. Shaffer*, 367 Mass. 508, 326 N.E.2d 880 (1975), the defendant, convicted of manslaughter in the shooting of her cohabitant, claimed the trial justice erred in failing to instruct the jury that she was not obligated to attempt retreat from her assailant in her own home. The Supreme Judicial Court dismissed her appeal and adhered to its "long-established rule that the right to use deadly force by way of self-defense is not available to one threatened until he has availed himself of all reasonable and proper means in the circumstances to avoid combat. . . ." We are aware that the Massachusetts Legislature altered the holding in *Shaffer* as it applies to unlawful intruders.

We find the rationale of *Shaffer* persuasive in that it affords due recognition to the value of human life while recognizing that the right of self-defense is born of necessity and should terminate when the necessity is no more.

Consequently, we are of the belief that even in the so-called co-occupant situation, no justification exists for departing from our long-established rule that when a person "is attacked by another under such circumstances as to lead him to apprehend peril to his life, or great bodily harm, he may kill his assailant, provided he cannot otherwise protect himself, as by retreating from danger, by warding off the attack by a weapon not deadly, by disabling his adversary without killing him, or in any other way preserving his own life and person. . . ."

Thus, the obligation to attempt retreat exists where one is assaulted in his or her own living quarters by his or her co-occupant. Therefore, the trial justice did not err in refusing to instruct the jury in the manner requested by Quarles. Accordingly, Quarles's appeal is denied and dismissed, and the judgment appealed from is affirmed.

QUESTIONS FOR DISCUSSION

1. Define the castle exception.
2. What is the rationale for the castle exception?
3. Do you agree with it?
4. Should anyone have to retreat in the face of an attack? Why or why not?
5. What reasons does the Rhode Island court give for rejecting the co-occupant castle exception?
6. Do you agree with them? Why or why not?

NOTE CASE

Leon Cooper and his brother, Robert Parker, lived with their mother, Alice Cooper. In the early part of August 1981, Parker unexpectedly left home for ten days. Early on the morning of August 12, he returned. He did not tell his mother or brother where he had been.

Parker stayed home for much of the day. Mrs. Cooper returned from work in the evening, and Cooper returned from his job shortly afterward. Cooper was carrying a pistol when he returned. The three were sitting in Mrs. Cooper's small living room when the two brothers began to quarrel after Cooper asked Parker where he had been during the past ten days.

Suddenly the quarrel escalated, and the two brothers found themselves standing in the middle of the living room, shouting at each other. Parker hit Cooper in the head with a small radio; Mrs. Cooper ran upstairs to call for help. She then heard a "pop." She went downstairs and saw Parker lying on the floor. Cooper said, "I have shot my brother," and "Mama, I am so sorry. I mean—" Cooper later told the police that he had just shot his brother, that his brother was hitting him with the radio and "I couldn't take it anymore and I just shot him."

Was Cooper entitled to the castle exception? In affirming the conviction, the court held:

[A]ll co-occupants, even those unrelated by blood and marriage, have a heightened obligation to treat each other with a degree of tolerance and respect. That obligation does not evaporate when one co-occupant disregards it and attacks another. We are satisfied, moreover, that an instruction that embraces the middle ground approach appropriately permits

the jury to consider the truly relevant question, i.e., whether a defendant, "if he safely could have avoided further encounter by stepping back or walking away, was actually or apparently in imminent danger of bodily harm." We hold that evidence that the defendant was attacked in his home by a co-occupant did not entitle him to an instruction that he had no duty whatsoever to retreat. The trial court did not err in refusing to give a castle doctrine instruction under the circumstances of this case. *Cooper v. United States*, 512 A.2d 1002 (D.C.1986)

Defense of Others

Historically, self-defense meant protecting both the individuals attacked and their immediate families. Although several jurisdictions still require a special relationship, the trend is definitely away from such a prescription. Several states that retain it have relaxed its meaning to include lovers and friends. Many states have abandoned the special relationship requirement altogether. They either write a special provision for defending others, which is the same as that for defending oneself, or they modify their self-defense statutes to read "himself or third persons."[19]

Whatever the limits, the defense-of-others defense requires that the "other" have the right to defend himself or herself in order for the defender to claim the defense. Therefore, where abortion rights protesters argued that they had the right to prevent abortions by violating the law because they were defending the right of unborn children to live, the court rejected the defense:

The "defense of others" specifically limits the use of force or violence in protection of others to situations where the person attacked would have been justified in using such force or violence to protect himself. In view of Roe [v. Wade] . . . and the provisions of the Louisiana abortion statute, defense of others as justification for the defendants' otherwise criminal conduct is not available in these cases. Since abortion is legal in Louisiana, the defendants had no legal right to protect the unborn by means not even available to the unborn themselves.[20]

Defense of Home and Property

The justifiable use of force is not limited to the protection of life and the prevention of bodily injury; it also extends to the protection of homes and property. The law regarding the defense of homes is deeply rooted in the common-law notion that "a man's home is his castle." As early as 1604, Sir Edward Coke, the great common-law judge, in his report of *Semayne's Case*, wrote:

The house of everyone is to him his castle and fortress, as well for his defense against injury and violence, as for his repose; and although the life of a man is a thing precious and favored in law . . . if thieves come to a man's house to rob him, or murder, and the owner or his servants kill any of the thieves in defense of himself and his house, it is not felony and he shall lose nothing.[21]

Perhaps the most quoted statement about the supreme value placed on the sanctity of homes came from the Earl of Chatham during a debate in the British Parliament in 1764:

The poorest man may in his cottage bid defiance to all the forces of the Crown. It may be frail; its roof may shake; the wind may blow through it; the storm may enter; the rain may enter; but the King of England may not enter; all his force dares not cross the threshold of the ruined tenement.

Sir William Blackstone, in his famous eighteenth century *Commentaries*, states that the common law allowed the use of force, including deadly force, to protect homes:

If any person attempts . . . to break open a house in the nighttime (which extends also to an attempt to burn it) and shall be killed in such attempt, the slayer shall be acquitted and discharged. This reaches not to . . . the breaking open of any house in the daytime, unless it carries with it an attempt of robbery.[22]

Nearly all states authorize the use of force to protect homes; some states go further and adopt provisions authorizing the use of force to protect personal property as well. Texas, for example, has enacted the following statute:

§ 9.42 Deadly Force to Protect Property
A person is justified in using deadly force against another to protect land or tangible, movable property:
1. if he would be justified in using force against the other under § 9.41 of this code; and
2. when and to the degree he reasonably believes the deadly force is immediately necessary:
　　A. to prevent the other's imminent commission of arson, burglary, robbery, aggravated robbery, theft during the nighttime, or criminal mischief during the nighttime; or
　　B. to prevent the other who is fleeing immediately after committing burglary, robbery, aggravated robbery, or theft during the nighttime from escaping with the property; and
3. he reasonably believes that:
　　A. the land or property cannot be protected or recovered by any other means; or
　　B. the use of force other than deadly force to protect or recover the land or property would expose the actor or another to a substantial risk of death of serious bodily injury.

The court dealt with a case of using deadly force to protect a home in *State v. Mitcheson*.

C A S E

Can He Kill to Defend His Home?

State v. Mitcheson,
560 P.2d 1120 (1977)

Defendant was convicted of murder in the second degree, and he appealed. The Supreme Court reversed and remanded the case.

CROCKETT, Justice:

FACTS

The defendant, Gary Alfred Mitcheson, was convicted of murder in the second degree for shooting Richard Herrera in the front yard of 432 South Fourth East, Price, Utah, at about 3:30 A.M. on February 7, 1976. He was sentenced to a term of five years to life in the state prison. On his appeal the point of critical concern is his charge that the trial court erred in refusing his request to instruct the jury on the defense of using force in the protection of one's habitation.

The deceased, Richard Herrera, sold his car (a 1967 Chevrolet van) to Alfred Mitcheson, defendant's father, on December 15, 1975. The original wheels and tires had been changed for what are called 'Mag Wheels' and tires, which have a wider tread. Some time after the father had taken possession of the van, a dispute arose between the parties over those wheels. The father, supported by the defendant, claimed that they had been included in the sale, but the deceased and his brother, Ernie Herrera, claimed they only agreed to loan the 'Mag Wheels' and tires temporarily.

On several occasions in January, 1976, the two brothers requested that the wheels and tires be returned, but the defendant and his father did not comply. On one of those occasions the Herrera brothers and some friends went to the father's home to remove the wheels. The father protested and called the police. When they arrived they told the Herreras, the deceased and his brother, to leave the wheels alone and that any disagreement should be settled by going to court.

A few days thereafter, on February 6, 1976, the defendant was parked in the van at a drive-in restaurant when the deceased came up to the van, opened the door and hit the defendant on the jaw and eye; and made threats to the defendant to the effect that I will 'put you under.' A couple of hours later the defendant and some of his friends went to the home of Jerry Giraud, where they saw the deceased's car parked. There was a conversation in which the defendant offered to fight the deceased, which was then refused. But, they agreed to meet in the town park and fight at 2:00 o'clock the next afternoon.

Defendant and his friend, Wendell Johnson, drove to his father's house, where the defendant obtained a rifle. He and Johnson then arranged for a poker game to be held at the home of defendant's sister, Debbie, and went there in the van where they proceeded to play cards. Still later that night, at about 3:30 A.M., the deceased, Richard Herrera, and some of his friends drove up to this house for the stated purpose of removing the wheels from the van. When they entered upon her premises Debbie told them to leave. They did not comply. A considerable commotion ensued, including her screaming at them to get off her premises. Defendant came to the doorway of the house with the rifle. He fired a shot and Richard Herrera fell with a bullet wound in his neck from which he shortly expired.

OPINION

The essence of the defense, and the basis for the requested instructions, was that the defendant was using the rifle as a backup resource in protection of the peace and security of his habitation. . . . The argument that the defendant was not entitled to that instruction is . . . that the sister's home was not his habitation. . . .

The pertinent statute is 762405, U.C.A.1953, which provides in part:

A person is justified in using force against another when and to the extent that he reasonably believes . . . necessary to prevent . . . other's unlawful entry into or attack upon his habitation; however, he is justified in the use of force which is intended to cause death or serious bodily injury only if:

> (1) The entry is made or attempted in a violent and tumultuous manner and he reasonably believes that the entry is attempted or made for the purpose of assaulting or offering personal violence to any person, dwelling or being therein. . . .

That statute has its roots in the ancient and honored doctrine of the common law that a man's home is his castle, and that even the peasant in his cottage, may peaceably abide within the protective cloak of the law, and no one, not even the king nor all his armies can enter to disturb him. See *Semayne's Case* (1604) 5 Coke 91, 77 Eng. Reprint 194, where it was stated that

> the house of everyone is to him his castle and fortress, as well for his defense against injury and violence, as for his repose; and although the life of a man is a thing precious and favored in law . . . if thieves come to a man's house to rob him, or murder, and the owner or his servants kill any of the thieves in defense of himself and his house, it is not felony and he shall lose nothing. . . .

In view of the salutary purpose of that statute, of preserving the peace and good order of society, it should be interpreted and applied in the broad sense to accomplish that purpose. Thus it would include not only a person's actual residence, but also whatever place he may be occupying peacefully as a substitute home or habitation, such as a hotel, motel, or even where he is a guest in the home of another; and so would apply to the defendant in his sister's home.
. . .

On the basis of what has been said herein, it is our opinion that if the requested instruction had been given and the jury had so considered the evidence, there is a reasonable likelihood that it may have had some effect upon the verdict rendered. Therefore the defendant's request should have been granted. Accordingly, it is necessary that the judgment be reversed and that the case be remanded for a new trial. [Upon reversal for error defendant is not entitled to go free, but to a new trial.] No costs awarded.

ELLETT, C.J., and MAUGHAN, WILKINS and HALL, JJ., concur.

QUESTIONS FOR DISCUSSION

1. What rule does the court adopt in the use of force to protect homes?
2. What facts bear on the question of justification here?
3. Does it make a difference that Mitcheson was defending his sister's house? Why or why not?

NOTE CASE

In 1986 Colorado enacted a "make my day law" for the protection of homes. § 18-1-704.5, 8B, C.R.S. (1986) provides:

1. The general assembly hereby recognizes that the citizens of Colorado have a right to expect absolute safety within their own homes.
2. . . . [A]ny occupant of a dwelling is justified in using any degree of physical force, including deadly physical force, against another person when that other person has made an unlawful entry into the dwelling, and when the occupant has a reasonable belief that such other person has committed a crime in the dwelling in addition to the uninvited entry, or is committing or intends to commit a crime against a person or property in addition to the uninvited entry, and when the occupant reasonably believes that such other person might use any physical force, however slight, against any occupant.
3. Any occupant of a dwelling using physical force, including deadly force, in accordance with the provisions in subsection (2) of this section shall be immune from criminal prosecution for the use of such force.
4. Any occupant of a dwelling using physical force, including deadly physical force, in accordance with the provisions of subsection (2) of this section shall be immune from any civil liability for injuries or death resulting from the use of such force.

When neighbors pounded on David and Pam Guenther's door, and Pam Guenther went outside the door and got into a struggle with one of the neighbors, David Guenther shot and killed two neighbors outside the front door with four shots from a Smith and Wesson .357 Magnum six-inch revolver. Did David Guenther use lawful force to protect his home? The court held:

In accordance with the explicit terms of the statute, we hold that § 18-1-704.5 provides the home occupant with immunity from prosecution only for force used against one who has made an unlawful entry into the dwelling, and that this immunity does not extend to force used against non-entrants. *People v. Guenther*, 740 P.2d 971 (Colo.1987)

EXECUTION OF PUBLIC DUTIES

Public executioners throw switches to electrocute condemned murderers; soldiers shoot and kill wartime enemies; police officers use force to make arrests or to take citizens' property pursuant to search warrants. In all these examples, individuals' lives, liberty, and property are intentionally taken away. Yet, none of these examples is a crime. Why? Because all the actors were doing their jobs, and the deprivations they caused were justified because they were carried out as public duties.

These examples illustrate the justification called execution of public duty. This defense is at least as old as the sixteenth century, as its common-law definition illustrates: "A public officer is justified in using reasonable force against the person of another, or in taking his property, when he acts pursuant to a valid law, court order, or process, requiring or authorizing him so to act."[23]

The values underlying the execution-of-public-duty defense are clear: Once the state legitimately formulates laws, citizens must obey them; the law takes precedence over citizens' property, their liberty, and even their lives. Therefore, the value in enforcing the law ranks higher than individual property, liberty, and life.

The public duty defense arouses most controversy over the power of the police to kill suspects. A furious debate has raged over whether, and under what circumstances, the police may lawfully kill fleeing suspects. Some say the defense should cover officers who "need" to kill in order to make arrests. Others insist that only protecting officers' or other innocent people's lives justifies killing—that police have only the defense of self-defense belonging to private citizens. Still others believe that officers cannot shoot at fleeing suspects if doing so endangers innocent lives.

At one time, state laws authorized police officers to kill when necessary to effect felony arrests, including those for property crimes. In 1985, however, the Supreme Court restricted the constitutionality of police use of deadly force under the Fourth Amendment search and seizure clause (see *Tennessee v. Garner*, excerpted later in this section). Furthermore, police departments have established rules that prescribe in detail when officers can use force, including deadly force, in arresting suspects.[24]

The argument favoring the police power to kill in order to arrest fleeing suspects is based not only on protecting lives but also on maintaining respect for law enforcement authority. One commentator said:

> I am convinced that only through truly effective power of arrest can law be satisfactorily enforced. Obviously until violators are brought before the courts the law's sanctions cannot be applied to them. But effectiveness in making arrests requires more than merely pitting the footwork of policemen against that of suspected criminals. An English director of public prosecutions once explained to me that the English police had no need to carry pistols because (1) no English criminal would think of killing a police officer, and (2) even if a suspected offender should outrun an officer in the labyrinth of London he could be found eventually in Liver-

pool or Birmingham. As the director put it, if a man offends in his own district everyone knows him, if he goes somewhere else everyone notices him.

[Without such power, he continued] we say to the criminal, "You are foolish. No matter what you have done you are foolish if you submit to arrest. The officer dare not take the risk of shooting at you. If you can outrun him, if you are faster than he is, you are free, and God bless you." I feel entirely unwilling to give that benediction to the modern criminal.[25]

The value of general obedience to the law rests on the reasonable assumption that life, liberty, and property mean little without order. The power to kill in order to make an arrest is therefore grounded not only on the value of life but also on the need for law observance in general. On the other hand, critics contend that the police power to kill creates social problems. Commenting on the troubled time of the late 1960s, United States Attorney General Ramsey Clarke wrote:

In these dog days of 1968, we have heard much loose talk of shooting looters. This talk must stop. The need is to train adequate numbers of police to prevent riots and looting altogether. Where prevention fails, looters must be arrested not shot. The first need in a civil disorder is to restore order. To say that when the looting starts, the shooting starts means either that shooting is preferable to arrest, or that there are [sic] not enough police protection, or the unpredictable nature of a disorder makes arrest impossible. Other techniques—including the use of tear gas—may be necessary. The use of deadly force is neither necessary, effective nor tolerable.

Far from being effective, shooting looters divides, angers, embitters, drives to violence. It creates the very problems its advocates claim is their purpose to avoid. Persons under the influence of alcohol killed 25,000 Americans in automobile accidents in 1967. Fewer than 250 people have died in all riots since 1964. Looters, as such, killed no one. Why not shoot drunken drivers? What is it that causes some to call for shooting looters when no one is heard to suggest the same treatment for a far deadlier and less controllable crime?

Is the purpose to protect property? Bank embezzlers steal ten times more money each year than bank robbers. Should we shoot embezzlers? What do the police themselves believe? It is the police to whom some would say, pull the trigger when looters are fleeing—perhaps dozens of looters fleeing toward a crowd; women, children; some making trouble, some committing crime, some trying to talk sense to a mob, to cool it.[26]

C A S E

Did He Use Reasonable Force to Execute the Arrest?

Tennessee v. Garner,
471 U.S. 1, 105 S.Ct. 1694,
85 L.Ed.2d 1 (1985)

Garner's father brought an action for wrongful death when a police officer shot and killed his young son who was fleeing the scene of a suspected burglary. The trial court awarded damages. The defendant city and police department appealed. Justice White delivered the opinion, joined by Justices Brennan, Marshall, Blackmun, Powell, and Stevens. Justice O'Connor filed a dissenting opinion, joined by Chief Justice Burger and Justice Rehnquist.

FACTS

At about 10:45 P.M. on October 3, 1974, Memphis Police Officers Elton Hymon and Leslie Wright were dispatched to answer a "prowler inside call." Upon arriving at the scene they saw a woman standing on her porch gesturing toward the adjacent house. She told them she had heard glass breaking and that "they" or "someone" was breaking in next door. While Wright radioed the dispatcher to say that they were on the scene, Hymon went behind the house. He heard a door slam and saw someone run across the back yard. The fleeing suspect, who was appellee-respondent's descendent, Edward Garner, stopped at a 6-feet-high chain link fence at the edge of the yard. With the aid of a flashlight, Hymon was able to see Garner's face and hands. He saw no sign of a weapon, and, though not certain, was "reasonably sure" and "figured" that Garner was unarmed. He thought Garner was 17 or 18 years old and about 5′5″ or 5′7″ tall. While Garner was crouched at the base of the fence, Hymon called out "police, halt" and took a few steps toward him. Garner began to climb over the fence. Convinced that if Garner made it over the fence he would elude capture, Hymon shot him. The bullet hit Garner in the back of the head. Garner was taken by ambulance to a hospital, where he died on the operating table. Ten dollars and a purse taken from the house were found on his body.

In using deadly force to prevent escape, Hymon was acting under the authority of a Tennessee statute and pursuant to Police Department policy. The statute provides that "[i]f, after notice of the intention to arrest the defendant, he either flee or forcibly resist, the officer may use all the necessary means to effect the arrest." Tenn. Code Ann. § 40-7-108 (1982). The Department policy was slightly more restrictive than the statute, but still allowed the use of deadly force in cases of burglary. The incident was reviewed by the Memphis Police Firearm's Review Board and presented to a grand jury. Neither took any action.

Garner's father then brought this action in the Federal District Court for the Western District of Tennessee, seeking damages under 42 U.S.C. § 1983 for asserted violations of Garner's constitutional rights. The complaint alleged that the shooting violated the Fourth, Fifth, Sixth, Eighth, and Fourteenth Amendments of the United States Constitution. It named as defendants Officer Hymon, the Police Department, its Director, and the Mayor and city of Memphis. After a 3-day bench trial, the District Court entered judgment for all defendants. It dismissed the claims against the Mayor and the Director for lack of evidence. It then concluded that Hymon's actions were authorized by the Tennessee statute, which in turn was constitutional. Hymon had employed the only reasonable and practicable means of preventing Garner's escape. Garner had "recklessly and heedlessly attempted to vault over the fence to escape, thereby assuming the risk of being fired upon."

The District Court . . . found that the statute, and Hymon's actions, were constitutional. The Court of Appeals reversed and remanded. . . .

OPINION

. . .

Whenever an officer restrains the freedom of a person to walk away, he has seized that person. . . . [T]here can be no question that apprehension by the use of deadly force is a seizure subject to the reasonableness requirement of the Fourth Amendment.

A police officer may arrest a person if he has probable cause to believe that person committed a crime. Petitioners and appellant argue that if this requirement is satisfied the Fourth Amendment has nothing to say about how that seizure is made. This submission ignores the many cases in which this Court, by balancing the extent of the intrusion against the need for it, has examined the reasonableness of the manner in which a search or seizure is conducted. . . .

The use of deadly force to prevent the escape of all felony suspects, whatever the circumstances, is constitutionally unreasonable. It is not better that all felony suspects die than that they escape. Where the suspect poses no immediate threat to the officer and no threat to others, the harm resulting from failing to apprehend him does not justify the use of deadly force to do so. It is no doubt unfortunate when a suspect who is in sight escapes, but the fact the police arrive a little late or are a little slower afoot does not always justify killing the suspect. A police officer may not seize an unarmed, nondangerous suspect by shooting him dead. The Tennessee statute is unconstitutional insofar as it authorizes the use of deadly force against such fleeing suspects. . . .

Officer Hymon could not reasonably have believed that Garner—young, slight, and unarmed—posed any threat. Indeed, Hymon never attempted to justify his actions on any basis other than the need to prevent escape. . . . [T]he fact that Garner was a suspected burglar could not, without regard to the other circumstances, automatically justify the use of deadly force. Hymon did not have probable cause to believe that Garner, whom he correctly believed to be unarmed, posed any physical danger to himself or to others.

DISSENT

For purposes of Fourth Amendment analysis, I agree with the Court that Officer Hymon "seized" Garner by shooting him. Whether that seizure was reasonable and therefore permitted by the Fourth Amendment requires a careful balancing of the important public interest in crime prevention and detection and the nature and quality of the intrusion upon legitimate interests of the individual. In striking this balance here, it is crucial to acknowledge that police use of deadly force to apprehend a fleeing criminal suspect falls within the "rubric of police conduct . . . necessarily [involving] swift action predicated upon the on-the-spot observations of the officer on the beat." . . .

The public interest involved in the use of deadly force as a last resort to apprehend a fleeing burglary suspect relates primarily to the serious nature of the crime. Household burglaries represent not only the illegal entry into a person's home, but also "pos[e] a real risk of serious harm to others." According to recent Department of Justice statistics, "[t]hree-fifths of all rapes in the home, three-fifths of all home robberies, and about a third of home aggravated and simple assaults are committed by burglars." . . .

Against the strong public interests justifying the conduct at issue here must be weighed the individual interests implicated in the use of deadly force by police officers. The majority declares that "[t]he suspect's fundamental interest in his own life need not be elaborated upon." This blithe assertion hardly provides an adequate substitute for the majority's failure to acknowledge the distinctive manner in which the suspect's interest in his life is even exposed to risk. For purposes of this case, we must recall that the police officer, in the course of investigating a nighttime burglary, had reasonable cause to arrest the suspect and ordered him to halt. The officer's use of force resulted because the suspected burglar refused to heed this command and the officer reasonably believed that there was no means short of firing his weapon to apprehend the suspect. . . . "[T]he policeman's hands should not be tied merely because of the possibility that the suspect will fail to cooperate with legitimate actions by law enforcement personnel." . . .

QUESTIONS FOR DISCUSSION

1. State all of the facts relevant to determining whether public duty justified the use of deadly force in this case.

2. Should the Fourth Amendment prohibit the use of deadly force to arrest property felons?

3. Is residential burglary simply a property crime?

4. Do you agree with the majority or dissent? Explain.

5. Will this rule embolden criminals? Defend your answer.

RESISTING UNLAWFUL ARREST

A problem related to the execution of public duty arises when citizens use force to resist arrest. Jurisdictions differ over whether individuals can use force at all in resisting arrest, and over how much force individuals may use to resist unlawful arrest. They range across this spectrum:

1. Individuals cannot use force against even plainclothes officers whom they know or believe to be officers.

2. Individuals can never use force against known police officers.

3. Individuals can use non deadly force against police officers.

4. If individuals use deadly force against officers, resisting unlawful arrest may reduce the charge from criminal homicide to a lesser degree of homicide.

Two policies underlie restricting citizens' use of force against police officers:

1. To encourage obedience to police.

2. To encourage other remedies to the use of force against police officers, such as civil lawsuits against the police, their departments, or the governmental units they serve.

The right to resist arrest has fluctuated over time. Historically, the common law of both England and the United States favored the right to resist arrest. Then, beginning in the 1960s, states began to limit, sometimes substantially, the right to resist arrest. By the late 1990s, the majority of states had restricted the right to resist arrest. The issue is still alive, however, because of an historical suspicion, if not outright hostility, to government power in the United States. The majority and dissenting opinions in the following extended excerpt from *State v. Valentine* graphically demonstrate the heated debate over the individual right to resist arrest.

C A S E

Did He Lawfully Resist Arrest?

State v. Valentine,
935 P.2d 1294 (Wash. 1997)

Ronald Valentine was convicted of assaulting police officers. He appealed. The Court of Appeals affirmed. The Washington supreme court granted review and affirmed.

ALEXANDER, Justice.

FACTS

In the early afternoon of May 16, 1990, in downtown Spokane, Spokane Police Officer Rick Robinson observed what he believed was a "suspicious subject on the corner at First and Jefferson." Upon making this observation, Robinson radioed another Spokane police officer, John Moore, and asked him if he knew the person standing at First and Jefferson "wearing a black coat." Moore proceeded to that location and observed a person wearing a black jacket enter a car. Although Moore was unable to immediately identify that person, he followed the car as the person drove it away.

According to Moore, the car soon made a turn without signaling. Moore, who was driving an unmarked car, advised Robinson over his radio that he was going to stop the car. He then attempted to do so by placing a rotating blue light on his dashboard, flashing his headlights, and honking his horn. While attempting to stop the automobile, Moore recognized that the driver of the car he was following was Ronald Valentine. [Moore testified at trial that he was acquainted with Valentine because he had cited him on two prior occasions for front license plate violations.] Moore broadcast over his police radio that he was following Valentine and that Valentine was not heeding Moore's efforts to stop him. Shortly thereafter, Valentine stopped his automobile and Moore pulled his car in behind him. Officer Robinson also pulled in behind Moore as did several other officers who had over-heard the radio broadcasts.

All of the police officers who arrived at the scene testified at trial. Their version of the events that transpired after the traffic stop varied dramatically from Valentine's version of events. Moore said that upon confronting Valentine he asked to see his license and registration. This, he indicated, prompted Valentine to ask, "Why?" Moore said that he then told Valentine that he was being cited for failing to signal for a turn. According to Moore, Valentine said that since Moore had given him a ticket a few days earlier, he had all the information that he needed. Moore said that he again asked for the driver's license and registration and Valentine responded by saying that "you . . . cops are just harassing me. I'm Black, and I'm tired of the harassment." After what Moore said was his third request of Valentine to produce his driver's license and registration, Valentine produced it.

Moore testified that he asked Valentine for his current address and that Valentine told Moore to "[l]ook it up." Moore then asked Valentine if he was going to cooperate and sign a citation and, according to Moore, Valentine said that he would not do so. Moore then informed Valentine that he was being placed under "arrest for failure to cooperate . . . [and] refusing to sign an infraction."

Moore also testified that after Valentine walked to the front of the car to show Moore that the car Valentine had been driving had a front license plate, Valentine returned to his car door, opened it, and started to reach inside the car. Moore said that he told Valentine to stay out of the car and grabbed Valentine's left arm to prevent him from reaching into the car. Robinson also claimed that he grabbed Valentine's right arm in a similar effort to keep Valentine from entering his car. Valentine, according to Moore, responded to their actions by spinning toward Moore and punching him in the side of the head. Robinson also claimed that he was hit in the ensuing skirmish.

Spokane Police Officers Jones, Webb, and Yates all testified that they joined the scuffle when Valentine began to struggle with Moore and Robinson. They said that they eventually subdued Valentine and forced him to the ground. Yates, who indicated that he had decided to assist Moore in effecting the traffic stop

when he heard over the radio that it was Valentine who was being pursued, testified that when he became involved in the fracas, he felt Valentine's hand on his gun butt. [Yates had been involved in a verbal confrontation with Valentine in a tavern the day before the incident leading to this appeal. Yates testified that the tavern incident "probably could have been" discussed with other officers at roll call, about two hours before the incident.] He said that in order to subdue Valentine, he had to apply a "carotid hold" to Valentine's neck. [The carotid hold is a hold applied to the neck area. It is designed to inhibit the supply of blood to the brain, and when it is applied correctly, the victim of the hold will lose consciousness.]

Valentine was eventually placed in handcuffs and was transported to jail. A nurse supervisor at the jail refused to admit Valentine because of his apparent injuries. Valentine was then taken to a hospital where Moore presented him with a citation for failing to signal for a turn. Valentine signed the citation. Valentine was later booked into the Spokane County Jail where he was charged by information with two counts of third degree assault, it being alleged that he assaulted Moore and Robinson while they were performing "official duties."

Valentine testified at trial on his own behalf. He claimed that because his turn signals were not functioning, he used hand signals to indicate his intention to turn. He also said that he stopped his car as soon as it was possible for him to do so. Valentine indicated that before reaching inside his car, he told Moore he was going to lock his car in order to protect some personal items. He denied that he told Moore to look up his address for himself. He also said that he did not throw the first punch, asserting that any blows he delivered were in self-defense and amounted to reasonable force to protect himself from an illegal arrest. Valentine contended that he would have signed a citation on the scene if he had been presented with one. Valentine was found guilty of assaulting Moore and not guilty of assaulting Robinson.

OPINION

Valentine asks us to decide whether the trial court erred in instructing the jury regarding the employment of force to resist an unlawful arrest. Instruction 17 reads as follows:

> A person unlawfully arrested by an officer may resist the arrest; the means used to resist an unlawful arrest must be reasonable and proportioned to the injury attempted upon the party sought to be arrested. The use of force to prevent an unlawful arrest which threatens only a loss of freedom, if you so find, is not reasonable.

. . .

In [*State v.*] *Rousseau*, [40 Wash.2d 92, 241 P.2d 447 (1952)] . . . we recited the common law rule prevalent in most jurisdictions at the time: "It is the law that a person illegally arrested by an officer may resist that arrest, even to the extent of the taking of life if his own life or any great bodily harm is threatened." . . .

In 1966, the right to resist an unlawful arrest was recognized in 45 out of 50 states. At that time the five states that had abrogated the right were Rhode Island, New Hampshire, Delaware, California, and New Jersey. Max Hochanadel & Harry W. Stege, Note, Criminal Law: The Right to Resist an Unlawful Arrest: An Out-Dated Concept?, 3 TULSA L.J. 40, 46 (1966). By 1983, however, 25 of those 45 states had revoked the common law rule either by statute or decision, and today, only 20 states have it in place, while resisting even an unlawful arrest is prohibited by law in 30 states. "[T]his common law principle has suffered a devastating deluge of criticism." *State v. Thomas*, 262 N.W.2d 607, 610 (Iowa 1978) (rule is "an anachronistic and dangerous concept"). Thus, the hold of the common law rule has weakened substantially in the last 30 years as jurisdiction after jurisdiction has modernized its jurisprudence to reflect the differences in criminal procedure in late twentieth century America as compared to early eighteenth century England. "[T]he trend in this country has been away from the old rule and toward the resolution of disputes in court." *Moreira*, 447 N.E.2d at 1226.

Courts addressing the question have set out many cogent and compelling reasons for consigning the common law rule to the dustbin of history. For example:

> While society has an interest in securing for its members the right to be free of unreasonable searches and seizures, society also has an inter-

est in the orderly resolution of disputes between its citizens and the government. (*United States v. Ferrone* (3d Cir.1971) 438 F.2d 381, 390.) Given such competing interests, we opt for the orderly resolution through the courts over what is essentially "street justice." *People v. Curtis*, 70 Cal.2d 347, 450 P.2d 33, 3637, 74 Cal.Rptr. 713 (1969)

. . .

We are of the opinion that the common law rule is outmoded in our modern society. A citizen, today, can seek his remedy for a policeman's unwarranted and illegal intrusion into the citizen's private affairs by bringing a civil action in the courts against the police officer and the governmental unit which the officer represents. The common law right of forceful resistance to an unlawful arrest tends to promote violence and increases the chances of someone getting injured or killed. *Fields v. State*, 178 Ind.App. 350, 382 N.E.2d 972, 975 (1978).

More important [than the existence of civil remedies], however, are the unwarranted dangers to civil order caused by this lingering artifact. Peace officers are today lethally armed and usually well trained to efficiently effect arrests. Resultantly, the resister's chances of success are seriously diminished unless he counters with equal or greater levels of force. The inevitable escalation of violence has serious consequences for both participants and innocent bystanders.

Briefly stated, a far more reasonable course is to resolve an often difficult arrest legality issue in the courts rather than on often hectic and emotion laden streets. Modern urbanized society has a strong interest in encouraging orderly dispute resolution. Confronting this is the outmoded common law rule which fosters unnecessary violence in the name of an obsolete self-help concept which should be promptly discarded.

We agree with all of these sentiments. Finally, we also associate ourselves with Judge Learned Hand, who said,

> The idea that you may resist peaceful arrest — and mind you, that is all it is — because you are

in debate about whether it is lawful or not, instead of going to the authorities which can determine, seems to me not a blow for liberty but, on the contrary, a blow for attempted anarchy. 35 A.L.I.PROC. 254 (1958).

In the final analysis, the policy supporting abrogation of the common law rule is sound. That policy was well enunciated by Division Two of the Court of Appeals in *State v. Westlund,* 13 Wash.App. 460, 467, 536 P.2d 20, 77 A.L.R.3d 270, review denied, 85 Wash.2d 1014 (1975), where the court said:

[T]he arrestee's right to freedom from arrest without excessive force that falls short of causing serious injury or death can be protected and vindicated through legal processes, whereas loss of life or serious physical injury cannot be repaired in the courtroom. However, in the vast majority of cases, as illustrated by the one at bar, resistance and intervention make matters worse, not better. They create violence where none would have otherwise existed or encourage further violence, resulting in a situation of arrest by combat. Police today are sometimes required to use lethal weapons for self-protection. If there is resistance on behalf of the person lawfully arrested and others go to his aid, the situation can degenerate to the point that what should have been a simple lawful arrest leads to serious injury or death to the arrestee, the police or innocent bystanders. Orderly and safe law enforcement demands that an arrestee not resist a lawful arrest and a bystander not intervene on his behalf unless the arrestee is actually about to be seriously injured or killed.

. . .

In sum, we hold that, although a person who is being unlawfully arrested has a right, as the trial court indicated in instruction 17, to use reasonable and proportional force to resist an attempt to inflict injury on him or her during the course of an arrest, that person may not use force against the arresting officers if he or she is faced only with a loss of freedom. We explicitly overrule *Rousseau* and other cases that are inconsistent with our holding in this case.

. . . [I]f the rule were, as the dissent suggests it should be, that a person being unlawfully arrested may always resist such an arrest with force, we would be inviting anarchy. While we do not, as the dissent appears to suggest, condone the unlawful use of state force, we can take note of the fact that in the often heated confrontation between a police officer and an arrestee, the lawfulness of the arrest may be debatable. To endorse resistance by persons who are being arrested by an officer of the law, based simply on the arrested person's belief that the arrest is unlawful, is to encourage violence that could, and most likely would, result in harm to the arresting officer, the defendant, or both. In our opinion, the better place to address the question of the lawfulness of an arrest that does not pose harm to the arrested person is in court and not on the street.

. . .

Affirmed.

DISSENT

SANDERS, Justice, dissenting.

Ronald Valentine was brutally beaten during the course of an unlawful arrest for a minor traffic infraction. Now this court affirms the criminal conviction of the victim despite the common law rule which clearly provides Valentine a viable legal defense. Mr. Valentine would not give up his liberty without a fight. Neither should we.

. . .

The facts as recounted by the majority are bad enough, yet understated. Even so they depict a bone-chilling, brutal, and nearly lethal beating of a fellow citizen for a minor traffic violation. But I would rejoin, to sustain a criminal conviction of the victim who was denied an instruction which simply would have allowed the jury to consider his defense is yet a greater outrage. Such refusal of the proposed jury instruction not only excuses the true offense perpetrated upon the victim but generalizes the wrong to all of us through its ill-conceived precedent.

. . .

Claiming a new-found enlightenment not apparent to legal generations which preceded it, the majority then opines that the established common law rule has outlived its usefulness in our brave new world where resistance to unlawful infliction of state coercive power is not only futile (Majority at 1302-03), but also invites "anarchy." Apparently the majority believes the unlawful use of state force is not anarchy but order. Yet I suggest such circumstances are not new, nor is the seeming futility of individual resistance to the overwhelming, yet still unlawful, police power of the state. It is an age-old tale. Mr. Valentine does not need courts to tell him who is going to win a physical confrontation with the police. But he does need this court to recognize and protect his legal rights.

Ultimately the majority's rule forbidding lawful resistance to unlawful state conduct specially privileges government agents in the wrong to the prejudice of citizens in the right. This special privilege is established notwithstanding the unquestioned and continuing right of a citizen to forcibly resist an assault against his person or a trespass on his property if committed by a private citizen. Thus, in a society of equals, those who violate their public trust by stepping beyond the boundaries of their lawful authority are privileged to become the usurping masters of the public they were originally entrusted to serve. Compare, e.g., *State v. Williams*, 81 Wash.App. 738, 74344, 916 P.2d 445 (1996) (one who is assaulted in a place he has a right to be has no duty to retreat and has a right to respond with force no matter how reasonable flight may be).

Finally, I offer my condolences to a majority which makes a criminal out of a victim under a circumstance which "causes [it] concern." The concurrence appears to appreciate exactly what is afoot but still will deny Mr. Valentine the benefit of his legal defense.

. . .

In America the tradition of resisting unlawful authority has been embraced from the early days of resisting imperial British power during the Revolution through the civil rights movement. . . . Traditionally, illegal, arbitrary abuse of state power has been regarded as even more threatening and deserving of resistance than the occasional street crime.

. . .

Justice Brandeis said much the same:

The maxim of unclean hands comes from courts of equity. But the principle prevails also in courts of law. Its common application is in

civil actions between private parties. Where the government is the actor, the reasons for applying it are even more persuasive. Where the remedies invoked are those of the criminal law, the reasons are compelling. *Olmstead v. United States*, 277 U.S. 438, 48384, 48 S.Ct. 564, 574, 72 L.Ed. 944 (1928) (Brandeis, J., dissenting).

Decency, security, and liberty alike demand that government officials shall be subjected to the same rules of conduct that are commands to the citizen. In a government of laws, existence of the government will be imperiled if it fails to observe the law scrupulously. Our government is the potent, the omnipresent teacher. For good or for ill, it teaches the whole people by its example. Crime is contagious. If the government becomes a lawbreaker, it breeds contempt for law; it invites every man to become a law unto himself; it invites anarchy. To declare that in the administration of the criminal law the end justifies the means—to declare that the government may commit crimes in order to secure the conviction of a private criminal—would bring terrible retribution. Against that pernicious doctrine this court should resolutely set its face. Id. at 485, 48 S.Ct. at 575 (Brandeis, J., dissenting).

. . .

Thomas Paine considered it common sense that

Society in every state is a blessing, but government even in its best state is but a necessary evil; in its worst state an intolerable one; for when we suffer, or are exposed to the same miseries by a government, which we might expect in a country without government, our calamities is [sic] heightened by reflecting that we furnish the means by which we suffer. Thomas Paine, Common Sense at 65 (Penguin Books 1976) (1776).

. . .

The Government of the State of Washington, as well, was "established to protect and maintain individual rights." Const. art. I, § 1. It was not established to do precisely the opposite.

The age-old rule which recognizes the right to re-sist unlawful assertions of state power is an important deterrent to tyranny. With the rule limited to cases where the police are exceeding and abusing their authority, the police officers involved in the excess should be deterred, knowing that their abuse may spark resistance.

This rule has equal application in the twentieth and twenty-first centuries to the extent it is rooted in political theory and human nature. In a well-known passage in The Gulag Archipelago, at 13 n. 5 (English ed. 1973), Aleksandr Solzhenitsyn wonders what would have happened had the countless victims of Stalin's arbitrary state power resisted and whether the officers serving under Stalin might have acted with less zeal had they known they could face legitimate resistance and even harm in effectuating their unlawful arrests. Solzhenitsyn suggests that resistance would have been an effective deterrent; had the victims resisted, "notwithstanding all of Stalin's thirst, the cursed machine would have ground to a halt!" He then concludes that "resistance should have begun right there, at the moment of the arrest itself." What, then, would Solzhenitsyn make of the majority's claim that this rule has outlived its usefulness because resistance to unlawful arrest when perpetrated by American authority is an act of futility, as the power of our state is so omnipotent that resistance is not only futile but should be condemned?

It may be true, as the majority posits, those who resist an unlawful arrest, like Valentine, will often be the worse for it physically; however, that is not to say that their resistance is unlawful. The police power of the state is not measured by how hard the officer can wield his baton but rather by the rule of law. Yet by fashioning the rule as it has, the majority legally privileges the aggressor while insulting the victim with a criminal conviction for justifiable resistance.

. . .

"[I]n the famous language of the Massachusetts Bill of Rights, the government of the commonwealth 'may be a government of laws and not of men.' For, the very idea that one man may be compelled to hold his life, or the means of living, or any material right essential to the enjoyment of life, at the mere will of another, seems to be intolerable in any country where freedom prevails, as being the essence of slavery itself." *Yick Wo v. Hopkins*, 118 U.S. 356, 370, 6 S.Ct. 1064, 1071, 30 L.Ed. 220 (1886).

QUESTIONS FOR DISCUSSION

Self-defense does not mean defense only against death or bodily injury. It also includes defending personal liberty. Resisting unlawful arrests is a good, but controversial, example.

1. Can citizens ever use force against the police, and if so, how much force can they use?

2. *State v. Valentine* represents the law in the now majority of states that have rejected the common law right to resist unlawful arrest.

3. Identify the competing interests involved in the right to resist arrest.

4. Summarize the arguments in favor of and against the right to resist arrest.

5. Do you agree that times have changed, or do we still need a rule that supports the right to resist arrest? Defend your answer.

CHOICE-OF-EVILS DEFENSE

The choice-of-evils defense, also known as the principle of necessity, has a long history in the law of Europe and the Americas. Throughout that history, the defense has generated heated controversy. The great thirteenth-century jurist of English and Roman law, Bracton, declared that what "is not otherwise lawful, necessity makes lawful." Other famous English commentators, such as Sir Francis Bacon, Sir Edward Coke, and Sir Matthew Hale in the sixteenth and seventeenth centuries, concurred with Bracton's judgment. The influential seventeenth-century English judge Hobart expressed the argument this way: "All laws admit certain cases of just excuse, when they are offended in letter, and where the offender is under necessity, either of compulsion or inconvenience." On the other side of the debate, the distinguished nineteenth-century English historian of criminal law and judge Sir James F. Stephen believed that the defense of necessity was so vague that judges could interpret it to mean anything they wanted. In the same vein, Glanville Williams, the modern criminal law professor, writes: "It is just possible to imagine cases in which the expediency of breaking the law is so overwhelmingly great that people may be justified in breaking it, but these cases cannot be defined beforehand."[27]

Early cases record occasional instances of defendants successfully pleading necessity as a defense to criminal liability. The most common example of the defense of necessity in the older cases is destroying houses in order to stop fires from spreading. In another example, as early as 1499, jurors could leave a trial without a judge's permission in order to avoid injury from a melee that broke out. In 1500, a prisoner successfully pleaded necessity to a charge of prison break because he was trying to avoid a fire that burned down the jail. In 1912, a man was acquitted on the defense of necessity when he burned a strip of the owner's strip heather in order to prevent a fire from spreading to his house.[28]

Perhaps the most famous case involving the defense of necessity is *The Queen v. Dudley and Stephens.* Dudley and Stephens, two adults with families, and Brooks, a youth of eighteen without family responsibilities, were lost in a lifeboat on the high seas without food or water, except for two cans of turnips and a turtle they caught in the sea on the fourth day. After twenty days (the last eight without food), perhaps a thousand miles from land and with virtually no hope of rescue, Dudley and Stephens—after failing to secure Brooks's agreement to cast lots—told Brooks that if no rescue vessel appeared by the next day, they were going to kill him for food. They explained to Brooks that his life was the most expendable, because Dudley and Stephens had family responsibilities whereas Brooks did not. The following day, no vessel appeared. After saying a prayer for him, Dudley and Stephens killed Brooks, who was too weak to resist. They survived on his flesh and blood for four days, when they were finally rescued. Dudley and Stephens were prosecuted, convicted, and sentenced to death for murder. They appealed, pleading the defense of necessity.

The judge, Lord Coleridge, in this famous passage, rejected the defense of necessity:

> [T]he temptation to act . . . here was not what the law ever called necessity. Nor is this to be regretted. Though law and morality are not the same, and many things may be immoral which are not necessarily illegal, yet the absolute divorce of law from morality would be of fatal consequence; and such divorce would follow if the temptation to murder in this case were to be held by law an absolute defense of it. It is not so. . . .
>
> To preserve one's life is generally speaking a duty, but it may be the plainest and the highest duty to sacrifice it. War is full of instances in which it is a man's duty not to live, but to die. The duty, in case of shipwreck, of a captain to his crew, of the crew to the passengers, of soldiers to women and children . . .; these duties impose on men the moral necessity, not of the preservation, but of the sacrifice of their lives for others. . . . It is not correct, therefore, to say that there is any absolute or unqualified necessity to preserve one's own life. . . .

It is not needful to point out the awful danger of admitting the principle contended for. Who is to be the judge of this sort of necessity? By what measure of the comparative value of lives to be measured? Is it to be strength, or intellect, or what? It is plain that the principle leaves to him who is to profit by it to determine the necessity which will justify him in deliberately taking another's life to save his own. In this case, the weakest, the youngest, the most unresisting, was chosen. Was it more necessary to kill him than one of the grown men? The answer must be "No" —

"So spake the Fiend, and with necessity,
The tyrant's plea, executed his devilish deeds."

It is not suggested that in this particular case, the deeds were "devilish," but it is quite plain that such a principle once admitted might be made the legal cloak for unbridled passion and atrocious crime.

Lord Coleridge sentenced them to death but expressed the hope that Queen Victoria would pardon them. The queen commuted their sentence to six months in prison.[29]

The Elements of the Choice-of-Evils Defense

The essence of the choice-of-evils defense consists of correctly choosing the lesser of two evils.

The *Model Penal Code* choice-of-evils provision reads as follows:

§ 3.02. Justification Generally: Choice of Evils.
1. Conduct that the actor believes to be necessary to avoid a harm or evil to himself or to another is justifiable, provided that:
    a. the harm or evil sought to be avoided by such conduct is greater than that sought to be prevented by the law defining the offense charged; and
    b. neither the Code nor other law defining the offense provides exceptions or defenses dealing with the specific situation involved; and
    c. a legislative purpose to exclude the justification claimed does not otherwise plainly appear.
2. When the actor was reckless or negligent in bringing about the situation requiring a choice of harms or evils or in appraising the necessity for his conduct, the justification afforded by this Section is unavailable in a prosecution

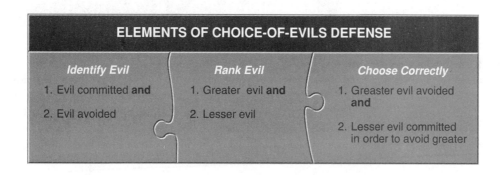

ELEMENTS OF CHOICE-OF-EVILS DEFENSE

Identify Evil	*Rank Evil*	*Choose Correctly*
1. Evil committed **and**	1. Greater evil **and**	1. Greater evil avoided **and**
2. Evil avoided	2. Lesser evil	2. Lesser evil committed in order to avoid greater

for any offense for which recklessness or negligence, as the case may be, suffices to establish culpability.

Some states, such as Illinois, New York, and Texas, have enacted necessity defense statutes that follow to some extent the *Model Penal Code* provision.[30]

The choice-of-evils defense provision in the *Model Penal Code* involves three analytical steps:

1. Identify the evils.
2. Rank the evils.
3. Choose between the evils.

Simply put, the choice-of-evils defense justifies choosing to do a lesser evil in order to avoid a greater evil. The choice of the lesser evil must be both imminent and necessary. Those who choose to do the lesser evil must reasonably believe their only choice is to cause the lesser evil right now in order to avoid the imminent danger of the greater evil.

The *Model Penal Code*'s provision extends the necessity principle to include:

1. destroying property to prevent spreading fire;
2. violating a speed limit to get a dying person to a hospital;
3. throwing cargo overboard to save a sinking vessel and its crew;
4. dispensing drugs without a prescription in an emergency; and
5. breaking and entering a mountain cabin to avoid freezing to death.

In all these instances, life, safety, and health are values superior to the strict property interests that actors violate to protect these superior interests.[31]

Since the *Model Penal Code* provided for a defense of necessity, 21 states have adopted choice-of-evil defense provisions.

Defining necessity is a major problem and therefore an obstacle to stating clearly how to apply it in real cases. The *Model Penal Code* provision does not leave the ranking of evils decision to individuals who claim its protection. Legislatures, or judges and juries at trial, must rank the evils. Once actors have made the "right" choice, the *Model Penal Code* provision either frees them entirely from criminal liability or considers the right choice a mitigating circumstance. The court applied the choice of evils defense in *People v. Alderson and others.*

C A S E

Did They Choose the Lesser Evil?

People v. Alderson and others,
144 Misc.2d 133, 540 N.Y.S.2d 948 (N.Y. 1989)

Alderson and nine other defendants were charged with criminal trespass in the third degree in connec-

tion with entering and remaining in office of Commissioner of the New York City Department of Health during a protest. Following a bench trial and motions for an order of dismissal, the Criminal Court of the City of New York rejected the defendants' defense of necessity, found the defendants guilty of trespass, and denied their motion to dismiss the charges.

LAURA E. DRAGER, Judge.

FACTS

The defendants are all members of an interest group called ACT UP which seeks to focus attention on the AIDS crisis. On July 19, 1988, Dr. Joseph announced a reduction in the estimated number of HIV-infected people in New York City from approximately 400,000 to 200,000. The primary cause for this reduction resulted from a decrease in the city's estimate of the number of gay men infected with the virus. Previously, relying on the 1948 Kinsey Report conclusion that "nationally, among white men, one in ten is 'more or less exclusively homosexual,'" the Department had estimated a New York City gay/bisexual population of from 250,000 to 500,000. Using several studies which had suggested that as many as 60% of the gay/bisexual men in the City were HIV-infected, the Department estimated that approximately 150,000 to 300,000 gay/bisexual men were infected.

However, the Department had since found this estimate unsupported by the actual number of known AIDS cases. Given what is known about the rate at which people infected with the virus develop AIDS, far more AIDS cases should have developed if the estimate was correct. As a result, the Department began to explore other methodologies to estimate the number of gay/bisexual men infected with the virus and on July 19, 1988 announced it had adapted a method developed in San Francisco. As a result of more specific information known about its gay/bisexual population, San Francisco had derived a figure representing the ratio between its gay/bisexual population infected with the virus and those with known AIDS cases.

The Department determined that the AIDS epidemics in New York and San Francisco bore sufficient similarities that New York could use the San Francisco ratio to determine the number of gay/bisexual men infected with the virus. Using this methodology, and accounting for a possible 15% underreporting of AIDS cases, the Department estimated between 46,000 to 76,000 gay/bisexual men in New York City

were infected with the virus, a substantial decrease from its previous estimate.

The conclusions reached by the Department were released to the public at a press conference held on July 19, 1988. The defendants each learned of the new figures through the media — in particular, from a series of three articles which appeared in the *New York Times* on July 19, 20 and 21, 1988. These articles raised serious concerns about the manner in which the figures were issued as well as the methodology used. Several community leaders and activists in the AIDS crisis were quoted as having deep reservations about the figures. They were also skeptical of the City's motivations, suggesting that the intent was to reduce funding for treatment of AIDS patients.

The articles specified some of the reasons for these concerns. First, the figures were issued only two months after the city had issued its master plan for AIDS services which had cited the old estimate. Second, there seemed to be little advance warning to community leaders of the impending change. Third, the figures were released at the same time that State Comptroller Edward J. Regan issued a report assailing the city for underestimating future health costs. The articles also suggested that the figures were suspect since they seemed to suggest that the city had only 100,000 gay/bisexual men in residence. [At trial, Dr. Joseph responded to these issues noting 1) the Master Plan concerned planning for actual AIDS cases and was not an epidemeology [sic] study as was now being issued; 2) the Department does not consult with community groups when it releases statistics and does not "negotiate" statistics; 3) the figures were not released in response to the State Comptroller's Report; and 4) the Department specifically sought to avoid an estimate of the gay population.]

On July 19 and 24 some of the defendants attended meetings held by ACT UP to discuss the figures and the concerns raised in the media reports. There was general disbelief as to the validity of applying a methodology developed for San Francisco to New York with its more diverse population, and a demonstration was scheduled for July 28 at the Department's building. According to the defendants, on July 27, the Department released a working paper (the "Report") setting forth its analysis resulting in the new estimate. Further, in an effort to dispel some of the confusion, Dr. Joseph spent approximately 15 minutes at a previously planned public forum answering questions about the Report, and then after he left for another meeting other Department representatives continued answering questions. Some of the defendants were present at that forum and found the answers did nothing to dispel their confusion.

On July 28, ACT UP held the previously planned demonstration at the Department. Several of the demonstrators—including some of the defendants—went to Dr. Joseph's private office and requested a meeting with him. Instead, they were offered a meeting with the Department's counsel and a public relations staff member. The demonstrators rejected the offer believing only a meeting with Dr. Joseph would be of any value. Members of ACT UP subsequently determined that further action was essential. They decided to hold what they called an unscheduled necessary meeting with Dr. Joseph in his office. They believed such action necessary to prevent loss of life that would result from a reduction of funding for AIDS health care which they believed would be the inevitable outcome of the Department's reduced estimate of infected gay men. The defendants further believed this action necessary because they would otherwise be unable to arrange a meeting with Dr. Joseph. Some of the defendants claimed they had been denied a meeting approximately six months before (although this occurred after these defendants had had a meeting with Dr. Joseph). One of the defendants (Mr. Quester) claimed he had tried to arrange a meeting after the figures were released but could not get through to Dr. Joseph's office by telephone.

On August 3, 1988, at approximately 3:00 P.M. the defendants entered Dr. Joseph's private office without an appointment, disrupting an ongoing meeting concerning an AIDS issue. The defendants arrived with a lawyer, observers, still photographers and a video camera. Some of the defendants wore signs saying "JOSEPH RESIGN." They were told by uniformed Security Officer Salome, a peace officer, not to enter. This order was ignored. Upon entering the office, although a few of the defendants announced that they were there to hold a meeting, most of the defendants within minutes began shouting at Dr. Joseph, calling

for his resignation. Dr. Joseph adjourned the meeting he had been holding.

The defendants were told by Sergeant Christine Harper, a peace officer and senior special officer with the Department of Health, that they were trespassing and if they did not leave they would be arrested. Subsequently, Charles Floyd, Director of Security for the Department of Health gave the same warning as did another individual with him. During the course of the action the defendants sat at Dr. Joseph's conference table and one defendant, Mr. Allan Robinson, sat behind Dr. Joseph's desk. Another defendant, Mr. Vance, banged on the conference table. At various times the defendants shouted abusive slogans. When Dr. Joseph sought to leave his office his way was blocked by some of the defendants (in particular, by Mr. David Robinson).

Arrests began within a few minutes after the defendants were told by Officer Harper that they were trespassing. However, a number of the defendants remained in the office until additional police could be called. During this time, Dr. Joseph, who had briefly left, returned to his office. Initially he sat at his desk. However, as the shouting and banging on the table continued, he moved to a seat at the conference table. As each defendant shouted a question or comment at him, Dr. Joseph looked at the person who spoke. Dr. Joseph never responded to any question but within a short time the shouting by the defendants subsided. They continued asking him questions about the reduced estimate to which Dr. Joseph gave no response. Dr. Joseph was present as arrests were made.

OPINION

The defendants argue that their action on August 3rd was justified to avoid the deaths of thousands of New Yorkers threatened by reduced funding for AIDS care that would result from the Department's new figures. Some of the defendants further believed their action justified because the Report in their view was unscientific, racist and heterosexist. The New York statutory embodiment of the necessity defense is found at P.L. § 35.05(2):

> . . . conduct which would otherwise constitute an offense is justifiable and not criminal when: . . .

2. Such conduct is necessary as an emergency measure to avoid an imminent public or private injury which is about to occur by reason of a situation occasioned or developed through no fault of the actor, and which is of such gravity that, according to ordinary standards of intelligence and morality, the desirability and urgency of avoiding such injury clearly outweigh the desirability of avoiding the injury sought to be prevented by the statute defining the offense in issue. The necessity and justifiability of such conduct may not rest upon considerations pertaining only to the morality and advisability of the statute, either in its general application or with respect to its application to a particular class of cases arising thereunder. Whenever evidence relating to the defense of justification under this subdivision is offered by the defendant, the court shall rule as a matter of law whether the claimed facts and circumstances would, if established, constitute a defense.

As required by statute, this court must decide preliminarily whether the evidence offered by the defendants, if found credible, supports the defense as a matter of law. The New York statute was influenced by the "choice of evils" provision of the *Model Penal Code* (ALI) at section 3.02. . . . [The section then quoted appears earlier in this chapter.]

The commentary to that provision notes:

This section . . . reflects the judgment that . . . a qualification on criminal liability, like the general requirements of culpability, is essential to the rationality and justice of the criminal law, and is appropriately addressed in a penal code. Under this section, property may be destroyed to prevent the spread of a fire. . . . Mountain climbers lost in a storm may take refuge in a house or may appropriate provisions. . . . A druggist may dispense a drug without the requisite prescription to alleviate grave distress in an emergency. A developed legal system must have better ways of dealing with such problems than to refer only to the letter of particular prohibitions, framed without reference to cases of this kind.

The *Model Penal Code* provision does not require that the evil sought to be avoided by the defendant be imminent. The drafters believed such a requirement "unduly emphasizes one ingredient in the judgment that is called for at the expense of others just as important." (American Law Institute *Model Penal Code*, Tentative Draft No. 8, p. 17).

The drafters of the New York provision believed a more stringent statute appropriate, thereby limiting the defense to "rare and highly unusual circumstances." This purpose was accomplished, by adding the requirement that the injury to be avoided be imminent.

It has been held that two elements must be met under the New York Statute for action to be found justifiable and not criminal:

First: Such conduct must be found to be necessary as an emergency measure to avoid an imminent public or private injury which is about to occur by reason of a situation occasioned or developed through no fault of the actor; and

Second: The injury is of such gravity that, according to ordinary standards of intelligence and morality, the desirability and urgency of avoiding such injury clearly outweigh the desirability of avoiding the injury sought to be prevented by the statute defining the offense in issue. *People v. Brown*, 70 Misc.2d 224, 2278, 333 N.Y.S.2d 342 (New York County 1972).

There has been an increasing trend in New York and throughout the country for protestors of various causes to rely on a justification defense to excuse what would otherwise be criminal action. Most comparable to the conduct of the defendants before this court are cases involving demonstrations at nuclear power energy plants, missile manufacturer sites, selective service offices and prisons. In none of the reported cases of these types has the necessity defense been sustained. The necessity defense has also been tried and generally rejected in anti-abortion protest cases too. However, the underpinnings for the court rulings are somewhat different than in other protest situations. The Supreme Court in *Roe v. Wade*, 410 U.S. 113, 93 S.Ct. 705, 35 L.Ed.2d 147 (1973), ruled and various state legislatures enacted laws specifically legalizing abortions. Where a legislature has made a determination of values, the necessity defense is inapplicable.

Several themes recur in the relevant case law. First, the actor must reasonably believe that his conduct is necessary to avoid an evil. "It is not enough that the actor believes that his behavior possibly may be conducive to ameliorating certain evils; he must believe it is 'necessary' to avoid the evils." *Model Penal Code* § 3.02, supra, p. 12. The Commentator went on to note that this requirement would therefore "create" significant barriers to the use of this defense in cases of illegal political protest. . . .

The second common theme in these cases is that the harm to be prevented must be imminent. In *People v. Brown*, 70 Misc.2d 224, 333 N.Y.S.2d 342 (New York County 1972) the defendants, inmates at the Manhattan House of Detention, took hostages in a prison uprising. The defendants claimed their action was in protest against and to publicize deplorable conditions. They further argued that previously filed grievances had been ignored. The court found that the defendants failed to offer proof that the injuries to be prevented were "about to occur" as required by the New York statute.

Third, and closely tied to the issue of imminence, is that the defense is unavailable where alternative options exist to the defendants. The Supreme Court, in *United States v. Bailey*, 444 U.S. 394, 100 S.Ct. 624, 62 L.Ed.2d 575 (1980), a prison escape case, said:

> . . . Under any definition of (the necessity defense) one principle remains constant: if there was a reasonable, legal alternative to violating the law, 'a chance both to refuse to do the criminal act and also to avoid the threatened harm,' the defense will fail.

. . .

A fourth common theme in these cases is that the action taken by the defendant must be reasonably designed to prevent the threatened greater harm. In this regard, the sincerity of the defendant's belief is not the determinative factor. In a Missouri case, defendants trespassed in the lobby of General Dynamics' corporate offices in the hopes of pressuring company executives into holding a meeting concerning the manufacture and deployment of Trident nuclear submarines. In denying the justification defense, the court noted "Any expectation that such a meeting would result in the discontinuance of the manufacture of nuclear weapon systems is more accurately described as fanciful optimism than reasonable."

Fifth, the necessity defense cannot be used to "excuse criminal activity intended to express the protestor's disagreement with positions reached by the lawmaking branches of the government." It is not for the courts to decide if an appropriate decision was made by the legislative or executive branches, among competing policy options. To extend the defense this far would violate the principle of separation of powers.

Turning to the facts in this case, this court finds that the defendants failed to offer evidence that would legally support the justification defense. The defendants offered no proof that the issuance of the Department's Report created an imminent emergency to anyone's life other than their personal beliefs that it might. They offered no proof that the Report would have any immediate impact on funding for AIDS cases by either the city or state; nor did they offer substantive proof that the Report would even have such impact in the future. The only evidence offered by the defense to prove this point was the testimony of Timothy Sweeney, Deputy Executive Director for Gay Men's Health Crisis ("GMHC"), who stated that the Report was likely to have an impact on AIDS funding in the future. However, Mr. Sweeney's testimony was necessarily speculative. The defense offered no evidence that any legislator or member of the executive branch of government had even suggested reducing AIDS funding as a result of the Report. [Indeed, Dr. Joseph testified that he was hoping to increase funding by expanding the types of cases entitled to assistance.]

Even if the defendants believed the Report contained erroneous conclusions which needed immediate correction, the action they took was not reasonably designed to accomplish this end. Trooping en masse uninvited into Dr. Joseph's office to attempt to hold a "meeting" while shouting "resign" and "murderer" are not actions that could reasonably have been thought to accomplish the goal of changing the Report. That goal might have been achieved, if warranted, by offering alternative expert research and reasoned objections to the analysis contained in the Report.

It is clear that lawful actions could have been undertaken by the defendants along these lines. For instance, they could have accepted the offer to meet with the Department's counsel on July 28 or they could have lobbied legislators to express their reservations about the Report. GMHC, an entity as concerned with the AIDS crisis and the accuracy of the Report as the defendants, elected to write a detailed letter to Dr. Joseph setting forth GMHC's concerns about the validity of the Report. The defendants could have done the same, but did not. [It is worth noting that even if the Report adversely affected AIDS funding, the defendants would still not have been justified in their action. The legislature and/or executive branches of government would, in that event, have made a policy determination. As has been noted before, the courts are not arbiters of competing public policies. The justification defense cannot be used to contest a disliked policy.]

Some of the defendants engaged in the action not only because they thought the Report would decrease government involvement in the AIDS crisis, but because they believed some of the ideas advanced in the Report were wrong. [For instance, some of the defendants believed—erroneously to the mind of the court—that the Report decreased the estimated gay/bisexual population of the city and the Report ignored gay black men altogether. All of the defendants objected to the application of a San Francisco based methodology to New York.] However, one cannot use the necessity defense to justify unlawful action intended to limit the advancement of ideas contrary to one's own. One's moral convictions alone can never be the basis for a justification defense.

Finally, the defendants also objected to the manner in which the Report was issued. Although the way the Report was released may have created some confusion, it did not in and of itself create an emergency as proven by the fact that the defendants did not enter Dr. Joseph's office for over two weeks after its issuance. It also merits consideration that no other AIDS activist organization found the type of action taken by the defendants a necessary response to the report.

Therefore, this court finds as a matter of law that the defendants failed to offer sufficient evidence for the trier of fact to consider the justification defense.

. . . This court does not doubt that the defendants entered Dr. Joseph's office with a moral conviction that their action was necessary and justified. But moral conviction is not a defense to criminal action. "(It) is commonly conceded that the exercise of a moral judgment based upon individual standards does not carry with it legal justification or immunity from punishment for breach of the law." *U.S. v. Kroncke*, 459 F.2d 697, 703 (8th Cir.1972) Civil disobedience has a well recognized place in the history of our country and the world, but those who engage in such actions must understand that unless the law they violate is unconstitutional they will bear the consequence of their actions.

For these reasons this court denies the motion for a trial order of dismissal and finds each of the defendants guilty of Criminal Trespass in the Third Degree. Further, each of the defendant's motions for a dismissal in the furtherance of justice is denied.

QUESTIONS FOR DISCUSSION

1. Identify the two evils in this case.
2. Rank them.
3. What, specifically, did the court say are the elements of the "choice of evils" defense?
4. Which of the elements of the defense did the court decide the facts in the case do not support?
5. Do you agree?
6. How does the court distinguish between civil disobedience and the defense of necessity?
7. Was this a case of civil disobedience or of necessity? Explain your answer, relying on the facts of the case.

NOTE CASE

The prosecution proved beyond a reasonable doubt by the use of radar readings that Dover was driving eighty miles per hour in a fifty-five-mile-per-hour zone. However, the court also found that the defendant, who is a lawyer, was not guilty on the grounds that his speeding violation was justified because he was late for a court hearing in Denver as a result of a late hearing in Summit County, Colorado.

A Colorado statute, § 42-4-1001(8)(a) provides:

The conduct of a driver of a vehicle which would otherwise constitute a violation of this section is justifiable and not unlawful when:

a. It is necessary as an emergency measure to avoid an imminent public or private injury which is about to occur by reason of a situation occasioned or developed through no conduct of said driver and which is of sufficient gravity that, according to ordinary standards of intelligence and morality, the desirability and urgency of avoiding the injury clearly outweigh the desirability of avoiding the consequences sought to be prevented by this section.

The Colorado Supreme Court reversed. It held:

In this case, the defendant did not meet the foundational requirements of § 42-4-1001(8)(a). He merely testified that he was driving to Denver for a 'court matter' and that he was late because of the length of a hearing in Summit County. No other evidence as to the existence of emergency as a justification for speeding was presented. The defendant did not present evidence as to the type or extent of the injury that he would suffer if he did not violate § 42-4-1001(1). He also failed to establish that he did not cause the situation or that his injuries would outweigh the consequences of his conduct. The record does not include evidence to establish a sufficient foundation to invoke the emergency justification defense provided by § 42-4-1001(8)(a). Since the defendant did not lay a proper foundation as to the existence of the defense, the prosecution was not required to prove beyond a reasonable doubt that the defendant was not justified in violating § 42-4-1001(1). § 18-1-407(2). The county court erred by finding the defendant not guilty because the defendant's speeding was justified because of an emergency. § 42-4-1001(8)(a). Accordingly, we reverse the district court and disapprove the ruling of the county court. *People v. Dover*, 790 P.2d 834 (Colo.1990)

Economic Necessity

The great French novel *Les Miserables*, by Victor Hugo, dealt with a timeless problem: whether it was right for a father to steal a loaf of bread to feed his starving children. That problem is not always fictitious, as *State v. Moe*, and the note case *State v. Celli* following it make clear. Because it requires balancing values, the necessity defense creates both ethical and social dilemmas. In *Moe*, the conflict was between hunger and theft, in *Celli*, between life and property, between breaking and entering or freezing to death. The natural thing to do in the situation is just what the defendants did.

Sharp disagreement has always existed over the defense of economic necessity in general and in particular the necessity of stealing in order to avert hunger. Conflicting comments abound throughout Anglo-American law regarding economic necessity. In the seventeenth century, in his *Maxims*, Francis Bacon asserted that stealing food in order to satisfy present hunger was not larceny. In *Leviathan*, written later in the century, Thomas Hobbes was more cautious, asserting that hungry people could take food during great famine if they could not get it either with money or through charity. In his *Pleas of the Crown*, Hawkins claimed that necessity was not a defense if hunger was due to the defendants' own unthriftiness. Late in the seventeenth century, Sir Matthew Hale stated the law as it is today; he rejected the defense altogether, because

1. the poor are already adequately cared for;

2. "men's properties would be under a strange insecurity, being laid open to other men's necessities, whereof no man can possibly judge, but the party himself"; and

3. pardons can resolve economic necessity cases.

Sir William Blackstone, in his widely used *Commentaries*, adopted the same rule and reasoning in the eighteenth century, and American law imported it from him. The doctrine has prevailed since then in both America and England.[32]

Blackstone and Hale have not persuaded everyone. Professor Glanville Williams assesses the defense of economic necessity this way:

> Although Hale and Blackstone settled the rule that economic necessity is no defense, their arguments were not impressive. The Crown's power of pardon really means the discretion of a politician who happens to be Home Secretary, and its existence is hardly a valid justification for what may otherwise be thought to be imperfect law. It is not a sincere argument to say that no one can judge the extremity of want, especially when the argument goes on to say that the Home Secretary can judge it. In fact, Blackstone's opinion would have the logical result of ruling out the whole defense of necessity in criminal law, including the defenses of self-defense and duress; yet Blackstone himself admitted them. The argument based upon the existence of the poor law has a much stronger foundation; but English social history does not suggest that the scale occurred after Blackstone's day, in the troubled years following the Napoleonic wars, when public assistance was kept at only just above starvation level, notwithstanding the desperate straits of the working classes and the growing wealth of farmers and landlords. It became clear at that time that no trust could be placed in the executive to look with sympathetic eye upon the defense of economic necessity. On the contrary, the hunger riots and machine breaking that inevitably followed from the mass misery were vindictively suppressed. If the judges of this period had had the courage to recognize famine as an excuse for stealing, they might have helped to bring the Government to a realization of the need for adequate public relief.
>
> Whatever the defects of the poor law in the past, it can hardly be doubted that the only satisfactory solution of the problem of economic necessity is through the provision of social services that prevent the question arising. Otherwise an impossible conflict is created between humanitarianism and social exigencies. No society, capitalist or communist, can tolerate a state of affairs in which the poorest are allowed to help themselves. The law must set its face against anarchy, but it can morally do so only on condition of itself making provision for the relief of extreme need.[33]

CASE

Is Economic Necessity a Defense?

State v. Moe,
174 Wash. 303, 24 P.2d 638 (1933)

The defendants were convicted of the crimes of grand larceny and riot. They appealed, claiming the defense of necessity. The supreme court affirmed their convictions. Justice Blake wrote the opinion for the court.

FACTS

In the afternoon of September 3, 1932, a large number of unemployed people, among whom were the appellants, gathered together and marched to the Red Cross commissary in the city of Anacortes. Their purpose was to make a demonstration in support of a demand for a greater allowance of flour than had theretofore been made by the relief committee. Not finding the chairman of the committee at the commissary, they dispatched a messenger for him. On being informed that the chairman could not leave his place of business, they then marched to his office.

All of the appellants were present during these movements, and they were present in the office of the chairman when the written demand was presented. The appellant Anderson, in fact, presented the demand, and seems to have been the principal spokesman for the people at the meeting in the chairman's office. The chairman advised them that it was impossible to comply with the demand, whereupon someone asked if that was final. Being informed that it was, several persons in the crowd said, in substance: "Very well, we'll get it." Up to this point the assemblage had been peaceable and lawful.

The crowd then left the chairman's office, and a large number of them (variously estimated from forty to seventy-five) proceeded to the Skaggs store, which they entered. Many of them helped themselves to groceries, which they took away without paying for them. The appellants were in the store during all of the time the groceries were being taken. . . . There is ample positive evidence of the . . . active participation [of Moe, Trafton, and Wollertz] in the offenses. The evidence is conflicting, but we can concern ourselves only as to whether there was sufficient evidence to take the case to the jury on both counts. In considering the evidence, it must be borne in mind that, when several people are engaged in perpetrating a crime, each is responsible for the acts of the others done in furtherance of the common purpose. So, as here, where a larceny is committed by a number of people by force and violence, all who participate are chargeable with the offenses of larceny and riot. This, even though some take the property without outward manifestations of force and violence, and others manifest force and violence, but take no property.

Measured by these rules, we find evidence that Wollertz left the store carrying groceries for which he did not pay. We find evidence that Moe and Trafton, by threat of physical violence, compelled the manager of the store to unlock and open the door, which he had closed and locked after the rioters entered. This evidence of larceny by Wollertz and of force and violence threatened by Moe and Trafton was sufficient to take the case to the jury on both counts as to all of them.

Contention is made that there was not sufficient evidence that the value of the groceries taken was in excess of $25. This contention is addressed rather to the weight and credibility of the evidence in that respect than to the absence of such proof. At least two witnesses, the manager of the store and one of his clerks, testified directly that, in the aggregate, more than $25 worth of groceries were taken by the rioters. This was sufficient to make a case of grand larceny for the jury.

Appellants offered to prove the conditions of poverty and want among the unemployed of Anacortes and Skagit county on and prior to September 3rd. This proof was offered for the purpose of showing a motive and justification for the raid on the Skaggs store and to show that the raid was spontaneous and not premeditated.

OPINION

Economic necessity has never been accepted as a defense to a criminal charge. The reason is that, were it ever countenanced, it would leave to the individual the right to take the law into his own hands. In larceny cases economic necessity is frequently invoked in mitigation of punishment, but has never been recognized as a defense.

Nor is it available as a defense to the charge of riot. The fact that a riot is spontaneous makes it none the less premeditated. Premeditation may, and frequently does, arise on the instant. A lawful assembly may turn into a riotous one in a moment of time over trivial incident or substantial provocation. When it does, those participating are guilty of riot, and neither the cause of the riot nor their reason for participation in it can be interposed as a defense. The causes, great or small, are available to the participants only in mitigation of punishment. The court did not err in rejecting the offer of proof. . . .

It is next contended that the prosecuting attorney was guilty of prejudicial misconduct, in his closing argument to the jury, by referring to appellants as radicals and communists. The court immediately instructed the jury to disregard the remark. However, we do not regard the remark as misconduct in the light of the facts developed and the arguments made by the appellants themselves.

During the examination of jurors on voir dire, appellants referred to themselves as militant members of labor organizations, and brought out the fact that two of their number were members of the Communist Party. One of the appellants, in his argument to the jury, said: "The groceries were taken, of course, but remember this, there is a higher law that says that a person holds his responsibility to himself first. There is a law of self-preservation, and how can you expect a man to go against the most fundamental urges — the most prominent is the quest for food. Even the cave man in days gone by must have food."

The remarks of the prosecutor, now complained of, were made in the course of an argument in answer to the tenets appellants themselves made of record, namely, that, acting under economic necessity, they had the right to disregard and violate the laws of the state. The full context of the prosecutor's argument in this respect was as follows:

> It is not a question with these people here as to whether a crime was committed. Mr. Moe has admitted to you that a crime was committed, so have the rest of them, but they say to you "There is a higher law" than the laws of the United States and the state of Washington and we are going to obey that higher law. Has the time come in this country and in our county when the laws of the United States and the laws of the state of Washington are to be ignored by a small group of radicals, and the country turned over to communism? . . . .

The judgments are affirmed as to appellants Moe, Trafton, and Wollertz.

QUESTIONS FOR DISCUSSION

1. Why did the court reject the defense of economic necessity? Was it for legal or political reasons?
2. What evils were balanced here?
3. Which is greater?
4. Was the danger from the greater evil imminent?
5. Did the defendants have alternatives?

NOTE CASE

On a cold winter day, Celli and his friend left Deadwood, South Dakota, hoping to hitchhike to Newcastle, Wyoming, to look for work. The weather turned colder, they were afraid of frostbite, and there was no place of business open for them to get warm. Their feet were so stiff from the cold that it was difficult for them to walk. They entered the only structure around, a cabin, breaking the lock on the front door. Celli immediately crawled into a bed to warm up, and defendant Brooks attempted to light a fire in the fireplace. They rummaged through drawers to look for matches, which they finally located and started a fire. Finally defendant Celli emerged from the bedroom, took off his wet moccasins, socks and coat, placed them near the fire, and sat down to warm himself. After warming up somewhat they checked the kitchen for edible food. That morning they had shared a can of beans, but had not eaten since. All they found was dry macaroni, which they could not cook because there was no water.

A neighbor noticed the smoke from the fireplace and notified the police. When the police entered the cabin, both defendants were warming themselves in front of the fireplace. The defendants were searched, but nothing belonging to the cabin owners was found. Do they have the defense of necessity? The trial court convicted them of fourth-degree burglary. The appellate court reversed on other grounds. *State v. Celli*, 263 N.W.2d 145 (S.D.1978)

CONSENT

The defense of consent is based on the value of individual autonomy and one of its offshoots — that individuals should be able to waive their rights. In other words, autonomous individuals have the right to suffer, or in the case of suicide, perhaps to kill themselves in order to prevent suffering. Individuals should have this right without the interference of a paternalistic government. In some crimes, consent is an element of the crime itself. In theft, for example, taking property without the owner's consent is central to the crime. In rape, too, consent eliminates the *mens rea*—rape requires the intent to have sexual penetration by force and without consent.

Sometimes, the same act may be criminal in one situation while it is appropriate in another. Grabbing another forcibly around the ankles and bringing him or her abruptly to the ground is assault if it happens between strangers on the street, but it generates thunderous approval from fans supporting the defensive team if it takes place on the playing field during the Super Bowl. A surgeon commits neither assault and battery by cutting into a patient's body nor murder if the patient dies.

When those who attack others attempt to justify their attacks by claiming that the consent of the victim is a defense to the attack, consent is considered a most controversial defense. In fact, the law either prohibits altogether or places severe limits to the defense of consent. In most Western countries, for example, individuals can take their own lives and inflict injuries on themselves without incurring criminal liability. But they cannot authorize others to kill them or beat them. Courts tend to recognize the defense only when

- No serious injury results from the consensual attack, such as when a slap in the face requires no medical treatment.

- Society widely accepts the risk of injury, such as in ice hockey, football, soccer, and boxing.

- The defendant's conduct has a beneficial result, such as when a doctor performs surgery.[34]

Of course, the consent must be both voluntary and knowing. That is, the consent must stem from the consenting party's own free will without compulsion or duress. The person consenting must be competent to consent; youth, intoxication, or mental abnormality might disable the consent. Consent obtained by fraud or deceit renders the consent ineffective. Finally, forgiveness by victims after defendants have committed crimes is not considered justified by consent. The court dealt with the defense of consent in *State v. Shelley*.

C A S E

Did He Consent to the Attack?

State v. Shelley,
929 P.2d 489 (Wash. 1997)

Shelley was convicted in the Superior Court, King County, of second-degree assault, arising out of an incident in which Shelley intentionally punched another basketball player during a game. Shelley appealed. The Court of Appeals affirmed the conviction.

GROSSE, Judge.

FACTS

. . .

On March 31, 1993, Jason Shelley and Mario Gonzalez played "pickup" basketball on opposing teams at the University of Washington Intramural Activities Building (the IMA). Pickup games are not refereed by an official; rather, the players take responsibility for calling their own fouls. During the course of three games, Gonzalez fouled Shelley several times. Gonzalez had a reputation for playing overly aggressive defense at the IMA. Toward the end of the evening, after trying to hit the ball away from Shelley, he scratched Shelley's face, and drew blood. After getting scratched, Shelley briefly left the game and then returned.

Shelley and Gonzalez have differing versions of what occurred after Shelley returned to the game. According to Gonzalez, while he was waiting for play in the game to return to Gonzalez's side of the court, Shelley suddenly hit him. Gonzalez did not see Shelley punch him. According to Shelley's version of events, when Shelley rejoined the game, he was running down the court and he saw Gonzalez make "a move towards me as if he was maybe going to prevent me from getting the ball." The move was with his hand up "across my vision." Angry, he "just reacted" and swung. He said he hit him because he was afraid of being hurt, like the previous scratch. He testified that Gonzalez continually beat him up during the game by fouling him hard.

A week after the incident, a school police detective interviewed Shelley and prepared a statement for Shelley to sign based on the interview. Shelley reported to the police that Gonzalez had been "continually slapping and scratching him" during the game. Shelley "had been getting mad" at Gonzalez and the scratch on Shelley's face was the "final straw." As the two were running down the court side by side, "I swung my right hand around and hit him with my fist on the right side of his face." Shelley asserted that he also told the detective that Gonzalez waved a hand at him just before Shelley threw the punch and that he told the detective that he was afraid of being injured. Gonzalez required emergency surgery to repair his jaw. Broken in three places, it was wired shut for six weeks. His treating physician believed that a "significant" blow caused the damage.

During the course of the trial, defense counsel told the court he intended to propose a jury instruction that: "A person legally consents to conduct that causes or threatens bodily harm if the conduct and the harm are reasonably foreseeable hazards of joint participation in a lawful, athletic contest or competitive sport." Although the trial court agreed that there were risks involved in sports, it stated that "the risk of being intentionally punched by another player is one

that I don't think we ever do assume." The court noted, "In basketball . . . you consent to a certain amount of rough contact. If they were both going for a rebound and Mr. Shelley's elbow or even his fist hit Mr. Gonzalez as they were both jumping for the rebound and Mr. Gonzalez'[s] jaw was fractured in exactly the same way . . . then you would have an issue." Reasoning that "our laws are intended to uphold the public peace and regulate behavior of individuals," the court ruled "that as a matter of law, consent cannot be a defense to an assault." The court indicated that Shelley could not claim consent because his conduct "exceed[ed] what is considered within the rules of that particular sport[:]"

> [C]onsent is to [sic] contact that is contemplated within the rules of the game and that is incidental to the furtherance of the goals of that particular game.

If you can show me any rule book for basketball at any level that says an intentional punch to the face in some way is a part of the game, then I would take another . . . look at your argument. I don't believe any such rule book exists.

Later Shelley proposed jury instructions on the subject of consent:

> An act is not an assault, if it is done with the consent of the person alleged to be assaulted. It is a defense to a charge of second degree assault occurring in the course of an athletic contest if the conduct and the harm are reasonably foreseeable hazards of joint participation in a lawful athletic contest or competitive sport.

The trial court rejected these and Shelley excepted. The trial court did instruct the jury about self-defense.

OPINION

First, we hold that consent is a defense to an assault occurring during an athletic contest. This is consistent with the law of assault as it has developed in Washington. A person is guilty of second degree assault if he or she "[i]ntentionally assaults another and thereby recklessly inflicts substantial bodily harm." One common law definition of assault recognized in

Washington is "an unlawful touching with criminal intent." At the common law, a touching is unlawful when the person touched did not give consent to it, and was either harmful or offensive. As our Supreme Court stated in *State v. Simmons,* "where there is consent, there is no assault." The State argues that because *Simmons* was a sexual assault case, the defense of consent should be limited to that realm. We decline to apply the defense so narrowly. Logically, consent must be an issue in sporting events because a person participates in a game knowing that it will involve potentially offensive contact and with this consent the "touchings" involved are not "unlawful."

Our review of the cases and commentary on the issue of consent reveals that although the defense of consent is applied in the realm of sexual assault, it has been sparingly applied by the courts in other areas. [*Model Penal Code and Commentaries* pt. 1, § 2.11 cmt. 2, at 396 (Official Draft & Revised Comments 1995); 2 Wayne R. LaFave & Austin W. Scott, Jr., *Substantive Criminal Law* § 7.15(e), at 31112 (1986); 1 Paul H. Robinson, *Criminal Law Defenses* §§ 23, 106(b) (1984); W.E. Shipley, *Annotation, Assault and Battery—Consent as Defense,* 58 A.L.R.3d 662, 664 (1974)] The rationale that courts offer in limiting it is that society has an interest in punishing assaults as breaches of the public peace and order, so that an individual cannot consent to a wrong that is committed against the public peace. Urging us to reject the defense of consent because an assault violates the public peace, the State argues that this principle precludes Shelley from being entitled to argue the consent defense on the facts of his case. In making this argument, the State ignores the factual contexts that dictated the results in the cases it cites in support.

When faced with the question of whether to accept a school child's consent to hazing or consent to a fight, [*People v. Lenti,* 44 Misc.2d 118, 253 N.Y.S.2d 9 (1964); *People v. Lucky,* 45 Cal.3d 259, 753 P.2d 1052, 247 Cal.Rptr. 1 (1988), cert. denied, 488 U.S. 1034, 109 S.Ct. 848, 102 L.Ed.2d 980 (1989); *State v. Hatfield,* 218 Neb. 470, 356 N.W.2d 872, 876 (1984)] or a gang member's consent to a beating, [*Helton v. State,* 624 N.E.2d 499, 514 (Ind.Ct.App.1993)] courts have declined to apply the defense. Obviously, these cases present "touchings" factually distinct from "touchings" occurring in athletic competitions.

If consent cannot be a defense to assault, then most athletic contests would need to be banned because many involve "invasions of one's physical integrity." [FN11] Because society has chosen to foster sports competitions, players necessarily must be able to consent to physical contact and other players must be able to rely on that consent when playing the game. This is the view adopted by the drafters of the *Model Penal Code:* There are, however, situations in which consent to bodily injury should be recognized as a defense to crime.... There is ... the obvious case of participation in an athletic contest or competitive sport, where the nature of the enterprise often involves risk of serious injury. Here, the social judgment that permits the contest to flourish necessarily involves the companion judgment that reasonably foreseeable hazards can be consented to by virtue of participation. [*Model Penal Code,* supra, § 2.11 cmt. 2, at 396]

The more difficult question is the proper standard by which to judge whether a person consented to the particular conduct at issue. The State argues that "when the conduct in question is not within the rules of a given sport, a victim cannot be deemed to have consented to this act." The trial court apparently agreed with this approach. Although we recognize that there is authority supporting this approach, we reject a reliance on the rules of the games as too limiting. Rollin M. Perkins in *Criminal Law* explains:

> The test is not necessarily whether the blow exceeds the conduct allowed by the rules of the game. Certain excesses and inconveniences are to be expected beyond the formal rules of the game. It may be ordinary and expected conduct for minor assaults to occur. However, intentional excesses beyond those reasonably contemplated in the sport are not justified. [Rollin M. Perkins & Ronald N. Boyce, *Criminal Law,* at 154 (3d ed. 1982)]

Instead, we adopt the approach of the *Model Penal Code* which provides that:

> (2) Consent to Bodily Injury. When conduct is charged to constitute an offense because it causes or threatens bodily injury, consent to such conduct or to the infliction of such injury is a defense if:

. . . .

(b) the conduct and the injury are reasonably foreseeable hazards of joint participation in a lawful athletic contest or competitive sport or other concerted activity not forbidden by law. [*Model Penal Code*, supra, § 2.11, at 393. See 1 Paul H. Robinson, *Criminal Law Defenses* § 23, at 80 & n. 13 (1984) and statutes cited therein; Robinson, supra, § 106(b), at 520.]

The State argues the law does not allow "the victim to 'consent' to a broken jaw simply by participating in an unrefereed, informal basketball game." This argument presupposes that the harm suffered dictates whether the defense is available or not. This is not the correct inquiry. The correct inquiry is whether the conduct of defendant constituted foreseeable behavior in the play of the game. Additionally, the injury must have occurred as a byproduct of the game itself. In construing a similar statutory defense, the Iowa court required a "nexus between defendant's acts and playing the game of basketball." In *State v. Floyd*, a fight broke out during a basketball game and the defendant, who was on the sidelines, punched and severely injured several opposing team members. Because neither defendant nor his victims were voluntarily participating in the game, the defense did not apply because the statute "contemplated a person who commits acts during the course of play, and the exception seeks to protect those whose acts otherwise subject to prosecution are committed in furtherance of the object of the sport." As the court noted in *Floyd*, there is a "continuum, or sliding scale, grounded in the circumstances under which voluntary participants engage in sport . . . which governs the type of incidents in which an individual volunteers (i.e., consents) to participate[.]" [*State v. Floyd*, 466 N.W.2d 919, 922 (Iowa.Ct.App.1990)]

The New York courts provide another example. In a football game, while tackling the defendant, the victim hit the defendant. After the play was over and all of the players got off the defendant, the defendant punched the victim in the eye. The court in *People v. Freer* held that this act was not consented to:

Initially it may be assumed that the very first punch thrown by the complainant in the course of the tackle was consented to by defendant. The act of tacking an opponent in the course of a football game may often involve "contact" that could easily be interpreted to be a "punch". Defendant's response after the pileup to complainant's initial act of "aggression" cannot be mistaken. Clearly, defendant intended to punch complainant. This was not a consented to act. *People v. Freer*, 86 Misc.2d 280, 381 N.Y.S.2d 976, 978 (1976).

As a corollary to the consent defense, the State may argue that the defendant's conduct exceeded behavior foreseeable in the game. Although in "all sports players consent to many risks, hazards and blows," there is "a limit to the magnitude and dangerousness of a blow to which another is deemed to consent." This limit, like the foreseeability of the risks, is determined by presenting evidence to the jury about the nature of the game, the participants' expectations, the location where the game has been played, as well as the rules of the game. Here, taking Shelley's version of the events as true, the magnitude and dangerousness of Shelley's actions were beyond the limit. There is no question that Shelley lashed out at Gonzalez with sufficient force to land a substantial blow to the jaw, and there is no question but that Shelley intended to hit Gonzalez. There is nothing in the game of basketball, or even rugby or hockey, that would permit consent as a defense to such conduct. Shelley admitted to an assault and was not precluded from arguing that the assault justified self-defense; but justification and consent are not the same inquiry.

. . .

We affirm.

QUESTIONS FOR DISCUSSION

1. According to the court, why can participants in a sport consent to conduct that would otherwise be a crime?

2. Why should they be allowed to consent to such conduct when in other situations, such as those enumerated in the note cases that follow, they cannot consent?

3. Should individuals be allowed to knowingly and voluntarily consent to the commission of crimes against them? Why or why not?

4. Why was Shelley not allowed the defense of consent in this case?

5. Do you agree with the court's decision? Relying on the relevant facts in the case, defend your answer.

NOTE CASES

1. Mrs. Brown, the victim, was an alcoholic. On the day of the alleged crime she indulged in some spirits, apparently to Mr. Brown's dissatisfaction. As per their agreement, defendant sought to punish Mrs. Brown by severely beating her with his hands and other objects. Brown was charged with atrocious assault and battery. He contended that he was not guilty of atrocious assault and battery because he and Mrs. Brown, the victim, had an understanding to the effect that if she consumed any alcoholic beverages (and/or became intoxicated), he would punish her by physically assaulting her. The trial court refused the defense of consent. Do you agree? In *State v. Brown*, 143 N.J. Super. 571, 364 A.2d 27 (1976), the New Jersey appellate court affirmed the conviction. The court wrote:

> . . . The laws . . . are simply and unequivocally clear that the defense of consent cannot be available to a defendant charged with any type of physical assault that causes appreciable injury. If the law were otherwise, it would not be conducive to a peaceful, orderly and healthy society. . . .
>
> This court concludes that, as a matter of law, no one has the right to beat another even though that person may ask for it. Assault and battery cannot be consented to by a victim, for the State makes it unlawful and is not a party to any such agreement between the victim and perpetrator. To allow an otherwise criminal act to go unpunished because of the victim's consent would not only threaten the security of our society but also might tend to detract from the force of the moral principles underlying the criminal law. . . .

Thus, for the reasons given, the State has an interest in protecting those persons who invite, consent to and permit others to assault and batter them. Not to enforce these laws which are geared to protect such people would seriously threaten the dignity, peace, health and security of our society.

2. Fransua and the victim were in a bar in Albuquerque. Fransua had apparently been drinking heavily that day and the previous day. Sometime around 3:00 P.M., after an argument, Fransua told the victim that if Fransua had a gun, he would shoot the victim. The victim then left the bar, went to his own automobile, removed a loaded pistol from the automobile, and returned to the bar. He came up to Fransua, laid the pistol on the bar, and made the following remark: "There is the gun. If you want to shoot me, go ahead." Fransua picked up the pistol, put the barrel next to the victim's head, and pulled the trigger, wounding him seriously.

Was Fransua guilty of aggravated battery or was the victim's consent a justification? In *State v. Fransua*, 85 N.M. 173, 510 P.2d 106, 58 A.L.R.3d 656 (App.Ct.1973), the court ruled that consent was not a defense. The court wrote:

> It is generally conceded that a state enacts criminal statutes making certain violent acts crimes for at least two reasons: One reason is to protect the persons of its citizens; the second, however, is to prevent a breach of the public peace. While we entertain little sympathy for either the victim's absurd actions or the defendant's equally unjustified act of pulling the trigger, we will not permit the defense of consent to be raised in such cases. Whether or not the victims of crimes have so little regard for their own safety as to request injury, the public has a stronger and overriding interest in preventing and prohibiting acts such as these. We hold that consent is not a defense to the crime of aggravated battery, irrespective of whether the victim invites the act and consents to the battery.

SUMMARY

In the defenses of justification, defendants admit their responsibility for their actions but maintain that special circumstances justify their conduct or its result. The defenses of justification examined in this chapter involve cases in which defendants are confronted with a dilemma—choosing between two evils. They kill or injure persons, or violate the property of another, in order to avoid an imminent greater evil, or do so because they are performing a public duty, defending their rights against government invasion, or carrying out an agreement with the consent of the "victim."

Theoretically, these evils—and the greater ones defended against—apply the general principle of necessity to specific crimes. Practically, however, neither legislators, judges, prosecutors, nor defense attorneys think in such broad, theoretical terms. Rather, they think in terms of specific defenses applicable to particular crimes. Hence, for example, they think in terms of self-defense as a defense to the specific crimes of criminal homicide, rape, and assault. They refer to the special defense of choice-of-evils defense, not to the general principle of necessity, when they deal with such cases as freezing people breaking into deserted cabins to keep warm.[35]

REVIEW QUESTIONS

1. Identify and briefly describe the three situations in which defenses to crimes arise.

2. Explain the theoretical and practical differences between the defenses of justification and the defenses of excuse.

3. Explain how an affirmative defense works.

4. Explain the relationship between motive and *mens rea*. How and why does motive affect punishment?

5. What is the common-law definition of self-defense?

6. What two purposes do not justify the use of force in self-defense?

7. When can one who has provoked an attack plead self-defense?

8. What two elements must defendants demonstrate in order to plead self-defense?

9. Distinguish between imminent and present danger.

10. Explain the retreat doctrine and the castle exception to the retreat doctrine.

11. Identify the conditions under which a person can use force to protect a third person.

12. When can a person use less than deadly force to protect homes and property and when can deadly force be used?

13. Under what conditions can a public official use force, including deadly force, against citizens?

14. How much force can a citizen use against a police officer and under what circumstances? What is the rationale for prohibiting the use of force against police officers?

15. Explain the principle of necessity. What are the elements in the *Model Penal Code*'s choice-of-evils defense?

16. Identify and describe the three steps in applying the choice-of-evils defense.

17. What five conditions in addition to self-defense does the *Model Penal Code* provide for the application of the choice-of-evils defense?

18. Define the defense of economic necessity, explain the conditions under which it has been applied, and summarize the arguments against the defense.

19. What two critical issues surround the defense of consent? Explain the situations in which consent is accepted as a defense to crime.

KEY TERMS

affirmative defense A defense in which the defendant bears the burden of production.

alibi A defense that places defendants in a different place at the time and scene of the crime.

burden of persuasion The responsibility to convince the fact finder of the truth of the defense.

burden of production The responsibility to introduce initial evidence to support a defense.

burden of proof The responsibility to produce the evidence to persuade the fact finder.

castle exception The principle stating that defenders have no need to retreat when attacked in their homes.

defenses Justifications and excuses to criminal liability.

excuse A defense admitting wrongdoing without criminal responsibility.

imperfect defense Defense reducing but not eliminating criminal liability.

justification A defense deeming acceptable under the circumstances what is otherwise criminal conduct.

mitigating circumstances Facts that reduce but do not eliminate culpability.

motive The reason why a defendant commits a crime.

objective test An external measure of reasonableness of belief; used to determine immediate or present danger of attack.

perfect defense A defense that leads to outright acquittal.

subjective test An internal or "honest belief" test used to determine immediate or present danger of attack.

Suggested Readings

1. George Fletcher, "Justification," in *Encyclopedia of Crime and Justice*, vol. 3, ed. Sanford H. Kadish (New York: Free Press, 1983), pp. 941–946. An excellent introduction to the theory of justification in criminal law. Fletcher describes and assesses the scope and criteria for justification, balancing evils, and the imminent risk requirement.

2. American Law Institute, *Model Penal Code and Commentaries*, vol. 2 (Philadelphia: American Law Institute, 1985), pp. 8–22. The most complete discussion of the principle of necessity by the foremost authorities on the subject. Although written primarily for lawyers, it is worth the serious student's effort.

3. George F. Dix, "Self-Defense," in *Encyclopedia of Crime and Justice*, vol. 3, pp. 946–953. A good general discussion of self-defense. Dix covers the main elements of self-defense, the defense by battered wives who attack their husbands, the retreat doctrine, the defense of others, and the use of force to resist arrest.

4. Rollin M. Perkins and Ronald N. Boyce, *Criminal Law*, 3d ed. (Mineola, N.Y.: Foundation Press, 1982), pp. 1074—1092. The authors thoroughly discuss the consent defense in criminal law. They describe both the legal effect of consent and the crimes to which consent is a defense. They also appraise arguments both for and against consent, as well as the law as it stands in several jurisdictions.

Notes

1. George Fletcher, *Rethinking Criminal Law* (Boston: Little, Brown, 1981), chap. 10; Rollin M. Perkins and Ronald N. Boyce, *Criminal Law*, ed. (Mineola, NY: Foundation Press, 1982), chs. 8–10; Thomas Morawetz, "Reconstructing the Criminal Defenses: The Significance of Justification," *Journal of Criminal Law and Criminology* 77 (1986):277.

2. Fletcher, *Rethinking Criminal Law*, p. 759; American Law Institute, *Model Penal Code and Commentaries*, vol. 2 (Philadelphia: American Law Institute, 1985), pt. I, p. 3.

3. See Arnold H. Loewy, *Criminal Law* (St. Paul, Minn.: West Publishing Co., 1987), pp. 192–204, for a brief introduction to the topics of burdens and amount of proof. Also, more thorough discussion appears in Wayne R. LaFave and Austin W. Scott, Jr., *Criminal Law*, 2d ed. (St. Paul, Minn.: West Publishing Com-

pany, 1986), pp. 51–56; *People v. Dover*, 790 P.2d 834 (Colo.1990).

4. *New York Times*, November 11, 1994.

5. Perkins and Boyce, *Criminal Law*, 926–932; Jerome Hall, *General Principles of Criminal Law*, 2d ed. (Indianapolis, Ind.: Bobbs-Merrill, 1960), pp. 86–88, 97–102; Carol Byrne, "Was Mercy in This Killing?" *Minneapolis Star and Tribune* (May 1, 1988), 1A; Carol Byrne, "An Old Man Starts a New Life — In Prison," *Minneapolis Star and Tribune* (June 5, 1988), p. 1A.

6. George P. Fletcher, *A Crime of Self-Defense: Bernhard Goetz and the Law on Trial* (New York: Free Press, 1988), Chapter 2, especially pp. 18–19.

7. Francis Wharton, *A Treatise on the Criminal Law of the United States* (Philadelphia: Kay and Brother, 1861), § 1020.

8. *State v. Goode*, 271 Mo. 43, 195 S.W. 1006 (1917); Perkins and Boyce, *Criminal Law*, pp. 1128–1129.

9. American Law Institute, *Model Penal Code and Commentaries*, vol. 2, pt. I, pp. 30–61; George P. Fletcher, *A Crime of Self-Defense*, pp. 18–27.

10. *New York Times* (January 14, 1989), p. 9.

11. Quoted in *New York Times* (January 23, 1989); also see Fletcher, *A Crime of Self-Defense*.

12. *State v. Schroeder*, 199 Neb. 822, 261 N.W.2d 759 (1978).

13. *People v. Williams*, 56 Ill.App.2d 159, 205 N.E.2d 749 (1965); American Law Institute, *Model Penal Code and Commentaries*, art. 3.04.

14. *People v. Johnson*, 2 Ill.2d 165, 117 N.E.2d 91 (1954).

15. 158 U.S. 550, 15 S.Ct. 962, 39 L.Ed. 1086 (1894); American Law Institute, *Model Penal Code and Commentaries*, vol. 3, pt. I, pp. 35–37.

16. Quoted in *Model Penal Code*, tentative draft no. 8 (Philadelphia: American Law Institute, 1958), pp. 79–80.

17. 117 Tenn. 430 100 S.W. 94 (1907).

18. *State v. Kennamore*, 604 S.W.2d 856 (Tenn.1980).

19. Ibid.

20. *State v. Aguillard*, 567 So.2d 674 (La.1990).

21. Quoted in *State v. Mitcheson*, 560 P.2d 1120 (Utah 1977), 1122.

22. Sir William Blackstone, *Commentaries on the Laws of England* (New York: Garland, 1978), pt. IV, p. 180.

23. LaFave and Scott, *Criminal Law*, p. 389.

24. *Mattis v. Schnarr*, 547 F.2d 1007 (8th Cir. 1976) judgment vacated 431 U.S. 171, 97 S.Ct. 1739, 52 L.Ed.2d 219 (1977). Catherine H. Milton et al., *Police Use of Deadly Force* (Washington, D.C.: The Police Foundation, 1977), contains a detailed discussion. See also Lawrence O'Donnell, Jr., *Deadly Force* (New York: Morrow, 1983), for a spirited attack on deadly force.

25. Quoted in American Law Institute, *Model Penal Code*, tentative draft no. 8, pp. 60–62.

26. Address delivered to National College of State Trial Judges, Chapel Hill, North Carolina, August 15, 1968. Quoted in Sanford Kadish and Manfred Paulson, *Criminal Law and Its Processes*, 3d ed. rev. (Boston: Little, Brown, 1975), pp. 541–542.

27. American Law Institute, *Model Penal Code and Commentaries*, vol. 3, pt. 1, p. 18; Quoted in Glanville Williams, *Criminal Law*, 2d ed. (London: Stevens & Sons, 1961), pp. 724–725.

28. Jerome Hall, *General Principles of Criminal Law*, pp. 425ff.

29. *The Queen v. Dudley and Stephens*, L.R. 14 Q.B.D. 273 (1883).

30. For a general introduction to this topic, see Edward Arnolds and Norman Garland, "The Defense of Necessity in Criminal Law: The Right to Choose the Lesser Evil," *The Journal of Criminal Law and Criminology* 65 (1974):291–293; see also American Law Institute, *Model Penal Code and Commentaries*, vol. 2, pt. 1, pp. 8–22.

31. American Law Institute, *Model Penal Code and Commentaries*, vol. 1, pt. 1, p. 18.

32. *The Queen v. Dudley and Stephens*, L.R. 14 Q.B.D. 273 (1883)

33. Williams, *Criminal Law*, pp. 735–736.

34. George P. Fletcher, *Rethinking Criminal Law*, p. 770; Perkins and Boyce, *Criminal Law*, pp. 1154–1160; Richard L. Binder, "The Consent Defense: Sports, Violence, and the Criminal Law," *The American Criminal Law Review* 13 (1975):235–248.

35. American Law Institute, *Model Penal Code and Commentaries*, vol. 2, pt. I, pp. 1–5.

CHAPTER SEVEN

Defenses to Criminal Liability: Excuses

CHAPTER MAIN POINTS

1. In excuse, defendants admit the wrongfulness of their actions but argue that under the circumstances they were not responsible.

2. The main defenses of excuse are duress, intoxication, mistake, age, entrapment, insanity, diminished capacity, and syndromes.

3. Duress excuses some crimes when defendants are in immediate danger of death or serious harm.

4. Voluntary intoxication never excuses criminal liability; involuntary intoxication is an excuse in crimes of specific intent if the involuntary intoxication impairs specific intent.

5. Mistakes of law never excuse criminal liability; honest and reasonable mistakes of fact sometimes excuse criminal liability; legal and factual mistakes are sometimes difficult to distinguish.

6. Age, either old or young, may excuse criminal liability if it impairs *mens rea*.

7. Entrapment is a defense to criminal liability if the government induces an otherwise law-abiding citizen to commit a crime he or she would not have committed.

8. Insanity is a legal concept; mental illness is a medical condition.

9. A mental disease or defect excuses criminal liability when it impairs *mens rea*.

10. The right-wrong test of insanity focuses on reason; the irresistible impulse test focuses on will; and the *Model Penal Code* test focuses on both reason and will.

11. Insanity is an affirmative defense.

12. Diminished capacity reduces but does not remove responsibility when mental disease or defect less than insanity impairs *mens rea*.

Were Laotian Cultural Norms an Excuse?

May Aphaylath, a Laotian refugee living in this country for approximately two years, intentionally killed his Laotian wife of one month because of his jealousy over his wife's ex-boyfriend. Under Laotian culture the conduct of the victim wife in displaying affection for another man and receiving phone calls from an unattached man brought shame on defendant and his family sufficient to trigger Aphaylath's actions.

INTRODUCTION

Practically speaking, the defenses of excuse, except for insanity, provide defendants the same opportunity as justification (see chapter 6) to avoid criminal liability. Defendants who successfully plead these defenses "walk." The defenses, however, relieve defendants of criminal liability by means of a different theory. Defendants who plead the defenses based on the principle of justification accept responsibility for their actions but claim that under the circumstances what they did was right. Those who plead the defenses based on the principle of excuse admit what they did was wrong but deny that they were responsible under the circumstances. The most common excuses, and the defenses based on them discussed in this chapter, are duress, intoxication, mistake, age, entrapment, insanity, diminished capacity, and various syndromes.

DURESS

Professor Hyman Gross admirably states the problem in the defense of duress:

Sometimes people are forced to do what they do. When what they are forced to do is wrong it seems that the compulsion ought to count in their favor. After all, we say, such a person wasn't free to do otherwise—he couldn't help himself, not really. No claim to avoid blame appeals more urgently to our moral intuitions, yet none presents more problems of detail. There are times, after all, when we ought to stand firm and run the risk of harm to ourselves instead of taking a way out that means harm to others. In such a situation we must expect to pay the price if we cause harm when we prefer ourselves, for then the harm is our fault even though we did not mean it and deeply regret it.[1]

At common law, the defense of duress consisted of

> ... threats or menaces, which induce a fear of death or other bodily harm, and which take away for that reason the guilt of many crimes and misdemeanors; at least before a human tribunal. But then that fear, which compels a man to do an unwarrantable action, ought to be just and well grounded ... [However,] though a man be violently assaulted, and hath no other possible means of escaping death, but by killing an innocent person; this fear and force shall not acquit him of murder; for he ought rather to die himself, than escape by the murder of an innocent.[2]

The defense of duress raises the following issues:

- What is the definition of duress?
- What crimes does duress excuse?
- When does duress have to occur?
- Is duress measured objectively or subjectively?

Theorists and scholars disagree over the definition of duress. The nineteenth-century English jurist and historian of the criminal law, Sir James F. Stephen, argued that duress should never excuse criminal liability because "it is at the moment when temptation is strongest that the law should speak most clearly and emphatically to the contrary." Stephen conceded that judges could moderate sentences in cases where offenders committed crimes under duress. Borrowing from the defense of necessity, American theorist Jerome Hall maintained that coercion should excuse only minor crimes committed under the threat of death. Professor Glanville Williams argued that duress should excuse criminal liability because the law has no effect on the choices of defendants when defendants are "in thrall to some power," such as duress.[3]

As for the kind of threat required to invoke the defense, states differ. Some permit only threats to kill, as for example when, with a loaded gun at another's head, a robber says, "If you do not take that purse from her, I'll pull this trigger!" Other states accept threats to do serious bodily harm: "If you don't steal that jacket for me, I'll break your kneecaps!" Threats to property—such as a threat to smash a car if another does not steal a stereo—do not amount to duress. Neither do threats to reputation. For example, "If you don't sell me some marijuana, I'll tell your boss you have AIDS," is not a sufficient threat to invoke the defense of duress. In some states, threats to harm others, such as to kill a mother, son, or lover, do not amount to duress.[4]

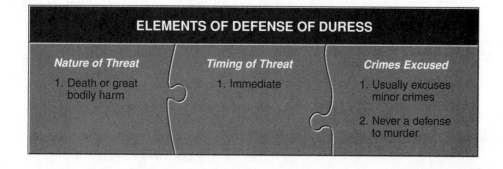

ELEMENTS OF DEFENSE OF DURESS

Nature of Threat	Timing of Threat	Crimes Excused
1. Death or great bodily harm	1. Immediate	1. Usually excuses minor crimes
		2. Never a defense to murder

The timing of the threat is important in most jurisdictions, but the degree of immediacy required varies from state to state. In Minnesota, for example, only threats of "instant death" qualify. In most states an imminent threat of death or serious bodily harm is enough. The definition of immediate threat is not always clear. For example, in *Regina v. Hudson*, a woman lied in court under oath (the crime of perjury) in order to provide Hudson with an alibi. Outside the courtroom Hudson had threatened to stab the woman if she did not lie in court. He sat in court while she committed the perjury. The trial court ruled that his threat was not immediate because he could not stab her at the moment she was lying in court. The appellate court disagreed:

> In the present case the threats of Hudson were likely to be no less compelling, because their execution could not be effected in the court room, if they could be carried out in the streets of Salford the same night. Insofar, therefore, as the [trial judge] ruled the threats were not sufficiently present and immediate to support the duress we think that he was in error.[5]

In some states, duress excuses all crimes except murder; in others, duress excuses only minor crimes. Some jurisdictions require that only the fear of instant death amounts to sufficient coercion; others accept an imminent fear of death or serious bodily harm.[6]

Jurisdictions also differ over whether to measure threats objectively or subjectively. Some states accept proof of the subjective, honest belief of defendants; others demand proof of their reasonable belief and honest belief. A few states speak of actual compulsion. Finally, courts do not always distinguish clearly between duress and the choice-of-evils defense (see chapter 6), recognizing a difficult-to-draw line between justification and excuse in duress. The New Hampshire Supreme Court dealt with the defense of duress in *State v. Daoud*.[7]

CASE

Was She Compelled to Drive While Intoxicated?

State v. Daoud,
679 A.2d 577 (N.H. 1996)

Daoud was convicted in the Superior Court, Hillsborough, of a second offense of driving while intoxicated, and she appealed. The Supreme Court affirmed the conviction but remanded the case for resentencing.

THAYER, Justice.

FACTS

... On August 24, 1993, the defendant and her boyfriend, John Hilane, spent the evening socializing with friends in Manchester. They went to a bar where the defendant consumed at least four mugs of beer. When the bar closed, the group decided to continue the party at a house nearby. At approximately 2:00 A.M., the defendant offered to drive a friend, Gina Lynch, home from the party. She wanted to take Lynch's car and leave it for her to use the following day, so she asked Hilane to pick her up. Hilane agreed and decided to follow the defendant because he did not know where Lynch lived. During the trip, however, he got lost and returned to the party. When the defendant realized that Hilane was not coming, she drove Lynch's car back to the party and confronted him. The couple argued. When they left the party later that night, Hilane decided to walk home and the defendant took her car.

The defendant was the first to arrive home. She was upset with Hilane and immediately began looking for a gun he kept in the apartment. When she could not find the gun, she concluded that Hilane had it with him. Thinking it would be safer to leave the apartment than to stay overnight, the defendant decided to drive to Massachusetts and live with Hilane's sister "until things cooled down." She took their daughter, placed her in the car, and left the apartment area.

Before heading to Massachusetts, however, she drove around the neighborhood looking for Hilane to make certain that he planned on returning home. The defendant met Hilane near the couple's apartment. After a brief exchange, which left the defendant feeling threatened, she drove off. She returned a few moments later, however, and the couple exchanged more words. At the time of the second conversation, the defendant was in her car and Hilane was on the balcony of their apartment. When the defendant drove off again, Hilane called the police, telling them that he believed the defendant was driving drunk with their child in the back seat. He provided police with a description of the car.

Officers David Connare and George Baker responded to Hilane's call. Using Hilane's description, they spotted the defendant's car and, based on their subsequent observations, concluded that the defendant was intoxicated. They arrested her and charged her with driving while intoxicated (DWI), second offense, and endangering the welfare of a child, see RSA 639:3 (1986).

Before trial, the State entered nolle prosequi on the charge of endangering the welfare of a child. The defendant then filed a notice of duress defense regarding the remaining DWI charge and, in subsequent motions, explained the theory of her defense. She argued that she drove away from her apartment under duress and that consequently her conduct was not voluntary as required by RSA 626:1, I (1986). To prove duress, the defendant planned to introduce evidence about battered woman's syndrome and evidence of prior abuse by Hilane.

At trial, the defendant formally requested that she be allowed to present a duress defense. The State objected, arguing that duress is not a defense in New Hampshire because it is not part of the Criminal Code, and that "the crime of driving while intoxicated does not have any requisite mental state . . . and since the defense of duress relates to a defendant's mental state, it is irrelevant in this case." Following the State's presentation of its evidence, the trial court ruled that a duress defense was not available to the defendant "under these circumstances and in view of the facts presented in the State's case and with regard to a charge of DWI." Accordingly, the court refused to allow the defendant to present evidence of duress. After two days of testimony, the jury returned a verdict of guilty.

OPINION

We begin with the defendant's assertion that duress is a statutory defense in New Hampshire. She argues that the defense is codified in the State's voluntary act statute, which excuses a defendant from criminal liability if the conduct upon which the liability is based is involuntary. See RSA 626:1, I. According to the defendant, Hilane's conduct on August 24, combined with his earlier abuse, forced her to leave the apartment under the influence of alcohol and therefore made her conduct involuntary. The defendant's argument is based on an overly broad reading of the voluntary act statute. RSA 626:1, I, provides, in relevant part, that "[a] person is not guilty of an offense unless . . . criminal liability is based on conduct that includes a voluntary act." In interpreting that language, "this court is the final arbiter of the intent of the legislature." We look to the words of the statute because they are the touchstone of the legislature's intent, and we construe those words according to their fair import and in a manner that promotes justice.

RSA 626:1, I, does not excuse criminal acts committed under duress. Nothing in the statute's language states that duress makes criminal conduct involuntary. Had the legislature intended to adopt that view, it could have done so explicitly. Moreover, RSA 626:1, I, is identical to the main section of the *Model Penal Code*'s voluntary act provision. Later sections of the *Model Penal Code* make clear that conduct is involuntary under section 2.01 only if it results from reflexes, convulsions, unconsciousness, sleep, hypnosis, or other circumstances that do not involve a volitional act. Duress is not included in that list. We believe that the similarity between the operative language in subsection 2.01(1) and RSA 626:1 indicates that they share a common meaning; neither treats conduct committed under duress as involuntary.

In support of her position, the defendant focuses on comments written by the 1969 commission charged with codifying New Hampshire's criminal laws. In discussing the voluntary act statute, the commission wrote that the statute "ought to be broad enough to preclude criminal liability under circumstances of duress." Report of Commission to Recommend Codification of Criminal Laws § 571:1 comment (1969). The defendant urges us to accept those comments as law. Although the comments of the commission may be useful in interpreting the Criminal Code, they are not law. Given our interpretation of the statutory language, we decline to adopt the commission's comment and conclude that the trial court did not err in refusing to allow the defendant to present a duress defense based on RSA 626:1, I.

Our conclusion is supported by other factors. First, commentators agree that duress does not make criminal conduct involuntary.... The commentators responsible for drafting the *Model Penal Code* ... expressed wide agreement that voluntary act statutes should only excuse criminal conduct where the "actor is moved by force, as distinguished from threat." See *Model Penal Code and Commentaries*, supra § 2.01, at 221. In addition, our prior cases convince us that duress cannot, as a matter of law, make criminal conduct involuntary within the meaning of RSA 626:1, I. When we have excused a defendant from criminal liability on the grounds that certain conduct was involuntary under RSA 626:1, I, we have emphasized that the defendant did not choose to commit the charged crime. See *State v. Akers*, 119 N.H. 161, 16263, 400 A.2d 38, 39 (1979) (defendant parents not guilty of violating a statute making them responsible for their children's illegal use of snowmobiles because they did not commit a voluntary act);

State v. Adelson, 118 N.H. 484, 487, 389 A.2d 1382, 1384 (1978) (company president not guilty of violating statute requiring him to make unemployment compensation contributions because company lacked funds to make payments at the time the payments became due); *Plummer*, 117 N.H. at 328, 374 A.2d at 436 (only when a defendant claims that his alcoholism constitutes a mental disease or insanity which renders him incapable of exercising his volition will he be permitted to present evidence of his condition under RSA 626:1, I).

In this case, the defendant chose to violate the law. After all, a person who commits a crime under duress "makes a choice" to violate the law, even though that choice is compelled. See *Model Penal Code and Commentaries*, supra § 2.09, at 372–74; Webster's Third New International Dictionary (unabridged ed. 1961) (defining "voluntary" as "proceeding from the will [or] produced in or by an act of choice"). Therefore, even if we accepted the defendant's claim that she acted under duress, we would still conclude that she committed a voluntary act when she drove away from her apartment. Under our case law, that choice put her beyond the scope of RSA 626:1, I. Accordingly, we hold that the trial court did not err in refusing to allow the defendant to present a duress defense based on RSA 626:1, I.

Having rejected the defendant's argument that the duress defense is codified in RSA 626:1, I, we now consider whether the duress defense is available to her under our common law. Although we have not yet recognized the common law duress defense, it is widely accepted that duress is an affirmative defense under the common law. It excuses a defendant from criminal liability despite the fact that he has committed each element of a crime, thereby overriding the elements of his offense. See *State v. Soucy*, 139 N.H. 349, 352, 653 A.2d 561, 564 (1995) ("A pure defense is a denial of an element of the offense, while an affirmative defense is a defense overriding the element[s].").

In New Hampshire, the burden is on the defendant to prove each element of an affirmative defense on a balance of the probabilities. When no reasonable juror could find that the defendant has met that burden, a trial court may withhold the defense from the jury. Based on the evidence presented in the State's case and the defendant's offer of proof, we conclude that no reasonable juror could have found that the defendant satisfied her burden of proving duress in this case. Accordingly, even assuming that duress is a common law affirmative defense in New Hampshire, the trial court properly prevented her from presenting evidence of duress.

At common law, "[d]uress was said to excuse criminal conduct where the actor was under an unlawful threat of imminent death or serious bodily injury, which threat caused the actor to engage in conduct violating the literal terms of the criminal law." Although jurisdictions define the specific elements of the defense differently, the United States Supreme Court has recognized that, regardless of the definition of the duress defense, "one principle remains constant: if there [is] a reasonable, legal alternative to violating the law, a chance both to refuse to do the criminal act and also to avoid the threatened harm, the defense will fail."

The State's evidence in this case demonstrated that the defendant had lawful alternatives to driving while intoxicated. For example, on crossexamination the defendant admitted that her telephone was working when she returned from the party. Therefore, she could have called a friend or a taxi and requested a ride away from her apartment. Moreover, Hilane testified that the defendant was friendly with almost all of her neighbors. Accordingly, before she drove away from her apartment, the defendant could have walked to a neighbor's apartment to seek shelter or call the police. Hilane never forced her to leave by car; nor did he prevent her from walking away.

The defendant's offer of proof did nothing to contradict that evidence. Instead, the defendant merely told the court that she would present evidence of battered woman's syndrome and evidence of prior abuse to show that the defendant was "in fear" when she left the apartment area in her car. She mentioned no evidence which could overcome the State's proof that she had lawful alternatives to violating the law. cf. *State v. O'Brien*, 132 N.H. 587, 591, 567 A.2d 582, 584 (1989) (defendant not entitled to competing harms defense because he had legal alternatives to driving an injured co-worker to the hospital while he was an habitual offender); *State v. Fee*, 126 N.H. 78, 8081, 489 A.2d 606, 608 (1985) (defendant not entitled to competing harms defense because he had legal alternatives to driving to his pharmacy under the influence of alcohol to investigate a burglar alarm). As a result, we hold that the defendant could not have met her burden of proving duress in this case. The trial court properly precluded the jury from hearing her evidence on duress. . . .

We agree with the State and the defendant that the trial court erred in denying the defendant's motion for pretrial incarceration credit. Accordingly, we remand the case to the trial court and order that the defendant's pretrial incarceration time be credited to her sentence.

Conviction affirmed; remanded for resentencing.

QUESTIONS FOR DISCUSSION

1. List all of the facts relevant to determining whether Daoud has the excuse of duress.

2. What test of duress does the court adopt in the case?

3. Do you agree that duress is a voluntary act?

4. What arguments does the court give to support its definition?

5. Do you favor the court's test? Defend your answer.

———————————◼️□———————————

One variation, or extension, to duress is the defense of superior orders. The United States Court of Military Appeals considered this problem in a famous case toward the end of the Vietnam War, *United States v. Calley*.

C A S E

Do Superior Orders Constitute Duress?

United States v. Calley,
46 C.M.R. 1131 (1973)

Calley was convicted of murder. He appealed. The conviction was affirmed.

FACTS

[D]uring midmorning on 16 March 1968 a large number of unresisting Vietnamese were placed in a ditch on the eastern side of My Lai and summarily executed by American soldiers. [According to PFC Meadlo], Meadlo . . . [as he] wandered back into the village alone . . . met his fire team leader, Specialist Four Grzesik. They took seven or eight Vietnamese to what he labeled a "ravine," where Lieutenant Calley, Sledge, and Dursi and a few other Americans were located with what he estimated as seventy-five to a hundred Vietnamese. Meadlo remembered also that Lieutenant Calley told him, "We got another job to do, Meadlo," and that the appellant started shoving people into the ravine and shooting them. Meadlo, in contrast to Dursi, followed the directions of his leader and himself fired into the people at the bottom of the "ravine." Meadlo then drifted away from the area but he doesn't remember where.

Specialist Four Grzesik found PFC Meadlo, crying and distraught, sitting on a small dike on the eastern edge of the village. He and Meadlo moved through the village, and came to the ditch, in which Grzesik thought were thirty-five to fifty dead bodies. Lieutenant Calley walked past and ordered Grzesik to take his fire team back into the village and help the following platoon in their search. He also remembered that Calley asked him to "finish them off," but he refused.

Specialist Four Turner saw Lieutenant Calley for the first time that day as Turner walked out of the village near the ditch. Meadlo and a few other soldiers were also present. Turner passed within fifteen feet of the area, looked into the ditch and saw a pile of ap-

proximately twenty bodies covered with blood. He also saw Lieutenant Calley and Meadlo firing from a distance of five feet into another group of people who were kneeling and squatting in the ditch. Turner recalled he then went north of the ditch about seventy yards, where he joined with Conti at a perimeter position. He remained there for over an hour, watching the ditch. Several more groups of Vietnamese were brought to it, never to get beyond or out of it. In all he thought he observed about ninety or a hundred people brought to the ditch and slaughtered there by Lieutenant Calley and his subordinates.

OPINION

There is no dispute as to the fact of killings by and at the instance of appellant at a ditch on the eastern edge of My Lai. Of the several bases for his argument that he committed no murder at My Lai because he was void of *mens rea*, appellant emphasized most of all that he acted in obedience to orders. . . .

An order of the type appellant says he received is illegal. Its illegality is apparent upon even cursory evaluation by a man of ordinary sense and understanding. [Calley argues] essentially that obedience to orders is a defense which strikes at *mens rea*; therefore in logic an obedient subordinate should be acquitted so long as he did not personally know of the order's illegality. [We do] not agree with the argument. Heed must be given not only to subjective innocence-through-ignorance in the soldier, but to the consequences for his victims. Also, barbarism tends to invite reprisal to the detriment of our own force or disrepute which interferes with the achievement of war aims, even though the barbaric acts were preceded by orders for their commission. Casting the defense of obedience to orders solely in subjective terms of *mens rea* would operate practically to abrogate those objective restraints which are essential to functioning rules of war. The court members, after being given correct standards, properly rejected any defense of obedience to orders.

We find no impediment to the findings that appellant acted with murderous *mens rea*, including premeditation. The aggregate of all his contentions against the existence of murderous *mens rea* is no more absolving than a bare claim that he did not suspect he did any wrong act until after the operation, and indeed is not convinced of it yet. This is no excuse in law.

Affirmed.

QUESTIONS FOR DISCUSSION

1. What is Calley's defense of superior orders based on?
2. Why does the court reject Calley's defense?

3. Assume that you are the prosecutor. Argue in favor of Calley's guilt.
4. Assume you are the defense attorney. Argue for Calley's acquittal.

The Nazi war criminals tried to use the same defense after World War II. In the famous Nuremberg trials, German officers attempted to defend Nazi atrocities against the Jews, claiming they were merely obeying their commanders' orders and were not criminally responsible for the people they killed. Their defenses were rejected for reasons similar to those that the court gave for its decision in *Calley*.

Brainwashing represents another attempt to extend the defense of duress. In the 1970s, a self-styled revolutionary group, the Symbionese Liberation Army (SLA), kidnapped heiress Patty Hearst and confined her for months. During that time, she and her abductors robbed a bank. In her highly publicized trial for armed robbery, Hearst argued that her captors pressured her for months, breaking down and overcoming her will. She had no mind of her own left, their beliefs became her beliefs, and thus her actions were their actions. Therefore, she argued, although what she did was wrong, she was not responsible for what she did because of the brainwashing.

Although the court denied Hearst's defense of brainwashing, the logic of the defense is clear. The *Model Penal Code* reporters have adopted the logic. They say that the *Model Penal Code*'s duress provision applies to brainwashing because coercion includes breaking down a person's will. Brainwashing is one form of breaking down a person's will.[8]

Puerto Rico has adopted a specific brainwashing defense statute that provides:

Whoever acts compelled by intimidation or violence shall not be held liable [and] [t]he concept of violence also includes the use of hypnotic means, narcotic substances, depressant or stimulant drugs, or other means or substances.[9]

Three rationales underlie the defense of duress.

1. Those who are forced to commit a crime do not act voluntarily; hence, there is no *actus reus*. This rationale does not apply to those who intentionally, recklessly, or negligently put themselves in a position where others can coerce them.

2. Subjection to the will of another negates *mens rea*. The criminal intent in cases of duress is more properly attributed to the person who coerces, not to the person coerced.

3. As a practical matter, the criminal law cannot force people to act irrationally against their own self-interest. Faced with enough pressure, people will always act to save their own lives even if that requires hurting someone else.

The only argument against the defense of duress is that denying the excuse of duress encourages people to resist the pressure to commit crimes.

INTOXICATION

Johnny James went quietly to his death by lethal injection . . . inside the Texas prison system's Huntsville Unit. He had been convicted of abducting two women, forcing them to perform sex acts on each other, then shooting them both in the head. One died, the other survived and identified him at trial.

In allowing James' execution, the courts turned a deaf ear to his claim that he had been too drunk to know what he was doing and did not deserve to die for the crime.[10]

The defense of intoxication, according to Professor George Fletcher, is "buffeted between two conflicting principles":

1. Accountability. Those who get drunk should take the consequences of their actions. Someone who gets drunk is liable for the violent consequences.

2. Culpability. Criminal liability and punishment depend on blameworthiness.[11]

The common-law approach focused on the first principle:

As to artificial, voluntarily contracted madness, by drunkenness or intoxication, which, depriving men of their reason, puts them in a temporary frenzy; our law looks upon this as an aggravation of the offense, rather than as an excuse for any criminal misbehavior.[12]

The Johnny James case illustrates that the common law principle is alive and well in 1997. John Gibeaut, who related the James case in an article entitled, "Sobering Thoughts," notes this contemporary emphasis on the principle of accountability in the subtitle to his article: "Legislatures and courts increasingly are just saying no to intoxication as a defense or mitigating factor." Between November 1996 and May 1997, at least ten states introduced bills that would abolish voluntary intoxication as a defense of excuse. According to a member of the Prosecution Function Committee of the American Bar Association's Criminal Justice Section, "The fight goes back to the ancient struggle over just how much free will one has."[13]

Critics worry that the attack on the defense of intoxication undermines the principle that the government bears the burden of proving every element in criminal cases be-

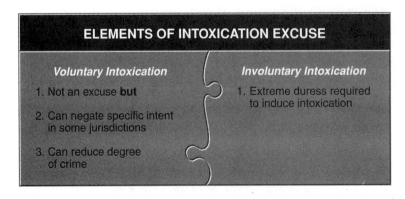

ELEMENTS OF INTOXICATION EXCUSE

Voluntary Intoxication	Involuntary Intoxication
1. Not an excuse **but**	1. Extreme duress required to induce intoxication
2. Can negate specific intent in some jurisdictions	
3. Can reduce degree of crime	

yond a reasonable doubt. This includes the venerable principle of *mens rea*. Supporters of the defense maintain that intoxicated people cannot form the intent required to commit common-law and statutory specific intent crimes, or, in the *Model Penal Code* terminology, crimes of purpose. Voluntary intoxication can impair the capacity to form either the purpose or the knowledge required to prove the *mens rea* of particular crimes. For example, a heavily intoxicated person may not have the capacity to premeditate—or in fact to have premeditated—a homicide; premeditation is part of the *mens rea* of most first-degree murders. However, intoxication may not have impaired the capacity to form, or to have in fact formed, the *mens rea* for manslaughter. Intoxication cannot negate recklessness or negligence.[14]

The attacks on the intoxication defense extend only to *voluntary* intoxication. Involuntary intoxication is an excuse to criminal liability. Involuntary intoxication includes cases in which defendants do not know they are taking intoxicants, or know but are forced to take them. In one case, a man took what his friend told him were "breath perfumer" pills; in fact, they were cocaine tablets. While under their influence, he killed someone. The court allowed the defense of intoxication. However, the defense of involuntary intoxication applies only to *extreme* duress. According to one authority, "a person would need to be bound hand and foot and the liquor literally poured down his throat, or . . . would have to be threatened with immediate serious injury."[15]

In another case where the defendant claimed involuntary intoxication, an eighteen-year-old youth was traveling with an older man across the desert. The man insisted that the youth drink some whiskey with him. When the youth declined, the man became abusive. The youth, fearing the man would put him out of the car in the middle of the desert without any money, drank the whiskey, became intoxicated, and killed the man. The court rejected a claim of involuntary intoxication because the older man had not compelled the youth "to drink against his will and consent."[16]

Apart from *mens rea*, even voluntary intoxication might negate *actus reus*. Hence, a man so intoxicated that he could not get an erection could not commit the required act of rape. This should not be taken to mean that defendants who voluntarily induce intoxication act involuntarily. Their voluntary act in drinking establishes voluntariness, even though when committing the crime charged they were "overwhelmed or overpowered by alcohol to the point of losing [their] . . . faculties or sensibilities" (see chapter 3).[17]

The United States Supreme Court dealt with the constitutionality of state statutes that eliminate the defense of voluntary intoxication in *Montana v. Egelhoff*.

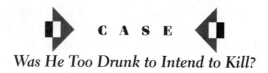

C A S E

Was He Too Drunk to Intend to Kill?

Montana v. Egelhoff,
116 S.Ct. 2013 (1996)

Steven Egelhoff was convicted of two counts of deliberate homicide, and he appealed. The Montana Supreme Court reversed. Montana petitioned for a writ of certiorari. The Supreme Court reversed. Justice SCALIA announced the judgment of the Court and delivered an opinion, in which THE CHIEF JUSTICE, Justice KENNEDY, and Justice THOMAS join. Justice Ginsburg filed an opinion concurring in the judgment. Justice O'Connor filed a dissenting opinion, in which Justices Stevens, Souter, and Breyer joined. Justice Souter filed a dissenting opinion, in which Justice Stevens joined.

FACTS

In July 1992, while camping out in the Yaak region of northwestern Montana to pick mushrooms, respondent made friends with Roberta Pavola and John Christenson, who were doing the same. On Sunday, July 12, the three sold the mushrooms they had collected and spent the rest of the day and evening drinking, in bars and at a private party in Troy, Montana. Some time after 9 P.M., they left the party in Christenson's 1974 Ford Galaxy station wagon. The drinking binge apparently continued, as respondent was seen buying beer at 9:20 P.M. and recalled "sitting on a hill or a bank passing a bottle of Black Velvet back and forth" with Christenson.

At about midnight that night, officers of the Lincoln County, Montana, sheriff's department, responding to reports of a possible drunk driver, discovered Christenson's station wagon stuck in a ditch along U.S. Highway 2. In the front seat were Pavola and Christenson, each dead from a single gunshot to the head. In the rear of the car lay respondent, alive and yelling obscenities. His blood-alcohol content measured .36 percent over one hour later. On the floor of the car, near the brake pedal, lay respondent's .38 caliber handgun, with four loaded rounds and two empty casings; respondent had gunshot residue on his hands.

Respondent was charged with two counts of deliberate homicide, a crime defined by Montana law as "purposely" or "knowingly" causing the death of another human being. Mont.Code Ann. § 455102 (1995). A portion of the jury charge, uncontested here, instructed that "[a] person acts purposely when it is his conscious object to engage in conduct of that nature or to cause such a result," and that "[a] person acts knowingly when he is aware of his conduct or when he is aware under the circumstances his conduct constitutes a crime; or, when he is aware there exists the high probability that his conduct will cause a specific result." Respondent's defense at trial was that an unidentified fourth person must have committed the murders; his own extreme intoxication, he claimed, had rendered him physically incapable of committing the murders, and accounted for his inability to recall the events of the night of July 12. Although respondent was allowed to make this use of the evidence that he was intoxicated, the jury was instructed, pursuant to Mont.Code Ann. § 452203 (1995), that it could not consider respondent's "intoxicated condition . . . in determining the existence of a mental state which is an element of the offense." App. to Pet. for Cert. 29a. The jury found respondent guilty on both counts, and the court sentenced him to 84 years' imprisonment.

The Supreme Court of Montana reversed. It reasoned (1) that respondent "had a due process right to present and have considered by the jury all relevant evidence to rebut the State's evidence on all elements of the offense charged," and (2) that evidence of respondent's voluntary intoxication was "clear[ly] . . . relevant to the issue of whether [respondent] acted knowingly and purposely." Because § 452203 prevented the jury from considering that evidence with regard to that issue, the court concluded that the State had been "relieved of part of its burden to prove beyond a reasonable doubt every fact necessary to constitute the crime charged," and that respondent had therefore been denied due process. We granted certiorari.

OPINION

The cornerstone of the Montana Supreme Court's judgment was the proposition that the Due Process Clause guarantees a defendant the right to present and have considered by the jury "all relevant evidence to rebut the State's evidence on all elements of the offense charged." Respondent does not defend this categorical rule; he acknowledges that the right to present relevant evidence "has not been viewed as absolute." That is a wise concession, since the proposition that the Due Process Clause guarantees the right to introduce all relevant evidence is simply indefensible. . . . Of course, to say that the right to introduce relevant evidence is not absolute is not to say that the Due Process Clause places no limits upon restriction of that right. But it is to say that the defendant asserting such a limit must sustain the usual heavy burden that a due process claim entails:

"[P]reventing and dealing with crime is much more the business of the States than it is of the Federal Government, and . . . we should not lightly construe the Constitution so as to intrude upon the administration of justice by the individual States. Among other things, it is normally 'within the power of the State to regulate procedures under which its laws are carried out,' . . . and its decision in this regard is not subject to proscription under the Due Process Clause unless 'it offends some principle of justice so rooted in the traditions and conscience of our people as to be ranked as fundamental.'" *Patterson v. New York*, 432 U.S. 197, 201–202, 97 S.Ct. 2319, 2322, 53 L.Ed.2d 281 (1977) (citations omitted).

Respondent's task, then, is to establish that a defendant's right to have a jury consider evidence of his voluntary intoxication in determining whether he possesses the requisite mental state is a "fundamental principle of justice."

Our primary guide in determining whether the principle in question is fundamental is, of course, historical practice. Here that gives respondent little support. By the laws of England, wrote Hale, the intoxicated defendant "shall have no privilege by this voluntarily contracted madness, but shall have the same judgment as if he were in his right senses." 1 M. Hale, Pleas of the Crown According to Blackstone and Coke, the law's condemnation of those suffering from dementia affectata was harsher still: Blackstone, citing Coke, explained that the law viewed intoxication "as an aggravation of the offence, rather than an excuse for any criminal misbehaviour." 4 W. Blackstone, Commentaries This stern rejection of inebriation as a defense became a fixture of early American law as well. The American editors of the 1847 edition of Hale wrote:

Drunkenness, it was said in an early case, can never be received as a ground to excuse or palliate an offence: this is not merely the opinion of a speculative philosopher, the argument of counsel, or the obiter dictum of a single judge, but it is a sound and long established maxim of judicial policy, from which perhaps a single dis-

senting voice cannot be found. But if no other authority could be adduced, the uniform decisions of our own Courts from the first establishment of the government, would constitute it now a part of the common law of the land."

In an opinion citing the foregoing passages from Blackstone and Hale, Justice Story rejected an objection to the exclusion of evidence of intoxication as follows:

This is the first time, that I ever remember it to have been contended, that the commission of one crime was an excuse for another. Drunkenness is a gross vice, and in the contemplation of some of our laws is a crime; and I learned in my earlier studies, that so far from its being in law an excuse for murder, it is rather an aggravation of its malignity." *United States v. Cornell*, 25 F. Cas. 650, 657–658 (No. 14,868) (CC R.I. 1820).

The historical record does not leave room for the view that the common law's rejection of intoxication as an "excuse" or "justification" for crime would nonetheless permit the defendant to show that intoxication prevented the requisite *mens rea*. . . .

Against this extensive evidence of a lengthy common-law tradition decidedly against him, the best argument available to respondent is the one made by his amicus and conceded by the State: Over the course of the 19th century, courts carved out an exception to the common law's traditional across-the-board condemnation of the drunken offender, allowing a jury to consider a defendant's intoxication when assessing whether he possessed the mental state needed to commit the crime charged, where the crime was one requiring a "specific intent." . . . [A]s late as 1878, the Vermont Supreme Court upheld the giving of the following instruction at a murder trial:

The voluntary intoxication of one who without provocation commits a homicide, although amounting to a frenzy, that is, although the intoxication amounts to a frenzy, does not excuse him from the same construction of his conduct, and the same legal inferences upon the question of premeditation and intent, as affecting the grade of his crime, which are applicable to a person entirely sober. *State v. Tatro*, 50 Vt. 483, 487 (1878).

. . .

On the basis of this historical record, respondent's amicus argues that "[t]he old common-law rule . . . was no longer deeply rooted at the time the Fourteenth Amendment was ratified." Brief for National Association of Criminal Defense Lawyers as Amicus Curiae 23. That conclusion is questionable, but we need not pursue the point, since the argument of amicus mistakes the nature of our inquiry. It is not the State which bears the burden of demonstrating that its rule is "deeply rooted," but rather respondent who must show that the principle of procedure violated by the rule (and allegedly required by due process) is "so rooted in the traditions and conscience of our people as to be ranked as fundamental." *Patterson v. New York*, 432 U.S., at 202, 97 S.Ct., at 2322. Thus, even assuming that when the Fourteenth Amendment was adopted the rule Montana now defends was no longer generally applied, this only cuts off what might be called an a fortiori argument in favor of the State. The burden remains upon respondent to show that the "new common law" rule—that intoxication may be considered on the question of intent—was so deeply rooted at the time of the Fourteenth Amendment (or perhaps has become so deeply rooted since) as to be a fundamental principle which that Amendment enshrined.

That showing has not been made. Instead of the uniform and continuing acceptance we would expect for a rule that enjoys "fundamental principle" status, we find that fully one-fifth of the States either never adopted the "new common-law" rule at issue here or have recently abandoned it. . . .

It is not surprising that many States have held fast to or resurrected the common-law rule prohibiting consideration of voluntary intoxication in the determination of *mens rea*, because that rule has considerable justification—which alone casts doubt upon the proposition that the opposite rule is a "fundamental principle." A large number of crimes, especially violent crimes, are committed by intoxicated offenders; modern studies put the numbers as high as half of all homicides, for example. See, e.g., Third Special Report to the U.S. Congress on Alcohol and Health from the Secretary of Health, Education, and Welfare 64 (1978); Note, Alcohol Abuse and the Law, 94 Harv. L.Rev. 1660, 1681–1682 (1981). Disallowing consideration of voluntary intoxication has the effect of increasing the punishment for all unlawful acts committed in that state, and thereby deters drunkenness or irresponsible behavior while drunk. The rule also serves as a specific deterrent, ensuring that those who prove incapable of controlling violent impulses while voluntarily intoxicated go to prison. And finally, the rule comports with and implements society's moral perception that one who has voluntarily impaired his own faculties should be responsible for the consequences.

. . .

There is, in modern times, even more justification for laws such as § 452203 than there used to be. Some recent studies suggest that the connection between drunkenness and crime is as much cultural as pharmacological—that is, that drunks are violent not simply because alcohol makes them that way, but because they are behaving in accord with their learned belief that drunks are violent. See, e.g., Collins, Suggested Explanatory Frameworks to Clarify the Alcohol Use/Violence Relationship, 15 Contemp. Drug Prob. 107, 115 (1988); Critchlow, The Powers of John Barleycorn, 41 Am. Psychologist 751, 754–755 (July 1986). This not only adds additional support to the traditional view that an intoxicated criminal is not deserving of exoneration, but it suggests that juries—who possess the same learned belief as the intoxicated offender—will be too quick to accept the claim that the defendant was biologically incapable of forming the requisite *mens rea*. Treating the matter as one of excluding misleading evidence therefore makes some sense.

In sum, not every widespread experiment with a procedural rule favorable to criminal defendants establishes a fundamental principle of justice. Although the rule allowing a jury to consider evidence of a defendant's voluntary intoxication where relevant to *mens rea* has gained considerable acceptance, it is of too recent vintage, and has not received sufficiently uniform and permanent allegiance to qualify as fundamental, especially since it displaces a lengthy common-law tradition which remains supported by valid justifications today.

. . .

The doctrines of *actus reus, mens rea*, insanity, mistake, justification, and duress have historically provided the tools for a constantly shifting adjustment of the tension between the evolving aims of the criminal law and changing religious, moral, philosophical, and medical views of the nature of man. This process of adjustment has always been thought to be the province of the States. *Powell v. Texas*, 392 U.S. 514, 535–536, 88 S.Ct. 2145, 2156, 20 L.Ed.2d 1254 (1968) (plurality opinion). [*Powell v. Texas* is excerpted in chapter 3 in the section on *actus reus*.]

The people of Montana have decided to resurrect the rule of an earlier era, disallowing consideration of voluntary intoxication when a defendant's state of mind is at issue. Nothing in the Due Process Clause prevents them from doing so, and the judgment of the Supreme Court of Montana to the contrary must be reversed.

It is so ordered.

CONCURRING OPINION

Justice GINSBURG, concurring in the judgment. [omitted]

DISSENT

Justice O'CONNOR, with whom Justice STEVENS, Justice SOUTER, and Justice BREYER join, dissenting.

The Montana Supreme Court unanimously held that Mont.Code Ann. § 452203 (1995) violates due process. I agree. Our cases establish that due process sets an outer limit on the restrictions that may be placed on a defendant's ability to raise an effective defense to the State's accusations. Here, to impede the defendant's ability to throw doubt on the State's case, Montana has removed from the jury's consideration a category of evidence relevant to determination of mental state where that mental state is an essential element of the offense that must be proved beyond a reasonable doubt. Because this disallowance eliminates evidence with which the defense might negate an essential element, the State's burden to prove its case is made correspondingly easier. The justification for this disallowance is the State's desire to increase the likelihood of conviction of a certain class of de-

fendants who might otherwise be able to prove that they did not satisfy a requisite element of the offense. In my view, the statute's effect on the criminal proceeding violates due process. . . .

. . .

Due process demands that a criminal defendant be afforded a fair opportunity to defend against the State's accusations. Meaningful adversarial testing of the State's case requires that the defendant not be prevented from raising an effective defense, which must include the right to present relevant, probative evidence. To be sure, the right to present evidence is not limitless; for example, it does not permit the defendant to introduce any and all evidence he believes might work in his favor, Crane, supra, at 690, 106 S.Ct., at 2146, nor does it generally invalidate the operation of testimonial privileges, *Washington v. Texas*, 388 U.S. 14, 23, n. 21, 87 S.Ct. 1920, 1925, n. 21, 18 L.Ed.2d 1019 (1967). Nevertheless, "an essential component of procedural fairness is an opportunity to be heard. That opportunity would be an empty one if the State were permitted to exclude competent, reliable evidence" that is essential to the accused's defense. Section 452203 forestalls the defendant's ability to raise an effective defense by placing a blanket exclusion on the presentation of a type of evidence that directly negates an element of the crime, and by doing so, it lightens the prosecution's burden to prove that mental-state element beyond a reasonable doubt.

. . .

I would afford more weight to principles enunciated in our case law than is accorded in the Court's opinion today. It seems to me that a State may not first determine the elements of the crime it wishes to punish, and then thwart the accused's defense by categorically disallowing the very evidence that would prove him innocent.

. . .

The Due Process Clause protects those "principle[s] of justice so rooted in the traditions and conscience of our people as to be ranked as fundamental." *Patterson v. New York*, 432 U.S., at 202, 97 S.Ct., at 2322. At the time the Fourteenth Amendment was ratified, the common-law rule on consideration of intoxication evidence was in flux. The Court argues that rejection of the historical rule in the

19th century simply does not establish that the "new common law" rule is a principle of procedure so "deeply rooted" as to be ranked "fundamental." But to determine whether a fundamental principle of justice has been violated here, we cannot consider only the historical disallowance of intoxication evidence, but must also consider the "fundamental principle" that a defendant has a right to a fair opportunity to put forward his defense, in adversarial testing where the State must prove the elements of the offense beyond a reasonable doubt. As concepts of *mens rea* and burden of proof developed, these principles came into conflict, as the shift in the common law in the 19th century reflects.

. . .

Justice SOUTER, dissenting. . . .

The plurality opinion convincingly demonstrates that when the Fourteenth Amendment's Due Process Clause was added to the Constitution in 1868, the common law as it then stood either rejected the notion that voluntary intoxication might be exculpatory, or was at best in a state of flux on that issue. That is enough to show that Montana's rule that evidence of voluntary intoxication is inadmissible on the issue of culpable mental state contravenes no principle " 'so rooted in the traditions and conscience of our people,' " as they stood in 1868, " 'as to be ranked as fundamental.' " But this is not the end of the due process enquiry. Justice Harlan's dissenting opinion in *Poe v. Ullman*, 367 U.S. 497, 542, 81 S.Ct. 1752, 1776, 6 L.Ed.2d 989 (1961), teaches that the "tradition" to which we are tethered "is a living thing." What the historical practice does not rule out as inconsistent with "the concept of ordered liberty," *Palko v. Connecticut*, 302 U.S. 319, 325, 58 S.Ct. 149, 152, 82 L.Ed. 288 (1937), must still pass muster as rational in today's world.

. . .

Justice BREYER, with whom Justice STEVENS joins, dissenting.

I join Justice O'CONNOR's dissent. As the dissent says, and as Justice SOUTER agrees, the Montana Supreme Court did not understand Montana's statute to have redefined the mental element of deliberate homicide. In my view, however, this circumstance is not simply happenstance or a technical matter that

deprives us of the power to uphold that statute. To have read the statute differently—to treat it as if it had redefined the mental element—would produce anomalous results. A statute that makes voluntary intoxication the legal equivalent of purpose or knowledge but only where external circumstances would establish purpose or knowledge in the absence of intoxication, is a statute that turns guilt or innocence not upon state of mind, but upon irrelevant external circumstances. An intoxicated driver stopped at an intersection who unknowingly accelerated into a pedestrian would likely be found guilty, for a jury unaware of intoxication would likely infer knowledge or purpose. An identically intoxicated driver racing along a highway who unknowingly sideswiped another car would likely be found innocent, for a jury unaware of intoxication would likely infer negligence. Why would a legislature want to write a statute that draws such a distinction, upon which a sentence of life imprisonment, or death, may turn? If the legislature wanted to equate voluntary intoxication, knowledge, and purpose, why would it not write a statute that plainly says so, instead of doing so in a roundabout manner that would affect, in dramatically different ways, those whose minds, deeds, and consequences seem identical? I would reserve the question of whether or not such a hypothetical statute might exceed constitutional limits.

QUESTIONS FOR DISCUSSION

1. If the degree of intoxication was as great as the facts say it was, was Egelhoff capable of forming the intent to commit murder?

2. Summarize the arguments of the plurality in favor of the power of states to abolish the defense of voluntary intoxication without violating the due process clause.

3. Summarize the arguments of the dissents that abolishing the defense of voluntary intoxication violates due process.

4. Which arguments persuade you?

5. Does your answer depend on the heinousness of the murder that Egelhoff committed?

6. Or does it depend on his capacity to form the intent to commit first degree murder?

7. Or does it depend on whether he was capable of committing the voluntary act (*actus reus*) of first degree murder?

8. Can you blame someone who is as intoxicated as Egelhoff was?

9. Which of the conflicting principles enunciated by Professor Fletcher at the outset of this section does the plurality adopt?

10. Which does the dissent adopt?

11. Do you agree with the majority or with the dissent?

Alcohol is the most widely used intoxicant, but it is not the only one qualifying defendants to claim the intoxication excuse. The *Model Penal Code* and most states define intoxication to include disturbing mental and physical capacities by introducing "substances" into the body. *State v. Hall* illustrates this point. Hall's friend gave him a pill containing LSD (lysergic acid diethylamide). Hall did not know this; he knew only that, as his friend assured him, it was only a "little sunshine" to make him feel "groovy." A car picked up the hitchhiking Hall. At that time, the drug caused Hall to hallucinate that the driver was a rabid dog. Under this sad delusion, he shot and killed the driver. The court recognized no legal distinction between the voluntary use of alcohol and the voluntary use of other intoxicants in determining criminal responsibility.[18]

MISTAKE

"Ignorance of the law is no excuse" is a concept with which almost everyone is familiar; most do not know, however, that this doctrine is no longer hard and fast, if it ever was. Ignorance of fact, on the other hand, has always excused criminal responsibility under some circumstances. Mistake of fact excuses criminal liability when it negates a material element in the crime. For example, if I take from a restaurant coatroom a coat that I believe is mine, I have not stolen the coat because I do not have the requisite *mens rea*: to deprive the owner of his or her property. The actor's mistake must be "honest" and "reasonable"; hence the proper way to state the defense is that an honest and reasonable mistake of fact excuses criminal responsibility. For example, if I take the coat because it is where I left mine an hour ago, it is the same color and size as mine, and no other coat hanging there resembles it, I have honestly and reasonably mistaken the coat for mine. (For a full discussion of mistake of fact in statutory rape, see chapter 9.)

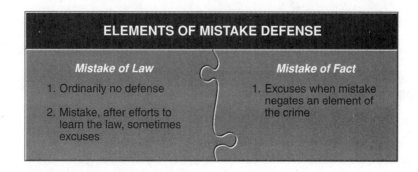

ELEMENTS OF MISTAKE DEFENSE

Mistake of Law

1. Ordinarily no defense

2. Mistake, after efforts to learn the law, sometimes excuses

Mistake of Fact

1. Excuses when mistake negates an element of the crime

Mistake of law does not ordinarily excuse criminal responsibility, for several reasons grounded in public policy. First, the state must determine what constitutes crime; individuals cannot define crimes for themselves. Second, the doctrine supposedly encourages citizens to know the law. Finally, nearly everyone could shield themselves behind the claim of ignorance because most people do not know the specifics of criminal statutes and court decisions interpreting them. Hence, the law presumes that everyone knows the law.[19]

Former Supreme Court justice and legal philosopher Oliver Wendell Holmes wrote that the

> . . . true explanation of the rule is the same as that which accounts for the law's indifference to a man's particular temperament, faculties, and so forth. Public policy sacrifices the individual to the general good. It is desirable that the burden of all should be equal, but it is still more desirable to put an end to robbery and murder. It is no doubt true that there are many cases in which the criminal could not have known that he was breaking the law, but to admit the excuse at all would be to encourage ignorance where the law-maker has determined to make men know and obey, and justice to the individual is rightly outweighed by the larger interests on the other side of the scales.[20]

Ignorance of the law, following reasonable efforts to learn it, sometimes excuses criminal liability. For example, a defendant conducted a lottery, relying on a statute that a state supreme court later ruled unconstitutional. The defendant's honest and reasonable belief that the lottery was lawful was an excuse, even though the supreme court later ruled that the lottery was unconstitutional. Furthermore, relying on an attorney's advice does not constitute an excuse to criminal liability. Hence, if I ask my lawyer if it is lawful to put a sign in my front yard and she tells me yes, and later the government prosecutes me for violating an ordinance prohibiting signs in residential areas, I have no defense of mistake. If I had instead asked the prosecutor, I might have an excuse; some states permit reliance on such officials, others do not.[21]

The distinction between law and fact, although important legally, is not easy to draw in practice. In *People v. Snyder*, the court addresses the defense of mistake and the problem in determining whether the defendant mistook the law or a fact.

C A S E

Did Her Mistake Excuse Her?

People v. Snyder,
32 Cal.3d 590, 186 Cal.Rptr. 485 (1982)

Snyder appealed from a judgment convicting her of possession of a concealable firearm by a convicted felon. Snyder pleaded the defense of mistake. The trial court denied the defense. The appeals court af-

firmed the conviction. Justice Richardson wrote the opinion for the court.

FACTS

At trial, defendant offered to prove the following facts supporting her theory of mistake: The marijuana possession charge resulted from a plea bargain not involving a jail or prison sentence. At the time the bargain was struck, defendant's attorney advised her that she was pleading guilty to a misdemeanor. Believing that she was not a felon, defendant thereafter had registered to vote, and had voted. On one prior occasion, police officers found a gun in her home but, after determining that it was registered to her husband, the officers filed no charges against defendant. The trial court refused to admit any evidence of defendant's mistaken belief that her prior conviction was a misdemeanor and that she was not a felon. The court also rejected proposed instructions requiring proof of defendant's prior knowledge of her felony conviction as an element of the offense charged.

OPINION

Penal Code § 12021, subdivision (a), provides:

> Any person who has been convicted of a felony under the laws of the . . . State of California . . . who owns or has in his possession or under his custody or control any pistol, revolver, or other firearm capable of being concealed upon the person is guilty of a public offense. . . .

The elements of the offense proscribed by § 12021 are conviction of a felony and ownership, possession, custody or control of a firearm capable of being concealed on the person. No specific criminal intent is required, and a general intent to commit the proscribed act is sufficient to sustain a conviction. With respect to the elements of possession or custody, it has been held that knowledge is an element of the offense.

Does § 12021 also require knowledge of one's legal status as a convicted felon? No case has so held. Penal Code § 26 provides that a person is incapable of committing a crime if he acted under a "mistake of fact" which disproves criminal intent. In this regard, the cases have distinguished between mistakes of fact and mistakes of law. As we stated in an early case:

> "It is an emphatic postulate of both civil and penal law that ignorance of a law is no excuse for a violation thereof. Of course it is based on a fiction, because no man can know all the law, but it is a maxim which the law itself does not permit any one to gainsay. . . .

> "The rule rests on public necessity; the welfare of society and the safety of the state depend upon its enforcement. If a person accused of a crime could shield himself behind the defense that he was ignorant of the law which he violated, immunity from punishment would in most cases result." Accordingly, lack of actual knowledge of the provisions of Penal Code § 12021 is irrelevant; the crucial question is whether the defendant was aware that she was engaging in the conduct proscribed by that section.

In the present case, defendant was presumed to know that it is unlawful for a convicted felon to possess a concealable firearm. (Pen.Code, § 12021.) She was also charged with knowledge that the offense of which she was convicted (former Health & Saf. Code, § 11531) was, as a matter of law, a felony. That section had prescribed a state prison term of from five years to life, and the express statutory definition of a "felony" is "a crime which is punishable with death or by imprisonment in the state prison." (Pen.Code, § 17, subd. (a).)

Thus, regardless of what she reasonably believed, or what her attorney may have told her, defendant was deemed to know under the law that she was a convicted felon forbidden to possess concealable firearms. Her asserted mistake regarding her correct legal status was a mistake of law, not fact. It does not constitute a defense to § 12021. . . .

We conclude that the trial court properly excluded evidence of defendant's asserted mistake regarding her status as a convicted felon.

The judgment is affirmed.

DISSENT

Broussard, Justice, dissenting. I dissent.

The two elements of a violation of Penal Code § 12021 are felony status and possession of a concealable firearm. While no specific criminal intent is required, a general criminal intent should be required as to both elements in accordance with long-settled rules of statutory interpretation, and an honest and reasonable mistake as to either element of the offense, however induced, should negate the requisite general criminal intent. Defendant's testimony if believed would have established an honest and reasonable mistaken belief that her prior offense was not a felony but a misdemeanor, and it was prejudicial error to refuse to admit the evidence and to refuse instructions on the mistake doctrine. . . .

During a lawful search of defendant and her husband's home in 1979, officers found one loaded handgun and two other handguns which were partially disassembled. In 1973 she had been convicted upon a guilty plea of sale of marijuana, a felony.

Defendant sought to testify that she believed that her marijuana possession conviction had been for a misdemeanor rather than a felony. She offered to testify that she had not been sentenced to jail or prison but was on probation for two years, that her attorney told her at the time of the plea bargain that she was pleading guilty to a misdemeanor, and that believing she was not a felon she had since registered to vote and voted. She also offered to testify that on a prior occasion, officers found a pistol in her home but that after determining the gun was registered to her husband, no charges were filed for possession of the gun. Other charges were filed but dismissed.

Her husband had also been convicted in 1973 of the same marijuana charge. The trial court refused to admit the evidence of defendant's mistaken belief that the prior conviction was a misdemeanor and that she was not a felon.

The court also rejected offered instructions to require knowledge of a prior felony conviction as an element of the offense, and to define "knowingly," to explain the effect of ignorance or mistake of fact disproving criminal intent. The instructions, if given, would have required the jury to find that defendant knew she was a felon as an element of the crime. . . .

Penal Code § 12021, subdivision (a) provides:

> Any person who has been convicted of a felony under the laws of the . . . State of California . . . who owns or has in his possession or under his custody or control any pistol, revolver, or other firearm capable of being concealed upon the person is guilty of a public offense. . . .

At common law an honest and reasonable belief in circumstances which, if true, would make the defendant's conduct innocent was held to be a good defense. The concept of *mens rea,* the guilty mind, expresses the principle that it is not conduct alone but conduct accompanied by certain mental states which concerns, or should concern, the law. . . .

The elements of the offense proscribed by § 12021 are conviction of a felony and ownership, possession, custody or control of a firearm capable of being concealed on the person. While no specific criminal intent is required, a general intent to commit the proscribed act is necessary. As to the element of possession or custody, it has been held that knowledge is an element of the offense. . . .

To hold otherwise is contrary to the settled California rule that a *mens rea* requirement is an "invariable" element of every crime unless excluded expressly or by necessary implication. Having established the rule, we must assume the Legislature is aware of it and acting in accordance with it, and the absence of any provision to establish strict liability must be read as reflecting legislative intent to require wrongful intent. . . .

In determining whether a defendant's mistaken belief disproves criminal intent pursuant to Penal Code § 26, the courts have drawn a distinction between mistakes of fact and mistakes of law. Criminal intent is the intent to do the prohibited act, not the intent to violate the law. "It is an emphatic postulate of both civil and penal law that ignorance of a law is no excuse for a violation thereof. Of course it is based on a fiction, because no man can know all the law, but it is a maxim which the law itself does not permit anyone to gainsay. . . . The rule rests on public necessity; the welfare of society and the safety of the state depend upon its enforcement. If a person accused of a crime could shield himself behind the defense that he was ignorant of the law which he violated, immunity from punishment would in most cases result." Accordingly, lack of knowledge of the provisions of Penal Code § 12021 is irrelevant; the crucial question is whether the defendant was aware that she was engaging in the conduct proscribed by that section. . . .

I am perplexed by the majority's apparent limitation of the mistake doctrine to would-be "moral leper[s]." The more heinous the crime the more reason to limit defenses, and the majority's suggested limitation appears to turn the usual relationship between law and morality upside down. Had the trial court in the instant case admitted the offered evidence and given the requested instruction, the jury could properly have concluded that defendant had a reasonable and good faith belief that her conviction was not a felony conviction. She was granted probation without jail or prison sentence.

Her attorney had advised her that the offense was a misdemeanor (It has been held that advice of counsel that prohibited conduct is lawful is not a defense because it would place the advice of counsel above the law.) and there were additional circumstances reflecting a good faith belief. Counsel's advice in the instant case is relevant to establish good faith; it does not in and of itself establish a defense.

The errors in excluding the offered evidence and refusing the offered instructions denied defendant the right to have the jury determine substantial issues material to her guilt and require reversal of the conviction. I would reverse the judgment.

QUESTIONS FOR DISCUSSION

1. Does the majority or dissent make clear what distinguishes mistakes of fact from mistakes of law?

2. Should it make any difference?

3. What arguments does the majority give for rejecting evidence of mistake in the case?

4. Why does the dissent reject them?

5. Should the defendant's reliance on her attorney's statements excuse her from liability? Why or why not?

6. Does the dissent have a point in stressing that "moral lepers" have a better chance at the defense than misdemeanants? Explain.

AGE

A four-year-old boy stabs his two-year-old sister in a murderous rage. Is this a criminal assault? What if the boy is eight? Twelve? Sixteen? Eighteen? At the other end of the age spectrum, what if he is eighty-five? At how early an age are people liable for criminal conduct? And when, if ever, does someone become too old for criminal responsibility? Age—both old and young—does affect criminal liability, sometimes to excuse it, sometimes to mitigate it, and sometimes even to aggravate it.

Ever since the early days of the English common law, immaturity has excused criminal liability. A rigid but sensible scheme for administering the defense was developed by the sixteenth century. The law divided people into three age groups—under 7 years; 7 to 14 years; over 14 years. Children under seven could not form criminal intent, that is, there was an **irrebuttable presumption** that they lacked the mental capacity to commit crimes. Between seven and fourteen, the presumption became a **rebuttable presumption**; that is, children were presumed to lack the capacity to form criminal intent. The prosecution could rebut the presumption by presenting evidence proving that defendants between seven and fourteen had in fact formed *mens rea*. The presumption of incapacity was strong at age seven but gradually weakened until it disappeared at age fourteen. At fourteen, children were conclusively presumed to have the mental capacity to commit crimes.

About half the states initially adopted the common-law approach but altered the specific ages within it. Some states excluded serious crimes—usually offenses carrying the death penalty or life imprisonment—from the scheme. Guided by the *Model Penal Code*, states have integrated the age of criminal responsibility with the jurisdiction of the juvenile courts. Some grant the juvenile court exclusive jurisdiction up to a specific age, usually between fifteen and sixteen. Then, from sixteen to eighteen (although occasionally up to twenty-one), juvenile court judges can transfer, or certify, cases to adult criminal courts. The number of cases certified has increased with the public recognition that youths can and do commit serious felonies. In *State v. K.R.L.*, the Washington state supreme court grappled with the capacity of an eight-year-old boy to form *mens rea*.[22]

C A S E

Too Young to Commit Burglary?

State v. K.R.L.,
67 Wash.App. 721, 840 P.2d 210 (Wash. App. 1992)

K.R.L., an eight-year-old boy, was convicted of residential burglary by the Superior Court, Clallam County, Grant S. Meiner, J., and he appealed. The Court of Appeals, Alexander, J., held that the state failed to overcome the presumption by clear and convincing evidence that defendant was incapable of committing residential burglary. Reversed.

ALEXANDER, Judge.

FACTS

In July 1990, K.R.L., who was then 8 years and 2 months old, was playing with a friend behind a business building in Sequim. Catherine Alder, who lived near the business, heard the boys playing and she instructed them to leave because she believed the area was dangerous. Alder said that K.R.L.'s response was belligerent, the child indicating that he would leave "in a minute." Losing patience with the boys, Alder said "[n]o, not in a minute, now, get out of there now." The boys then ran off. Three days later, during daylight hours, K.R.L. entered Alder's home without her permission. He proceeded to pull a live goldfish from her fishbowl, chopped it into several pieces with a steak knife and "smeared it all over the counter. He then went into Alder's bathroom and clamped a "plugged in" hair curling iron onto a towel.

Upon discovering what had taken place, Alder called the Sequim police on the telephone and reported the incident. A Sequim police officer con-

tacted K.R.L.'s mother and told her that he suspected that K.R.L. was the perpetrator of the offense against Alder. K.R.L.'s mother confronted the child with the accusation and he admitted to her that he had entered the house. She then took K.R.L. to the Sequim Police Department where the child was advised of his constitutional rights by a Sequim police officer. This took place in the presence of K.R.L.'s mother who indicated that she did not believe "he really understood." K.R.L. told the police officer that he knew it was wrong to enter Alder's home. [The statement given by K.R.L. to the officer was not offered by the State to prove guilt. Initially, the State took the position that K.R.L. fully understood those rights and that he had made a free and voluntary waiver of rights. Defense counsel objected to the admission of the statements and eventually the State withdrew its offer of the evidence, concluding that the evidence was cumulative in that K.R.L.'s admissions were already in evidence through the testimony of his mother.]

K.R.L. was charged in Clallam County Juvenile Court with residential burglary, a class B felony. At trial, considerable testimony was devoted to the issue of whether K.R.L. possessed sufficient capacity to commit that crime. The juvenile court judge heard testimony in that regard from K.R.L.'s mother, Catherine Alder, two school officials, a Sequim policeman who had dealt with K.R.L. on two prior occasions as well as the incident leading to the charge, one of K.R.L.'s neighbors and the neighbor's son.

K.R.L.'s mother, the neighbor, the neighbor's son and the police officer testified to an incident that had occurred several months before the alleged residential burglary. This incident was referred to by the police officer as the "Easter Candy Episode." Their testimony revealed that K.R.L. had taken some Easter candy from a neighbor's house without permission. As a consequence, the Sequim police were called to investigate. K.R.L. responded to a question by the investigating officer, saying to him that he "knew it was wrong and he wouldn't like it if somebody took his candy." The same officer testified to another incident involving K.R.L. This was described as the "joyriding incident," and it occurred prior to the "Easter Candy Episode." It involved K.R.L. riding the bicycles of two neighbor children without having their permission to do so. K.R.L. told the police officer that he "knew it was wrong" to ride the bicycles.

The assistant principal of K.R.L.'s elementary school testified about K.R.L.'s development. He said that K.R.L. was of "very normal" intelligence. K.R.L.'s first grade teacher said that K.R.L. had "some difficulty" in school. He said that he would put K.R.L. in the "lower age academically." K.R.L.'s mother testified at some length about her son and, in particular, about the admissions he made to her regarding his entry into Alder's home. Speaking of that incident, she said that he admitted to her that what he did was wrong "after I beat him with a belt, black and blue." She also said that her son told her "that the Devil was making him do bad things."

The juvenile court rejected the argument of K.R.L.'s counsel that the State had not presented sufficient evidence to show that K.R.L. was capable of committing a crime. It found him guilty, saying:

> [F]rom my experience in my eight, nine years on the bench, it's my belief that the so-called juvenile criminal system is a paper tiger and it's not going to be much of a threat to Mr. [K.R.L.], so I don't think that for that reason there is a whole lot to protect him from.

OPINION

There is only one issue — did the trial court err in concluding that K.R.L. had the capacity to commit the crime of residential burglary? [Residential burglary is defined in RCW 9A.52.025 as: "A person is guilty of residential burglary if, with intent to commit a crime against a person or property therein, the person enters or remains unlawfully in a dwelling.... " RCW 9A.04.050 speaks to the capability of children to commit crimes and, in pertinent part, provides:

> Children under the age of eight years are incapable of committing crime. Children of eight and under twelve years of age are presumed to be incapable of committing crime, but this presumption may be removed by proof that they have sufficient capacity to understand the act or neglect, and to know that it was wrong.

This statute applies in juvenile proceedings.

Because K.R.L. was 8 years old at the time he is alleged to have committed residential burglary, he was presumed incapable of committing that offense. The burden was, therefore, on the State to overcome that presumption and that burden could only be removed by evidence that was "clear and convincing." Thus, on review we must determine if there is evidence from which a rational trier of fact could find capacity by clear and convincing evidence. There are no reported cases in Washington dealing with the capacity of 8-year-old children to commit crimes. That is not too surprising in light of the fact that up to age 8, children are deemed incapable of committing crimes. Two cases involving older children are, however, instructional. In *State v. Q.D.* . . . our Supreme Court looked at a case involving a child who was charged with committing indecent liberties. In concluding that there was clear and convincing circumstantial evidence that the child understood the act of indecent liberties and knew it to be wrong, the court stressed the fact that the child was only 3 months shy of age 12, the age at which capacity is presumed to exist. The court also placed stock in the fact that the defendant used stealth in committing the offense as well as the fact that she had admonished the victim, a 4½-year-old child whom she had been babysitting, not to tell what happened.

In another case, *State v. S.P.*, 49 Wash.App. 45, 746 P.2d 813 (1987), rev'd on other grounds, 110 Wash.2d 886, 756 P.2d 1315 (1988), Division One of this court upheld a trial judge's finding that a child, S.P., had sufficient capacity to commit the crime of indecent liberties. In so ruling, the court noted that (1) S.P. was 10 years of age at the time of the alleged acts; (2) S.P. had had sexual contact with two younger boys during the prior year; (3) in treatment for the earlier incident, S.P. acknowledged that sexual behavior was wrong; (4) S.P. was aware that if convicted on the present charge, detention could result; and (5) experts concluded that S.P. had an extensive knowledge of sexual terms and understood the wrongfulness of his conduct toward the victims.

None of the factors that the courts highlighted in the two aforementioned cases is present here. Most notably, K.R.L. is considerably younger than either of the children in the other two cases. In addition, we know almost nothing about what occurred when K.R.L. went into Alder's home. Furthermore, there was no showing that he used "stealth" in entering Alder's home. We know only that he entered her home in daylight hours and that while he was there he committed the act. Neither was there any showing that K.R.L. had been previously treated for his behavior, as was the case in *State v. S.P.*

The State emphasizes the fact that K.R.L. appeared to appreciate that what he did at Alder's home and on prior occasions was wrong. When K.R.L. was being beaten "black and blue" by his mother, he undoubtedly came to the realization that what he had done was wrong. We are certain that this conditioned the child, after the fact, to know that what he did was wrong. That is a far different thing than one appreciating the quality of his or her acts at the time the act is being committed.

In arguing that it met its burden, the State placed great reliance on the fact that K.R.L. had exhibited bad conduct several months before during the so-called "Easter Candy" and "Joyriding" incidents. Again, we do not know much about these incidents, but it seems clear that neither of them involved serious misconduct and they shed little light on whether this child understood the elements of the act of burglary or knew that it was wrong. In *State v. Q.D.*, our

Supreme Court emphasized that a capacity determination must be made in reference to the specific act charged. If the State shows no more than a general understanding of the justice system, the State does not meet its burden of showing an understanding of the act and knowledge that it was wrong. Indeed, the court indicated that an understanding of the wrongfulness of one crime does not alone establish capacity in regard to another crime.

Here, we have a child of very tender years—only two months over 8 years. While the State made a valiant effort to show prior bad acts on the part of the child, an objective observer would have to conclude that these were examples of behavior not uncommon to many young children. Furthermore, there was no expert testimony in this case from a psychologist or other expert who told the court anything about the ability of K.R.L. to know and appreciate the gravity of his conduct. Although two school officials testified, one of them said K.R.L. was of an age lower than 8, "academically." In short, there is simply not enough here so that we can say that in light of the State's significant burden, there is sufficient evidence to support a finding of capacity.

Reversed.

QUESTIONS FOR DISCUSSION

1. Was the trial judge or the supreme court of Washington right in the ruling on the capacity of K.R.L. to form criminal intent?

2. Back up your answer with facts from the case.

3. Did K.R.L. know what he was doing intellectually yet not sufficiently *appreciate* what he was doing?

4. What facts support this conclusion?

5. Should it matter whether he appreciated what he did so long as he knew what he did? Explain your answer.

Youth does not always excuse criminal responsibility or mitigate the punishment; sometimes it aggravates conduct. For example, seventeen-year-old Muñoz was convicted of possessing a switchblade under a New York City ordinance that prohibited youths under twenty-one from carrying such knives. Had Muñoz been over twenty-one, what he did would not have been a crime.[23]

At the other end of the spectrum, old age can also affect the capacity to commit crimes. Consider the incident described by the prosecutor in the following case excerpt.

C A S E

Too Old to Commit Crimes?

A prosecutor related the following tragedy.[24]

> You have this married couple, married for over 50 years, living in a retirement home. The guy sends his wife out for bagels and while the wife can still get around she forgets and brings back onion rolls. Not a capital offense, right? Anyway, the guy goes berserk and he axes his wife; he kills the poor woman with a Boy Scout-type axe! What do we do now? Set a high bail? Prosecute? Get a conviction and send the fellow to prison? You tell me! We did nothing. The media dropped it quickly and, I hope, that's it.

QUESTIONS FOR DISCUSSION

1. Which alternatives available to the prosecutor would you choose?

2. What about an old age defense?

3. In an English case, *Regina v. Kemp*, a respectable old man, who had never been in trouble, beat his wife. The old man, Kemp, suffered from arteriosclerosis, or hardening of the arteries, a disease that affects mental capacity. The condition caused him to assault his wife. Although the court did not permit his old age to excuse him, the judges did permit his arteriosclerosis to prove he was insane. The jury found Kemp not guilty but insane. Is Kemp entitled to the defense of old age? Defend your answer.[25]

ENTRAPMENT

Entrapment consists of government agents inducing individuals to commit crimes that they otherwise would not commit. Under limited circumstances entrapment is a defense to crimes, that is, it results in the dismissal of the criminal prosecution generated by the entrapment. The defense of entrapment was not recognized in American courts until the twentieth century. In 1864, the New York Supreme Court explained why courts rejected the defense:

> Even if inducements to commit crime could be assumed to exist in this case, the allegation of the defendant would be but the repetition of the pleas as ancient as the world, and first interposed in Paradise: "The serpent beguiled me and I did eat." That defense was overruled by the great Lawgiver, and whatever estimate we may form, or whatever judgment pass upon the character or conduct of the tempter, this plea has never since availed to shield crime or give indemnity to the culprit, and it is safe to say that under any code of civilized, not to say Christian ethics, it never will.[26]

In 1904, another court summed up this attitude toward entrapment:

> We are asked to protect the defendant, not because he is innocent, but because a zealous public officer exceeded his powers and held out a bait. The courts do not look to see who held out the bait, but to see who took it.[27]

The earlier attitude had its basis in an indifference to government inducements to commit crimes. After all, "once the crime is committed, why should it matter what particular incentives were involved and who offered them?" Attitudes have shifted from indifference to both a "limited sympathy" toward entrapped defendants and a growing intolerance of government inducements to entrap otherwise law-abiding people.[28]

The present law of entrapment attempts to balance criminal predisposition and law enforcement practices. That is, it aims to catch the habitual criminal but not at the expense of the otherwise law-abiding person. The entrapment defense did not come about because of the difficulties in apprehending violent criminals or other crimes with complaining victims. Rather, it arose because the police find it particularly difficult to detect consensual crimes or crimes without complaining victims, mainly in cases of illicit drugs, gambling, pornography, prostitution, and official wrongdoing.

The use of government inducement as a law enforcement tool is neither new nor limited to the United States. However, the practice is associated with some highly unsavory characters. Ancient tyrants and modern dictators alike have relied on government agents to induce innocent people to commit crimes (the infamous *agents provocateurs*) so that these autocrats can silence and destroy their political opponents. From the days of Henry VIII to the era of Hitler and Stalin, to the dictators of our own time, most of the world's police states have utilized government informers to encourage dissidents to admit their disloyalty.

Unfortunately, inducement is not simply a tool of dictators in the oppression of their opponents. In all societies and political systems, the tactic creates the risk that law-abiding people will commit crimes they would not commit in the absence of the inducement. Furthermore, government enticement flouts the essential purposes of government. The great Victorian British Prime Minister William Gladstone wisely admonished government to make it easy to do right and difficult to do wrong. Moreover, inducement to criminality flies in the face of the entreaty of the Lord's Prayer to "lead us not into temptation, but deliver us from evil."[29]

Law enforcement encouragement occurs when the following conditions are present: law enforcement officers

1. Pretend they are victims.

2. Intend to entice suspects to commit crimes.

3. Communicate the enticement to suspects.

4. Influence the decision to commit crimes.[30]

Encouragement requires the simulation of reality. Officers present the opportunity to commit a crime when agents are available to gather evidence to prove the guilt of those who receive the encouragement. Usually, it is not enough for officers to simply present an opportunity to commit crimes, or even to request that targets commit crimes. Officers must actively encourage the commission of crimes because most individuals about to commit crimes are wary of strangers. Active encouragement includes such tactics as

- Making repeated requests to commit a crime.

- Forming personal relationships with suspects.

- Appealing to personal considerations.

- Promising benefits from committing the crime.
- Supplying contraband.
- Helping to obtain contraband.[31]

Encouragement becomes entrapment when the encouraging behavior crosses the line from acceptable to *un*acceptable encouragement. Entrapment is a defense to crime; it is not a constitutional right. The Court has held that Congress, in the enactment of criminal statutes, did not intend to permit government agents to lure innocent citizens into committing crimes so that government can punish them. In many jurisdictions, entrapment is an *affirmative defense*, meaning that in order to introduce the defense, defendants must show some evidence of entrapment. Thereafter, the burden may shift to the prosecution to prove that defendants were not entrapped. The jury— or the judge in trials without juries—decides whether officers in fact entrapped defendants. Until recently in federal courts and in some state courts, defendants who denied that they had committed the crime with which they were charged could not use the entrapment defense.

Most state and all federal courts have adopted the subjective test of entrapment. The subjective test focuses on the predisposition of defendants to commit crimes. According to this view, the only defendants who can claim the defense of entrapment are those who initially had no desire to commit crimes but whom the government induced into criminality. The crucial question in the subjective test is, Where did criminal intent originate? If it originated with the defendant, then the government could not have entrapped the defendant. If it originated with the government, then the government entrapped the defendant. For example, in the leading case of *Sherman v. United States*, Kalchinian, a government informant and undercover agent, met Sherman in a drug treatment center. He struck up a friendship with Sherman and eventually asked Sherman to get him some heroin. Sherman, an addict, first refused. Following persistent begging and pleading that extended over several weeks, Sherman finally relented and supplied Kalchinian with the requested heroin. The police promptly arrested Sherman. The Supreme Court ruled that the intent originated with the government. Sherman was in treatment for his addiction—hence, hardly predisposed to commit a drug offense, according to the Court.[32]

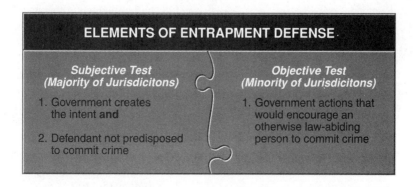

ELEMENTS OF ENTRAPMENT DEFENSE

Subjective Test (Majority of Jurisdicitons)
1. Government creates the intent **and**
2. Defendant not predisposed to commit crime

Objective Test (Minority of Jurisdicitons)
1. Government actions that would encourage an otherwise law-abiding person to commit crime

Once defendants have shown some evidence that the government agent induced the defendant to commit the crime, the government can prove disposition by showing one of the following circumstances:

- Prior convictions for similar offenses.
- Defendant's willingness to commit similar offenses.
- Defendant's display of some criminal expertise in carrying out the offense.
- Defendant's ready ability to commit the crime.

As this list indicates, proving predisposition can depend on either the character of defendants or their past and present conduct. The United States Supreme Court applied the predisposition test of entrapment in *Jacobson v. United States.*

CASE

Did the Government Entrap Jacobson?

Jacobson v. United States, 503 U.S. 540, 112 S.Ct. 1535, 118 L.Ed.2d 174 (1992)

Keith Jacobson was indicted for violating a provision of the Child Protection Act of 1984, which criminalizes the knowing receipt through the mails of a "visual depiction [that] involves the use of a minor engaging in sexually explicit conduct. . . ." Jacobson asserted the defense of entrapment. Jacobson was found guilty after a jury trial. The court of appeals affirmed his conviction. The Supreme Court reversed. Justice White wrote the opinion of the Court, in which Justices Blackmun, Stevens, Souter, and Thomas, joined. Justice O'Connor filed a dissenting opinion, in which Chief Justice Rehnquist and Justices Kennedy and Scalia joined.

FACTS

In February 1984, petitioner, a 56-year-old veteran-turned-farmer who supported his elderly father in Nebraska, ordered two magazines and a brochure from a California adult bookstore. The magazines, entitled Bare Boys I and Bare Boys II, contained photographs of nude preteen and teenage boys. The contents of the magazines startled petitioner, who testified that he had expected to receive photographs of "young

men 18 years or older." On cross-examination, he explained his response to the magazines:

PROSECUTOR: . . . [Y]ou were shocked and surprised that there were pictures of very young boys without clothes on, is that correct?

JACOBSON: Yes, I was.

PROSECUTOR: Were you offended? . . .

JACOBSON: I was not offended because I thought these were a nudist type publication. Many of the pictures were out in a rural or outdoor setting. There was—I didn't draw any sexual connotation or connection with that.

The young men depicted in the magazines were not engaged in sexual activity, and petitioner's receipt of the magazines was legal under both federal and Nebraska law. Within three months, the law with respect to child pornography changed; Congress passed the Act illegalizing the receipt through the mails of sexually explicit depictions of children. In the very month that the new provision became law, postal inspectors found petitioner's name on the mailing list of the California bookstore that had mailed him Bare Boys I and II. There followed, over the next 2½ years, repeated efforts by two Government agencies, through five fictitious organizations and a bogus pen pal, to explore petitioners' willingness to break the new law by ordering sexually explicit photographs of children through the mail.

The Government began its efforts in January 1985 when a postal inspector sent petitioner a letter supposedly from the American Hedonist Society, which in fact was a fictitious organization. The letter included a membership application and stated the Society's doctrine: that members had the "right to read what we desire, the right to discuss similar interests with those who share our philosophy, and finally that we have the right to seek pleasure without restrictions being placed on us by outdated puritan morality." Petitioner enrolled in the organization and returned a sexual attitude questionnaire that asked him to rank on a scale of one to four his enjoyment of various sexual materials, with one being "really enjoy," two being "enjoy," three being "somewhat enjoy," and four being "do not enjoy." Petitioner ranked the entry "[p]re-teen sex" as a two, but indicated that he was opposed to pedophilia.

For a time, the Government left petitioner alone. But then a new "prohibited mail specialist" in the Postal Service found petitioner's name in a file, and in May 1986, petitioner received a solicitation from a second fictitious consumer research company, "Midlands Data Research," seeking a response from those who "believe in the joys of sex and the complete awareness of those lusty and youthful lads and lasses of the neophite [sic] age." The letter never explained whether "neophite" referred to minors or young adults. Petitioner responded: "Please feel free to send me more information. I am interested in teenage sexuality. Please keep my name confidential."

Petitioner then heard from yet another Government creation, "Heartland Institute for a New Tomorrow" (HINT), which proclaimed that it was "an organization founded to protect and promote sexual freedom and freedom of choice. We believe that arbitrarily imposed legislative sanction restricting your sexual freedom should be rescinded through the legislative process." The letter also enclosed a second survey. Petitioner indicated that his interest in "[p]re-teen sex-homosexual" material was above average, but not high. In response to another question, petitioner wrote: "Not only sexual expression but freedom of the press is under attack. We must be ever vigilant to counter attack right wing fundamentalists who are determined to curtail our freedoms."

HINT replied, portraying itself as a lobbying organization seeking to repeal "all statutes which regulate sexual activities, except those laws which deal with violent behavior, such as rape. HINT is also lobbying to eliminate any legal definition of 'the age of consent.'" These lobbying efforts were to be funded by sales from a catalog to be published in the future "offering the sale of various items which we believe you will find to be both interesting and stimulating." HINT also provided computer matching of group members with similar survey responses; and, although petitioner was supplied with a list of potential "pen pals," he did not initiate any correspondence.

Nevertheless, the Government's "prohibited mail specialist" began writing to petitioner, using the pseudonym "Carl Long." The letter employed a tactic known as "mirroring," which the inspector described as "reflect[ing] whatever the interests are of the person we are writing to." Petitioner responded at first, indicating that his interest was primarily in "male-male items." Inspector "Long" wrote back: "My interests too are primarily male-male items. Are you satisfied with the type of VCR tapes available? Personally, I like the amateur stuff better if its [sic] well produced as it can get more kinky and also seems more real. I think the actors enjoy it more."

Petitioner responded: "As far as my likes are concerned, I like good looking young guys (in their late teens and early 20's) doing their thing together." Petitioner's letters to "Long" made no reference to child pornography. After writing two letters, petitioner discontinued the correspondence. By March 1987, 34 months had passed since the Government obtained petitioner's name from the mailing list of the California bookstore, and 26 months had passed since the Postal Service had commenced its mailings to petitioner. Although petitioner had responded to surveys and letters, the Government had no evidence that petitioner had ever intentionally possessed or been exposed to child pornography. The Postal Service had not checked petitioner's mail to determine whether he was receiving questionable mailings from persons—other than the Government—involved in the child pornography industry. At this point, a second Government agency, the Customs Service, included petitioner in its own pornography sting, "Operation Borderline," after receiving his name on lists submitted by the Postal Service. Using the name of a fictitious Canadian company called "Produit Outaouais," the Customs Service mailed petitioner a brochure advertising photographs of young boys engaging in sex. Petitioner placed an order that was never filled. The Postal Service also continued its efforts in the Jacobson case, writing to petitioner as the "Far Eastern Trading Company Ltd." The letter began:

> As many of you know, much hysterical nonsense has appeared in the American media concerning "pornography" and what must be done to stop it from coming across the borders. This brief letter does not allow us to give much comment; however, why is your government spending millions of dollars to exercise international censorship while tons of drugs, which make yours the world's most crime ridden country, are passed through easily?

The letter went on to say:

> [W]e have devised a method of getting these to you without prying eyes of U.S. Customs seizing your mail. . . . After consultations with American solicitors, we have been advised that once we have posted our material through your system, it cannot be opened for any inspection without authorization of a judge.

The letter invited petitioner to send for more information. It also asked petitioner to sign an affirmation that he was "not a law enforcement officer or agent of the U.S. Government acting in an undercover capacity for the purpose of entrapping Far Eastern Trading Company, its agents or customers." Petitioner responded. A catalogue was sent, and petitioner ordered Boys Who Love Boys, a pornographic magazine depicting young boys engaged in various sexual activities. Petitioner was arrested after a controlled delivery of a photocopy of the magazine. When petitioner was asked at trial why he placed such an order, he explained that the Government had succeeded in piquing his curiosity:

> Well, the statement was made of all the trouble and the hysteria over pornography and I wanted to see what the material was. It didn't describe the — I didn't know for sure what kind of sexual action they were referring to in the Canadian letter. . . .

In petitioner's home, the Government found the Bare Boys magazines and materials that the Government had sent to him in the course of its protracted investigation, but no other materials that would indicate the petitioner collected or was actively interested in child pornography.

Petitioner was indicted for violating 18 U.S.C. §2552(a)(2)(A). The trial court instructed the jury on the petitioner's entrapment defense, petitioner was convicted, and a divided Court of Appeals for the Eighth Circuit, sitting en banc, affirmed, concluding that "Jacobson was not entrapped as a matter of law." We granted certiorari.

OPINION

There can be no dispute about the evils of child pornography or the difficulties that laws and law enforcement have encountered in eliminating it. Likewise, there can be no dispute that the Government may use undercover agents to enforce the law. "It is well settled that the fact that officers or employees of the Government merely afford opportunities or facilities for the commission of the offense does not defeat the prosecution. Artifice and stratagem may be employed to catch those engaged in criminal enterprises." *Sorrells v. United States* (1932); *Sherman v. United States* (1958), *United States v. Russell* (1973). In their zeal to enforce the law, however, Government agents may not originate a criminal design, implant in an innocent person's mind the disposition to commit a criminal act, and then induce commission of the crime so that the Government may prosecute. Where the Government has induced an individual to break the law and the defense of entrapment is at issue, as it was in this case, the prosecution must prove beyond reasonable doubt that the defendant was disposed to commit the criminal act prior to first being approached by Government agents. . . .

Had the agents in this case simply offered petitioner the opportunity to order child pornography through the mails, and petitioner — who must be presumed to know the law — had promptly availed himself of this criminal opportunity, it is unlikely that his entrapment defense would have warranted a jury instruction. But that is not what happened here. By the time petitioner finally placed his order, he had already been the target of 26 months of repeated mailings and communications from Government agents and fictitious organizations. Therefore, although he had become predisposed to break the law by May 1987, it is our view that the Government did not prove that this predisposition was independent and not the product of the attention that the Government had directed at petitioner since January 1985.

The prosecution's evidence of predisposition falls into two categories: evidence developed prior to the Postal Service's mail campaign, and that developed during the course of the investigation. The sole piece of preinvestigation evidence is petitioner's 1984 order and receipt of the Bare Boys magazines. But this is scant if any proof of petitioner's predisposition to commit an illegal act, the criminal character of which a defendant is presumed to know. It may indicate a predisposition to view sexually-oriented photographs that are responsive to his sexual tastes; but evidence that merely indicates a generic inclination to act within a broad range, not all of which is criminal, is of little probative value in establishing predisposition. Furthermore, petitioner was acting within the law at the time he received these magazines. Receipt through the mails of sexually explicit depictions of children for noncommercial use did not become illegal under federal law until May 1984, and Nebraska had no law that forbade petitioner's possession of such material until 1988. Neb.Rev.Stat. §28-813.01 (1989).

Evidence of predisposition to do what once was lawful is not, by itself, sufficient to show predisposition to do what is now illegal, for there is a common understanding that most people obey the law even when they disapprove of it. This obedience may reflect a generalized respect for legality or the fear of prosecution, but for whatever reason, the law's prohibitions are matters of consequence. Hence, the fact that petitioner legally ordered and received the Bare Boys magazines does little to further the Government's burden of proving that petitioner was predisposed to commit a criminal act. This is particularly true given petitioner's unchallenged testimony that he did not know until they arrived that the magazines would depict minors.

The prosecution's evidence gathered during the investigation also fails to carry the Government's burden. Petitioner's responses to the many communications prior to the ultimate criminal act were at most indicative of certain personal inclinations, including a predisposition to view photographs of preteen sex and a willingness to promote a given agenda by supporting lobbying organizations. Even so, petitioner's responses hardly support an inference that he would commit the crime of receiving child pornography through the mails. Furthermore, a person's inclinations and "fantasies . . . are his own and beyond the reach of the government. . . ." On the other hand, the strong argument inference is that, by waving the banner of individual rights and disparaging the legitimacy and constitutionality of efforts to restrict the availability of sexually explicit materials, the Government not only excited petitioner's interest in sexually explicit materials banned by law but also exerted substantial pressure on petitioner to obtain and read such material as part of a fight against censorship and the infringement of individual rights. . . .

Petitioner's ready response to these solicitations cannot be enough to establish beyond reasonable doubt that he was predisposed, prior to the Government acts intended to create predisposition, to commit the crime of receiving child pornography through the mails. The evidence that petitioner was ready and willing to commit the offense came only after the Government had devoted 2½ years to convincing him that he had or should have the right to engage in the very behavior proscribed by law. Rational jurors could not say beyond a reasonable doubt that petitioner possessed the requisite predisposition prior to the Government's investigation and that it existed independent of the Government's many and varied approaches to petitioner. As was explained in *Sherman*, where entrapment was found as a matter of law, "the Government [may not] pla[y] on the weaknesses of an innocent party and beguil[e] him into committing crimes which he otherwise would not have attempted."

Law enforcement officials go too far when they "implant in the mind of an innocent person the disposition to commit the alleged offense and induce its commission in order that they may prosecute." Like the *Sorrel[l]s* court, we are unable to conclude that it was the intention of the Congress in enacting this statute that its processes of detection and enforcement should be abused by the instigation by government officials of an act on the part of persons otherwise innocent in order to lure them to its commission and to punish them.

When the Government's quest for convictions leads to the apprehension of an otherwise law-abiding citizen who, if left to his own devices, likely would have never run afoul of the law, the courts should intervene.

Because we conclude that this is such a case and that the prosecution failed, as a matter of law, to adduce evidence to support the jury verdict that petitioner was predisposed, independent of the Government's acts and beyond a reasonable doubt, to violate the law by receiving child pornography through the mails, we reverse the Court of Appeals' judgment affirming the conviction of Keith Jacobson.

It is so ordered.

DISSENT

Justice O'Connor, with whom the chief justice and Justice Kennedy join, and with whom Justice Scalia joins except as to Part II, dissenting.

Keith Jacobson was offered only two opportunities to buy child pornography through the mail. Both times, he ordered. Both times, he asked for opportunities to buy more. He needed no Government agent to coax, threaten, or persuade him; no one played on his sympathies, friendship, or suggested that his committing the crime would further a greater good. In fact, no Government agent even contacted him face-to-face. The Government contends that from the enthusiasm with which Mr. Jacobson responded to the chance to commit a crime, a reasonable jury could permissibly infer beyond a reasonable doubt that he was predisposed to commit the crime. I agree. . . .

Today, the Court holds that Government conduct may be considered to create a predisposition to commit a crime, even before any Government action to induce the commission of the crime. In my view, this holding changes entrapment doctrine. Generally, the inquiry is whether a suspect is predisposed before the government induces the commission of the crime, not before the Government makes initial contact with him. There is no dispute here that the Government's questionnaires and letters were not sufficient to establish inducement; they did not even suggest that Mr. Jacobson should engage in any illegal activity. . . . Yet the Court holds that the Government must prove not only that a suspect was predisposed to commit the crime before the opportunity to commit it arose, but also before the Government came on the scene.

The rule that preliminary Government contact can create a predisposition has the potential to be misread by lower courts as well as criminal investigators as requiring that the Government must have sufficient evidence of a defendant's predisposition before it ever seeks to contact him. Surely the Court cannot intend to impose such a requirement, for it would mean that the Government must have a reasonable suspicion of criminal activity before it begins an investigation, a condition that we have never before imposed.

The Court denies that its new rule will affect run-of-the-mill sting operations, and one hopes that it means what it says. Nonetheless, after this case, every defendant will claim that something the Government agent did before soliciting the crime "created" a predisposition that was not there before. For example, a bribe taker will claim the description of the amount of money available was so enticing that it implanted a disposition to accept the bribe later offered. A drug buyer will claim that the description of the drug's purity and effects was so tempting that it created the urge to try it for the first time. . . .

The crux of the Court's concern in this case is that the Government went too far and "abused" the "processes of detection and enforcement" by luring an innocent person to violate the law. Consequently, the Court holds that the Government failed to prove beyond a reasonable doubt that Mr. Jacobson was predisposed to commit the crime. It was, however, the jury's task, as the conscience of the community, to decide whether or not Mr. Jacobson was a willing participant in the criminal activity here or an innocent dupe. The jury is the traditional "defense against arbitrary law enforcement." . . . There is no dispute that the jury in this case was fully and accurately instructed on the law of entrapment, and nonetheless found Mr. Jacobson guilty. Because I believe there was sufficient evidence to uphold the jury's verdict, I respectfully dissent.

QUESTIONS FOR DISCUSSION

1. What specific facts demonstrate that the government induced Keith Jacobson to order the child pornography?

2. What evidence demonstrates that Jacobson was predisposed to commit the crime?

3. Why did the Court reverse the conviction even though the jury convicted him?

4. What does the dissent mean when it says that the majority has changed the law of entrapment?

5. Do you agree with criticism that the Court's decision ties the hands of law enforcement officers? Defend your answer.

INSANITY

The insanity defense commands great public and scholarly attention. But both the public and, surprisingly, many criminal defense attorneys grossly misunderstand the operation and the effects of the insanity defense. Contrary to widespread belief, few defendants plead the insanity defense (only a few thousand a year, according to the largest empirical study ever conducted of the insanity defense). Moreover, again contrary to common belief, most fail in the defense, and the few who succeed do not go free but go to maximum-security prisons. The case of Lorena Bobbitt, a woman who successfully pleaded insanity to a charge of cutting off her husband's penis and who was free a mere five weeks after the verdict, was known throughout the world because CNN televised the trial. Not known at all to the public is the case of John Smith, who tried to drive a Greyhound bus out of the New York City Port Authority bus terminal in 1980, crashed, and was acquitted of grand larceny charges "by reason of insanity," and is still confined at the Manhattan Psychiatric Center on Ward's Island in New York City. CNN may have made Lorena Bobbitt a household word throughout the world and no one but the lawyers, doctors, and hospital staff may know of John Smith, but his case is far more typical of insanity defense cases.[33]

Defendants rarely plead insanity because they have too much to lose whether they fail or succeed. Contrary to widely held beliefs, and unlike all other defenses discussed up to this point, a successful insanity plea does not lead to automatic freedom. Take the typical verdict of "not guilty by reason of insanity." Once juries find that defendants were insane when they committed the crimes, special proceedings take place in which the court decides whether they still require custody for their own and society's safety. In other words, successful insanity pleas bestow upon the government the authority to incarcerate without conviction. Persons found not guilty by reason of insanity rarely go free immediately; some never go free. Courts nearly always commit them to maximum-security hospitals, institutions virtually indistinguishable from prisons. Not surprisingly, then, only a few defendants resort to the insanity plea. The few who do plead insanity—nearly all charged with capital crimes or crimes subject to life imprisonment—rarely succeed. During 1991, for example, 60,432 individuals were indicted in Baltimore, Maryland. Of these, only 190 entered a plea of insanity, and all but eight dropped the plea before trial.[34]

Insanity excuses criminal liability because it impairs *mens rea*. Punishing insane persons does not serve the major objectives of criminal law. If defendants were so mentally diseased that they could not form *mens rea*, then they are not blameworthy, and retribution is out of order. Neither would it deter either the defendant or other mentally ill people who cannot form *mens rea*. Also, the government can invoke its civil commitment authority to incapacitate and treat mentally ill persons without calling upon the criminal law to control them.

Insanity is a legal concept, not a medical term. What psychiatry calls mental illness may or may not conform to the law's definition of insanity. Mental illness alone does not prove insanity, and only insanity excuses criminal responsibility. Psychiatrists testify in courts to aid fact finders in determining whether defendants are legally insane, not to prove they are mentally ill. The verdict "guilty but mentally ill" makes this point clear. In that verdict, used in some jurisdictions, the jury can find that defendants were not insane but were mentally ill when they committed crimes. These defendants receive criminal sentences and go to prison, but they may require, and are supposed to receive, treatment for their mental illness while in prison.[35]

Jurisdictions determine insanity according to two primary tests:

1. The right-wrong test.

2. The substantial capacity test.

Both tests require looking at defendants' mental capacity, but they differ in what they emphasize about that capacity. The right-wrong test focuses on the intellect, or cognition—what defendants know. The substantial capacity test focuses not only on knowledge but also on the emotional dimension to understanding—defendants' appreciation of what they did. Freud expressed this distinction in his phrase "there is knowing, and there is *knowing!*" A child knows intellectually that stealing is wrong but does not fully appreciate, or feel, its significance. The substantial capacity test also stresses volition, or defendants' will to control their actions. Defendants may know that what they are doing is wrong but lack the will to control their actions.

Right-Wrong Test

The **M'Naghten rule,** or **right-wrong test,** focuses narrowly on the intellectual capacity of defendants to know what they are doing and to distinguish right from wrong. In *Rex v. Porter,* the trial judge explained the right-wrong test in these instructions to the jury:

> I wish to draw your attention to some general considerations affecting the question of insanity in the criminal law in the hope that by so doing you may be helped to grasp what the law prescribes. The purpose of the law in punishing people is to prevent others from committing a like crime or crimes. Its prime purpose is to deter people from committing offenses. It may be that there is an element of retribution in the criminal law, so that when people have committed offenses the law considers that they merit punishment, but its prime purpose is to preserve society from the depredations of dangerous and vicious people.
>
> Now, it is perfectly useless for the law to attempt, by threatening punishment, to deter people from committing crimes if their mental condition is such that they cannot be in the least influenced by the possibility or probability of subsequent punishment; if they cannot understand what they are doing or cannot understand the ground upon which the law proceeds.
>
> The law is not directed, as medical science is, to curing mental infirmities. The criminal law is not directed, as the civil law of lunacy is, to the care and custody of people of weak mind whose personal property may be in jeopardy through someone else taking a hand in the conduct of their affairs and their lives. This is quite a different thing from the question, what utility there is in the punishment

of people who, at a moment, would commit acts which, if done when they were in sane minds, would be crimes.

What is the utility of punishing people if they be beyond the control of the law for reasons of mental health? In considering that, it will not perhaps, if you have ever reflected upon the matter, have escaped your attention that a great number of people who come into a Criminal Court are abnormal. They would not be there if they were the normal type of average everyday people. Many of them are very peculiar in their dispositions and peculiarly tempered. That is markedly the case in sexual offences. Nevertheless, they are mentally quite able to appreciate what they are doing and quite able to appreciate the threatened punishment of the law and the wrongness of their acts, and they are held in check by the prospect of punishment. It would be very absurd if the law were to withdraw that check on the ground that they were somewhat different from their fellow creatures in mental make-up or texture at the very moment when the check is most needed.

You will therefore see that the law, in laying down a standard of mental disorder sufficient to justify a jury in finding a prisoner not guilty on the ground of insanity at the moment of offence, is addressing itself to a somewhat difficult task. It is attempting to define what are the classes of people who should not be punished although they have done actual things which in others would amount to crime. It is quite a different object to that which the medical profession has in view or other departments of the law have in view of defining insanity for the purpose of the custody of the person's property, capacity to make a will, and the like.[36]

The right-wrong test, although it has deep historical antecedents, derived its present form from the famous English M'Naghten case. In 1843, Daniel M'Naghten suffered the paranoid delusion that the prime minister, Sir Robert Peel, had masterminded a conspiracy to kill M'Naghten. M'Naghten shot at Peel in delusional self-defense but killed Peel's secretary, Edward Drummond, by mistake. Following his trial for murder, the jury returned a verdict of not guilty by reason of insanity. On appeal, England's highest court, the House of Lords, formulated the right-wrong test, or M'Naghten rule. According to the rule, the court designed a two-pronged insanity test:

1. The defendant must suffer from a disease or defect of the mind, and

2. the disease or defect must cause the defendant either to not know the nature and quality of the criminal act or to not know that the act was wrong.[37]

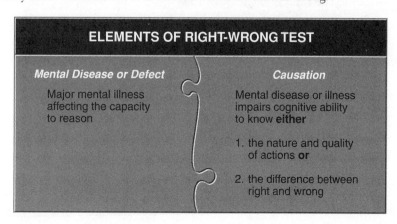

ELEMENTS OF RIGHT-WRONG TEST

Mental Disease or Defect

Major mental illness affecting the capacity to reason

Causation

Mental disease or illness impairs cognitive ability to know **either**

1. the nature and quality of actions **or**

2. the difference between right and wrong

The right-wrong test, as the House of Lords formulated it, creates several difficulties. First, what mental diseases or defects does the phrase "a disease or defect of the mind" include? All formulations include severe psychoses, such as the paranoia from which M'Naghten himself suffered, and schizophrenia. Virtually all also include severe mental retardation affecting cognition. They exclude neuroses and/or personality disorders, particularly psychopathic and sociopathic personalities—those who engage in repeated criminal or antisocial conduct.[38]

The word "know" also creates problems. Most statutes and decisions say it means pure intellectual awareness: cognition. Others include more than intellectual awareness; nearly everyone possesses intellectual awareness. Hence, some statutes bring within the compass of knowing the ability to understand or appreciate, meaning to grasp an act's true significance. The appreciation and understanding requirements add an emotional, affective, or feeling dimension to the intellectual dimension of the cognition requirement. Some jurisdictions do not define the term, leaving it to juries to define it by applying it to the facts of specific cases.

The following example captures the meaning of not knowing the "nature and quality of the criminal act," as M'Naghten defined that phrase: If a man believes he is squeezing lemons when in fact he is strangling his wife, he clearly does not know the nature and quality of his act. Some hold that the phrase means knowing right from wrong. A few go further, contending that it refers to more than knowing the nature of the physical act. One court, for example, required "true insight" into the act's consequences. This does not mean that defendants must believe the act is wrong. M'Naghten himself knew that he was killing, but he thought the killing was justified.

The word "wrong" itself has created problems in the definition of the right-wrong test. Some jurisdictions require that defendants did not know their conduct was legally wrong; others interpret "wrong" to mean that defendants did not know their conduct was morally wrong. Consider the person who kills another person under the insane delusion that his subsequent conviction and execution for the murder will save the human race. The person knew that killing was legally, but not morally, wrong. If "wrong" means "legal," the person is guilty; if it means "moral," he is insane. Some jurisdictions adopt an objective test to determine moral wrongfulness: Do defendants lack the capacity to know that their conduct violated the prevailing moral standard of the community? Others adopt a subjective test: Do defendants know the conduct was wrong by their own moral standards? The court in *State v. Crenshaw* applied the right-wrong test.[39]

C A S E

Too Insane to Be Guilty?

State v. Crenshaw,
98 Wash.2d 789, 659 P.2d 488 (1983)

Crenshaw was convicted of first-degree murder. He appealed. The Washington supreme court affirmed. Justice Brachtenback wrote the opinion for the court.

FACTS

While defendant and his wife were on their honeymoon in Canada, petitioner was deported as a result of his participation in a brawl. He secured a motel room in Blaine, Washington and waited for his wife to join him. When she arrived 2 days later, he immediately thought she had been unfaithful — he sensed "it wasn't the same Karen. She'd been with someone else."

Petitioner did not mention his suspicions to his wife, instead he took her to the motel room and beat her unconscious. He then went to a nearby store, stole a knife, and returned to stab his wife 24 times, inflicting a fatal wound. He left again, drove to a nearby farm where he had been employed and borrowed an ax. Upon returning to the motel room, he decapitated his wife with such force that the ax marks cut into the concrete floor under the carpet and splattered blood throughout the room.

Petitioner then proceeded to conceal his actions. He placed the body in a blanket, the head in a pillowcase and put both in his wife's car. Next, he went to a service station, borrowed a bucket and sponge, and cleaned the room of blood and fingerprints. Before leaving, petitioner also spoke with the motel manager about a phone bill, then chatted with him for awhile over a beer.

When Crenshaw left the motel he drove to a remote area 25 miles away where he hid the two parts of the body in thick brush. He then fled, driving to the Hoquiam area, about 200 miles from the scene of the crime. There he picked up two hitchhikers, told them of his crime, and enlisted their aid in disposing of his wife's car in a river. The hitchhikers contacted the police and Crenshaw was apprehended shortly thereafter. He voluntarily confessed to the crime.

The defense of not guilty by reason of insanity was a major issue at trial. Crenshaw testified that he followed the Muscovite religious faith, and that it would be improper for a Muscovite not to kill his wife if she committed adultery. Crenshaw also has a history of mental problems, for which he has been hospitalized in the past. The jury, however, rejected petitioner's insanity defense, and found him guilty of murder in the first degree.

OPINION

The insanity defense is not available to all who are mentally deficient or deranged; legal insanity has a different meaning and a different purpose than the concept of medical insanity. A verdict of not guilty by reason of insanity completely absolves a defendant of any criminal responsibility. Therefore, "the defense is available only to those persons who have lost contact with reality so completely that they are beyond any of the influences of the criminal law."

Petitioner assigned error to insanity defense instruction 10 which reads:

> Insanity existing at the time of the commission of the act charged is a defense. For a defendant to be found not guilty by reason of insanity you must find that, as a result of mental disease or defect, the defendant's mind was affected to such an extent that the defendant was unable to perceive the nature and quality of the acts with which the defendant is charged or was unable to tell right from wrong with reference to the particular acts with which defendant is charged.
>
> What is meant by the terms "right and wrong" refers to knowledge of a person at the time of committing an act that he was acting contrary to the law.

Petitioner contends . . . that the trial court erred in defining "right and wrong" as legal right and wrong rather than in the moral sense.

First, in discussing the term "moral" wrong, it is important to note that it is society's morals, and not the individual's morals, that are the standard for judging moral wrong under *M'Naghten*. If wrong meant moral wrong judged by the individual's own conscience, this would seriously undermine the criminal law, for it would allow one who violated the law to be excused from criminal responsibility solely because, in his own conscience, his act was not morally wrong.

This principle was emphasized by Justice Cardozo:

> The anarchist is not at liberty to break the law because he reasons that all government is wrong. The devotee of a religious cult that enjoins polygamy or human sacrifice as a duty is not thereby relieved from responsibility before the law.

There is evidence on the record that Crenshaw knew his actions were wrong according to society's standards, as well as legally wrong. Dr. Belden testified:

> I think Mr. Crenshaw is quite aware on one level that he is in conflict with the law *and with*

people. However, this is not something that he personally invests his emotions in. [italics ours]

We conclude that Crenshaw knew his acts were morally wrong from society's viewpoint and also knew his acts were illegal. His personal belief that it was his duty to kill his wife for her alleged infidelity cannot serve to exculpate him from legal responsibility for his acts.

We also find that, under any definition of wrong, Crenshaw did not qualify for the insanity defense under *M'Naghten*; therefore, any alleged error in that definition must be viewed as harmless.

Here, any error is harmless for two alternate reasons. First, Crenshaw failed to prove an essential element of the defense because he did not prove his alleged delusions stemmed from a mental defect; second, he did not prove by a preponderance of the evidence that he was legally insane at the time of the crime.

In addition to an incapacity to know right from wrong, *M'Naghten* requires that such incapacity stem from a mental disease or defect. RCW 9A.12.010. Assuming, arguendo, that Crenshaw did not know right from wrong, he failed to prove that a mental defect was the cause of this inability.

Petitioner's insanity argument is premised on the following facts:

(1) he is a Muscovite and Muscovites believe it is their duty to assassinate an unfaithful spouse;

(2) he "knew," without asking, that his wife had been unfaithful when he met her in Blaine and this was equivalent to an insane delusion; and

(3) at other times in his life, he had been diagnosed as a paranoid personality and had been committed to mental institutions.

A conscientious application of the *M'Naghten* rule demonstrates, however, that these factors do not afford petitioner the sanctuary of the insanity defense.

To begin, petitioner's Muscovite beliefs are irrelevant to the insanity defense, because they are not insane delusions. Some notion of morality, unrelated to a mental illness, which disagrees with the law and mores of our society is not an insane delusion.

Nor was petitioner's belief that his wife was unfaithful an insane delusion. Dr. Trowbridge, a psychiatrist, explained:

A man suspects his wife of being unfaithful. Certainly such suspicions are not necessarily delusional, even if they're ill based. Just because he suspected his wife of being unfaithful doesn't mean that he was crazy.

Certainly when a man kills his wife he doesn't do it in a rational way. No one ever does that rationally. But that is not to suggest that every time a man kills his wife he was [sic] insane.

Finally, evidence of prior commitments to mental institutions is not proof that one was legally insane at the time the criminal act was committed.

Those who are commonly regarded as "odd" or "unsound" or even "deranged" would not normally qualify [for the insanity defense]. Many, if not most, mentally ill persons presently being treated in the mental institutions of this state who are there under the test of "likelihood of serious harm to the person detained or to others," would not meet the *M'Naghten* test, if charged with a crime.

Thus, petitioner does not establish the necessary connection between his criminal acts and his psychological problems to qualify for the insanity defense.

In addition, the preponderance of the evidence weighs against finding Crenshaw legally insane. All of the psychological experts, save one, testified that defendant was not insane at the time of the murder. The only doctor who concluded defendant (petitioner) was legally insane, Dr. Hunger, was a psychologist who had not examined petitioner for a year and a half.

Given the various qualifications of the experts, the time they spent with the petitioner, and the proximity in time of their examinations to the murder, the testimony does not establish by a preponderance of the evidence that petitioner was legally insane at the time of the murder.

Furthermore, in addition to the expert testimony, there was lay testimony that petitioner appeared rational at the time of the killing. After cleaning the motel room, Crenshaw resolved a phone bill dispute with the manager, then shared a beer with him without arousing any suspicion in the manager's mind. Also, the woman who gave him the ax testified as to his behavior the day before the murder.

Well, he seemed very normal or I certainly wouldn't have handed him an ax or a hoe. He was polite, he done his work. He didn't, I wasn't afraid of him or anything. I mean we were just out there working and I certainly wouldn't have handed him an ax or anything like that if I would have thought that there was anything even remotely peculiar about him.

And, with specific reference to the time when petitioner borrowed the ax to decapitate his wife:

Q: Did he seem rational to you?
A: Oh, yes, he was very nice.
Q: Did he seem coherent when he spoke to you?
A: Oh, yes.
Q: Did he appear to be sane to you then?
A: Yes.

Thus, at the same time that he was embroiled in the act of murdering his wife, he was rational, coherent, and sane in his dealings with others.

Finally, evidence of petitioner's calculated execution of the crime and his sophisticated attempts to avert discovery support a finding of sanity. Crenshaw performed the murder methodically, leaving the motel room twice to acquire the knife and ax necessary to perform the deed. Then, after the killing he scrubbed the motel room to clean up the blood and remove his fingerprints. Next, he drove 25 miles to hide the body in thick brush in a remote area. Finally, he drove several hundred miles and ditched the car in a river.

Such attempts to hide evidence of a crime manifest an awareness that the act was legally wrong. Moreover, petitioner testified that he did these things because he "didn't want to get caught."

To summarize thus far, we find no error in instruction 10 for the following reasons:

1. As we interpret the *M'Naghten* case, it was not improper for the trial court to instruct with reference to the law of the land, under the facts of this case;

2. because the concept of moral wrong refers to the mores of society and not to the individual's morals, "moral" wrong is synonymous with "legal" wrong with a serious crime such as this one, therefore, instructing in terms of legal wrong did not alter the meaning of the *M'Naghten* rule;

3. any error was harmless because

   (a) Crenshaw did not show that at the time of the crime his mind was affected as a result of a mental disease or defect and without this essential element the insanity defense was not available to him, and

   (b) an overwhelming preponderance of the evidence supports the finding that Crenshaw was not legally insane when he killed his wife. We thus conclude that the additional statement in instruction 10 was not improper, or, at the very least, that it was harmless error.

Affirmed.

QUESTIONS FOR DISCUSSION

1. Do you agree that moral wrong and legal wrong are the same?

2. Should the test be whether Crenshaw knew he was breaking the law or that he knew it was wrong in the general sense?

3. What would you do with Crenshaw?

4. Do you think it is possible to be objective about Crenshaw's insanity?

5. Or does the brutal way he killed his wife make you want to call him a criminal, no matter what his state of mind?

6. Do you see how this can create serious problems with the insanity defense?

The right-wrong test has generated protracted argument. Critics mainly contend that modern developments in both law and psychiatry have rendered the test obsolete. This criticism loomed especially large during the 1950s, when many social reformers relied on Freudian psychology to cure a wide spectrum of individual and social ills. *Durham v. United States* reflects psychiatry's influence on criminal law generally and on the insanity defense particularly. With regard to the right-wrong test, the court said:

> The science of psychiatry now recognizes that a man is an integrated personality and that reason, which is only one element in that personality, is not the sole determinant of his conduct. The right-wrong test, which considers knowledge or reason alone, is therefore an inadequate guide to mental responsibility for criminal behavior.[40]

Borrowing from a New Hampshire rule formulated in 1871 and still in effect in that state, the *Durham* court formulated a broad insanity definition reflecting the influence of psychiatry. According to the **Durham rule,** or **product test,** acts that are the products of mental disease or defect excuse criminal liability. The court aimed to broaden the concept of insanity beyond the purely intellectual knowledge in the right-wrong test to deeper areas of cognition and will. Only New Hampshire (where the test originated), the federal court of appeals for the District of Columbia (which decided Durham), and Maine ever adopted the product test. The federal court and Maine have since abandoned the test, leaving it in effect only in New Hampshire.[41]

M'Naghten's defenders contend that the product test misses the point of legal insanity. They maintain that the right-wrong test should not substitute mental illness for insanity. Rather, it is an instrument to determine which mental states ought to relieve persons of criminal responsibility. Two articulate defenders put it this way:

> It is always necessary to start any discussion of *M'Naghten* by stressing that the case does not state a test of psychosis or mental illness. Rather, it lists conditions under which those who are mentally diseased will be relieved from criminal responsibility. Thus, criticism of *M'Naghten* based on the proposition that the case is premised on an outdated view of mental disease is inappropriate. The case can only be criticized justly if it is based on an outdated view of the mental conditions that ought to preclude application of criminal sanction.[42]

Other critics contend that the *M'Naghten* rule focuses too narrowly on intellectual knowledge of right and wrong in cognition, neglecting the deeper emotional components necessary to full appreciation of conduct. Furthermore, considering only cognition excludes volition—whether defendants can control their behavior even though they fully appreciate, both intellectually and emotionally, that they are acting wrongfully. These critics say that criminal law acts inappropriately if it excuses only those who do not know or appreciate what they are doing while punishing those who cannot stop themselves from doing what they know is wrong. We can neither blame nor deter those who cannot conform their conduct to what the law requires. The law of civil commitment can protect society from them and treat them without resorting to criminal sanctions.

M'Naghten's supporters contend that the law should presume everyone has some control because operating on that assumption deters more potential offenders. Therefore, the insanity defense ought to include only those who

1. did not know what they were doing; or
2. did know what they were doing but did not know it was wrong, assuming that they can choose right if they know what right is.

Irresistible Impulse Test

Several jurisdictions have supplemented the right-wrong test with the irresistible impulse test in an effort to deal with the volition problem. **Irresistible impulse** requires

> a verdict of not guilty by reason of insanity if it is found that the defendant has a mental disease which kept him from controlling his conduct. Such a verdict is called for even if the defendant knew what he was doing and that it was wrong.[43]

Although the irresistible impulse test predates *M'Naghten* (it goes back to at least 1834 in England), the leading American case was decided in 1877. In *Parsons v. State*, the court held that when defendants plead insanity, juries should determine the following:

1. At the time of the crime was the defendant afflicted with "a disease of the mind"?
2. If so, did the defendant know right from wrong with respect to the act charged? If not, the law excuses the defendant.
3. If the defendant did have such knowledge, the law will still excuse the defendant if two conditions concur:
   a. if mental disease caused the defendant to so far lose the power to choose between right and wrong and to avoid doing the alleged act that the disease destroyed the defendant's free will, and
   b. if the mental disease was the sole cause of the act.[44]

Despite broadening the right-wrong defense, critics maintain that the irresistible impulse supplement still restricts the insanity defense too much. It includes only impulsive acts, ignoring mental disease "characterized by brooding and reflection." Defenders deny this. Courts do not tell juries that they must limit their findings to sudden and unplanned impulses; juries can consider any evidence showing that defendants lack control owing to mental disease. Critics also claim that the irresistible requirement implies that defendants must lack control totally. In practice, however, juries do acquit defendants who have some control; rarely do juries demand an utter lack of control.

Other critics claim that the irresistible impulse test includes too much. By permitting people who lack control to escape criminal liability, the test unduly curtails the deterrent purposes of criminal law. For example, the jury acquitted John Hinckley, Jr., on the grounds that Hinckley was insane when he attempted to assassinate former president Ronald Reagan in order to gain the attention of actress Jodie Foster. Shortly after Hinckley's trial, Harvard criminal law professor Charles Nesson wrote:

> [T]o many Mr. Hinckley seems like a kid who had a rough life and who lacked the moral fiber to deal with it. This is not to deny that Mr. Hinckley is crazy but to recognize that there is a capacity for craziness in all of us. Lots of people have tough lives, many tougher than Mr. Hinckley's, and manage to cope. The Hinckley verdict let those people down. For anyone who experiences life as a struggle to act responsibly in the face of various temptations to let go, the Hinckley verdict is demoralizing, an example of someone who let himself go and who has been exonerated because of it.[45]

Defenders claim that empirical research has not demonstrated the effectiveness of deterrence; hence, the law should not base the insanity defense on it. Finally, opponents who are disillusioned with the rehabilitative ideal argue that the state should not engage in hopeless efforts to treat and cure the mentally diseased (see the discussion on deterrence in chapter 2).

Since the attempted murder of former President Reagan, several jurisdictions have abolished the irresistible impulse defense on the ground that juries cannot accurately distinguish between irresistible and merely unresisted impulses. Unresisted impulses should not excuse criminal conduct. The federal statute abolishing irresistible impulse in federal cases provides as follows:[46]

> It is an affirmative defense to a prosecution under any Federal statute that, at the time of the commission of the acts constituting the offense, the defendant, as a result of a severe mental disease or defect, was unable to appreciate the nature and quality or the wrongfulness of his acts. Mental disease or defect does not otherwise constitute a defense.[47]

Substantial Capacity Test

The right-wrong test, either supplemented by the irresistible impulse test or not, was the rule in most states until the 1960s, after which the *Model Penal Code*'s **substantial capacity test** became the majority rule. During the 1970s, and since the 1980s, following John Hinckley's trial, the pure right-wrong test (unencumbered by the emotional component of understanding, irresistible impulse, or both) has enjoyed a resurgence.[48]

The *Model Penal Code* provision resulted from efforts to remove objections to both the *M'Naghten* rule and the irresistible impulse test while preserving the legal nature of both tests. It emphasizes the qualities in insanity that affect culpability: the intellectual (cognitive) and emotional (affective) components of understanding, and will (volition).

The *Model Penal Code* requires that defendants lack "substantial," not total, mental capacity. Both the right-wrong and irresistible impulse tests are ambiguous on this point, leading some to maintain that both require total lack of knowledge and control. Hence, persons who know right and wrong minimally and whose will to resist is slightly intact are insane, according to the code provision:

> A person is not responsible for criminal conduct if at the time of such conduct as a result of mental disease or defect he lacks substantial capacity either to appreciate the criminality [wrongfulness] of his conduct or to conform his conduct to the requirements of law.[49]

The use of "appreciate" instead of "know" makes clear that mere intellectual awareness does not constitute culpability. The code includes affective or emotional compo-

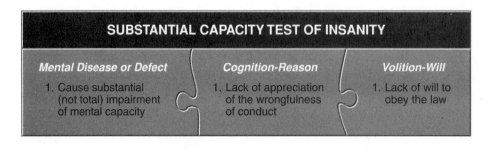

SUBSTANTIAL CAPACITY TEST OF INSANITY

Mental Disease or Defect	*Cognition-Reason*	*Volition-Will*
1. Cause substantial (not total) impairment of mental capacity	1. Lack of appreciation of the wrongfulness of conduct	1. Lack of will to obey the law

nents of understanding. The phrase "conform his conduct" removes the requirement of a "sudden" lack of control. In other words, the code provision eliminates the suggestion that losing control means losing it on the spur of the moment, as the irresistible impulse test unfortunately implies. The code's definition of "mental disease or defect" excludes psychopathic personalities, habitual criminals, and antisocial personalities from the defense.

Until the return to right-wrong, the substantial capacity test had replaced it as the majority rule. The history of the insanity defense in California illustrates this historical pattern:

1. The original adoption of the *M'Naghten* rule.

2. Then the shift to the *Model Penal Code* substantial capacity test.

3. Then a return to the *M'Naghten* right-wrong test.

In California, the return to the right-wrong test was effected by an initiative that the electorate approved in 1982. *People v. Skinner* raised the issue of whether the insanity test approved by the electorate reverted to an even stricter test of insanity, the wild beast test in effect before 1850. In 1724, Judge Tracy instructed an English jury in *Rex v. Arnold*:

> If a man be deprived of his reason and consequently of his intention he cannot be guilty. . . . [I]t is not every kind of frantic humour . . . that points him out to be such a madman as is to be exempted from punishment: it must be a man that is totally deprived of his understanding and memory, and doth not know what he is doing, no more than infant, than a brute, or a wild beast, such a one is never the object of any punishment.[50]

C A S E

Was He Insane?

**People v. Skinner,
39 Cal.3d 765, 217 Cal.Rptr. 685,
704 P.2d 752 (1985)**

Skinner was convicted of second-degree murder, being determined legally sane, and he appealed. The California Supreme Court reversed, finding Skinner not guilty by reason of insanity, without further hearing on the sanity issue. Justice Groddin wrote the opinion for the court.

FACTS

. . . Defendant strangled his wife while he was on a day pass from the Camarillo State Hospital at which he was a patient. [Psychiatric testimony included] the opinion . . . that defendant suffered from either classical paranoic schizophrenia, or schizo-affective illness with significant paranoid features. A delusional product of this illness was a belief held by the defendant that the marriage vow "till death do us part" bestows on a marital partner a God-given right to kill the other partner who has violated or was inclined to violate the marital vows, and that because the vows reflect the direct wishes of God, the killing is with complete moral and criminal impunity. The act is not wrongful because it is sanctified by the will and desire of God. . . .

OPINION

For over a century prior to the decision in *People v. Drew* (1978), California courts framed this state's definition of insanity, as a defense in criminal cases, upon the two-pronged test adopted by the House of Lords in *M'Naghten's Case* . . . [owing to mental disease or defect, defendant

(1) did not know the nature and quality of the act he was doing or

(2) if he did know it, he did not know that it was wrong].

Over the years the *M'Naghten* test became subject to considerable criticism and was abandoned in a number of jurisdictions. In *Drew* this court followed suit, adopting the test for mental incapacity proposed by the American Law Institute. . . .

In June 1982 the California electorate adopted an initiative measure . . . which . . . for the first time established a statutory definition of insanity. . . . It is apparent from the language of § 25(b) that it was designed to eliminate the *Drew* test and to reinstate the prongs of the *M'Naghten* test. However, the section uses the conjunctive "and" instead of the disjunctive "or" to connect the two prongs. Read literally, therefore, § 25(b) would do more than reinstate the *M'Naghten* test. It would strip the insanity defense from an accused who, by reason of mental disease, is incapable of knowing that the act he was doing was wrong. That is, in fact, the interpretation adopted by the trial court in this case. . . .

The judge stated that under the *Drew* test of legal insanity defendant would qualify as insane, and also found that "under the right-wrong prong of § 25(b), the defendant would qualify as legally insane; but under the other prong, he clearly does not." Concluding that by the use of the conjunctive "and" in § 25(b), the electorate demonstrated an intent to establish a stricter test of insanity than the *M'Naghten* test, and to "virtually eliminate" insanity as a defense, the judge found that defendant had not established that he was legally insane. . . .

In this context we must determine whether the trial court's conclusion . . . was correct, and if not, whether the court's finding that defendant met the "right-wrong" aspect of the test requires reversal. . . .

For more than a century after . . . the *M'Naghten* test [was adopted in this state], although sometimes stated in the conjunctive, [it] was in fact applied so as to permit a finding of insanity if either prong of the test was satisfied. . . . [T]he insanity defense reflects a fundamental legal principle common to the jurisprudence of this country and to the common law of England that criminal sanctions are imposed only on persons who act with wrongful intent in the commission of a *malum in se* offense. Since 1850 the disjunctive *M'Naghten* test of insanity has been accepted as the rule by which the minimum cognitive function which constitutes wrongful intent will be measured in this state. As such it is itself among the fundamental principles of our criminal law. Had it been the intent of the drafters . . . or of the electorate which adopted it both to abrogate the more expansive ALI-*Drew* test and to abandon that prior fundamental principle of culpability for crime, we would anticipate that this intent would be expressed in some more obvious manner than the substitution of a single conjunctive in a lengthy initiative provision. . . .

Applying § 25(b) as a conjunctive test of insanity would erase that fundamental principle. It would return the law to that which preceded *M'Naghten*, a test known variously as the "wild beast test" and as the "good and evil" test under which an accused could be found insane only if he was "totally deprived of his understanding and memory, and doth not know what he is doing, no more than an infant, than a brute, or a wild beast. . . ." We find nothing in the language . . . [of the initiative], or in any other source from which the intent of the electorate may be divined which indicates that such a fundamental, far-reaching change in the law of insanity as that was intended. . . .

We conclude . . . that § 25(b) reinstated the M'Naghten test as it was applied in California prior to Drew as the test of legal insanity in criminal prosecutions in this state. . . .

The judgment is reversed and the superior court is directed to enter a judgment of not guilty by reason of insanity. . . .

DISSENT

Byrd, Chief Justice.

In June of 1982, the voters adopted a ballot measure which radically altered the test for criminal insanity in this state. . . . I cannot ignore the fact that they adopted language which unambiguously requires the accused to demonstrate that "he or she was incapable of knowing or understanding the nature and quality of his or her act *and* of distinguishing right from wrong at the time of the commission of the offense" [emphasis added]. There is nothing in the statute . . . or in the ballot arguments that implies that the electorate intended "and" to be "or." However unwise that choice, it is not within this court's power to ignore the expression of popular will and rewrite the statute.

Since appellant failed to establish his insanity under the test enunciated in Penal Code § 25, subdivision (b), I cannot join the decision of my brethren.

QUESTIONS FOR DISCUSSION

1. Did the electorate make its position clear by using "and" rather than "or," as Chief Justice Byrd argued in her dissent?

2. Or is the majority right in arguing that the electorate should have made the statute clearer?

3. How could the statute be more precise?

4. Do you think the court violated the electorate's intent by interpreting the provision to mean "or"?

5. Now that you have had the chance to consider right-wrong, irresistible impulse, substantial capacity, and the California statutory initiative, what definition of insanity do you favor? Explain.

Burden of Proof

The defense of insanity not only poses definition problems but also gives rise to difficulties in application. Authorities disagree and critics hotly debate who must prove insanity, and how convincingly. The burden-of-proof question received public attention and generated hostility among both the public and criminal justice professionals when the jury acquitted John Hinckley, Jr., in the shooting of former President Reagan and three others. Federal law required that the government prove Hinckley's sanity beyond a reasonable doubt. Thus, if Hinckley's lawyers could raise a doubt in jurors' minds about his sanity, the jury had to acquit. Even though the jury may have thought Hinckley was sane, if they were not convinced beyond a reasonable doubt that he was, then they had to acquit. That is what happened: They thought he was sane but had their doubts, so they acquitted.

The result was not only criticism but also swift legislative action. The Comprehensive Crime Control Act of 1984 shifted the burden of proof from the government's having to prove sanity beyond a reasonable doubt to defendants' having to prove they were insane by clear and convincing evidence.[51]

The *Model Penal Code* rejects this standard, and so do most states. The *Model Penal Code* adopts the standard of affirmative defenses. Sanity and responsibility are presumed unless the defense offers some evidence to show that defendants are insane. Once the sanity presumption is overcome by some evidence, then under the *Model Penal Code* provision, prosecutors must prove the defendants sane beyond a reasonable doubt. Prosecutors need not prove sanity, however, unless defendants raise the issue. Insanity is also an affirmative defense under the new federal rule.

Some jurisdictions require proof beyond a reasonable doubt. Others accept proof by a preponderance of the evidence. There is a trend in favor of shifting the burden to defendants and making that burden heavier. This is both because Hinckley's trial generated antagonism toward the insanity defense and because of growing hostility toward rules that the public believes coddle criminals.[52]

The insanity defense has only one purpose in criminal law. No matter how advanced psychiatry becomes, no matter who must prove it and by how much, the insanity defense is primarily a legal, not a medical question: Has a mental disease or defect, however defined, sufficiently altered defendants' mental states to excuse their crimes?

DIMINISHED CAPACITY

Some defendants suffer from mental diseases or defects that do not affect their mental capacity sufficiently to make them insane. They may still have a defense, however, if the mental disease or defect impairs their capacity to form *mens rea*. Theoretically, this defense ought to apply to all crimes, if impaired mental capacity raises a reasonable doubt about the capacity to form *mens rea*. In practice, however, jurisdictions severely restrict the use of diminished capacity.

Some jurisdictions prohibit all evidence of mental impairment short of insanity. In these jurisdictions, defendants are either sane or insane. For example, California, in the wake of public hostility to mental impairment excuses, enacted the following provision to replace its diminished capacity provision:

> The defense of diminished capacity is hereby abolished. In a criminal action . . . evidence concerning an accused person's intoxication, mental illness, disease, or defect shall not be admissible to show or negate capacity to form the particular purpose, intent, motive, malice aforethought, knowledge, or other mental state required for the commission of the crime charged. . . . Notwithstanding the foregoing, evidence of diminished capacity or of a mental disorder may be considered by the court at the time of sentencing or other disposition or commitment.[53]

At the other extreme, the *Model Penal Code* provision admits evidence of impaired mental capacity to negate *mens rea* in all crimes. For example, under the *Model Penal Code*, if a mental disease or defect not serious enough to amount to insanity causes a defendant to believe the television she took belonged to her, the belief caused by the impairment would negate the specific intent to take "another's property" that larceny *mens rea* requires.

The few jurisdictions that permit evidence of diminished capacity take a middle ground. They restrict its use to crimes of more than one degree that require specific intent—almost always murder. A defendant in these jurisdictions can introduce evidence that a mental disease or defect negates the capacity to form the specific intent to premeditate a homicide but not the general intent to kill. Hence, the defendant could not commit first-degree murder, requiring premeditation, but could commit second-degree murder, requiring the general intent to kill. Some states go further, permitting mental impairment to reduce murder to manslaughter if a mental disease or defect generated the required heat of passion in manslaughter (see chapter 8 on homicide).[54]

C A S E

Was His Diminished Capacity a Defense?

State v. Gallegos,
628 P.2d 999 (Colo. 1981)

Gallegos was convicted of second-degree murder. He appealed. The Colorado supreme court affirmed. Justice Quinn wrote the opinion for the court.

FACTS

The defendant, Leroy Joe Gallegos, was charged with murder in the first degree after deliberation. The charge arose out of the shooting death of the defendant's wife on December 19, 1977. The prosecution's evidence established that the defendant and his wife were living apart and on the night of the homicide he visited her about a possible reconciliation. After a prolonged argument during which she accused him of incompetence and sexual inadequacy he shot her five times with a pistol.

The defense presented opinion evidence from two psychiatrists and a psychologist that the defendant was afflicted with minimal brain dysfunction and an associated explosive personality disorder with paranoid features. Minimal brain dysfunction was described as a biochemical imbalance in the brain that prevents a person from maintaining control over his bodily functions and emotional impulses, especially in situations of stress. The expert witnesses expressed the opinion that the defendant's condition rendered him incapable of forming the specific intent to kill at the time of the shooting of his wife. The defendant offered no testimony specifically addressing his capacity to act "knowingly" at the time of the homicide, although some of the expert testimony described the shooting as beyond the defendant's control. The trial court submitted the case to the jury on the charge of first-degree murder after deliberation and on the lesser offenses of murder in the second degree and manslaughter upon sudden heat of passion. The jury was instructed that the requisite culpability for first-degree murder and manslaughter was the specific intent to cause the death of

another, and that the culpable mental state for second-degree murder was knowingly causing the death of another. The instructions on the affirmative defense of impaired mental condition were as follows:

Instruction No. 13
The evidence presented in this case has raised the issue of the affirmative defense of impaired mental condition. The prosecution, therefore, has the burden of proving to your satisfaction beyond a reasonable doubt the guilt of the defendant as to that issue as well as all of the elements of the crime charged. If, after consideration of the evidence concerning the affirmative defense, along with all the other evidence, you are not convinced beyond a reasonable doubt of the guilt of the defendant then you must return a verdict of not guilty.

Instruction No. 14
It is an affirmative defense to the crime of murder in the first degree and manslaughter that the defendant, due to an impaired mental condition, did not have the capacity to form the specific intent required by the offense.

OPINION

Under the Colorado Criminal Code issues relating to lack of responsibility are affirmative defenses. One may be relieved of criminal responsibility on the grounds of insufficient age, insanity, impaired mental condition, or intoxication.

The statutory categorization of a matter as an affirmative defense has consequences for the prosecution's burden of proof. Under the Colorado Criminal Code once the issue of an affirmative defense is raised, the prosecution must prove the guilt of the defendant beyond a reasonable doubt as to that issue as well as all other elements of the offense.

Second-degree murder is defined as causing "the death of a person knowingly." By statute, offenses with the culpability requirement of "knowingly" are deemed to be general, rather than specific, intent crimes. § 18–3–102(2), C.R.S. 1973 (1978 Repl. Vol. 8) states that "[d]iminished responsibility due to lack of mental capacity is not a defense to murder in the second degree." A diminished responsibility attributable to a lack of mental capacity is the statutory equivalent of the affirmative defense of impaired mental condition in § 18–1–803, C.R.S.1973 (1978 Repl. Vol. 8), which provides:

> Evidence of an impaired mental condition though not legal insanity may be offered in a proper case as bearing upon the capacity of the accused to form the specific intent if such an intent is an element of the offense charged.

Thus, § 18–3–103(2) merely makes explicit with respect to second-degree murder what already is implicit in § 18–1–803: the affirmative defense of diminished responsibility due to impaired mental condition is not an affirmative defense to the general intent crime of second-degree murder.

The record before us establishes that the defendant's psychiatric and psychological experts testified without restriction to the defendant's mental status. Each witness expressed the opinion that at the time of the shooting the defendant was incapable not only of forming an intent to kill but also of exercising any control over his actions. One psychiatrist described the shooting as "an act based on a chemical brain disorder" rather than "a wilful, voluntary act." When this opinion evidence was admitted, the trial court did not caution the jury to consider it in relation to the specific intent crimes of first-degree murder and manslaughter only. One must conclude, therefore, that it was admitted and considered as to all offenses, including second-degree murder.

Jury's guilty verdict reinstated.

QUESTIONS FOR DISCUSSION

1. Should Gallegos's brain dysfunction and the chemical imbalance resulting from it reduce his liability?

2. If so, is it right to reduce the sentence to only second-degree murder?

3. Do you agree that it is possible to intend something, but not as much, when you are somewhat incapacitated? Or do you believe the rule should be that either you intended to kill or you did not? In other words, do you believe that "sort of" intending something is not possible? The difficulty in applying the rule and the objections raised to deciding who is "sort of" responsible have led California to abolish its diminished capacity defense.

NOTE CASE

Schiro v. Clark, 963 F.2d 962 (7th Cir. 1992)

Thomas Schiro was serving a three-year suspended sentence for robbery at a halfway house. While in the work-release program, Schiro worked across the street from Laura Luebbehusen's home. At approximately 7:00 P.M. on February 4, Schiro went to an Alcoholics Anonymous meeting. Instead of staying for his 8:00 P.M. meeting, Schiro went to a liquor store and stole an alcoholic beverage. He took the liquor with him and went to see "quarter movies," which were characterized as hard core pornography. At approximately 9:30 P.M. Schiro went to Ms. Luebbehusen's door and asked if he could use her phone on the pretext that his car would not start. After he pretended to use the phone, Schiro asked to use the bathroom. When he came out of the bathroom Schiro was exposed and Luebbehusen became frightened. In an attempt to calm her, Schiro told Luebbehusen that he did not want to hurt her, that he was gay, and that he was just trying to win a bet that he could "get it on" with a woman. Schiro went through the small apartment looking for drugs and money. He came back with drugs and two dildos. Schiro told Luebbehusen to drink some liquor and take drugs as he did. Schiro also told Luebbehusen to insert a dildo into his anus but he found that very painful. Luebbehusen told Schiro that she was gay, that she had been raped as a child, that she had never had sex before, and that she did not want to have sex. Schiro then raped her. When Schiro left the room, Luebbehusen tried to leave but Schiro pulled her back in the house, dragged her by her hair, told her not to try to leave again, and raped her a second time. When the liquor ran out, Schiro took her with him to get some more. When they returned to Luebbehusen's home Schiro raped her a third time and then passed out on the couch. When Schiro woke up, Luebbehusen was dressed and headed out the door. Luebbehusen told Schiro that she would not turn him in and was just going to find her girlfriend. Schiro wouldn't let her leave and Schiro believed that she then fell asleep. At that time Schiro decided that he had to kill her so that she couldn't report the rapes. Schiro hit her on the head with a vodka bottle until it shattered. Luebbehusen was fighting Schiro. He picked up an iron and beat her with it. She was still fighting him when he strangled her to death. He then dragged her body from the bedroom to the living room where he performed vaginal and anal intercourse on the corpse and chewed on several parts of her body. When Schiro left Luebbehusen's house he took one of the plastic dildos with him and threw it in the trash behind a tavern. Schiro also took gloves that he had been wearing so as not to leave any fingerprints. He gave the gloves to his girlfriend Mary Lee who washed them, cut them in little pieces and threw them away.

Schiro was convicted of murder and rape and the jury recommended a life sentence. The trial judge instead sentenced Schiro to death. Schiro argued that he should receive life imprisonment instead of the death penalty because of a mitigating circumstance, namely that

> he was a sexual sadist and that his extensive viewing of rape pornography and snuff films rendered him unable to distinguish right from wrong. In support of this assertion, his expert witness, Edward Donnerstein, testified that after a short exposure to aggressive pornography "nonrapist populations . . . begin to endorse myths about rape." "They begin to say that women enjoy being raped and they begin to say that using force in sexual encounters is okay. Sixty percent of the subjects will also indicate that if not caught they would commit the rape themselves."

In addition to Mr. Donnerstein's testimony that pornography generally encourages men to commit acts of violence against women, one of defendant's other expert witnesses testified that Schiro's viewing of pornography actually encouraged him to commit the acts of violence at issue in this case. Dr. Frank Osanka testified that Schiro viewed pornographic films from age six, and throughout his childhood and his adulthood, that led him to be aroused by women's pain and taught him techniques of rape.

A written autobiographical statement of petitioner's which was read to the jury is perhaps most telling: "I can remember when I get horny from looking at girly books and watching girly shows that I would want to go

rape somebody. Every time I would jack off before I come I would be thinking of rape and the women I had raped and remembering how exciting it was. The pain on their faces. The thrill, the excitement."

At closing argument Schiro's counsel relied on Dr. Osanka and Mr. Donnerstein to support his claim that "the pattern is clear, premature exposure to pornography and continual use with more violent forms created one thing, created a person who no longer distinguishes between violence and rape, or violence and sex."

Schiro contended either that pornography is a mitigating factor akin to intoxication or mental disease or defect which rendered him unable to appreciate the criminality of his conduct, or that pornography caused him to suffer from sexual sadism, which in turn rendered him unable to appreciate the wrongfulness of his conduct. . . .

Was Schiro's sexual sadism a mitigating factor? No, according to both the trial court and the U.S. Court of Appeals for the Seventh Circuit. According to the Court of Appeals

> Judge Rosen rejected the arguments on the basis that defendant was sadistic, not psychotic or insane, and on the basis that he was able to appreciate the wrongfulness of his conduct. Clearly, Indiana may determine that sadism (or voyeurism, exhibitionism, and necrophilia as also claimed) does not amount to a mental disease or defect which warrants reduced punishment. This is particularly so because the primary manifestation of these conditions is criminal, antisocial conduct and under Indiana law "[t]he terms 'mental disease or defect' do not include an abnormality manifested only by repeated criminal or otherwise anti social conduct." Moreover, the trial judge could permissibly find from the evidence both that Schiro understood the criminality of his conduct and that pornography is not a mental disease or defect which would permit a finding of insanity.

The troubling aspect of Schiro's defense is that his argument that pornography reduced his capacity to understand the criminality of his conduct, if successful, would not only excuse him from imposition of the death penalty but further excuse him for his criminal conduct altogether on the basis that he was not guilty by reason of insanity. Under Schiro's theory pornography would constitute a legal excuse to violence against women.

SYNDROMES

Since the 1970s, a range of "syndromes" affecting mental states have led to novel defenses in criminal law. The most bizarre of these include the policeman's, love, fear, chronic brain, and holocaust syndromes. Law professor and famous defense attorney Alan Dershowitz has written a highly critical book (*The Abuse Excuse and Other Cop-Outs, Sob Stories, and Evasions of Responsibility*) that lists dozens of what he calls "abuse excuses, cop-outs, sob stories, and other evasions of responsibility." Dershowitz worries that these excuses are "quickly becoming a license to kill and maim." His is probably a needless worry because defendants rarely plead these excuses, and except for a few notorious cases picked up by television and the newspapers, defendants rarely succeed when they do plead syndromes and other "abuse excuses."[55]

When San Francisco city official Dan White was tried for killing his fellow official Harvey Milk and Mayor George Moscone, the defense introduced the junk food syndrome, popularly called the "Twinkie defense." White's lawyer argued that junk food diminished White's mental faculties. One psychiatrist testified as follows concerning White's frequent depressions:

> During these spells he'd become quite withdrawn, quite lethargic. He would retreat to his room. Wouldn't come to the door. Wouldn't answer the phone. And during these periods he found that he could not cope with people. Any confrontations would cause him to kind of become argumentative. Whenever he felt things were not going right he would abandon his usual program of exercise and good nutrition and start gorging himself on junk foods. Twinkies, Coca Cola.
>
> Mr. White had always been something of an athlete, priding himself on being physically fit. But when something would go wrong he'd hit the high sugar stuff. He'd hit the chocolate and the more he consumed the worse he'd feel, and he'd respond to his ever-growing depression by consuming even more junk food. The more junk food he consumed, the worse he'd feel. The worse he'd feel, the more he'd gorge himself.

The defense argued that these depressions, which junk food aggravated, sufficiently diminished White's capacity to reduce his responsibility. The jury returned a verdict of manslaughter, and White was sentenced to a relatively short prison term. After his release from prison, he committed suicide. No one has ventured to blame his suicide on junk food. During the White case, much public comment—most of it negative—was directed at the Twinkie defense. Despite that derision, substantial evidence exists to suggest that white sugar does indeed diminish capacity. Whether or not it does so to sufficiently reduce responsibility is a highly controversial and far-from-settled question.[56]

Defendants have, with limited success, relied on the battered spouse syndrome to justify killing spouses in self-defense, even though the defendants were not in imminent danger (see chapter 6).

Occasionally, women have used premenstrual syndrome (PMS) to excuse their crimes. In a New York case, Shirley Santos called the police, telling them, "My little girl is sick." The medical team in the hospital emergency room diagnosed the welts on the girl's legs and blood in her urine as the results of child abuse. The police arrested Santos, who explained, "I don't remember what happened. . . . I would never hurt my baby . . . I just got my period." At a preliminary hearing, Santos asserted PMS as a complete defense to assault and endangering the welfare of a child, both felonies. She admitted beating her child but argued that she had blacked out owing to PMS, hence she could not have formed the intent to assault or endanger her child's welfare. After lengthy plea bargaining, the prosecutor dropped the felony charges and Santos pleaded guilty to the misdemeanor of harassment. Santos received no sentence, not even probation or a fine, even though her daughter spent two weeks in the hospital from the injuries. The plea bargaining prevented a legal test of the PMS defense in this case. Nevertheless, the judge's leniency suggests that PMS affected the outcome informally.[57]

Three difficulties ordinarily stand in the way of proving the PMS defense:

1. Defendants must prove that PMS is a disease; little medical research exists to demonstrate that it is.

2. The defendant must suffer from PMS; rarely do medical records document the condition.

3. The PMS must cause the mental impairment that excuses the conduct; too much skepticism still surrounds PMS to expect ready acceptance that it excuses criminal conduct.[58]

The years since the Vietnam War have revealed that combat soldiers suffered more lasting and serious casualties than physical injury. The war took a heavy emotional and mental toll on the veterans. The effects have created what some call a "mental health crisis which has had a dramatic impact on the incidence of major crime." Medical research has established a complex relationship between the stress of the combat tour in guerilla type, as opposed to conventional, warfare and later antisocial conduct. At the same time, lawyers have begun to consider the effect the Vietnam Vet syndrome has on criminal responsibility.

C A S E

Did Vietnam Vet Syndrome Excuse His Crime?[59]

A man had been charged with assaulting a group of police officers who had been summoned to investigate a call that a man (the defendant) was wandering about in a park late at night. The police reports indicated that when the officers arrived in the park they could hear someone thrashing about in the wooded area. While attempting to follow the sounds they were suddenly confronted by the defendant who was carrying a large log as if it were a rifle. The officers reported that the man did not respond to their orders and seemed to be in a drunken and incoherent rage. The man charged toward the officers, wounded two of them, and was finally subdued and arrested.

A series of discussions with the defendant revealed that he was a Vietnam combat veteran who had a post-military history of job-related difficulties and marital discord. His wife related that he had begun within the last few years to suffer from periods of depression which were usually punctuated by episodes of excessive drinking, explosive violence, and recurrent nightmares. He had apparently been in the midst of such a period on the date of the incident and had spent a few hours drinking in a bar just prior to stopping in the park on his way home. When asked why he had stopped in the park, he responded that he was unsure but thought that he had needed some fresh air to "clear his head." He professed to have no recollection of the attack on the police and attributed it to his drunken condition.

The extensive medical investigation disclosed that the defendant was, at the time of the incident, engulfed in a delusional flashback in which he genuinely believed he was once again in the jungles of Vietnam. He perceived the police officers to be enemy soldiers who were ... ambushing ... his patrol [based on a real experience from Vietnam in which a friend of his was killed.] As a result of this information, the medical experts were able to testify that although it was clear that he "knew the nature and quality of his acts" in the sense that he knew he was attacking someone, it was equally clear that he "did not know that those acts were wrong" since, in his mind, he was not attacking police officers but was attacking enemy soldiers. The defendant was accordingly found to be not guilty by reason of insanity. [The defendant was hospitalized shortly after his arrest for two months, then was released but continued out-patient therapy until the trial.] On the basis of his response to this treatment, the court ... conclude[d] that the defendant no longer constituted a danger and could therefore be placed on probation, with a condition that he continue his therapy.

QUESTIONS FOR DISCUSSION

1. Would you recommend that your state allow the Vietnam Vet defense? Why or why not?

2. If you did allow the defense, should this vet fall under it?

3. Is he too dangerous to be free?

4. Do you think probation with treatment properly serves the aims of the criminal law? Why or why not?

5. What disposition in this case do you recommend?

Occasionally, defendants have also sought to excuse their criminal liability by means of what might be called a **cultural norms defense.** This defense is based on the claim that criminal behavior in the United States is normal behavior in an immigrant's homeland. Therefore, although what they may have done is wrong, they are not responsible for acting according to their cultural norms.

C A S E

Was Laotian Culture an Excuse?

People v. Aphaylath,
68 N.Y.2d 945, 502 N.E.2d 998,
510 N.Y.S.2d 83 (1986)

Defendant was convicted of second-degree murder, and he appealed. The Supreme Court, Appellate Division, affirmed. Defendant appealed. The Court of Appeals reversed.

FACTS

Defendant, a Laotian refugee living in this country for approximately two years, was indicted and tried for the intentional murder of his Laotian wife of one month. At trial, defendant attempted to establish the affirmative defense of extreme emotional disturbance to mitigate the homicide (Penal Law § 125.25[1][a] on the theory that the stresses resulting from his status of a refugee caused a significant mental trauma, affecting his mind for a substantial period of time, simmering in the unknowing subconscious and then inexplicably coming to the fore. (*People v. Patterson,* 39 N.Y.2d 288, 303, 383 N.Y.S.2d 573, 347 N.E.2d 898) Although the immediate cause for the defendant's loss of control was his jealousy over his wife's apparent preference for an ex-boyfriend, the defense argued that under Laotian culture the conduct of the victim wife in displaying affection for another man and receiving phone calls from an unattached man brought shame on defendant and his family sufficient to trigger defendant's loss of control.

OPINION

The defense was able to present some evidence of the Laotian culture through the cross-examination of two prosecution witnesses and through the testimony of defendant himself, although he was hampered by his illiteracy in both his native tongue and English. Defendant's ability to adequately establish his defense was impermissibly curtailed by the trial court's exclusion of the proffered testimony of two expert witnesses concerning the stress and disorientation encountered by Laotian refugees in attempting to assimilate into the American culture. It appears from the record before us that the sole basis on which the court excluded the expert testimony was because "neither one was going to be able to testify as to anything specifically relating to this defendant". It is unclear from this ruling whether the Trial Judge determined that she had no discretion to allow the testimony because the experts had no knowledge of this particular defendant or that she declined to exercise her discretion because of the experts' lack of knowledge of the defendant or his individual background and characteristics. Under

either interpretation, however, the exclusion of this expert testimony as a matter of law was erroneous because the admissibility of expert testimony that is probative of a fact in issue does not depend on whether the witness has personal knowledge of a defendant or a defendant's particular characteristics. Whether or not such testimony is sufficiently relevant to have probative value is a determination to be made by the Trial Judge in the exercise of her sound discretion.

Accordingly, because the court's ruling was not predicated on the appropriate standard and the defendant may have been deprived of an opportunity to put before the jury information relevant to his defense, a new trial must be ordered.

QUESTIONS FOR DISCUSSION

1. Should defendants be allowed the "opportunity to put before the jury information" about cultural norms? Why or why not?

2. A variation of the cultural norms defense is what Alan Dershowitz calls the "urban survival syndrome." This excuse is that some neighborhoods are so dangerous as to require living by the motto, "Kill or be killed." In one Texas case, a lawyer used the defense. Although it did not produce a "not guilty" verdict, it nevertheless caused a hung jury.[60] Should the conditions of your neighborhood excuse your criminal liability? Act as both prosecutor and defense attorney and argue your case.

SUMMARY

The general defenses to criminal liability rest on two rationales. In justification (see chapter 6), defendants admit responsibility but maintain that under the circumstances they did the right thing. Self-defense is the primary justification, but a general defense called necessity also exists in most jurisdictions. In excuse, defendants admit they did the wrong thing but deny responsibility under the circumstances. The main excuses are duress, intoxication, mistake, age, entrapment, insanity, diminished capacity, and syndromes. The line between justification and excuse is not clearly drawn, and some defenses fall outside the principles altogether, such as entrapment based on the objective theory of controlling government misconduct.

Whatever their theoretical underpinning, most defenses have the same practical effect—acquittal. But not always. Defenses can also work to reduce the degree of an offense or to reduce the offense to a lesser, related offense. In some cases, defenses offer an opportunity to lighten a penalty attached to a particular crime because of mitigating circumstances. Finally, the insanity defense can lead to confinement in a mental hospital rather than incarceration. Whatever their specific consequences, the general defenses to criminal liability are based on the idea that the special circumstances of necessity, human frailty, and human imperfection ought to lessen the harshness of the criminal law. In this sense, the defenses are companions to the general principles of criminal liability outlined in chapter 3. The principles of liability, justification, and excuse work together to ensure that criminal law works fairly and according to well-defined principles, so that the state does not punish persons if circumstances surrounding otherwise criminal conduct justify or excuse that conduct.

REVIEW QUESTIONS

1. Distinguish between the defenses of justification and the defenses of excuse.

2. How does the defense of insanity differ from the other defenses?

3. According to Professor Hyman Gross, what is the problem with the defense of duress?

4. State and explain the elements of common-law duress.

5. List and briefly explain the differing resolutions to the five main issues in the defense of duress.

6. Explain the defenses of superior orders and brainwashing.

7. Identify and describe the three rationales for the defense of duress.

8. Explain the circumstances under which intoxication is, and is not, a defense of excuse.

9. Explain when mistake is, and is not, a defense of excuse.

10. When is age an excuse for criminal liability, and why?

11. Define entrapment, then identify and explain the three main tests for determining when entrapment is a defense to criminal liability.

12. Explain the extent to which the insanity defense is used and is successful, then describe the consequences of successful insanity pleas.

13. Identify the tests of insanity.

14. State the major elements of each of the tests of insanity.

15. Compare and contrast the tests of insanity as they relate to the importance of reason, affect, and will.

16. Explain different ways in which the burden of proof works in insanity cases.

17. Define diminished capacity. Under what conditions is it a defense to criminal liability? Explain the extent and limits of the defense.

18. Explain the impact of various syndromes on the defenses of excuse in criminal law.

KEY TERMS

entrapment government actions that induce individuals to commit crimes that they otherwise would not commit.

diminished capacity Mental capacity less than "normal" but more than "insane."

***Durham* rule, or product test** An insanity test to determine whether a crime was a product of mental disease or defect.

irrebuttable presumption A conclusive assumption that requires a finding of a presumed fact once the fact is introduced into evidence.

irresistible impulse Impairment of the will that makes it impossible to control the impulse to do wrong.

***M'Naghten* rule, or right-wrong test** A defense pleading insanity due to mental disease or defect that impairs the capacity to distinguish right from wrong.

rebuttable presumption An assumption of fact that can be overturned upon sufficient proof.

substantial capacity test Insanity due to mental disease or defect impairing the substantial capacity either to appreciate the wrongfulness of conduct or to conform behavior to the law.

Suggested Readings

1. Telford Taylor, *Nuremberg and Vietnam: An American Tragedy* (New York: Quadrangle, 1970). Discusses the superior orders defense as Taylor tells the stories of the Nuremberg trials and the Calley case. This is an interesting book, written for the general public.

2. David G. Bromley and James T. Richardson, *The Brainwashing/Deprogramming Controversy: Sociological, Psychological, Legal, and Historical Perspectives* (New York: Edwin Mellen Press, 1983). Discusses brainwashing from a multidisciplinary perspective, covering many topics relevant to the defense of brainwashing.

3. Peter Meyer, *The Yale Murder* (New York: Empire Books, 1982). A compelling narrative relating the "fatal romance" of Yale student Richard Herrin and Bonnie Garland. Meyer gives a detailed account of the trial, the insanity plea, the jury deliberations, and the verdict. Written for the general reader, this is an excellent journalistic account revealing much about the insanity plea.

4. Joseph Livermore and Paul Meehl, "The Virtues of M'Naghten," *Minnesota Law Review* 51 (1967):800. A well-argued, articulate defense of the right-wrong test. Although intended for specialists, it is well worth the novice's efforts.

5. Mike Weiss, *Double Play: The San Francisco City Hall Killings* (Reading, Mass.: Addison-Wesley, 1984). A detailed account of former San Francisco city supervisor Dan White's shooting of Mayor George Moscone and fellow supervisor Harvey Milk in San Francisco City Hall, and of the trial that followed. Weiss gives an excellent description of the diminished capacity defense, which came to be called the Twinkie defense because it was based on the argument that White's excessive use of junk foods, particularly those containing white sugar, led to his erratic behavior.

Notes

1. Hyman Gross, *A Theory of Criminal Justice* (New York: Oxford University Press, 1978), p. 276.

2. William Blackstone, *Commentaries on the Laws of England* (New York: Garland Publishing, 1978), pt. IV, p. 30.

3. Jerome Hall, *General Principles of Criminal Law*, 2d ed. (Indianapolis, Ind.: Bobbs-Merrill, 1960), pp. 437–444; Glanville Williams, *Criminal Law: The General Part*, 2d ed. rev. (London: Stevens and Sons, 1961), pp. 765–766; American Law Institute, *Model Penal Code and Commentaries*, vol. 1, pt. I, 372–373.

4. American Law Institute, *Model Penal Code and Commentaries*, vol. 1, pt. I, pp. 380–381.

5. *Regina v. Hudson*, 2 All E.R. 244 (1971).

6. American Law Institute, *Model Penal Code and Commentaries*, vol. 1, pt. I, pp. 368–380.

7. Gross, *A Theory of Criminal Justice*, 276–292; Wayne R. LaFave and Austin W. Scott, Jr., *Criminal Law* (St. Paul, Minn.: West Publishing Co., 1972), pp. 434–439; George Fletcher, *Rethinking Criminal Law* (Boston: Little, Brown and Co., 1978), pp. 429–435.

8. American Law Institute, *Model Penal Code and Commentaries*, vol. 1, pt. I, p. 376.

9. P. R. tit. 33, 3098.

10. Related in John Gibeaut, "Sobering Thoughts: Legislatures and courts increasingly are just saying no to intoxication as a defense or mitigating factor," *American Bar Association Journal*, May 1997, 56.

11. Fletcher, *Rethinking Criminal Law*, p. 846.

12. Blackstone, *Commentaries*, pt. IV, pp. 25–26.

13. Gibeaut, "Sobering Thoughts," pp. 56–57.

14. American Law Institute, *Model Penal Code and Commentaries*, vol. 1, pt. I, pp. 350–366, surveys most of these arguments; *State v. Hall*, 214 N.W.2d 205 (Iowa 1974).

15. *People v. Penman*, 271 Ill. 82, 110 N.E. 894 (1915) Hall, *General Principles of Criminal Law*, p. 540.

16. *Burrows v. State*, 38 Ariz. 99, 297 P. 1029 (1931).

17. *Powell v. Texas*, 392 U.S. 514, 88 S.Ct. 2145, 20 L.Ed.2d 1254 (1968); American Law Institute, *Model*

Penal Code and Commentaries, vol. 1, pt. I, 353; *Commonwealth v. Reiff*, 489 Pa. 12, 413 A.2d 672 (1980).

18. 214 N.W.2d 205 (Iowa 1974).

19. Rollin M. Perkins and Ronald N. Boyce, *Criminal Law*, 3d ed. (Mineola, N.Y.: Foundation Press, 1982), p. 1030.

20. Oliver Wendell Holmes, Jr., *The Common Law* (Boston: Little, Brown, and Company, 1963), p. 41.

21. *Brent v. State*, 43 Ala. 297 (1869) (lottery); *Ostrosky v. State*, 704 P.2d 786 (Alaska App. 1985) (game laws); *Hopkins v. State*, 193 Md. 489, 69 A.2d 456 (1949) (sign).

22. American Law Institute, *Model Penal Code and Commentaries*, vol. 1, pt. I, pp. 273–279.

23. *People v. Munoz*, 22 Misc.2d 1078, 200 N.Y.S.2d 957 (1960).

24. Taken from Fred Cohen, *Criminal Law Bulletin* 21 (1985):9.

25. *Regina v. Kemp*, 3 All. E.R. 249 (1956).

26. *Board of Commissioners v. Backus*, 29 How. Pr. 33, 42 (1864).

27. *People v. Mills*, 178 N.Y. 274, 70 N.E. 786, 791 (1904).

28. Paul Marcus, "The Development of Entrapment Law," *Wayne Law Review* 33 (1986):5.

29. Jonathan C. Carlson, "The Act Requirement and the Foundations of the Entrapment Defense," *Virginia Law Review* 73 (1987):1011.

30. *United States v. Jenrette*, 744 F.2d 817 (D.C.Cir.1984) (one of the Abscam cases); "Gershman, Abscam, the Judiciary, and the Ethics of Entrapment," *Yale Law Journal* 91 (1982):1565 (history of Abscam); L. Tiffany and others, *Detection of Crime* (Boston: Little, Brown and Co., 1967) (quote defining encouragement).

31. Wayne R. LaFave and Jerold H. Israel, *Criminal Procedure* (St. Paul: West Publishing Co., 1984), 1:412–13.

32. 356 U.S. 369, 78 S.Ct. 819, 2 L.Ed.2d 848 (1958).

33. Rorie Sherman, "Insanity Defense: A New Challenge," *The National Law Journal*, March 28, 1994, 1, p. 24.

34. American Law Institute, *Model Penal Code and Commentaries*, vol. 1, pt. I, pp. 182–183; Jeffrey S. Janofsky, Mitchell H. Dunn, Erik J. Roskes and others, "Insanity defense pleas in Baltimore City: An analysis of outcome," *American Journal of Psychiatry*, 153 (1996): 1464–1468.

35. Mich. Stat. Ann. § 28.1059(1).

36. 55 Comm. L.R. 182, 186–188 (1933).

37. *M'Naghten's Case*, 8 Eng.Rep. 718 (1843).

38. Herbert M. Fingarette, *The Meaning of Criminal Insanity* (Berkeley: University of California, 1972), contains a full treatment of the subject. A good introduction is Abraham S. Goldstein, "Insanity," in *Encyclopedia of Crime and Justice*, ed. Sanford Kadish (New York: Free Press, 1983), pp. 735–742; American Law Institute, *Model Penal Code and Commentaries*, vol. 1, pt. I, pp. 174–176.

39. *People v. Schmidt*, 110 N.E. 945 (1915).

40. 214 F.2d 862 (D.C.Cir.1954).

41. 18 U.S.C.A. § 17 adopted the right-wrong test; *United States v. Brawner*, 471 F.2d 969 (D.C.Cir.1972) rejected the *Durham* rule for that circuit; adopted by Maine Rev. Stat. Ann. tit. 15, § 102 (1964), superseded by Maine Rev. Stat. Ann. tit. 17–A, § 58 adopting the substantial capacity test.

42. Joseph Livermore and Paul Meehl, "The Virtues of M'Naghten," *Minnesota Law Review* 51 (1967):800.

43. LaFave and Scott, *Criminal Law*, p. 283.

44. 2 So. 854 (Ala.1877).

45. "A Needed Verdict: Guilty but Insane," *New York Times* (July 1, 1982), p. 29.

46. See Slovenko, "The Insanity Defense in the Wake of the Hinckley Trial," *Rutgers Law Journal* 14 (1983):373.

47. 18 U.S.C.A. § 17.

48. Robert F. Schopp, "Returning to *M'Naghten* to Avoid Moral Mistakes: One Step Forward, or Two Steps Backward for the Insanity Defense?" *Arizona Law Review* 30 (1988):135.

49. *Model Penal Code*, § 4.01(1).

50. *Rex v. Arnold*, 16 Howell State Trials, pp. 695, 764–765 (Eng.1724), quoted in Perkins and Boyce, *Criminal Law*, p. 951.

51. Federal Criminal Code and Rules (St. Paul, Minn.: West Publishing Co., 1988), § 17(b).

52. American Law Institute, *Model Penal Code and Commentaries*, vol. 2, pt. I, p. 226.

53. California Penal Code, § 25 (b); (c).

54. *People v. Colavecchio*, 11 A.D.2d 161, 202 N.Y.S.2d 119 (1960) (mental disease negatives the specific intent to take another's property).

55. Alan Dershowitz, *The Abuse Excuse and Other Cop-Outs, Sob Stories, and Evasions of Responsibility* (Boston: Little, Brown and Company, 1994), p. 3.

56. Mike Weiss, *Double Play: The San Francisco City Hall Killings* (Reading, Mass.: Addison-Wesley, 1984), pp. 349–350.

57. "Not Guilty Because of PMS?" *Newsweek* (November 8, 1982):111.

58. [author?]"Premenstrual Syndrome: A Criminal Defense," *Notre Dame Law Review* 59 (1983):263–269.

59. "In Defense of the Defenders: The Vietnam Vet Syndrome," John R. Ford, *Criminal Law Bulletin* 19 (1983):434–443.

60. Dershowitz, *Abuse Excuse*, p. 73.

CHAPTER EIGHT

Crimes Against Persons I: Criminal Homicide

CHAPTER MAIN POINTS

1. The law of criminal homicide involves the most complex grading in the criminal law.

2. The law of criminal homicide applies the general principles of *actus reus, mens rea,* and causing a particular result to causing the death of another person.

3. The *actus reus* of criminal homicide requires the killing of another live human being.

4. Definitions of "live human being" raise fundamental moral, legal, and policy issues in specifying both when life begins and when it ends.

5. Criminal homicide refines the general principle of *mens rea* to the highest degree in criminal law; *mens rea* is the most important ingredient in grading the kinds and degrees of criminal homicides.

6. First-degree murders include premeditated, deliberate killings as well as, in some states, particularly brutal murders and some felony murders.

7. According to the modern law of homicide, premeditated killings do not require long-term planning; even a few seconds satisfies the requirement in most states.

8. Second-degree murder is a catchall category, including all criminal homicides that are neither manslaughter nor first-degree murders.

9. Felony murder causes problems of determining what felonies to include and of determining the relationship between the felony and the death of a person that occurs during the commission of the felony.

10. Establishing *mens rea* and causation are major problems in applying murder statutes to corporations.

11. In nearly all states, words are never regarded as adequate provocation to reduce murder to voluntary manslaughter.

12. Involuntary manslaughter is criminal homicide committed without the intent to kill or inflict serious bodily harm; it includes reckless and grossly criminally negligent homicides and, in some states, deaths that occur during the commission of some misdemeanors.

13. Some states have adopted special vehicular homicide statutes that require something less than gross criminal negligence and for which both the penalty and stigma are milder than for manslaughter.

Did He Murder His Wife?

Schnopps and his wife were having marital problems. Among the problems was that his wife was having an affair with a man at work. Schnopps found out about the affair. Mrs. Schnopps moved out of the house, taking their children with her. Schnopps asked his wife to come to their home and talk over their marital difficulties. Schnopps told his wife that he wanted his children at home, and that he wanted the family to remain intact. Schnopps cried during the conversation, and begged his wife to let the children live with him and to keep their family together. His wife replied, "No, I am going to court, you are going to give me all the furniture, you are going to have to get the Hell out of here, you won't have nothing." Then, pointing to her crotch, she said, "You will never touch this again, because I have got something bigger and better for it."

On hearing those words, Schnopps claims that his mind went blank, and that he went "berserk." He went to a cabinet and got out a pistol he had bought and loaded the day before, and he shot his wife and himself. Schnopps survived the shooting but his wife died.

INTRODUCTION

Crimes against persons threaten three fundamental values—life, liberty, and privacy. Chapter 9 analyzes crimes against persons that fall short of death—criminal sexual conduct, nonsexual assaults and batteries, and crimes against free movement, including kidnapping and false imprisonment. These crimes far outnumber criminal homicide, the subject of this chapter. Criminal homicide includes a number of crimes that consist of conduct that causes the death of another human being. Criminal homicide is unique among all other offenses. Death is a harm of a wholly different order than all of the other crimes that make up the subject matter of chapters 9 through 12. To be sure, criminal harms to property and harms to persons other than death may be irreversible. However, these injuries are to worldly things—bodies and property. Causing death, on the other hand, deprives another human being of life itself. According to Professor George P. Fletcher,

> Killing another human being is not only a worldly deprivation; in the Western conception of homicide, killing is an assault on the sacred, natural order. In the Biblical view, the person who slays another was thought to acquire control over the blood—the life force—of the victim. The only way that this life force could be returned to God, the origin of all life, was to execute the slayer himself. In this conception of crime and punishment, capital execution for homicide served to expiate the desecration of the natural order.[1]

Most of the law of criminal homicide is devoted to defining and grading its seriousness. Hence, the common questions regarding criminal homicide: Is this murder first- or second-degree? Is that unlawful killing murder or manslaughter? Is this manslaughter voluntary or involuntary? One might wonder, "Why so much concern over distinguishing among the various types of criminal homicide?" "Does it really matter? Certainly not to the victim—who is already and always dead!" But it does make a difference. For purposes of determining the seriousness of—and therefore the punishment for—killing another person, these definitions play a vital role.

The degrees of criminal homicide—the most complex grading in all of criminal law—depend mainly on three elements:

1. *Mens rea.*

2. *Actus reus.*

3. Special circumstances.

The most common element used to grade criminal homicide is *mens rea*. The law of criminal homicide contains the most complex *mens rea* in all of criminal law. There are purposeful, knowing, reckless, and negligent criminal homicides, the four states of mind outlined and analyzed in chapter 3. But the law of criminal homicide further refines purposeful killings into premeditated and deliberate purposeful killings in order to aggravate murder to first-degree. Proof of an especially brutal *actus reus* can also aggravate murder to first-degree. In addition to *mens rea* and *actus reus*, special circumstances, known as circumstance elements, are used to grade criminal homicides. The best-known circumstance—provocation to kill in the sudden heat of passion—mitigates what would otherwise be first-degree murder to voluntary manslaughter. A range of special aggravating and mitigating circumstances spelled out in statutes determine whether first-degree murder is capital murder. In states with the death penalty, these circumstances determine whether murderers receive the death penalty. In states without the death penalty, they determine whether the murderer receives life imprisonment without parole.[2]

ELEMENTS OF CRIMINAL HOMICIDE

Homicide—killing another live human being—took three forms at common law:

1. *justifiable homicides*, such as self-defense, capital punishment, and police use of deadly force;

2. *excusable homicides*, such as those caused by accident or insanity; and

3. *criminal homicides*, namely, all homicides that were neither justified nor excused.

Criminal Homicide *Mens Rea*

Mens rea is the most common element used to grade criminal homicides. In fact, criminal homicide law refines *mens rea* to a higher degree than in any other crime. There are purposeful, knowing, reckless, and negligent criminal homicides. Purposeful killings are ordinarily—but not always—graded the most serious, and negligent killings are ordinarily graded the least serious.

The law of criminal homicide divides intentional killings into several additional categories. Premeditated deliberate murder (first-degree murder) is a more serious killing than killing suddenly in the heat of passion (second-degree murder). Both of these purposeful killings are graded more seriously than reckless killings, and reckless killings are more serious than negligent killings. In addition, some surrounding circumstances can aggravate—and others mitigate—purposeful, reckless, and negligent homicides. The mental element combined with special material surrounding circumstances provides the basis for grading criminal homicide.

Criminal Homicide *Actus Reus*

The *actus reus* of criminal homicide consists of taking the life of another live human being. Defining "live human being" requires the determination of both when life begins and when it ends. Defining life at its extremes is both a theoretical and policy problem, even though, as a practical matter, most cases do not involve victims at the edges of the normal life cycle. Both courts and legislatures have defined the beginning of life to include the period before birth. Some statutes say that life begins at conception; others say that only "viable fetuses," such as those twenty-eight weeks past conception, are live human beings. Still other jurisdictions retain the common-law criminal homicide definition "born alive."[3]

The Beginning of Life. Fetal death statutes (laws defining when life begins for purposes of the law of criminal homicide) have generated heated debate over whether

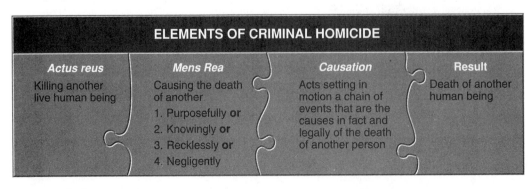

ELEMENTS OF CRIMINAL HOMICIDE

Actus reus	*Mens Rea*	*Causation*	*Result*
Killing another live human being	Causing the death of another 1. Purposefully **or** 2. Knowingly **or** 3. Recklessly **or** 4. Negligently	Acts setting in motion a chain of events that are the causes in fact and legally of the death of another person	Death of another human being

abortion is criminal homicide. However, fetal death statutes and abortion differ fundamentally. Whatever personal values concern abortion, the procedure involves the medical termination of a pregnancy with the mother's consent. Fetal death statutes deal with killing a fetus without the mother's consent outside normal medical practice. For this reason, many who oppose making abortion a form of criminal homicide at the same time support fetal death statutes because such statutes are directed toward third persons who, without the consent of the mothers and without medical skill, injure or kill fetuses. Furthermore, a statute that made medically performed abortions criminal homicides would surely violate the Constitution, according to the United States Supreme Court in *Roe v. Wade*. In *Roe v. Wade*, the Court upheld the right of mothers to terminate their pregnancies under some conditions.[4]

The debate over fetal death statutes can get quite complicated and almost always gets entangled with the emotional issue of abortion. In Minnesota, for example, two groups in the legislature vied to enact different statutes. One group hoped to make fetal death equivalent to homicide. Another, trying to separate fetal death from abortion, drafted a bill to punish people who injure or kill fetuses while committing other crimes. The impetus for passing this version stemmed from two types of cases:

1. When perpetrators injure or kill fetuses while they are assaulting pregnant women; and

2. When pregnant women get killed or injured in automobile crashes.

The final version of the Minnesota fetal death defined a live fetus as "the unborn offspring of a human being conceived but not yet born."

It cannot be stressed enough that defining the beginning of life is neither a purely medical nor a purely legal problem. The definition must ultimately rest more upon religious, moral, and ethical values than upon technical legal rules and medical science. And that is as it should be. Public policy requires that legislators determine when life in its earliest—and latest—stages is sufficiently valuable that taking it amounts to criminal homicide. No amount of medical knowledge or skill in the techniques of law can answer this question. One art student captured the dilemma in a poster. Under a drawing of a just-fertilized egg inside a happy, laughing fourteen-year-old girl is a caption that reads, "Which life is worth more?" The Minnesota statute did not resolve this dilemma, as its opinion and dissents make clear in *State v. Merrill*.[5]

C A S E

Did He Kill an "Unborn Child"?

State v. Merrill,
450 N.W.2d 318 (Minn.1990)

Merrill was indicted for the first- and second-degree murder of Gail Anderson and also for the first- and second-degree murder of her "unborn child." The trial court denied Merrill's motion to dismiss the charges.

Simonett, Justice.

FACTS

On November 13, 1988, Gail Anderson died from gunshot wounds allegedly inflicted by the defendant. An autopsy revealed Ms. Anderson was pregnant with a 27- or 28-day-old embryo. The coroner's office concluded that there was no abnormality which would have caused a miscarriage, and that death of the embryo resulted from the death of Ms. Anderson. At this stage of development, a 28-day-old embryo is 4- to 5-millimeters long and, through the umbilical cord, completely dependent on its mother. The Anderson embryo was not viable. Up to the eighth week of development, it appears that an "unborn child" is referred to as an embryo; thereafter it is called a fetus. The evidence indicates that medical science generally considers a fetus viable at 28 weeks following conception although some fetuses as young as 20 or 21 weeks have survived.

The record is unclear in this case whether either Ms. Anderson or defendant Merrill knew she was pregnant at the time she was assaulted. Defendant was indicted for the death of Anderson's "unborn child" under two statutes entitled, respectively, "Murder of an Unborn Child in the First Degree" and "Murder of an Unborn Child in the Second Degree."

These two statutes, enacted by the legislature in 1986, followed precisely the language of our murder statutes, except that "unborn child" is substituted for "human being" and "person." The term "unborn child" is defined as "the unborn offspring of a human being conceived, but not yet born." Minn.Stat. § 609.266(a) (1988).

[COURT NOTE: "Minn.Stat. § 609.2661 (1988), provides in part: Whoever does any of the following is guilty of murder of an unborn child in the first degree and must be sentenced to imprisonment for life: (1) causes the death of an unborn child with premeditation and with intent to effect the death of the unborn child or of another; . . .

Minn.Stat. § 609.2662 (1988), provides in part:

Whoever does either of the following is guilty of murder of an unborn child in the second degree and may be sentenced to imprisonment for not more than 40 years: (1) causes the death of an unborn child with intent to effect the death of that unborn child or another, but without premeditation; . . ."]

OPINION

This legislative approach to a fetal homicide statute is most unusual and raises the constitutional questions certified to us. Of the 17 states that have codified a crime of murder of an unborn, 13 create criminal liability only if the fetus is "viable" or "quick." Additionally, two noncode states have expanded their definition of common-law homicide to include viable fetuses [Massachusetts and South Carolina]. Arizona and Indiana impose criminal liability for causing the death of a fetus at any stage, as does Minnesota, but the statutory penalty provided upon conviction is far less severe. Ariz.Rev.Stat.Ann. § 13–1103(A)(5) (1989) (5-year sentence); Ind.Code Ann. § 35–42–1–6 (Burns 1985) (2-year sentence).

Before discussing the Minnesota statutes, three preliminary observations must be made. First, to challenge successfully the constitutional validity of a statute, the challenger bears the very heavy burden of demonstrating beyond a reasonable doubt that the statute is unconstitutional.

Second, there are no common-law crimes in this state. Minnesota is a code state, i.e., the legislature has exclusive province to define by statute what acts constitute a crime. *State v. Soto*, 378 N.W.2d 625, 627 (Minn.1985).

And, third, the role of the judiciary is limited to deciding whether a statute is constitutional, not whether it is wise or prudent legislation. We do not sit as legislators with a veto vote, but as judges deciding whether the legislation, presumably constitutional, is so.

I.

Defendant first contends that the unborn child homicide statutes violate the Equal Protection Clause. Defendant premises his argument on *Roe v. Wade*, 410 U.S. 113, 93 S.Ct. 705, 35 L.Ed.2d 147 (1973), which, he says, holds that a nonviable fetus is not a person. He then argues that the unborn child criminal statutes have impermissibly "adopted a classification equating viable fetuses and nonviable embryos with a person." . . .

The state's interest in protecting the "potentiality of human life" includes protection of the unborn child, whether an embryo or a nonviable or viable fetus, and it protects, too, the woman's interest in her unborn child and her right to decide whether it shall be carried in utero. The interest of a criminal assailant in terminating a woman's pregnancy does not outweigh the woman's right to continue the pregnancy. In this context, the viability of the fetus is "simply immaterial" to an equal protection challenge to the feticide statute.

We conclude that sections 609.2661(1) and 609.2662(1) do not violate the Fourteenth Amendment by failing to distinguish between a viable and a nonviable fetus.

II.

A more difficult issue, as the trial court noted, is whether the unborn child criminal statutes are so vague as to violate the Due Process Clause of the Fourteenth Amendment. Defendant claims the statutes are unconstitutionally vague because they fail to give fair warning of the prohibited conduct and because they encourage arbitrary and discriminatory enforcement. . . .

A.

Defendant first contends that the statutes fail to give fair warning to a potential violator. Defendant argues it is unfair to impose on the murderer of a woman an additional penalty for murder of her unborn child when neither the assailant nor the pregnant woman may have been aware of the pregnancy. . . .

In this case, defendant seems to be arguing that an intent to kill the mother is not transferable to the fetus because the harm to the mother and the harm to the fetus are not the same. We think, however, the harm is substantially similar. The possibility that a female homicide victim of childbearing age may be pregnant is a possibility that an assaulter may not safely exclude. We conclude, however, that the statutes provide the requisite fair warning.

B.

Defendant next contends that the unborn child criminal statutes are fatally vague because they do not define the phrase "causes the death of an unborn child." As a result, defendant argues, the statutes invite or permit arbitrary and discriminatory enforcement. Defendant argues that the statute leaves uncertain when "death" occurs, or, for that matter, when "life" begins. . . .

Some background is necessary to put the issue in its proper perspective. In 1985 this court, in *State v. Soto*, 378 N.W.2d 625 (Minn.1985), held that when the legislature referred to the death of a "human being" in the homicide statutes, the term "human being" was being used in its well-established common-

law sense of a person born alive. Consequently, we held that the homicide statutes did not apply to the death of an 8-month-old fetus yet unborn. The legislature was free, of course, if it wished to do so, to create a crime to cover feticide. Traditionally, the crime of feticide imposed criminal liability for the death of a "viable" fetus, that is, a fetus at that stage of development which permits it to live outside the mother's womb, or a fetus that has "quickened," that is, which moves within the mother's womb.

Apparently in response to *Soto*, the legislature has enacted criminal statutes to cover feticide. In so doing, it has enacted very unusual statutes which go beyond traditional feticide, both in expanding the definition of a fetus and in the severity of the penalty imposed. The statutes in question impose the criminal penalty for murder on whoever causes the death of "the unborn offspring of a human being conceived, but not yet born." Whatever one might think of the wisdom of this legislation, and notwithstanding the difficulty of proof involved, we do not think it can be said the offense is vaguely defined. An embryo or nonviable fetus when it is within the mother's womb is "the unborn offspring of a human being."

Defendant argues, however, that to cause the death of an embryo, the embryo must first be living; if death is the termination of life, something which is not alive cannot experience death. In short, defendant argues that causing the death of a 27-day-old embryo raises the perplexing question of when "life" begins, as well as the question of when "death" occurs.

The difficulty with this argument, however, is that the statutes do not raise the issue of when life as a human person begins or ends. The state must prove only that the implanted embryo or the fetus in the mother's womb was living, that it had life, and that it has life no longer. To have life, as that term is commonly understood, means to have the property of all living things to grow, to become. It is not necessary to prove, nor does the statute require, that the living organism in the womb in its embryonic or fetal state be considered a person or a human being. People are free to differ or abstain on the profound philosophical and moral questions of whether an embryo is a human being, or on whether or at what stage the embryo or fetus is ensouled or acquires "personhood."

These questions are entirely irrelevant to criminal liability under the statute. Criminal liability here requires only that the genetically human embryo be a living organism that is growing into a human being. Death occurs when the embryo is no longer living, when it ceases to have the properties of life.

Defendant wishes to argue that causing the death of a living embryo or nonviable fetus in the mother's womb should not be made a crime. This is an argument, however, that must be addressed to the legislature. Our role in the judicial branch is limited solely to whether the legislature has defined a crime within constitutional parameters. Indeed, in this case, our role is further limited to answering only the two specific questions certified to us for a ruling. We answer both questions no.

Certified questions answered.

DISSENT

Wahl and Keith, J.J., dissent. Kelley, Justice (concurring in part, dissenting in part):

. . . It cannot be gainsaid that few topics today compel as fierce public debate and evoke the passionate convictions of as many of our citizens as does the issue of when "life" in a fetus begins. In view of the stridency of that debate, it appears conceivable, perhaps even predictable, that two juries having the same evidence could arrive at the same factual conclusions, but due to divergent and strongly held beliefs arrived at a dissimilar legal result.

By way of example, in the case before us, one jury sharing a common viewpoint of when life commences could find the defendant guilty of fetal murder, whereas another whose members share the view that life was nonexistent in a 26- to 28-day-old embryo, could exonerate the appellant.

The likelihood of discriminatory enforcement is further enhanced when the discretionary charging function possessed by a grand jury is considered. The decision to charge must be concurred in by only a majority of the panel. Thus, the decision to charge or not may well pivot on the personal philosophical and moral tenets of a majority of the potential panel—a majority whose beliefs may vary from grand jury panel to grand jury panel. . . . I think the proper forum for defining life's onset and its cessation in these feticide statutes is the legislature. . . .

Wahl, Justice (dissenting).

The trial court . . . noted that "the Minnesota crimes against unborn children statutes represent the most sweeping legislative attempt in the country to criminalize actions of third parties which harm fetuses and embryos." . . .

Defendant is charged with murder of an unborn child in the first degree carrying a sentence of life imprisonment, Minn.Stat. § 609.2661(1), and murder of an unborn child in the second degree, carrying a sentence of imprisonment for not more than 40 years, Minn.Stat. § 609.2662(1). These statutes track, respectively, the language and sentences of murder in the first degree, Minn.Stat. § 609.185(1) (1988), and murder in the second degree, Minn.Stat. § 609.19(1) (1988), with one exception. In both §§ 609.2661(1) and 609.2662(1), the actor, to be guilty of murder and to be sentenced for murder, must cause the death, not of a human being, but of an unborn child. An unborn child is the unborn offspring of a human being conceived, but not yet born. Minn.Stat. § 609.266(a) (1988). Thus an unborn child can be a fertilized egg, an embryo, a nonviable fetus or a viable fetus.

The law with regard to murder is clear. Murder is the "unlawful killing of a human being by another. . . ." *Black's Law Dictionary* 918 (5th ed. 1979). The term murder implies a felonious homicide, which is the wrongful killing of a human being. A nonviable fetus is not a human being, nor is an embryo a human being, nor is a fertilized egg a human being. None has attained the capability of independent human life. Each has the potentiality of human life. In this potential human life the state has an important and legitimate interest—an interest which becomes compelling at viability. Only at viability does the fetus have the "capability of meaningful life outside the mother's womb." . . .

The underlying rationale of [*Roe v.*] *Wade* . . . is that until viability is reached, human life in the legal sense has not come into existence. Implicit in *Wade* is the conclusion that as a matter of constitutional law the destruction of a non-viable fetus is not a taking of human life. It follows that such destruction cannot constitute murder or other form of homicide, whether committed by a mother, a father (as here), or a third person. . . .

The fundamental right involved in the case before us as far as defendant is concerned is his liberty. He is charged with two counts of murder of a woman who was 26 to 28 days pregnant at the time of her death. For the death of the 28-day embryo he is further charged with murder of an unborn child in the first degree and murder of an unborn child in the second degree for which he may be sentenced to life imprisonment and 40 years. The state does not have a compelling interest in this potential human life until the fetus becomes viable. . . .

QUESTIONS FOR DISCUSSION

1. What objections did the defendant make to the unborn child homicide statutes?

2. How does the majority answer these objections?

3. Why does the dissent disagree with the majority?

4. Isn't the statute perfectly clear—that life begins at conception? Why does it therefore give the court so much difficulty?[6]

5. Do you agree that the penalties should be the same for killing embryos? Fetuses? Born babies? Adults? Why or why not?

6. Who should resolve these questions? Legislatures? Courts? Public opinion polls? Doctors? Lawyers? Priests, ministers, and rabbis?

The End of Life. Determining when life ends has become increasingly complex as organ transplants and sophisticated artificial life support mechanisms make it possible to maintain some vital life signs. To kill a dying person, to accelerate a person's death, or to kill a "worthless" person are clearly homicide under current law. Under these general rules, a doctor who with requisite *mens rea* kills another person by removing a vital organ too soon has committed criminal homicide. Anyone who kills another by purposely disconnecting a respirator has also committed criminal homicide.[7]

Historically, *alive* meant breathing and having a heartbeat. The concept of brain death has gained prominence over the past several years, with implications not only for medicine and morals but also for criminal law. If artificial supports alone maintain breathing and heartbeat while brain waves remain minimal or flat, brain death has occurred. The Uniform Brain Death Act provides that an individual who has suffered irreversible cessation of all brain functions, including those of the brain stem, is dead.[8]

More difficult are cases involving individuals with sufficient brain functions to sustain breathing and heartbeat but nothing more, such as patients in a deep coma because of serious injury. They may breathe and their hearts may beat, even without artificial support, but they are not alive for criminal law purposes. Troubling cases arise in which patients in deep coma have been described by medical specialists as "vegetables" but regain consciousness and live for a considerable time afterward. A Minneapolis police officer was shot and written off for dead after more than a year of deep coma, but then regained consciousness and lived several years. Reports of other such cases appear from time to time.

C A S E

Were They "Dead"?

People v. Eulo,
63 N.Y.2d 34, 482 N.Y.S.2d 436, 472
N.E.2d 286 (1984)

Cooke, Chief Judge. Eulo was indicted for second-degree murder. Following a jury trial he was convicted of manslaughter. He appealed. The appellate court affirmed his conviction. In a second case, Bonillo was indicted for second-degree murder and was convicted of first-degree manslaughter. He appealed and the appellate court affirmed his conviction.

People v. Eulo

FACTS

On the evening of July 19, 1981, defendant and his girlfriend attended a volunteer firemen's fair in Kings Park, Suffolk County. Not long after they arrived, the two began to argue, reportedly because defendant was jealous over one of her former suitors, whom they had seen at the fair. The argument continued through the evening; it became particularly heated as the two sat in defendant's pick-up truck, parked in front of the home of the girlfriend's parents. Around midnight, defendant shot her in the head with his unregistered handgun.

The victim was rushed by ambulance to the emergency room of St. John's Hospital. A gunshot wound to the left temple causing extreme hemorrhaging was apparent. A tube was placed in her windpipe to enable artificial respiration and intravenous medication was applied to stabilize her blood pressure.

Shortly before 2:00 A.M., the victim was examined by a neurosurgeon, who undertook various tests to evaluate damage done to the brain. Painful stimuli were applied and yielded no reaction. Various reflexes were tested and, again, there was no response. A further test determined that the victim was incapable of spontaneously maintaining respiration. An electroencephalogram (EEG) resulted in "flat," or "isoelectric," readings indicating no activity in the part of the brain tested.

Over the next two days, the victim's breathing was maintained solely by a mechanical respirator. Her heartbeat was sustained and regulated through medication. Faced with what was believed to be an imminent cessation of these two bodily functions notwithstanding the artificial maintenance, the victim's parents consented to the use of certain of her organs for transplantation.

On the afternoon of July 23, a second neurosurgeon was called in to evaluate whether the victim's brain continued to function in any manner. A repetition of all of the previously conducted tests led to the same diagnosis: the victim's entire brain had irreversibly ceased to function. This diagnosis was reviewed and confirmed by the Deputy Medical Examiner for Suffolk County and another physician.

The victim was pronounced dead at 2:20 P.M. on July 23, although at that time she was still attached to a respirator and her heart was still beating. Her body was taken to a surgical room where her kidneys, spleen, and lymph nodes were removed. The mechanical respirator was then disconnected, and her breathing immediately stopped, followed shortly by a cessation of the heartbeat.

Defendant was indicted for second degree murder. After a jury trial, he was convicted of manslaughter. The Appellate Division unanimously affirmed the conviction, without opinion.

People v. Bonilla

FACTS

At approximately 10:30 P.M. on February 6, 1979, a New York City police officer found a man lying faceup on a Brooklyn street with a bullet wound to the head. The officer transported the victim in his patrol car to the Brookdale Hospital, where he was placed in an intensive care unit. Shortly after arriving at the hospital, the victim became comatose and was unable to breathe spontaneously. He was placed on a respirator and medication was administered to maintain his blood pressure.

The next morning, the victim was examined by a neurologist. Due to the nature of the wound, routine tests were applied to determine the level, if any, of the victim's brain functions. The doctor found no reflex reactions and no response to painful stimuli. The mechanical respirator was disconnected to test for spontaneous breathing. There was none, and the respirator was reapplied. An EEG indicated an absence of activity in the part of the brain tested. In the physician's opinion, the bullet wound had caused the victim's entire brain to cease functioning.

The following day, the tests were repeated and the same diagnosis was reached. The victim's mother had been informed of her son's condition and had consented to a transfer of his kidneys and spleen. Death was pronounced following the second battery of tests and, commencing at 9:25 P.M., the victim's kidneys and spleen were removed for transplantation. The respirator was then disconnected, and the victim's breathing and heartbeat stopped.

An investigation led to defendant's arrest. While in police custody, defendant admitted to the shooting. He was indicted for second degree murder and criminal possession of a weapon. A jury convicted him of the weapons count and of first degree manslaughter. The conviction was affirmed by a divided Appellate Division.

OPINION

. . . Death has been conceptualized by the law as, simply, the absence of life: "Death is the opposite of life; it is the termination of life." But, while erecting death as a critical milepost in a person's legal life, the law has had little occasion to consider the precise point at which a person ceases to live. Ordinarily, the precise time of death has no legal significance. . . .

Within the past two decades, machines that artificially maintain cardiorespiratory functions have come into widespread use. This technical accomplishment has called into question the universal applicability of the traditional legal and medical criteria for determining when a person has died.

These criteria were cast into flux as the medical community gained a better understanding of human physiology. It is widely understood that the human brain may be anatomically divided, generally, into three parts: the cerebrum, the cerebellum, and the brain stem. The cerebrum, known also as the "higher brain," is deemed largely to control cognitive functions such as thought, memory, and consciousness. The cerebellum primarily controls motor coordination. The brain stem, or "lower brain," which itself has three parts known as the midbrain, pons, and medulla, controls reflexive or spontaneous functions such as breathing, swallowing, and "sleep-wake" cycles.

In addition to injuries that directly and immediately destroy brain tissue, certain physical traumas may indirectly result in a complete and irreversible cessation of the brain's functions. For example, a direct trauma to the head can cause great swelling of the brain tissue, which, in turn, will stem the flow of blood to the brain. A respiratory arrest will similarly cut off the supply of oxygen to the blood and, hence, the brain. Within a relatively short period after being deprived of oxygen, the brain will irreversibly stop functioning. With the suffocation of the higher brain all cognitive powers are lost and a cessation of lower brain functions will ultimately end all spontaneous bodily functions.

Notwithstanding a total irreversible loss of the entire brain's functioning, contemporary medical techniques can maintain, for a limited period, the operation of the heart and the lungs. Respirators or ventilators can substitute for the lower brain's failure to maintain breathing. This artificial respiration, when combined with a chemical regimen, can support the continued operation of the heart. This is so because, unlike respiration, the physical contracting or "beating" of the heart occurs independently of impulses from the brain: so long as blood containing oxygen circulates to the heart, it may continue to beat and medication can take over the lower brain's limited role in regulating the rate and force of the heartbeat.

It became clear in medical practice that the traditional "vital signs"—breathing and heartbeat—are not independent indicia of life, but are, instead, part of an integration of functions in which the brain is dominant. As a result, the medical community began to consider the cessation of brain activity as a measure of death.

The movement in law towards recognizing cessation of brain functions as criteria for death followed this medical trend. The immediate motive for adopting this position was to ease and make more efficient the transfer of donated organs. Organ transfers, to be successful, require a "viable, intact organ." Once all of a person's vital functions have ceased, transferable organs swiftly deteriorate and lose their transplant value. The technical ability to artificially maintain respiration and heartbeat after the entire brain has ceased to function was sought to be applied in cases of organ transplant to preserve the viability of donated organs. . . .

Professional and quasi-governmental groups (including the American Bar Association, the American Medical Association, the President's Commission for the Study of Ethical Problems in Medicine and Biomedical and Behavioral Research, and the National Conference of Commissioners on Uniform State Laws) have jointly indorsed a single standard that includes both cardiorespiratory and brain-based criteria. The recommended standard provides:

An individual who has sustained either (1) irreversible cessation of circulatory and respiratory functions, or (2) irreversible cessation of all functions of the entire brain, including the brain stem, is dead. A determination of death must be made in accordance with accepted medical standards.

In New York, the term "death," although used in many statutes, has not been expressly defined by the Legislature. This raises the question of how this court may construe these expressions of the term "death" in the absence of clarification by the Legislature. When the Legislature has failed to assign definition to a statutory term, the courts will generally construe that term according to "its ordinary and accepted meaning as it was understood at the time." . . .

We hold that a recognition of brain-based criteria for determining death is not unfaithful to prior judicial definitions of "death," as presumptively adopted in the many statutes using that term. Close examination of the common-law conception of death and the traditional criteria used to determine when death has occurred leads inexorably to this conclusion.

Courts have not engaged in a metaphysical analysis of when life should be deemed to have passed from a person's body, leaving him or her dead. Rather, they have conceptualized death as the absence of life, unqualified and undefined. On a practical level, this broad conception of death as "the opposite of life" was substantially narrowed through recognition of the cardiorespiratory criteria for determining when death occurs. Under these criteria, the loci of life are the heart and the lungs: where there is no breath or heartbeat, there is no life. Cessation manifests death.

Considering death to have occurred when there is an irreversible and complete cessation of the functioning of the entire brain, including the brain stem, is consistent with the common-law conception of death (see *Commonwealth v. Golston*, 373 Mass. 249, 254, 366 N.E.2d 744 [treated as a note case later in the chapter]). Ordinarily, death will be determined according to the traditional criteria of irreversible cardiorespiratory repose. When, however, the respiratory and circulatory functions are maintained by mechanical means, their significance, as signs of life, is at best ambiguous. Under such circumstances, death may nevertheless be deemed to occur when, according to accepted medical practice, it is determined that the entire brain's function has irreversibly ceased. . . .

[I]n each case, the order of the Appellate Division should be affirmed. . . . Order affirmed.

QUESTIONS FOR DISCUSSION

1. What facts indicate death in the cases?

2. What facts indicate the victims were still alive?

3. What determines death, according to the court's criteria?

4. How would you define death for purposes of the law of homicide?

5. Is putting another in a deep coma murder?

6. The underlying idea in brain death is that insufficient activity exists to appreciate life. Do you agree?

7. What about killing other people in somewhat similar circumstances?

8. What about persons who are born so retarded or so seriously brain damaged that they cannot ever hope to perform life's most basic tasks? Are they "live" human beings?

9. What about psychotics so deep in paranoia that they have no lucid intervals? Are such tragic persons "alive" in a meaningful sense?

10. How would you define death for homicide purposes?

As was true for defining when life begins, defining death need not be fastened to traditional legal doctrine or medical practice. Definitions that satisfy the purposes of criminal law should rather depend on the underlying values that homicide statutes are meant to preserve. Resolving definition problems therefore requires policymakers and legislators to grapple with how to determine what worth they ultimately attribute to continuing life for the critically and hopelessly injured, the gravely mentally ill, and other victims of advanced disease and life's vicissitudes.

CAUSING ANOTHER'S DEATH

The element in homicide that requires the prosecution to prove beyond a reasonable doubt that defendants caused the death of another can create difficulties. Some killers never touch their victims but still cause their deaths. For example, if I invite my blind enemy to step over a precipice he cannot see, and he dies, I have caused his death. If I expose my helpless child to freezing temperatures, I have killed her. Such bizarre incidents rarely occur.[9]

More commonly, death stems from several causes. In some cases, victims do not die immediately after brutal attacks. One man beaten almost to death was taken to a hospital where, in a delirious state, he pulled life support plugs and died. Another victim was so stunned from a beating that he stumbled in front of a speeding car and was killed. Factual cause exists in these killings because the assailants set in motion chains of events that ended in the victims' deaths. Whether the assailants legally caused their victims' deaths depends on whether it is fair, just, and expedient to impose liability for criminal homicide (see chapter 3). In *Commonwealth v. Golston*, the court ruled that even if a doctor's negligence contributed to the victim's death, Golston's brutal attack with a baseball bat amounted to enough evidence for the jury to find Golston's actions the legal cause of death.[10]

The ancient **year-and-a-day rule,** still followed in some states today, mandates that no act occurring more than one year and one day before death constitutes the legal cause of death for purposes of the law of criminal homicide. According to the year-and-a-day rule, the law conclusively presumes that death was due to "natural causes," not the defendant's acts. The rigid common-law formulation of this rule does not conform to modern medical realities. The case of *State v. Minster* deals with this problem.

C A S E

What Caused the Death?

State v. Minster,
302 Md. 240, 486 A.2d 1197 (1985)

Minster was indicted for first-degree murder. The trial court dismissed the indictment, invoking the year-and-a-day rule. The state appealed. The supreme court upheld the dismissal.

Couch, J.

FACTS

. . . On July 8, 1982, Minster shot the victim, Cheryl Dodgson, in the neck. As a result of the shooting, Ms. Dodgson became a quadriplegic. Minster was charged in Prince George's County Circuit Court with attempted first degree murder, assault with intent to murder, assault and battery and use of a handgun in a crime of violence. He was brought to trial in April of 1983.

Minster was convicted of attempted first degree murder and the use of a handgun in a crime of violence. He was sentenced to 20 years imprisonment for attempted murder and received a 10 year concurrent sentence for the handgun violation. The Court of Special Appeals affirmed his conviction in an unreported per curiam opinion.

On October 3, 1983, Ms. Dodgson died from injuries the State contends resulted directly from Minster's actions on July 8, 1982 one year and eighty-seven days before the victim's death. One month after Ms. Dodgson's death, Minster was indicted for first degree murder. The Circuit Court for Prince George's County dismissed the indictment because the death of Ms. Dodgson occurred more than a year and a day after the shooting. Judge Johnson [the trial judge] noted that *State v. Brown*, 21 Md.App. 91, 318 A.2d 257 (1974), which held that the year and a day rule was valid in Maryland, barred the indictment. The State appealed the dismissal to the Court of Special Appeals. We granted certiorari prior to consideration by the Court of Special Appeals in order to address an issue of public importance.

OPINION

The State's issue is simply stated: should the prosecution of Minster for the murder of Cheryl Dodgson be barred by the year-and-a-day rule. It argues that the common law rule is now archaic and, in light of medical advances in life-saving techniques, there is no sound reason for retaining the rule today. Minster argues that there are legitimate justifications for the rule's continued application; moreover, because of the number of alternatives available to replace the year-and-a-day rule, a change in the rule should be left to the legislature.

In *Brown*, this identical issue came before the Court of Special Appeals. . . . The Court held that the rule was part of our common law and, although no Maryland case had previously addressed the issue, the rule was "in full force and effect in Maryland." In addition, "if change is to be made in the rule it should be by the General Assembly because expression and

weighing of divergent views, consideration of potential effect, and suggestion of adequate safeguards, are better suited to the legislative forum." We are in accordance with this view.

We agree with Minster that there are a number of sound justifications for retaining this rule. As Chief Judge Orth stated in Brown,

> [a]bolition of the rule may well result in imbalance between the adequate protection of society and justice for the individual accused, and there would remain a need for some form of limitation on causation.

Justice Musmanno, who dissented from the judicial abrogation of the rule in *Commonwealth v. Ladd*, 402 Pa. 164, 166 A.2d 501 (1960), stated this concern more fully:

> Dorothy Pierce, the alleged victim, died of pneumonia. It is possible, of course, that her weakened condition, due to the alleged hurt received thirteen months before, made her more susceptible to the attack of pneumonia. On the other hand, there is the likely possibility that the pneumonia had no possible connection with the injury allegedly inflicted by the defendant.
>
> Suppose that the pneumonia occurred two years after the physical injury, would it still be proper to charge the defendant with murder? If a murder charge can be brought two years after a blow has been struck, will there ever be a time when the Court may declare that the bridge between the blow and death has now been irreparably broken? May the Commonwealth indict a man for murder when the death occurs ten years after the blow has fallen? Twenty years? Thirty years? One may search the majority opinion through every paragraph, sentence, clause, phrase and comma, and find no answer to this very serious question. The majority is content to open a Pandora's box of interrogation and let it remain unclosed, to the torment and possible persecution of every person who may have at one time or another injured another. I don't doubt that an "expert" of some kind can be found to testify that a slap in the face was the cause of a death fifteen years later.
>
> If there is one thing which the criminal law must

be, if it is to be recognized as just, it must be specific and definitive. We are reminded of the oft-cited explanation for the rule's existence: "[I]f he die[d] after that time [of a year and a day], it cannot be discerned, as the law presumes, whether he died of the stroke or poison, etc. or of a natural death; and in the case of life, the rule of law ought to be certain." 3 Coke, *Institutes of the Laws of England* at 52 (1797)

In addition, a person charged with attempted first degree murder (as was the case here) can be sentenced to life imprisonment. Moreover, a sentencing judge may always consider the seriousness of the injury to, or the subsequent death of, the victim. The only additional conceivable punishment a first degree murder conviction entails is the death penalty.

We do not believe this distinction is a sufficient reason to rescind a common law rule which has existed for over seven hundred years. [COURT NOTE: The rule has been traced back to the Statutes of Gloucester (1278) in the reign of King Edward I.]

Assuming, arguendo, that we abrogate this rule, with what do we replace it? In *People v. Stevenson*, 416 Mich. 383, 331 N.W.2d 143 (1982), the court addressed the identical issue we address today. Five alternatives to the rule were offered to that court:

1. The Court could retain the year and a day rule.

2. The Court could modify the rule by extending the span of time, for example, to three years and a day. California Penal Code § 194.

3. The Court could extend the rule to any length of time it chooses, perhaps two years, five years, or ten years.

4. The Court could change the rule from an irrebuttable presumption to a rebuttable one, but with a higher burden of proof. Cf., *Serafin v. Serafin*, 401 Mich. 629, 258 N.W.2d 461 (1977), requiring clear and convincing evidence.

5. Finally, the Court could simply abolish the rule entirely, leaving the issue of causation to the jury in light of the facts and arguments in each particular case.

Similarly, in *State v. Young*, 77 N.J. 245, 390 A.2d 556 (1978), the justices were split between three alternatives: four justices favoring abrogation, two jus-

tices favoring retention, and one justice favoring a compromise "three years and a day" rule. In fact, two jurisdictions, California and Washington, have enacted a three year and a day rule.

Thus we find there is a great difference of opinion surrounding the appropriate length of the period after which prosecution is barred and some doubt whether the rule should exist at all. Consequently, we believe it is the legislature which should mandate any change in the rule, if indeed any change is appropriate in Maryland. The legislature may hold hearings on this matter; they can listen to the testimony of medical experts; and they may determine the viability of this rule in modern times.

We also observe that if there is any discernible trend towards abrogation of the year and a day rule, the trend is towards abrogation by act of the legislature, not the judiciary. Of the thirteen jurisdictions which had enacted the year and a day rule by statute in 1941, only four jurisdictions retain the rule today. In addition, in two jurisdictions (New York and Oregon) the judiciary has held that the legislature abrogated the rule by failing to include it in the comprehensive revision of the state's Criminal Code. Thus, in eleven jurisdictions the rule has been abrogated by legislative action or omission. In contrast, judicial abrogation has occurred in only five jurisdictions.

[COURT NOTE: "The statistical breakdown of the above analysis is as follows:

A. Jurisdictions legislatively retaining the rule—California, Idaho, Nevada and South Carolina (reckless manslaughter by vehicle).

B. Jurisdictions legislatively abrogating the rule—Arizona, Arkansas, Colorado, Delaware, Illinois, Montana, North Dakota, Texas, and Utah.

C. Jurisdictions judicially abrogating the rule—Massachusetts, Michigan, New Jersey, Ohio and Pennsylvania."]

We recognize the cogency of the State's argument concerning medical advances in lifesaving techniques, and we are aware that other courts have been persuaded by this argument. Yet recent decisions have affirmed the viability of the year and a day rule, and, by our count, the rule remains extant in twenty-six states.

In sum, we uphold the application of the year and

a day rule in Maryland. Accordingly, we affirm the trial court's dismissal of the indictment. Judgment affirmed; costs to be paid by appellant.

QUESTIONS FOR DISCUSSION

1. What reasons does the court give for maintaining the year-and-a-day rule?

2. Do they make sense in the 1990s? Why or why not?

3. Why does the court believe that if Maryland wishes to change the year-and-a-day rule, the legislature should make the change?

4. Do you agree?

5. Is it important that this rule has existed for more than seven hundred years? Does its longevity argue in favor of keeping this rule or rejecting it?

TYPES AND DEGREES OF CRIMINAL HOMICIDE

Criminal homicide falls into two general categories — murder and manslaughter. These in turn are subdivided into several further categories. Nearly all distinctions among these categories depend on the killer's mental state.[11]

At common law, the English judge Sir Edward Coke defined murder as

> [w]hen a man of sound memory and of the age of discretion unlawfully kills any reasonable creature in being, and under the King's peace, with malice aforethought, either express or implied by the law, the death taking place within a year and a day.[12]

In the sixteenth century, when Lord Coke wrote this definition of murder, malice aforethought was a vague term that spanned a broad range of states of mind, only one of which clearly fits our modern definitions of premeditated (planned in advance) and deliberate (the classic killings "in cold blood"). The typical sixteenth-century cases of this type of murder were those in which someone lay in wait to kill, or poisoned another person. But at common law, malice aforethought also included, and sometimes still includes today, the:

1. Intent to kill.
2. Intent to inflict serious bodily harm.
3. Intent to commit dangerous felonies.
4. Intent to resist arrest by force.
5. Creation of a greater than reckless risk of death or serious bodily harm (so-called "depraved heart murder," such as shooting into a crowd of people).

First-Degree Murder

The common law did not recognize degrees of murder; all criminal homicides were capital felonies. Pennsylvania was the first state to depart from the common law, enacting in 1794 the first statute that divided murder into degrees. The Pennsylvania statute provided that

> all murder, which shall be perpetrated by means of poison, lying in wait, or by any other kind of willful, deliberate or premeditated killing, or which shall be com-

mitted in the perpetration, or attempt to perpetrate any arson, rape, robbery or burglary shall be deemed murder in the first degree; and all other kinds of murder shall be deemed murder in the second degree.[13]

The reason for creating first degree murder was to confine the death penalty (at the time prescribed for all murders) to particularly heinous killings. Most states followed the practice of grading first-degree murder as capital murder. As states abolished the death penalty, first-degree murder became a life imprisonment felony.

Capital murder has attracted particular attention because of Supreme Court opinions regarding the constitutionality of the death penalty. The Supreme Court has ruled that capital punishment does not violate the Eighth Amendment's prohibition against cruel and unusual punishments. However, the way the death penalty is administered may violate both the cruel and unusual punishments clause and the due process clauses of the Fifth and Fourteenth amendments to the United States Constitution. Therefore, the Court has carefully scrutinized the administration of death penalty statutes. For example, the Court has ruled that mandatory death penalty statutes are not constitutional unless courts and juries take into account specific aggravating and mitigating circumstances and do so according to strict procedural safeguards. As a result, most states that prescribe the death penalty for murder have statutes outlining the aggravating and mitigating circumstances that qualify convicted murderers for the death penalty.[14]

Premeditated, Deliberate Murder. Most statutes define first-degree murder as the premeditated, deliberate killing of another person. **Premeditated killings** are planned in advance. **Deliberate killings** are "coldblooded," that is, they are carefully considered, not like voluntary manslaughter which is a sudden killing "in the heat of passion."[15]

Courts are not consistent in their definitions of premeditation and deliberation. A few courts require that defendants must have taken substantial time to formulate a well-laid plan to kill. According to one court:

> A verdict of murder in the first degree . . . [on a theory of willful, deliberate, and premeditated killing] is proper only if the slayer killed "as a result of careful thought and weighing of considerations; as a deliberate judgment or plan; carried on coolly and steadily, according to a preconceived design."[16]

The majority of courts, however, virtually eliminate the element of advanced planning by holding that premeditation includes killings that take place even instantly after forming the intent to kill. One judge said that a defendant premeditated when the

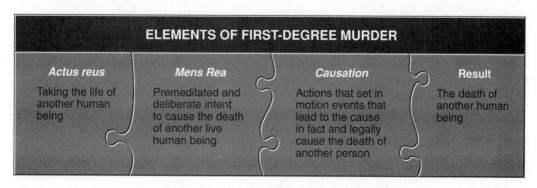

ELEMENTS OF FIRST-DEGREE MURDER

Actus reus	*Mens Rea*	*Causation*	Result
Taking the life of another human being	Premeditated and deliberate intent to cause the death of another live human being	Actions that set in motion events that lead to the cause in fact and legally cause the death of another person	The death of another human being

intent to kill arose "at the very moment the fatal shot was fired." Other courts require sufficient maturity or mental health (or both) to appreciate fully what it means to plan to kill in advance of doing so. The Idaho Supreme Court dealt with the meaning of premeditated murder in the capital murder case of *State v. Snowden*.[17]

C A S E

Did He "Premeditate" the Killing?

State v. Snowden,
79 Idaho 266, 313 P.2d 706 (1957)

Snowden pleaded guilty to first-degree murder. The trial judge sentenced him to death. He appealed to the Idaho supreme court. Justice McQuade delivered the opinion. The supreme court affirmed.

FACTS

Defendant Snowden had been playing pool and drinking in a Boise pool room early in the evening. With a companion, one Carrier, he visited a club near Boise, then went to nearby Garden City. There the two men visited a number of bars, and defendant had several drinks. Their last stop was the HiHo Club. Witnesses related that while defendant was in the HiHo Club he met and talked to Cora Lucyle Dean. The defendant himself said he hadn't been acquainted with Mrs. Dean prior to that time, but he had "seen her in a couple of the joints up town." He danced with Mrs. Dean while at the HiHo Club. Upon departing from the tavern, the two left together.

In statements to police officers, that were admitted in evidence, defendant Snowden said after they left the club Mrs. Dean wanted him to find a cab and take her back to Boise, and he refused because he didn't feel he should pay her fare. After some words, he related: "[S]he got mad at me so I got pretty hot and I don't know whether I back handed her there or not. And, we got calmed down and decided to walk across to the gas station and call a cab."

They crossed the street, and began arguing again. Defendant said: "She swung and at the same time she kneed me again. I blew my top." Defendant said he pushed the woman over beside a pickup truck which was standing near a business building. There he pulled his knife—a pocket knife with a two-inch blade—and cut her throat.

The body, which was found the next morning, was viciously and sadistically cut and mutilated. An autopsy surgeon testified the voice box had been cut, and that this would have prevented the victim from making any intelligible outcry. There were other wounds inflicted while she was still alive—one in her neck, one in her abdomen, two in the face, and two on the back of the neck. The second neck wound severed the spinal cord and caused death. There were other wounds all over her body, and her clothing had been cut away. The nipple of the right breast was missing. There was no evidence of a sexual attack on the victim; however, some of the lacerations were around the breasts and vagina of the deceased. A blood test showed Mrs. Dean was intoxicated at the time of her death.

Defendant took the dead woman's wallet. He hailed a passing motorist and rode back to Boise with him. There he went to a bowling alley and changed clothes. He dropped his knife into a sewer, and threw the wallet away. Then he went to his hotel and cleaned up again. He put the clothes he had worn that evening into a trash barrel.

OPINION

By statute, murder is defined as the unlawful killing of a human being with malice aforethought. Degrees of murder are defined by statute as follows:

All murder which is perpetrated by means of poison, or lying in wait, torture, or by any other kind of wilful, deliberate and premeditated killing, or which is committed in the perpetration of, or attempt to perpetrate arson, rape, robbery, burglary, kidnapping or mayhem, is murder of the first degree. All other murders are of the second degree.

The defendant admitted taking the life of the deceased. The principal argument of the defendant pertaining to . . : [premeditation] is that the defendant did not have sufficient time to develop a desire to take the life of the deceased, but rather this action was instantaneous and a normal reaction to the physical injury which she had dealt him. . . . The test to determine if the killing was willful, deliberate, and premeditated has been set out in *State v. Shuff* . . . :

> The unlawful killing must be accompanied with a deliberate and clear intent to take life, in order to constitute murder of the first degree. The intent to kill must be the result of deliberate premeditation. It must be formed upon the pre-existing reflection, and not upon a sudden heat of passion sufficient to preclude the idea of deliberation. . . .

The Supreme Court of Arizona held in the case of *Macias v. State*:

> There need be no appreciable space of time between the intention to kill and the act of killing. They may be as instantaneous as successive thoughts of the mind. It is only necessary that the act of killing be preceded by a concurrence of will, deliberation, and premeditation on the part of the slayer, and, if such is the case, the killing is murder in the first degree.

In the present case, the trial court had no other alternative than to find the defendant guilty of willful, deliberate, and premeditated killing with malice aforethought in view of the defendant's acts in deliberately opening up a pocket knife, next cutting the victim's throat, and then hacking and cutting until he had killed Cora Lucyle Dean and expended himself. The full purpose and design of defendant's conduct was to take the life of the deceased. . . .

[Snowden objected to the imposition of the death penalty. Idaho provides the following punishment for murder:]

Every person guilty of murder in the first degree shall suffer death or be punished by imprisonment in the state prison for life, and the jury may decide which punishment shall be inflicted. . . .

The trial court could have imposed life imprisonment, or, as in the instant case, sentenced the defendant to death. It is abuse of discretion we are dealing with, and in particular the alleged abuse of discretion in prescribing the punishment for murder in the first degree as committed by the defendant. To choose between the punishments of life imprisonment and death there must be some distinction between one homicide and another. This case exemplifies an abandoned and malignant heart and sadistic mind, bent upon taking human life. It is our considered conclusion, from all the facts and circumstances, the imposition of the death sentence was not an abuse of discretion by the trial court. The judgment is affirmed.

QUESTIONS FOR DISCUSSION

1. The Idaho Supreme Court upheld the trial court's finding that Snowden premeditated Dean's death. In fact, in a part of the opinion not included here, the court approved the trial judge's death sentence over life imprisonment because it was satisfied that Snowden clearly premeditated Dean's murder. Do you agree?

2. If you were defining premeditation in a criminal statute, would you say it is sufficient that the deed followed instantly upon the intention?

3. What practical meaning does premeditation have according to that definition?

4. Do you think the court used premeditation as an "excuse" to make it possible to sentence Snowden to death for the especially brutal way he murdered Dean? (When you read about second-degree murder, rethink how you defined premeditation in first-degree murder.)

5. As for the sentence, do you find any mitigating circumstances, such as Snowden's intoxication, Dean's provocation, and Snowden's quick response to Dean's provocation?

Not everyone agrees that premeditated killings constitute the worst murders. According to James F. Stephen, a nineteenth-century English judge and criminal law reformer:

> As much cruelty, as much indifference to the life of others, a disposition at least as dangerous to society, probably even more dangerous, is shown by sudden as by premeditated murders. The following cases appear to me to set this in a clear light. A, passing along the road, sees a boy sitting on a bridge over a deep river and, out of mere wanton barbarity, pushes him into it and so drowns him. A man makes advances to a girl who repels him. He deliberately but instantly cuts her throat. A man civilly asked to pay a just debt pretends to get the money, loads a rifle and blows out his creditor's brains. In none of these cases is there premeditation unless the word is used in a sense as unnatural as "aforethought" in "malice aforethought," but each represents even more diabolical cruelty and ferocity than that which is involved in murders premeditated in the natural sense of the word.[18]

The British Home Office's remarks to the Royal Commission on Capital Punishment contained the observation that

> [a]mong the worst murders are some which are not premeditated, such as murders committed in connection with rape, or murders committed by criminals who are interrupted in some felonious enterprise and use violence without premeditation, but with a reckless disregard of the consequences to human life. There are also many murders where the killing is clearly intentional, unlawful and unaccompanied by any mitigating circumstances, but where there is no evidence to show whether there was or was not premeditation. For the foregoing reasons, we deem ourselves constrained to reject the determinants of first degree murder suggested by existing law. The question then is whether it is possible to construct a more satisfactory delineation of the class of murders to which the capital sanction ought to be confined insofar as it is used at all.[19]

Heinous or Atrocious Murder. Some murder statutes focus on the act of killing, defining first degree murders as those that demonstrate a particularly brutal *actus reus*. In heinous or atrocious first-degree murder, the killer not only means to kill but also does it in an especially brutal manner. Atrocious murder usually appears as an aggravating circumstance that qualifies a murderer for the death penalty or life imprisonment without parole. The court considered the "heinous" or "atrocious" aggravating circumstances in *Smith v. State.*

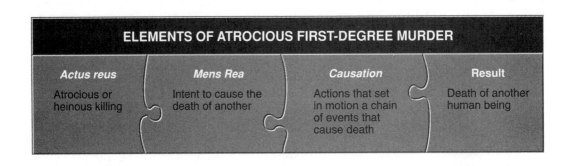

ELEMENTS OF ATROCIOUS FIRST-DEGREE MURDER			
Actus reus	*Mens Rea*	*Causation*	**Result**
Atrocious or heinous killing	Intent to cause the death of another	Actions that set in motion a chain of events that cause death	Death of another human being

CASE

Was the Murder Atrocious?

Smith v. State,
727 P.2d 1366 (Okl. 1986)

Lois Nadean Smith was convicted in the District Court of Sequoyah County, of first-degree murder and was sentenced to death. The Oklahoma supreme court affirmed the conviction and sentence.

Bussey, Judge.

FACTS

The evidence shows that the appellant, her son Greg, and Teresa Baker picked up Cindy Baillee at a Tahlequah motel early on the morning of July 4, 1982. Baillee had been Greg's girlfriend, but allegedly had made threats to have him killed. As the group drove away from the motel, appellant confronted Ms. Baillee with rumors that she had arranged for Greg's murder. When Ms. Baillee denied making any threats or arrangements, appellant choked the victim and stabbed her in the throat with a knife found in the victim's purse. The car traveled to the home of Jim Smith, the appellant's ex-husband and Greg's father in Gans, Oklahoma. Present at the house were Smith and his wife Robyn. She left shortly after the group arrived.

While at the Smith house, appellant forced Ms. Baillee to sit in a recliner chair. She then threatened to kill Ms. Baillee, and taunted her with a pistol. Finally, appellant fired a shot into the recliner, near Ms. Baillee's head. She then fired a series of shots at Ms. Baillee, and the wounded victim fell to the floor. As Greg Smith reloaded the pistol, appellant laughed while jumping on the victim's neck. Appellant took the pistol from Greg and fired four more bullets into the body. A subsequent autopsy showed Ms. Baillee had been shot five times in the chest, twice in the head, and once in the back. Five of these gunshot wounds were fatal. The knife wound was also potentially fatal.

An expert in blood spatter analysis testified blood stains on the blouse worn by appellant proved circumstantially that she had fired the fatal shots. Evidence also was presented by the State that appellant directed her companions to dispose of some evidence and arranged an alibi story for them. Appellant testified on her own behalf that Teresa Baker actually shot and killed Ms. Baillee. She claimed Ms. Baker killed the victim because of jealousy over Greg.

OPINION

... We find that the aggravating circumstance of "heinous, atrocious, or cruel" is ... supported. The victim was first choked, then stabbed in the throat, then taken to a house where she continued to beg for her life while the appellant tormented her with a revolver by shooting it into the chair in which the victim sat, and by alternately pointing it at her head and stomach until the first bullet wounds were inflicted. When the victim fell to the floor, the appellant jumped on her neck until the reloaded pistol was handed back to the appellant who discharged all six rounds into the helpless victim.... The judgment and sentence is affirmed.

QUESTIONS FOR DISCUSSION

1. What facts amounted to atrocious and heinous, according to the court?
2. What about the facts makes them atrocious? That they were planned? That Smith got pleasure from them? That they were brutal? That they had no motive? That they were totally unprovoked?
3. What penalty would you attach to this crime? Why?
4. Does it deserve the most severe punishment the law allows? Why or why not?

NOTE CASES

1. About 2 P.M. on Sunday, August 24, 1975, a white man about thirty-four years old came out of a store and walked toward his car. Golston, a nineteen-year-old African American man, tiptoed up behind the

victim and hit him on the head with a baseball bat. A witness testified to the sound made by Golston's blow to the victim's head: "Just like you hit a wet, you know, like a bat hit a wet baseball, that's how it sounded." Golston then went into a building, changed his clothes, and crossed the street to the store, where he worked. When asked why he had hit the man, Golston replied, "For kicks." The victim later died. Was this atrocious murder, a form of first-degree murder that qualified Golston for the death penalty? According to the court, it was.

> [T]here was evidence of great and unusual violence in the blow, which caused a four-inch cut on the side of the skull. . . . [T]here was also evidence that after he was struck the victim fell to the street, and that five minutes later he tried to get up, staggered to his feet and fell again to the ground. He was breathing very hard and a neighbor wiped vomit from his nose and mouth. Later, according to the testimony, the defendant said he did it, "For kicks."
>
> There is no requirement that the defendant know that his act was extremely atrocious or cruel, and no requirement of deliberate premeditation. A murder may be committed with extreme atrocity or cruelty even though death results from a single blow. Indifference to the victim's pain, as well as actual knowledge of it and taking pleasure

in it, is cruelty; and extreme cruelty is only a higher degree of cruelty. *Commonwealth v. Golston*, 373 Mass. 249, 366 N.E.2d 744 (1977)

2. On February 15, 1982, Duest, carrying a knife in the waistband of his pants, boasted that he was going to a gay bar to "roll a fag." Duest was later seen at a predominantly gay bar with John Pope. Pope and Duest left the bar and drove off in Pope's gold Camaro. Several hours later, Pope's roommate returned home and found the house unlocked, the lights on, the stereo on loud, and blood on the bed. The sheriff was contacted. Upon arrival, the deputy sheriff found Pope on the bathroom floor in a pool of blood with multiple stab wounds. Duest was found and arrested on April 18, 1982. He was tried and found guilty of first-degree murder. In accordance with the jury's advisory recommendation, the trial judge imposed the death sentence. Duest argued that this was not a particularly heinous or atrocious killing. The court wrote:

> We disagree with the defendant. The evidence presented at trial shows that the victim received eleven stab wounds, some of which were inflicted in the bedroom and some inflicted in the bathroom. The medical examiner's testimony revealed that the victim lived some few minutes before dying. *Duest v. State*, 462 So.2d 446 (Fla.1985)

Second-Degree Murder

Second-degree murder, a catchall offense, includes all criminal homicides that are neither first-degree murder nor manslaughter. One good way to think of murder is to think of the "typical" murder as second-degree. Then, some circumstances, like those outlined above in the section on first-degree murder, can aggravate second-degree murder to first-degree. Other circumstances, outlined later in the section on voluntary manslaughter, can reduce second-degree murder to manslaughter. Second-degree murders include killing:

- without premeditation,
- with the intent to inflict serious bodily injury but not death,
- with "depraved heart," that is without the intent to kill but with extreme recklessness that shows a wanton disregard for human life,
- without any intent to kill or injure but where death occurs during the commission of some felonies.

The court examined the *mens rea* of second-degree murder in *People v. Thomas*.

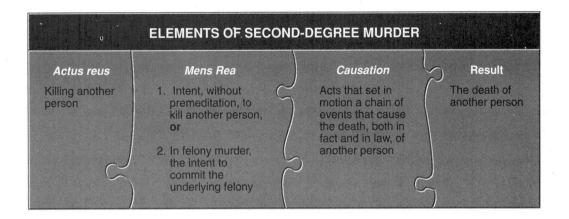

ELEMENTS OF SECOND-DEGREE MURDER

Actus reus	Mens Rea	Causation	Result
Killing another person	1. Intent, without premeditation, to kill another person, **or** 2. In felony murder, the intent to commit the underlying felony	Acts that set in motion a chain of events that cause the death, both in fact and in law, of another person	The death of another person

C A S E

Did He Intend to Kill?

People v. Thomas,
85 Mich.App. 618, 272 N.W.2d 157 (1978)

Thomas was charged with second-degree murder. The jury convicted him of involuntary manslaughter. The trial judge sentenced Thomas to five to fifteen years in prison. Thomas appealed. Presiding judge D. E. Holbrook, Jr., wrote the opinion for the court. The conviction was affirmed.

FACTS

The victim, a 19-year-old male "catatonic schizophrenic," was at the time of his death a resident of Oak Haven, a religious practical training school. When it appeared he was not properly responding to ordinary treatment, defendant, the work coordinator at Oak Haven, obtained permission from the victim's parents to discipline him if such seemed necessary. Thereafter defendant, together with another supervisor at Oak Haven, took decedent to the edge of the campus, whereupon decedent's pants were taken down, following which he was spanked with a rubber hose. Such disciplinary session lasted approximately 15 to 30 minutes. During a portion thereof decedent's hands were tied behind his back for failure to cooperate.

Following the disciplinary session aforesaid, defendant testified that the young man improved for awhile but then commenced to backslide. Defendant again received permission from decedent's parents to subject him to further discipline. On September 30, 1976, defendant again took decedent to the approximate same location, removed his pants, bound his hands behind him with a rope looped over a tree limb and proceeded to beat him with a doubled-over rubber hose. This beating lasted approximately 45 minutes to an hour. While the evidence conflicted, it appears that the victim was struck between 30 to 100 times. The beating resulted in severe bruises ranging from the victim's waist to his feet. Decedent's roommate testified that decedent had open bleeding sores on his thighs. On the date of death, which was nine days after the beating, decedent's legs were immobile. At no time did defendant obtain medical attention for the victim.

Defendant admitted he had exercised poor judgment, after seeing the bruises, in continuing the discipline. He further testified that in the two days following the discipline, decedent seemed to be suffering from the flu, but by Sunday was up and walking and was in apparent good health until one week following the beating, when decedent became sick with nausea and an upset stomach. These symptoms continued for two days, when decedent died.

As a result of the autopsy, one Dr. Clark testified that the bruises were the result of a trauma and that decedent was in a state of continuous traumatization because he was trying to walk on his injured legs. Dr. Clark testified that decedent's legs were swollen to possibly twice their normal size. He further testified that the actual cause of death was acute pulmonary edema, resulting from the aspiration of stomach contents. Said aspiration caused a laryngeal spasm, causing decedent to suffocate on his own vomit. Although pulmonary edema was the direct cause of death, Dr. Clark testified that said condition usually had some underlying cause and that, while there were literally hundreds of potential underlying causes, it was his opinion that in the instant case the underlying cause was the trauma to decedent's legs.

In explaining how the trauma ultimately led to the pulmonary edema, Dr. Clark testified that the trauma to the legs produced "crush syndrome" or "blast trauma," also known as "tubular necrosis." "Crush syndrome" is a condition caused when a part of the body has been compressed for a long period of time and then released. In such cases, there is a tremendous amount of tissue damage to the body part that has been crushed. When the compression is relieved, the tissues begin to return to their normal position, but due to the compression, gaps appear between the layers of tissues, and these areas fill up with blood and other body fluids, causing swelling. In the present case, Dr. Clark estimated that about 10–15% of decedent's entire body fluids were contained in the legs, adding an additional ten pounds in weight to the normal weight of the legs and swelling them to twice their normal size. This extra blood and body fluid decreased the amount of blood available for circulation in the rest of the body and would cause the person to become weak, faint and pass out if he attempted to sit up or do other activities. Decedent was sitting up when he died.

It was Dr. Clark's opinion that the causal connection between the trauma and death was more than

medically probable and that it was "medically likely." He further testified he could say with a reasonable degree of medical certainty that the trauma to the legs was the cause of death. . . .

OPINION

. . . Appellant claims that the prosecution failed to establish the malice element of second-degree murder. We disagree. Malice or intent to kill may be inferred from the acts of the defendant. In *People v. Morrin,* . . . Justice Levin, stated that the intent to kill may be implied where the actor actually intends to inflict great bodily harm or the natural tendency of his behavior is to cause death or great bodily harm. In the instant case defendant's savage and brutal beating of the decedent is amply sufficient to establish malice. He clearly intended to beat the victim and the natural tendency of defendant's behavior was to cause great bodily harm. . . .

Affirmed.

QUESTIONS FOR DISCUSSION

1. Although the jury found Thomas guilty of involuntary manslaughter, the Michigan court of appeals ruled that the jury could have found Thomas guilty of second-degree murder because the facts supported the conclusion that Thomas intended to "inflict great bodily harm" on the deceased. Intending to beat someone within an inch of his or her life is not different enough from intending to beat someone to death to grade the two crimes differently. Do you agree that it is murder if Thomas intended only to beat the deceased severely?

2. Was Thomas's state of mind with respect to the death purposeful, reckless, or negligent?

3. What facts would you use to support your answer?

4. Does this case mean that reckless homicide is murder? Explain.

5. Do you think it should be?

Reckless murder, which has largely replaced the old "depraved heart" murder, is another form of second-degree murder. Reckless murder involves deaths that result from individuals' purposely or consciously creating substantial and unjustifiable risks that someone will either die or suffer serious injury. In one case, for example, a man, intending to unload his gun, shot it into the air. The bullets penetrated an airplane passing overhead, killing one of the passengers. The man intended neither to kill nor even to harm anyone. In fact, it was the last thing he contemplated when he emptied his gun. Most analysts agree that this kind of death should result in liability for some kind of criminal homicide. But they disagree over whether it ought to be murder. To some analysts, murder *mens rea* should be limited strictly to the specific intent or purpose to kill. Despite these objections, "depraved heart" or reckless killing remains murder in most jurisdictions, although only in the second degree.

Felony Murder

In most jurisdictions, deaths that occur during the commission, or attempted commission, of some felonies are **felony murder.** The felonies that qualify deaths that occur during their commission as felony murder include arson, rape, robbery, burglary, kidnapping, mayhem, and sexual molestation of a child. Felony murder can be either first- or second-degree murder, depending on the jurisdiction or the felony. For example, first-degree felony murder might include deaths that occur during the commission of all felonies. Or, deaths that occur during the commission of rape and armed robbery might qualify as first-degree murder while deaths that occur during the commission of assault or reckless driving might rank as second-degree felony murder.[20]

Felony murder does not require the intent either to kill or to inflict serious bodily harm. In fact, most felony murderers do not intend either to kill or to injure their victims. Most often, felony murders are deaths that occur either recklessly or negligently in the course of the commission of a felony. The intent to commit the felony substitutes for the intent to kill. For example, if a robber fires a gun during the robbery and kills a convenience store clerk without the intent to kill, the intent to rob is sufficiently blameworthy to satisfy the *mens rea* of felony murder. Analytically, the robber has acted purposely with respect to the robbery and either knowingly or recklessly with respect to the death of the clerk.

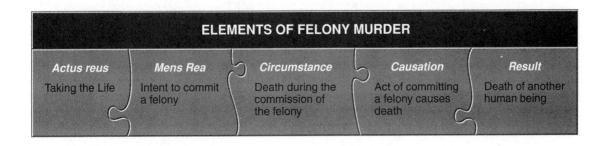

ELEMENTS OF FELONY MURDER

Actus reus	Mens Rea	Circumstance	Causation	Result
Taking the Life	Intent to commit a felony	Death during the commission of the felony	Act of committing a felony causes death	Death of another human being

The felony murder doctrine is supposed to accomplish several policy goals:

- *Deter offenders:* The added threat of a murder conviction is supposed to prevent would-be felons from committing felonies that can lead to death.

- *Reduce violence:* The threat of a murder conviction is supposed to curtail the use of violence during the commission of felonies by inducing felons to act more carefully during robberies and other felonies fraught with the risk of injury and death.

- *Punish wrongdoers:* People who intentionally commit felonies, creating high risks of death or injury while they do so, should suffer the most serious possible consequences for their actions.

Research has not demonstrated that the rule either deters dangerous felons or reduces the number of deaths during the commission of felonies. Four states—Ohio, Hawaii, Michigan, and Kentucky—have abolished felony murder. Other states have restricted felony murder to deaths that were foreseeable during the commission of the underlying felony. In *State v. Noren*, during a robbery, Noren punched his victim three times in the head so hard that Noren's knuckles bled. The victim was extremely drunk, which Noren knew. The court decided that the victim's death was foreseeable. In the course of its opinion, the court explained why felony murder is limited to foreseeable deaths. According to the court,

> The statutory requirement that death be a probable consequence of a felony is intended to limit felony-murder liability to situations where the defendant's conduct creates some measure of foreseeable risk of death. Under the predecessor felony-murder statute, a defendant committed murder when death resulted from the commission of any felony. This rule was modified because it imposed severe criminal sanctions without considering the moral culpability of the defendant. . . . [Therefore,] the acts causing death must be inherently dangerous to life. We apply this test to felony-murder because it requires a high degree of foreseeability, thereby implicitly requiring greater culpability than lesser grades of homicide. Our supreme court applied this standard under the predecessor felony-murder statute when it stated that the act constituting the felony must be in itself dangerous to life.[21]

Problems arise when someone who is not the felon causes a death during a felony. The someone who actually does the killing might be the victim, police officers, or even a co-felon. Some states exclude from felony murder deaths caused by third persons. For example, when a resisting victim shot and killed one of two burglars, the surviving burglar was not guilty of the felony murder of the burglar whom the victim killed. Similarly, when a cabdriver and a police officer shot and killed one of two men attempting to rob the driver, the surviving attempted robber was not guilty of felony murder. Some states, however, do not apply the third-party exclusion to resisting victims. For example, in one case the victim of a felonious assault returned fire and killed one of the assailants; the dead assailant's co-felon was convicted of felony murder.[22]

Felony murder applies only to deaths that happen during the commission of *dangerous* felonies. For example, the California Supreme Court held that a chiropractor was not guilty of felony murder when he fraudulently treated a cancer patient with chiropractic and the patient died. The court ruled that although a felony, fraud was not a "dangerous" felony. The Rhode Island Supreme Court examined the meaning of "dangerous felonies" in *State v. Stewart*.[23]

C A S E

Did She Commit an "Inherently Dangerous" Felony?

State v. Stewart,
663 A.2d 912 (Md. 1995)

Twenty-year-old Tracy Stewart was convicted in the Superior Court, Providence County, of second-degree felony murder. She appealed. The Supreme Court affirmed the conviction.

WEISBERGER, Chief Justice.

FACTS

On August 31, 1988 twenty-year-old Tracy Stewart (Stewart or defendant) gave birth to a son, Travis Young (Travis). Travis's father was Edward Young, Sr. (Young). Stewart and Young, who had two other children together, were not married at the time of Travis's birth. [Subsequent to her trial, Stewart married Young. Several months later she filed for divorce.] Travis lived for only fifty-two days, dying on October 21, 1988, from dehydration.

During the week prior to Travis's death, Stewart, Young, and a friend, Patricia McMasters (McMasters), continually and repeatedly ingested cocaine over a two- to three-consecutive-day period at the apartment shared by Stewart and Young. The baby, Travis, was also present at the apartment while Stewart, Young, and McMasters engaged in this cocaine marathon. Young and McMasters injected cocaine intravenously and also smoked it while Stewart ingested the cocaine only by smoking it. The smoked cocaine was in its strongest or base form, commonly referred to as "crack." When the three exhausted an existing supply of cocaine, they would pool their money and Young and McMasters would go out and buy more with the accumulated funds. The primary source of funds from which the three obtained money for this cocaine spree was Stewart's and McMasters's Aid to Families with Dependent Children (AFDC) checks. Stewart and McMasters had each just received the second of their semimonthly AFDC checks. They both cashed their AFDC checks and gave money to Young, which he then used to purchase more co-

caine. After all the AFDC funds had been spent on cocaine and the group had run out of money, McMasters and Young committed a robbery to obtain additional money to purchase more cocaine.

The cocaine binge continued uninterrupted for two to three days. McMasters testified that during this time neither McMasters nor Stewart slept at all. McMasters testified that defendant was never far from her during this entire two- to three-day period except for the occasions when McMasters left the apartment to buy more cocaine. During this entire time, McMasters saw defendant feed Travis only once. Travis was in a walker, and defendant propped a bottle of formula up on the walker, using a blanket, for the baby to feed himself. McMasters testified that she did not see defendant hold the baby to feed him nor did she see defendant change Travis's diaper or clothes during this period.

Ten months after Travis's death defendant was indicted on charges of second-degree murder, wrongfully causing or permitting a child under the age of eighteen to be a habitual sufferer for want of food and proper care (hereinafter sometimes referred to as "wrongfully permitting a child to be a habitual sufferer"), and manslaughter. The second-degree-murder charge was based on a theory of felony murder. The prosecution did not allege that defendant intentionally killed her son but rather that he had been killed during the commission of an inherently dangerous felony, specifically, wrongfully permitting a child to be a habitual sufferer. Moreover, the prosecution did not allege that defendant intentionally withheld food or care from her son. Rather the state alleged that because of defendant's chronic state of cocaine intoxication, she may have realized what her responsibilities were but simply could not remember whether she had fed her son, when in fact she had not.

At defendant's trial both the prosecution and the defense presented expert medical witnesses who testified concerning what they believed to be the cause of Travis's death. The experts for both sides agreed that the cause of death was dehydration, but they strongly disagreed regarding what caused the dehydration. The prosecution expert witnesses believed that the dehydration was caused by insufficient intake of food and water, that is, malnutrition. The defense expert witnesses, conversely, believed that the dehydration was caused by a gastrointestinal virus known as gastroenteritis which manifested itself in an overwhelming expulsion of fluid from the baby's body.

The defendant was found guilty of both second-degree murder and wrongfully permitting a child to be a habitual sufferer. A subsequent motion for new trial was denied. This appeal followed. . . .

OPINION

. . . At the pretrial hearing on the motion to dismiss, defendant argued that the law in Rhode Island is moving toward the approach used in California to determine if a felony is inherently dangerous. This approach examines the elements of a felony in the abstract. . . . In denying the motion to dismiss, the trial justice stated that "[n]othing . . . in my examination of Rhode Island case law, leads the Court to conclude that the Rhode Island Supreme Court is moving toward the California concept." Rather than determine if the crime of wrongfully permitting a child to be a habitual sufferer was inherently dangerous in the abstract, the trial justice ruled that the state would have the opportunity to prove at trial that the crime was inherently dangerous in the manner that it was committed. The trial justice committed no error in so ruling. . . .

The defendant moved for judgment of acquittal . . . at the close of the state's case and again at the close of all the evidence. In regard to the felony-murder charge defendant claimed that the evidence was insufficient to prove (1) that the crime of wrongfully permitting a child to be a habitual sufferer is an inherently dangerous felony and (2) that defendant intentionally committed the crime of wrongfully permitting a child to be a habitual sufferer. The motions for judgment of acquittal were denied on both grounds. The defendant claims that the denial of her motions for judgment of acquittal was reversible error.

Rhode Island's murder statute, § 11231, enumerates certain crimes that may serve as predicate felonies to a charge of first-degree murder. A felony

that is not enumerated in § 11231 can, however, serve as a predicate felony to a charge of second-degree murder. Thus the fact that the crime of wrongfully permitting a child to be a habitual sufferer is not specified in § 11231 as a predicate felony to support a charge of first-degree murder does not preclude such crime from serving as a predicate to support a charge of second-degree murder.

In Rhode Island, second-degree murder has been equated with common-law murder. At common law, where the rule is unchanged by statute, "[h]omicide is murder if the death results from the perpetration or attempted perpetration of an inherently dangerous felony." To serve as a predicate felony to a charge of second-degree murder, a felony that is not specifically enumerated in § 11231 must therefore be an inherently dangerous felony.

The defendant contends that wrongfully permitting a child to be a habitual sufferer is not an inherently dangerous felony and cannot therefore serve as the predicate felony to a charge of second-degree murder. In advancing her argument, defendant urges this court to adopt the approach used by California courts to determine if a felony is inherently dangerous. This approach requires that the court consider the elements of the felony "in the abstract" rather than look at the particular facts of the case under consideration. With such an approach, if a statute can be violated in a manner that does not endanger human life, then the felony is not inherently dangerous to human life. Moreover, the California Supreme Court has defined an act as "inherently dangerous to human life when there is 'a high probability that it will result in death.'"

In [*People v.*] *Caffero*, [207 Cal.App.3d 678, 68384, 255 Cal.Rptr. 22, 25 (1989)] . . . a two-and-one-half-week-old baby died of a massive bacterial infection caused by lack of proper hygiene that was due to parental neglect. The parents were charged with second-degree felony murder and felony-child-abuse, with the felony-child-abuse charge serving as the predicate felony to the second-degree-murder charge. Examining California's felony-child-abuse statute in the abstract, instead of looking at the particular facts of the case, the court held that because the statute could be violated in ways that did not endanger human life, felony-child abuse was not inherently dangerous to human life. By way of example, the court noted that a fractured limb, which comes within the ambit of the felony-child-abuse statute, is unlikely to endanger the life of an infant, much less of a seventeen-year-old. . . . Because felony-child-abuse was not inherently dangerous to human life, it could not properly serve as a predicate felony to a charge of second-degree felony murder.

The defendant urges this court to adopt the method of analysis employed by California courts to determine if a felony is inherently dangerous to life. . . . We decline defendant's invitation to adopt the California approach in determining whether a felony is inherently dangerous to life and thus capable of serving as a predicate to a charge of second-degree felony murder. We believe that the better approach is for the trier of fact to consider the facts and circumstances of the particular case to determine if such felony was inherently dangerous in the manner and the circumstances in which it was committed, rather than have a court make the determination by viewing the elements of a felony in the abstract. We now join a number of states that have adopted this approach. . . .

The proper procedure for making such a determination is to present the facts and circumstances of the particular case to the trier of fact and for the trier of fact to determine if a felony is inherently dangerous in the manner and the circumstances in which it was committed. This is exactly what happened in the case at bar. The trial justice instructed the jury that before it could find defendant guilty of second-degree murder, it must first find that wrongfully causing or permitting a child to be a habitual sufferer for want of food or proper care was inherently dangerous to human life "in its manner of commission." This was a proper charge. By its guilty verdict on the charge of second-degree murder, the jury obviously found that wrongfully permitting a child to be a habitual sufferer for want of food or proper care was indeed a felony inherently dangerous to human life in the circumstances of this particular case.

. . .

. . . [W]e are of the opinion that the evidence offered by the state was sufficient to prove beyond a reasonable doubt each of the elements of second-degree felony murder, including that the crime of wrongfully

permitting a child to be a habitual sufferer was an inherently dangerous felony in its manner of commission. The defendant's motions for judgment of acquittal on the felony-murder charge on the ground that wrongfully permitting a child to be a habitual sufferer is not an inherently dangerous felony were properly denied.

The theory of felony murder is that a defendant does not have to have intended to kill one who dies during the course of certain statutorily enumerated felonies, or other inherently dangerous felonies, in order to be charged with murder. The intent to commit the underlying felony will be imputed to the homicide, and a defendant may thus be charged with murder on the basis of the intent to commit the underlying felony.

The defendant claims that the evidence presented at trial failed to establish that she intentionally committed the crime of wrongfully permitting a child to be a habitual sufferer. She claims that absent an intent to commit this felony, it cannot serve as a predicate to support a charge of second-degree felony murder because there would then be no intent to be imputed from the underlying felony to the homicide. We agree with defendant that intent to commit the underlying felony is a necessary element of felony murder. However, we believe the circumstances surrounding the events preceding Travis's death support a finding that defendant did indeed intentionally permit her son to be a habitual sufferer for want of food or proper care.

The defendant's addiction to and compulsion to have cocaine were the overriding factors that controlled virtually every aspect of her life. She referred to the extended periods that she was high on cocaine as "going on a mission." Although she was receiving public assistance and did not have much disposable income, she nevertheless spent a great deal of money on cocaine, including her AFDC money. She shoplifted and traded the stolen merchandise for cocaine. She stole food because she had used the money that she should have been using to purchase food to purchase cocaine. The compulsion to have cocaine at any cost took precedence over every facet of defendant's life including caring for her children.

Although defendant did not testify at trial, she did testify before the grand jury. A redacted tape of her grand jury testimony was admitted into evidence and played for the jury at trial. During the days preceding Travis's death, defendant had been on a two- to three-day cocaine binge, a mission, as she referred to it. Her grand jury testimony indicated that she knew that during such periods she was unable to care for her children properly. The defendant testified that whenever she would go on a mission, her mother, who lived only a few houses away, would take and care for the children. This testimony evinced a knowledge on the part of defendant that she was incapable of properly caring for her children during these periods of extended cocaine intoxication. In addition, defendant was prone to petit mal seizures, which were exacerbated by her cocaine use. During such seizures she would "black out" or "[go] into a coma state." She testified before the grand jury that she was aware that taking cocaine brought on more seizures and that the weekend before Travis died she had in fact blacked out and "went into a coma state."

Despite her grand jury testimony to the contrary, Travis remained with defendant at her apartment during the entire two- to three-day binge. He died two or three days later. The defendant's repeated voluntary and intentional ingestion of crack cocaine while her seven-week-old son was in her care, [,] in addition to her testimony that she knew that she was incapable of properly caring for her children during these extended periods of cocaine intoxication, support a finding that she intentionally permitted her son to be a habitual sufferer for want of food and proper care. We make the distinction between a finding that defendant intentionally deprived her son of food and proper care, which even the state does not allege, and a finding that defendant intentionally permitted her son to be a habitual sufferer for want of food or proper care, which we find to be supported by the evidence adduced at trial.

. . .

Two or three days after the cocaine binge had ended, defendant went to McMasters's apartment and informed her that Travis had died that morning. The defendant was carrying a bag containing cans of baby formula and asked McMasters if she knew where she (defendant) could exchange the unused formula for cocaine. McMasters told defendant that she did not know where the formula could be exchanged for co-

caine but suggested that she take it to a local supermarket to get a cash refund. McMasters then accompanied defendant to a supermarket in Pawtucket where they attempted to return the formula for cash. They were unsuccessful in this attempt, however, because they did not have a receipt for the formula and store policy dictated that no cash refunds be given for returns without a receipt for the merchandise. The defendant told the assistant store manager that her baby had just died, and the manager gave defendant $20 out of his own pocket because he felt sorry for her. The defendant used this $20 to purchase cocaine. The defendant and McMasters then went to McMasters's apartment and smoked cocaine. . . .

[I]n order for the crime of wrongfully permitting a child to be a habitual sufferer to serve as a predicate felony to a charge of second-degree felony murder, the accused must have had the intent to commit the underlying felony. Although it is true that the trial justice did not specifically instruct the jury that in order to find defendant guilty of second-degree murder, it must find as one of the elements of the crime that she intentionally caused or permitted her son to be a habitual sufferer for want of food or proper care, we believe that the instructions given were substantially equivalent. The trial justice instructed the jury that it must find that defendant wrongfully, that is, without legal justification or without legal excuse, caused or permitted Travis to be a habitual sufferer. She also instructed that it must find that defendant knew or was aware beforehand that there was a likelihood that Travis's life would be endangered as a result of permitting or causing him to be a habitual sufferer for want of food or proper care. We believe that these two instructions in combination, requiring that the jury find that defendant had no legal justification or no legal excuse for causing her son to be a habitual sufferer and also requiring that the jury find that defendant knew or was aware beforehand that causing or permitting her son to be a habitual sufferer for want of food or proper care was likely to endanger his life, were the functional equivalent to an instruction requiring the jury to find that defendant intentionally caused or permitted her son to be a habitual sufferer. "This failure to distinguish between intent . . . and knowledge is probably of little consequence in many areas of the law, as often there is good reason for imposing liability whether the defendant desired or merely knew of the practical certainty of the results." LaFave and Scott, *Substantive Criminal Law*, § 3.5(b) at 305 (1986); see also *Model Penal Code* § 2.02 cmt. 2 at 234 (1985) (the "distinction [between acting purposely and knowingly] is inconsequential for most purposes of liability; acting knowingly is ordinarily sufficient"). The trial justice committed no error in refusing to give the requested instruction.

For the foregoing reasons the defendant's appeal is denied and dismissed, and the judgment of conviction is affirmed. The papers in the case may be remanded to the Superior Court.

QUESTIONS FOR DISCUSSION

1. Explain the California approach of determining "inherently dangerous felony" in the abstract.

2. Why did the Rhode Island court reject the California approach?

3. What test did the Rhode Island court use in determining whether the felony of wrongfully permitting a child to suffer is inherently dangerous?

4. In your opinion, which is the better test? Why?

5. List all of the facts in this case relevant to determining whether Tracy Stewart was guilty of felony murder.

6. Assume you are a defense attorney in California. Relying on the relevant facts, argue that Stewart is not guilty of felony murder.

7. Assume you are a prosecutor in Rhode Island. Relying on the facts, argue that Stewart is guilty of felony murder.

NOTE CASES

1. Cline, Smith, and Bragg got together to "do drugs." Cline had illegally obtained phenobarbital tablets and the three shared them. Bragg seemed unable to get high on them, so he asked for more, which Cline readily supplied. Later in the evening, after taking a total of 52 tablets, Bragg lapsed into unconsciousness. A few days later, Bragg died from a central nervous system depression caused by barbiturate intoxication. The state of California prosecuted Cline for felony murder, and he was convicted. Cline maintained that the underlying felony—illegal use of narcotics—was not inherently dangerous to human life.

On appeal, the California Supreme Court held:

A homicide that is a direct causal result of the commission of a felony inherently dangerous to human life (other than the six felonies enumerated in Pen.Code, § 189) constitutes at least second-degree murder. However, there can be no deterrent where the felony is not inherently dangerous, since the potential felon will not anticipate that any injury or death might arise solely from the fact that he will commit the felony. . . . The crucial issue that must be resolved in this appeal is, as pointed out by both parties, whether the felony of furnishing a restricted dangerous drug in violation of § 11912 of the Health and Safety Code is inherently dangerous to human life.

The trial judge found that defendant's act in furnishing a restricted dangerous drug to the deceased in violation of law was inherently dangerous to human life. His finding in this respect is amply supported by the evidence. It was the uncontroverted testimony of the pathologist that the consumption of phenobarbital in unknown strength was dangerous to human life. There was clear evidence that within a period of one-half hour this drug was consumed in considerable quantity by Bragg in defendant's presence and with his knowledge. Even defendant admitted that the deceased consumed 15 of these pills within one-half hour. It is also significant that the Legislature has defined this type of drug as "dangerous." (Health & Saf.Code, § 11901.) *People v. Cline*, 75 Cal.Rptr. 459 (1969)

2. Lee Swatsenbarg had been diagnosed by the family physician as suffering from terminal leukemia. Unable to accept impending death, the twenty-four-year-old Swatsenbarg unsuccessfully sought treatment from a variety of traditional medical sources. He and his wife then began to participate in Bible study, hoping that through faith Lee might be cured. Finally, on the advice of a mutual acquaintance who had heard of defendant's ostensible successes in healing others, Lee turned to defendant for treatment.

During the first meeting between Lee and defendant, the latter described his method of curing cancer. This method included consumption of a unique "lemonade," exposure to colored lights, and a brand of vigorous massage administered by defendant. Defendant remarked that he had successfully treated "thousands" of people, including a number of physicians. He suggested the Swatsenbargs purchase a copy of his book, *Healing for the Age of Enlighten-ment.* If after reading the book Lee wished to begin defendant's unorthodox treatment, defendant would commence caring for Lee immediately. During the thirty days designated for the treatment, Lee would have to avoid contact with his physician.

Lee read the book, submitted to the conditions delineated by defendant, and placed himself under defendant's care. Defendant instructed Lee to drink the lemonade, salt water, and herb tea, but consume nothing more for the ensuing thirty days. At defendant's behest, the Swatsenbargs bought a lamp equipped with some colored plastic sheets, to bathe Lee in various tints of light. Defendant also agreed to massage Lee from time to time, for an additional fee per session.

Rather than improve, within two weeks Lee's condition began rapidly to deteriorate. He developed a fever and was growing progressively weaker. Defendant counseled Lee that all was proceeding according to plan and convinced the young man to postpone a bone marrow test urged by his doctor. During the next week Lee became increasingly ill. He was experiencing severe pain in several areas, including his abdomen, and vomiting frequently. De-

fendant administered "deep" abdominal massages on two successive days, each time telling Lee he would soon recuperate. Lee did not recover as defendant expected, however, and the patient began to suffer from convulsions and excruciating pain. He vomited with increasing frequency. Despite defendant's constant attempts at reassurance, the Swatsenbargs began to panic when Lee convulsed for a third time after the latest abdominal massage.

Three and a half weeks into the treatment, the couple spent the night at defendant's house, where Lee died of a massive hemorrhage of the mesentery in the abdomen. The evidence presented at trial strongly suggested the hemorrhage was the direct result of the massages performed by defendant.

Did the defendant commit a felony murder? In deciding that he did not, the California Supreme Court noted:

> the few times we have found an underlying felony inherently dangerous (so that it would support a conviction of felony murder), the offense has been tinged with malevolence totally absent from the facts of this case. *People v. Burroughs,* 35 Cal.3d 824, 201 Cal.Rptr. 319, 678 P.2d 894 (1984)

Corporate Murder

Like individuals, corporations can face charges of criminal homicide. Prosecutors have charged several corporations with criminal homicide, even murder in a few cases. Probably the most publicized corporate murder case involved three young women who were killed on an Indiana highway when their Ford Pinto exploded after being struck from behind by another vehicle. The explosion followed several other similar incidents involving Pintos that led to grisly deaths. Published evidence revealed that Ford may have known that the Pinto gas tanks were not safe but took the risk that they would not explode and injure or kill anyone. Following the three young women's deaths, the state of Indiana indicted Ford Motor Company for reckless homicide, charging that Ford had recklessly authorized, approved, designed, and manufactured the Pinto and allowed the car to remain in use with defectively designed fuel tanks. These tanks, the indictment charged, killed the three young women in Indiana. For a number of reasons not related directly to whether corporations can commit murder, the case was later dismissed.[24]

In another case that drew wide public attention during the 1980s, Autumn Hills Convalescent Centers, a corporation that operated nursing homes, went on trial for charges that it had murdered an eighty-seven-year-old woman by neglect. David Marks, a Texas assistant attorney general, said, "From the first day until her last breath, she was unattended to and allowed to lie day and night in her own urine and waste." The case attracted attention because of allegations that as many as sixty elderly people had died from substandard care at the Autumn Hills nursing home near Galveston, Texas. The indictment charged that the company had failed to provide nutrients, fluids, and incontinent care for Mrs. Breed and neglected to turn and reposition her regularly to combat bedsores. One prosecution witness testified that Mrs. Breed's bed was wet constantly and the staff seldom cleaned her. The corporation defended against the charges, claiming that Mrs. Breed had died from colon cancer, not improper care.[25]

Most state criminal codes apply to corporate criminal homicide the same as they apply to other crimes committed for the corporation's benefit. Specifically, both corporations and high corporate officers acting within the scope of their authority and for the benefit of a corporation can commit murder. Practically speaking, however, prosecutors rarely charge corporations or their officers with criminal homicide, and convictions rarely follow.

The reluctance to prosecute corporations for murder, or for any homicide requiring the intent to kill or inflict serious bodily injury, is due largely to the hesitation to view corporations as persons. Although theoretically the law clearly makes that possible, in practice prosecutors and courts have drawn the line at involuntary manslaughter, a crime whose *mens rea* is negligence and occasionally recklessness. As for corporate executives, the reluctance to prosecute stems from vicarious liability and the questions it raises about culpability (see chapter 4). It has been difficult to attribute deaths linked with corporate benefit to corporate officers who were in charge generally but did not order or authorize a killing, did not know about it, or even did not want it to happen.

Only in egregious cases that receive widespread public attention, such as the Pinto and nursing home cases mentioned earlier, do prosecutors risk acquittal by trying corporations and their officers for criminal homicide. In these cases, prosecutors do not hope to win the case in traditional terms, meaning to secure convictions. Business law professor William J. Maakestad says:

> At this point, success of this type of corporate criminal prosecution is defined by establishing the legitimacy of the case. If you can get the case to trial, you have really achieved success.[26]

People v. O'Neil involves one of the few prosecutions of a corporation and its officers for murder.

► ◄ C A S E ► ◄
Did They "Murder" Their Employee?

People v. O'Neil,
194 Ill.App.3d 79, 141 Ill.Dec. 44,
550 N.E.2d 1090 (1990)

Following a joint bench trial, individual defendants Steven O'Neil, Charles Kirschbaum, and Daniel Rodriguez, agents of Film Recovery Systems, Inc. (Film Recovery), were convicted of the murder of Stefan Golab, a Film Recovery employee, from cyanide poisoning stemming from conditions in Film Recovery's plant in Elk Grove Village, Illinois. Corporate defendants Film Recovery and its sister corporation Metallic Marketing Systems, Inc. (Metallic Marketing), were convicted of involuntary manslaughter in the same death. O'Neil, Kirschbaum, and Rodriguez each received sentences of 25 years' imprisonment for murder. O'Neil and Kirschbaum were also each fined $10,000 with respect to the murder convictions. Corporate defendants Film Recovery and Metallic Marketing were each fined $10,000 with respect to the convictions for involuntary manslaughter. The defendants appealed, and the appellate court reversed the convictions.

Justice Lorenz wrote the opinion for the court.

FACTS

. . . In 1982, Film Recovery occupied premises at 1855 and 1875 Greenleaf Avenue in Elk Grove Village. Film Recovery was there engaged in the business of extracting, for resale, silver from used x-ray and photographic film. Metallic Marketing operated out of the same premises on Greenleaf Avenue and owned 50% of the stock of Film Recovery. The recovery process was performed at Film Recovery's plant located at the 1855 address and involved "chipping" the film product and soaking the granulated pieces in large open bubbling vats containing a solution of water and sodium cyanide. The cyanide solution caused silver contained in the film to be released. A continuous flow system pumped the silver laden solution into polyurethane tanks which contained electrically charged stainless steel plates to which the separated silver adhered. The plates were removed from the tanks to another room where the accumulated silver was scraped off. The remaining solution was pumped out of the tanks and the granulated film, devoid of silver, shoveled out.

On the morning of February 10, 1983, shortly after he disconnected a pump on one of the tanks and began to stir the contents of the tank with a rake, Stefan Golab became dizzy and faint. He left the production area to go rest in the lunchroom area of the plant. Plant workers present on that day testified Golab's body had trembled and he had foamed at the mouth. Golab eventually lost consciousness and was taken outside of the plant. Paramedics summoned to the plant were unable to revive him. Golab was pronounced dead upon arrival at Alexian Brothers Hospital.

The Cook County medical examiner performed an autopsy on Golab the following day. Although the medical examiner initially indicated Golab could have died from cardiac arrest, he reserved final determination of death pending examination of results of toxicological laboratory tests on Golab's blood and other body specimens. After receiving the toxicological report, the medical examiner determined Golab died from acute cyanide poisoning through the inhalation of cyanide fumes in the plant air.

Defendants were subsequently indicted by a Cook County grand jury. The grand jury charged defendants O'Neil, Kirschbaum, Rodriguez, Pett, and Mackay with murder, stating that, as individuals and as officers and high managerial agents of Film Recovery, they had, on February 10, 1983, knowingly created a strong probability of Golab's death. Generally, the indictment stated the individual defendants failed to disclose to Golab that he was working with substances containing cyanide and failed to advise him about, train him to anticipate, and provide adequate equipment to protect him from, attendant dangers involved. The grand jury charged Film Recovery and Metallic Marketing with involuntary manslaughter stating that, through the reckless acts of their officers, directors, agents, and others, all acting within the scope of their employment, the corporate entities had, on February 10, 1983, unintentionally killed Golab. Finally, the grand jury charged both individual and corporate defendants with reckless conduct as to 20 other Film Recovery employees based on the same conduct alleged in the murder indictment, but expanding the time of that conduct to "on or about March 1982 through March 1983."

Proceedings commenced in the circuit court in January 1985 and continued through the conclusion of trial in June of that year. In the course of the 24-day trial, evidence from 59 witnesses was presented, either directly or through stipulation of the parties. That testimony is contained in over 2,300 pages of trial transcript. The parties also presented numerous exhibits including photographs, corporate documents and correspondence, as well as physical evidence.

On June 14, 1985, the trial judge pronounced his judgment of defendants' guilt. The trial judge found that "the mind and mental state of a corporation is the mind and mental state of the directors, officers and high managerial personnel because they act on behalf of the corporation for both the benefit of the corporation and for themselves." Further, "if the corporation's officers, directors and high managerial personnel act within the scope of their corporate responsibilities and employment for their benefit and for the benefit of the profits of the corporation, the corporation must be held liable for what occurred in the work place."

Defendants filed timely notices of appeal, the matters were consolidated for review, and arguments were had before this court in July 1987. . . .

OPINION

. . .

We find it helpful to set out the pertinent statutory language of the offenses for which the defendants were convicted. The Criminal Code of 1961 defines murder as follows:

A person who kills an individual without lawful justification commits murder if, in performing the acts which cause the death: He knows that such acts create a strong probability of death or great bodily harm to that individual[.] (Ill.Rev.Stat.1981, ch. 38, par.9–1(a)(2).)

Involuntary manslaughter is defined as:

A person who unintentionally kills an individual without lawful justification commits involuntary manslaughter if his acts whether lawful or unlawful which cause the death are such as are likely to cause death or great bodily harm to some individual, and he performs them recklessly [.] (Ill.Rev.Stat.1981, ch. 38, par. 9–3(a).)

Reckless conduct is defined as:

A person who causes bodily harm to or endangers the bodily safety of an individual by any means, commits reckless conduct if he performs recklessly the acts which cause the harm or endanger safety, whether they otherwise are lawful or unlawful. Ill.Rev.Stat.1981, ch. 38, par. 12–5(a).

. . .

. . . [I]n Illinois, a corporation is criminally responsible for offenses "authorized, requested, commanded, or performed by the board of directors or by a high managerial agent acting within the scope of his employment." (Ill.Rev.Stat.1981, ch. 38, par. 5–4(a)(2).) A high managerial agent is defined as "an officer of the corporation, or any other agent who has a position of comparable authority for the formulation of corporate policy or the supervision of subordinate employees in a managerial capacity." (Ill.Rev.Stat. 1981, ch. 38, par. 5–4(c)(2).) Thus, a corporation is criminally responsible whenever any of its high managerial agents possess the requisite mental state and is responsible for a criminal offense while acting within the scope of his employment. . . .

. . .

Evidence at trial indicated Golab died after inhaling poisonous cyanide fumes while working in a plant operated by Film Recovery and its sister corporation Metallic Marketing where such fumes resulted from a process employed to remove silver from used x-ray and photographic film. The record contains substantial evidence regarding the nature of working conditions inside the plant. Testimony established that air inside the plant was foul smelling and made breathing difficult and painful. Plant workers experienced dizziness, nausea, headaches, and bouts of vomiting. There is evidence that plant workers were not informed they were working with cyanide. Nor were they informed of the presence of, or danger of breathing, cyanide gas. Ventilation in the plant was poor. Plant workers were given neither safety instruction nor adequate protective clothing. Finally, testimony established that defendants O'Neil, Kirschbaum, and Rodriguez were responsible for operating the plant under those conditions. For purposes of our disposition, we find further elaboration on the evidence unnecessary. Moreover, although we have determined evidence in the record is not so insufficient as to bar retrial, our determination of the sufficiency of the evidence should not be in any way interpreted as a finding as to defendants' guilt that would be binding on the court on retrial.

Reversed and remanded.

Coccia, P.J., and Murray, J., concur.

QUESTIONS FOR DISCUSSION

1. What are the relevant facts in determining whether the corporation and the individuals were guilty of murder or involuntary manslaughter?

2. Why did the court reverse and remand the case?

3. On remand, would you find the defendants guilty of murder? Explain your answer.

4. Do you agree that it is inconsistent to find that the corporation had one state of mind and the individuals another?

5. Do you see why vicarious liability is a difficult ground upon which to rest a criminal homicide conviction?

Following the conviction in the original trial, then attorney Richard M. Daley said the verdicts meant that employers who knowingly expose their workers to dangerous conditions leading to injury or even death can be held criminally responsible for the results of their actions. Ralph Nader, consumer advocate lawyer, said:

> The public is pretty upset with dangerously defective products, bribery, toxic waste, and job hazards. The polls all show it. The verdict today will encourage other prosecutors and judges to take more seriously the need to have the criminal law catch up with corporate crime.

Professor John Coffee, Columbia University Law School, said, "When you threaten the principal adequately, he will monitor the behavior of his agent." A California deputy district attorney put it more bluntly: "A person facing a jail sentence is the best deterrent against wrongdoing." Joseph E. Hadley, Jr., a corporate lawyer who specializes in health and safety issues, said the decision would not send shock waves through the corporate community: "I don't think corporate America should be viewed as in the ballpark with these folks. This was a highly unusual situation, but now people see that where the egregious situation occurs, there could be a criminal remedy."

Robert Stephenson, a lawyer defending another corporation, said, "I don't believe these statutes [murder and aggravated battery] were ever meant to be used in this way."

Utah's governor, Scott M. Matheson, refused to extradite Michael T. McKay, a former Film Recovery vice-president then living in Utah, because he was an "exemplary citizen who should not be subjected to the sensational charges in Illinois."[27]

6. Which of the preceding statements best describes what you think is proper policy regarding corporate executive murder prosecutions? Defend your answer.

Summary of Murder

Murder includes all killings committed with malice. Malice, as it applies to murder, has a broader meaning than hate or spite. It includes several mental states—the intent to kill, the intent to do serious bodily harm, killing with a depraved heart, and the intent to commit a serious felony.

Murder is divided into degrees. First-degree murder includes

1. purposeful, premeditated, and deliberate killings,

2. atrocious or cruel murder,

3. some felony murders.

Second-degree murder is a catchall category that includes all criminal homicides that are neither first-degree murder nor manslaughter. The principal second-degree murders include

1. intentional killings that are neither premeditated nor deliberate,

2. deaths resulting from the intent to inflict great bodily injury,

3. some felony murders,

4. deaths that occur while resisting lawful arrest.

MANSLAUGHTER

Manslaughter, like second-degree murder, is a catchall offense that includes all homicides that are neither murder, nor are justified or excused. The criminal law divides manslaughter into two categories: voluntary and involuntary. A third type of manslaughter, negligent homicide, includes deaths that occur during automobile accidents. At common law, manslaughter meant "the unlawful killing of another, without malice either express or implied . . . either voluntarily, upon a sudden heat; or involuntarily, but in the commission of some unlawful act."[28]

Voluntary Manslaughter

Voluntary manslaughter is the intentional killing of another live human being under extenuating circumstances. One extenuating circumstance is imperfect self-defense, that is, the intentional killing of another in the honest—but not reasonable—belief that self-defense required the use of deadly force (see chapter 6). The circumstance of honest belief in the need to use deadly force can reduce murder to voluntary manslaughter even if the use of deadly force is not justified enough to constitute self-defense. According to one court, "A person is guilty of voluntary manslaughter, if, in taking another's life, he believes that he is in danger of losing his own life or suffering great bodily harm but his belief is unreasonable."[29]

Provocation is the most common extenuating circumstance that reduces murder to voluntary manslaughter. While the criminal law aims to bridle passions and build self-control, at the same time it does not ignore the frailty of human nature. Hence, an intentional killing that the victim provoked, while still a serious felony, falls into a lower grade of felony than murder. The law of voluntary manslaughter does not reward individuals who give in to their rages by freeing those individuals. It does, however; reduce murder to the somewhat less serious felony of voluntary manslaughter. It does so only under carefully prescribed conditions defined by the adequate provocation rule. These conditions include killings

1. upon adequate provocation,

2. during the "heat of passion,"

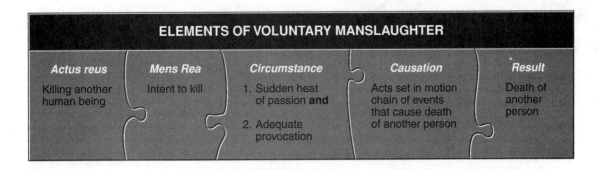

ELEMENTS OF VOLUNTARY MANSLAUGHTER

Actus reus	Mens Rea	Circumstance	Causation	Result
Killing another human being	Intent to kill	1. Sudden heat of passion **and** 2. Adequate provocation	Acts set in motion chain of events that cause death of another person	Death of another person

3. without time for the passion to "cool off,"

4. where a causal connection links the provocation, the passion, and the fatal act.[30]

The law of voluntary manslaughter recognizes only *adequate* provocation. Adequate provocation means the provocations that the law allows, by means of the **adequate provocation rule.** Not everyone who flies into a rage and suddenly kills someone has committed voluntary manslaughter instead of murder. The main provocations the law regards as adequate to reduce murder to manslaughter include

- mutual combat, that is, fighting,
- battery,
- assault,
- trespass,
- some informational words,
- adultery.

Only serious fights amount to adequate provocation; scuffles do not qualify. The fight must generate a sudden passion without reasonable time to cool off before the killing. And the death must be causally linked to the fight and the passion. Some batteries—but not all offensive touching (see chapter 9)—are considered legally adequate provocation. Pistol whipping on the head, striking hard with fists in the face, and "staggering" body blows qualify as adequate provocation. Mere slaps or shoves do not.

Assault in which the assailant establishes no body contact is sometimes adequate provocation. In one case, a man shot at the defendant and missed him. The defendant was so enraged that he shot his assailant in the back as the assailant ran away. The initial assault, although not enough to qualify the defendant's action as self-defense, was regarded as sufficiently provocative to reduce murder to manslaughter.[31]

Insulting gestures by themselves are not adequate provocation. They are, however, if they indicate an intent to attack with deadly force. So, using a well-known obscene gesture is not adequate provocation, but waving a gun around in a threatening manner can be. Trespasses are adequate provocation only if trespassers invade the homes of slayers and put the slayers in danger.[32]

In *State v. Watson*, the court examined the well-established proposition that words are never adequate provocation that can reduce murder to voluntary manslaughter.

C A S E

Are Words Adequate Provocation?

State v. Watson,
287 N.C. 147, 214 S.E.2d 85 (1975)

Watson was convicted of second-degree murder and was sentenced to life imprisonment. He appealed, arguing that he was legally provoked. The conviction was affirmed. Justice Copeland delivered the opinion.

FACTS

At the time of this incident, defendant, a black, was twenty-years-old. He was serving a twenty-five year prison sentence on judgment imposed at the October, 1972, Session of Rockingham County Superior Court upon his plea of guilty to second-degree murder. The decedent Samples, was white. Neither Samples' age nor the basis for his incarceration appears from the record. The defendant was called "Duck" by his fellow prisoners in I-Dorm. Samples, the decedent, was known as "Pee Wee." Although Samples was referred to as "Pee Wee," there appeared to be no relation between this nickname and his physical size. In fact, he was a strong man who worked out daily with weights.

The "hearsay" among the residents of I-Dorm was to the effect that Watson and Samples were "swapping-out." "Swapping-out" is a prison term that means two inmates are engaging in homosexual practices. Generally, prisoners that are "swapping-out" try to hide the practice from their fellow inmates. In particular, they try to hide it from any "home-boys" that may be in their particular unit. A "home-boy," in the prison vernacular, is a fellow inmate from one's own hometown or community. One of the State's witnesses, Johnny Lee Wilson, a resident of I-Dorm on the date of the offense, was Samples' "home-boy".

It appears that Watson and Samples had been "swapping-out" for several months. Approximately a month or so prior to the date of the killing, Watson and Samples had engaged in a "scuffle" while working in the prison kitchen. This appears to have been nothing more than a fist-fight. Samples was the winner. Although it is by no means clear from the record, it appears that this "scuffle" arose out of Samples' suspicion that Watson had been "swapping-out" with another prisoner.

At approximately 4:30 P.M. on the afternoon of the killing, Johnny Lee Wilson, Samples' "home-boy," saw Watson and Samples sitting together on a bunk in the back of I-Dorm. At this time, "they were close talking, they were close." Apparently, assuming that they were about to "swap-out," and not wanting to embarrass Samples, Wilson quickly turned around and left the dorm.

Shortly before the lights were to be dimmed (10:00 P.M.), Watson and Samples began to argue. After several minutes, Watson got up and walked across the aisle, a distance of approximately seven feet, to his bunk. Samples subsequently followed him and renewed the dispute. At this time, both parties were seated on Watson's bottom bunk. During the course of the renewed argument, Samples was verbally abusing Watson and challenging him to fight. At one

point, he said: "Nigger, nigger, you're just like the rest of them." He also told Watson that he was too scared to fight him and that all he was going to do was tremble and stay in his bunk. Finally, Samples made several derogatory and obscene references to Watson's mother. The prisoners refer to this as "shooting the dove." Generally, when a prisoner "shoots the dove," he expects the other party to fight. At this point, Watson told Johnny Lee Wilson, whose bunk was nearby on Watson's side of the room: "You better get your home-boy straightened out before I f— him up." Responding to this statement, Samples said: "Why don't you f— me up if that's what you want to do. All you're gonna do is tremble, nigger."

As Samples was making the above quoted statement, he was walking over to Wilson's bunk. Samples borrowed a cigarette from Wilson and then proceeded to his own bed. He got up in his bunk (top) and was more or less half sitting up with his back propped up against the wall. At this point, he renewed the argument with Watson, who was still in his bottom bunk on the opposite side of the room. He called Watson a "nigger" and "a black mother f—." While this was going on, Watson, without saying a word, either walked or ran across the aisle between the two rows of bunks and violently and repeatedly stabbed Samples with a kitchen-type paring knife. According to the State's witnesses, this occurred approximately two (2) to ten (10) minutes after Samples had left Watson's bed.

After summarizing the evidence, and prior to fully instructing on first-degree murder, the court stated: "[L]et me say here, that mere words will not form a justification or excuse for a crime of this sort." In instructing the jury on voluntary manslaughter, the court stated:

> [T]he defendant must satisfy you that this passion was produced by acts of Samples which the law regards as adequate provocation. This may consist of anything which has a natural tendency to produce such passion in a person of average mind and disposition. However, words and gestures alone, where no assault is made or threatened, regardless of how insulting or inflammatory those words or gestures may be, does not constitute adequate provocation for the taking of a human life.

OPINION

[After reviewing several voluntary manslaughter decisions, the court wrote:] These decisions establish the following rules as to the legal effect of abusive language:

(1) Mere words, however abusive, are never sufficient legal provocation to mitigate a homicide to a lesser degree; and

(2) A defendant, prosecuted for a homicide in a difficulty that he has provoked by the use of language "calculated and intended" to bring on the encounter, cannot maintain the position of perfect self-defense unless, at a time prior to the killing, he withdrew from the encounter within the meaning of the law.

These two rules are logically consistent and demonstrate that abusive language will not serve as a legally sufficient provocation for a homicide in this State.

These well-settled rules are clearly controlling in the instant case. Hence, if defendant had provoked an assault by the deceased through the use of abusive language and had thereafter killed the deceased, then it would have been for the jury to determine if the language used by defendant, given the relationship of the parties, the circumstances surrounding the verbal assertions, etc., was "calculated and intended" to bring on the assault. If the jury had found this to be the case, then defendant would not have had the benefit of the doctrine of perfect self-defense, even though the deceased instigated the actual physical attack. But, here there was no evidence that defendant killed the deceased in self-defense. In fact, all of the evidence tends to show that the fatal attack was brought on by the continued verbal abuses directed toward defendant by the deceased. Under these circumstances, there was no basis for a jury determination of whether any of the words were "calculated and intended" to bring on the difficulty.

At this point, we note that in those few jurisdictions that permit abusive language to mitigate the degree of homicide, the majority hold that the words are only deemed sufficient to negate premeditation, thereby reducing the degree of homicide from first to second. Most of these courts reason that since the deceased had made no attempt to endanger the life of

the accused, the action of the latter in meeting the insulting remarks with sufficient force (deadly or otherwise) to cause the death of the former, was beyond the bounds of sufficient retaliation to constitute sufficient provocation to reduce the homicide to manslaughter. See Annot., 2 A.L.R.3d 1292, 1308–10 (1965). Although we expressly decline to adopt this minority view, we note that the jury in the instant case apparently applied the same reasoning and found defendant guilty of second-degree murder. Thus, even if the minority rule applied in this State, defendant would not be entitled to a new trial as a result of the instructions here given.

Defendant contends that the trial court committed prejudicial error in charging the jury as follows:

Now, ladies and gentlemen of the jury, this case is to be tried by you under the laws of the State of North Carolina, and not upon the rules and regulations and customs and unwritten code that exists within the walls of the North Carolina Department of Correction. I can't charge you on that law because I don't know that law. I think I know this one, and this is the law that you are trying this case under.

Defendant argues that this instruction "tends to discount as a matter of law all of the factual information" that the jury was "entitled to consider, not as law, but as a part of the factual background situation within which the incident took place." We find nothing in the charge to support such an inference. During the course of the trial, several of the State's witnesses (either present or former prison inmates) testified about a "prison code," i.e., a set of unwritten rules developed by the prisoners themselves. For example, one of the State's witnesses made the following statements on cross-examination:

In the prison system, if Watson had not fought after Samples had called him nigger, nigger, and talked about his mother, I guess, you know, everybody else probably would be jugging at him. What I mean by "jugging at him," I mean, messing with him, you know. Taking advantage of the fact that he won't stand up for himself. It is important that you stand up for yourself in the system because if you don't, somebody might get you down in the shower, you know. You might get dead-ended. It means if you don't take up for yourself, everybody picks on you.

Apparently, standing up for oneself was a vital part of this so-called "prison code." In this context, the import of the above instruction was clearly to inform the jurors that the case—like all other criminal cases tried in the North Carolina General Courts of Justice—had to be tried under the laws of this State and not upon any unwritten prisoners' code that existed within the walls of North Carolina's prisons. It is certainly not error for a trial judge to so instruct a jury. Furthermore, it appears that defendant's conduct even constituted a violation of the prisoner's code. We refer to the following redirect testimony of the same witness previously quoted above: "Standing up for yourself in the prison system would not necessarily include using a knife. He could have run over there and fought with bare fists, that would have been standing up for himself."

Defendant's contention under this assignment is without merit. Therefore, it is overruled. Affirmed.

QUESTIONS FOR DISCUSSION

1. List the specific provocations that prompted Watson to kill Samples.

2. The court states flatly that words are never adequate provocation to reduce murder to manslaughter, although they may be adequate to reduce murder from first to second degree. Do you think this is a good rule for this case?

3. Especially, is it good when the prison code called on Watson to stand up for himself or be mistreated in the future?

4. In fact, if the unwritten prison code does call for him to stand up for himself, was it the words or fears for his personal safety that provoked him?

5. If you were the judge, would you have interpreted the provocation rule differently? Why or why not?

NOTE CASE

Mark Harcar was beaten to death on October 26, 1990, near Tony's Meat Market in Streator, Illinois. William Vietti, a friend of the victim, testified that he was with Mark on the day he was killed. Vietti met Mark at the market at about 5 P.M. They spent the evening drinking beer and burning boxes and papers from the market. The market, owned by members of the Harcar family, was being remodeled. Vietti brought eight to twelve beers with him to the market and bought three additional twelve-packs of beer during the course of the evening. Jeffrey Harcar, the victim's 14-year old nephew, arrived around 10:15 P.M. Jeffrey did not see his uncle drinking beer, but he thought that Vietti was drunk.

Jeffrey Harcar and Vietti both testified regarding an incident involving two black women who walked by the market that evening. According to Jeffrey, as the women walked by, Vietti said, "Maybe we can get a B.J. from these two girls." Vietti walked up to the women and said something that Jeffrey could not hear. Jeffrey then heard one of the women say that they did not like being called niggers. Vietti left the women and they continued to walk down the street.

According to Vietti, Mark Harcar said to him, "There's two for you" as the women walked by, and then yelled out, "How about a blow job, mama?" Vietti approached the women and they asked, "What's his [Mark's] problem?" Vietti told them that Mark didn't like blacks. One of the women shook Vietti's hand, and he returned to the trash fire where Mark and Jeffrey were standing.

Both Jeffrey Harcar and Vietti agreed that after Vietti returned from talking to the women, Mark Harcar got into Vietti's truck and followed the women. At one point, the women moved from the street to a path that had been a sidewalk and yelled at Mark not to run them over. Mark later turned around and returned to the market and the women continued on their way.

Gwendolyn Patterson testified that she and Earl Phillips were in Streator on October 26, 1990, drinking and socializing with Alice Phillips. At about 10 P.M. the three of them, along with Jessie Phillips, drove to a tavern where the women got out and the men drove away. Patterson and Alice Phillips were unable to enter the tavern because they did not have membership cards so they walked through town looking for Earl or for someone to give them a ride. As they walked past the meat market around 10:30 P.M., one of two men standing outside the market called out, "You niggers." One of the men approached and Patterson asked him why they had called them niggers. The man said that the other man had called out to them, not him. Patterson and the man shook hands and she and Alice Phillips continued to walk down the street. The second man soon drove up behind them in a truck and the women left the street running into a yard. Patterson picked up a brick and told the man that she would throw it through his windshield if he tried to run them over. The man pulled into a vacant lot across the street and, according to Patterson, said, "You nigger bitches come through here again, you're as good as dead." The man, whom Patterson identified as Mark Harcar, then drove back to the meat market.

Patterson further testified that she and Alice later found someone to give them a ride to look for Earl Phillips. On the way, they stopped at a liquor store and bought some beer and whiskey. They eventually found Earl and some other people, including Earnest and Walter Merritte, outside an apartment in Streator. Patterson had known the Merrittes for about eight years. She told the group about the incident at the meat market and a number of people, including Patterson, the Merrittes and Alice, Earl and Jessie Phillips, got into two cars and drove to the market at about 11 or 11:30 P.M.

Vietti testified that when he saw the two cars drive up to the market, he told Mark Harcar that they were outnumbered and that they should go inside the market. According to Vietti, Harcar said "f— it", grabbed a piece of conduit, and began walking in the direction of the cars. Vietti went inside the market and locked the door.

Gwendolyn Patterson and Earl Phillips testified that after parking the cars, they walked toward the market along with the Merrittes and Alice Phillips. Patterson picked up a four-foot long stick and saw Mark Harcar approaching with a shovel in his hands. Walter Merritte asked Harcar why he had tried to run the women over. Harcar denied it. Patterson became angry, insisted Harcar had tried to run them over and swung the stick at Harcar, which he blocked with the shovel. Patterson then saw Harcar get hit with a beer can and fall to the ground. Earl Phillips testified that the can was thrown by Earnest Merritte. After Harcar fell, Patterson jumped on top of him and began hitting him with her fists. Walter Merritte told Earl Phillips to pull Patterson off of Harcar. Walter Merritte then began hitting Harcar in the side with the shovel that Harcar had dropped when he fell. Earnest Merritte, meanwhile, was kicking Harcar in the back. During this time, Harcar was lying on his side, covering up his head with his hands and forearms.

Earl Phillips further testified that Gregory Ennis appeared on the scene, picked up a wire milk crate and used it to beat Harcar in the head. Earl stated that he hadn't seen Ennis earlier that evening and didn't know where Ennis had come from. Patterson claimed that she had seen Ennis earlier in the day at Alice Phillips' house but she did not see him at any time later that day. Patterson stated that she did not know that Ennis had been involved in the beating until the next morning when Ennis told her that he had beaten Harcar in the head with an iron crate.

According to Patterson, the beating ended when she and Alice Phillips told the Merrittes to stop. Patterson thought that the entire incident lasted three or four minutes. Earl Phillips testified that the beating stopped when Earnest Merritte stepped between Ennis and Walter Merritte and told them that that was enough. Earl thought that the incident lasted 11 or 12 minutes.

The jury found both defendants guilty of first degree murder. At the sentencing hearing, the trial court found that the defendants' conduct was brutal and heinous and indicative of wanton cruelty. The court referred to the photographs of the victim presented at trial and noted that it had never seen anyone beaten more viciously. The court found that no mitigating factors were present and, after discussing the factors in aggravation, sentenced Walter Merritte to natural life imprisonment and Earnest Merritte to a term of 80 years imprisonment.

Were the defendants adequately provoked? No, according to the Illinois Court of Appeal. The court reasoned:

> Defendants next contend that a new sentencing hearing is required because the trial court failed to consider a mitigating factor and improperly relied upon two aggravating factors. Defendants first argue that Harcar's insults, threats and attempt to run over Patterson and Alice Phillips, which defendants were told of shortly before the beating, were strong provocation which should have been considered as a mitigating factor. The trial court found that any provocation had occurred "quite sometime" prior to the beating and that the defendants were only "second-hand recipients" of the provocation.
>
> . . . When considering whether an individual has acted under serious provocation sufficient to reduce the offense of first degree murder to second degree murder, the only categories of serious provocation recognized by our courts are substantial physical injury or assault, mutual quarrel or combat, illegal arrest and spousal adultery. Mere words, no matter how abusive or indecent, are not considered serious provocation. The facts presented here clearly do not rise to the level of serious provocation. *People v. Merritte*, 611 N.E.2d 24 (1993)

Some jurisdictions have taken the view that the law does not require a "specific type of provocation." In

People v. Berry, for example, Rachael Berry, over an extended period of time taunted her husband with her love for another man. Finally, one evening after Rachael and Berry came home from a movie where they had petted heavily, Rachael said she wanted to have sexual intercourse. But when they got into bed, she announced she had changed her mind because "I am saving myself for Yako, so I don't think I will." Berry became so enraged that he choked Rachael. The California Supreme Court held:

In the present condition of our law it is left to the jurors to say whether the facts and circumstances in evidence are sufficient to lead them to believe that the defendant did, or to create a reasonable doubt in their minds as to whether or not he did, commit his offense under the heat of passion. . . . There is no specific type of provocation required. . . . [V]erbal provocation may be sufficient. . . .[33]

According to the common law **paramour rule,** a husband who caught his wife in the act of adultery had adequate provocation to kill: "There could be no greater provocation than this." Many cases have held that it is voluntary manslaughter for a husband to kill his wife, her paramour, or both in the first heat of passion following the sight of the wife's adultery." Some statutes went further than the common-law rule and called paramour killings justifiable homicide. The paramour rule did not apply to both spouses. Wives could not claim it; only husbands benefited from it. Also, the rule applied only to cases in which husbands caught their wives in the act of adultery. Husbands who killed upon learning second hand of the adultery instead of witnessing it when it occurred were not entitled to the benefit of the rule. The case of *Commonwealth v. Schnopps* deals with adultery as adequate provocation.[34]

CASE

Did She Adequately Provoke Him?

Commonwealth v. Schnopps,
383 Mass. 178, 417 N.E.2d 1213 (1981)

Schnopps was convicted of the first-degree murder of his estranged wife and of unlawfully carrying a firearm. He appealed. The Supreme Judicial Court of Massachusetts held that the evidence was sufficient to require an instruction on voluntary manslaughter, and the refusal to give such an instruction was reversible error. The judgment of the trial court was reversed, the verdict set aside, and the case remanded for a new trial. The appeal from the judgment on the firearms conviction was dismissed. Justice Abrams wrote the opinion for the court.

FACTS

On October 13, 1979, Marilyn R. Schnopps was fatally shot by her estranged husband, George A. Schnopps. A jury convicted Schnopps of murder in the first degree, and he was sentenced to the mandatory term of life imprisonment. Schnopps claims that the trial judge erred by refusing to instruct the jury on voluntary manslaughter. We agree. We reverse and order a new trial.

Schnopps testified that his wife had left him three weeks prior to the slaying. He claims that he first became aware of problems in his fourteen-year marriage at a point about six months before the slaying. According to the defendant, on that occasion he took his wife to a club to dance, and she spent the evening dancing with a coworker. On arriving home, the defendant and his wife argued over her conduct. She told him that she no longer loved him and that she wanted a divorce. Schnopps became very upset. He admitted that he took out his shotgun during the course of this argument, but he denied that he intended to use it. During the next few months, Schnopps argued frequently with his wife. The defendant accused her of seeing another man, but she steadfastly denied the accusations. On more than one occasion Schnopps threatened his wife with physical harm. He testified he never intended to hurt his wife but only wanted to scare her so that she would end the relationship with her coworker.

One day in September, 1979, the defendant became aware that the suspected boy friend used a "signal" in telephoning Schnopps' wife. Schnopps used the signal, and his wife answered the phone with "Hi, Lover." She hung up immediately when she recognized Schnopps' voice. That afternoon she did not return home. Later that evening, she informed Schnopps by telephone that she had moved to her mother's house and that she had the children with her. She told Schnopps she would not return to their home. Thereafter she "froze [him] out," and would not talk to him. During this period, the defendant spoke with a lawyer about a divorce and was told that he had a good chance of getting custody of the children, due to his wife's "desertion and adultery."

On the day of the killing, Schnopps had asked his wife to come to their home and talk over their marital difficulties. Schnopps told his wife that he wanted his children at home, and that he wanted the family to remain intact. Schnopps cried during the conversation, and begged his wife to let the children live with him and to keep their family together. His wife replied, "No, I am going to court, you are going to give me all the furniture, you are going to have to get the Hell out of here, you won't have nothing." Then, pointing to her crotch, she said, "You will never touch this again, because I have got something bigger and better for it."

On hearing those words, Schnopps claims that his mind went blank, and that he went "berserk." He went to a cabinet and got out a pistol he had bought and loaded the day before, and he shot his wife and himself. When he "started coming to" as a result of the pain she asked him to summon help. The victim

was pronounced dead at the scene, and the defendant was arrested and taken to the hospital for treatment of his wound.

OPINION

The issue raised by Schnopps' appeal is whether in these circumstances the judge was required to instruct the jury on voluntary manslaughter. Instructions on voluntary manslaughter must be given if there is evidence of provocation deemed adequate in law to cause the accused to lose his self control in the heat of passion, and if the killing followed the provocation before sufficient time had elapsed for the accused's temper to cool. A verdict of voluntary manslaughter requires the trier of fact to conclude that there is a causal connection between the provocation, the heat of passion, and the killing.

Schnopps argues that "[t]he existence of sufficient provocation is not foreclosed absolutely because a defendant learns of a fact from oral statements rather than from personal observation," and that a sudden admission of adultery is equivalent to a discovery of the act itself, and is sufficient evidence of provocation. Schnopps asserts that his wife's statements constituted a "peculiarly immediate and intense offense to a spouse's sensitivities." He concedes that the words at issue are indicative of past as well as present adultery. Schnopps claims, however, that his wife's admission of adultery was made for the first time on the day of the killing, and hence the evidence of provocation was sufficient to trigger jury consideration of voluntary manslaughter as a possible verdict.

The Commonwealth quarrels with the defendant's claim, asserting that the defendant knew of his wife's infidelity for some months, and hence the killing did not follow immediately upon the provocation. Therefore, the Commonwealth concludes, a manslaughter instruction would have been improper. The flaw in the Commonwealth's argument is that conflicting testimony and inferences from the evidence are to be resolved by the trier of fact, not the judge. . . .

Reversed and remanded for new trial on manslaughter issue.

QUESTIONS FOR DISCUSSION

1. The paramour rule was adopted to cover cases where husbands found their wives in bed with other men. The provocation was the sight of the adultery itself.

Thus, the passion was immediately connected to the adulterous act. If you were a juror, could you in good conscience say that Schnopps was adequately provoked?

2. If so, was it the adultery that provoked him or the provocative words his wife used to describe her adulterous relationship?

3. Do you think the prohibition against provocative words makes sense?

4. f you were writing a manslaughter law, how would you treat cases like Schnopps?

NOTE CASE

Jerry Elder and Lynn Mallas had an intimate relationship, but were never married. Mallas broke off the relationship and moved out of Elder's apartment some time in March or April of 1990. On June 2, 1990, Elder saw Mallas, her two year old daughter Angela, and her fiance, Tom Wicks, in an automobile. Elder, in a rented car, followed them to Wicks' apartment. Elder blocked Mallas's exit from the car, and they exchanged words. As Mallas tried to get past him, Elder shot her twice in the back, killing her in front of her two year old daughter. After seeing that Mallas was shot, Wicks fled on foot. Elder chased after Wicks and caught up to him when Wicks tripped and fell in a nearby field. Elder then shot Wicks in the chest. Wicks rolled onto his stomach, and Elder shot him again in the back. After Elder fled the scene, Wicks managed to return to his apartment and tell a neighbor to call the police. Wicks was seriously injured, but he survived.

Elder was convicted of first degree murder and of attempted first degree murder and sentenced to 60 years in prison. Elder claims that he was entitled to a second degree murder conviction (second degree murder has replaced manslughter in Illinois) because of adequate provocation. Do you agree? According to the Illinois Supreme Court:

. . . In Illinois, only four categories of provocation have been recognized as sufficiently serious to reduce the crime of first degree murder to second degree murder. They are: (1) substantial physical injury or assault; (2) mutual quarrel or combat; (3) illegal arrest; and (4) adultery with the offender's spouse. The defendant has the burden of establishing some evidence of serious provocation, or the trial court may properly deny a second degree murder instruction.

The facts of this case do not fall under any of the four categories of serious provocation recognized in Illinois. The first three categories clearly do not apply. Under the fourth category, there is obviously no evidence of adultery with the offender's spouse since the defendant and the victim were not married.

The defendant argues that this last category should be expanded to include the "special relationship" between the defendant and the victim. . . . [A]lthough Mallas and the defendant had previously enjoyed an intimate relationship, that relationship had ended two months before the homicide occurred. Additionally, there is no evidence in this case to suggest that the defendant was acting under a "sudden and intense passion". In fact, the evidence here suggests that the defendant literally stalked the murder victim. The defendant carried a loaded gun and followed Mallas in a rented car. This conduct suggests that he was not suddenly provoked when he shot Mallas, but rather that he was completing a contemplated plan. The trial court's decision not to instruct the jury on second degree murder was proper. *State v. Elder*, 579 N.E.2d 420 (Ill.App. 1991)

Adequate provocation means *reasonable* provocation. But reasonable to whom? Reasonableness can mean reasonable in the statistical sense; that is, how would the majority of people react under similar circumstances? Or, it can mean reasonable in a normative sense; that is, how should the person react under the circumstances, or how does the law expect people to react in these circumstances?

Sometimes defendants in special circumstances argue that the standard should be whether the circumstances would have provoked a reasonable person in their special category. In *People v. Washington*, for example, Merle Francis Washington shot his homosexual partner following a lover's quarrel, brought on by the unfaithfulness of the victim, Owen Wilson Brady. The court instructed the jury on provocation as follows:

[T]he jury was instructed that to reduce the homicide from murder to manslaughter upon the ground of sudden quarrel or heat of passion, the conduct must be tested by the ordinarily reasonable man test. Defendant argues without precedent that to so instruct was error because, "Homosexuals are not at present a curiosity or a rare commodity. They are a distinct third sexual class between that of male and female, are present in almost every field of endeavor, and are fast achieving a guarded recognition not formerly accorded them. The heat of their passions in dealing with one another should not be tested by standards applicable to the average man or the average woman, since they are aberrant hybrids, with an obvious diminished capacity.

Defendant submits that since the evidence disclosed that he was acting as a servient homosexual during the period of his relationship with the victim, that his heat of passion should have been tested, either by a standard applicable to a female, or a standard applicable to the average homosexual, and that it was prejudicial error to instruct the jury to determine his heat of passion defense by standards applicable to the average male."

We do not agree:

In the present condition of our law it is left to the jurors to say whether or not the facts and circumstances in evidence are sufficient to lead them to believe that the defendant did, or to create a reasonable doubt in their minds as to whether or not he did, commit his offense under a heat of passion. The jury is further to be admonished and advised by the court that this heat of passion must be such a passion as would naturally be aroused in the mind of an ordinarily reasonable person under the given facts and circumstances, and that, consequently, no defendant may set up his own standard of conduct and justify or excuse himself because in fact his passions were aroused, unless further the jury believe that the facts and circumstances were sufficient to arouse the passions of the ordinarily reasonable man. Thus no man of extremely violent passion could so justify or excuse himself if the exciting cause be not adequate, nor could an excessively cowardly man justify himself unless the circumstances were such as to arouse the fears of the ordinarily courageous man. Still further, while the conduct of the defendant is to be measured by that of the ordinarily reasonable man placed in identical circumstances, the jury is properly to be told that the exciting cause must be such as would naturally tend to arouse the passion of the ordinarily reasonable man.[35]

Voluntary manslaughter requires not only adequate or reasonable provocation but also actual provocation. This means that the legally adequate provocation must also actually provoke the defendant. The provocation rule contains both objective and subjective dimensions. The provocations that the law recognizes as adequate make up the objective side of provocation; that these provocations in fact provoke the defendant is the subjective side.

At common law, and in most modern statutes, voluntary manslaughter requires killing in the "sudden heat of passion" with no "cooling off" period. The actual time between provocation and killing, whether seconds, hours, or even days, depends upon the facts of the individual case. Courts usually apply an objective test: Would a reasonable person under the same circumstances have had time to cool off? If defendants had reasonable time for their murderous rages to subside, the law views their killings as murders even if the provocations were adequate to reduce those killings to manslaughter had they taken place immediately following the provocations.

Using the same objective test, the time for cooling off may be considerable. In one case, a man's wife told him her father had raped her. The court ruled that the husband's passion had not reasonably cooled even after he walked all night to his father-in-law's house and killed him the next day! The court said the heinous combination of incest and rape was sufficient to keep a reasonable person in a murderous rage for at least several days.[36]

To prove voluntary manslaughter, the prosecution must prove a causal link between the provocation, passion, and killing. It is not voluntary manslaughter if I intend to kill an enemy, and, just as I am about to execute my intent, I find him in bed with my wife and use that as my excuse to kill. The provocation must cause the passion that leads to the killing.

Voluntary manslaughter, in summary, consists of the following elements:

1. intentional or purposeful killings that

2. occur in a sudden heat of passion

3. without time to cool off and that are

4. caused by reasonable and actual provocation.

Involuntary Manslaughter

Involuntary manslaughter is a form of criminal homicide in which the killers did not intend to cause the death of their victims. In involuntary manslaughter, deaths result from either reckless or negligent legal acts, or during the commission of illegal acts. The **misdemeanor manslaughter rule** addresses the latter case: According to this rule, if death occurs during the commission of a misdemeanor, the misdemeanant has committed involuntary manslaughter. The misdemeanor manslaughter rule is the counterpart to the felony-murder doctrine. Courts vary as to the kinds of unlawful acts that qualify for the misdemeanor manslaughter doctrine. Most include breaches of public order, injuries to persons or property, and offenses against public decency and morals. Examples include nonfelonious assault, carrying a concealed weapon, driving illegally, and illegally dispensing drugs.

The court applied the misdemeanor manslaughter rule in *Commonwealth v. Feinberg.*

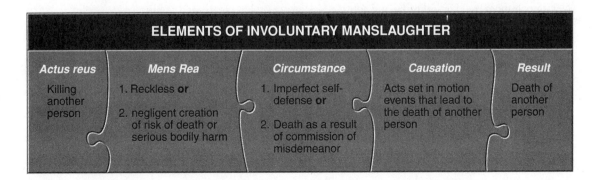

ELEMENTS OF INVOLUNTARY MANSLAUGHTER				
Actus reus	*Mens Rea*	*Circumstance*	*Causation*	*Result*
Killing another person	1. Reckless **or** 2. negligent creation of risk of death or serious bodily harm	1. Imperfect self-defense **or** 2. Death as a result of commission of misdemeanor	Acts set in motion events that lead to the death of another person	Death of another person

C A S E

Did He "Kill" the Victims?

Commonwealth v. Feinberg, 433 Pa. 558, 253 A.2d 636 (1969)

Feinberg was convicted of involuntary manslaughter in the Quarter Sessions Court, Philadelphia County. The Superior Court affirmed the conviction. Feinberg appealed. The Pennsylvania Supreme Court affirmed the conviction.

Justice Jones wrote the opinion for the court.

FACTS

Appellant Max Feinberg owned and operated a cigar store in the skid-row section of Philadelphia. One of the products he sold was Sterno, a jelly-like substance composed primarily of methanol and ethanol and designed for cooking and heating purposes. Sterno was manufactured and sold in two types of containers, one for home use and one for industrial use. Before September, 1963, both types of Sterno contained approximately 3.75% Methanol, or wood alcohol, and 71% Ethanol, or grain alcohol; of the two types of alcohols, methanol is far more toxic if consumed internally. Beginning in September of 1963, the Sterno company began manufacturing a new type of industrial Sterno which was 54% Methanol. The cans containing the new industrial Sterno were identical to the cans containing the old industrial Sterno except in one crucial aspect: on the lids of the new 54% Methanol Sterno were imprinted the words 'Institutional Sterno. Danger. Poison. For use only as a Fuel. Not for consumer use. For industrial and commercial use. Not for home use.' A skull and crossbones were also lithographed on the lid. The carton in which the new Sterno cans were packaged and shipped did not indicate that the contents differed in any respect from the old industrial Sterno.

According to its records, Sterno Corporation sent only one shipment of the new Sterno to the Philadelphia area; that shipment went to the Richter Paper Company and was received on December 17, 1963. Charles Richter, president of the firm, testified that

his company, in turn, made only one sale of the new industrial Sterno, and that was to appellant. Richter testified that his records indicated that appellant received the Sterno on December 21 and, since Richter had not opened any of the cartons, he was unaware that he was selling appellant a new type of industrial Sterno. On December 27, Richter received a call from appellant informing him that the cartons contained a new type of Sterno and that appellant wished to return the portion of his order that he had not sold. The unused cartons were picked up by Richter's deliveryman the next day.

Meanwhile, between December 21 and December 28, appellant had sold approximately 400 cans of the new industrial Sterno. Between December 28 and December 30, thirty-one persons died in the skid-row area as a result of methanol poisoning. In many of the cases the source of the methanol was traced to the new industrial Sterno. Since appellant was the only retail outlet of this type of Sterno in Philadelphia, he was arrested and indicted on thirty-one counts charging involuntary manslaughter and on companion bills charging violations of the Pharmacy Act (Act of September 27, 1961, P.L. 1700, § 1 et seq., 63 P.S. § 390—1 et seq.)

[COURT NOTE: Section 9 of the Act, dealing with poisons, states in pertinent part:

(a) Poison means and includes the compositions of the following schedules: Schedule 'B.'

(12) Methyl alcohol or formaldehyde, and preparations containing one per centum or more of these compounds, except when used as a preservative and not sold to the general public.

(d) No person shall sell, distribute or furnish, either directly or indirectly, except on prescription, any poisons enumerated in Schedules 'A' and 'B' . . . unless there is affixed a poison label to the package, box, bottle or paper, in which the poison is contained. The word 'poison' shall be distinctly shown on said label, together with the name of said place of business of the seller, all of which shall be printed in red ink. In addition the name of such poison shall be printed or written thereupon in clear print. (e) No person shall sell, distribute or furnish any poison named in Schedule 'A' or 'B' . . . unless on inquiry it is found that the person desiring it is aware of its poisonous character and it satisfactorily appears that the poison is to be used for a legitimate purpose.

(i) Any person violating any of the provisions of this section is guilty of a misdemeanor. . . .]

Appellant was convicted on seventeen counts of involuntary manslaughter and on twenty-five counts of violating the Pharmacy Act by Judge Charles L. Guerin, sitting without a jury. Judge Guerin held that appellant had violated the Pharmacy Act and that, therefore, he was guilty of a misdemeanor-manslaughter in each of the seventeen cases. Five of the manslaughter convictions were appealed to the Superior Court which affirmed four of them, although on a different theory. *Commonwealth v. Feinberg*, 211 Pa.Super. 100, 234 A.2d 913 (1967). In writing for a six-judge majority, Judge Montgomery held that appellant had not violated the Pharmacy Act and, therefore, was not guilty of a misdemeanor-manslaughter, but that the evidence justified the conclusion that appellant was guilty of involuntary manslaughter. Judge Hoffman dissented, maintaining that the Superior Court should not affirm the convictions on the grounds of involuntary manslaughter when the trial court had apparently rested its decision solely on the violation of the Pharmacy Act.

OPINION

[The parts of the opinion deciding that Feinberg did not violate the Pharmacy Act are omitted.]

The second issue in this case is whether appellant is guilty of involuntary manslaughter in each or any of the four appeals presently before us. The Penal Code defines involuntary manslaughter as a death 'happening in consequence of an unlawful act, or the doing of a lawful act in an unlawful way. . . .' (Act of June 24, 1939, P.L. 872, § 703, 18 P.S. § 4703) Since we have determined that appellant did not violate the Pharmacy Act in selling the new industrial Sterno, the second portion of this statutory definition must be controlling.

When a death results from the doing of an act lawful in itself but done in an unlawful manner, in order to sustain a conviction for manslaughter the Commonwealth must present evidence to prove that the defendant acted in a rash or reckless manner. The conduct of the defendant resulting in the death must be such a departure from the behavior of an ordinary and prudent man as to evidence a disregard of human life or an indifference to the consequences. Furthermore, there must be a direct causal relationship between the defendant's act and the deceased's death. . . .

We have searched in vain for cases from this Commonwealth involving factual situations similar to the one now before us. We have, however, found four cases from other jurisdictions which are on point. In the leading case, *Thiede v. State*, 106 Neb. 48, 182 N.W. 570 (1921), the defendant gave the deceased moonshine containing methanol, the drinking of which resulted in his death. While noting that the defendant had violated the state prohibition laws, the court refused to rest the manslaughter conviction on this statutory violation, holding that the manufacturing and distribution of moonshine was merely *malum prohibitum* and not malum per se. The court continued,

> We cannot go so far as to say that (dispensing moonshine), prompted perhaps by the spirit of good-fellowship, though prohibited by law, could ever, by any resulting consequence, be converted into the crime of manslaughter; but, where the liquor by reason of its extreme potency or poisonous ingredients, is dangerous to use as an intoxicating beverage, where the drinking of it is capable of producing direct physical injury, other than as an ordinary intoxicant, and of perhaps endangering life itself, the case is different, and the question of negligence enters; for, if the party furnishing the liquor knows, or was apprised of such facts that he should have known, of the danger, there then appears from his act a recklessness which is indifferent to results. Such recklessness in the furnishing of intoxicating liquors, in violation of law, may constitute such an unlawful act as, if it results in causing death, will constitute manslaughter.

We conclude, after studying the record, that appellant fits within the blackletter rule laid down in *Thiede* and that the Commonwealth has made out all the elements necessary to warrant a conviction for involuntary manslaughter.

First, the record establishes that appellant sold the Sterno with the knowledge that at least some of his customers would extract the alcohol for drinking purposes. Witnesses for the Commonwealth testified that when they purchased the Sterno from appellant, they would merely say 'make one' or hold up fingers to indicate how many cans they wanted; one witness testified that appellant referred to the Sterno as shoe polish and on one occasion shouted to him on the street asking how he and his wife were making out with their shoe polish; finally, the witnesses testified that appellant asked them to conceal the Sterno under their coats when leaving his store. Such conduct does not square with the conclusion that appellant was merely selling the Sterno for cooking and heating purposes. Second, appellant was aware, or should have been aware, that the Sterno he was selling was toxic if consumed. The new industrial Sterno was clearly marked as being poisonous. Even the regular Sterno is marked 'Caution. Flammable. For Use only as a Fuel' and if consumed internally may have serious consequences.

Furthermore, when appellant was informed about the first deaths from methanol poisoning, he told the boy who worked in his shop to tell any police who came around that there was no Sterno in the store. Appellant also told police that he had never purchased any Sterno from the Richter Paper Company. This evidence indicates to us that appellant was aware that he was selling the Sterno for an illicit purpose.

Appellant presses several contentions for our consideration. First, he claims that the Commonwealth has not established the necessary causal link between the sale of the Sterno and the deaths. We cannot agree. First, appellant sold the Sterno knowing, or having reason to know, that some of his customers would consume it. Second, some of his customers did consume the new industrial Sterno and died as a result. The Commonwealth's expert toxicologist testified that in several of the cases death could only have resulted from consumption of the new as opposed to the regular Sterno. Since appellant was the only retail outlet for the new Sterno in Philadelphia, these persons must have died from drinking Sterno purchased in appellant's store.

Third . . . the defendant [cannot be] held criminally responsible for the deceased's death . . . [unless there is a] direct causal connection between the defendant's act . . . and the deceased's death. The court in *Thiede*, in answering an argument similar to the one now made by appellant, stated: 'Defendant contends that the drinking of liquor, by deceased was his voluntary act and served as an intervening cause, breaking the causal connection between the giving of the liquor by defendant and the resulting death. The drinking of the liquor, in consequence of defendant's act, was, however, what the defendant contemplated. Deceased, it is true, may have been negligent in drinking, but, where the defendant was negligent, then the contributory negligence of the deceased will be no defense in a criminal action.'

Appellant next criticizes the following sentence in Judge Montgomery's opinion:

> In the light of the recognized weaknesses of the purchasers of the product, and appellant's greater concern for profit than with the results of his actions, he was grossly negligent and demonstrated a wanton and reckless disregard for the welfare of those whom he might reasonably have expected to use the product for drinking purposes.'

Appellant argues that the Superior Court is here imposing an inequitable burden on sellers of Sterno by requiring them to recognize the 'weaknesses' of their customers. Appellant has exaggerated the import of this sentence. The Superior Court was not imposing a duty on all sellers of Sterno to determine how their customers will use the product. The Court was merely saying that if a seller of Sterno is aware that the purchaser is an alcoholic and will use Sterno as a source of alcohol, then the seller is grossly negligent and wantonly reckless in selling Sterno to him. We do not think this imposes an intolerable burden on sellers of Sterno.

Finally, appellant maintains that in at least one of the four convictions, the evidence indicated that the deceased purchased the Sterno from appellant's helper and that appellant had not sanctioned the sale. Appellant maintains that he cannot receive a prison sentence for such vicarious liability, citing *Commonwealth v. Koczwara*, 397 Pa. 575, 155 A.2d 825 (1959), cert. denied, 363 U.S. 848, 80 S.Ct. 1624, 4 L.Ed. 1731 (1960). In that case, this Court struck down a three-month prison sentence meted out for a second violation of the liquor code where it appeared that the defendant's bartender had sold liquor to minors without the knowledge or consent of the defendant. *Koczwara* is presently inapposite. While appellant may not have been present when some of the Sterno was sold, there is ample evidence in the record that he was aware of and condoned such sales.

We have carefully reviewed the evidence in each of the four cases before us and are convinced that the Commonwealth has met its burden of proof in each case. In three of the cases there is direct testimony that the deceased drank a beverage made from industrial Sterno purchased from the appellant and died as a result.

[COURT NOTE: "In the case of Juanita Williams, her common law husband testified that he purchased three unlabeled cans of Sterno from appellant's store on December 24 and took them home where his wife mixed the contents with water. That night they both drank the mixture. Mrs. Williams died the next day and Mr. Williams eventually became blind. In the cases of John Streich, and James Newsome, a John Woods testified that he purchased Sterno around this time from appellant's store and drank the contents along with the two deceased. Woods became sick immediately and was taken to the hospital where his stomach was pumped — apparently saving his life. The next day Streich and Newsome were found dead."]

In the fourth case the evidence is more circumstantial. The deceased died of methanol poisoning which would be consistent with the consumption of only the new as opposed to the regular Sterno. An empty can of the industrial Sterno was found near his body. Appellant's employee identified the deceased as a regular customer of appellant but could not be certain if the deceased had purchased Sterno between December 21 and December 28. We feel, however, that there is sufficient circumstantial evidence to affirm this conviction also.

. . . In his opinion at the close of the trial, Judge Guerin made the following remarks

There is an abundance of evidence in this case which satisfies me beyond a reasonable doubt that the conduct of the defendant with respect

to all Bills of Indictment now remaining before me for disposition caused the death of the individuals named in the respective indictments. He proceeded without due caution. He was engaged in a business of selling a poisonous substance. He knew or should have known of the poisonous nature of the substance because in the majority, indeed, if not in all of the cases the container of the poisonous substance contained upon the lid thereof a warning in the shape of lettering stating that the contents were poison and containing the indication of danger which is known to all of us from early childhood, the familiar skull and crossbones.

In conclusion, we find that Judge Guerin did, in fact, consider the issue of involuntary manslaughter and did find appellant guilty of involuntary manslaughter.

Orders affirmed.

CONCURRING OPINION

ROBERTS, Justice (concurring).

Although I join in the opinion of the Court, I believe it is necessary to emphasize the controlling considerations which support the Court's holding that this case is an appropriate one for criminal sanctions. There can be little question that the record before us not only supports the findings of the court below but leads to the almost unalterable conclusion that appellant knew (or should have known) of the toxic nature of the product he was selling and knew of the exact use to which the Sterno would be put. Appellant was dealing with a product which when taken internally clearly was a dangerous instrumentality. By selling it to the persons to whom he sold it, knowing that they would use it in a way that was certain to cause serious harm to themselves, appellant exhibited the indifference to and reckless disregard for human life that is the classic element of the involuntary manslaughter offense. No causation problem is presented by the allegedly 'intervening' acts of the victims, since those acts are exactly what appellant knew would take place when he sold the Sterno to these customers.

In my view, it is crucial that this record presents no question whether appellant investigated — or was obligated to investigate — the use to which his customers would put the product. It is clear that appellant knew that the skid-row alcoholics to whom he dispensed the

Sterno would extract the alcohol for drinking purposes. As the majority correctly points out, our decision and the decisions below did not impose 'a duty on all sellers of Sterno to determine how their customers will use the product. The Court was merely saying that if a seller of Sterno is aware that the purchaser is an alcoholic and will use Sterno as a source of alcohol, then the seller is grossly negligent and wantonly reckless selling Sterno to him.'

QUESTIONS FOR DISCUSSION

1. What definition does the court give for involuntary manslaughter?

2. Is the *mens rea* negligence? Recklessness? Gross negligence? Or something else?

3. What are the relevant facts in the case to determine whether Feinberg was guilty of involuntary manslaughter?

4. If you were deciding the case, how would you define the *mens rea*?

5. Do the facts support a conviction, according to your definition?

6. Do you think the facts might support a *mens rea* more culpable than either negligence or recklessness, such as knowledge or even purpose?

7. What facts might support such a conclusion?

NOTE CASE

Dr. Youngkin wrote a prescription for three-grain-size tablets of Tuinal (twice the normal dosage of the barbiturate) for one of his patients, seventeen-year-old Barbara Fedder. She died of an overdose of Tuinal and the state charged and convicted Dr. Youngkin of involuntary manslaughter. The indictment charged that Fedder died as a "direct result of the reckless and grossly negligent manner in which he [Dr. Youngkin] prescribed the drug Tuinal." One pharmacist testified that

the decedent came into his store on one occasion, about a month before her death, in such a dazed and stuporous condition that she had to hold onto the cash register to maintain her balance. Leery of selling the decedent a prescription that would enhance her stuporous stage, the pharmacist telephoned appellant, described to him Ms. Fedder's condition, and queried whether it was advisable to fill the prescription in those circumstances. Appellant's response to the pharmacist was "fill the damn thing."

In upholding the conviction, the court held:

Our review of the evidence leads us to the conclusion that there was sufficient evidence to prove each element of involuntary manslaughter. The evidence indicates that appellant prescribed Tuinal to the decedent in quantities and frequencies termed irresponsible and totally inappropriate in the circumstances. The frequency with which the prescriptions were written should have suggested that the decedent was abusing Tuinal. Moreover, this fact was specifically brought to appellant's attention by a pharmacist who called appellant alarmed over the decedent's physical condition. However, appellant chose to ignore these indications of abuse and continued to prescribe the drug to decedent. In these circumstances the record supports and justifies the jury's conclusion that appellant consciously disregarded a substantial and unjustifiable risk, which disregard involved a gross deviation from the standard of conduct a reasonable person would have observed. *Commonwealth v. Youngkin*, 285 Pa.Super. 417, 427 A.2d 1356 (1981)

Negligent Homicide

Involuntary manslaughter includes not only reckless killings but also criminally negligent homicide. **Negligent homicides** are unintentional killings in which actors should have known they were creating substantial and unjustified risks of death by conduct that grossly deviated from ordinary care. The common law did not recognize these types of killings as involuntary manslaughters. However, statutes have brought within the scope of criminal law a variety of deaths caused by criminal negligence — criminal neg-

ELEMENTS OF NEGLIGENT HOMICIDE

Actus reus	Mens Rea	Circumstance	Causation	Result
Actions that cause the death of another person	Negligent creation of risk of death or serious bodily harm	Negligence in 1. use of firearms **or** 2. handling explosives **or** 3. practicing medicine **or** 4. operating vehicles	Actions that set in motion a chain of events leading to the death of another person	Death of another person

ligence homicide — including negligently using firearms, handling explosives, allowing vicious animals to run free, practicing medicine, and operating trains, planes, ships, and highway vehicles.

The most common criminal negligent homicide is death caused by negligent driving. Most states require gross negligence to convict drivers in fatal accidents. **Gross criminal negligence** is

> very great negligence or absence of even slight care, but as not equivalent to wanton and willful wrong. . . . Gross negligence is substantially and appreciably higher in magnitude than ordinary negligence.[37]

A few states have adopted special vehicular homicide statutes that reduce the culpability required in driving deaths to something less than gross negligence. According to one court,

> [b]y the enactment of this [vehicular homicide] statute, the Legislature obviously intended to create a lesser offense than involuntary manslaughter . . . where the negligent killing was caused by the operation of a vehicle. . . . Therefore, this statute was intended to apply only to cases where the negligence is of a lesser degree than gross negligence.[38]

Under this scheme, if drivers' reckless or grossly negligent driving causes death, they have committed involuntary manslaughter. If the death resulted from less than gross negligence, but more than the ordinary negligence required for civil liability, the driver has committed vehicular homicide.

In effect, then, three degrees of negligence govern liability in negligent homicides:

1. Gross negligence for liability in involuntary manslaughter;

2. Less than gross but still criminal negligence for liability in vehicular homicide;

3. Ordinary carelessness for civil liability in wrongful death actions.

A fine line separates the gross negligence and recklessness required for involuntary manslaughter, and the criminal (but not gross) negligence required for vehicular homicide liability. Nevertheless, courts and numerous statutes use the distinction anyway. Fact finders, whether juries or judges, are left to apply the definition or standard to the particular facts of the cases before them. Hence, although criminal recklessness, gross and lesser criminal negligence, and ordinary negligence are difficult to quantify, they nonetheless determine how to grade conduct resulting in death.

The reason for the complex grading of vehicular homicide is practical. Juries are frequently reluctant to convict drivers in fatal car accident cases of manslaughter. They are more willing to convict the drivers of vehicular homicide because the penalties are milder and the stigma less than they are for convictions for manslaughter. In line with this thinking, some states have included vehicular homicide in their motor vehicle or traffic codes, rather than placing it in the criminal code sections.[39]

Neither legislatures, courts, nor juries extend the same leniency to fatal accidents involving drunken drivers. Thirteen states have, in fact, called deaths resulting from drunk driving murder. In *State v. Gibson*, the Louisiana Court of appeal dealt with both the elements of vehicular homicide and the proper sentence for it.[40]

C A S E

Was She Guilty of Vehicular Homicide?

State v. Gibson,
1997 WL 209702 (1997 La.App. 3 Cir.)

Bridgette Gibson was charged by a grand jury with vehicular homicide, a violation of La.R.S. 14:32.1. A trial by jury was held on September 24, 1996, with the jury returning a verdict of guilty as charged. The defendant was subsequently sentenced to serve a term of nine years at hard labor, with one year of the sentence being without the benefit of probation, parole, or suspension of sentence. Additionally, she was ordered to participate in a court-approved substance abuse program and a court-approved driver improvement program. After her motion to reconsider sentence was denied, the defendant appealed her conviction and sentence. The Court of Appeal affirmed.

PETERS, Judge.

FACTS

The automobile accident giving rise to this criminal charge occurred on Interstate Highway 49 (I49) in Opelousas, Louisiana, in the early evening of March 17, 1996. A vehicle being driven north on I49 by the defendant crossed the grassy median separating the north and south lanes of the interstate, became airborne, and collided with a southbound vehicle being driven by Miranda Marie Ross, a twenty-year old nursing student. Ms. Ross was pronounced dead at the scene. The defendant had been drinking heavily before the accident, and three hours after the accident, her blood-alcohol concentration was 0.17 percent by weight based upon grams of alcohol per 100 cubic centimeters of blood. It is not disputed that the defendant was under the influence of alcohol at the time of the accident.

There is also little dispute concerning the events leading up to the accident. On the afternoon of the accident the defendant met her friend, Michelle Roberts, in Opelousas at Ms. Roberts's mother's home, and the two women began an evening of riding around and consuming alcohol. According to Ms. Roberts, the defendant arrived with a beer in her hand. Ms. Roberts testified that she and the defendant first traveled to the defendant's home to put oil in the defendant's car. A party was in progress next door, and the two women were given a cup of gin. This gin was mixed with a bottle of Thunderbird wine purchased at an Opelousas service station, and the two women consumed the mixture as they drove around. Their travels next took them to Washington, Louisiana, where they attended a local fair and visited with the defendant's father, Chief of Police John Offord. Despite Chief Offord's warning not to drink and drive, the two women purchased a fifth of Thunderbird wine before leaving Washington and consumed it as they continued their travels. According to Ms. Roberts, another fifth of Thunderbird wine was purchased at a service station in Sunset, Louisiana, and a final bottle of the wine was purchased in Lafayette, Louisiana.

According to Ms. Roberts, the two women were drinking from large mugs which each held one-half of a fifth of wine and as they purchased the wine, they would pour it into the mugs and throw away the bottles. Ms. Roberts testified that she and the defendant were sharing the alcohol equally and that by the time they reached Gerard Park in Lafayette, they had drunk all but the fourth fifth of wine. According to Ms. Roberts, they then consumed the last of the alcohol at the park and proceeded toward home because the defendant was scheduled to be home before dark to help her daughter make a poster for school. Ms. Roberts admitted that she was "drunk" when the two women left the Lafayette park.

The defendant testified that she did not have a beer in her possession when she met Ms. Roberts and that she only had one beer before that time. Additionally, she testified that she only had a "taste" of the gin. While not agreeing entirely with Ms. Roberts's testimony, the defendant did admit that she helped to consume at least a pint and two fifths of Thunderbird wine from the time she and Ms. Roberts began their spree until the time of the accident. Despite her consumption of this wine, she testified that she did not have as much to drink as Ms. Roberts because she had not refilled her glass every time Ms. Roberts had refilled hers. She did acknowledge that immediately before the accident, she felt "woozy," which to her meant that she was not sober but was not drunk either.

Neither the defendant nor Ms. Roberts had an explanation for the accident. Ms. Roberts testified that she was sleepy and had begun to doze. She recalled that the defendant was traveling in the left lane of the interstate and was northbound. Immediately before the accident, she felt the automobile vibrate but did not recall crossing the median or striking the victim's vehicle. In fact, after feeling the vibration, the next thing she remembered was being upside down in the wrecked vehicle and held up only by her seat belt.

Jarrett Deville of Scott, Louisiana, was an eyewitness to the accident, which, according to him, occurred just as it was turning dark. He was traveling south on I49, and Ms. Ross had gradually passed him in the left lane immediately before the accident. Mr. Deville testified that he observed vehicle lights in the northbound lane of I49 "kinda moving erratically . . . . from side to side, going up and down, kinda going in and out the lane." He further testified that he observed the defendant's vehicle leave the northbound roadway, reenter the northbound roadway, exit again, and finally cross over the median. According to Mr. Deville, when the vehicle crossed over the median, it went airborne and crashed into the windshield of Ms. Ross's vehicle. Mr. Deville testified that immediately after the accident, the defendant expressed to him that she thought that Ms. Ross had hit her. Mr. Deville did not observe any other cars in the vicinity of the defendant before the collision, and the defendant did not complain to him of any mechanical or tire failure that may have caused the collision.

. . .

Dr. Sylvan Manuel, the coroner for St. Landry Parish, testified concerning Ms. Ross's fatal injuries and also concerning how alcohol affects perception. It was his professional opinion that alcohol, as a depressant, could make someone react slowly and could give a false sense of confidence which could cause a person to take chances she would not ordinarily take. Regarding whether the defendant's level of intoxication could have been a contributing factor to the collision, Dr. Manuel stated: "It's my professional opinion that from the cops, I learned from them, and what I saw this morning, that this lady with a .17 alcohol could have done all of this. . . . I would expect it, it wouldn't be unusual for her to do this." He further testified that he would have expected the defendant's level of intoxication to be a contributing factor in the accident.

. . .

OPINION

In her appeal, the defendant asserts four assignments of error:

1. The state failed to prove beyond a reasonable doubt that the defendant's blood-alcohol concentration combined with her operation of a vehicle to cause the death of the victim; therefore, the jury verdict finding the defendant guilty of vehicular homicide fails to meet the legal standard for sufficiency of the evidence.

2. [Not included in this excerpt.]

3. The trial court erred in failing to balance its expressed sympathy for the victim with acceptable penal goals in sentencing the defendant.

4. The sentence imposed by the trial court is unconstitutionally excessive and constitutes cruel and unusual punishment.

For the reasons set forth below, we find these assignments to be without merit and affirm the defendant's conviction and sentence.

The defendant first contends that the state failed to prove beyond a reasonable doubt that her blood-alcohol concentration, combined with her operation of the vehicle, caused the death of Miranda Marie Ross. . . . The crime of vehicular homicide is defined by La.R.S. 14:32.1, which reads in pertinent part as follows:

A. Vehicular homicide is the killing of a human being caused proximately or caused directly by an offender engaged in the operation of, or in actual physical control of, any motor vehicle, aircraft, vessel, or other means of conveyance whether or not the offender had the intent to cause death or great bodily harm whenever any one of the following conditions exists:

  (1) The operator is under the influence of alcoholic beverages as determined by chemical tests administered under the provisions of R.S. 32:662.

  (2) The operator's blood alcohol concentration is 0.08 percent or more by weight based upon grams of alcohol per one hundred cubic centimeters of blood.

  (3) The operator is under the influence of any controlled dangerous substance listed in Schedule I, II, III, IV, or V as set forth in R.S. 40:964.

The Louisiana Supreme Court has held that "under the vehicular homicide statute, the state, in order to convict, must prove that an offender's unlawful blood alcohol concentration combined with his operation of a vehicle to cause the death of a human being." *State v. Taylor*, 463 So.2d 1274, 1275 (La.1985). "It is insufficient for the state to prove merely that the alco-

hol consumption 'coincides' with the accident." *State v. Archer*, 619 So.2d 1071, 1074 (La.App. 1 Cir.), writ denied, 626 So.2d 1178 (La.1993).

While acknowledging that her blood-alcohol concentration exceeded the limits of La.R.S. 14:32.1(2), the defendant contends that she left the roadway, not because she was under the influence of alcohol, but because she was trying to pick up a cassette tape off of the floor of her vehicle. In her testimony, she speculated that she "probably ran off the road or something" as she tried to retrieve the tape.

After viewing the evidence in the light most favorable to the prosecution, we conclude that any rational trier of fact could have found the essential elements of vehicular homicide proven beyond a reasonable doubt. The state established beyond a reasonable doubt that a human being was killed, that the death was caused directly by the defendant's operation of a motor vehicle, and that the defendant's blood alcohol-concentration exceeded 0.08 percent by weight based upon grams of alcohol per 100 cubic centimeters of blood. Additionally, we find that the state proved beyond a reasonable doubt that the defendant's intoxication or alcohol level was a contributing factor of the accident. The trial court found no evidence of the involvement of any other factor, such as a third vehicle, mechanical failure, or a highway condition that would have been an intervening cause. We agree with that determination.

. . .

The last two assignments of error relate to the defendant's sentence. The defendant claims that the trial court erred in failing to balance its expressed sympathy for the victim with acceptable penal goals in sentencing her and that the sentence imposed is unconstitutionally excessive and constitutes cruel and unusual punishment.

La.R.S. 14:32.1(B) provides:

Whoever commits the crime of vehicular homicide shall be fined not less than two thousand dollars nor more than fifteen thousand dollars and shall be imprisoned with or without hard labor for not less than two years nor more than fifteen years. At least one year of the sentence of imprisonment shall be imposed without benefit of probation, parole, or suspension of sentence. The court shall require the offender to participate in a court-approved substance abuse or a court-approved driver improvement program, or both.

Thus, the defendant's nine-year sentence was in the mid to high range of the applicable sentence for this crime.

We find that the case sub judice [under adjudication] is very similar to *State v. Trahan*, 93 1116 (La.App. 1 Cir. 5/20/94); 637 So.2d 694, wherein the defendant received three concurrent ten-year terms at hard labor after being convicted of three counts of vehicular homicide. The defendant was considered a first felony offender, having never received even a speeding ticket, but the trial court found his lack of remorse and lack of interest in the victims to be aggravating factors. The twenty-two-year-old defendant had a three-year-old son, and his wife was expecting another child. The court found it extremely disturbing that the defendant was observed drinking at a bar and driving away while on bail, awaiting trial on the case. The sentences were affirmed on appeal.

In the case sub judice, the defendant admitted that she had driven while drinking before this incident, and between arraignment and trial, she was arrested and pled no contest to disturbing the peace by being drunk. During sentencing, the trial court stated:

Some of the factors that I've had to consider in reaching the sentence that I am getting ready to impose upon the defendant, were not only . . . the horror of the offense. The statute creates the intoxication level at .08. In this case my recollection is that the intoxication level was .17, which is double the level provided by the statute. The evidence was also to the effect . . . that I believe that this was the results of a test that was given I want to say two or three hours after the incident. It doesn't take a rocket scientist to figure out. I know they've got a formula. I'm not smart enough to work the formula or even to quote the formula, but there is a formula that would certainly indicate to me that the .17 was obviously higher than that at the time of this accident. There is information in the file that is what I call the inherent contradiction in the life of the defendant. Ms. Gibson is thirty-three years of age. She's married and has four young minor children. Apparently, a bright young person; two years of college education, graduated, and I guess it's coincidental also, graduated in the top of her class in nursing at T.H. Harris. Yet, she's had no meaningful employment since 1986. Apparently she's had some problems with alcohol, beer, wine, gin. Also, apparently some trial and error with marijuana. Ms. Gibson, you've also apparently had some problem with alcohol since this incident. Although it was not a traffic matter, apparently a disturbing the peace that you entered a plea of guilty to.

The supreme court recently reversed this court's vacation of a nine-year sentence for vehicular homicide and reinstated the sentence in *State v. Cook*, 952784 (La.5/31/96); 674 So.2d 957, cert. denied, U.S., 117 S.Ct. 615, 136 L.Ed.2d 539 (1996). In that case, the defendant was a single mother, maintained gainful employment, and had no prior felony conviction specifically related to alcohol abuse or operation of a vehicle.

In *State v. Green*, 418 So.2d 609 (La.1982), the court found that concurrent sentences of three years at hard labor for two counts of negligent homicide, a five-year felony offense, were not excessive, although the defendant was a hardworking single mother with no criminal record.

The defendant's sentence is in the mid to high range of sentencing possibilities and is not excessive considering the circumstances of the crime. The defendant had been drinking almost all day, then drove from Opelousas to Lafayette and back even after being warned to not drink and drive by her father. She remembers nothing of the accident. The impact was so great that Ms. Ross was killed instantly and the engine and transmission flew out of the defendant's car. The defendant's lack of remorse and failure to refrain from drinking further justify the sentence. Therefore, the defendant's assignments of error relative to the sentence are without merit.

For the foregoing reasons, we affirm the defendant's conviction and sentence.

AFFIRMED.

QUESTIONS FOR DISCUSSION

1. Identify the elements of vehicular homicide in the Louisiana statute.

2. List all of the facts relevant to determining whether the prosecution proved each of the elements of vehicular homicide.

3. According to these facts, why did the court uphold Bridgette Gibson's conviction and sentence?

4. Assume you are the prosecutor. Argue for the conviction and sentence.

5. Assume you are Gibson's attorney. Argue for her acquittal, or at least a lesser sentence.

NOTE CASES

1. David Fleming drove his car on Virginia's George Washington Memorial Parkway between 70 and 100 mph in a 45-mph zone. At times he crossed the median of the divided highway to avoid police officers pursuing him and drove around the traffic coming in the opposite direction. Eventually he lost control of his vehicle, striking head on a car traveling in the opposite direction, killing the occupant. At the time of the collision he was traveling between 70 mph and 80 mph in a 30-mph zone. Police dragged Fleming from the wreckage of his car. At the hospital, his blood alcohol level was 0.315! In affirming Fleming's conviction for murder—not manslaughter—the court held:

   > Malice aforethought . . . is the distinguishing characteristic which, when present, makes a homicide murder rather than manslaughter. Whether malice is present or absent must be inferred by the jury from the whole facts and circumstances surrounding the killing. Proof of the existence of malice does not require a showing that the accused harbored hatred or ill will against the victim or others. Neither does it require proof of an intent to kill or injure. Malice may be established by evidence of conduct which is "reckless and wanton and a gross deviation from a reasonable standard of care, of such a nature that a jury is warranted in inferring that defendant was aware of a serious risk of death or serious bodily harm." To support a conviction for murder, the government need only have proved that defendant intended to operate his car in the manner in which he did with a heart that was without regard for the life and safety of others.

   We conclude that the evidence regarding defendant's conduct was adequate to sustain a finding by the jury that defendant acted with malice aforethought. . . . The difference between malice, which will support conviction for murder, and gross negligence, which will permit conviction only for manslaughter, is one of degree rather than kind. In the vast majority of vehicular homicides, the accused has not exhibited such wanton and reckless disregard for human life as to indicate the presence of malice on his part. In the present case, however, the facts show a deviation from established standards of regard for life and the safety of others that is markedly different in degree from that found in most vehicular homicides. In the average drunk driving homicide, there is no proof that the driver has acted while intoxicated with the purpose of wantonly and intentionally putting the lives of others in danger. Rather, his driving abilities were so impaired that he recklessly put others in danger simply by being on the road and attempting to do the things that any driver would do. In the present case, however, danger did not arise only by defendant's determining to drive while drunk. Rather, in addition to being intoxicated while driving, defendant drove in a manner that could be taken to indicate depraved disregard of human life, particularly in light of the fact that because he was drunk his reckless behavior was all the more dangerous. *United States v. Fleming,* 739 F.2d 945 (4th Cir. 1984)

2. Miller's semi tractor trailer collided with a vehicle, killing the driver and her two passengers. The roads were dry and in good condition; no drivers were drinking. An inspection of the truck, however, revealed defective brakes and failure by Miller to conduct regular brake checks of his truck, as federal regulations and state law required. A grand jury indicted Miller with vehicular homicide. A trial judge dismissed the indictment because of insufficient evidence of "gross negligence." The trial court found:

   > The only conduct pointed to is Defendant's failure to inspect his brakes as required by Statute and Regulation which would have, presumably, revealed 50 percent braking capacity. Based upon the above principles of law the court finds that there is insufficient evidence to establish the offenses charged. . . . Because the court has determined that the evidence does not rise to the level

necessary to support a charge of gross negligence against Defendant, . . . the Indictment against Defendant [is] dismissed.

On appeal, the Minnesota Supreme Court affirmed the dismissal:

Gross negligence is substantially and appreciably higher in magnitude than ordinary negligence. It is materially more want of care than constitutes simple inadvertence. It is an act or omission respecting legal duty of an aggravated character as distinguished from a mere failure to exercise ordinary care. . . . But it is something less than the willful, wanton and reckless conduct which renders a defendant who has injured another liable to the latter even though guilty of contributory negligence, or which renders a defendant in rightful possession of real estate liable to a trespasser whom he has injured. *State v. Miller*, 471 N.W.2d 380 (Minn.App.1991)

SUMMARY

The following outline summarizes the complicated and intricate elements in criminal homicide.

I. Criminal homicide is divided into two main categories: murder and manslaughter.

II. Murder requires taking another's life with malice aforethought.

  A. The precise points at which life begins and ends for purposes of criminal homicide are difficult to determine.

  B. Malice aforethought includes five distinct mental states—the specific intent or purpose to do one of the following:

  1. Kill another person,

  2. Seriously injure another person,

  3. Forcibly resist a lawful arrest,

  4. Commit specified dangerous felonies,

  5. Create a higher than criminally reckless risk of death or serious bodily injury.

  C. Murder is divided into two degrees.

  1. First-degree murder:

    a. Premeditated, deliberate killings,

    b. Killings that take place while committing dangerous felonies (in some states),

    c. Particularly brutal or cruel murders (in some states).

  2. Second-degree murder:

    a. Killings resulting from the intent to do serious bodily injury,

    b. Killings resulting from the resisting of lawful arrest,

    c. Killings taking place during the commission of less serious felonies.

III. Manslaughter is either voluntary or involuntary.

  A. Voluntary manslaughter is the intentional killing of another in the following circumstances:

  1. Under provocation, where such provocation

    a. is actual and adequate,

    b. occurs in the heat of passion,

    c. occurs before an adequate cooling off period.

2. Where defendants believe they acted in self-defense but where it was unreasonable to do so.
   B. Involuntary manslaughter is the killing of another person unintentionally, either
      1. recklessly or
      2. with gross criminal negligence
      3. while committing certain misdemeanors.
   C. Negligent homicide is causing death by less than gross negligence. It is usually deaths related to the operation of vehicles.

REVIEW QUESTIONS

1. Relate each of the elements of criminal homicide to each of the general principles of criminal liability.

2. What are the problems with defining life for purposes of the law of criminal homicide?

3. Explain all of the types of *mens rea* associated with the law of criminal homicide and what effect *mens rea* has on the law of criminal homicide.

4. What is included within the definition of first-degree murder? Relate the kinds of first-degree murders to the general principles of criminal liability involved in each type.

5. According to the modern law of homicide, what are the definitions of premeditated killings and deliberate killings?

6. Define the types and the elements of second-degree murder.

7. Define and discuss the problems and limitations associated with felony murder.

8. What are the main problems with applying murder statutes to corporations?

9. Identify and describe the elements of voluntary manslaughter and relate them to the general principles of criminal liability.

10. Identify and describe the elements of involuntary manslaughter and relate them to the general principles of criminal liability.

11. Identify and describe the elements of vehicular homicide and relate them to the general principles of criminal liability.

KEY TERMS

adequate provocation rule The rule that only certain defined circumstances will reduce murder to voluntary manslaughter.

capital murder First-degree murders for which the penalty is either death or life imprisonment.

criminal negligence homicides Deaths resulting from action actors should have known, but did not know, would cause death or serious bodily harm.

deliberate The requirement in murder *mens rea* that killings must be committed with a cool, reflecting mind.

felony-murder doctrine The rule that deaths occurring during the commission of felonies are murders.

fetal death statutes Laws defining when life begins for purposes of the law of criminal homicide.

first-degree murder Premeditated, deliberate killings and other particularly heinous capital murders.

gross criminal negligence Very great negligence; actions without even slight care but not amounting to intentional or conscious wrongdoing.

homicide The killing of one live human being by another.

involuntary manslaughter Criminal homicides caused either by recklessness or gross criminal negligence.

malice aforethought The common law designation for murder *mens rea* that covered a broad range of states of mind.

misdemeanor manslaughter rule The rule that deaths occurring during the commission of misdemeanors are manslaughter.

negligent homicide Unintentional killings in which actors should have known they were creating substantial and unjustified risks of death by conduct that grossly deviated from ordinary care.

paramour rule The rule that a husband's witnessing his wife in the act of adultery is adequate provocation to reduce murder to manslaughter.

premeditated The requirement in first-degree murder *mens rea* that killings must be planned in advance.

reckless or **"depraved heart" murder** Deaths resulting from purposely or consciously creating sub-

stantial and unjustifiable risks that someone will either die or suffer serious injury.

second-degree murder A catchall offense including killings that are neither manslaughter nor first-degree murder.

voluntary manslaughter Intentional killings committed in the sudden heat of passion upon adequate provocation.

year-and-a-day rule The rule that no act occurring more than one year and one day before death is the legal cause of death.

Suggested Readings

1. Rollin M. Perkins and Ronald N. Boyce, *Criminal Law*, 3d ed. (Mineola, N.Y.: Foundation Press, 1982), pp. 46–151. Thoroughly covers criminal homicide, using many cases and examples to illustrate the complicated elements in criminal homicide. In addition, Perkins and Boyce discuss new developments in the law, including the *Model Penal Code* approach to negligent homicide.

2. George Fletcher, *Rethinking Criminal Law* (Boston: Little, Brown, 1978), chaps. 4 and 5. Fletcher takes a critical look at criminal homicide, stressing the uniqueness of homicide as a crime because of its irreversibility. He goes into the philosophical underpinnings of homi-

cide law. These chapters enhance much of what Fletcher says in this text about various homicides, including the *mens rea* and circumstances surrounding them.

3. American Law Institute, *Model Penal Code and Commentaries*, vol. 1 (Philadelphia: American Law Institute, 1980), pt. II, pp. 1–90. This volume develops the *Model Penal Code*'s reconstruction of homicide law, doing away with degrees and replacing them with three classifications: murder, manslaughter, and negligent homicide. It is a thorough, thought-provoking discussion, well worth the serious student's efforts.

Notes

1. George Fletcher, *Rethinking Criminal Law* (Boston: Little, Brown and Company, 1978), 235–236.

2. Rollin M. Perkins and Ronald N. Boyce, *Criminal Law*, 3d ed. (Mineola, N.Y.: Foundation Press, 1982), 46–150.

3. Ibid., 49–53.

4. 410 U.S. 113, 93 S.Ct. 705, 35 L.Ed.2d 147 (1973); American Law Institute, *Model Penal Code and Commentaries*, vol. 1 (Philadelphia: American Law Institute, 1980), pt. II, 11–13, maintains that abortion and fetal death statutes should be kept distinct.

5. I am grateful to Randall Rogers, the poster's creator, for this idea.

6. Minnesota Statutes Annotated § 609.266(a).

7. *State v. Fierro*, 124 Ariz. 182, 603 P.2d 74, 77–78 (1979); Perkins and Boyce, *Criminal Law*, 48–49.

8. American Law Institute, *Model Penal Code and Commentaries*, vol. 1, pt. II, 10–11, discusses this and summarizes recent legislation on the subject.

9. Perkins and Boyce, *Criminal Law*, 822–824.

10. 373 Mass. 249, 366 N.E.2d 744 (1977).

11. American Law Institute, *Model Penal Code and Commentaries*, vol. 1, pt. II, 6–7.

12. Quoted in American Law Institute, *Model Penal Code and Commentaries*, vol. 1, pt. 11, 14.

13. Pa. Laws of 1794, ch. 257, §§ 1,2 (1794); Herbert Wechsler and Jerome Michael discuss this development thoroughly in "A Rationale of the Law of Homicide I," *Columbia Law Review* 37 (1937):703–717.

14. *Gregg v. Georgia*, 428 U.S. 153, 96 S.Ct. 2909, 49 L.Ed.2d 859 (1976); *Proffitt v. Florida*, 428 U.S. 242, 96 S.Ct. 2960, 49 L.Ed.2d 913 (1976); *Woodson v. North Carolina*, 428 U.S. 280, 96 S.Ct. 2978, 49 L.Ed.2d 944 (1976).

15. *Goodman v. State*, 573 P.2d 400 (Wyo.1977); Perkins and Boyce, *Criminal Law*, 131–134.

16. Quoted in *People v. Anderson*, 70 Cal.2d 15, 73 Cal.Rptr. 550, 447 P.2d 942 (1968).

17. *State v. Hall*, 54 Nev. 213, 13 P.2d 624 (1932) (intent formed when shot fired); *People v. Wolff*, 61 Cal.2d 795, 40 Cal.Rptr. 271, 394 P.2d 959 (1964).

18. Sir James F. Stephen, *History of the Criminal Law* (New York: Burt Franklin, 1973), 94.

19. "Minutes of Evidence," *Report* 12, 174–175.

20. *State v. Weisengoff*, 85 W.Va. 271, 101 S.E. 450 (1919) (accidental death); Jerome Hall, "The Substantive Law of Crimes — 1187–1936," *Harvard Law Review* 50 (1937):616, 642.

21. 125 Wis.2d 204, 371 N.W.2d 381 (1985).

22. *State v. Crane*, 247 Ga. 779, 279 S.E.2d 695 (1981) (victim shooting burglar); *Campbell v. State*, 293 Md. 438, 444 A.2d 1034 (1982) (victim cabdriver and police officer); *State v. O'Dell*, 684 S.W.2d 453 (Mo.App.1984) (victim of felonious assault).

23. *People v. Phillips*, 64 Cal.2d 574, 51 Cal.Rptr. 225, 414 P.2d 353 (1966).

24. Francis T. Cullen, William J. Maakestad, and Gray Cavender, *Corporate Crime under Attack: The Ford Pinto Case and Beyond* (Cincinnati, Ohio: Anderson Publishing Company, 1987).

25. "Texas Nursing Home on Trial in Death," *New York Times* (October 1, 1985); and (March 18, 1986), 11.

26. "Business and the Law," *New York Times* (March 5, 1985), 30; and (May 19, 1985).

27. "Three Executives Convicted of Murder for Unsafe Workplace Conditions," *New York Times* (June 14, 1985), 1, 9.

28. Sir William Blackstone, *Commentaries* (University of Chicago Press, 1979), IV:191.

29. *People v. Davis*, 33 Ill.App.3d 105, 337 N.E.2d 256 (1975); also *State v. Grant*, 418 A.2d 154 (Me.1980); but to the contrary see *State v. Tuzon*, 118 Ariz. 205, 575 P.2d 1231 (1978).

30. Perkins and Boyce, *Criminal Law*, 85.

31. *Beasley v. State*, 64 Miss. 518, 8 So. 234 (1886).

32. Perkins and Boyce, *Criminal Law*, 95–96.

33. *People v. Berry*, 18 Cal.3d 509, 134 Cal.Rptr. 415, 556 P.2d 777 (1976).

34. *Manning's Case*, 83 Eng. Rep. 112 (1793); *Palmore v. State*, 283 Ala. 501, 218 So.2d 830 (1969) (husband killed wife); *Dabney v. State*, 113 Ala. 38, 21 So. 211 (1897) (husband killed both wife and paramour).

35. *People v. Washington*, 58 Cal.App.3d 620, 130 Cal.Rptr. 96 (1976).

36. *State v. Flory*, 40 Wyo. 184, 276 P. 458 (1929).

37. *State v. Miller*, 471 N.W.2d 380 (Minn.App.1991), 382, surveys the definitions of gross negligence adopted by courts around the country.

38. *People v. Campbell*, 237 Mich. 424, 212 N.W. 97 (1927).

39. Perkins and Boyce, *Criminal Law*, 116–118.

40. James B. Jacobs, *Drunk Driving: An American Dilemma* (Chicago: University of Chicago Press, 1989), 86.

CHAPTER NINE

Crimes Against Persons II: Criminal Sexual Conduct and Others

CHAPTER MAIN POINTS

1. Sex offenses cover a broad spectrum, including everything from violent assaults to nonviolent private sex between consenting adults.

2. Rape is both a violent crime and a sexual violation.

3. Criminal sexual conduct statutes have expanded traditional rape law, making sexual violations, no matter what their nature, gender-neutral crimes.

4. Violence is not always required in rape and related offenses; immaturity and other conditions sometimes substitute for it.

5. Battery is the crime of offensive physical contact.

6. Assault is either an attempted battery or a threatened battery.

7. Injury and the use of weapons aggravate simple battery and assault.

8. False imprisonment is the misdemeanor of illegal detention against the victim's will.

9. Kidnapping is the use of force or fear of force to move or keep in secret another person beyond the reach of help from the law or friends.

Did He Rape Her?

A female college student left her class, went to her dormitory room where she drank a martini, and then went to a lounge to await her boyfriend. When her boyfriend failed to appear, she went to another dormitory to find a friend, Earl Hassel. She knocked on the door, but received no answer. She tried the doorknob and, finding it unlocked, entered the room and discovered a man sleeping on the bed. She first believed the man to be Hassel, but he turned out to be Hassel's roommate, Robert Berkowitz. Berkowitz asked her to stay for a while and she agreed. He requested a backrub and she declined. He suggested that she sit on the bed, but she declined and sat on the floor.

Berkowitz then moved to the floor beside her, lifted up her shirt and bra and massaged her breasts. He then unfastened his pants and unsuccessfully attempted to put his penis in her mouth. They both stood up, and he locked the door. He returned to push her onto the bed, and removed her undergarments from one leg. He then penetrated her vagina with his penis. After withdrawing and ejaculating on her stomach, he stated, "Wow, I guess we just got carried away," to which she responded, "No, we didn't get carried away, you got carried away."

INTRODUCTION

Crimes against persons threaten three fundamental values—life, liberty, and privacy. The law of homicide, the subject of chapter 8, examined the special criminal conduct that threatens life itself. The crimes against persons examined in this chapter encompass **405** a range of conduct that does not take life itself but injures persons, invades their sexual integrity, infringes on their privacy and liberty, and frightens and exploits vulnerable victims. These crimes include a wide range of harms to people, including violence and coercion, threats, putting others in fear, deception, and taking advantage of positions of trust and authority in order to exploit others.

Criminal sexual conduct shares much with other crimes against persons, but both the law and society treat sex offenses as especially serious. Criminal sexual conduct, particularly when it includes force, stands only slightly below murder in both public recognition and law as the most serious crime against a person. One indication of this special recognition is that criminal sexual conduct is a serious crime even if the victim suffers no physical injury. The reason is that criminal sexual conduct violates intimacy in a way that physical injury does not. Even offensive sexual touchings, such as pinching buttocks or fondling breasts, bear the mark of a special violation. Offensive sexual contacts short of rapes are universally regarded by the law and society as more serious than other offensive touching found in the law of battery. An unwanted erotic caress can offend more than an insulting spit in the face.[1]

Criminal sexual conduct and homicide are clearly regarded as the most serious crimes against persons. But a range of other offenses against persons far outnumber criminal homicide and criminal sexual conduct. Nonsexual assault and battery are among the most common crimes recorded by the police and reported by victims of crime. Kidnapping and its relative false imprisonment, although not among the most numerous of the crimes committed against persons, nevertheless threaten two fundamental values in a free society—the liberty and privacy of individuals.

CRIMINAL SEXUAL CONDUCT

Historically, only two forms of sexual conduct were recognized by the criminal law—rape and sodomy. At common law, rape meant forced heterosexual penetration and sodomy meant consensual homosexual conduct. Modern court opinions have relaxed the strict definitions of rape, and statutes have expanded criminal sexual conduct so that now it embraces a wide range of nonconsensual penetrations and contacts that fall short of violence. Furthermore, public attention and criminal justice agencies have gone beyond their prior narrow focus on rape by strangers—the classic case of the stranger, an evil man, who jumps from the shadows and attacks a defenseless woman on a dark street at night. Another type of rape—long unacknowledged, and therefore virtually unknown save by its victims and perpetrators—that reflects more the social reality of criminal sexual conduct, has come to public attention. Public attention in turn has brought changes in both the law of rape and the criminal justice response to it. This is rape of women by men they know. The overwhelming number of rapes occur within relationships—as when men rape their employees, their dates, their fellow workers, and their wives. In one survey of women who did not report rapes to the police, more than 80 percent indicated that they were raped by men they knew. In three separate surveys of college women, one in five reported being "physically forced" to have sexual intercourse by her date. Another aspect of the social reality of rape is that a substantial number of rapes are committed against men.[2]

History of Rape

Rape, an ancient common-law felony, was punishable by death in Anglo-Saxon England. The common law defined rape as the carnal knowledge (sexual intercourse) by a man with force and without the consent of a woman who was not his wife. This definition limited common-law rape in the following ways:

1. Only men could rape; minors or women could not.

2. Rape included only vaginal intercourse, not anal intercourse or fellatio.

3. Men could rape only women, not other men or boys.

4. Men could not rape their wives.

5. Rape required force.

6. Rape had to occur against the woman's will, or without her consent, unless she was a minor or otherwise incompetent.[3]

The common law required proof beyond a reasonable doubt of all of these elements because, as Lord Hale, the highly regarded seventeenth-century lawyer and legal scholar of the criminal law, noted:

> It must be remembered, that it is an accusation to make, hard to be proved, and harder to be defended by the party accused, though innocent. . . . [T]he heinousness of the offence many times transporting the judge and jury with so much indignation, that they are overhastily carried to the conviction of the person accused thereof, by the confident testimony of sometimes false and malicious witnesses.[4]

The common law allowed rape victims to testify against accused rapists, leaving the jury to determine the credibility of the victim witnesses. However, credibility depended on three conditions regarding the victim, all of them difficult, and often impossible, to satisfy:

1. "Good fame," meaning the chastity of the victim.

2. Prompt reporting of the rape by the victim.

3. Corroboration of the rape by witnesses other than the victim.

Blackstone, the leading eighteenth-century authority on the common law in both England and the American colonies, asserted that even prostitutes could be of good fame,

---

ELEMENTS OF COMMON-LAW RAPE

Actus reus	*Mens Rea*	*Circumstance*
1. Sexual penetration **by**	1. Intent to sexually penetrate by force or the threat of force without consent	Non-consent of the victim
2. Force or threat of force		

but then seemed to have made the assertion meaningless by adding the warning that if the victim

> be of evil fame, and stand unsupported by others; if she concealed the injury for any considerable time after she had opportunity to complain; if the place where the fact was alleged to be committed, was where it was possible she might have been heard, and she made no outcry; these and the like circumstances carry a strong, but not conclusive, presumption that her testimony is false or feigned.[5]

From the seventeenth century in England to the 1970s in the United States, the law of rape concentrated on the element of consent. Women had to show by their resistance to the unwanted sexual advances against them that they did not consent. According to an early frequently cited case, *Reynolds v. States*:

> [V]oluntary submission by the woman, while she has power to resist, no matter how reluctantly yielded, removes from the act an essential element of the crime of rape. . . . if the carnal knowledge was with the consent of the woman, no matter how tardily given, or how much force had theretofore been employed, it is not rape.[6]

The rule that women had to show that they did not consent by proving that they resisted the advances against them is a requirement peculiar to the law of rape. In other crimes where lack of consent is at least an implied element of the crime, passive acceptance is not considered consent. Robbery, for example, requires taking another's property by force or threat of force, yet the law of robbery does not require victims to resist in order to prove the material element of force. Entering a house because the door was unlocked is still trespass; owners do not have to prove they did not consent to the entry. According to Lani Anne Remick,

> Although there are other crimes for which nonconsent is an element, only in rape is proof of a lack of consent insufficient to prove nonconsent. A common defense to a charge of auto theft, for example, is that the car's owner consented to the defendant's use of the vehicle. A mere showing that the owner never gave the defendant permission to take the car is enough to defeat this defense; no showing that the owner actually told the defendant not to take the car is necessary. In rape law, however, the "default" position is consent. Proof of the absence of affirmative indications by the victim is not enough to defeat a consent defense; instead, the prosecution must show that the alleged victim indicated to the defendant through her overt actions and/or words that she did not wish to participate in sexual activity with him. Thus, "[t]he law presumes that one will not give away that which is his to a robber, but makes no similar presumption as to the conduct of women and rapists." In fact, quite the opposite is true: in the context of sexual activity the law presumes consent. For example, proving both that a woman did not verbally consent and that her actions consist of lying still and not moving does not raise a presumption of nonconsent but of consent. Only through evidence of some sort of overt behavior such as a verbal "no" or an attempt to push away the defendant can the prosecution meet its burden of proving nonconsent.[7]

The amount of resistance required to prove lack of consent has changed over time. From the nineteenth century until the 1950s, the **utmost resistance standard** prevailed; it required that women use all the power at their command to physically resist. In *Brown v. State*, the victim, a sixteen-year-old virgin, testified that her neighbor grabbed her, tripped her to the ground, and forced himself on her.

> I tried as hard as I could to get away. I was trying all the time to get away just as hard as I could. I was trying to get up; I pulled at the grass; I screamed as hard as I could, and he told me to shut up, and I didn't, and then he held his hand on my mouth until I was almost strangled.

The jury convicted the neighbor of rape. On appeal, the Wisconsin Supreme Court reversed because the victim had not adequately demonstrated that she did not consent.

> Not only must there be entire absence of mental consent or assent, but there must be the most vehement exercise of every physical means or faculty within the woman's power to resist the penetration of her person, and this must be shown to persist until the offense is consummated.[8]

In another case, the Nebraska Supreme Court put the matter even more strongly:

> [T]he general rule is that a mentally competent woman must in good faith resist to the utmost with the most vehement exercise of every physical means or faculty naturally within her power to prevent carnal knowledge, and she must persist in such resistance as long as she has the power to do so until the offense is consummated.[9]

Strict as the utmost resistance standard was, the law did not require physical resistance in all cases. Intercourse with women who were incapacitated by intoxication, mental deficiency, or insanity was regarded as rape regardless of whether the perpetrator used force or the victim consented. Sexual penetration obtained by fraud was not rape either, but only fraud as to the nature of the act. For example, if a doctor told a woman he needed to insert an instrument into her vagina for treatment but in fact was engaging in intercourse, the law did not recognize her consent. On the other hand, if a woman consented to sexual intercourse because a doctor convinced her that it was good for her health, the law recognized this consent because the woman was defrauded only as to the benefits, not as to the act of sexual intercourse (see the discussion in chapter 11 on fraud in the inducement). Finally, sexual intercourse with a minor who consented and did not resist was rape.[10]

By the 1950s, courts had begun to replace the utmost resistance test with a less stringent standard that favored victims more than the old test. Called the **reasonable resistance standard,** it measures resistance by the amount required by the totality of the circumstances in individual cases. For example, the Virginia Supreme Court ruled that a "woman is not required to resist to the utmost of her physical strength if she reasonably believes that resistance would be useless and result in serious bodily injury."[11]

During the 1970s and 1980s, major reforms took place in the law of rape. In the procedural law of rape, many states abolished the requirement that in order to convict a defendant of rape, the prosecution has to provide corroboration for the testimony of the victim. In addition, most states enacted rape shield statutes, which prohibit the exposure of women's sexual pasts in rape prosecutions and trials. Many states also relaxed the requirement that prohibited prosecution unless women promptly report rapes. Finally, a few states have abolished the marital exception.

States have also made changes in the substantive law of rape. Criminal sexual conduct statutes have shifted the emphasis from the consent of the victim by failing to resist to the force of the rapist in effecting penetration. The Pennsylvania Superior Court, for example, ruled that the common-law emphasis on lack of consent had "worked to the unfair disadvantage of the woman who, when threatened with violence, chose quite rationally to submit to her assailant's advances rather than risk death or serious bodily injury."[12]

The *Model Penal Code* provision eliminated consent as an element in rape because of its "disproportionate emphasis upon objective manifestations by the woman." However, the drafters of the code also recognized that a complex relationship exists between force and consent. Unlike the acts in all other criminal assaults, the drafters noted, under ordinary circumstances victims may desire the physical act in rape — sexual intercourse:

> This unique feature of the offense requires drawing a line between forcible rape on the one hand and reluctant submission on the other, between true aggression and desired intimacy. The difficulty in drawing this line is compounded by the fact that there will often be no witness to the event other than the participants and that their perceptions may change over time. The trial may turn as much on an assessment of the motives of the victim as of the actor.[13]

Criminal sexual conduct statutes have replaced rape statutes and expanded the definition of sex offenses to include all sexual penetrations: vaginal, anal, and oral. In addition, they have created a lesser offense of criminal sexual contact that falls short of penetration. Under criminal sexual conduct statutes, sex offenses are gender-neutral; men can commit criminal sexual conduct against men or women, and women can commit criminal sexual conduct against women or men.[14]

THE ELEMENTS OF RAPE

Most states define rape as sexual activity with another person by force and without the other person's consent. Thus, rape in most jurisdictions consists of four elements:

1. The *actus reus* of sexual penetration between perpetrator and victim.
2. The *actus reus* of the use of force, or the threat of force, by the perpetrator as the means to accomplish the sexual penetration.
3. The circumstance of nonconsent of the victim.
4. The *mens rea* of engaging in sexual activity by force or threat of force without the consent of the victim.

The *Actus Reus* of Rape

The rape *actus reus* consists of two elements:

1. sexual penetration
2. by force or the threat of force.

Sexual penetration has never meant full sexual intercourse to emission. The common-law phrase "penetration however slight" also describes the modern requirement. For example, a defendant who "put his fingers between folds of skin over her vagina, but [did] not insert his fingers . . ." satisfied the penetration requirement.[15]

Courts have adopted two standards to determine whether the force element of rape *actus reus* is satisfied:

1. Extrinsic force standard.

2. Intrinsic force standard.

According to the **extrinsic force standard,** some force in addition to that required to accomplish the penetration is required. The amount of force required varies according to the circumstances of particular cases. The *Model Penal Code* focuses on the "objective manifestations of aggression by the actor." Force that "compels" the victim to "submit" satisfies the rape *actus reus*. According to the **intrinsic force standard,** the *actus reus* of rape requires only the amount of force necessary to accomplish the penetration. The court dealt with the force element of the rape *actus reus* in *State in the interest of M.T.S.*[16]

C A S E

Did He Use Force to Rape?

State in the Interest of M.T.S., 609 A.2d 1266 (N.J. 1992)

M.T.S. was found delinquent for committing sexual assault and he appealed. The Superior Court reversed and the state's petition for certification was granted. The Supreme Court reversed.

HANDLER, J.

FACTS

On Monday, May 21, 1990, fifteen-year-old C.G. was living with her mother, her three siblings, and several other people, including M.T.S. and his girlfriend. A total of ten people resided in the three-bedroom townhome at the time of the incident. M.T.S., then age seventeen, was temporarily residing at the home with the permission of C.G.'s mother; he slept downstairs on a couch. C.G. had her own room on the second floor. At approximately 11:30 P.M. on May 21, C.G. went upstairs to sleep after having watched television with her mother, M.T.S., and his girlfriend. When C.G. went to bed, she was wearing underpants, a bra, shorts, and a shirt. At trial, C.G. and M.T.S. offered very different accounts concerning the nature of

their relationship and the events that occurred after C.G. had gone upstairs. The trial court did not credit fully either teenager's testimony.

C.G. stated that earlier in the day, M.T.S. had told her three or four times that he "was going to make a surprise visit up in [her] bedroom." She said that she had not taken M.T.S. seriously and considered his comments a joke because he frequently teased her. She testified that M.T.S. had attempted to kiss her on numerous other occasions and at least once had attempted to put his hands inside of her pants, but that she had rejected all of his previous advances.

C.G. testified that on May 22, at approximately 1:30 A.M., she awoke to use the bathroom. As she was getting out of bed, she said, she saw M.T.S., fully clothed, standing in her doorway. According to C.G., M.T.S. then said that "he was going to tease [her] a little bit." C.G. testified that she "didn't think anything of it"; she walked past him, used the bathroom, and then returned to bed, falling into a "heavy" sleep within fifteen minutes. The next event C.G. claimed to recall of that morning was waking up with M.T.S. on top of her, her underpants and shorts removed. She said "his penis was into [her] vagina." As soon as C.G. realized what had happened, she said, she immediately slapped M.T.S. once in the face, then "told him to get off [her], and get out." She did not scream or cry out. She testified that M.T.S. complied in less than one minute after being struck; according to C.G., "he jumped right off of [her]." She said she did not know how long M.T.S. had been inside of her before she awoke.

C.G. said that after M.T.S. left the room, she "fell asleep crying" because "[she] couldn't believe that he did what he did to [her]." She explained that she did not immediately tell her mother or anyone else in the house of the events of that morning because she was "scared and in shock." According to C.G., M.T.S. engaged in intercourse with her "without [her] wanting it or telling him to come up [to her bedroom]." By her own account, C.G. was not otherwise harmed by M.T.S.

At about 7:00 A.M., C.G. went downstairs and told her mother about her encounter with M.T.S. earlier in the morning and said that they would have to "get [him] out of the house." While M.T.S. was out on an errand, C.G.'s mother gathered his clothes and put them outside in his car; when he returned, he was told that "[he] better not even get near the house." C.G. and her mother then filed a complaint with the police.

According to M.T.S., he and C.G. had been good friends for a long time, and their relationship "kept leading on to more and more." He had been living at C.G.'s home for about five days before the incident occurred; he testified that during the three days preceding the incident they had been "kissing and necking" and had discussed having sexual intercourse. The first time M.T.S. kissed C.G., he said, she "didn't want him to, but she did after that." He said C.G. repeatedly had encouraged him to "make a surprise visit up in her room."

M.T.S. testified that at exactly 1:15 A.M. on May 22, he entered C.G.'s bedroom as she was walking to the bathroom. He said C.G. soon returned from the bathroom, and the two began "kissing and all," eventually moving to the bed. Once they were in bed, he said, they undressed each other and continued to kiss and touch for about five minutes. M.T.S. and C.G. proceeded to engage in sexual intercourse. According to M.T.S., who was on top of C.G., he "stuck it in" and "did it [thrust] three times, and then the fourth time

[he] stuck it in, that's when [she] pulled [him] off of her." M.T.S. said that as C.G. pushed him off, she said "stop, get off," and he "hopped off right away."

According to M.T.S., after about one minute, he asked C.G. what was wrong; she replied with a backhand to his face. He recalled asking C.G. what was wrong a second time, and her replying, "how can you take advantage of me or something like that." M.T.S. said that he proceeded to get dressed and told C.G. to calm down, but that she then told him to get away from her and began to cry. Before leaving the room, he told C.G., "I'm leaving . . . I'm going with my real girlfriend, don't talk to me . . . I don't want nothing to do with you or anything, stay out of my life . . . don't tell anybody about this . . . it would just screw everything up." He then walked downstairs and went to sleep.

On May 23, 1990, M.T.S. was charged with conduct that if engaged in by an adult would constitute second-degree sexual assault of the victim, contrary to N.J.S.A. 2C:142c(1). . . .

Following a two-day trial on the sexual assault charge, M.T.S. was adjudicated delinquent. After reviewing the testimony, the court concluded that the victim had consented to a session of kissing and heavy petting with M.T.S. The trial court did not find that C.G. had been sleeping at the time of penetration, but nevertheless found that she had not consented to the actual sexual act. Accordingly, the court concluded that the State had proven second-degree sexual assault beyond a reasonable doubt. On appeal, following the imposition of suspended sentences on the sexual assault and the other remaining charges, the Appellate Division determined that the absence of force beyond that involved in the act of sexual penetration precluded a finding of second-degree sexual assault. It therefore reversed the juvenile's adjudication of delinquency for that offense.

OPINION

The issues in this case are perplexing and controversial. We must explain the role of force in the contemporary crime of sexual assault and then define its essential features. We then must consider what evidence is probative to establish the commission of a sexual assault. The factual circumstances of this case expose the complexity and sensitivity of those issues and underscore the analytic difficulty of those seemingly-straightforward legal questions.

Under New Jersey law a person who commits an act of sexual penetration using physical force or coercion is guilty of second degree sexual assault. The sexual assault statute does not define the words "physical force." The question posed by this appeal is whether the element of "physical force" is met simply by an act of nonconsensual penetration involving no more force than necessary to accomplish that result.

That issue is presented in the context of what is often referred to as "acquaintance rape." The record in the case discloses that the juvenile, a seventeen-year-old boy, engaged in consensual kissing and heavy petting with a fifteen-year-old girl and thereafter engaged in actual sexual penetration of the girl to which she had not consented. There was no evidence or suggestion that the juvenile used any unusual or extra force or threats to accomplish the act of penetration.

The trial court determined that the juvenile was delinquent for committing a sexual assault. The Appellate Division reversed the disposition of delinquency, concluding that nonconsensual penetration does not constitute sexual assault unless it is accompanied by some level of force more than that necessary to accomplish the penetration.

The New Jersey Code of Criminal Justice, N.J.S.A. 2C:142c(1), defines "sexual assault" as the commission "of sexual penetration" "with another person" with the use of "physical force or coercion." An unconstrained reading of the statutory language indicates that both the act of "sexual penetration" and the use of "physical force or coercion" are separate and distinct elements of the offense. Neither the definitions section of N.J.S.A. 2C:141 to 8, nor the remainder of the Code of Criminal Justice provides assistance in interpreting the words "physical force." The initial inquiry is, therefore, whether the statutory words are unambiguous on their face and can be understood and applied in accordance with their plain meaning. The answer to that inquiry is revealed by the conflicting decisions of the lower courts and the arguments of the opposing parties. The trial court held that "physical force" had been established by the sexual penetration of the victim without her consent. The Appellate Division believed that the statute requires some amount of force more than that necessary to accomplish penetration.

The parties offer two alternative understandings of the concept of "physical force" as it is used in the statute. The State would read "physical force" to entail any amount of sexual touching brought about involuntarily. A showing of sexual penetration coupled with a lack of consent would satisfy the elements of the statute. The Public Defender urges an interpretation of "physical force" to mean force "used to overcome lack of consent." That definition equates force with violence and leads to the conclusion that sexual assault requires the application of some amount of force in addition to the act of penetration.

. . .

. . . [P]rereform rape law in New Jersey, with its insistence on resistance by the victim, greatly minimized the importance of the forcible and assaultive aspect of the defendant's conduct. Rape prosecutions turned then not so much on the forcible or assaultive character of the defendant's actions as on the nature of the victim's response. "[I]f a woman assaulted is physically and mentally able to resist, is not terrified by threats, and is not in a place and position that resistance would have been useless, it must be shown that she did, in fact, resist the assault." Under the pre-reform law, the resistance offered had to be "in good faith and without pretense, with an active determination to prevent the violation of her person, and must not be merely passive and perfunctory." That the law put the rape victim on trial was clear.

. . .

[T]he New Jersey Code of Criminal Justice [reformed the law of rape in 1978. Among other things, it changed the name of rape to "sexual assault," extended the range of penetrations included in the definition of sexual assault, and made sexual assault gender neutral]. The Code does not refer to force in relation to "overcoming the will" of the victim, or to the "physical overpowering" of the victim, or the "submission" of the victim. It does not require the demonstrated nonconsent of the victim. As we have noted, in reforming the rape laws, the Legislature placed primary emphasis on the assaultive nature of the crime, altering its constituent elements so that they focus exclusively on the forceful or assaultive conduct of the defendant.

The Legislature's concept of sexual assault and the role of force was significantly colored by its understanding of the law of assault and battery. As a general matter, criminal battery is defined as "the unlawful application of force to the person of another." 2 Wayne LaFave & Austin Scott, *Criminal Law*, § 7.15 at 301 (1986). The application of force is criminal when it results in either (a) a physical injury or (b) an offensive touching. Id. at 30102. Any "unauthorized touching of another [is] a battery." *Perna v. Pirozzi*, 92 N.J. 446, 462, 457 A.2d 431 (1983). Thus, by eliminating all references to the victim's state of mind and conduct, and by broadening the definition of penetration to cover not only sexual intercourse between a man and a woman but a range of acts that invade another's body or compel intimate contact, the Legislature emphasized the affinity between sexual assault and other forms of assault and battery. . . . We are thus satisfied that an interpretation of the statutory crime of sexual assault to require physical force in addition to that entailed in an act of involuntary or unwanted sexual penetration would be fundamentally inconsistent with the legislative purpose to eliminate any consideration of whether the victim resisted or expressed nonconsent.

We note that the contrary interpretation of force — that the element of force need be extrinsic to the sexual act — would not only reintroduce a resistance requirement into the sexual assault law, but also would immunize many acts of criminal sexual contact short of penetration. The characteristics that make a sexual contact unlawful are the same as those that make a sexual penetration unlawful. An actor is guilty of criminal sexual contact if he or she commits an act of sexual contact with another using "physical force" or "coercion." N.J.S.A. 2C:143(b). That the Legislature would have wanted to decriminalize unauthorized sexual intrusions on the bodily integrity of a victim by requiring a showing of force in addition to that entailed in the sexual contact itself is hardly possible.

Because the statute eschews any reference to the victim's will or resistance, the standard defining the role of force in sexual penetration must prevent the possibility that the establishment of the crime will turn on the alleged victim's state of mind or responsive behavior. We conclude, therefore, that any act of sexual penetration engaged in by the defendant without the

affirmative and freely-given permission of the victim to the specific act of penetration constitutes the offense of sexual assault. Therefore, physical force in excess of that inherent in the act of sexual penetration is not required for such penetration to be unlawful. The definition of "physical force" is satisfied under N.J.S.A. 2C:142c(1) if the defendant applies any amount of force against another person in the absence of what a reasonable person would believe to be affirmative and freely-given permission to the act of sexual penetration.

. . .

Our understanding of the meaning and application of "physical force" under the sexual assault statute indicates that the term's inclusion was neither inadvertent nor redundant. The term "physical force," like its companion term "coercion," acts to qualify the nature and character of the "sexual penetration." Sexual penetration accomplished through the use of force is unauthorized sexual penetration. That functional understanding of "physical force" encompasses the notion of "unpermitted touching" derived from the Legislature's decision to redefine rape as a sexual assault. As already noted, under assault and battery doctrine, any amount of force that results in either physical injury or offensive touching is sufficient to establish a battery. Hence, as a description of the method of achieving "sexual penetration," the term "physical force" serves to define and explain the acts that are offensive, unauthorized, and unlawful.

. . .

Today the law of sexual assault is indispensable to the system of legal rules that assures each of us the right to decide who may touch our bodies, when, and under what circumstances. The decision to engage in sexual relations with another person is one of the most private and intimate decisions a person can make. Each person has the right not only to decide whether to engage in sexual contact with another, but also to control the circumstances and character of that contact. No one, neither a spouse, nor a friend, nor an acquaintance, nor a stranger, has the right or the privilege to force sexual contact. See "Definition of Forcible Rape," supra, 61 Va.L.Rev. at 1529 (arguing that "forcible rape is viewed as a heinous crime primarily because it is a violent assault on a person's bodily security, particularly degrading because that person is forced to submit to an act of the most intimate nature").

We emphasize as well that what is now referred to as "acquaintance rape" is not a new phenomenon. Nor was it a "futuristic" concept in 1978 when the sexual assault law was enacted. Current concern over the prevalence of forced sexual intercourse between persons who know one another reflects both greater awareness of the extent of such behavior and a growing appreciation of its gravity. Notwithstanding the stereotype of rape as a violent attack by a stranger, the vast majority of sexual assaults are perpetrated by someone known to the victim. Acquaintance Rape, supra, at 10. One respected study indicates that more than half of all rapes are committed by male relatives, current or former husbands, boyfriends or lovers. Diana Russell, The Prevalence and Incidence of Forcible Rape and Attempted Rape of Females, 7 Victimology 81 (1982). Similarly, contrary to common myths, perpetrators generally do not use guns or knives and victims generally do not suffer external bruises or cuts. Acquaintance Rape, supra, at 10. Although this more realistic and accurate view of rape only recently has achieved widespread public circulation, it was a central concern of the proponents of reform in the 1970s.

The insight into rape as an assaultive crime is consistent with our evolving understanding of the wrong inherent in forced sexual intimacy. It is one that was appreciated by the Legislature when it reformed the rape laws, reflecting an emerging awareness that the definition of rape should correspond fully with the experiences and perspectives of rape victims. Although reformers focused primarily on the problems associated with convicting defendants accused of violent rape, the recognition that forced sexual intercourse often takes place between persons who know each other and often involves little or no violence comports with the understanding of the sexual assault law that was embraced by the Legislature. Any other interpretation of the law, particularly one that defined force in relation to the resistance or protest of the victim, would directly undermine the goals sought to be achieved by its reform.

. . .

The Appellate Division was correct in recognizing that a woman's right to end intimate activity without penetration is a protectable right the violation of which can be a criminal offense. However, it misperceived the purpose of the statute in believing that the only way that right can be protected is by the woman's unequivocally-expressed desire to end the activity. The effect of that requirement would be to import into the sexual assault statute the notion that an assault occurs only if the victim's will is overcome, and thus to reintroduce the requirement of nonconsent and victim resistance as a constituent material element of the crime. Under the reformed statute, a person's failure to protest or resist cannot be considered or used as justification for bodily invasion.

We acknowledge that cases such as this are inherently fact sensitive and depend on the reasoned judgment and common sense of judges and juries. The trial court concluded that the victim had not expressed consent to the act of intercourse, either through her words or actions. We conclude that the record provides reasonable support for the trial court's disposition.

Accordingly, we reverse the judgment of the Appellate Division and reinstate the disposition of juvenile delinquency for the commission of second degree sexual assault. For reversal and reinstatement—Chief Justice WILENTZ, and Justices CLIFFORD, HANDLER, POLLOCK, O'HERN, GARIBALDI and STEIN—7. Opposed—None.

QUESTIONS FOR DISCUSSION

1. List all of the facts relevant to determining whether M.T.S. satisfied the force element of the *actus reus* of sexual assault under the New Jersey statute.

2. What reasons does the court give for adopting the intrinsic force standard?

3. Do you agree that intrinsic force is sufficient to satisfy the force element? Defend your answer.

NOTE CASES

1. A female college student left her class, went to her dormitory room where she drank a martini, and then went to a lounge to await her boyfriend. When her boyfriend failed to appear, she went to another dormitory to find a friend, Earl Hassel. She knocked on the door, but received no answer. She tried the

doorknob and, finding it unlocked, entered the room and discovered a man sleeping on the bed. The complainant originally believed the man to be Hassel, but it turned out to be Hassel's roommate, Robert Berkowitz. Berkowitz asked her to stay for a while and she agreed. He requested a backrub and she declined. He suggested that she sit on the bed, but she declined and sat on the floor.

Berkowitz then moved to the floor beside her, lifted up her shirt and bra and massaged her breasts. He then unfastened his pants and unsuccessfully attempted to put his penis in her mouth. They both stood up, and he locked the door. He returned to push her onto the bed, and removed her undergarments from one leg. He then penetrated her vagina with his penis. After withdrawing and ejaculating on her stomach, he stated, "Wow, I guess we just got carried away," to which she responded, "No, we didn't get carried away, you got carried away."

Did Berkowitz use force in accomplishing the penetration? No, said the Pennsylvania court which applied the extrinsic force standard. According to the court:

> In regard to the critical issue of forcible compulsion, the complainant's testimony is devoid of any statement which clearly or adequately describes the use of force or the threat of force against her. In response to defense counsel's question, "Is it possible that [when Appellee lifted your bra and shirt] you took no physical action to discourage him," the complainant replied, "It's possible." When asked, "Is it possible that [Appellee] was not making any physical contact with you . . . aside from attempting to untie the knot [in the drawstrings of complainant's sweatpants]," she answered, "It's possible." She testified that "He put me down on the bed. It was kind of like—He didn't throw me on the bed. It's hard to explain. It was kind of like a push but not—I can't explain what I'm trying to say." She concluded that "it wasn't much" in reference to whether she bounced on the bed, and further detailed that their movement to the bed "wasn't slow like a romantic kind of thing, but it wasn't a fast shove either. It was kind of in the middle." She agreed that Appellee's hands were not restraining her in any manner during the actual penetration, and that the weight of his body on top of her was the only force applied. She testified that at no time did Appellee verbally threaten her. The complainant did testify that she sought to leave the

room, and said "no" throughout the encounter. As to the complainant's desire to leave the room, the record clearly demonstrates that the door could be unlocked easily from the inside, that she was aware of this fact, but that she never attempted to go to the door or unlock it.

> As to the complainant's testimony that she stated "no" throughout the encounter with Appellee, we point out that, while such an allegation of fact would be relevant to the issue of consent, it is not relevant to the issue of force. . . . [W]here there is a lack of consent, but no showing of either physical force, a threat of physical force, or psychological coercion, the "forcible compulsion" requirement under 18 Pa.C.S. § 3121 is not met.

> Moreover, we find it instructive that in defining the related but distinct crime of "indecent assault," the Legislature did not employ the phrase "forcible compulsion" but rather chose to define indecent assault as "indecent contact with another . . . without the consent of the other person." The phrase "forcible compulsion" is explicitly set forth in the definition of rape under 18 Pa.C.S. § 3121, but the phrase "without the consent of the other person," is conspicuously absent. The choice by the Legislature to define the crime of indecent assault utilizing the phrase "without the consent of the other" and to not so define the crime of rape indicates a legislative intent that the term "forcible compulsion" under 18 Pa.C.S. § 3121, be interpreted as something more than a lack of consent. Moreover, we note that penal statutes must be strictly construed to provide fair warning to the defendant of the nature of the proscribed conduct. 1 Pa.C.S.A. § 1928; 18 Pa.C.S.A. § 104.

> Reviewed in light of the above described standard, the complainant's testimony simply fails to establish that the Appellee forcibly compelled her to engage in sexual intercourse as required under 18 Pa.C.S. § 3121. Thus, even if all of the complainant's testimony was believed, the jury, as a matter of law, could not have found Appellee guilty of rape. Accordingly, we hold that the Superior Court did not err in reversing Appellee's conviction of rape. *Commonwealth v. Berkowitz*, 641 A.2d 1161 (Pa. 1994)

2. Pat, the twenty-one-year-old prosecuting witness, went to a bar with a friend to "have a few drinks." She met Eddie Rusk. They struck up a conversation, learning that they were both separated from their

spouses and that they both had children. Pat eventually told Eddie she had to leave because it was a weeknight and she had to get up early with her baby. Rusk asked Pat for a ride home. She agreed, but told him, "I'm just giving you a ride home, you know, as a friend, not anything to be, you know, thought of other than a ride." He said, "Oh, o.k." When they got to his building, in a part of town she did not know, he asked her to come up to his apartment. She declined. He asked again. She declined again. He reached over, turned off the key, removed the key from the ignition, got out of the car, walked around to Pat's side, and said, "Now, will you come up?" Pat, frightened, went up to the apartment. After sitting for a few minutes, Rusk excused himself and went into the bathroom. He returned about five minutes later. He sat beside her and turned off the light. She asked if she could go. He said he wanted her to stay. He asked her to get on the bed with him, and pulled her by the arms onto the bed and began to undress her. She took off her pants when he asked her to. She removed his pants, because "he asked me to do it." Pat explained what happened next:

> I was still begging him to please let, you know, let me leave. I said, "you can get a lot of other girls down there, for what you want," and he just kept saying, "no"; and then I was really scared, because I can't describe, you know, what was said. It was more the look in his eyes; and I said, at that point—I didn't know what to say; and I said, "If I do what you want, will you let me go without

killing me?" Because I didn't know, at that point, what he was going to do; and I started to cry; and when I did, he put his hands on my throat, and started lightly to choke me; and I said, "If I do what you want, will you let me go?" And he said, yes, and at the same time, I proceeded to do what he wanted me to.

Pat also testified that Rusk made her perform oral sex and then vaginal intercourse.

Did Eddie rape Pat? The rape statute in the state required intercourse "by force or threat of force against the will and without consent." On appeal, in affirming Eddie Rusk's rape conviction, the appellate court wrote:

> [I]t is readily apparent to us that the trier of fact could rationally find that the elements of force and nonconsent had been established and that Rusk was guilty of the offense beyond a reasonable doubt. Of course, it was for the jury to observe the witnesses and their demeanor, and to judge their credibility and weigh their testimony. Quite obviously, the jury . . . believed Pat's testimony. . . .
>
> Just where persuasion ends and force begins in cases like the present is essentially a factual issue, to be resolved in light of the controlling legal precepts. That threats of force need not be made in any particular manner in order to put a person in fear of bodily harm is well established. Indeed, conduct, rather than words, may convey threat. . . . *State v. Rusk*, 424 A.2d 720 (1981)

The threat of force can also satisfy the rape *actus reus*. Courts consider a number of factors in determining whether particular threats satisfy the force element. The threat of force must show that:

1. The victim was placed in real fear of imminent and serious bodily harm.

2. The fear was objectively reasonable under the circumstances.

Specific verbal threats, such as threats to kill, seriously injure, or kidnap either the victim or another clearly satisfy the requirement. But the threat need not consist of express words or even the brandishing of a weapon. In determining if the fear is reasonable, courts might consider the following factors:

- The respective ages of the perpetrator and the victim.

- The physical sizes of the perpetrator and the victim.

- The mental condition of the perpetrator and the victim.

- The physical setting of the assault.

- The position of authority, domination, or custodial control of the perpetrator over the victim.[17]

Neither actual force nor the threat of force is required in cases where perpetrators obtain consent fraudulently, or when a minor, a mentally deficient, or an insane person consents. In these cases, the act of penetration itself suffices (as described [or discussed?] in the following section, on consent).

The Element of Nonconsent

The nonconsent element requires that the prosecution prove beyond a reasonable doubt that victims did not consent. Failure to prove nonconsent results in acquittal. The nonconsent element establishes a legal presumption that victims have consented unless the state can prove otherwise. As we have already noted in the section on the history of rape law, unlike virtually every other crime, consent is the "default position." It is easy to confuse the force element with that of nonconsent because evidence of force frequently is also evidence of nonconsent. However, they are distinct elements, one of *actus reus*, the other of a material circumstance. According to the National Institute of Justice and Law Enforcement, "the perpetrator could use all the force imaginable and no crime would be committed if the state could not prove additionally that the victim did not consent."[18]

Proof of nonconsent does not require the prosecution to prove that victims "announce their consent to engage in sexual penetration." According to the court in *State in re M.T.S.*

> Permission to engage in an act of sexual penetration can be and indeed often is indicated through physical actions rather than words. Permission is demonstrated when the evidence, in whatever form, is sufficient to demonstrate that a reasonable person would have believed that the alleged victim had affirmatively and freely given authorization to the act.[19]

The Utah supreme court dealt with the element of nonconsent in *State ex rel J.F.S.*

CASE

Did She Consent?

State ex rel. J.F.S.,
803 P.2d 1254 (Utah 1990)

J.F.S. appealed from a juvenile court adjudication finding him delinquent. His adjudication was based upon convictions of an offense which, if he were an adult, would have been rape, in violation of Utah Code Ann. § 76 5402 (1989), a first degree felony. J.F.S. claimed that the evidence was insufficient to

support the finding that he committed rape and attempted rape. The Utah Supreme Court affirmed the finding of delinquency.

BILLINGS, Judge:

FACTS

In 1989, J.F.S. was fifteen years old and attending high school in Utah. Fifteen year-old P.A. was a friend and classmate of J.F.S. On Halloween day 1989, a friend told J.F.S. that P.A. found him attractive. As a result, J.F.S. approached P.A. After talking for a while, J.F.S. and P.A. arranged to meet at school that evening so they could go trick or treating together.

P.A. had moved to Utah in August of 1989 and was temporarily living with her aunt. On Halloween evening, P.A. asked her aunt to drop her off at school, and she and J.F.S. met as planned. Shortly thereafter, the two started walking down a pathway behind the school on their way to a friend's house. According to P.A.'s version of the events that evening, when the couple passed the high school swimming pool and pump room, J.F.S. pushed P.A. into the pump room through an opening in the side wall, and started to fondle her. As J.F.S. fondled and kissed P.A. she ducked away from him, and exited the pump room through the opening in the wall. P.A. began walking away from the pump room, while reminding J.F.S. of his girlfriend, R.G. As she was walking away, J.F.S. took hold of P.A. and forced her back into the pump room through an unlocked door. P.A. testified she was scared and did not want to go into the pump room. P.A. held on to the sides of the doorway in order to keep from being forced into the room. When J.F.S. "nudged" her, she lost her footing and grip on the doorway and stumbled into the pump room. After J.F.S. shut the door, he held P.A. against the door and began kissing and fondling her. P.A. testified that she kept telling him "no" and that they "were friends," but J.F.S. didn't respond. J.F.S. continued to fondle her and began to undo her pants. P.A. then testified that she was on the ground and J.F.S. had his hands down her pants. J.F.S. pulled down her pants and underwear and lay on top of her, holding her arms and straddling her. P.A. struggled, hitting him once in order to make him stop. J.F.S. then forced P.A. to have intercourse.

J.F.S. had told some friends earlier that he might have sex with P.A. that evening. His friends stayed near the school and tried several times to look into the pump room. At trial one of J.F.S.'s friends, K.J., testified that he could hear voices coming from the pump room, but the words were distorted by the sound of the pump. Although K.J. could not tell what P.A. and J.F.S. were saying, he testified that P.A. did not call for help. When asked why she did not call out to J.F.S.'s

friends for help, P.A. said she didn't cry out because the boys were "running around and laughing" and "if they knew what was going on they thought it was a joke."

After J.F.S. forced P.A. to have intercourse, he asked her if she had any diseases. She answered no and said she had never had sex before. After she put her clothes back on, P.A. called her friend, A.S., from the telephone located in the pump room. At this time, P.A. did not mention the events of the evening.

After the incident, J.F.S. and P.A. left the pump room and P.A. went to a convenience store, where she bought ice cream and telephoned her cousin to come pick her up. P.A. testified that she did not report the rape because she "felt dirty" and "didn't think anybody would believe her," and was leaving the next day to go live with her parents in Maryland.

On the morning P.A. was to leave for Maryland, the friend she called from the pump room, A.S., came to P.A.'s house to retrieve some clothing. When A.S. asked P.A. how she was doing, P.A. began shaking and crying and said that she hated J.F.S. When A.S. asked why, P.A. said that he was "forceful" and showed A.S. bruises on her arms, which were in the shape of a hand.

Shortly after she moved to Maryland, P.A. reported the incident to the principal of the Utah high school after he called and told her he had heard rumors that J.F.S. had been bragging in the boys' locker room about his conquest. P.A. said she had not told her parents what had happened until after the phone call because she was "embarrassed."

J.F.S. was charged with rape. . . . At trial J.F.S. testified that . . . P.A. consented to the sexual activities. He claimed P.A. had sexual intercourse with him willingly. . . . [T]he juvenile court found J.F.S. had committed rape. The court found J.F.S. had planned the rape, and P.A. had withdrawn from any consensual participation long before the rape occurred. . . .

On appeal, J.F.S. claims there was insufficient evidence to support his conviction of rape of P.A. . . . While we note defendant's concern that rape is easy to charge but hard to defend and that his case has some unusual aspects, we emphasize that this court is not reviewing the case de novo, but after a full trial on the merits in which the juvenile court judge found J.F.S. had committed rape. . . . We will reverse the juvenile court's findings only if they are "against the clear weight of the evidence" or this court "reaches a definite and firm conviction that a mistake has been made. . . ."

OPINION

Under Utah law, a person commits rape when he or she has "sexual intercourse with another person, not [their] spouse, without the victim's consent." Utah Code Ann. § 765402 (1989).

In the present case, J.F.S. does not deny that he had sexual intercourse with P.A., but claims P.A. consented to the act. Utah has long held that consent as a defense to a charge of rape is a highly fact sensitive issue, where great deference should be afforded to the fact finder. *State v. Herzog*, 610 P.2d 1281 (Utah 1980); *State v. Studham*, 572 P.2d 700 (Utah 1977). In *Herzog*, for example, the defendant claimed there was insufficient evidence to support the jury's rape verdict. As in this case, the defendant alleged the victim had consented to sexual intercourse. A jury found the act nonconsensual, and convicted the defendant of rape. In upholding the conviction, the Utah Supreme Court stated: "[t]he determination of whether . . . consent was present or absent in any given case is factual in nature, and is thus a matter for determination by the finder of fact." *Herzog*, 610 P.2d at 1283. See also *Studham*, 572 P.2d at 701 ("Most crimes are committed in such secrecy as can be effected, and that is particularly so [in rape]. . . . Therefore the question of guilt or innocence often depends upon the weighing of the credibility of the victim against the accused.").

In 1989, the consent provisions of the Utah rape and sexual abuse statutes were modified, and the defense of consent significantly narrowed. Focusing on the changes relevant to rape, the new statute eliminates the requirement that the victim "earnestly resist" the assailant, and adds specific circumstances which will rebut an allegation of consent. Utah Code Ann. § 765406 (1990) provides in relevant part:

> An act of sexual intercourse, rape, attempted rape . . . is without consent of the victim under any of the following circumstances:
> (1) the victim expresses lack of consent through words or conduct;

> (2) the actor overcomes the victim through the actual application of physical force or violence.

Utah appellate courts have yet to address this new statutory definition of "without consent."

J.F.S. argues that because the evening began as a date and preliminary consensual kissing and fondling occurred, it follows that P.A. consented to intercourse within the statutory meaning. J.F.S. also claims P.A.'s failure to cry out, her delayed reporting and the lack of physical evidence prove P.A. consented to sexual intercourse. Utah authority supports a contrary conclusion.

The fact that preliminary consensual kissing and fondling occurred does not, as J.F.S. claims, negate P.A.'s claim that she did not consent to sexual intercourse. In *State v. Myers*, 606 P.2d 250 (Utah 1980), a jury convicted the defendant of rape, and subsequently the trial judge arrested judgment. The trial judge found that the victim, who willingly engaged in kissing and fondling with the defendant, had "practically invited what had happened to her." The Utah Supreme Court reversed the trial court's decision and ordered the verdict reinstated, stating: The view so expressed seems to suggest that if a woman is "friendly" in accepting the proffered hospitality of a man . . . , and engages in "necking," that is, kissing and hugging, and that this persists over a period of time, she loses her right to protest against further advances the man may desire to force upon her; and thereby subjects herself to such advances and should be deemed to consent to intercourse if he, but not she, so desires. Neither this Court nor the law will justify any such conclusion. See also *State v. Herzog*, 610 P.2d 1281, 1283 (Utah 1980) ("One does not surrender the right to refuse sexual intimacy by the act of accepting another's company, or even by encouraging and accepting romantic overtures.").

Similarly, P.A.'s failure to cry out and her delayed reporting do not establish that P.A. consented to sexual intercourse with J.F.S. In *State v. Lovato*, 702 P.2d 101, 108 (Utah 1985), the defendant asserted that "the failure of the complainant to attempt escape or to cry for help when opportunities presented themselves adds to the improbability of her version of the incident." In affirming the defendant's conviction of sexual abuse, the Utah Supreme Court stated:

[T]he mere failure to make an . . . outcry does not render a conviction unsupportable and [w]hether an outcry should have been made, depends upon how practical and effective it might have been.

J.F.S. was a friend, someone P.A. trusted. When J.F.S. pushed P.A. into the pump house and began the assault, she was undoubtedly surprised and confused. Further, as the rape progressed P.A. testified that she did not cry out because the only people within hearing distance, J.F.S.'s fifteen year-old male friends, were "running around and laughing," and if they "knew what was going on they thought it was a joke." Given the circumstances, P.A. could have reasonably concluded that any type of outcry would have been useless.

Furthermore, P.A.'s delay in reporting the rape does not necessarily prove she consented to sexual intercourse. The Utah Supreme Court, faced with a similar argument in *State v. Archuleta*, 747 P.2d 1019, 102124 (Utah 1987), rejected the proposition that a victim's delay in reporting rape is inconsistent with a claim of lack of consent. P.A.'s delayed reporting is not inconsistent with her claim that she was raped. The embarrassment and shame that is characteristic of rape victims prevents many victims from reporting the incident. P.A., a young, sexually inexperienced teenager, testified that she felt "dirty" and embarrassed about what had happened. P.A. also did not think anyone would believe her, an attitude apparently common in date rape situations where the victim may have initially willingly gone with the perpetrator. See note 6, supra. Given P.A.'s guilty feelings, her embarrassment, age, lack of sexual experience and that she was moving to another state the next day, we find her delay in reporting was not necessarily inconsistent with the judge's finding of lack of consent.

Finally, defendant argues that because of the lack of physical evidence there was insufficient evidence to support his rape conviction. However, lack of physical evidence does not necessarily mean there is insufficient evidence to support a conviction of rape. In *Archuleta*, a jury found the defendant guilty of raping a mentally impaired woman. In reviewing defendant's claim that there was not enough evidence to establish lack of consent beyond a reasonable doubt, the Utah

Supreme Court stated: "[T]he principal evidence supporting the conviction in this case consisted of the victim's testimony, there being no decisively corroborating physical evidence. We again decline to adopt the position that the testimony of a rape victim, without more, cannot support a conviction."

Rape is a crime in which corroborating evidence is usually unavailable. As one commentator persuasively notes:

> In most [rape] cases, there are no witnesses. The event cannot be repeated for the tape recorder—as bribes or drug sales are. There is no contraband—no drugs, money, no stolen goods. Unless the victim actively resists, her clothes may be untorn and her body unmarked. Medical corroboration may establish the fact of penetration, but that only proves that the victim engaged in intercourse—not that it was nonconsensual or that this defendant was the man involved. Moreover, the availability of medical corroboration turns not only on prompt and appropriate treatment by police and medical personnel but, in the first instance, on the victim not doing what interviews find to be the most immediate response of many rape victims: bathing, douching, brushing her teeth, or gargling. On the surface, at least, rape appears to be a crime for which corroboration may be uniquely absent. Estrich, Rape, 95 Yale L.J. 1087, 1175 (1986).

We conclude the evidence supports the juvenile court's finding that P.A. did not consent to intercourse with J.F.S. After listening to J.F.S. and P.A. testify and observing their demeanor, the juvenile court judge explicitly found P.A. to be the more credible witness. P.A. testified that J.F.S. pushed her into the pump room. When she tried to get away, J.F.S. went after her and forced her back into the room. P.A. kept telling J.F.S. "no" and that they "were friends," but J.F.S. didn't respond. Instead, J.F.S. continued fondling her and pulling down her pants and underwear. P.A. struggled, and hit him in order to make him stop. Nevertheless, J.F.S. continued. He straddled P.A., held her down, and forced her to have intercourse.

P.A.'s story is further corroborated by A.S. The next day when A.S. asked P.A. how she was doing, P.A. started crying and shaking. P.A. told A.S. that she hated J.F.S. because he had been forceful and showed A.S. bruises on her arm. We do not believe the juvenile court's finding of lack of consent was against the clear weight of evidence and conclude the facts in the record adequately support the conclusion that P.A. expressed her lack of consent through words and conduct, as required by section 765406(1), and/or that J.F.S. overcame P.A. through the application of physical force as provided by section 765406(2).

[Affirmed.]

QUESTIONS FOR DISCUSSION

1. Exactly how does the Utah supreme court define lack of consent?

2. How did the defense wish to define the element of nonconsent?

3. Which is the better definition? Explain your answer.

4. List all of the facts relevant to determining whether the state proved nonconsent.

5. Do you think that the state proved nonconsent beyond a reasonable doubt? Defend your answer.

Statutory Rape

Statutory rape, or sexual penetration of persons under the age of consent, requires neither force in the *actus reus* nor intent to penetrate sexually in the *mens rea*. Nonconsent is not an element in statutory rape. Immaturity substitutes for force in all jurisdictions, and minors cannot legally consent to sexual intercourse. A few states, such as California and Alaska, however, do permit the defense of reasonable mistake of age. The defense applies only if a man reasonably believes his victim is over the age of consent. California initiated the defense of honest mistake in *People v. Hernandez.*

C A S E

Is Reasonable Belief She Was Eighteen a Defense to Statutory Rape?

People v. Hernandez,
61 Cal.2d 529, 39 Cal.Rptr. 361,
393 P.2d 673 (1964)

Hernandez was found guilty of statutory rape. The California supreme court reversed the decision. Justice Peek wrote the opinion for the court.

FACTS

The undisputed facts show that the defendant and the prosecuting witness were not married and had been companions for several months prior to January 3,

1961, the date of the commission of the alleged offense. Upon that date the prosecutrix was 17 years and 9 months of age and voluntarily engaged in an act of sexual intercourse with defendant.

OPINION

The sole contention raised on appeal is that the trial court erred in refusing to permit defendant to present evidence going to his guilt for the purposes of showing that he had in good faith a reasonable belief that the prosecutrix was 18 years or more of age.... [D]efendant relies upon Penal Code, § 20, which provides that "there must exist a union, or joint operation of act and intent, or criminal negligence" to constitute the commission of a crime. He further relies upon § 26 of that code which provides that one is not capable of committing a crime who commits an act under an ignorance or mistake of fact which disapproves any criminal intent. Thus the sole issue relates to the question of intent and knowledge entertained by the defendant at the time of the commission of the crime charged.

Consent of the female is often an unrealistic and unfortunate standard for branding sexual intercourse a crime as serious as forcible rape. Yet the consent standard has been deemed to be required by important policy goals. We are dealing here, of course, with statutory rape where, in one sense, the lack of consent of the female is not an element of the offense. In a broader sense, however, the lack of consent is deemed to remain an element but the law makes a conclusive presumption of the lack thereof because she is presumed too innocent and naive to understand the implications and nature of her act. The law's concern with her capacity or lack thereof to so understand is explained in part by a popular conception of the social, moral and personal values which are preserved by the abstinence from sexual indulgence on the part of a young woman. An unwise disposition of her sexual favor is deemed to do harm both to herself and the social mores by which the community's conduct patterns are established. Hence the law of statutory rape intervenes in an effort to avoid such a disposition. This goal, moreover, is not accomplished by penalizing the naive female but by imposing criminal sanctions against the male, who is conclusively presumed to be responsible for the occurrence.

The assumption that age alone will bring an understanding of the sexual act to a young woman is of doubtful validity. Both learning from the cultural group to which she is a member and her actual sexual experiences will determine her level of comprehension. The sexually experienced 15-year-old may be far more acutely aware of the implications of sexual intercourse than her sheltered cousin who is beyond the age of consent. A girl who belongs to a group whose members indulge in sexual intercourse at an early age is likely to rapidly acquire an insight into the rewards and penalties of sexual indulgence.

Nevertheless, even in circumstances where a girl's actual comprehension contradicts the law's presumption, the male is deemed criminally responsible for the act, although himself young and naive and responding to advances which may have been made to him.

[COURT NOTE: "The inequitable consequences to which we may be led are graphically illustrated by the following excerpt from *State v. Snow* (Mo.1923) 252 S.W. 629 at page 632:

> We have in this case a condition and not a theory. This wretched girl was young in years but old in sin and shame. A number of callow youths, of otherwise blameless lives . . . fell under her seductive influence. They flocked about her, . . . like moths about the flame of a lighted candle and probably with the same result. The girl was a common prostitute . . . The boys were immature and doubtless more sinned against than sinning. They did not defile the girl. She was a mere 'cistern for foul toads to knot and gender in.' Why should the boys, misled by her, be sacrificed? What sound public policy can be subserved by branding them as felons? Might it not be wise to ingraft an exception in the statute?"]

The law as presently constituted does not concern itself with the relative culpability of the male and female participants in the prohibited sexual act. Even when the young woman is knowledgeable it does not impose sanctions upon her. The knowledgeable young man, on the other hand, is penalized and there are none who would claim that under any construction of the law this should be otherwise. However, the issue raised by the rejected offer of proof in the instant case goes to the culpability of the young man who acts without knowledge that an essential factual element exists and has, on the other hand, a positive, reasonable belief that it does not exist.

The primordial concept of *mens rea*, the guilty mind, expresses the principle that it is not conduct alone but conduct accompanied by certain specific mental states which concerns, or should concern the law. . . .

Statutory rape has long furnished a fertile battleground upon which to argue that the lack of knowledgeable conduct is a proper defense. . . . [The court here notes that when statutory rape originated, the age of consent was 10, but that most states have raised it to at least 16.]

[COURT NOTE: "When the law declares that sexual intercourse with a girl under the age of ten years is rape, it is not illogical to refuse to give any credence to the defense, 'I thought she was older, and I therefore did not believe that I was committing a crime when I had sexual intercourse with her.' . . . But when age limits are raised to sixteen, eighteen, and twenty-one, when the young girl becomes a young woman, when adolescent boys as well as young men are attracted to her, the sexual act begins to lose its quality of abnormality and physical danger to the victim. Bona fide mistakes in the age of girls can be made by men and boys who are no more dangerous than others of their social, economic and educational level. . . . Even if the girl looks to be much older than the age of consent fixed by the statute, even if she lies to the man concerning her age, if she is a day below the statutory age sexual intercourse with her is rape. The man or boy who has intercourse with such girl still acts at his peril. The statute is interpreted as if it were protecting children under the age of ten. (Ploscowe, Sex and the Law (1951) at pages 184 and 185.)"]

There can be no dispute that a criminal intent exists when the perpetrator proceeds with utter disregard of, or in the lack of grounds for, a belief that the female has reached the age of consent. But if he participates in a mutual act of sexual intercourse, believing his partner to be beyond the age of consent, with reasonable grounds for such belief, where is his criminal intent? In such circumstances he has not consciously taken any risk. Instead he has subjectively eliminated the risk by satisfying himself on reasonable evidence that the crime cannot be committed. If it occurs that he has been misled, we cannot realistically conclude that for such reason alone the intent with which he undertook the act suddenly becomes more heinous. . . .

At common law an honest and reasonable belief in the existence of circumstances, which, if true, would make the act for which the person is indicted an innocent act, has always been held to be a good defense. . . . So far as I am aware it has never been suggested that these exceptions do not equally apply to the case of statutory offenses unless they are excluded expressly or by necessary implication.

Our departure . . . is in no manner indicative of a withdrawal from the sound policy that it is in the public interest to protect the sexually naive female from exploitation. No responsible person would hesitate to condemn as untenable a claimed good faith belief in the age of consent of an "infant" female whose obviously tender years preclude the existence of reasonable grounds for that belief. However, the prosecutrix in the instant case was but three months short of 18 years of age and there is nothing in the record to indicate that the purposes of the law as stated in *Ratz* can be better served by foreclosing the defense of a lack of intent. This is not to say that the granting to consent by even a sexually sophisticated girl known to be less than the statutory age is a defense.

We hold only that in the absence of a legislative direction otherwise, a charge of statutory rape is defensible wherein a criminal intent is lacking. . . . The judgment is reversed.

QUESTIONS FOR DISCUSSION

1. What reasons does the court give for the majority view that mistake is no defense to statutory rape?

2. Why did the court decide to change that rule and permit mistake as a defense to statutory rape?

3. Which rule do you favor?

4. If you would permit mistake, would you have a cutoff age, such as the court's reference to age ten?

5. What age would you choose as a proper cutoff point?

6. Do you think the court is right in saying that the defense of mistake should apply to all crimes? (See the discussion in chapter 7 on mistake.)

7. In *State v. Randolph*, Randolph argued that the state of Washington should adopt the rule of the *Hernandez* case. The court declined:

   It may well be . . . that "(c)urrent social and moral values make more realistic the California view that a reasonable and honest mistake of age is a valid defense to a charge of statutory rape. . . ." Nevertheless, statutory rape . . . is a recognized judicial exception to the general rule that a mistake of fact is a defense to a criminal charge. We therefore disagree with the view expressed in Hernandez that such exception may not be sustained except by legislation so directing; rather, we believe the converse, that the exception must be sustained unless the legislature decides otherwise.... We do not think the predatory nature of man has changed in the last decade. If mistake of fact is to be the standard of permissive conduct, the legislature is the appropriate forum to indulge in that decision.[20]

Do you agree? Why or why not?

NOTE CASE

On the evening of [April 14, 1985, Navarette,] ... the victim, and a third person had been drinking and driving around Ogallala, Nebraska. The defendant, who was 22 years of age, purchased the beer which was consumed by the defendant, the victim, and the third person. The victim was only 15 years of age, although he was within approximately 6 weeks of his 16th birthday.

At about midnight the defendant and the victim were at the defendant's home. The third person had gone home. The victim was feeling the effect of the beer and went into the defendant's bedroom so that he could lie down on the bed. He awakened sometime later and found the defendant on the bed beside him. The defendant spoke with the victim for a while and then placed his hand on the victim's penis. Later the defendant put his penis in the victim's mouth and then into the victim's anus. The victim again fell asleep.

When he did awaken he returned to his home but did not enter the house. The victim sat in his father's pickup truck for about an hour and then decided to report the incident to the police...."

In upholding Navarette's conviction, against Navarette's argument that to deny him the defense of mistake and remove *mens rea* as an element of statutory rape violated the Constitution, the court wrote:

> The defendant ... contends that the statute under which he was prosecuted, § 28–319(1)(c), is unconstitutional because consent and reasonable mistake concerning the victim's age are not defenses. The statute in this respect is similar to ones on statutory rape in which consent is not a defense. "[M]istake or lack of information as to the victim's chastity is no defense to the crime of statutory rape." We have expressly rejected the "California Rule." ...
>
> The majority of the cases hold that a defense of reasonable mistake is not constitutionally required. It is not violative of due process for the Legislature, in framing its criminal laws, to cast upon the public the duty of care or extreme caution. Nor is it unfair to require one who gets perilously close to an area of proscribed conduct to take the risk that he may cross over the line. *People v. Navarette*, 221 Neb. 171, 376 N.W.2d 8 (1985)

The *Mens Rea* of Rape

The *actus reus* in forcible rape implies that the defendant intends to effect sexual penetration by force or threat. In *Regina v. Morgan*, a widely publicized English case, four companions were drinking in a bar. When they failed to "find some women," Morgan invited the other three to come home with him to have sexual intercourse with his wife. Morgan told the others not to worry if she struggled because she was "kinky"; the struggle "turned [her] on." The trial court convicted the men, and the intermediate appellate court upheld the conviction. The House of Lords, England's highest appeal court, overturned the conviction because the defendants lacked the *mens rea*. Rape requires the specific intent to have sexual intercourse by force and without consent. Because the men believed Morgan's wife wanted the struggle, they could not have formed that intent.[21]

Regina v. Morgan generated a storm of debate. Although England has adhered to the specific intent requirement, American statutes and decisions barely mention intent, except in attempted rape where intent is the essence of the crime. Where courts face the intent question, they vary in their response. The Maine Supreme Judicial Court ruled that forcible rape requires no showing of *mens rea*; it is a strict liability crime:

[C]ertain crimes are defined to expressly include a culpable state of mind and others are not. The more forceful or egregious sexual conduct, including rape compelled by force, is defined without reference to the actor's state of mind. The legislature, by carefully defining the sex offenses in the criminal code, and by making no reference to a culpable mental state for rape, clearly indicated that rape compelled by force or threat requires no culpable state of mind.[22]

Other courts have adopted a reckless or negligent standard with regard to the sexual penetration, saying that rapists must be either aware that they are risking coerced sexual intercourse or should know that their victims have not consented. Against the argument that rape constitutes a crime too serious with penalties too harsh for the law to impose liability for reckless or negligent rape, law professor Susan Estrich responds:

If inaccuracy or indifference to consent is "the best that this man can do" because he lacks the capacity to act reasonably, then it might well be unjust and ineffective to punish him for it. . . . More common is the case of the man who could have done better but did not; heard her refusal or saw her tears, but decided to ignore them. The man who has the inherent capacity to act reasonably but fails to has, through that failure, made a blameworthy choice for which he can justly be punished. The law has long punished unreasonable action which leads to the loss of human life as manslaughter—a lesser crime than murder, but a crime nonetheless. . . . The injury of sexual violation is sufficiently great, the need to provide that additional incentive pressing enough, to justify negligence liability for rape as for killing.[23]

In some cases, the defendant may not even intend a sexual assault, and yet satisfy the criminal sexual conduct *mens rea*. In *State v. Bonds*, Bonds got into an altercation with another tenant in his rooming house. When she confronted him, Bonds grabbed the nipple of his victim's left breast "intending to hurt her, not to violate her sexually." In upholding his conviction the court held that the intent to injure by contacting victims' intimate parts satisfies the criminal sexual conduct *mens rea*.[24]

Criminal Sexual Conduct with Children

In the past twenty-five years, child sex abuse has drawn much attention. Several notorious cases came to light, leading researchers to conclude that many people in trust positions with authority over children—parents, teachers, counselors, ministers, and others—were abusing their authority by sexually violating the children under their care. The law has long taken a strong stance against such activity, as made clear not only by statutory rape but also by statutes concerning deviate sex and corruption of minors.

New developments are taking place, however, to strengthen existing law and even to create new authority to punish child sex abuse. In some cases, penalties are being made harsher for child sex abuse, and rules are being changed to make it easier for children to testify against perpetrators and to extend the law's reach beyond sexual intercourse to broad-ranging offensive touching.

It is too soon either to tell how far these developments will go or to know just where to draw the line between appropriately demonstrating affection to children and making unwanted and otherwise harmful sexual advances. Harsh penalties and fear of prosecutions ought not to offset advances made over the past three or four decades in releasing repressed healthy desires to demonstrate affection toward children. The issue is sensitive but important. It will take time to learn how to encourage healthy, affectionate demonstrations while responding to damaging sexual advances with proper legislation, prosecution, and punishment.

Marital Rape Exception

According to the **marital rape exception,** it is not a crime for a husband to rape his wife. The reasons for the exception include the following:

1. When a woman marries, she consents to sex at her husband's demand.
2. Permitting rape within marriage encourages unhappy wives to make false charges against their husbands.
3. The intervention of criminal law into marital problems hinders reconciliation during marital difficulties.[25]

However warmly criminal policymakers embraced these arguments in the past, modern civil rights and feminist movements have attacked them savagely. In essence, the argument is that women are not possessions and that simply because women consent to marriage their husbands are not granted the right to "sex on demand." Marriage is increasingly coming to mean an equal partnership. Hence, sex practices must be negotiated and mutually agreed upon.

Hostility to the marital rape exception has resulted in significant changes in the law of marital rape. According to the National Clearinghouse on Marital and Date Rape, marital rape is now a crime in every state. Some states, however, have weakened the effect of these new laws. They have replaced the marital exception with a "marital rape law allowance." The marital rape allowance creates a lesser crime for wife rape than for other rapes. In *People v. Liberta*, New York's highest court, the Court of Appeals, dealt with whether the marital rape exception violates the U.S. Constitution.[26]

C A S E

Is the Marital Rape Exception Constitutional?

People v. Liberta,
64 N.Y.2d 152, 485 N.Y.S.2d 207, 474 N.E.2d 567 (1984)

Following remand, defendant was convicted of first-degree rape and first-degree sodomy, and he appealed. The Supreme Court, Appellate Division, affirmed, and defendant appealed. The Court of Ap-

peals, New York's highest court, affirmed the conviction. Judge Wachter wrote the opinion of the court.

FACTS

Defendant Mario Liberta and Denise Liberta were married in 1978. Shortly after the birth of their son, in October of that year, Mario began to beat Denise. In early 1980 Denise brought a proceeding in the Family Court in Erie County seeking protection from the defendant. On April 30, 1980 a temporary order of protection was issued to her by the Family Court. Under this order, the defendant was to move out and remain away from the family home, and stay away from Denise. The order provided that the defendant could visit with his son once each weekend.

On the weekend of March 21, 1981, Mario, who was then living in a motel, did not visit his son. On Tuesday, March 24, 1981 he called Denise to ask if he could visit his son on that day. Denise would not allow the defendant to come to her house, but she did agree to allow him to pick up their son and her and take them both back to his motel after being assured that a friend of his would be with them at all times. The defendant and his friend picked up Denise and their son and the four of them drove to defendant's motel.

When they arrived at the motel the friend left. As soon as only Mario, Denise, and their son were alone in the motel room, Mario attacked Denise, threatened to kill her, and forced her to perform fellatio on him and to engage in sexual intercourse with him. The son was in the room during the entire episode, and the defendant forced Denise to tell their son to watch what the defendant was doing to her.

The defendant allowed Denise and their son to leave shortly after the incident. Denise, after going to her parents' home, went to a hospital to be treated for scratches on her neck and bruises on her head and back, all inflicted by her husband. She also went to the police station, and on the next day she swore out a felony complaint against the defendant. On July 15, 1981 the defendant was indicted for rape in the first degree and sodomy in the first degree.

OPINION

Section 130.35 of the Penal Law provides in relevant part that "A male is guilty of rape in the first degree when he engages in sexual intercourse with a female * * * by forcible compulsion". "Female", for purposes of the rape statute, is defined as "any female person who is not married to the actor" (Penal Law, s 130.00, subd. 4). Section 130.50 of the Penal Law provides in relevant part that "a person is guilty of sodomy in the

first degree when he engages in deviate sexual intercourse with another person * * * by forcible compulsion". "Deviate sexual intercourse" is defined as "sexual conduct between persons not married to each other consisting of contact between the penis and the anus, the mouth and penis, or the mouth and the vulva" (Penal Law, s 130.00, subd. 2). Thus, due to the "not married" language in the definitions of "female" and "deviate sexual intercourse", there is a "marital exemption" for both forcible rape and forcible sodomy. The marital exemption itself, however, has certain exceptions. For purposes of the rape and sodomy statutes, a husband and wife are considered to be "not married" if at the time of the sexual assault they "are living apart * * * pursuant to a valid and effective: (i) order issued by a court of competent jurisdiction which by its terms or in its effect requires such living apart, or (ii) decree or judgment of separation, or (iii) written agreement of separation" (Penal Law, § 130.00, subd. 4). . . .

The defendant's constitutional challenges to the rape and sodomy statutes are premised on his being considered "not married" to Denise and are the same challenges as could be made by any unmarried male convicted under these statutes. The defendant's claim is that both statutes violate equal protection because they are underinclusive classifications which burden him, but not others similarly situated. . . .

As noted above, under the Penal Law a married man ordinarily cannot be convicted of forcibly raping or sodomizing his wife. This is the so-called marital exemption for rape. . . . The assumption . . . that a man could not be guilty of raping his wife, is traceable to a statement made by the 17th century English jurist Lord Hale, who wrote: "[T]he husband cannot be guilty of a rape committed by himself upon his lawful wife, for by their mutual matrimonial consent and contract the wife hath given up herself in this kind unto her husband, which she cannot retract" (1 Hale, *History of Pleas of the Crown*, p. 629). Although Hale cited no authority for his statement it was relied on by State Legislatures which enacted rape statutes with a marital exemption and by courts which established a common-law exemption for husbands. . . .

Presently, over 40 States still retain some form of marital exemption for rape. While the marital exemption is subject to an equal protection challenge, because it classifies unmarried men differently than married men, the equal protection clause does not prohibit a State from making classifications, provided the statute does not arbitrarily burden a particular group of individuals. Where a statute draws a distinction based upon marital status, the classification must be reasonable and must be based upon "some ground of difference that rationally explains the different treatment."

We find that there is no rational basis for distinguishing between marital rape and nonmarital rape. The various rationales which have been asserted in defense of the exemption are either based upon archaic notions about the consent and property rights incident to marriage or are simply unable to withstand even the slightest scrutiny. We therefore declare the marital exemption for rape in the New York statute to be unconstitutional. . . .

Because the traditional justifications for the marital exemption no longer have any validity, other arguments have been advanced in its defense. The first of these recent rationales, which is stressed by the People in this case, is that the marital exemption protects against governmental intrusion into marital privacy and promotes reconciliation of the spouses, and thus that elimination of the exemption would be disruptive to marriages. While protecting marital privacy and encouraging reconciliation are legitimate State interests, there is no rational relation between allowing a husband to forcibly rape his wife and these interests. The marital exemption simply does not further marital privacy because this right of privacy protects consensual acts, not violent sexual assaults (see *Griswold v. Connecticut*, 381 U.S. 479, 485–486, 85 S.Ct. 1678, 1682–1683). Just as a husband cannot invoke a right of marital privacy to escape liability for beating his wife, he cannot justifiably rape his wife under the guise of a right to privacy. . . .

The final argument in defense of the marital exemption is that marital rape is not as serious an offense as other rape and is thus adequately dealt with by the possibility of prosecution under criminal statutes, such as assault statutes, which provide for less severe punishment. The fact that rape statutes exist, however, is a recognition that the harm caused by a forcible rape is different, and more severe, than the

harm caused by an ordinary assault. Under the Penal Law, assault is generally a misdemeanor unless either the victim suffers "serious physical injury" or a deadly weapon or dangerous instrument is used (Penal Law, §§ 120.00, 120.05, 120.10). Thus, if the defendant had been living with Denise at the time he forcibly raped and sodomized her he probably could not have been charged with a felony, let alone a felony with punishment equal to that for rape in the first degree.

Moreover, there is no evidence to support the argument that marital rape has less severe consequences than other rape. On the contrary, numerous studies have shown that marital rape is frequently quite violent and generally has more severe, traumatic effects on the victim than other rape. . . .

Under the Penal Law only males can be convicted of rape in the first degree. . . . Rape statutes historically applied only to conduct by males against females, largely because the purpose behind the proscriptions was to protect the chastity of women and thus their property value to their fathers or husbands. New York's rape statute has always protected only females, and has thus applied only to males (see Penal Law, § 130.35; 1909 Penal Law, § 2010; 1881 Penal Code, tit. X, ch. II, § 278). Presently New York is one of only 10 jurisdictions that does not have a gender-neutral statute for forcible rape.

A statute which treats males and females differently violates equal protection unless the classification is substantially related to the achievement of an important governmental objective. This test applies whether the statute discriminates against males or against females. The People bear the burden of showing both the existence of an important objective and the substantial relationship between the discrimination in the statute and that objective. This burden is not met in the present case, and therefore the gender exemption also renders the statute unconstitutional.

The first argument advanced by the People in support of the exemption for females is that because only females can become pregnant the State may constitutionally differentiate between forcible rapes of females and forcible rapes of males. This court and the United States Supreme Court have upheld statutes which subject males to criminal liability for engaging in sexual intercourse with underage females without the converse being true (*Michael M. v. Sonoma County Superior Ct.*, 450 U.S. 464, 101 S.Ct. 1200, 67 L.Ed.2d 437). The rationale behind these decisions was that the primary purpose of such "statutory rape" laws is to protect against the harm caused by teenage pregnancies, there being no need to provide the same protection to young males.

There is no evidence, however, that preventing pregnancies is a primary purpose of the statute prohibiting forcible rape, nor does such a purpose seem likely. Rather, the very fact that the statute proscribes "forcible compulsion" shows that its overriding purpose is to protect a woman from an unwanted, forcible, and often violent sexual intrusion into her body. Thus, due to the different purposes behind forcible rape laws and "statutory" (consensual) rape laws, the cases upholding the gender discrimination in the latter are not decisive with respect to the former, and the People cannot meet their burden here by simply stating that only females can become pregnant.

The People also claim that the discrimination is justified because a female rape victim "faces the probability of medical, sociological, and psychological problems unique to her gender". This same argument, when advanced in support of the discrimination in the statutory rape laws, was rejected by this court in *People v. Whidden* (51 N.Y.2d at p. 461, 434 N.Y.S.2d 937, 415 N.E.2d 927, supra), and it is no more convincing in the present case. "[A]n '"archaic and overbroad" generalization' * * * which is evidently grounded in long-standing stereotypical notions of the differences between the sexes, simply cannot serve as a legitimate rationale for a penal provision that is addressed only to adult males."

Finally, the People suggest that a gender-neutral law for forcible rape is unnecessary, and that therefore the present law is constitutional, because a woman either cannot actually rape a man or such attacks, if possible, are extremely rare. Although the "physiologically impossible" argument has been accepted by several courts, it is simply wrong. The argument is premised on the notion that a man cannot engage in sexual intercourse unless he is sexually aroused, and if he is aroused then he is consenting to intercourse. "Sexual intercourse" however, "occurs upon any penetration, however slight" (Penal Law, § 130.00); this degree of contact can be achieved without a male being aroused and thus without his consent.

As to the "infrequency" argument, while forcible sexual assaults by females upon males are undoubtedly less common than those by males upon females this numerical disparity cannot by itself make the gender discrimination constitutional. Women may well be responsible for a far lower number of all serious crimes than are men, but such a disparity would not make it permissible for the State to punish only men who commit, for example, robbery.

To meet their burden of showing that a gender-based law is substantially related to an important governmental objective the People must set forth an "'exceedingly persuasive justification'" for the classification, which requires, among other things, a showing that the gender-based law serves the governmental objective better than would a gender-neutral law. The fact that the act of a female forcibly raping a male may be a difficult or rare occurrence does not mean that the gender exemption satisfies the constitutional test. A gender-neutral law would indisputably better serve, even if only marginally, the objective of deterring and punishing forcible sexual assaults. The only persons "benefited" by the gender exemption are females who forcibly rape males. As the Supreme Court has stated, "[a] gender-based classification which, as compared to a gender-neutral one, generates additional benefits only for those it has no reason to prefer cannot survive equal protection scrutiny."

Accordingly, we find that section 130.35 of the Penal Law violates equal protection because it exempts females from criminal liability for forcible rape. . . . [A]ffirmed.

QUESTIONS FOR DISCUSSION

1. Why did Lord Hale say that men could not rape their wives?

2. What are the modern reasons for the marital rape exception?

3. Why does the court reject them?

4. Do you agree that these are not good reasons? Why or why not?

5. Do you agree that the marital rape exception violates the equal protection clause? Why or why not?

6. How far should courts go in trying to determine what legislatures meant when they wrote statutes?

7. Do you think the U.S. Supreme Court would agree with the New York court that the marital rape exception violates the equal protection clause of the Fourteenth Amendment? Why or why not? (Review the section on equal protection in chapter 2.)

Criminal Sexual Conduct Statutes

In the 1970s a combination of civil rights activists, feminists, and some criminal law reformers raised a strong and unified voice for abolishing existing rape and other sex laws. In their place, they recommend that legislatures create new, gender-neutral offenses that would emphasize the violent over the erotic aspects of sexual assault. Some states have done this, enacting what are called criminal sexual conduct laws. One of the earliest and best known of these laws is Michigan's 1974 statute which provides:

> 1st degree: This consists of "sexual penetration," defined as sexual intercourse, cunnilingus, fellatio, anal intercourse, "or any other intrusion, however slight, of any part of a person's body or of any object into the genital or anal openings of another person's body." In addition one of the following must have occurred:
> 1. the defendant must have been armed with a weapon;
> 2. force or coercion was used and the defendant was aided by another person; or
> 3. force or coercion was used and personal injury to the victim was caused.
>
> 2nd degree: This consists of "sexual contact," defined as the intentional touching of the victim's or actor's personal parts or the intentional touching of the clothing covering the immediate area of the victim's intimate parts, for purposes of sexual arousal or gratification. "Intimate parts" is defined as including the primary genital area, groin, inner thigh, buttock, or breast. In addition, one of the circumstances required for 1st degree criminal sexual conduct must have existed.
>
> 3rd degree: This consists of sexual penetration accomplished by force or coercion.
>
> 4th degree: This consists of sexual contact accomplished by force or coercion.[27]

As the Michigan statute indicates, the new legislation purports to cover all offensive and violent sexual penetration and contact without regard to victims' and perpetrators' gender. Under the Michigan statute, what crime did the women in the following true incident commit?

> Police have received a complaint from a man stating he was raped by two women. According to the complaint, the twenty-four-year-old man was driving home when he stopped to help two women who appeared to be having car trouble. He said that as he approached them, one of the women pointed a gun at him and told him to get into the back seat of their car. He said the women bound his hands with rope, pulled a ski mask over his head, and drove "about half an hour" to a house at an undetermined location. There, he said, they forced him

into a bedroom and "used his body repeatedly" for "several hours." He told police he was driven back, unharmed, to his own car late that night. He gave police a sketchy description of the two women.[28]

Grading Rape

Most statutes divide rape into two degrees: simple or second-degree rape, and aggravated or first-degree rape. Aggravated rape involves at least one of the following:

- The victim suffers serious bodily injury.
- A stranger commits the rape.
- The rape occurs in connection with another crime.
- The rapist is armed.
- The rapist has accomplices.
- The victim is a minor and the rapist is several years older.

All other rapes are simple rapes for which the penalties are less severe. The criminal sexual conduct statutes have added more degrees in order to accommodate the distinction between penetration and contact. Aggravated penetration constitutes first-degree criminal sexual conduct, aggravated contact second degree, simple criminal penetration third degree, and simple criminal contact fourth degree.

Summary of Rape and Criminal Sexual Conduct

Rape, a special assault, entails the specific purpose to have sexual intercourse by force and against the victim's will. Traditionally, and to a large extent even today, only men who try to force vaginal intercourse on women who are not their wives can commit rape. Changing moral, sexual, and social values, combined with civil rights and feminist pressures, have led most states to modify their rape laws during the 1970s and 1980s. Some have enacted criminal sexual conduct statutes. The criminal sexual conduct statutes shift the emphasis away from the sexual nature of the offenses and toward their assaultive aspects. They also make rape a gender-neutral crime in which a range of sexual penetrations and contacts, whether committed by or against men or women, are considered criminal sexual conduct. Other states have made more modest changes. All states have abolished the marital rape exception. Many have changed old evidence rules such as the requirement of corroboration and the admission of victims' prior sexual history.

ASSAULT AND BATTERY

Assault and battery, although frequently combined in statutes, were distinct offenses at common law. A **battery** is an unjustified offensive touching. Central to the *actus reus* of battery is body contact. An **assault** is either an attempted or a threatened battery. Assault differs from battery—it requires no physical contact; an assault is complete before the offender touches the victim.

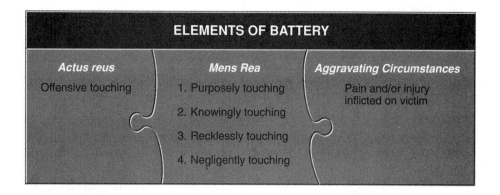

ELEMENTS OF BATTERY

Actus reus	Mens Rea	Aggravating Circumstances
Offensive touching	1. Purposely touching	Pain and/or injury inflicted on victim
	2. Knowingly touching	
	3. Recklessly touching	
	4. Negligently touching	

The Elements of Battery

The *actus reus* of battery consists of unjustified offensive touching. Corporal punishment that parents or other guardians inflict to "discipline" those under their legal authority, although offensive, is not battery because the law justifies it. Unjustified offensive touching covers a wide spectrum. Brutal attacks with baseball bats, kicking with heavy boots, and staggering blows with fists obviously fall within its scope. At the other extreme, spitting in the face of someone you want to insult satisfies the *actus reus* of battery.[29]

Existing law does not clearly specify the battery *mens rea*. At common law, battery was an injury inflicted "willfully or in anger." Modern courts and statutes extend battery *mens rea* to include reckless and negligent contacts. Most jurisdictions either include reckless and negligent injuring within the scope of battery or create a separate offense to that effect. Louisiana, for example, provides that "inflicting any injury upon the person of another by criminal negligence" constitutes "negligent injuring." The *Model Penal Code* removes the *mens rea* confusion by defining battery to include "purposely, recklessly, or negligently caus[ing] bodily injury," or "negligently caus[ing] bodily injury . . . with a deadly weapon." The court in *State v. Glenn* dealt with the required *mens rea* of assault and battery.[30]

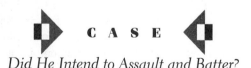

C A S E

Did He Intend to Assault and Batter?

State v. Glenn,
1997 WL 340753 (S.C.App. 1997)

HOWELL, J.

David L. Glenn appealed from his conviction for assault and battery with intent to kill. The South Carolina supreme court affirmed.

FACTS

Sara LeCroy lives approximately four miles from Interstate 85 on Old Dobbins Bridge Road in Anderson County. Glenn lives in the same area as LeCroy. In March 1994, LeCroy removed a white porcelain toilet from her house and placed it in her yard behind the mailbox. LeCroy and her daughter-in-law placed potting soil in the toilet and planted flowers in it. On Saturday night, April 9, 1994, the toilet was still in LeCroy's yard. Sometime after midnight that night, LeCroy was awakened by a loud car or truck "taking off." The next morning, the toilet was gone.

At approximately 2:00 A.M. on Sunday, April 10, 1994, Gene Allen was traveling northbound on Interstate 85. He was driving a tractor trailer from Gainesville, Georgia, to Sagamore Beach, Massachusetts. As he approached an interstate overpass at the five-mile marker in Anderson County, Allen saw two young white males and a car on the overpass. One of the men was standing at the front of the car, while the other was standing at the rear of the car on the passenger side. As Allen was coming to the overpass, his vehicle was hit by a large white object, coming through the windshield and roof of the tractor. Although Allen was severely injured, he managed to stop his rig. Allen testified that he never actually saw the object before it hit his truck; however, the record makes clear that the object was a toilet containing some fertilizer or potting soil.

Allen's truck was towed from the scene by a local towing company. The trucking company then picked up the truck and returned it to its terminal in Norcross, Georgia.

After hearing about the incident, Larry Duckett, Glenn's cousin, contacted the victim and the police, telling them that Glenn was the only person in the community that Duckett thought might be capable of committing the crime. Duckett reached this conclusion because, sometime during the previous year, Glenn told Duckett that he had been throwing items at moving vehicles. According to Duckett, Glenn thought his pranks were funny. Glenn also told Duckett that he wondered what it would feel like to kill someone.

. . . Samuel Duckett, Larry's brother, also testified. In response to the solicitor's question about whether Glenn told Samuel that he had a desire to throw things into moving vehicles, Samuel responded:

No, it ain't exactly like a craving, like he wanted to do something like this or something. He didn't really, you know, like was put like [sic] a big desire or anything to do something like this. It's just something spur of the moment.

OPINION

. . .

. . . Glenn argues the trial court erred in denying his motion for directed verdict. Glenn contends his motion for directed verdict should have been granted because the State failed to prove that Glenn acted with malice. Glenn also argues that the State failed to establish that Glenn acted willfully and with a specific intent to kill. . . . [W]e disagree.

Assault and battery with intent to kill (ABIK) is the unlawful act of a violent nature to the person of another with malice aforethought, either express or implied. *State v. Foust*, S.C., 479 S.E.2d 50 (1996). Assault and battery with intent to kill contains all the elements of murder except the actual death of the person assaulted. Before a person can be convicted of ABIK, the jury must be satisfied beyond a reasonable doubt that if the party assaulted had died from the injury, the defendant would have been guilty of murder. Accordingly, ABIK requires an intent to kill accompanied with malice. With respect to the intent to kill, it is sufficient for the State to show a general intent as opposed to a specific intent to kill.

In this case, we conclude that the evidence as outlined above was sufficient to allow the jury to conclude that Glenn acted with malice and with an intent to kill. Clearly, the jury could have reasonably inferred that Glenn acted with malice, particularly in light of the evidence establishing that Glenn waited on the overpass for a motorist to pass by and then intentionally dropped a heavy item onto the moving vehicle. See, e.g., *State v. Bell*, 305 S.C. 11, 406 S.E.2d 165 (1991) (Malice is the doing of a wrongful act intentionally and without just cause or excuse.), cert. denied, 502 U.S. 1038 (1992); *State v. Johnson*, 291 S.C. 127, 128, 352 S.E.2d 480, 481 (1987) ("Malice has been defined as the wrongful intent to injure another and indicates a wicked or depraved spirit intent on doing wrong.").

The evidence was likewise sufficient to support a finding that Glenn acted with an intent to kill. In *State v. Hayes*, 272 S.C. 256, 250 S.E.2d 342 (1979), overruled in part on other grounds, *State v. Doctor*, 306 S.C. 527, 413 S.E.2d 36 (1992), the defendant was convicted of assault and battery with intent to kill as a result of injury to a passing motorist who was struck by a brick thrown by the defendant from an overpass onto the interstate. With respect to the element of intent to kill, the Supreme Court agreed with the trial court's conclusion that the act was of such gross recklessness as to be tantamount to intent. Thus, the Court held that the intent to kill could be inferred from the surrounding circumstances. The evidence presented in this case establishes a similar act of gross recklessness and, therefore, is sufficient to support a finding that Glenn intended to kill. See also *Foust*, S.C. at, 479 S.E.2d at 52, n. 4 (Evidence of the character of the means or instrument used, the manner in which it was used, the purpose to be accomplished, and resulting wounds or injuries are admissible to show the intent with which an assault was committed.). The trial court, therefore, did not err by denying Glenn's motion for directed verdict.

Accordingly, for the foregoing reasons, the judgment below is hereby AFFIRMED.

QUESTIONS FOR DISCUSSION

1. How does the court define the *mens rea* of assault and battery with the intent to kill.

2. List all of the facts relevant to determining whether Glenn satisfied the *mens rea* of assault and battery with the intent to kill.

3. How would you define the *mens rea* of assault and battery with intent to kill?

4. Do you think that Glenn committed assault and battery with the intent to kill? Defend your answer.

NOTE CASE

Cheryl thought her live-in boyfriend, Harrod, was at work and invited her other boyfriend, Calvin, over. Unknown to Cheryl, Harrod had left work, gone to a back room in the house, and fallen asleep. Harrod awoke and discovered Calvin. When Calvin refused to leave, Harrod threw a hammer at him, Calvin ducked, and the hammer hit the wall just over Harrod's baby son's crib. Of course Harrod assaulted Calvin, but did he assault his baby Christopher, whom he did not intend to hurt and who had no idea his father threw a hammer at him? The Maryland Court of Special Appeals, reversing Harrod's conviction for assault against Christopher, held that attempted battery assault required the specific intent to harm Christopher, which Harrod lacked. *Harrod v. State*, 65 Md.App. 128, 499 A.2d 959 (1985)

Battery requires some injury, at least of an emotional nature in most jurisdictions. These emotional harm batteries and batteries resulting in minor physical injury are misdemeanors in most jurisdictions. Batteries resulting in serious bodily injury are felonies. The *Model Penal Code* departs from existing law by requiring at least some bodily injury; offensive touching itself is not a crime. Supporters of the code admit that insulting touching causes real psychological and emotional suffering but maintain that tort law and informal sanctions more appropriately deal with those harms.

Some codes include provisions regarding specific harms. Recent injuries surrounding pit bulls prompted the Minnesota legislature to enact the following provision:

Section 609.26. A person who causes great or substantial bodily harm to another by negligently or intentionally permitting any dog to run uncontrolled off the owner's premises, or negligently failing to keep it properly confined is guilty of a petty misdemeanor. . . .

Subd. 3. If proven by a preponderance of the evidence, it shall be an affirmative defense to liability under this section that the victim provoked the dog to cause the victim's bodily harm.[31]

Injuries and deaths resulting from drug abuse have led the same legislature to enact the following provision:

> 609.228 Whoever proximately causes great bodily harm by, directly or indirectly, unlawfully selling, giving away, bartering, delivering, exchanging, distributing, or administering a controlled substance . . . may be sentenced to imprisonment for not more than ten years or to payment of a fine of not more than $20,000, or both.[32]

The *Model Penal Code* grades bodily harm offenses as follows:

> § 211.1
> 2. Bodily injury is a felony when
>   a. such injury is inflicted purposely or knowingly with a deadly weapon; or
>   b. serious bodily injury is inflicted purposely, or knowingly or recklessly under circumstances manifesting extreme indifference to the value of human life.
>   c. except as provided in paragraph (2), bodily injury is a misdemeanor, unless it was caused in a fight or scuffle entered into by mutual consent, in which case it is a petty misdemeanor.

The Elements of Assault

Assault includes two types of offense: attempted batteries and threatened batteries. **Attempted battery assault** focuses on the objective dimension to the offense, the *actus reus*. As in other attempts, attempted battery requires a specific intent to commit a battery and, in most jurisdictions, substantial steps toward carrying out the attempt without actually completing it (see chapter 5).

Threatened battery assault focuses on the subjective dimension—the *mens rea* and the fear placed in the victim by the assaulter. **Threatened battery assault,** sometimes called intentional scaring, requires only that actors intend to frighten their victims, thus expanding assault beyond attempted battery. Even absent the intent to physically injure, the intent to frighten victims into believing the actor will hurt them satisfies the threatened battery assault requirement.

Victims' awareness is critical in threatened battery assault. Specifically, victims must fear an immediate battery, and that fear must be reasonable. Words alone are not assaults; threatening gestures must accompany them. This requirement is not always just. For example, what if an assailant approaches from behind a victim, saying, "Don't

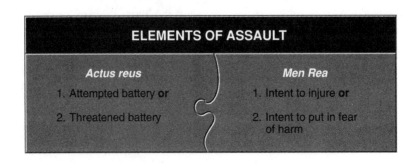

ELEMENTS OF ASSAULT

Actus reus	*Men Rea*
1. Attempted battery **or**	1. Intent to injure **or**
2. Threatened battery	2. Intent to put in fear of harm

move, or I'll shoot!" These words produce a reasonable fear that injury is imminent, yet they are not an assault.

Conditional threats are not immediate. The conditional threat, "I'd punch you out if you weren't a kid," is not immediate because it is conditioned on the victim's age. Therefore, no threatened battery assault has taken place. In a few jurisdictions, a present ability to carry out the threat must exist. But in most, even a person who approaches a victim with a gun he knows is unloaded, points the gun at the victim, and pulls the trigger (intending only to frighten his victim) has committed threatened battery.[33]

Both threatened and attempted battery assaults address two somewhat distinct harms. Attempted battery assault deals with an incomplete or inchoate physical injury. Threatened battery assault is directed at a present psychological or emotional harm: the victim's fear. In attempted battery assault, therefore, a victim's awareness is immaterial; in threatened battery assault, it is crucial.

The *Model Penal Code* deals with threatened and attempted battery assaults as follows:

§ 211.1 Simple Assault.
A person is guilty of assault if he:
    a. attempts to cause bodily injury to another; or
    b. attempts by physical menace to put another in fear of imminent serious bodily harm.
Simple assault is a misdemeanor unless committed in a fight or scuffle entered into by mutual consent, in which case the assault is a petty misdemeanor.

Historically, all assaults were misdemeanors. However, modern statutes have created several aggravated assaults that are felonies. Most common are assaults with the intent to commit violent felonies (murder, rape, and robbery, for example), assaults with deadly weapons (such as guns and knives), and assaults on police officers. In *Commonwealth v. Sexton*, the court dealt with the difficult problem of defining just what kinds of objects "deadly weapon" includes.

C A S E

Was the Pavement a Deadly Weapon?

Commonwealth v. Sexton,
680 N.E.2d 23 (Mass. 1997)

Everett Sexton was convicted of assault and battery by means of a dangerous weapon and wilful and malicious destruction of property. On appeal, the Appeals Court reversed his conviction. The Massachusetts Supreme Judicial Court granted the Commonwealth's application for further appellate review and affirmed the conviction by the Superior Court.
    FRIED, Justice.

FACTS

On the evening of August 28, 1992, Jeffrey Czyzewski and a female companion went to a bar in Holyoke. At the bar, Czyzewski played a game of pool with the wife of Donald Sexton. Czyzewski briefly left the pool table. On his return, he accused Sexton's wife of cheating by moving the pool balls during his absence. Ending the game, Czyzewski left the pool table and was thereafter approached three separate times by an agitated Donald Sexton, who demanded an apology.

Czyzewski testified that after the second request, the defendant, Everett Sexton, the brother of Donald Sexton, approached Czyzewski and said that he would stand by his brother if anything happened. On the third occasion, Donald Sexton smashed a beer bottle on the bar, but was restrained before he could threaten Czyzewski further. Following this incident, the defendant, his brother, and his brother's wife left the bar.

Shortly thereafter, Czyzewski and his companion went out to the parking lot and got into their car. Immediately a van pulled up alongside them and the defendant, his brother, and a third man got out. The defendant and his brother kicked in the window on the passenger side where Czyzewski was sitting. The defendant reached through the shattered window to grab Czyzewski, attempting to pull him through the window. At that moment, Czyzewski's companion was able to start the car and drove out of the parking lot. As they pulled out, the Sextons said, "Let's go get him," and returned to the van to follow Czyzewski. Because their car was about to run out of gas, Czyzewski and his companion were forced to return to the parking lot, with the van following behind. Czyzewski left the vehicle and Donald Sexton, the defendant, and their companion left their van. The defendant and his brother immediately approached Czyzewski; they began to push and shove him. The defendant restrained Czyzewski by lifting Czyzewski's jacket over his head and the brothers threw Czyzewski to the ground. On the ground, Donald Sexton banged Czyzewski's head against the pavement a number of times while the defendant repeatedly kicked him. The beating was interrupted by the bar owner and another man. The Sexton brothers left before the police arrived.

OPINION

. . .

This case presents an issue of first impression, in that we have not previously addressed whether stationary objects can be considered dangerous weapons in Massachusetts. The statute, G.L. c. 265, § 15A, does not define the term "dangerous weapon," but we have stated previously that there are things which are dangerous per se and those which are dangerous as used. We have defined the former class as "instru-

mentalit[ies] designed and constructed to produce death or great bodily harm." In the latter class are things which become dangerous weapons because they are "used in a dangerous fashion." In such cases it is generally "a question for the fact finder whether the instrument was so used in a particular case." In evaluating different situations, the determination has invariably turned on "use," and our courts have repeatedly held that ordinarily innocuous items can be considered dangerous weapons when used in an improper and dangerous manner. See *Commonwealth v. Scott*, 408 Mass. 811, 822–823, 564 N.E.2d 370 (1990) (gag); *Commonwealth v. Barrett*, 386 Mass. 649, 655–656, 436 N.E.2d 1219 (1982) (aerosol spray can); *Commonwealth v. Appleby*, 402 N.E.2d 1051 (riding crop); *Commonwealth v. Tarrant*, 367 Mass. 411, 418, 326 N.E.2d 710 (1975) (German shepherd dog); *Commonwealth v. Farrell*, 78 N.E.2d 697 (lighted cigarettes); *Commonwealth v. Mercado*, 24 Mass.App.Ct. 391, 395, 509 N.E.2d 300 (1987) (baseball bat); *Commonwealth v. LeBlanc*, 3 Mass.App.Ct. 780, 780, 334 N.E.2d 647 (1975) (automobile door swung knocking police officer down). Our courts have also noted, with approval, decisions in other jurisdictions which have found otherwise innocent items to fit this classification when used in a way which endangers another's safety. See *United States v. Loman*, 551 F.2d 164, 169 (7th Cir.), cert. denied, 433 U.S. 912, 97 S.Ct. 2982, 53 L.Ed.2d 1097 (1977) (walking stick); *United States v. Johnson*, 324 F.2d 264, 266 (4th Cir. 1963) (chair brought down upon victim's head); *People v. White*, 212 Cal.App.2d 464, 465, 28 Cal.Rptr. 67 (1963) (a rock); *Bennett v. State*, 237 Md. 212, 216, 205 A.2d 393 (1964) (microphone cord wrapped around victim's neck); *People v. Buford*, 69 Mich.App. 27, 30, 244 N.W.2d 351 (1976) (dictum) (automobile, broomstick, flashlight and lighter fluid may all be dangerous weapons as used).

We do not agree with the Appeals Court that, to be a dangerous weapon, the defendant must be able to wield the item at issue, nor do we think it relevant that the pavement was present as part of the environment in which the defendant chose to participate in this assault. Prior to the Appeals Court's decision in *Commonwealth v. Shea*, supra, the only explicit restriction on our use-based categorization of dangerous weapons held that human teeth and other parts of the human body were not dangerous weapons because they are not "instrumentalities apart from the defendant's person." *Commonwealth v. Davis*, 406 N.E.2d 417. In *Shea*, a case in which the defendant pushed two women from his boat and sped off, leaving them five miles off shore, the Appeals Court found that, while "the ocean can be and often is dangerous, it cannot be regarded in its natural state as a weapon within the meaning of § 15A," because "in its natural state [it] cannot be possessed or controlled." *Commonwealth v. Shea*, 644 N.E.2d 244. We believe that this is too narrow a reading of the instrumentality and use language we have employed when we have defined dangerous weapons as "an instrument or instrumentality which, because of the manner in which it is used, or attempted to be used, endangers the life or inflicts great bodily harm." *Commonwealth v. Farrell*, 78 N.E.2d 697. While one might not be able to possess the ocean or exercise authority over it in a traditional sense, *Commonwealth v. Shea*, 644 N.E.2d 244, one could certainly use it to inflict great harm, such as by holding another's head underwater.

Likewise, it is obvious that one could employ concrete pavement, as the defendant and his brother did here, to cause serious bodily harm to another by banging the victim's head against the hard surface. As the Commonwealth points out, there would be no problem in convicting a defendant of assault and battery by means of a dangerous weapon if he used a broken slab of concrete to bludgeon his victim. We see no reason to hold that such a conviction cannot stand merely because the instrumentality in question is a fixed thing at the time of its dangerous use.

A number of other jurisdictions which have considered this question have also held that an object's stationary character does not prevent its use as a dangerous weapon. *United States v. Murphy*, 35 F.3d 143, 147 (4th Cir.1994), cert. denied, 513 U.S. 1135, 115 S.Ct. 954, 130 L.Ed.2d 897 (1995) (steel cell bars); *State v. Brinson*, 337 N.C. 764, 766, 448 S.E.2d 822 (1994) (cell bars and floor); *People v. O'Hagan*, 176 A.D.2d 179, 179, 574 N.Y.S.2d 198 (1991) (cell bars); *People v. Coe*, 165 A.D.2d 721, 722, 564 N.Y.S.2d 255 (1990) (plate glass window); State v. Reed, 101 Or.App. 277, 279–280, 790 P.2d 551 (1990) (sidewalk); *People v. Galvin*, 65 N.Y.2d 761, 762–763, 492 N.Y.S.2d

25, 481 N.E.2d 565 (1985) (same). As North Carolina recognized, an item's dangerous propensities "often depend entirely on its use," and not its mobility, for "[w]hether the pitcher hits the stone or the stone hits the pitcher, it will be bad for the pitcher." *State v. Reed*, 790 P.2d 551, quoting Cervantes, *Don Quixote*, Part II, ch. 43 (1615). We hold that one who intentionally uses concrete pavement as a means of inflicting serious harm can be found guilty of assault and battery by means of a dangerous weapon.

Finally, we agree with the Appeals Court that the jury were presented with sufficient evidence to find that the defendant possessed the requisite intent and knowledge to be guilty of assault and battery by means of a dangerous weapon under a joint venture theory. From the defendant's statements and actions it is apparent that he possessed the intent to engage in an assault and battery with his brother. While he may not initially have had knowledge that his brother intended to use the pavement to effectuate the attack, as the Appeals Court noted, "there is no need to prove an anticipatory compact between the parties to establish joint venture," if, "at the climactic moment the parties consciously acted together in carrying out the criminal endeavor." *Commonwealth v. Young*, 35 Mass.App.Ct. 427, 435, 621 N.E.2d 1180 (1993). The defendant continuously kicked and punched Czyzewski while his brother repeatedly slammed Czyzewski's head into the pavement. At no time during this conflict did the defendant seek to withdraw.

The conviction of assault and battery by means of a dangerous weapon is affirmed. So ordered.

QUESTIONS FOR DISCUSSION

1. Exactly what does the court mean by the distinction between things that are dangerous *per se* and things that are dangerous as used?

2. What is the problem with including stationary objects within the meaning of the term deadly weapon?

3. Do you agree with the court that the pavement is a dangerous weapon? Defend your answer.

4. How many of the many objects that the court lists from other cases cited in the opinion do you think are deadly weapons?

5. How would you define the term?

The *Model Penal Code* includes a comprehensive assault and battery statute, integrating, rationalizing, and grading assault and battery. It takes into account *actus reus, mens rea*, circumstance elements, and intended harm. Note the careful attention paid to these critical elements:

§ 211.2

A person is guilty of aggravated assault if he:

a. attempts to cause serious bodily injury to another, or causes such injury purposely, knowingly or recklessly under circumstances manifesting extreme indifference to the value of human life; or

b. attempts to cause or purposely or knowingly causes bodily injury to another with a deadly weapon.

Aggravated assault under paragraph (a) is a felony of the second degree; aggravated assault under paragraph (b) is a felony of the third degree.

§ 211.3

A person commits a misdemeanor if he recklessly engages in conduct which places or may place another person in danger of death or serious bodily injury. Recklessness and danger shall be presumed where a person knowingly points a firearm at or in the direction of another, whether or not the actor believed the firearm to be loaded.

FALSE IMPRISONMENT

False imprisonment is a harm to two fundamental rights:

1. Liberty: the right to come and go as we please, sometimes called the right of locomotion.
2. Privacy: the right to be left alone by the government.

Some states have enacted false imprisonment statutes to protect against invasions of these rights. For example, in California "the unlawful violation of the personal liberty of another" is a misdemeanor carrying a one-year jail term.[34]

False imprisonment is a specific intent crime. Prosecutors must prove that defendants meant to take away their victims' liberty forcibly and unlawfully. The *Model Penal Code* provides that such restraint, if done knowingly, is sufficient to prove false impris-

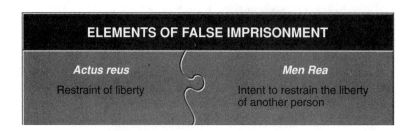

ELEMENTS OF FALSE IMPRISONMENT

Actus reus	*Men Rea*
Restraint of liberty	Intent to restrain the liberty of another person

onment. Motive is ordinarily not material in such cases. For example, if police officers make unlawful arrests, they can be prosecuted for false imprisonment even if they believed the arrests were lawful. Whether the error concerning an arrest was reckless, negligent, or merely honest causes problems.

Most forcible detentions or confinements are considered false imprisonment under existing law. This does not include restraints authorized by law, however, as when police officers make lawful arrests, parents restrict their children's activities, or victims detain their victimizers. False imprisonment does not require long detentions, nor does it include all detentions. The standard for criminal false imprisonment is somewhat higher than the civil requirement, which is satisfied by any confinement, however short.

The *Model Penal Code* requires the restraint to "interfere substantially with the victim's liberty." Although physical force often accomplishes the detention, it is not essential; threatened force is enough. Hence, the threat, "If you don't come with me, I'll break your arm," suffices. Even nonthreatening words occasionally qualify, such as when a police officer who has no right to do so orders someone on the street into a squad car, asserting, "You're under arrest."

KIDNAPPING

Like false imprisonment, kidnapping invades privacy and takes away liberty. Kidnapping is essentially an aggravated form of false imprisonment. As such, all kidnappings include the lesser offense of false imprisonment. Originally, kidnapping was the "forcible abduction or stealing away of man, woman or child from their own country." Although kidnapping was only a misdemeanor, Blackstone called it a "heinous crime" because "it robs the king of his subjects, banishes a man from his country, and may in its consequences be productive of the most cruel and disagreeable hardships."[35]

Until the twentieth century, kidnapping was a capital offense in some jurisdictions in the United States, mainly as a result of events during the first half of the century. During Prohibition (1919 to 1933), kidnapping was prevalent in the organized crime world. One gang member might abduct a rival, "take him for a ride," and kill him. Much more frequently, rivals were captured and held hostage for ransom. Before long, law-abiding citizens were being abducted, especially the spouses and children of wealthy and otherwise prominent citizens.

The most famous early case was the ransom kidnap and murder of Charles Lindbergh's son. Lindbergh was an aviator who captured Americans' hearts and imaginations when he flew solo across the Atlantic Ocean. Kidnapping was only a misdemeanor in New Jersey in 1932 when the crime occurred. The tremendous sympathy that Lindbergh's popular hero status generated and the public outrage toward what was perceived as a rampant increase in random kidnappings of America's "pillars of wealth and virtue" led legislatures to enact harsh new kidnapping statutes. These statutes are largely in force today, even though they were passed in an emotional overreaction to a few notorious cases.[36]

Another widely publicized case breathed new life into these harsh statutes. In 1974, Patricia Hearst, heiress to newspaper tycoon William Randolph Hearst, was kidnapped.

The case met with public outrage, not only because of sympathy for the prominent Hearst family but also because of shock at the psychological and physical dimensions of the crime. The kidnappers were self-styled revolutionaries calling themselves the Symbionese Liberation Army. One of the SLA's first demands was that William Randolph Hearst distribute $1 million in food to the poor of California. Later on, much to her parents' and the public's horror, Patricia Hearst converted to the SLA, participating in bank robberies to raise money for the "revolution." This all happened during a time when radicalism and violence were much feared and when the Vietnam War protest and airline hijackings for terrorist political purposes were very much on the public's mind. Hence, the public saw not only Patty Hearst's capture and her family's deep trauma but also a threat to destroy American society.

The Hearst case brought kidnapping's heinous side into bold relief. It drew together in one story capture and detention, terror, violence, and political radicalism. The details were trumpeted sensationally every day in newspapers and on radio and television. Hope that existing harsh and sweeping kidnapping legislation would be reflectively reassessed vanished in this inflamed, emotional atmosphere. President Nixon expressed his hope—a hope that many others shared—that the Supreme Court would not declare capital punishment for kidnapping to be unconstitutional. Then California Governor Reagan reflected the deep public outrage against kidnapping when he wished aloud that the kidnappers' demand for a free food program would set off a botulism epidemic among the poor.

Like false imprisonment, the offense from which it descended, kidnapping is a crime against personal liberty. At common law its main elements were

1. seizing,

2. confining, and

3. carrying away (asporting)

4. another person

5. by force, threat of force, fraud, or deception.

The critical difference between false imprisonment and kidnapping is the carrying away, or asportation, of victims. Since at least the eighteenth century, as Blackstone makes clear, carrying a victim into a foreign country where no friends or family could give aid and comfort, and the law could not protect the victim, added a particularly terrifying dimension to kidnapping. In the early days, the victim had to be carried at least as far as another county and usually into a foreign country.

Modern interpretations leave the asportation requirement virtually meaningless. The famous case of *People v. Chessman* illustrates how broadly asportation is interpreted by courts faced with especially revolting cases. Caryl Chessman was a multiple rapist who, in one instance, forced a young woman to leave her car and get into his, which was only twenty-two feet away. The court held that asportation's mere fact, not its distance, determined kidnapping. They upheld Chessman's conviction for kidnapping, a capital crime in California. After many years of fighting the decision, Chessman eventually was executed.[37]

Modern statutes in some states have removed the asportation requirement, usually replacing it with the requirement that kidnappers intend to confine, significantly restrain, or hold their victims in secret. The Wisconsin statute, for example, defines a kid-

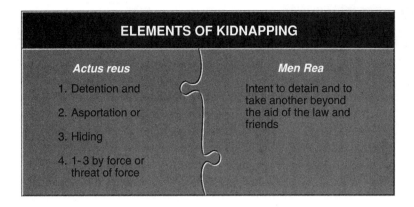

napper as one who "seizes or confines another without his consent and with intent to cause him to be secretly confined." Whatever the changes, the heart of the crime remains to "isolate the victim from prospect of release or friendly intervention." The court dealt with the meaning of asportation in the carjacking case of *People v. Allen.*[38]

Did He Move Her a "Substantial" Distance?

People v. Allen,
64 Cal.Rptr.2d 497 (1997)

Tyrone Allen was convicted in the Superior Court, City and County of San Francisco, of, among other offenses, carjacking and kidnapping of a person under the age of 14. He appealed. The Court of Appeal, affirmed the conviction for kidnapping.

RUVOLO, Associate Justice.

FACTS

On August 7, 1995, May SunYoung and her family lived at 2951 Treat Street in San Francisco. That morning, Ms. SunYoung was on her way to take her 7-year old daughter, Kirstie, to summer camp and stopped her automobile briefly in the driveway to close her garage door manually as she was backing out onto the street.

As Ms. SunYoung closed her garage door, a man approached her from behind and said, "Excuse me, can you do me a favor?" While turning around she saw the man later identified as appellant getting into her vehicle, whose engine was still running. He then locked the car doors. Kirstie was still in the vehicle with her seatbelt on and began crying. Because the driver's side window was rolled down about seven inches, Ms. SunYoung put her arms through the window and struggled with appellant in an attempt to reach the ignition key and turn off the engine.

Appellant then released the parking brake, put the vehicle in reverse, and backed out of the driveway with Kirstie inside and Ms. SunYoung running alongside the vehicle still attempting to reach the ignition key. The vehicle backed across Treat Street, which was a two-lane road with two parking lanes, until it hit the opposite curb and came to a stop. Appellant estimated the vehicle movement was 30–40 feet. While respondent now claims this estimate to be "speculation," both sides at different times suggested that the distance moved was approximately 5 car lengths, or

50 feet. Appellant exited the vehicle, threw the car keys onto the ground, shoved Ms. SunYoung against a fence, and ran down the street carrying her purse which had been left in the vehicle. Shortly thereafter, a neighbor on Treat Street several blocks away saw a man run by. In response to the neighbor's attempts to stop the man, the fleeing suspect stated, "Stay back, I got a gun." After a brief struggle, the man ran off but was later apprehended by San Francisco police officers and identified as appellant.

The jury instruction given regarding the simple kidnapping count was CALJIC No. 9.52, which sets forth the elements of kidnapping of a person under 14 years of age as follows: "Every person who unlawfully and with physical force or by any other means of instilling fear moves any other person under 14 years of age without her consent for a substantial distance, that is, a distance more than slight or trivial, is guilty of the crime of kidnapping . . . ." (Pen. Code, § 208, subd. (b); all further statutory references are to the Penal Code unless otherwise indicated.)

OPINION

The only element of the crime for which appellant asserts there was insufficient evidence and inadequate jury instructions is asportation. For "simple" kidnapping, that is, a kidnapping not elevated to a statutory form of "aggravated" kidnapping, the movement needed must be "substantial," or a distance that is more than "trivial, slight, or insignificant."

Appellant . . . argues that his conviction for simple kidnapping must be reversed because the minimum distance requirement for asportation is not met. He asserts the movement of Ms. SunYoung's vehicle 30–50 feet down her driveway and across Treat Street with Kirstie inside as a matter of law cannot be "substantial," or a distance that is more than "trivial, slight or insignificant."

Appellant is correct that under most cases decided pre-1981 which have examined only the actual distance involved, the movement here would not meet the legal test of substantiality. In *People v. Brown* (1974) 11 Cal.3d 784, 114 Cal.Rptr. 426, 523 P.2d 226 (Brown), after breaking into the victim's residence, the defendant forced the victim to accompany him through a search of her house for her husband. When the victim's husband was not found, the defendant

moved the victim outside and along a passageway next to the house until a neighbor's intervention caused the defendant to abandon the victim and flee alone. The total distance the victim was moved was unascertained. The Supreme Court held the asportation of the victim was insufficient to satisfy the "substantial" requirement and was no more than trivial. . . .

. . . [T]hose cases which have considered the quality and character of the movement in addition to its absolute distance have weighed the purpose for the movement, whether it posed an increased risk of harm to the victim, and the "context of the environment in which the movement occurred." Purposes for movement found to be relevant have been those undertaken to facilitate the commission of a further crime, to aid in flight, or to prevent detection. We believe these factors are appropriate considerations. "Substantiality" implies something more than only measured distance. While "slight" is consistent with a quantitative analysis, the term "trivial" is a qualitative term suggestive of the conclusion that more is envisioned in determining whether a kidnapping occurs than simply how far the victim is moved. The legal requirement for asportation is satisfied by a finding of either. (CALJIC No. 9.52.)

In so holding, we conclude that while in absolute footage the distance moved here may have been empirically short, it was of a character sufficient to justify a finding of "substantiality" by the jury. The movement, in part, was plainly made to prevent Ms. SunYoung from regaining possession of her vehicle and to facilitate appellant's flight from the area with Kirstie. In addition to evasion of capture, the vehicle was moved from a position of relative safety onto a thoroughfare. The boundary crossed was significant because it placed Kirstie at greater risk of injury. We confirm these factors, coupled with the distance traveled, are sufficient to satisfy the "substantial movement" requirement for the crime of simple kidnapping.

. . .

[Affirmed.]

DISSENT

KLINE, Presiding Justice, concurring and dissenting opinion.

. . .

The majority essentially concedes the movement in this case does not meet the legal test of substantiality if only actual distance is considered. In light of this, I need not belabor the manifest insufficiency of the evidence to satisfy the asportation requirement properly applicable to simple kidnapping.

It deserves emphasis, however, that movement as short a distance as that shown here — 30 to 40 feet — has never been held to satisfy the asportation requirement of kidnapping. Indeed, considerably greater distances have often been held insufficient. As the majority opinion points out, movement of 90 feet, nearly three times the distance the victim in this case was moved, was held insufficient in *People v. Green* (1980) 27 Cal.3d 1, 164 Cal.Rptr. 1, 609 P.2d 468, where the Supreme Court noted that "[t]he shortest distance this court has ever held to be 'substantial' for this purpose was a full city block."

People v. Brown (1974) 11 Cal.3d 784, 114 Cal.Rptr. 426, 523 P.2d 226 also dramatically demonstrates that the movement in the present case must be deemed trivial as a matter of law. The defendant in *Brown* had gone to the victim's residence in search of her husband, whose name he had discovered in the home of his estranged wife. He forced the victim to accompany him in a search of the house for her husband. When a neighbor who heard the victim scream telephoned and asked if she needed help, the defendant dragged her out of the house and along a narrow passageway between her house and the house next door. A neighbor then ordered the defendant to release the victim and told him the police were on their way. Defendant released her and fled. "All in all he had taken her approximately 40 to 75 feet from the back door of her house." A unanimous Supreme Court had little difficulty concluding that "[t]he asportation of the victim within her house and for a brief distance outside the house must be regarded as trivial." "[U]nder the particular facts of this case," the court said, "the movement of the victim did not constitute a forcible taking 'into another part of the same county' and . . . the conviction of simple kidnapping must be reversed."

The movement in the present case is about half the distance which in *Brown* was held "trivial." Further, the victim in *Brown* was moved out of one area, the house, into another; and the movement of the victim was much more clearly intentional than that here, as it is not even clear appellant knew a child was in the vehicle when he moved it across the street.

I think it unreasonable to conclude that, when it enacted Penal Code section 207, the Legislature contemplated that backing up a car 30 to 40 feet across a street constitutes asportation "into another part of the same county" within the meaning of that statute. It must be remembered that the only definition of kidnapping that appears in the California Penal Code is that which appears in section 207. As the Supreme Court has noted on several occasions, the verb "kidnaps" used in section 209 (as well as in other statutes prescribing increased punishments for aggravated kidnappings, such as section 208 and 209.5) means kidnapping as defined in section 207. When the Legislature enacted section 209.5 in 1993 it not only adopted the section 207 definition of kidnapping, but explicitly incorporated into the new statute the "substantial distance" requirement imposed by the courts. (Pen.Code, § 209.5, subd. (b).) The Legislature must be deemed to have been aware of the distances considered by the courts too "slight" or "trivial" to satisfy this requirement. . . .

The fact that the Legislature punished aggravated kidnapping more severely than simple kidnapping has nothing to do with the distance the victim is moved but only to the greater harm to which the victim is exposed when a kidnapping is related to certain other serious offenses. If the Legislature felt aggravated kidnapping required movement over a greater distance than would suffice for simple kidnapping it would not have adopted the section 207 definition of kidnapping in an aggravated kidnapping statute, as it has, nor applied to aggravated kidnapping the same substantial distance requirement applicable to simple kidnapping, as it also has done. (Pen.Code, § 290.5, subd. (b).)

I agree that by moving the child in the vehicle across the street appellant committed a crime other than carjacking and the various other offenses of which he was properly convicted; that crime was not kidnapping, however, but false imprisonment (Pen. Code, § 236), which does not require any movement. . . . As the Supreme Court has repeatedly observed, "the Legislature did not intend to apply criminal sanctions [for any form of kidnapping] where the 'slightest movement' is involved."

Because the asportation in this case was trivial within the meaning of the applicable case law, I would reverse the judgment of conviction of simple kidnapping for lack of evidentiary support. I agree that in all other respects the judgment should be affirmed.

QUESTIONS FOR DISCUSSION

1. What test did the court establish in order to determine the distance required to satisfy the asportation element of the kidnapping *actus reus*?

2. What reasons does the majority give to support its definition of asportation?

3. How does the dissent's definition differ from that of the majority?

4. What reasons does the dissent give for its definition?

5. Do you agree with the majority or the dissent's definition of asportation? Defend your answer.

Kidnapping is usually divided into two degrees: simple and aggravated. The most common aggravating circumstances include kidnapping for the purpose of:

- Sexual invasions.
- Obtaining a hostage.
- Obtaining ransom.
- Robbing the victim.
- Murdering the victim.
- Blackmail.
- Terrorizing victims.
- Obtaining political aims.

The penalty for aggravated kidnapping is usually life imprisonment and, until recently, occasionally even death.

Since the 1970s, a new form of kidnapping has come into prominence. With increasing numbers of families separating and with the growing participation of both parents in child rearing, noncustodial parents are no longer willing to endure long periods without seeing their children. In fact, some cannot accept the noncustodial role. They take desperate measures to get their children, often illegally. The court dealt with such a kidnapping in *State v. McLaughlin*.

C A S E

Did He Abduct the Children?

State v. McLaughlin,
125 Ariz. 505, 611 P.2d 92 (1980)

McLaughlin was convicted of child abduction. He appealed. The conviction was affirmed. Justice Hays delivered the opinion.

FACTS

On February 18, 1977, Dr. Stephen Zang, a physician and attorney admitted to practice in both Arizona and Nevada, obtained a default divorce from his spouse, Cheryl Zang, in Las Vegas, Nevada. Pursuant to the terms of the dissolution, Dr. Zang was awarded custody of the two minor children of the marriage, subject to a right of visitation; however, the decree provided for subsequent review of the custody issue upon termination of the school semester. On February 20, 1977, Dr. Zang and the children moved to Arizona and shortly thereafter he had the Nevada decree entered on the Arizona dockets. Although the record at this point is unclear, the transcripts do establish the existence of a written order of the Maricopa County Superior Court granting custody of the children to Dr. Zang and suspending the visitation rights of his former spouse.

Apparently dissatisfied with the custody decrees, Ms. Zang allegedly decided to covertly remove the children from Arizona and her husband's possession. In furtherance of this scheme, she contacted appellant, the owner and operator of the local security guard service, requesting protection from interference by Dr. Zang. Although again the record is not clear, it is apparent that appellant was shown at least the Nevada decree of dissolution and possibly the order of the Arizona court.

On the morning of October 12, 1977, appellant, along with two employee security guards, met with Ms. Zang and a male companion at a Phoenix restaurant in order to finalize plans to remove the Zang children from their Tempe school. Appellant outlined the proposed course of action on a napkin which was subsequently introduced into evidence. In essence, the strategy involved the blocking of Dr. Zang's driveway with a purportedly inoperative automobile and the removal of the children from the schoolyard at the first appropriate moment. Ms. Zang wore a blond wig, sunglasses and a security guard shirt supplied her by appellant as a method of concealing her identity from school officials.

Pursuant to the scheme, appellant, a guard and Ms. Zang proceeded to the school, arriving at approximately 10:30 A.M. Appellant approached the school's principal, informed her that he was seeking a younger cousin and inquired regarding the lunch hour of the second grade. Nothing more occurred until noon recess, when Ms. Zang, accompanied by one of appellant's guards, removed one of her children from the lunch line and directed him towards a waiting auto. It was only the immediate pursuit of the child's teacher

and a nearby resident which prevented the successful completion of the plan and forced the parties to await the arrival of police.

OPINION

On appeal, appellant alleges that he has violated no law. He contends that jurisdiction in the Nevada divorce proceedings was fraudulently obtained and that any decree issued pursuant thereto was void and without effect. Based upon this premise, appellant would have us hold that there could thus have been no attempt at removing the youngster from a "person having lawful charge of the child" within the meaning A.R.S. § 13–841 (1956) of our previous Criminal Code. In our opinion, however, although the record before us is void of evidence other than defendant's testimony regarding the validity or invalidity of the Nevada decree, we find this contention of little significance.

A.R.S. § 13–841 provides in part:

A person who maliciously, forcibly or fraudulently takes or entices away a child under the age of seventeen years with intent to detain and conceal the child from its parent, guardian or other person having lawful charge of the child, shall be punished by imprisonment.

The . . . language establishes clearly the *mens rea* sufficient for conviction of child abduction. There must be an intent to detain and conceal the minor from a person in lawful control. In this regard, it must thus suffice if the accused knows that he is removing the child from the custody of one who appears to have lawful custody.

[Conviction affirmed.]

QUESTIONS FOR DISCUSSION

1. Do you think McLaughlin was guilty of child abduction?

2. Should Cheryl Zang be prosecuted, too?

3. How serious a crime do you think child abduction is under these circumstances?

4. Is it simple kidnapping, aggravated kidnapping, or a separate, less serious offense when parents kidnap their own children?

SUMMARY

Homicide and criminal sexual conduct are the most serious crimes against persons, threatening life, liberty, and privacy. Criminal sexual conduct includes the ancient common-law crimes of rape and sodomy as well as a range of other criminal sexual penetrations and contacts. Originally, rape was a crime against strangers, limited to the forcible penetration of the vagina of a woman by a man not her husband. Sodomy was directed at all other sexual penetrations and contacts, including mainly oral and anal sex, both heterosexual and homosexual. Although criminal homicide and criminal sexual conduct comprise the most serious crimes against persons, they are not the only crimes against persons. Measured in sheer numbers, assault and battery far outnumber homicides and criminal sexual conduct. Although often considered one crime, battery and assault are separate offenses. Batteries are offensive touching, ranging from severe beatings to insulting contacts. Assaults are attempted batteries or threatened batteries, in which no physical contact is required to complete the crime.

Another harm to persons covered by criminal law is deprivation of liberty. Short detentions without asportations are misdemeanors called false imprisonment. More serious detentions accompanied by asportation are kidnappings, ancient offenses generally associated with carrying off important persons for ransom. Aggravated kidnapping generally involves some circumstance that generates public outrage, such as kidnappings accompanied by rape, murder, and terror. Related to simple kidnapping is child abduction, a growing phenomenon as noncustodial parents are unwilling to accept separation from their children.

Restraints on liberty take three forms under existing criminal law. The misdemeanor of false imprisonment is a brief detention without asportation, the penalty for which is generally a fine or a short jail term. Simple kidnapping is a significant detention accompanied by asportation, however slight. The penalty for simple kidnapping is usually up to ten years' imprisonment. Aggravated kidnapping is reserved for cases touching off the most public outrage: kidnappings associated with murder, rape, ransom, blackmail, and terror. For aggravated kidnapping, the penalty is severe: usually life imprisonment and occasionally even death, at least until recently.

REVIEW QUESTIONS

1. What values in a free society do crimes against persons threaten?

2. Identify, compare, and contrast the main crimes against persons.

3. Compare the classical stereotype of rape and the social reality of criminal sexual conduct.

4. To what conditions was common-law rape limited?

5. According to Lord Hale, what was the justification for requiring proof of the conditions in question 4?

6. Upon what three conditions did the credibility of common-law rape charges depend?

7. What element of rape was most important until the 1970s?

8. Summarize the main changes in the law of rape that took place during the 1970s and 1980s.

9. Describe the *actus reus* of rape.

10. Describe the "storm of debate" over the *mens rea* of rape generated by *Regina v. Morgan*.

11. Summarize the majority and the California rule regarding statutory rape.

12. Summarize some of the problems connected with strengthening the laws regarding criminal sexual conduct against children.

13. Identify the three main reasons for the marital rape exception.

14. Identify and briefly describe the main provisions of the Michigan criminal sexual conduct statute and explain how it differs from traditional rape law.

15. List the main circumstance elements that can raise simple rape to aggravated rape.

16. State the *actus reus*, the *mens rea*, and the harm in battery.

17. What is the essential difference between assault and battery?

18. Identify and describe the two kinds of assault.

19. What are the basic interests that false imprisonment and kidnapping threaten?

20. Identify the elements of false imprisonment and kidnapping.

21. Contrast false imprisonment and kidnapping.

KEY TERMS

assault An attempt to commit a battery, or intentionally putting another in fear.

attempted battery assault The crime of assault that focuses on *actus reus*.

battery Offensive bodily contact.

carnal knowledge Sexual intercourse.

constructive force A substitute for actual force in rape cases.

marital rape exception The rule that husbands cannot rape their wives.

reasonable resistance standard The requirement that women must use the amount of resistive force required by the totality of the circumstances surrounding sexual assault.

statutory rape Carnal knowledge with a person under the age of consent whether or not accomplished by force.

threatened battery assault The crime of assault that focuses on the *mens rea*.

utmost resistance standard The requirement that rape victims must use all the physical strength they have to prevent penetration.

Suggested Readings

1. Rollin M. Perkins and Ronald N. Boyce, *Criminal Law,* 3d ed. (Mineola, N.Y.: Foundation Press, 1982), pp. 197–224 and 453–477. The authors discuss all matters in this chapter, including recent developments in the law.

2. American Law Institute, *Model Penal Code and Commentaries,* vol. 1 (Philadelphia: American Law Institute, 1980), pt. II, pp. 273–439. Summarizes the legal points and the debate surrounding revision of rape laws. It is worth reading for the arguments raised for and against various definitions of the sex offenses.

3. Battelle Law and Justice Study Center, *Forcible Rape: A National Survey* (Washington, D.C.: National Institute

of Law Enforcement and Criminal Justice, March 1977). An excellent study of how rape is viewed by criminal justice professionals and how rape law is enforced. This work shows rape law in action as opposed to what the books say rape law should be. It develops some important points concerning prosecutors' attitudes toward rape victims.

4. Susan Estrich, *Real Rape* (Cambridge, Mass.: Harvard University Press, 1987). A stimulating history and critique of rape law in the United States with particular attention to rape by acquaintances. The author writes forcefully and convincingly, stimulating readers to think about the definition and enforcement of rape laws.

Notes

1. For the feminist position regarding the special significance of the sexual component in rape, see Diana Russell, *The Politics of Rape: The Victim's Perspective* (New York: Stein and Day, 1975); Anra Medea and Kathleen

Thompson, *Against Rape* (New York: Farrar, Straus and Giroux, 1974).

2. Linda S. Williams, "The Classic Rape: When Do Victims Report?" *Social Problems* 31 (April 1984):464;

Diana E. H. Russell, *Sexual Exploitation* (Beverly Hills, Calif.: Sage, 1984); Judy Foreman, "Most Rape Victims Know Assailant, Don't Report to Police, Police Report Says," *Boston Globe* (April 16, 1986), p. 27; *Parade Magazine* (September 22, 1985), p. 10; Lani Anne Remick, "Read Her Lips: An Argument for a Verbal Consent Standard in Rape," *University of Pennsylvania Law Review*, 141(1993):1103; Richie McMullen, *Male Rape: Breaking the Silence on the Last Taboo* (London: Gay Men Press, 1990).

3. Sir William Blackstone, *Commentaries* (University of Chicago Press, 1979), book IV, p. 210.

4. Quoted in Blackstone, *Commentaries*, p. 215.

5. Ibid., pp. 213–214.

6. *Reynolds v. State*, 27 Neb. 90, 42 N.W. 903, 904 (1889).

7. Remick, "Read Her Lips," p. 1111.

8. 127 Wis. 193, 106 N.W. 536, 538 (1906).

9. *Casico v. State*, 147 Neb. 1075, 25 N.W.2d 897, 900 (1947).

10. *State v. Ely*, 114 Wash. 185, 194 P. 988 (1921) (fraud as to nature of the act); *Moran v. People*, 25 Mich. 356 (1872) (told intercourse beneficial).

11. *Satterwhite v. Commonwealth*, 201 Va. 478, 111 S.E.2d 820 (1960).

12. *Commonwealth v. Mlinarich*, 345 Pa.Super. 269, 498 A.2d 395, 397 (1985).

13. American Law Institute, *Model Penal Code and Commentaries*, vol. 1 (Philadelphia: American Law Institute, 1980), pt. II, pp. 279–281.

14. For example, see Minnesota Statutes Annotated § 609.341, subd. 12 (St. Paul, Minn.: West Publishing Company, 1987).

15. *State v. Shamp*, 422 N.W.2d 520 (Minn.App.1988).

16. *Model Penal Code and Commentaries*, vol. 1, pt. II, 281; Joshua Mark Fried, "Forcing the Issue: An Analysis of the Various Standards of Forcible Compulsion in Rape," *Pepperdine Law Review* 23 (1996):120, 123–127.

17. Daphne Edwards, "Acquaintance Rape and the 'Force' Element: When 'No' is Not Enough," *Golden Gate Law Review*, 26 (1996):241, 260–261.

18. National Institute of Law Enforcement and Criminal Justice, *Forcible Rape—An Analysis of Legal Issues* 5 (March 1978) (forcible rape).

19. *Commonwealth v. Berkowitz*, 609 A.2d 1266 (Pa. 1994), 1277.

20. *People v. Randolph*, 12 Wash.App. 138, 528 P.2d 1008 (1974).

21. *Regina v. Morgan*, [1975] 2. W.L.R. 923 (H.L.).

22. *State v. Reed*, 479 A.2d 1291, 1296 (Me.1984).

23. Estrich, *Real Rape*, pp. 97–98.

24. *State v. Bonds*, 165 Wis.2d 27, 477 N.W.2d 265 (1991).

25. *Model Penal Code and Commentaries*, vol. 1, pt. II, pp. 42–44.

26. N.Y. Penal Law 130.00(4) (1975): New Jersey Stat.Ann. 2C:14–2 (1979): Oregon Rev. Code §§ 163.365, 163.375 (1977); statistics from J. C. Barden, "Marital Rape: Drive for Tougher Laws Is Pressed," *New York Times* (May 13, 1987), p. 10; Note, "To Have and to Hold: The Marital Rape Exception and the Fourteenth Amendment," *Harvard Law Review* 99 (1986):1255 (insisting that marital rape exceptions violate equal protection guarantees of all women); Dorothy Q. Thomas, "Women's Human Rights: From Visibility to Accountability," *St. John's Law Review*, 69 (1995): 217, 230 (reference to National Clearing House on Marital and Date Rape).

27. M.C.L.A. § 750(a) through (g).

28. Unidentified source.

29. *State v. Humphries*, 21 Wash.App. 405, 586 P.2d 130 (1978).

30. Louisiana Stat.Ann.—Rev. Stat. tit. 17—A, 14.39 (1974); American Law Institute, *Model Penal Code*, tentative draft no. 11.

31. Ibid.

32. Minn.Stat.Ann. § 609.26 (1987) (1989 Cumulative Supplement).

33. *Encyclopedia of Crime and Justice* (New York: Free Press, 1983), 1:89.

34. West's Ann. Cal. Penal Code § 236 (St. Paul, Minn.: West Publishing Company, 1988).

35. Blackstone, *Commentaries*, book IV, p. 219.

36. *State v. Hauptmann*, 115 N.J.L. 412, 180 A. 809 (1935).

37. 38 Cal.2d 166, 238 P.2d 1001 (1951).

38. *Model Penal Code and Commentaries*, vol. II, pp. 211–212.

CHAPTER TEN

Crimes Against Habitation: Burglary and Arson

CHAPTER OUTLINE

CHAPTER MAIN POINTS

1. Burglary and arson protect both personal security and property.

2. The harm in burglary stems from intrusions on homes and other structures.

3. The harm in arson is damage and destruction to homes and other property.

4. The structures subject to burglary and arson cover a broad spectrum.

5. Burglary is a specific intent crime.

6. Arson is a general intent crime.

Did He Burglarize the Apartment?

An apartment manager was visited by a man who said he was looking to rent a one bedroom apartment. The manager showed the man the community room and the laundry facilities. She then took the man to a one bedroom, upper level apartment that had been vacant for approximately one month. She unlocked the door with her master keys and walked into the kitchen. As she turned around to face the man she saw he had a gun pointed at her. The man instructed her to do as she was told. He ordered her to walk down a hallway into the bedroom. There, he pushed her down on the floor, tied a scarf around her mouth and placed her in hand cuffs. He removed her boots, slacks and pantyhose. He then tied her ankles together with the pantyhose and fondled her. The man took her keys and asked for money. When she was sure he had left the apartment, the manager escaped to another apartment and called the police.

INTRODUCTION

The ancient English proverb, "A man's home is his castle," is not merely a popular belief. Two common-law felonies, burglary and arson, were created to protect where people lived. Common-law burglary protected dwellings from intruders in the night. Arson guarded against those who "maliciously and willfully" burned another person's home. Crimes against habitation are not merely property offenses, although to be sure homes have monetary value. Perhaps the best way to express a home's additional value is in the expression "A house is not a home." A house is the material thing worth money; a home is the haven of refuge where security and privacy from the outside world are possible. Modern burglary and arson have grown far beyond their common-law origin of protecting homes. Now, all kinds of structures and even vehicles fall within their scope. But at their core remain two harms considered serious by most people—intrusions and destruction or damage.

BURGLARY

The famous seventeenth-century English jurist Sir Edward Coke defined common-law burglary as follows:

> A felon, that in the night breaketh and entereth into the mansion house of another, with intent to kill some reasonable creature, or to commit some other felony within the same, whether his felonious intent be executed or not.[1]

The principal elements in Lord Coke's definition are:

1. breaking and entering
2. of dwellings
3. in the nighttime
4. with the intent to commit a felony
5. inside the dwelling.

The sentiment that a man's home is his castle ran deep in English culture. Under the common law, homes deserved and received the law's special protection. Not even the king's majesty and power could thwart this protection. According to Lord Pitt's famous speech in the British House of Commons:

> The poorest man may in his cottage bid defiance to all the forces of the Crown. It may be frail—its roof may shake—the wind may blow through it—the storm may enter—but the King of England cannot enter—all his force dares not cross the threshold of the ruined tenement.

Reflecting that idea, debate over unreasonable searches and seizures in homes began long before the Fourth Amendment to the United States guaranteed protection against them. In 1575, for example, an irate burgess from Colchester (an English town from which many American settlers originated) successfully challenged the right of Queen Elizabeth's officers to enter his home to search for seditious libels against a local public figure. When the officers tried to enter the burgess's front door without a warrant, he met them, armed with a sword. The burgess warned that officers who had earlier tried to come in without a warrant were heavily fined in the Queen's court for trespass. At this announcement, the officers disbanded, leaving the burgess alone for the time being.

The definition of burglary has varied greatly over the centuries. Medieval burglary was a broad offense that protected any place likely to attract people (churches, houses, even walled towns) against intrusions, no matter what their purpose. Sometime in the sixteenth century, the offense started to resemble Lord Coke's narrower definition. The more general trespass from medieval times became the nighttime invasion of a home to commit a felony. Burglary was a felony, punishable by death. Mere intrusions into homes without the intention to commit further crimes inside were lumped with other trespasses. Trespass was a misdemeanor, punishable by fines.

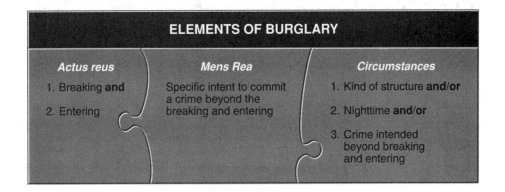

ELEMENTS OF BURGLARY

Actus reus	*Mens Rea*	*Circumstances*
1. Breaking **and**	Specific intent to commit a crime beyond the breaking and entering	1. Kind of structure **and/or**
2. Entering		2. Nighttime **and/or**
		3. Crime intended beyond breaking and entering

THE ELEMENTS OF BURGLARY

From Lord Coke's time to modern times, burglary gradually returned to its medieval origins. Both legislation and judicial decisions have broadened its sixteenth-century meaning. Consequently, burglary has come to include the following elements:

1. Breaking and entering, but also simply remaining in,

2. homes, but also any structure with four walls and a roof, and even most vehicles,

3. at any time of day or night

4. with the intent to commit felonies, but also almost any crime.

Burglary *Actus Reus*

The *actus reus* of burglary consists of two elements—breaking and entering. At one time, breaking probably meant a violent entry, but very early on it came to include much more than knocking down doors and smashing windows. Although it did not go so far as to include merely walking through an open door, breaking became nothing more than a technicality. In the eighteenth century, the common-law authority Sir William Blackstone wrote that breaking included "picking a lock, or opening it with a key; nay, by lifting up the latch of a door, or unloosing any other fastening which the owner has provided." Even if an outer door was left open and the felon entered through it, it was called breaking if an inner door had to be loosened to get in.

By the twentieth century, the common-law element of breaking had become a mere technicality. Entering structures in an unusual manner, such as through a chimney, was considered a constructive breaking. So was opening a door for an accomplice. Some retreat from constructive breaking has prevented the total elimination of the breaking requirement. The *Model Penal Code* provides that

> [a] person is guilty of burglary if he enters a building or occupied structure, or separately secured or occupied portion thereof, with purpose to commit a crime therein, unless the premises are at the time open to the public or the actor is licensed to enter. It is an affirmative defense to prosecution for burglary that the building or structure was abandoned.

A number of states have adopted the code's recommended **unprivileged entry** definition of burglary *actus reus.*[2]

Entering, like breaking, has a broad meaning in burglary law. From about 1650, partial entry was enough to satisfy the requirement. One burglar "entered" a house because his finger was inside the windowsill when he was caught. In another case, an intruder who assaulted an owner on the owner's threshold "entered" the house because his pistol crossed over the doorway. In Texas a man who never got inside a building at all, but who fired a gun into it intending to injure an occupant, "entered" by means of the bullet.[3]

Some statutes remove the entering element entirely by providing that *remaining* in a structure satisfies the *actus reus* requirement of burglary. Hence, it is burglary to go into a department store during business hours and wait in a rest room until the store closes, with the intent to steal jewelry. If the remaining requirement is carried to its logical extreme, however, injustices result. For example, suppose I am invited into my friend's house, and after I am inside I notice that she has some valuable antiques. If I decide to put the antiques in my pocket when she leaves the room, I have satisfied the remaining requirement. Other states, such as North Carolina, do not even require that burglars get inside structures; it is enough that they tried. Hence, one man who got a door ajar but never set foot inside was convicted because burglary does not require entering or remaining, according to the North Carolina statute. To some criminal law reformers, substituting remaining for breaking and entering badly distorts burglary's core idea—nighttime intrusions into homes.[4]

The *Model Penal Code* and several jurisdictions take a middle ground between having strict entry requirements and eliminating entry requirements altogether. They have adopted a surreptitious remaining element. **Surreptitious remaining** means entering lawfully but with the purpose to remain inside until it is not lawful to be there, in order to commit a crime. This requirement distinguishes between invited guests and potential criminals who enter lawfully but remain in order to commit crimes.

Dwelling Requirement

A material circumstance in burglary concerns what broken-into, entered, or remained-in structures qualify as "dwellings." Modern law goes far beyond the common-law definition of dwelling. The structures included in burglary today stand somewhere between the sweeping medieval "any place where people are likely to congregate" and the very narrow sixteenth-century "dwelling." Even in the sixteenth century, however, dwelling did not mean only fully constructed standard houses; it meant any place in which a person lived, no matter how poorly constructed or squalid. In one case, the dwelling was "a sheet stretched over poles and fastened to boards nailed to posts for sides, being closed at one end and having an old door at the other."[5]

Any structure intended for sleeping in regularly was considered a dwelling at common law. Most modern burglary statutes cover a broad, sometimes almost limitless, spectrum. Definitions such as "any structure" or "any building" are common. Many statutes also include vehicles. One writer who surveyed the subject concluded that any structure with "four walls and a roof" was included. This sweeping definition has led to bizarre results. In California, for example, a person who breaks into a car and steals something from the glove compartment has committed burglary, a crime punishable by up to fifteen years in prison. If, however, the person steals the entire car, including its contents, the crime is only grand larceny, for which the maximum penalty is ten years.[6]

The *Model Penal Code* definition aims at limiting burglary to *occupied* structures. The reason for this definition, according to the Reporter, is that it covers "intrusions that are typically the most alarming and dangerous." According to *Model Penal Code* Section 221.0, "occupied structure" means any structure, vehicle, or place adapted for overnight accommodations of persons, or for carrying on business therein, whether or not a person is actually present. A few states follow the *Model Penal Code* approach and limit burglary to occupied structures, whether or not people are present when the burglary occurs. The Ohio Court of Appeals dealt with the problem of defining "occupied structure" in the unpublished opinion of *State v. Burns.*[7]

C A S E

Did He Burglarize an "Occupied" Apartment?

State v. Burns,
1997 WL 152074 (Ohio App. 6 Dist. 1997)

Robert Burns was found guilty of aggravated burglary and other felonies. He appealed and the Ohio Court of Appeals affirmed.

FACTS

On January 8, 1996, an apartment manager of a one hundred thirty-eight unit complex in Maumee, Ohio was visited by a man who said he was looking to rent a one bedroom apartment. The manager showed the man the community room and the laundry facilities. She then took the man to a one bedroom, upper level apartment that had been vacant for approximately one month. She unlocked the door with her master keys and walked into the kitchen. As she turned around to face the man she saw he had a gun pointed at her. The man instructed her to do as she was told. He ordered her to walk down a hallway into the bedroom. There, he pushed her down on the floor, tied a scarf around her mouth and placed her in hand cuffs. He removed her boots, slacks and pantyhose. He then tied her ankles together with the pantyhose and fondled her. The man took her keys and asked for money. When she was sure he had left the apartment, the manager escaped to another apartment and called the

police. The manager identified appellant as the man who had attacked her.

A jury found appellant guilty of aggravated burglary, aggravated robbery, kidnaping and gross sexual imposition. The jury further found that the state had proven the specification that appellant used a firearm in the commission of these offenses. The court sentenced appellant to twelve to twenty-five concurrent years for aggravated burglary, aggravated robbery and kidnaping. He received a consecutive three to five year term of imprisonment for the offense of gross sexual imposition and a three year term of imprisonment for the firearm specification. The firearm specification sentence was ordered to be served consecutively to all the other sentences. In total, appellant was sentenced to not less than eighteen years nor more than thirty-three years.

OPINION

On appeal, appellant asserts . . . [that] the convictions are against the manifest weight of the evidence. The standard of review for manifest weight arguments is as follows:

An appellate court's function when reviewing the sufficiency of the evidence to support a criminal conviction is to examine the evidence admitted at trial to determine whether such evidence, if believed, would convince the average mind of the defendant's guilt beyond a reasonable doubt. The relevant inquiry is whether, after viewing the evidence in a light most favorable to the prosecution, any rational trier of fact could have found the essential elements of the crime proven beyond a reasonable doubt.

Appellant presents one argument for this court to consider. Appellant contends the state failed to prove the elements of aggravated burglary in that a vacant apartment is not an "occupied structure" pursuant to R.C. 2911.11. The elements of aggravated burglary, a violation of R.C. 2911.11 are as follows:

"(A) No person, by force, stealth, or deception, shall trespass in an occupied structure, as defined in section 2909.01 of the Revised Code, or in a separately secured or separately occupied portion thereof, with purpose to commit therein any theft offense, as defined in section 2913.01 of the Revised Code, or any felony, when any of the following apply:
"(1) The offender inflicts, or attempts or threatens to inflict physical harm on another;
"(2) The offender has a deadly weapon or dangerous ordnance, as defined in section 2923.11 of the Revised Code, on or about his person or under his control;
"(3) The occupied structure involved is the permanent or temporary habitation of any person, in which at the time any person is present or likely to be present."

R.C. 2909.01(C) defines occupied structure as:

"any house, building, outbuilding, watercraft, aircraft, railroad car, truck, trailer, tent, or other structure, vehicle, or shelter, or any portion thereof, to which any of the following applies:
"(1) It is maintained as a permanent or temporary dwelling, even though it is temporarily unoccupied and whether or not any person is actually present."

The court's jury instruction regarding "occupied structure" mirrored the above definition.

The Tenth District Court of Appeals addressed a similar issue in *State v. Green* (1984), 18 Ohio App.3d 69. The court stated:

"[I]t is obvious that the General Assembly, in adopting the definition of 'occupied structure' found in R.C. 2909.01, intended to broaden the concept of the offense of burglary from one of an offense against the security of habitation, to one concerned with the serious risk of harm created by the actual or likely presence of a person in a structure of any nature. In that context, it is noteworthy that the General Assembly utilized the word 'maintained' in division (A), as opposed to 'occupied,' although it did use that latter word in division (B), which deals with structures other than dwellings. We believe that the distinction between 'maintained' and 'occupied' is significant, in the sense that the former alludes more to the character or type of use for which the dwelling is intended to be subjected, whereas the latter is more closely related to the actual use to which the structure is presently being subjected.

"Thus, a structure which is dedicated and intended for residential use, and which is not presently occupied as a person's habitation, but, which has neither been permanently abandoned nor vacant for a prolonged period of time, can be regarded as a structure 'maintained' as a dwelling within the meaning of division (A). In this context, then, division (A) includes a dwelling whose usual occupant is absent on prolonged vacation, a dwelling whose usual occupant is receiving longterm care in a nursing home, a summer cottage, or a residential rental unit which is temporarily vacant. In all these examples, even though the dwelling is not being presently occupied as a place of habitation, that situation is temporary, and persons are likely to be present from time to time to look after the property to help 'maintain' its character as a dwelling."

Applying this analysis to the instant case, we conclude that there was sufficient evidence to support a finding that the apartment at issue was an "occupied structure" as that term is used in R.C. 2911.11. Accordingly, appellant's sole assignment of error is found not well-taken.

On consideration whereof, the court finds that appellant was not prejudiced or prevented from having a fair trial, and the judgment of the Lucas County Court of Common Pleas is affirmed. It is ordered that appellant pay the court costs of this appeal.

QUESTIONS FOR DISCUSSION

1. List all of the facts relevant to deciding whether Burns broke and entered an "occupied structure."
2. How did the Ohio Court of Appeals define "occupied structure"?
3. What policy interests does this definition promote?
4. Do you agree that Burns committed burglary of an occupied structure? Explain your answer.

The "of Another" Element

Another circumstance element in burglary stems from the common-law requirement that burglars break and enter the dwelling of *another*. Modern law has expanded the common-law definition. For example, landlords can burglarize their tenants' apartments. And, in *Jewell v. State*, the court dealt with the problem of whether you can burglarize your own home.

C A S E

Did He Burglarize His Own Home?

Jewell v. State,
672 N.E.2d 417 (Ind.App. 1996)

Barry L. Jewell, after a jury trial, was convicted of burglary with a deadly weapon resulting in serious bodily injury, a class A felony, and battery resulting in serious bodily injury, a class C felony. Jewell was sentenced to an aggregate term of 48 years imprisonment. After a retrial Jewell appealed. The Indiana Court of Appeals affirmed.

ROBERTSON, Judge.

FACTS

. . . [I]n 1989, Bridget Fisher, who later married Jewell and changed her name to Bridget Jewell, purchased a home on contract in her maiden name from her relatives. Bridget and Jewell lived in the house together on and off before and after they married in

1990. Jewell helped fix the house up, and therefore, had some "sweat equity" in the house.

Jewell and Bridget experienced marital difficulties and dissolution proceedings were initiated. Jewell moved out of the house and Bridget changed the locks so that Jewell could not reenter. At a preliminary hearing in the dissolution proceedings, Bridget's attorney informed Jewell that Bridget wanted a divorce and wanted Jewell to stop coming by the house. Jewell moved into a friend's house, agreeing to pay him $100.00 per month in rent and to split the utility expenses.

Bridget resumed a romantic relationship with her former boyfriend, Chris Jones. Jewell told a friend that he wanted to get Jones in a dark place, hit him over the head with a 2x4 (a board), and cut his "dick" off. Jewell confronted Jones at his place of employment and threatened to kill him if he were to continue to see Bridget. Jewell was observed on numerous occasions watching Bridget's house. Jewell used a shortwave radio to intercept and listen to the phone conversations on Bridget's cordless phone.

At approximately 4:00 A.M. on the morning of June 13, 1991, Jewell gained entry to Bridget's house through the kitchen window after having removed a window screen. Bridget and Jones were inside sleeping. Jewell struck Jones over the head with a 2x4 until he was unconscious, amputated Jones' penis with a knife, and fed the severed penis to the dog. Bridget awoke and witnessed the attack, but she thought she was having a bad dream and went back to sleep. Bridget described the intruder as the same size and build as Jewell and as wearing a dark ski mask similar to one she had given Jewell. She observed the assailant hit Jones on the head with a board, and stab him in the lower part of his body.

A bloody 2x4 was found at the scene. The sheets on the bed where Bridget and Jones had been sleeping were covered in blood. Bridget discovered that one of her kitchen knives was missing. However, the police did not preserve the sheets or take blood samples and permitted Bridget to dispose of the sheets. A police officer involved explained that the possibility that any of the blood at the crime scene could have come from anyone other than Jones had not been considered.

Jones' severed penis was never found and he underwent reconstructive surgery. His physicians fashioned him a new penis made from tissue and bone taken from his leg. Jones experienced complications and the result was not entirely satisfactory.

. . .

OPINION

. . .

Jewell attacks the sufficiency of evidence supporting his conviction of Burglary, which is defined as:

A person who breaks and enters the building or structure of another person, with intent to commit a felony in it, commits burglary. Ind. Code 354321

Jewell argues he was improperly convicted of breaking into his own house.

When reviewing the sufficiency of the evidence, we neither reweigh the evidence nor judge the credibility of witnesses. Rather, we examine only the evidence most favorable to the judgment, along with all reasonable inferences to be drawn therefrom, and if there is substantial evidence of probative value to support the conviction, it will not be set aside. It is for the fact-finder to resolve conflicts in the evidence and determine which witnesses to believe.

The Burglary statute's requirement that the dwelling be that "of another person" is satisfied if the evidence demonstrates that the entry was unauthorized. *Ellyson v. State*, 603 N.E.2d 1369, 1373 (Ind. Ct.App.1992). In *Ellyson*, we held a husband was properly convicted of burglary for breaking into the house in which he and his estranged wife had lived previously with the intent of raping his wife. We noted that dissolution proceedings had been initiated and that wife alone controlled access to the home. We upheld the husband's burglary conviction even though he may have had a right to possession of the house co-equal with his wife at the time of the breaking and entering.

In the present case, Bridget had purchased the house in her own name before the marriage. When she and Jewell experienced marital difficulties, Jewell moved out and Bridget changed the locks to prevent Jewell from reentering the house. Bridget alone controlled access to the house. Jewell entered the house at 4:00 A.M. through the kitchen window after having removed the screen. The evidence supports the conclusion that the entry was unauthorized; and, therefore, we find no error. . . .

Judgment affirmed.

QUESTIONS FOR DISCUSSION

1. List all of the facts relevant to determining whether Jewell burglarized his own home.

2. How does the state of Indiana define the "of another" element?

3. How did the court arrive at the conclusion that Jewell did not burglarize his own home?

4. What is the reason for the "unauthorized entry" requirement?

5. Do you agree with it? Defend your answer.

The "Nighttime" Element

At common law, burglaries had to take place at night. The requirement of the circumstance of nighttime was based on three considerations. First, darkness facilitates committing crimes. Second, darkness hampers identifying suspects. Finally, and perhaps most important, nighttime intrusions alarm victims more than do daytime intrusions. At least eighteen states retain the nighttime requirement specifically. Most recent statutory revisions have continued to regard nighttime intrusions as an aggravating circumstance. Some statutes, however, have eliminated the nighttime requirement entirely.

Burglary *Mens Rea*

Burglary is a specific intent crime. That is, to satisfy the *mens rea* of burglary, the prosecution must prove two elements:

1. The intent to commit the *actus reus* of breaking and entering or remaining;
2. The intent to commit a crime once inside the structure broken into, entered, or remained in.

In other words, burglars must intend not only to invade the structure of another but also to commit additional crimes once inside.

As in the other burglary elements, the list of crimes burglars must intend to commit has expanded since the sixteenth century. In Lord Coke's time, the intended crime had to be serious: murder or another heinous felony. Although some law books emphasized violent felony, the cases almost all involved breaking and entering in order to steal.

Modern statutes also concentrate on intrusions to commit theft. Many define the *mens rea* to include intruding with the intent to commit "a felony or any larceny." Under these statutes, even petty theft is burglary. Hence, to enter a store intending to steal a ballpoint pen is burglary. Some jurisdictions extend the burglary *mens rea* still further, making it burglary to intrude with the intent to commit "any crime," "any public offense," and sometimes "any misdemeanor."[8]

It is not necessary to *complete* or even attempt the intended crime in order to commit burglary. It is enough that an intent to commit the additional crime exists at the moment the entry takes place. Hence, if I break into my enemy's house intending to murder him, change my mind just inside the front door, and return home without hurting anyone, I have committed burglary. The *mens rea* of intending to commit murder is present. Burglary is complete at the moment the intrusion occurs, so long as the intent to commit an additional crime is present. Completing the intended crime, although not an element in burglary, is evidence of *mens rea*. For example, if I am caught leaving a house with my arms loaded with valuable silver, jurors can infer that I entered the house in order to steal the silver.

GRADING BURGLARY

Because burglary is so broadly defined in most jurisdictions, many states divide it into several degrees. In Minnesota, for example, first-degree burglary preserves the sixteenth-century emphasis on burglary of dwellings, if another is present, if the burglar possesses a weapon, or if the burglar assaults a person within the building. Burglary of a dwelling, a bank, or a pharmacy dealing in controlled substances constitutes second-degree burglary. Third-degree burglary includes burglary of any building with an intent to steal or commit any felony or gross misdemeanor. Fourth-degree burglary includes burglary of a building with an intent to commit a misdemeanor other than theft.[9]

Despite efforts to grade burglary into degrees that reflect the broad spectrum it covers, most burglary statutes do not eliminate possible injustices. This is true in large part because burglary punishes the intrusion and not the crime for which the intrusion took place. In many cases, the penalty for burglary is much harsher than the penalty for the intended crime. The difference between a five-year sentence and a twenty-year sentence sometimes depends upon the largely metaphysical question of whether a thief intended to steal before or after entering a building.

Rationale of Burglary Law

For several centuries following 1500, burglary protected primarily security in the home from nighttime intruders. Common-law burglary did not protect other buildings considered mere real estate. Dwellings were guarded by the worst penalty—death—because burglary was a capital offense. Homes were almost sacred at common law. Invaders who threatened defenseless, sleeping families and their treasured possessions at night were specters still feared in the 1990s.

Securing homes from nighttime intruders, however, far from explains burglary's rationale under present law. Two common features in modern burglary statutes indicate that burglary aims to protect additional interests. First, trespass statutes cover the intrusion itself. Burglary requires the *mens rea* of additional criminal purpose. Second, although first-degree burglary always includes dwellings, nearly all statutes require harm, threatened harm, or the victims' presence to accompany the intrusion. Furthermore, statutes usually require other aggravating circumstances for first-degree burglary, such as an intent to commit a violent crime or an actual assault upon a person. Modern burglary, therefore, protects more than people's homes. More accurately, burglary statutes are supposed to protect homes and people, or perhaps still more precisely, people's security in their homes.

Modern burglary statutes protect at least three basic interests in society: homes, persons, and property. But what do the statutes protect these interests from? Just as burglary law protects more than one interest, it protects against more than one harm. The paramount and most ancient is intrusion itself. The misdemeanor trespass protects intrusion without further criminal purpose, a social harm widely regarded as deserving at least minor punishment. Property owners who regularly file complaints against strangers, and even against their own neighbors, resemble in that respect their sixteenth-century and even medieval ancestors who prosecuted their neighbors for trespassing even without intending to commit further crimes.

Criminal trespass is not only very old but also appears to be worldwide. The Japanese criminal code, for example, condemns "intrusion upon a habitation," defined to include human habitations, structures, or vessels, or the refusal to leave on demand, punishable by a fine or up to three years' imprisonment. Nearly all countries similarly punish intruders even when they do not intend to commit additional crimes.

Burglary reaches beyond the trespass itself. It strikes at potential harms resulting from the intrusion, specifically those that could result if intruders accomplish further criminal purposes. This unfulfilled intention lies at the core of modern burglary statutes. In this sense, burglary is an inchoate offense, an "attempt" to commit the crime the burglar intruded in order to commit.

The following possible statute might solve some of the problems of current burglary law:

1. Anyone who unlawfully enters the dwelling of another shall be subject to a fine and/or imprisonment of up to one year.

2. Anyone who, in the course of any crime punishable by one year's imprisonment or more
   a. enters the dwelling of another in which there is a person at the time, or
   b. is armed with a deadly weapon, or so arms himself, or uses or attempts to use explosives, or
   c. commits assault or otherwise injures another, or
   d. is accompanied by confederates actually present, shall be subject to a penalty that shall not be more than double the penalty for the crime committed.

This example statute accomplishes several things. First, it separates security in homes from protecting life and property. It also takes into account elements usually included in present burglary statutes as aggravating circumstances, but it makes penalties dependent upon the crime committed rather than the trespass inherent in burglary. Attempt is removed entirely, leaving burglary's inchoate dimension to the specific attempted crime intruders intend to commit.

This solution, therefore, has many merits, but it is probably too radical. Burglary is an offense too deeply ingrained in English and American law to eradicate.

ARSON

Burglary and other criminal trespasses are directed at *invasions* of homes and other structures. Arson, on the other hand, aims at *damage* or *destruction* to homes and other buildings.

History and Rationale

[I]f any person shall wittingly, and willingly set on fire any dwelling house, meeting house, store house or any out house, barn, stable, stack of hay, corn or wood, or any thing of like nature, whereby any dwelling house, meeting house or store house, cometh to be burnt shall be put to death, and to forfeit so much of his lands, goods, or chattels, as shall make full satisfaction, to the victim.[10]

This 1652 Massachusetts Bay Colony statute making arson a capital offense demonstrates clearly that the colonists considered arson a serious crime. Today, arson still poses a serious threat to life and property in America.

Arson kills hundreds and injures thousands of people annually. It damages and destroys more than a billion dollars in property and in lost taxes and lost jobs. It has also significantly increased insurance rates throughout the United States. Most states prescribe harsh penalties for arson. In North Dakota and Hawaii, the maximum penalty is ten years. In other states, such as Texas and Alabama, arson is punishable by life imprisonment.

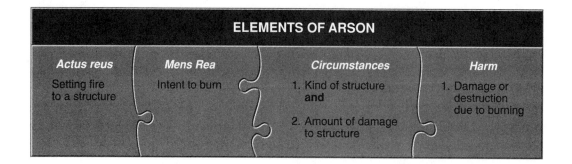

Burning: The Arson *Actus Reus*

At common law, burning meant actually setting on fire. Merely setting a fire was not enough; the fire had to reach the structure and burn it. This did not mean the structure had to burn to the ground. Once it was ignited, then however slight the actual burning, arson was complete. Modern statutes generally adopt the common-law rule, and devote great efforts to determining whether smoke merely blackened or discolored buildings, whether fire scorched them, or whether fire burned only the exterior material or the wood under it.

The *Model Penal Code* revises the common law, providing that "starting a fire," even if the fire never touches the structure aimed at, satisfies the burning requirement. The drafters justify expanding the common-law rule on the ground that no meaningful difference separates a fire that has already started but has not yet reached the basic structure and a fire that has reached the structure but has not yet done any real damage to it.[11]

Burning also includes explosions, even though the phrase "set on fire" does not generally mean "to explode." Many statutes state explicitly that explosions are burnings for the purposes of arson law. Explosions are included on tthe idea that they threaten equally—perhaps more—the lives, property, and security that arson was designed to protect.

C A S E

Did He Burn the House?

Lynch v. State,
175 Ind. App. III, 370 N.E.2d 401 (1977)

Lynch was convicted of first-degree arson. He appealed. Judge Buchanan delivered the opinion.

FACTS

In the early morning hours of June 18, 1975, a man identified as Lynch was seen throwing a burning object at the residence of Mr. and Mrs. Estel Barnett (Barnett). Immediately after the object struck the house flames engulfed the side of the residence. The flames lasted for several minutes and then died out. The fire department was not called.

The Barnetts, who were awakened by a passing neighbor, investigated and discovered a bottle containing flammable liquid with a cotton or cloth wick protruding from the opening. A "burn trail" extended from the lawn approximately ten feet to the house.

Damage to the building's aluminum siding consisted of blistering and discoloration of the paint. The amount of the damage was Ninety-one and 29/100 ($91.29) Dollars. No other part of the house was damaged.

OPINION

The phrase "sets fire to" in the First Degree Arson statute means something less than an actual burning and therefore is not synonymous with the word "burn." The gist of Lynch's position is that he is not guilty of arson because "sets fire to" and "burns" as used in the First Degree Arson statute are synonymous, and no "burning" took place, i.e., the house was not consumed.

The statute, Ind. Code § 35-16-1-1 [10-801], provides:

> Arson in the First Degree. Any person who willfully and maliciously sets fire to or burns, or causes the setting of fire to or the burning, or who aids, counsels or procures the setting of fire to or the burning of any dwelling house, rooming house, apartment house or hotel, finished or unfinished, occupied or unoccupied; or any kitchen, shop, barn, stable, garage or other outhouse, or other building that is part or parcel of any dwelling house, rooming house, apartment house or hotel, or belonging to or adjoining thereto, finished or unfinished, occupied or unoccupied, such being the property of another; or being insured against loss or damage by fire and such setting of fire to or burning, or such causing, aiding, counseling or procuring such setting of fire to or such burning, being with intent to prejudice or fraud the insurer; or such setting of fire to or burning or such causing, aiding, counseling or procuring such setting of fire to or such burning being with intent to defeat, prejudice or fraud the present or prospective property rights of his or her spouse, or co-owner, shall be guilty of arson in the first degree, and, upon conviction thereof, shall be imprisoned in the state prison not less than five [5] years nor more than twenty [20] years, to which may be added a fine not to exceed two thousand dollars [$2,000].

Observe that the drafter used the disjunctive word "or" in separating the phrase "sets fire to" from the word "burns." If we construe "or" in its "plain, or ordinary and usual, sense" as we are bound to do, it separates two different things. "Sets fire to" and "burns" are not synonymous in this context. Traditionally the common law rigidly required an actual burning. The fire must be actually communicated to the object to such an extent as to have taken effect upon it.

Other jurisdictions have recognized the distinction between "sets fire to" and "burns" as two different concepts. To "set fire to" a structure is to "place fire upon," or "against" or to "put fire in connection with" it. It is possible to set fire to a structure which, by reason of the sudden extinction of the fire, will fail to change the characteristics of the structure. Nevertheless, it has been "set fire to."

Unlike Lynch, then, we cannot conclude that he is not guilty of first degree arson because there was no burning of the house. He set fire to the house by causing a flammable substance to burn thereon causing a scorching or blistering of the paint which was an integral part of the structure. The composition of the structure was changed. No more was necessary.

Thus the modern construction of statutory terms we are interpreting is that they are not synonymous, each having a separate, independent meaning, thereby eliminating any ambiguity. The judgment is affirmed.

QUESTIONS FOR DISCUSSION

1. The court ruled that "burn" and "set fire to" are two different concepts; and that Lynch may not have burned the house, but he did set fire to it. Does it make a difference, really, whether Lynch burned or set fire to the house?

2. Does the *Model Penal Code* provision apply here?

3. Which is the better rule, the court's or the code's?

4. How much destruction would you require if you were writing an arson statute?

Arson *Mens Rea*

Most arson statutes follow the common-law *mens rea* requirement that arsonists maliciously and willfully burn or set fire to buildings. Some courts call the arson *mens rea* general intent. Here is one example:

> Arson is a crime of general, rather than specific, criminal intent. The requirement that defendant act "willfully and maliciously" does not signify that defendant must have actual subjective purpose that the acts he does intentionally shall produce either (1) a setting afire or burning of any structure or (2) damage to or destruction of said structure. So long as defendant has actual subjective intention to do the act he does and does it in disregard of a conscious awareness that such conduct involves highly substantial risks that will be set afire, burned or caused to be burned — notwithstanding that defendant does not "intend" such consequences in the sense that he has no actual subjective purpose that his conduct produce them — defendant acts "willfully and maliciously."[12]

Under modern decisions, such as that just quoted, defendants do not have to intend specifically to destroy buildings they set on fire or burn. It is generally considered enough if they intend to start a fire but do not intend, indeed do not even want, to burn a structure. In other words, the purpose requirement refers to the act in arson (burning or setting fire to buildings) and not to the harm (burning down or destroying buildings). Hence, a prisoner who burned a hole in his cell to escape was guilty of arson because he purposely started the fire. So, too, was a sailor who lit a match to find his way into a dark hold in a ship in order to steal rum. The criminal purpose in arson, then, is an intent or purpose to start a fire, even if there is no intent to burn a specific structure.

Burning property to defraud an insurer raises a special *mens rea* concern. The *Model Penal Code* divides arson into two degrees, according to defendants' culpability. Most culpable are defendants who intend to destroy buildings and not merely set fire to or burn them; these are first-degree arsonists. Second-degree arsonists are defendants who set buildings on fire for other purposes. For example, if I burn a wall with an acetylene torch because I want to steal valuable fixtures attached to the wall, I am guilty of second-degree arson for "recklessly" exposing the building to destruction even though I meant only to steal fixtures.[13]

Property in Arson

Common-law arson, like common-law burglary, protected dwellings. Modern arson law, like modern burglary law, has vastly expanded the types of structures it protects. It almost always means more than homes and sometimes even includes personal property.

The trend in modern legislation is to divide arson into three degrees. Most serious (first-degree arson) is burning homes or other occupied structures (such as schools, offices, and churches) where there is possible danger to human life. Second-degree arson includes setting fire to, or burning, unoccupied structures and perhaps vehicles (such as boats and automobiles). Third-degree arson includes setting fire to or burning personal property.

Because arson originally aimed to protect security in dwellings, setting fire to one's house was not arson. This is true in only a narrow sense today, because arson is a crime against possession and occupancy, not strictly against ownership. Hence, where owners are not in possession or do not occupy their own property, they can commit arson against it. For example, if I am a landlord and set fire to my house in order to hurt my enemy who leases it from me, I have committed arson because, although I own the house, I have transferred occupancy to my tenant enemy.

More important than this somewhat bizarre example is the significant number of owners who burn their property to collect insurance. Under common-law arson, such burnings were not arson if owners were in possession. The opportunities this provided to owners for defrauding insurance companies led to revision of the common-law rule. In most jurisdictions today, a specific provision makes it arson to burn property, whoever owns it, if done to defraud insurers.

Summary of Arson

Arson is a serious threat to at least three fundamental social interests: life, security, and property. The *actus reus* of arson consists of burning or setting fire to—however slightly—many structures, including houses, vehicles, and even personal property. First-degree arson includes burning homes and other occupied structures, second-degree includes burning unoccupied structures, and third-degree includes setting fire to personal property. The arson *mens rea* is general intent, meaning intent to burn but not necessarily to destroy. That is, arson requires purpose with respect to the act but generally recklessness with respect to destroying the building. Those who mean to destroy buildings are more culpable than those who recklessly destroy buildings.

One difficult problem with arson is that arsonists act for a variety of motives. There are those so consumed by rage that they burn down their enemies' homes. There are the pyromaniacs, whose neurotic or even psychotic compulsion drives them to set buildings on fire for thrill. Then there are the more rational, but equally deadly, defendants who burn down their own buildings or destroy their own property to collect insurance. Finally, the most deadly and difficult arsonist to catch is the professional torch who commits arson for hire.

Evidence indicates that professional arsonists are growing in numbers. Some even contend that arson rings are a multimillion-dollar business. Statutory provisions may not grade arson according to motive, but motive probably ought to affect sentencing. The difference between an enraged enemy and a pyromaniac on the one hand, and a calculating property owner or professional arsonist on the other, is clear.

SUMMARY

Burglary and arson are both aimed at protecting homes, other occupied structures, vehicles, and many other valuable properties. Their definitions have expanded since the sixteenth century, although signs are that statutes are limiting and grading both more stringently. Both felonies protect three basic social interests: personal security, homes, and property. Burglary's harm to these interests results from intrusion; arson's harm results from damage and destruction.

The *actus reus* in burglary generally includes entering another's property without privilege. Whether done at night, to homes, or to occupied structures, violence or harm to occupants aggravates the offense. The *actus reus* in arson is setting fire to or burning various structures. In some cases, it even means throwing a lighted match at a structure. The *mens rea* in burglary is the specific intent to intrude in order to commit a crime. The *mens rea* in arson is the general intent to burn or set fire to various structures.

REVIEW QUESTIONS

1. Define and give examples of the elements of breaking and entering in the law of burglary.

2. Trace the changes in the definition of burglary since medieval times.

3. What interests does the law of burglary protect?

4. Identify the criteria used to grade burglary.

5. Of what does the *actus reus* of arson consist?

6. What structures does arson include?

7. Identify the criteria used to grade arson.

KEY TERMS

surreptitious remaining Entering a structure lawfully with the intent to commit a crime inside.

unprivileged entry Entering a structure without right, license, or permission.

Suggested Readings

1. American Law Institute, *Model Penal Code and Commentaries*, vol. 2 (Philadelphia: American Law Institute, 1980), pt. II, pp. 3–94. The most detailed, up-to-date survey of arson and burglary and all the offenses related to them. It compares various recent statutory developments, argues for reforms in the law, suggests grading the crimes, and includes model provisions for them. Meant for professionals, it is still worth the serious student's effort.

2. Rollin M. Perkins and Ronald N. Boyce, *Criminal Law*, 3d ed. (Mineola, N.Y.: Foundation Press, 1982), chap. 3. This book extensively surveys arson and burglary. It includes a good history, thoroughly analyzes the material elements in both arson and burglary, and analyzes recent changes in the law.

3. Wayne R. LaFave and Austin W. Scott, Jr., *Handbook on Criminal Law* (St. Paul, Minn.: West Publishing Co., 1972). A good analysis of burglary's material elements.

5. James Inciardi, "The Adult Firesetter: A Typology," *Criminology* 8 (August 1970): 145–155. A sociologist's effort to divide arsonists into types using considerably more detail than appears in this text. Inciardi discusses not only the professional torch, the pyromaniac, and the businesspeople who burn down buildings to collect insurance, but also adolescent thrill seekers, revenge-seeking firesetters, political arsonists, and others. This is an excellent article that puts arson into a broader context than a strictly legal one.

Notes

1. Sir Edward Coke, *The Third Part of the Institutes of the Laws of England* (London: 1797), p. 63.

2. American Law Institute, *Model Penal Code and Commentaries* (Philadelphia: American Law Institute, 1985), § 221.1.

3. *Rex v. Bailey*, Crown Cases Reserved (1818); Matthew Hale, *Pleas of the Crown*, London: 1670 553; *Nalls v. State*, 219 S.W. 473 (Tex.Cr.App.1920).

4. *State v. Myrick*, 306 N.C. 110, 291 S.E.2d 577 (1982).

5. Rollin M. Perkins and Ronald N. Boyce, *Criminal Law*, 3d ed. (Mineola, N.Y.: Foundation Press, 1982), p. 201.

6. Note, "Statutory Burglary: The Magic of Four Walls and a Roof," *University of Pennsylvania Law Review* 100 (1951):411.

7. American Law Institute, *Model Penal Code and Commentaries*, vol. 2, pt. II, 72, 6.

8. Note, "Statutory Burglary," p. 420.

9. Minn.Stat.Ann 609.52 (1987).

10. William Whitmore, ed., *The Colonial Laws of Massachusetts* (Boston: 1887), p. 52.

11. *Model Penal Code and Commentaries*, vol. 2, pt. II, p. 3.

12. *State v. O'Farrell*, 355 A.2d 396, 398 (Me.1976).

13. *Crow v. State*, 136 Tenn. 333, 189 S.W. 687 (1916); *Regina v. Harris*, 15 Cox C.C. 75 (1882).

C H A P T E R   E L E V E N

Crimes Against Property

C H A P T E R   O U T L I N E

CHAPTER MAIN POINTS

1. Understanding property crimes depends more on history than on logic.

2. All property crimes originated in the ancient felony of larceny, which covered only wrongfully taking the property of others.

3. Consolidated theft statutes combine wrongful takings, conversion, and deceptions leading to property misappropriations.

4. Theft law aims to protect property possession and ownership.

5. Forgery and uttering statutes protect not only property but also confidence in the authenticity of documents, which fosters smoothly operating business transactions in modern society.

6. Robbery and extortion are crimes not only against property but also against persons.

Did He Receive Stolen Property?

A 1992 Chevrolet Astrovan automobile was stolen from a mobile home park in Spalding County. The van was subsequently utilized in a drive-by shooting on August 28, 1996. Later on the same day, Corporal Bradshaw of the Spalding County Sheriff's Department observed the van and recognized it as being similar to one that was reported stolen, as well as one that was reported as being involved in a drive-by shooting a few hours earlier. Corporal Bradshaw followed the van and could see four to five black males inside; he could not determine who was driving. While Corporal Bradshaw was following the van, the van abruptly turned into a driveway, where two or three men jumped out of the van and ran from the scene. Without the driver, the van, which was left in the "drive" mode, rolled backwards into the patrol car. Then, two young men, one of whom was the appellant, attempted to exit the van through the passenger door but were caught by Corporal Bradshaw before they could flee and were arrested at the scene.

The arresting officer was never able to determine who the driver had been or who had been in control of the stolen vehicle. The car keys were never found. When questioned by an investigator after receiving Miranda warnings, C.W. stated that he had only been along for a ride and did not know that the van was stolen. At the hearing, appellant's co-defendant, D.L.S., testified that C.W. had only gone for a ride in the van and did not have control of the vehicle at any time.

INTRODUCTION

Crimes against property include invasion, damage, destruction, and misappropriation. Burglary and arson, examined in chapter 10, are directed at invading, damaging, and destroying property. The crimes of misappropriation, whether temporary or permanent, include many offenses with a long history. In fact, understanding theft—the general term used to describe the crimes of property **misappropriation**—depends more on history than on logic. The major crimes of misappropriation include larceny, embezzlement, false pretenses, receiving stolen property, robbery, and extortion. Whatever the variations in their elements, all aim at the same misdeed: the wrongful taking and use of someone else's property. For that reason, several states have consolidated at least some of these crimes into one general theft offense.

HISTORY OF THEFT

Larceny is the oldest crime against property. All other misappropriation of property offenses stem from this ancient crime. Larceny developed in the common law as a protection of the ancient Anglo-Saxons' most valuable possession—livestock. People on the American frontier placed a similar value on cattle and horses. The disgrace attached to offenders against these valuable possessions still lingers in the epithet "horse thief," used today to signify a dishonest or untrustworthy person.[1]

In the beginning, the threat to peace and order created by taking another's valuable possessions was regarded as at least equal to, and probably even more important than, the misappropriation involved. People who took other people's property by stealth or force were therefore considered evil. On the other hand, cheaters were considered clever; they did not deserve the law's condemnation. Owners foolish enough to put their property into the hands of untrustworthy others did not deserve the law's support. Hence, larceny punished only those who got possession by stealth or force. Early on, larceny by force grew into a separate offense called robbery, a felony that violated both person and property.[2]

As society grew more complex, common-law larceny by stealth was too crude and simple to protect the many personal possessions and other valuable objects that clever people could get into their hands. Complex urban, commercial, and industrial society with its banks, businesses, services, and concentrated populations created a need to rely on others to carry on transactions of daily life. Owners and possessors transferred property to others voluntarily—for safekeeping, for shipping, for repair or storage—trusting caretakers to carry out the purpose for which the property was handed over.

Ordinary larceny did not cover the acquisition of property by means of abusing trust relationships, such as when owners turned over property for delivery to another person. In these cases, owners relinquished possession voluntarily. Hence, the element of taking in the *actus reus* of larceny was missing. This gap in the law led legislatures and judges to create additions to larceny and to new property offenses that would respond to the increased reliance on others in property transactions.[3]

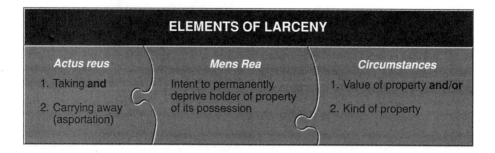

ELEMENTS OF LARCENY

Actus reus	*Mens Rea*	*Circumstances*
1. Taking **and**	Intent to permanently deprive holder of property of its possession	1. Value of property **and/or**
2. Carrying away (asportation)		2. Kind of property

LARCENY

For at least five hundred years, larceny has included five elements:

1. wrongfully taking and

2. carrying away

3. the property

4. of another

5. with the intent to permanently deprive the holder of its possession.

Larceny is a crime directed primarily at possession, not necessarily ownership. Furthermore, larceny aims at punishing specifically those who intend permanent, not temporary, possession.

Larceny *Actus Reus*

The larceny *actus reus* consists of two elements:

1. Taking.

2. Carrying away; also called **asportation.**

The element of taking requires control, if only brief control. Taking includes such direct actions as picking a pocket, lifting objects from a shop, or stealing a car. Some indirect takings also qualify. For example, suppose I see an unlocked bicycle that does not belong to me parked outside a shop. I offer to sell the bicycle to an unsuspecting passerby for forty dollars. He accepts my offer, pays me the money, and gets on the bicycle. In most states, as soon as the passerby gets on the bicycle, I have taken it, even though I never touched it. For another example, suppose I obtain money by threat. Even if I never actually touch the money, I have still taken it.

Carrying away, or asportation, means that property is moved from the place it was taken. Carrying a short distance satisfies the asportation requirement; even a few inches are enough. The word carry is not used in its ordinary sense; you can "carry away" in the legal sense what you cannot in fact carry. Hence, riding a horse away, driving a car off, leading a cow away, and pulling or pushing heavy objects away all satisfy the element of "carrying away" for purposes of the *actus reus* of larceny. All that is required is that the property actually move from where the taking occurred. A man who picked a pocket but got the money only partway out was not guilty, because he did not carry the money away. Another man who tried to steal a barrel also was not guilty, because he had only turned the barrel on its side so he could pick it up more easily. Still another who tried to walk off with an item that unbeknownst to her was chained to the counter has taken but not "carried away" the item.

Larceny violates possession, and it requires that actors wrongfully dispossess property. In the language of the common law, "There must be a trespass in the taking." Problems arise when a person who takes and carries away another person's property already lawfully possesses that property. Common examples are repair shop operators who have items in their possession, parking lot attendants who have their customers' car keys, and bank tellers who are authorized to handle money. In the ordinary sense of possession, all these persons possess another's property. Therefore, they could not *wrongfully* "take and carry away" the property because they already possess it.

The law does not define possession as simple possession alone. Instead, it looks to the nature of possession, drawing a distinction between mere custody for a particular purpose (such as when an employee possesses goods only to work on them) and legal possession (such as when someone leases a car, owns a television set, or rents a washing machine). Custodians for particular purposes can wrongfully take and carry away property they have in their possession, thereby committing larceny. Lawful possessors, however, cannot commit larceny if they take and carry away property in their possession. Possessors cannot larcenously take what they already possess.

Possession is a technical concept, involving both complex history and property law questions. Distinguishing between mere custody and lawful possession is not simple, but three rules elucidate the meaning of **trespassory taking.**

1. Employees do not possess their employers' goods; they have custody of the goods.

2. Those who hand over their personal property for repairs in their presence do not relinquish possession.

3. Money given to tellers or others for change does not transfer possession, only custody.

The court in *People v. Olivo* dealt with the element of taking.

C A S E

Did the Shoplifters Wrongfully Take the Property?

People v. Olivo,
52 N.Y. 2d 309, 438 N.Y.S.2d 242,
420 N.E. 2d 40 (1981)

Olivo and the other defendants were convicted of petit larceny. They appealed. Chief Judge Cooke delivered the opinion.

FACTS

In *People v. Olivo*, the defendant was observed by a security guard in the hardware area of a department store. Initially conversing with another person, defendant began to look around furtively when his acquaintance departed. The security agent continued to observe and saw defendant assume a crouching position, take a set of wrenches and secret it in his clothes. After again looking around, defendant began walking toward an exit, passing a number of cash registers en route. When defendant did not stop to pay for the merchandise, the officer accosted him a few feet from the exit. In response to the guard's inquiry, he denied having the wrenches, but as he proceeded to the security office, defendant removed the wrenches and placed them under his jacket. At trial, defendant testified that he had placed the tools under his arm and was in line at a cashier when apprehended. The jury returned a verdict of guilty on the charge of petit larceny. The conviction was affirmed by Appellate Term.

In *People v. Gasparik*, defendant was in a department store trying on a leather jacket. Two store detectives observed him tear off the price tag and remove a "sensormatic" device designed to set off an alarm if the jacket were carried through a detection machine. There was at least one such machine at the exit of each floor. Defendant placed the tag and the device in the pocket of another jacket on the merchandise rack. He took his own jacket, which he had been carrying with him, and placed it on a table. Leaving his own jacket, defendant put on the leather jacket and walked through the store, still on the same floor, bypassing several cash registers. When he headed for the exit from that floor, in the direction of the main floor, he was apprehended by security personnel. At trial, defendant denied removing the price tag and the sensormatic device from the jacket, and testified that he was looking for a cashier without a long line when he was stopped. The court, sitting without a jury, convicted defendant of petit larceny. Appellate Term affirmed 102 Misc.2d 487, 425 N.Y.S.2d 936.

In *People v. Spatzier*, defendant entered a bookstore on Fulton Street in Hempstead carrying an attaché case. The two co-owners of the store observed the defendant in a ceiling mirror as he browsed through the store. They watched defendant remove a book from the shelf, look up and down the aisle, and place the book in his case. He then placed the case at his feet and continued to browse. One of the owners approached defendant and accused him of stealing the book. An altercation ensued and when defendant allegedly struck the owner with the attaché case, the case opened and the book fell out. At trial, defendant denied secreting the book in his case and claimed that the owner had suddenly and unjustifiably accused him of stealing. The jury found defendant guilty of petit larceny, and the conviction was affirmed by the Appellate Term.

OPINION

These cases present a recurring question in this era of the self-service store which has never been resolved by this court: may a person be convicted of larceny for shoplifting if the person is caught with goods while still inside the store? For reasons outlined below, it is concluded that a larceny conviction may be sustained, in certain situations, even though the shoplifter was apprehended before leaving the store.

The primary issue in each case is whether the evidence, viewed in the light most favorable to the prosecution, was sufficient to establish the elements of larceny as defined by the Penal Law. To resolve this common question, the development of the common-law crime of larceny and its evolution into modern statutory form must be briefly traced.

Larceny at common law was defined as a trespassory taking and carrying away of the property of another with intent to steal it. The early common-law courts apparently viewed larceny as defending society against breach of the peace, rather than protecting individual property rights, and therefore placed heavy emphasis upon the requirement of a trespassory taking.

As the reach of larceny expanded, the intent element of the crime became of increasing importance, while the requirement of a trespassory taking became less significant. As a result, the bar against convicting a person who had initially obtained lawful possession of property faded. In *King v. Pear*, for instance, a defendant who had lied about his address and ultimate destination when renting a horse was found guilty of larceny for later converting the horse. Because of the fraudulent misrepresentation, the court reasoned, the defendant had never obtained legal possession. Thus, "larceny by trick" was born.

Later cases went even further, often ignoring the fact that a defendant had initially obtained possession lawfully, and instead focused upon his later intent. The crime of larceny then encompassed, not only situations where the defendant initially obtained property by a trespassory taking, but many situations where an individual, possessing the requisite intent, exercised control over property inconsistent with the continued right of the owner. During this evolutionary process, the purpose served by the crime of larceny obviously shifted from protecting society's peace to general protection of property rights.

Modern penal statutes generally have incorporated these developments under a unified definition of larceny (see e.g., American Law Institute, *Model Penal*

Code [Tent Draft No. 1], § 206.1 [theft is appropriation of property of another, which includes unauthorized exercise of control]). Case law, too, now tends to focus upon the actor's intent and the exercise of dominion and control over the property. Indeed, this court has recognized, in construing the New York Penal Law, that the "ancient common-law concepts of larceny" no longer strictly apply.

This evolution is particularly relevant to thefts occurring in modern self-service stores. In stores of that type, customers are impliedly invited to examine, try on, and carry about the merchandise on display. Thus in a sense, the owner has consented to the customer's possession of the goods for a limited purpose.

That the owner has consented to that possession does not, however, preclude a conviction for larceny. If the customer exercises dominion and control wholly inconsistent with the continued rights of the owner, and the other elements of the crime are present, a larceny has occurred. Such conduct on the part of a customer satisfies the "taking" element of the crime.

It is this element that forms the core of the controversy in these cases. The defendants argue, in essence, that the crime is not established, as a matter of law, unless there is evidence that the customer departed the shop without paying for the merchandise.

Although this court has not addressed the issue, case law from other jurisdictions seems unanimous in holding that a shoplifter need not leave the store to be guilty of larceny. This is because a shopper may treat merchandise in a manner inconsistent with the owner's continued rights — and in a manner not in accord with that of prospective purchaser — without actually walking out of the store.

Under these principles, there was ample evidence in each case to raise a factual question as to the defendants' guilt. In *People v. Olivo*, defendant not only concealed goods in his clothing, but he did so in a particularly suspicious manner. And, when defendant was stopped, he was moving towards the door, just three feet short of exiting the store.

In *People v. Gasparik*, defendant removed the price tag and sensor device from a jacket, abandoned his own garment, put the jacket on and ultimately headed for the main floor of the store. Removal of the price tag and sensor device, and careful concealment of those items, is highly unusual and suspicious conduct for a shopper. Coupled with defendant's abandonment of his own coat and his attempt to leave the floor, those factors were sufficient to make out a prima facie case of taking.

In *People v. Spatzier*, defendant concealed a book in an attaché case. Unaware that he was being observed in an overhead mirror, defendant looked furtively up and down the aisle before secreting the book. In these circumstances, given the manner in which defendant concealed the book and his suspicious behavior, the evidence was not insufficient as a matter of law.

In sum, in view of the modern definition of the crime of larceny, and its purpose of protecting individual property rights, a taking of property in the self-service store context can be established by evidence that a customer exercised control over merchandise wholly inconsistent with the store's continued rights. Quite simply, a customer who crosses the line between the limited right he or she has to deal with merchandise and the store owner's rights may be subject to prosecution for larceny. Such a rule should foster the legitimate interests and continued operation of self-service shops, a convenience which most members of the society enjoy.

Accordingly, in each case, the order of the Appellate Term should be affirmed.

QUESTIONS FOR DISCUSSION

1. The court says that originally larceny stressed possession, but modern convenience shopping requires that the emphasis shift to intent. Do you see why the court says this?

2. Under strict taking and carrying away requirements, do you think these defendants committed larceny?

3. Is the court right in adopting a rule that does not require shoplifters to leave the store before they have "taken" the property?

4. What rule would you adopt?

Possessors who voluntarily give up possession because they were tricked into giving their property up are victims of larceny by trick. The trick substitutes for the taking. Hence, if I lend a valuable watch to a friend who says he is only going to borrow it for the evening but who intends to sell it to a jeweler, my "friend" has wrongfully taken possession from me. Do not confuse larceny by trick with acquiring property by false pretenses. False pretenses requires a transfer of ownership or title, not simply a shift in possession (see the section below on obtaining property by false pretenses).

The "Property" Element

Not all property is subject to common-law larceny. Common-law larceny applied only to personal property. Real estate and anything attached to it, stocks and bonds, services and labor were not defined as property for purposes of larceny. Larceny law does not follow the old rhyme, "Finders keepers, losers weepers." Owners who lose their money or other property retain its possession for the purposes of larceny law. Hence, those who take and carry away lost money or other property commit larceny, assuming they do so with requisite intent.

Modern statutes have drastically altered the property element. Texas, for example, has expanded the scope of common-law property to include:

1. Real property.

2. Tangible or intangible personal property including anything severed from the land.

3. Documents, including money, that represent or embody anything of value.

4. Theft of service, including labor or professional services; telecommunication, public utility, and transportation services; lodging, restaurant services, and entertainment; and the supply of a motor vehicle or other property for use.[4]

The value of property usually determines the seriousness of the crime: the higher the value of the misappropriated property, the more serious the larceny. But the method of acquiring the property also affects the seriousness of the crime. Grand larceny, a felony punishable by one year or more in prison, includes property exceeding a dollar amount, typically between $100 and $400. Property worth less than the designated amount for grand larceny is usually included in the misdemeanor of petty larceny, which is punishable by less than one year in jail or a fine, or both. The dividing line between grand and petty larceny differs from state to state. In South Carolina, for example, the critical amount is only $1,000; in Pennsylvania it is $2,000.[5]

Market value does not always determine the gravity of theft. Pickpocketing, for example, is always a felony, and so is taking property from someone's home. These cases involve more interests than mere property; harms to both persons and habitation are present. Moreover, taking property from a person by force is robbery, a serious felony discussed later in this chapter. In most jurisdictions, taking and carrying away certain items is also a felony, no matter what the value of the items. These items vary depending on the interests in particular jurisdictions. In Texas, for example, stealing natural oil, no matter what the value, is grand larceny. California provides that grand larceny includes property valued in excess of $400. However, it is also grand larceny to steal avocados, olives, citrus or deciduous fruits, vegetables, artichokes, nuts, or other farm crops worth more than $100.[6]

Larceny *Mens Rea*

The *mens rea* of common-law larceny is the intent to permanently deprive the rightful possessor of the property taken and carried away. Therefore, larceny is a specific intent crime. For example, suppose I see a lawn mower on my neighbor's lawn, and I believe it is the one I loaned him last month, but it is in fact his. If I take the mower and sell it, I have not committed larceny because I did not intend to keep his lawn mower.

Temporary misappropriations do not constitute common-law larceny. Modern statutes have filled that gap in common-law larceny by making some temporary misappropriations separate crimes. A typical case is joyriding, or taking a vehicle to drive for a short time only, fully intending to return it to its rightful possessor. The joyrider lacks the larceny *mens rea*—the intent to permanently deprive the owner of possession. Joyriding statutes make it a less serious offense than larceny to take and carry away another's vehicle with the intent to temporarily dispossess the vehicle's rightful possessor.[7]

Finally, taking property that actors believe is theirs is not larceny. Called the **claim of right,** this defense removes the *mens rea* requirement to intend to permanently dispossess rightful possessors. Most jurisdictions permit claim of right as a defense to larceny.[8]

Summary of Larceny

Larceny, the ancient common-law felony, consists of four elements:

1. Wrongful taking and
2. wrongful carrying away of
3. someone else's property with
4. intent to permanently dispossess the property's rightful possessor.

Modern statutes in most states have modified common law, but the common-law elements remain important. These jurisdictions have added a number of other misappropriations that follow the common-law development. Some jurisdictions have consolidated several misappropriations into general theft statutes. The principal misappropriations consolidated into **theft** include embezzlement and obtaining property by false pretenses.

EMBEZZLEMENT

Historically, it was not a larcenous taking if a possessor voluntarily parted with property. For example, carriers, or persons hired to deliver owners' goods to third parties, could not "take" the goods while they were in the carriers' possession. Similarly, bank employees who removed money from an account could not "take" the money, because the owner had voluntarily deposited it. That such clearly wrongful appropriations were originally not criminal shows that larceny is an ancient crime predating carriers, banks, and other modern institutions. Statutes have altered common-law larceny so that those who acquire property lawfully—parking lot attendants, dry cleaners, auto repair people, and bank tellers—and then convert it to their own use commit embezzlement.

Embezzlers do not "take" property because they already possess it lawfully. In other words, they cannot wrongfully take what they already lawfully possess. **Conversion**

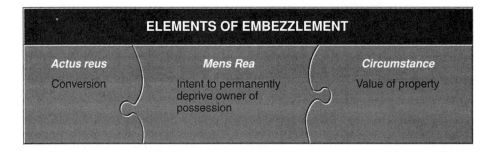

ELEMENTS OF EMBEZZLEMENT

Actus reus	Mens Rea	Circumstance
Conversion	Intent to permanently deprive owner of possession	Value of property

replaces taking in embezzlement. Conversion can occur only after someone acquires possession lawfully. Embezzlers acquire possession for a specific purpose—to repair a watch, to dry-clean clothes, and so on—and then convert the property to an unlawful purpose, usually for their own use or profit. Embezzlers stand in a position of trust (technically called a fiduciary relationship) with rightful possessors; they possess property only for the purpose for which the rightful permanent possessor transferred it. Conversion breaches this trust.

Embezzlers, that is, people who converted property lawfully but temporarily in their possession for a specific purpose, did not exist when larceny originated. They became important as society grew more complex. Larceny's trespassory taking requirement prevented the punishment of those who abused their trust and misappropriated property entrusted to them. Hence, the English Parliament created embezzlement during the period when temporary possessors (legally known as bailees) were becoming common. With the onset of banking, industrialization, and modern society, many more types of embezzlement were possible, and conversion became an increasingly common form of the misappropriation of other people's property. Under modern theft statutes, whether embezzlement and larceny or theft, either taking and carrying away (larceny) or conversion (embezzlement) satisfies the *actus reus* of theft.

FALSE PRETENSES—
STEALING BY DECEIT

Larceny requires a *trespassory* taking, and embezzlement requires the *conversion* of property rightfully in the converter's possession. But what about owners who part with possession because they are deceived into giving up title or ownership? Embezzlement covers only those who temporarily have a lawful right to possess and then convert property to their own use. Those who obtain property by false pretenses (often called stealing by deceit in modern law) have no right to possess it, and yet they do not "take" the property because owners willingly gave it to them. False pretenses fills the gap between larcenous takings and embezzlement that is created by deceitful misappropriation.

The *actus reus* in false pretenses replaces taking in larceny. It requires first an actual false representation, such as a promise to deliver something one cannot or does not intend to ever deliver. The law often expresses this as falsely representing a material past or existing fact. The false pretenses *mens rea* requires the specific intent to obtain title or ownership by deceit and lies—the false pretenses. A circumstance element in false

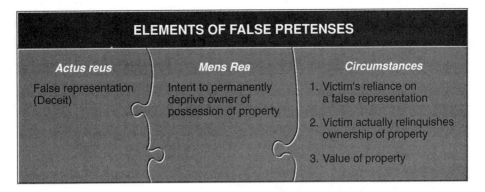

<pre>
ELEMENTS OF FALSE PRETENSES
</pre>

Actus reus | **Mens Rea** | **Circumstances**

False representation (Deceit)

Intent to permanently deprive owner of possession of property

1. Victim's reliance on a false representation

2. Victim actually relinquishes ownership of property

3. Value of property

pretenses is that victims must part with the possession and ownership because they believe and rely on the false representation. Suppose someone promises me he is a financial wizard when in fact he is only saying so to get my money. If I rely on his promise and transfer my money to him for investment, then the fake financial wizard obtained my money by false pretenses. Finally, the victim must actually part with the property. Note the difference between obtaining property through false pretenses and through larceny by trick. In larceny by trick, the possessor must part with possession. In false pretenses, the owner must part with title or ownership.

The law on obtaining property by false pretenses aims to protect owners from several harms inflicted by cheaters and con artists who misappropriate their wealth. Early on, English criminal law tried to protect against false weights and measures because they hindered trade. It was not until 1757, however, that individuals who privately cheated other individuals out of property were made criminals. In that year, the English Parliament made it a misdemeanor to "obtain [by false pretenses] from any person or persons, money, goods, wares, or merchandizes."[9]

The extension of criminal law to include cheating has not gone without criticism. Some critics base their attack on a general reluctance to use the criminal law in any but the most extreme situations. Others feel little sympathy with victims. Taking their cue from the ancient commercial doctrine of caveat emptor ("Let the buyer beware"), these critics believe that "fools and their money are soon parted." Such criticisms are especially effective against the view that duping the public is a crime even when no one loses property. This dimension to false pretenses—humiliating and making fools of people—deserves serious attention that cannot be given here. Suffice it to say that despite objections, criminal law protects property from misappropriations based on lying, cheating, deception, and other forms of false pretenses, at least under some circumstances.

Until the last twenty years, larceny, embezzlement, and obtaining property by false pretenses were distinct offenses in most criminal codes. Although all three involved misappropriation, the taking in larceny, the conversion in embezzlement, and the fraud in false pretenses were considered sufficiently different to require separate treatment under criminal codes. This view was largely due to the histories of these crimes, rather than to logic. The law regarding trespassory taking (first), conversion (later), and false pretense (last) created problems as society grew more complex during English and American history. Supreme Court justice Oliver Wendell Holmes put it simply: "In law a page of history is worth a volume of logic." The court applied the law of false pretenses in *State v. Watson.*

C A S E

Did He Attempt to Steal by Deceit?

State v. Watson,
1997 WL 342497 (Mo.App. W.D. 1997)

Following a jury trial before the Circuit Court, Clay County, Andre Watson was convicted of attempted stealing by deceit and was sentenced to one year in the county jail. He appealed. The Court of Appeals affirmed the conviction.

ULRICH, Chief Judge, Presiding Judge.

FACTS

In June 1995, Andre Watson was employed by A.B. May Sales and Service Company, a heating and air retailer, as an installer's helper. A.B. May purchases furnaces, air conditioners, humidifiers, and other parts used to repair and maintain equipment from Comfort Products, a distributor in Missouri and Kansas for Carrier Heating and Air. A.B. May places its orders with Comfort Products over the telephone using a purchase order system. Purchase order numbers are generated by A.B. May at the time an order is placed.

Bobbie Brakenbury, an employee of Comfort Products, received an order by telephone from a man named "Brian" on June 6, 1995. The man said he worked for A.B. May. The man placed an order for six condensing units, six furnaces, six coils, and six humidifiers. The caller ascribed A.B. May purchase order number 9400 to the order. The cost of the order was approximately $12,000.

Later, Ms. Brakenbury discovered that the coils ordered by the man did not match the size of the furnaces. She called A.B. May and asked to speak with "Brian." There was no employee at A.B. May named "Brian," however, so Ms. Brakenbury spoke with Trent Bryant who normally places the equipment orders for A.B. May. Mr. Bryant informed her that purchase order number 9400 was assigned to Lennox, another vendor, and not Comfort Products. The order was then "put on hold" until the validity of the order was determined.

Mr. Watson was working on an installation job in Prairie Village as an installer's helper on the same day. Just before lunch, the installer and Mr. Watson determined what additional parts they would need to complete the job. Mr. Watson was then sent to acquire the parts. During the lunch hour, Mr. Watson was involved in an automobile accident and did not return to work.

The next day, June 7, 1995, Mr. Watson arrived at Comfort Products requesting to pick up the six systems ordered by Brian. The warehouse manager, Thomas Dunmire, recognized Mr. Watson because he had been to Comfort Products on many occasions to get parts and equipment. Mr. Watson drove an A.B. May truck and was dressed in shorts and an A.B. May shirt with the name "Bill" printed on it.

Because the order was on hold, Mr. Dunmire informed Mr. Watson that there was a problem with the paper work and that he would have to wait a few minutes. Mr. Watson made a phone call, said he would be back in fifteen minutes, and departed. He did not return.

In the meantime, Ms. Brakenbury called Shane Coughlin, the chief financial officer at A.B. May, to confirm the order. Because the purchase order number was assigned to a different vendor and the cost of the order was approximately ten times larger than the normal $1500 order to Comfort Products, appropriate authority at Comfort Products concluded the order was not legitimate. Further inquiry at A.B. May disclosed that no one at the company was authorized to purchase six air conditioners and furnaces from Comfort Products on June 6 or 7, 1995.

Mr. Watson did not return to work at A.B. May except for part of a day on June 15, 1995. Attempts by A.B. May personnel to contact Mr. Watson by telephone failed. Ultimately, Mr. Watson was charged with attempted stealing by deceit. At trial, Mr. Watson testified in his own defense. He claimed that on June 7, 1995, he was at home recuperating from the automobile accident that occurred the previous day.

OPINION

. . .

Mr. Watson was convicted of attempted stealing by deceit. "A person is guilty of attempt to commit an offense when, with the purpose of committing the offense, he does any act which is a substantial step towards the commission of the offense." § 564.011.1, RSMo 1994. The crime of stealing is committed if a person "appropriates property or services of another with the purpose to deprive him thereof, either without his consent or by means of deceit or coercion." § 570.030.1, RSMo 1994. Deceit is defined as "purposely making a representation which is false and which the actor does not believe to be true and upon which the victim relies, as to a matter of fact, law, value, intention or other state of mind." § 570.010(6), RSMo 1994.

Mr. Watson contends that the evidence was insufficient to prove that he had the intent to deceive or that he knew or should have known that he did not have authority to pick up the furnaces and air conditioners. The subjective intent of a defendant to deceive may be proven by circumstantial evidence. The evidence presented in this case showed that an invalid order for six systems consisting of furnaces, air conditioners, coils, and humidifiers was placed with Comfort Products on June 6, 1995, by a man who identified himself as "Brian" from A.B. May. A.B. May did not have an employee named Brian on June 6, 1995, and no A.B. May employee had authority on June 6 or 7, 1995, to purchase six systems. The purchase order number provided was 9400, and the value of the six systems was about $12,000.00.

The evidence also established that Mr. Watson was working in Prairie Village for A.B. May on June 6 and was asked by his supervisor to order parts to complete the job and to get them. He did not return to work that day because he was involved in an automobile accident.

The next day, Mr. Watson arrived at Comfort Products to obtain six systems that included six furnaces, six coils and six air conditioners. He wore an A.B. May shirt with the name "Bill" printed on it and was not wearing the pants that are the normal uniform A.B. May employees wear. He was informed that the order was "on hold" because of a problem with the paper work. Mr. Watson left and did not return. Mr. Watson did not return to work at A.B. May except for part of June 15.

This evidence was sufficient for a reasonable juror to have concluded that Mr. Watson made a substantial act to steal six systems by deceit. From the evidence, a reasonable inference could have been drawn that Mr. Watson knowingly made a false representation that he had A.B. May's authorization to acquire the furnaces and air conditioners from Comfort Products. The trial court, therefore, did not err in overruling Mr. Watson's motion for judgment of acquittal at the close of all the evidence.

The judgment of conviction is affirmed.

QUESTIONS FOR DISCUSSION

1. The critical issue in the case is determining whether Watson intended to deceive Comfort Products in order to get the air conditioning equipment. In other words, did he use false pretenses to get the merchandise?

2. He argued that he did know he lacked the authority to purchase the merchandise. Does the evidence presented convince you that he meant to deceive Comfort Products in order to get the merchandise?

CONSOLIDATED THEFT STATUTES

Critics have long recommended reforming the law of larceny, embezzlement, and false pretenses to conform more to logic than to history. They believe that misappropriating property, whether by stealth, conversion, or deception, represents different dimensions to one general harm. In 1962, the *Model Penal Code* included a consolidated theft provision, one that most states now follow. The most common statutes consolidate larceny, embezzlement, and false pretenses into one offense called theft.

Consolidated theft statutes eliminate the largely artificial need to decide whether property was "taken and carried away," "converted," or "swindled," as traditional larceny, embezzlement, and false pretense statutes require. Joining the offenses deals more realistically with the social problem in all three: criminal property misappropriations.

Some statutes are even more ambitious than those that simply consolidate larceny, embezzlement, and false pretenses. The *Model Penal Code*, for example, has a single theft article that covers not only larceny, embezzlement, and false pretenses but also extortion, blackmail, and receiving stolen property. Thus, the code houses all nonviolent misappropriations in one provision. Only robbery—because it involves violence or its threat against persons—falls under a separate provision. Other consolidated theft statutes include some or all of the following thefts: taking, conversion, deception, extortion, lost property, receiving stolen property, theft of services, failure to make required deposits, and unauthorized vehicle use.[10]

California's consolidated theft statute provides that

> every person who shall feloniously steal the personal property of another, or who shall fraudulently appropriate property which has been entrusted to him, or who shall knowingly and designedly, by any false or fraudulent representation or pretense, defraud any other person of money, labor or real or personal property, shall be guilty of theft.[11]

Commenting on the provision, the California Supreme Court wrote:

> Included within § 484 is not only the offense of taking personal property (larceny), but also "embezzlement," theft by trick and device, and theft by false pretenses [of both personal and real property].[12]

Consolidated theft statutes reflect only in part the response of criminal law to the rapidly developing opportunities to misappropriate property. The term property itself has become too restrictive to describe what constitutes value subject to misappropriation in the late twentieth century. Electronics has created not only new value but also new methods to misappropriate it. For example, new legislation dealing with new devices used to misappropriate telephone long-distance services. The misappropriation of **intellectual property**—information and services stored in and transmitted to and from electronic data banks—is a rapidly developing area of property crimes.

Some states have attempted to deal with computer crimes by expanding the interpretation of the elements of the common-law crimes of larceny, embezzlement, and false pretenses. In *Hancock v. Texas*, the court ruled that computer programs are property for purposes of larceny. Most states have found this means inadequate to deal with computer crimes. Hence, virtually every state has enacted specific statutes directed at computer crimes. The Arkansas legislature stated its purpose for enacting a specific computer crime statute:

> It is found and determined that computer-related crime poses a major problem for business and government; that losses for each incident of computer-related

crime are potentially astronomical; that the opportunities for computer-related crime in business and government through the introduction of fraudulent records into a computer system, the unauthorized use of computers, alteration or destruction of computerized information or files, and the stealing of financial instruments, data, and other assets, are great; that computer-related crime has a direct effect on state commerce; and that, while various forms of computer-related crime might possibly be the subject of criminal charges based on other provisions of law, it is appropriate and desirable that a statute be enacted which deals directly with computer-related crime.[13]

California has adopted the following elaborate computer theft statute:

§ 502. Definitions; computer system or network; intentional access to defraud or extort or to obtain money, property or services with false or fraudulent intent, representations or promises; malicious access, alteration, deletion, damage or disruption; violations; penalty; civil action

a. For purposes of this section:

1. "Access" means to instruct, communicate with, store data in, or retrieve data from, a computer system or computer network.

2. "Computer system" means a device or collection of devices, excluding pocket calculators which are not programmable and capable of being used in conjunction with external files, one or more of which contain computer programs and data, that performs functions, including, but not limited to, logic, arithmetic, data storage and retrieval, communication, and control.

3. "Computer network" means an interconnection of two or more computer systems.

4. "Computer program" means an ordered set of instructions or statements, and related data that, when automatically executed in actual or modified form in a computer system, causes it to perform specified functions.

5. "Data" means a representation of information, knowledge, facts, concepts, or instructions, which are being prepared or have been prepared, in a formalized manner, and are intended for use in a computer system or computer network.

6. "Financial instrument" includes, but is not limited to, any check, draft, warrant, money order, note, certificate of deposit, letter of credit, bill of exchange, credit or debit card, transaction authorization mechanism, marketable security, or any computer system representation thereof.

7. "Property" includes, but is not limited to, financial instruments, data, computer programs, documents associated with computer systems and computer programs, or copies thereof, whether tangible or intangible, including both human and computer system readable data, and data while in transit.

8. "Services" includes, but is not limited to, the use of the computer system, computer network, computer programs, or data prepared for computer use, or data contained within a computer system, or data contained within a computer network. . . .

b. Any person who intentionally accesses or causes to be accessed any computer system or computer network for the purpose of (1) devising or executing any scheme or artifice to defraud or extort, or (2) obtaining money, property, or services with false or fraudulent intent, representations, or promises, is guilty of a public offense.

c. Any person who maliciously accesses, alters, deletes, damages, destroys or disrupts the operation of any computer system, computer network, computer program, or data is guilty of a public offense.

d. Any person who intentionally and without authorization accesses any computer system, computer network, computer program, or data, with knowledge that the access was not authorized, shall be guilty of a public offense. This subdivision shall not apply to any person who accesses his or her employer's computer system, computer network, computer program, or data when acting within the scope of his or her employment.

e. Any person who violates any provision of subdivision (b) or (c) unless specified otherwise, is punishable by a fine not exceeding ten thousand dollars ($10,000), or by imprisonment in the state prison for 16 months, or two or three years, or by both such fine and imprisonment, or by a fine not exceeding five thousand dollars ($5,000), or by imprisonment in the county jail not exceeding one year, or by both such fine and imprisonment.

f. (1) A first violation of subdivision (d) which does not result in injury is an infraction punishable by a fine not exceeding two hundred fifty dollars ($250).

2. A violation of subdivision (d) which results in an injury, or a second or subsequent violation of subdivision (d) with no injury, is a misdemeanor punishable by a fine not exceeding five thousand dollars ($5,000), or by imprisonment in the county jail not exceeding one year, or by both such fine and imprisonment.

3. As used in this subdivision, "injury" means any alteration, deletion, damage, or destruction of a computer system, computer network, computer program, or data caused by the access, or any expenditure reasonably and necessarily incurred by the owner or lessee to verify that a computer system, computer network, computer program, or data was not altered, deleted, damaged, or destroyed by the access.

g. In addition to any other civil remedy available, the owner or lessee of the computer system, computer network, computer program, or data may bring a civil action against any person convicted under this section for compensatory damages, including any expenditure reasonably and necessarily incurred by the owner or lessee to verify that a computer system, computer network, computer program, or data was not altered, damaged, or deleted by the access. For the purposes of actions authorized by this subdivision, the conduct of an unemancipated minor shall be imputed to the parent or legal guardian having control or custody of the minor, pursuant to the provisions of § 1714.1 of the Civil Code. In any action brought pursuant to this subdivision, the court may award attorney's fees to a prevailing plaintiff.

h. This section shall not be construed to preclude the applicability of any other provision of the criminal law of this state which applies or may apply to any transaction.[14]

The court in *State v. Smith* applied the law of theft to stealing computer software.

C A S E

Did He "Take" the Software?

State v. Smith,
798 P.2d 1146 (Wash. 1990)

John Smith was convicted of the theft of a copyrighted computer software package by the Superior Court, Thurston County. He appealed. The Washington Court of Appeals and the Washington Supreme Court affirmed the conviction.

DOLLIVER, Justice.

FACTS

On December 20, 1985, defendant John P. Smith contacted Micro Focus, Incorporated and inquired into purchasing a software package called "Professional Cobal". At the time, defendant was a student at The Evergreen State College (TESC). After Micro-Focus informed defendant he could not examine the software free of charge, he agreed to purchase it C.O.D. The marketing representative who took defendant's order testified that defendant represented himself as being a professor at TESC, thereby entitling him to a 20 percent discount off the $3,000 market price of the program.

On December 23, 1985, the United Parcel Service (UPS) attempted to deliver the program to defendant at TESC. The UPS driver spoke with the campus police sergeant who informed him the address on the package was actually student housing rather than an on-campus office address. The driver eventually located the correct address and delivered the program and instruction manual to defendant. Both the program and the manual were copyrighted. Defendant wrote a personal check to MicroFocus for the purchase in the amount of $2,407, even though the account upon which the check was issued had a balance of only $472.52. Defendant also maintained another bank account which had a balance of approximately $7,062 at the time. Almost immediately after receiving the program, defendant made a copy of it and the instruction manual.

Defendant testified that the following morning he realized the program did not work on his computer.

At some point after this, defendant called his bank and stopped payment on the check he had written to MicroFocus. Defendant then returned the items to MicroFocus, marking the package with the notation, "Unauthorized purchase, returned."

After investigation into the attempted misdelivery of the MicroFocus package, the campus police sergeant at TESC obtained a warrant to search defendant's apartment. During the execution of the warrant, officers uncovered multiple complete sets of the MicroFocus software defendant had ordered and returned, as well as a copy of the instruction manual which accompanied the software. These items, plus copies of additional programs defendant had ordered from other manufacturers but then returned, were seized and later produced at trial.

Defendant was charged in Thurston County Superior Court under RCW 9A.56.030(1)(a) and RCW 9A.56.020(1)(a) or (1)(b) with one count of first degree theft. Before trial, defendant moved to dismiss the charge, arguing federal copyright law preempted the State's jurisdiction to prosecute him for the offense. The trial court denied the motion. Defendant did not renew his motion. Defendant also moved to suppress reference to a charge for welfare fraud pending against him in Jefferson County. The trial court granted the motion contingent upon defendant not opening the subject up.

During trial, defendant admitted he had received five other software packages in the mail, paid for them, and then later stopped payment on the checks. He also testified to having made backup copies for all of the ordered programs but one, which he stated could not be copied. Defendant testified his original intention was to keep each of the programs he ordered, but he returned them because he later realized none of them ran properly on his computer. He also testified he copied the programs because the software manuals suggested doing this in case the master program was damaged or destroyed. He testified he copied the manuals in order to protect himself from theft or other loss. Although he kept copies of the materials after returning them to the manufacturers, he testified he never intended to use them.

When defendant was questioned about receiving the goods at a discount, he testified he had told a college official that he "understood how the system worked and how to manipulate it", but what he meant was that he was getting software at a wholesale price rather than the retail price and thereby "cutting out the middle man." Defendant also testified he merely told MicroFocus that he was "with" TESC and not that he was a professor there.

The jury found defendant guilty as charged. The defendant appealed to the Court of Appeals. In an unpublished opinion, the Court of Appeals affirmed the trial court. We granted review and affirm, although in part for reasons other than those set out by the Court of Appeals.

OPINION

. . .

RCW 9A.56.030(1) defines first degree theft as follows:

A person is guilty of theft in the first degree if he commits theft of:

(a) Property or services which exceed(s) one thousand five hundred dollars in value; or

(b) Property of any value taken from the person of another.

"Theft", according to RCW 9A.56.020(1), means:

(a) To wrongfully obtain or exert unauthorized control over the property or services of another or the value thereof, with intent to deprive him of such property or services; or

(b) By color or aid of deception to obtain control over the property or services of another or the value thereof, with intent to deprive him of such property or services . . .

Subsection (a) is known as theft by taking while subsection (b) is known as theft by deception. Here, defendant was charged under both subsections (a) and (b). "Deprive", in addition to its common meaning, also includes making "unauthorized use or an unauthorized copy of records, information, data, trade secrets, or computer programs . . ." RCW 9A.56.010(5).

We . . . find erroneous the Court of Appeals' conclusion that theft by taking requires a trespass. . . . Trespass is not required for statutory theft by taking. "The Legislature may define crimes. Where it does so, its statutory definition may supersede common law." Both this court and the Court of Appeals have affirmed convictions for theft by taking under RCW 9A.56.020(1)(a) without requiring evidence of a trespass. See *State v. Britten*, 46 Wash.App. 571, 731 P.2d 508 (1986) (involving theft by taking which occurred in a department store); *State v. Komok*, supra (also involving theft in a department store). *Vargas* and any other decision inferring the contrary is disapproved. As we find theft by taking as defined by statute does not include the common-law element of trespass, the contention of the Court of Appeals and defendant that there was insufficient evidence to convict under the taking statute is not valid. There was sufficient evidence for conviction of theft either by taking (RCW 9A.56.020(1)(a)) or deception (RCW 9A.56.020(1)(b)).

. . .

The Court of Appeals is affirmed.

QUESTIONS FOR DISCUSSION

1. How has the Washington statute modified the elements of common-law larceny?

2. Is it possible to define modern theft without referring to common-law larceny? Explain.

RECEIVING STOLEN PROPERTY

In some circumstances, it is a crime not only to take, convert, and acquire the property of others by deception but also to receive property after it has been criminally misappropriated. Called receiving stolen property, this offense aims to protect against those

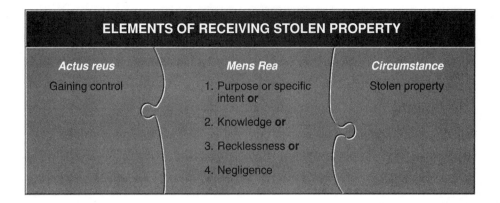

who stand to benefit from misappropriations even though they did not wrongfully acquire others' property. "Benefit" does not mean simply monetary profit; receiving stolen property includes not only fences (those who trade in stolen property), but also, for example, students who steal university equipment because they need calculators, typewriters, recorders, and other equipment. Large-scale fence operations, however, account for most traffic in stolen property.

Fences have the facilities to buy, store, and market property. As go-betweens, they are as indispensable as their counterparts in legitimate operations are to farmers, manufacturers, and other producers. Large-city fences trade a remarkably large volume and variety in stolen property, ranging from narcotics and weapons to appliances and computers and even clothes. Receiving stolen property is aimed primarily at these large-scale operations.

The *actus reus* in receiving stolen property requires that property taken, converted, or acquired by deception come into the receiver's control for at least a short period. It does not mandate that the receiver personally possess the property. Hence, if I buy a stolen fur from a fence who hands it directly to my friend, I have received the fur. If my friend then gives the fur to her friend, my friend has also received the stolen fur. Included in the definition of the *actus reus* are fences as well as friends who hide stolen goods temporarily for thieves.

A material element in receiving stolen property is that the property must in fact have been criminally misappropriated—that is, taken, converted, or acquired by deception. Hence, if I think I am hiding stolen weapons but in fact the weapons were not stolen, I have not received stolen weapons.

Mens rea is difficult to establish in receiving stolen property. The culpability required varies among the states. Some jurisdictions require actual knowledge that the goods are stolen. In other jurisdictions, an honest belief that the goods are stolen suffices. In all jurisdictions, this knowledge may be inferred from surrounding circumstances, as in receiving goods from a known thief or buying goods at a fraction of their real value (for example, buying a new twelve-speed bicycle for thirty-five dollars.) Some jurisdictions reduce the *mens rea* to recklessness or even negligence. This lowered culpability requirement is often directed at likely fences, usually junk dealers and pawn shop operators.

In addition to knowledge that property was stolen, *mens rea* requires that receivers intend to permanently dispossess rightful possessors. Hence, police officers who knowingly accept stolen property and secretly place it on suspected fences in order to catch them have not received stolen property because they intend to possess it only temporarily.

C A S E

Did He Receive the Stolen Car?

Hurston v. State,
414 S.E.2d 303 (Ga. App. 1991)

Illya Hurston and Demetrious Reese were convicted by a jury of theft by receiving stolen property before the Rockdale County Superior Court. Hurston appealed the denial of his motion for a new trial. The Court of Appeals affirmed.

ANDREWS, Judge.

FACTS

. . . [A] silver 1986 Pontiac Fiero belonging to Stella Burns was stolen from a parking lot at Underground Atlanta on June 11, 1989, between 10:35 and 11:05 P.M. Two Rockdale County sheriff's deputies observed a silver Fiero at a convenience store later that night at approximately 1:20 A.M. Hurston's co-defendant, Reese, was driving the car and appellant was slumped in the passenger seat. The deputies became suspicious because of the late hour, the cautious manner in which Reese was walking after exiting the car, and the fact that Hurston appeared to be hiding, and decided to follow the Fiero. When Reese drove away from the store with the deputies following in their marked car, he crossed the centerline of the highway. The deputies, who by this time had ascertained from computer records that the car was stolen, turned on the blue lights and siren of their automobile. Reese refused to stop, drove away from the deputies at a speed in excess of 100 miles per hour and attempted at one point to run the police vehicle into a wall. The deputies pursued the Fiero until Reese lost control and wrecked in a field. Reese ran from the scene and was pursued and apprehended by one deputy. Another officer apprehended Hurston,

who had gotten out of the car immediately after the accident and appeared to be ready to run.

At trial, Hurston testified that he spent the day at his former girl friend's home watching television with her and a friend of hers. Later in the day, the friend called her boyfriend, Reese, whom Hurston testified he had never met, to join them. Hurston testified Reese came to the house and stayed for awhile, left for several hours, and then returned and invited Hurston to ride in the Fiero with him to a relative's home. Hurston recalled that he was suspicious about the ownership of the vehicle because Reese, a teenager, seemed too young to own such a nice car, but that in response to his inquiry Reese stated that the car belonged to his cousin. Hurston testified that after they left the convenience store and Reese saw the deputies in pursuit, he began to speed, and admitted to Hurston for the first time that the car was stolen. Hurston's trial testimony differed somewhat from an earlier statement he gave regarding the evening's events.

Burns, the vehicle's owner, testified that the vehicle was driven without keys and that the steering wheel had been damaged, which was consistent with it having been stolen. She testified that various papers, including the car registration and business cards bearing the owner's name and address, had been removed from the glove compartment and were on the floor of the car; that grass, mud, food, drink and cigarettes were scattered in the car; and that a picture of her daughter was displayed on a visor. Hurston denied noticing the personal items or the damaged steering wheel.

OPINION

OCGA § 1687(a) provides: "[a] person commits the offense of theft by receiving stolen property when he receives, disposes of, or retains stolen property which he knows or should know was stolen unless the property is received, disposed of, or retained with intent to restore it to the owner. 'Receiving' means acquiring possession or control. . . ."

"Unexplained possession of recently stolen property, alone, is not sufficient to support a conviction for receiving stolen property but guilt may be inferred from possession in conjunction with other evidence of knowledge. Guilty knowledge may be inferred from circumstances which would excite suspicion in the mind of an ordinary prudent man." "Possession, as we know it, is the right to exercise power over a corporeal thing. . . ." Furthermore, " '[i]f there is any evidence of guilt, it is for the jury to decide whether that evidence, circumstantial though it may be, is sufficient to warrant a conviction.' "

Construed most favorably for the State, there was sufficient evidence for a jury to find Hurston guilty of receiving stolen property. First, there was sufficient evidence for a jury to find that Hurston knew, or should have known, that the vehicle was stolen. At trial, Hurston admitted that he doubted that the vehicle belonged to Reese. There was evidence from which the jury could reasonably have concluded that Hurston was aware during the two hours that he spent in the small vehicle that it was stolen, in that the vehicle was being driven without keys, the steering wheel was damaged and the interior was disorderly, which was inconsistent both with Reese's ownership of the vehicle and with his explanation that he borrowed it from a relative. Hurston's suspicious behavior at the convenience store and his attempt to flee also indicated that he knew the vehicle was stolen.

There was also evidence from which the jury could conclude that Hurston possessed, controlled or retained the vehicle. Although Hurston was only a passenger in the vehicle, the inquiry does not end here, for in some circumstances, a passenger may possess, control or retain a vehicle for purposes of OCGA § 1687. Here, there was sufficient evidence that Hurston exerted the requisite control over the vehicle in that Reese left Hurston alone in the car with the vehicle running when he went into the convenience store.

" 'Questions as to reasonableness are generally to be decided by the jury which heard the evidence and where the jury is authorized to find that the evidence,

though circumstantial, was sufficient to exclude every reasonable hypothesis save that of guilt, the appellate court will not disturb that finding, unless the verdict of guilty is unsupportable as a matter of law.'

. . .

Judgment affirmed.

DISSENT

SOGNIER, C.J., and McMURRAY, P.J., dissent.
SOGNIER, Chief Judge, dissenting.

I respectfully dissent, for I find the evidence was insufficient to establish the essential element of "receiving" beyond a reasonable doubt.

"A person commits the offense of theft by receiving stolen property when he receives, disposes of, or retains stolen property which he knows or should know was stolen. . . . 'Receiving' means acquiring possession or control . . . of the property." OCGA § 1687(a). Here, the record is devoid of evidence that appellant exercised or intended to exercise any dominion or control over the car or that he ever acquired possession of it. See *Patterson v. State*, 159 Ga.App. 290, 294, 283 S.E.2d 294 (1981); accord *Owens v. State*, 192 Ga.App. 335, 340(1)(b), 384 S.E.2d 920 (1989). The "mere presence" of a defendant in the vicinity of stolen goods "furnishes only a bare suspicion" of guilt, and thus is insufficient to establish possession of stolen property. *Williamson v. State*, 134 Ga.App. 329, 331–332, 214 S.E.2d 415 (1975). Evidence that a defendant was present as a passenger in a stolen automobile, without more, is insufficient to establish possession or control. *Williamson*, supra; see *Davis v. State*, 154 Ga.App. 599, 269 S.E.2d 494 (1980); accord *Abner v. State*, 196 Ga.App. 752–753, 397 S.E.2d 36 (1990) (conviction for theft by receiving automobile upheld where defendant was in actual possession of car). I disagree with the majority that the circumstantial evidence that appellant, the automobile passenger, was observed to be "slumped" in the seat while Reese parked the car and entered a store was sufficient to constitute the type of "other incriminating circumstances" that would authorize a rejection of the general principle that "the driver of the [stolen] automobile [is] held prima facie in exclusive possession thereof." . . .

Moreover, the evidence also did not meet the standard required for a conviction based on circumstantial evidence—i.e., that the evidence exclude every reasonable hypothesis except the guilt of the accused. The only evidence offered by the State to connect appellant to the stolen car was that he was a passenger in the car several hours after it was stolen. In response, appellant offered his explanation of his activities. "While neither the jury nor this court is required to accept these explanations, in the absence of any other valid explanation, we cannot ignore the only explanation offered. [Cit.] [I] conclude that there is no circumstantial evidence of guilt on which to base a conviction beyond a reasonable doubt." Accordingly, I would reverse. . . .

QUESTIONS FOR DISCUSSION

1. Identify all of the facts relevant to determining whether Hurston received stolen property.

2. State the elements of receiving stolen property according to the Georgia statute.

3. What reasons do the dissenting judges give for their dissent?

4. Do you agree with the dissent or the majority? Defend your answer.

NOTE CASE

A 1992 Chevrolet Astrovan automobile was stolen from a mobile home park in Spalding County. The van was subsequently utilized in a drive-by shooting on August 28, 1996. Later on the same day, Corporal Bradshaw of the Spalding County Sheriff's Department observed the van and recognized it as being similar to one that was reported stolen, as well as one that was reported as being involved in a drive-by shooting a few hours earlier. Corporal Bradshaw followed the van and could see four to five black males inside; he could not determine who was driving. While Corporal Bradshaw was following the van, the van abruptly turned into a driveway, where two or three men jumped out of the van and ran from the scene. Without the driver, the van, which was left in the "drive" mode, rolled backwards into the patrol car. Then, two young men, one of whom was the appellant, attempted to exit the van through the passenger door but were caught by Corporal Bradshaw before they could flee and were arrested at the scene.

The arresting officer was never able to determine who the driver had been or who had been in control of

the stolen vehicle. The car keys were never found. When questioned by an investigator after receiving Miranda warnings, C.W. stated that he had only been along for a ride and did not know that the van was stolen. At the hearing, appellant's co-defendant, D.L.S., testified that C.W. had only gone for a ride in the van and did not have control of the vehicle at any time.

The juveniles were charged with theft by receiving stolen property because they had been in the stolen vehicle. They were tried in Spalding County Juvenile Court on October 23, 1996. The juvenile court judge determined that C.W. was delinquent and sentenced him to 90 days in custody. Appellant timely appealed, asserting that the adjudication of delinquency was contrary to the law and to the evidence.

Did C.W. receive the stolen van? No, according to the Georgia Court of Appeals. The court wrote:

Mere proximity to stolen property is insufficient to establish possession or control. *Williamson v. State*, 134 Ga.App. 329, 331, 214 S.E.2d 415 (1975). In a similar vein, riding in a stolen van or automobile as a passenger does not support a conviction for theft by receiving unless the accused also, at some point, acquires possession of or controls the vehicle, i.e., has " 'the right to exercise power over a corporeal thing,' [cit.]" Therefore, one cannot be convicted of the crime of receiving stolen property absent exercise of control over the stolen goods, or if one is a passenger, intentionally aiding and abetting the commission of the crime.

. . . [N]o evidence was presented by the State that the appellant ever retained, disposed of, acquired possession of, or controlled the stolen van, nor was any evidence presented of any affirmative act by appellant that rose to the level of aiding and abetting the crime. The undisputed evidence indicates that the appellant got into the van while it was driven by an acquaintance, known as "Rat," and that Rat previously had acquired the van from a "Geek Monster," i.e., a crack addict, who apparently traded the van for cocaine. Appellant denied ever driving the van, an assertion supported by his co-defendant, D.L.S. In addition, there was no evidence that appellant ever exercised control over the van, i.e., determined where it would go, who it would transport, etc., or that the appellant otherwise actively aided and abetted the crime. All evidence indicates that appellant was simply along for the ride. While appellant admitted being in the van while another passenger shot at an acquaintance in a drive-by shooting, appellant was not charged with being an accessory to that offense. Therefore, lacking evidence that the appellant ever possessed or controlled the van under OCGA § 1687(a) or affirmatively acted as a party to the crime under OCGA § 16220(b), his adjudica-

tion of delinquency for the offense of theft by receiving stolen property must be reversed.

Judgment reversed. *In the Interest of C.W., a child*, 485 S.E.2d 561, (Ga.App. 1997)

FORGERY AND UTTERING

The crime of **forgery** includes making false legal documents or altering existing ones — such as checks, deeds, stocks, bonds, and credit cards. **Uttering** means to pass false documents on to others. Forgery and uttering both misappropriate and destroy property. They harm not only the individuals directly involved but also society in general. Because day-to-day business in modern society relies on legal instruments for its smooth and efficient operation, impairing confidence in the authenticity of those instruments can lead to serious disruption in business, commercial, and financial transactions. It is this general harm, as much as individual losses, that forgery and uttering laws are designed to protect against.

Forgery

The subject matter of forgery is false writing. Documents subject to forgery make up a long list, because the law defines fraudulent or false writings broadly. Many forgeries, such as forged checks, clearly and directly misappropriate property. These forgeries are obviously property offenses. Other forgeries are not so obviously harms to property. For example, a university might lose more reputation than property from forged diplomas. Injury to reputation and impairment of normal transactions make forgery more than a mere property offense.

California's approach to forgery is found in the California Penal Code, § 470.

Every person who, with intent to defraud, signs the name of another person, or of a fictitious person, knowing that he has no authority so to do, or falsely makes, alters, forges, or counterfeits, any charter, letters patent, deed, lease, indenture, writing obligatory, will, testament, codicil, bond, covenant, bank bill or note, post note, check, draft, bill of exchange, contract, promissory note, due bill for the payment of money or property, receipt for money or property, passage ticket, trading stamp, power of attorney, or any certificate of any share, right, or interest in the stock of any corporation or association, or any controller's warrant for the payment of money at the treasury, county order or warrant, or request for the payment of money, or the delivery of goods or chattels of any kind, or for the delivery of any instrument of writing, or acquittance, release, or receipt for money or goods, or any acquittance, release, or discharge of any debt, account, suit, action, demand, or other thing, real or personal, or any transfer or assurance of money, certificates of shares of stock, goods, chattels, or other property whatever, or any letter of attorney, or other power to receive money, or to receive or transfer certificates of shares of stock or annuities, or to let, lease, dispose of, alien, or convey

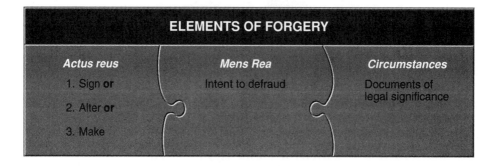

ELEMENTS OF FORGERY

Actus reus	*Mens Rea*	*Circumstances*
1. Sign **or**	Intent to defraud	Documents of legal significance
2. Alter **or**		
3. Make		

any goods, chattels, lands, or tenements, or other estate, real or personal, or any acceptance or endorsement of any bill of exchange, promissory note, draft, order, or any assignment of any bond, writing obligatory, promissory note, or other contract for money or other property; or counterfeits or forges the seal or handwriting of another; or utters, publishes, passes, or attempts to pass, as true and genuine, any of the above named false, altered, forged, or counterfeited matters, as above specified and described, knowing the same to be false, altered, forged, or counterfeited, with intent to prejudice, damage, or defraud any person; or who, with intent to defraud, alters, corrupts, or falsifies any record of any will, codicil, conveyance, or other instrument, the record of which is by law evidence, or any record of any judgment of a court or the return of any officer to any process of any court, is guilty of forgery.[15]

California's is not the only approach to defining forgery. Other states do not list documents by name; instead, they use phrases such as "any writing," "any writing having legal efficacy or commonly relied on in business or commercial transactions," or "any written instrument to the prejudice of another's right." Either approach, however, indicates the legislatures' intention to cover written documents broadly.

When the *Model Penal Code* drafters wrote a sweeping forgery definition, they aimed the code's forgery provision against three harms: the harms of direct property loss, damage to reputation, and impaired business and commercial confidence. Except in grading forgery, the code abandons a significant traditional requirement: that a forged document must have legal or evidentiary significance. Hence, it includes doctors' prescriptions, identification cards, diaries, and letters, not just deeds, wills, contracts, stocks, and bonds. Furthermore, documents are not the only subject matter of forgery. Coins, tokens, paintings, and antiques also fall within its scope. In fact, says the commentary to this provision, "Anything which could be falsified in respect of 'authenticity' can be the subject of forgery."[16]

Defenders of the *Model Penal Code* provision maintain that the grave harms caused by forgery and the difficulty in drawing meaningful distinctions between various forms of forgery justify the sweeping phrase, "any writing or object." Even critics admit that those who forge checks or fake antiques may respond more to deterrence and rehabilitation than do other criminals. There is no clear evidence that this is so, however, and some critics remain uneasy over all-encompassing forgery provisions.

Making a false document or altering an authentic one constitutes the forgery *actus reus*. Contrary to the apparent logic of the *Model Penal Code* provision, most jurisdictions limit forgery to the making of false writings that have apparent legal significance. "Making" means making documents, in whole or in part, or altering an authentic document in any material part. Hence, if I make out and sign a check on someone else's account or a nonexistent account, with no intent to back the check myself, I have forged it because I falsified the whole check. Most existing forgery laws require that either the whole document or some material part be falsified.

Merely presenting false information on an otherwise authentic document is not forgery. Hence, if I change only the amount on a check made out and signed by the checking account's owner, I have not committed forgery because the check itself is valid. Similarly, if a properly authorized payroll clerk alters payrolls by adding hours, it is not forgery because the payroll is still valid. However, both I and the payroll clerk may have obtained property under false pretenses. Furthermore, checks drawn on insufficient funds are not forgeries for two reasons. First, they are not false; second, unless the intention to back the checks is missing, they do not have the requisite forgery *mens rea*.

Forgery is a specific intent crime. It requires the forger to falsely write, intending to defraud others with the writing. It is not necessary to intend to defraud specific individuals; a general purpose to fraudulently use the falsified document suffices. Furthermore, forgery does not require the falsifier to intend to obtain money fraudulently. Intending to secure any advantage will do. Hence, a letter of recommendation intended to gain membership in a desirable professional organization satisfies the forgery *mens rea*.

Once documents are falsified or altered with proper fraudulent intent, forgery is complete. Forgers need not actually gain from their falsifications and fraudulent intent. The reason is that the harm of forgery lies in undermining confidence in the authenticity of documents and the consequent disruption created by such undermined confidence.

Uttering

Uttering does not require making false writings or materially altering authentic ones. Rather, it means knowingly or consciously passing or using forged documents with the specific intent to defraud. Forgery means the making of false documents in order to defraud, even if the forger never defrauds anyone. Uttering, on the other hand, means

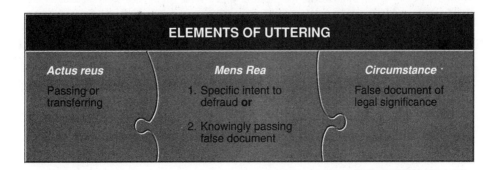

ELEMENTS OF UTTERING

Actus reus	Mens Rea	Circumstance
Passing or transferring	1. Specific intent to defraud **or** 2. Knowingly passing false document	False document of legal significance

passing or using documents that someone else may have falsified—even if the utterer never altered anything on the documents—and intending to defraud others with those instruments. Forgery and uttering are thus two distinct offenses. Forgery is directed at making and altering documents in order to defraud. Uttering is directed at passing and using forged documents in order to defraud.

ROBBERY AND EXTORTION

Robbery and extortion are more than property crimes; they are also crimes against persons, and as such they constitute aggravated property crimes. In fact, they are violent or threatened violent thefts. They are therefore more serious than ordinary thefts and usually carry much heavier penalties.

Robbery

The principal elements of **robbery** include

1. taking and
2. carrying away
3. the property of others
4. from their person or in their presence
5. by immediate force or threatened immediate force
6. with the intent to permanently dispossess the rightful possessor.

Hence, robbery consists of forcible theft from another person. It is an aggravated theft because actual threatened physical harm accompanies the misappropriation of property.

Any force beyond that needed to take and carry away property satisfies the force requirement. Picking a pocket is ordinary, although aggravated, larceny and not robbery because picking pockets requires only enough force to remove the pocket's contents. But even a slight mishandling of the victim (such as shoving) makes the crime robbery, if the mishandling secures the property. Determining just how much force satisfies the requirement is a problem in robbery, because the amount of force distinguishes between robbery and the less serious larcenies from the person, of which picking pockets is most common.

Some jurisdictions require the use of no force. Under the Arkansas Criminal Code, for example, robbery is committed "if with the purpose of committing a theft or resisting apprehension immediately thereafter . . . [the criminal] employs or threatens to immediately employ physical force upon another." Under that statute, a defendant who stole a roast in a grocery store and, when caught just beyond the checkout stand, injured the apprehending officer, was found guilty of robbery, not larceny.[17]

Robbery does not require actual force; threatened force ordinarily suffices. In addition, robbers need not threaten victims themselves; threats to family members qualify as well. However, robbers must threaten to kill, or at least to do great bodily injury. Threats to property, except perhaps to a dwelling house, do not satisfy the threatened force requirement.

Most jurisdictions require that robbers threaten to use force immediately, not at some time in the future. Furthermore, victims must relinquish their property because they

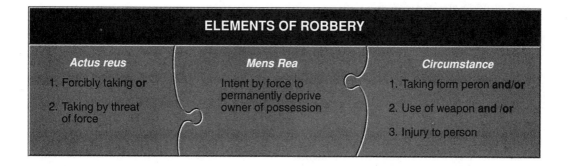

ELEMENTS OF ROBBERY

Actus reus	Mens Rea	Circumstance
1. Forcibly taking **or**	Intent by force to permanently deprive owner of possession	1. Taking form peron **and/or**
2. Taking by threat of force		2. Use of weapon **and /or**
		3. Injury to person

honestly and reasonably fear robbers' threats. Critics maintain that honest fear ought to suffice. Whether robbery requires real, honest, or reasonable fear (or a combination) bears directly on the extent to which criminal law ought to punish potential harm. The court in *State v. Curley* dealt with the element of force.

C A S E

Did He Commit Robbery?

State v. Curley,
1997 WL 242286 (N.M.App. 1997)

Erwin Curley was convicted in the District Court of robbery. He appealed. The Court of Appeals reversed and remanded for new trial.

   PICKARD, Judge.

FACTS

The victim was walking out of a mall with her daughter when Defendant grabbed her purse and ran away. The victim described the incident as follows: "I had my purse on my left side . . . and I felt kind of a shove of my left shoulder where I had my purse strap with my thumb through it and I kind of leaned—was pushed—toward my daughter, and this person came and just grabbed the strap of my purse and continued to run." The victim used the words "grab" or "pull" to describe the actual taking of the purse and "shove" or "push" to describe what Defendant did as he grabbed or "pulled [the purse] from her arm and hand." However, there was also evidence that the victim's thumb

was not through the strap of the purse, but was rather on the bottom of the purse. The purse strap was not broken, and the victim did not testify that she struggled with Defendant for the purse in any way or that any part of her body offered any resistance or even moved when the purse was pulled from her arm and hand. Defendant presented evidence that he was drunk and did not remember the incident at all.

OPINION

Robbery is theft by the use or threatened use of force or violence. NMSA 1978, § 30162 (Repl.Pamp.1994). Because the words "or violence" refer to the unwarranted exercise of force and do not substantively state an alternative means of committing the offense, we refer simply to "force" in this opinion. The force must be the lever by which the property is taken. Although we have cases saying in dictum that even a slight amount of force, such as jostling the victim or snatching away the property, is sufficient, we also have cases in which a taking of property from the person of a victim has been held not to be robbery, see *State v. Sanchez*, 78 N.M.

284, 285, 430 P.2d 781, 782 (Ct.App.1967) (wallet taken from victim's pocket while victim was aware that the defendant was taking the wallet).

A defendant is entitled to a lesser-included-offense instruction when there is some evidence to support it. There must be some view of the evidence pursuant to which the lesser offense is the highest degree of crime committed, and that view must be reasonable. Thus, in this case, to justify giving Defendant's larceny instruction, there must be some view of the evidence pursuant to which force sufficient to constitute a robbery was not the lever by which Defendant removed the victim's purse.

Defendant contends that such evidence exists in that the jury could have found that Defendant's shoving of the victim was part of his drunkenness, and then the purse was taken without force sufficient to constitute robbery. We agree. We are persuaded by an analysis of our own cases, as well as cases from other jurisdictions, that the applicable rule in this case is as follows: when property is attached to the person or clothing of a victim so as to cause resistance, any taking is a robbery, and not larceny, because the lever that causes the victim to part with the property is the force that is applied to break that resistance; however, when no more force is used than would be necessary to remove property from a person who does not resist, then the offense is larceny, and not robbery.

In our cases where we have not found sufficient force to be involved, the victim did not resist the property being taken from his person. See, e.g., *Sanchez*, 78 N.M. at 285, 430 P.2d at 782 (defendant took wallet from victim's pants, but force was not lever by which wallet was taken); see also *State v. Aldershof*, 220 Kan. 798, 556 P.2d 371, 372, 376 (1976) (purse lifted from victim's lap while she sat at a table). On the other hand, the evidence of a snatching of a purse was sufficient to establish robbery in *State v. Clokey*, 89 N.M. 453, 553 P.2d 1260 (1976), but the issue in that case was not whether there was evidence justifying a lesser-included-offense instruction.

The general rule from other jurisdictions is stated in 4 Charles E. Torcia, *Wharton's Criminal Law* Section 465, at 4749 (15th ed. 1996) that a mere snatching of property from a victim is not robbery unless the property is attached to the person or clothes of the owner so as to afford resistance. A minority position is represented by the analysis in *Commonwealth v. Jones*, 362 Mass. 83, 283 N.E.2d 840, 844 (1972). There, the court held that the values sought to be protected by the crime of robbery, as opposed to larceny, are equally present when any property is taken from a person as long as that person is aware of the application of force which relieves the person of property and the taking is therefore, at least to some degree, against the victim's will. See also *Commonwealth v. Ahart*, 37 Mass.App. Ct. 565, 641 N.E.2d 127, 131 (the snatching of a purse necessarily involves the use of force), certs. denied, 419 Mass. 1101, 644 N.E.2d 225 (1994).

The minority rule adopted by Massachusetts, however, appears inconsistent with our earlier cases. Pursuant to the Massachusetts rule, any purse snatching not accomplished by stealth would be robbery. We are not inclined to overrule cases such as Sanchez, in which we held that the taking of a wallet accompanied by just so much force as is necessary to accomplish the taking from a person who was not resisting was not robbery. Rather, we adhere to what we perceive to be the majority rule.

According to the majority rule, robbery is committed when attached property is snatched or grabbed by sufficient force so as to overcome the resistance of attachment. In cases such as this one, where one view of the facts appears to put the case on the border between robbery and larceny, it is necessary to further explore what is meant by the concept of "the resistance of attachment." Our exploration is informed by the interests protected by the two crimes.

In *Fuentes*, 119 N.M. at 106, 108, 888 P.2d at 988, 990, we said that robbery is a crime "primarily" directed at protecting property interests. That statement, however, was made in the context of contrasting the crime of robbery with the crime of assault, which is directed exclusively toward protecting persons. In this case, contrasting the crime of robbery with the crime of larceny, we could similarly say that robbery is directed "primarily" at protecting persons inasmuch as larceny is directed exclusively at protecting property interests. In truth, it is probably inaccurate to say that the crime of robbery is directed "primarily" at either personal or property interests. That is because it is directed at both interests. See Torcia, supra, § 454 at 5 ("By definition, then, robbery may be classified not only as an offense against property but also as an offense against the person."). It is the aspect of the offense that is directed against the person which distinguishes the crime of robbery from larceny and also justifies an increased punishment. See W. LaFave & A. Scott, Jr., *Substantive Criminal Law* § 8.11 at 437 (2d ed. 1986). Thus, "the resistance of attachment" should be construed in light of the idea that robbery is an offense against the person, and something about that offense should reflect the increased danger to the person that robbery involves over the offense of larceny.

LaFave and Scott state:

The great weight of authority, however, supports the view that there is not sufficient force to constitute robbery when the thief snatches property from the owner's grasp so suddenly that the owner cannot offer any resistance to the taking. On the other hand, when the owner, aware of an impending snatching, resists it, or when, the thief's first attempt being ineffective to separate the owner from his property, a struggle for the property is necessary before the thief can get possession thereof, there is enough force to make the taking robbery. Taking the owner's property by stealthily picking his pocket is not taking by force and so is not robbery; but if the pickpocket or his confederate jostles the owner, or if the owner, catching the pickpocket in the act, struggles unsuccessfully to keep possession, the pickpocket's crime becomes robbery. To remove an article of value, attached to the owner's person or clothing, by a sudden snatching or by stealth is not robbery unless the article in question (e.g., an earring, pin or watch) is so attached to the person or his clothes as to require some force to effect its removal.

Thus, it would be robbery, not larceny, if the resistance afforded is the wearing of a necklace around one's neck that is broken by the force used to remove it and the person to whom the necklace is attached is aware that it is being ripped from her neck. On the other hand, it would be larceny, not robbery, if the resistance afforded is the wearing of a bracelet, attached by a thread, and the person to whom the bracelet is attached is not aware that it is being taken until she realizes that it is gone.

While the difference . . . might appear to be the amount of force necessary to break the necklace or string, respectively, that is not how we distinguish the cases. Subtle differences in the amount of force used, alone, is neither a clear nor reasonable basis to distinguish the crime of robbery from that of larceny. However, if we remember that the reason for the distinction in crimes is the increased danger to the person, then an increase in force that makes the victim aware that her body is resisting could lead to the dangers that the crime of robbery was designed to alleviate. A person who did not know that a bracelet was being taken from her wrist by the breaking of a string would have no occasion to confront the thief, thereby possibly leading to an altercation. A person who knows that a necklace is being ripped from her neck might well confront the thief. As stated in the Florida cases, the law is well settled that snatching a purse or picking a pocket is "not robbery if no more force or violence is used than is necessary to remove the property from a person who does not resist."

We now apply these rules to the facts of this case. Although the facts in this case are simply stated, they are rich with conflicting inferences. Either robbery or larceny may be shown, depending on the jury's view of the facts and which inferences it chooses to draw.

In the light most favorable to the State, Defendant shoved the victim to help himself relieve her of the purse, and the shove and Defendant's other force in grabbing the purse had that effect. This view of the facts establishes robbery, and if the jury believed it, the jury would be bound to find Defendant guilty of robbery.

However, there is another view of the facts. Defendant contends that the evidence that he was drunk allows the jury to infer that the shove was unintentional and that the remaining facts show the mere snatching of the purse, thereby establishing larceny. Two issues are raised by this contention that we must address: (1) is there a reasonable view of the evidence pursuant to which the shove was not part of the robbery? and (2) even disregarding the shove, does the remaining evidence show only robbery?

We agree with Defendant that the jury could have inferred that the shove was an incidental touching due to Defendant's drunkenness. Defendant's testimony of his drunkenness and the lack of any testimony by the victim or any witness that the shove was necessarily a part of the robbery permitted the jury to draw this inference. Once the jury drew the inference that the shove was independent of the robbery, the jury could have found that Defendant formed the intent to take the victim's purse after incidentally colliding with her. Alternatively, the jury could have found that Defendant intended to snatch the purse without contacting the victim and that the contact (the shove) was not necessary to, or even a part of, the force that separated the victim from her purse. The victim's testimony (that she felt "kind of a shove" and then Defendant grabbed her purse) would allow this inference. Thus, the jury could have found that the shove did not necessarily create a robbery.

The question would then remain, however, whether the grabbing of the purse was still robbery because more force was used than would have been necessary to remove the purse if the victim had not resisted. Under the facts of this case, in which the victim did not testify that she held the strap tightly enough to resist and in which there was some evidence that she was not even holding the strap, we think that there was a legitimate, reasonable view of the evidence that, once the shove is eliminated from consideration, Defendant used only such force as was necessary to remove the purse from a person who was not resisting. Under this view of the facts, Defendant took the purse by surprise from a person who was not resisting, and not by force necessary to overcome any resistance. Therefore, the trial court should have given Defendant's tendered larceny instructions.

. . .

Accordingly, Defendant's conviction is reversed and remanded for a new trial.

IT IS SO ORDERED.

QUESTIONS FOR DISCUSSION

1. List all of the facts relevant to determining whether the purse snatching was a robbery.

2. State both the majority and the minority rule regarding the element of force in purse snatching.

3. In your opinion, which is the better rule? Defend your answer. See the note case below.

NOTE CASE

About 7:30 P.M., June 10, 1994, two elderly women, Nancy Colantonio and Vera Croston, returned in Croston's 1981 Chevrolet Citation automobile to their home at 36 Webster Street, Haverhill. Croston, upon entering the driveway, located by the side of the stairs leading to the porch and front door, stopped the car to let Colantonio out. Colantonio walked up the stairs. She felt someone snatch her purse from under her arm. She was stunned. Turning, she saw the back of a man running down Webster Street in the direction of Summer Street. She said she couldn't believe what she was seeing.

Was Zangari guilty of purse snatching? Yes, according to the Appeals Court of Massachusetts. The court wrote:

"[W]here the snatching or sudden taking of property from a victim is sufficient to produce awareness, there is sufficient evidence of force to permit a finding of robbery." In pickpocketing, which is accomplished by sleight of hand, such evidence is lacking. The difference accounts for the perceived greater severity of the offense of unarmed robbery in contrast with larceny. The [minority rule followed in Massachusetts] . . . was firmly adopted in the face of contrary authority in some States. It seems that a division continues to the present although, as usual, one can anticipate that a classification of jurisdictions may falter somewhat when the decisions are examined in detail. Judgment affirmed. *Commonwealth v. Zangari*, 677 N.E.2d 702 (Mass. App. 1997).

———————————◼◻————————————

Most states have divided robbery into degrees according to injury done and force or threat used. New York, for example, grades robbery into three degrees. Robbers commit first-degree robbery if they carry deadly weapons, seriously injure victims, threaten the

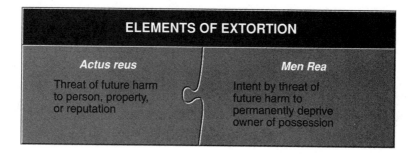

ELEMENTS OF EXTORTION

Actus reus	*Men Rea*
Threat of future harm to person, property, or reputation	Intent by threat of future harm to permanently deprive owner of possession

immediate use of dangerous instruments, or display what "appears to be a pistol, revolver, shotgun, machine gun or other firearm." In other words, play weapons suffice. Second-degree robbery occurs if robbers rob with accomplices, cause any injury, or display "what appears to be a pistol, revolver, rifle, shotgun, machine gun or firearm." Third-degree robbery is unarmed robbery or "forcible stealing"; that is, it occurs when the actor "uses or threatens the immediate use of force upon another person."[18]

Extortion

At common law, extortion applied only to public officials who used their influence illegally to collect fees. Most modern extortions were not known at common law, although unusually extreme threats to gain property (such as a threat to accuse another of sodomy) were considered robbery. Statutory extortion, or blackmail, resembles robbery in that it involves forcibly misappropriating property. It is distinguished from robbery by time. Generally, robbery is a threat to harm someone immediately. **Extortion,** on the other hand, involves threats to do future harm. The line between extortion and robbery is often very fine, making it difficult to distinguish between the two offenses.

Threats sufficient to constitute extortion include those:

1. To inflict bodily harm in the future (remember that robbery requires an immediate threat).
2. To do damage to property.
3. To expose victims to shame or ridicule.

Extortion requires the specific intent to obtain property by threats such as those just described. Some jurisdictions require that actors actually acquire the desired property to complete extortion. Others call it extortion if actors make threats with a present intention to carry them out. In these jurisdictions, victims must actually be put in fear. Under this definition, extortion is an inchoate offense. It is a completed crime against persons, however, because fear completes the harm. The court applied the elements of extortion to a threat against the victim if she told the police about a prior beating in *People v. Pena.*

C A S E

Did She Extort Her Silence?

People v. Pena,
1997 WL 411307 (Mich.App. 1997)

Following a jury trial, Pena was convicted of extortion. She was sentenced to ninety months to twenty years' imprisonment. Pena appealed as of right. The Michigan Court of Appeals affirmed but remanded for articulation of the reasons for the sentence imposed for the extortion conviction or for resentencing.

PER CURIAM.

FACTS

This case arises from an incident in which the victim was beaten by defendant, Tricia Lynn Alcock and Liz Ontiveros. Some days before the incident, the victim and some of her friends had stopped to get some gasoline, when defendant and some girls pulled alongside them in a car, "jumped out and came up to" the victim, and made some remarks to her. The victim and her friends drove away.

On a subsequent day, while the victim was walking home from high school, defendant, Ontiveros, Nicky Rivera, and an unidentified girl passed by her in a car. The victim had previously heard that the girls in the car were going to "jump" her, so she changed direction and walked along another street. The car turned, drove past the victim, and stopped in front of the victim. Defendant, Ontiveros, and the unidentified girl got out of the car. According to the victim, defendant said that someone told her that the victim had called her a bitch and that she was going to "jump" the victim. Defendant then punched the victim in the face, the victim fell, and defendant, Ontiveros and the unidentified girl began punching and kicking the victim. Moments after the assailants stopped beating the victim, a police officer approached the victim and took her complaint regarding the incident. The other girls told the police officer that the victim had thrown something at their car. No arrests were made.

Some days later, the victim, Sharon Stueller and Cynthia Mann were stopped in a car waiting for a friend, Germayne Kelly. After Kelly got into the car, the victim looked around and saw defendant, Alcock and Natalie Garza standing on a corner. Defendant and Alcock ran toward the car. Stueller was unable to restart the car to drive away. Defendant and Alcock were eventually able to enter the car. According to Mann, Alcock hit the victim in the face more than twice. The victim did not hit defendant or Alcock, but attempted to stay in the car. The victim indicated that defendant and Alcock grabbed her arms and hair and pulled her out of the car. While the victim was on the ground, defendant, Alcock and Garza kicked and punched the victim in the face, head, arms and chest. At some point, Alcock and Garza moved away while defendant held the victim by her hair and said "Are you done? Are you done?" Defendant then punched the victim's face twice more. Defendant told the victim to leave and pushed her back toward the car. The victim testified that, during the beating, defendant indicated that the victim had "snitched" to the police about her.

Mann corroborated the victim's account of the fight. Mann also testified that defendant told the victim that she would kill her if she said anything else to the police. After the fight, Mann observed that the victim's face was swollen and her eyes were black and blue, puffy, and bloodshot. Stueller confirmed that a white female and a Mexican female ran toward the car, pulled the victim out of the car, and kicked the victim in the head; but she could not identify them. Stueller did hear one of the attackers threaten to kill the victim if she called the police again. Stueller observed that the victim was bruised and that the victim's eyes "were bleeding blood."

Detective Michael Van Horn of the Michigan State Police saw the victim two days following the incident and described her appearance as follows:

> On her chest, on her wrist, and basically her right eye was pretty much swollen shut. There was a lot of blood in the white part of the eye. There was bruises up on the top of her forehead, and I could see little red bumps where it

looked like her hair had been pulled out from the roots on her head. A lot of facial swelling. There was still some blood—dry blood in her nose—in her nasal area.

OPINION

Defendant argues that her extortion conviction should be reversed because the extortion statute does not contemplate the behavior for which she was convicted. The extortion charge related to defendant's threat of harm, at the conclusion of the last beating, that defendant would kill the victim if she said anything else to the police (apparently about the previous assault). . . . The extortion statute, M.C.L. § 750.213; MSA 28.410, provides in pertinent part:

> Any person who shall . . . orally . . . maliciously threaten any injury to the person . . . with intent to compel the person so threatened to do or refrain from doing any act against his will, shall be guilty of a felony, punishable by imprisonment in the state prison not more than 20 years . . .

When a defendant is charged with extortion arising out of a compelled action or omission, a conviction may be secured upon the presentation of proof of the existence of a threat of immediate, continuing, or future harm.

In *People v. Atcher*, 65 Mich.App 734, 738–739; 238 NW2d 389 (1975), this Court affirmed the defendant's conviction for extortion where the defendant had attempted to prevent a witness from testifying in a misdemeanor assault and battery case against a third party. The decision in *Atcher* did not disapprove of the prosecutor's emphasizing the seriousness of the defendant's action of intimidating a witness, notwithstanding the fact that the testimony that the defendant sought to discourage was related to misdemeanor assault and battery.

Contrary to defendant's claim, threatening a victim with harm if he or she reports a crime to the police does not equate to a "minor threat." Rather, we conclude that the demand by defendant that the victim not talk to the police was an offense contemplated by the extortion statute as the act demanded was of such consequence or seriousness as to apply the statute.

. . .

Defendant's remaining arguments concern the validity of her sentences. She first contends that the trial court failed to articulate sufficient reasons for the sentence imposed for the extortion conviction. To facilitate appellate review, the sentencing court must articulate on the record the criteria considered and the reasons for the sentence imposed.

In imposing sentence for the conviction for extortion, the trial court stated: As to Count III, extortion, it is the sentence of this Court that she serve no less than 7½ to no more than 20 years in a state prison. . . .

Although the trial court asserted that the sentence was imposed because it was proportional to the circumstances of the offense and the offender, the court did not offer any explanation of why the particular sentence imposed was appropriate under the circumstances of this case. Because the trial court did not explain the criteria that it considered, we do not have an adequate record to review this issue. We therefore remand for an articulation of the reasons for the sentence imposed or for resentencing.

. . .

Defendant further argues that her minimum sentence of 7½ years' imprisonment for the extortion conviction is excessive and disproportionate. The extortion statute provides for a maximum penalty of twenty years' imprisonment, M.C.L. § 750.213; MSA 28.410, while the statute for assault with intent to do great bodily harm provides for a maximum penalty of ten years, M.C.L. § 750.84; MSA 28.279. Defendant contends that, notwithstanding that extortion carries a longer sentence than assault with intent to do great bodily harm, "based on the evidence produced at trial the assault was arguably the more serious offense" in the present case. Defendant cites no authority for this argument, but relies on the fact that the threat giving rise to the extortion conviction related to prosecution of a misdemeanor. As previously discussed, however, extortion may properly be viewed as a serious crime worthy of severe punishment even when the threat relates to interfering with the prosecution of a misdemeanor. Nevertheless, because the trial court did not articulate its reasons for the imposition of the sentence for the extortion conviction, we do not have an adequate basis for reviewing this argument.

. . .

Affirmed, but remanded for articulation of the reasons for the sentence imposed for the extortion conviction or for resentencing. . . .

QUESTIONS FOR DISCUSSION

1. List all of the facts relevant to determining whether Pena committed the crime of extortion.

2. What is the definition of extortion according to the Michigan statute?

3. What problem did the facts of this case create for proving extortion?

4. Do you agree that the facts in this case amount to extortion? Defend your answer.

SUMMARY

Property misappropriation crimes originated in the ancient felony of larceny, which protected against wrongfully taking other people's possessions. Separate offenses were created primarily to keep pace with society's increasing complexity, which presented new ways to misappropriate property. Over time, the law changed piecemeal to keep pace with social and economic realities. Embezzlement protected against the wrongful conversion of property; false pretenses against deceitful misappropriations; receiving stolen property against aiding in stolen goods traffic; forgery and uttering against creating, altering, and passing false documents; and extortion against acquiring property by threatening harm in the future. These crimes responded to new ways to misappropriate property, as well as to the expanding list of larcenable items. Their creation testifies to the way criminal misappropriation law developed over the past four hundred years. History, not logic, explains the distinctions between various misappropriation offenses.

In the past twenty years, consolidated theft statutes have made criminal property misappropriation more rational. They join together what used to be larceny, embezzlement, and false pretenses into a new offense called theft. They are based on the idea that whether culprits take, convert, or use deception to acquire other people's property, misappropriation is still the core evil that the separate statutes aim to combat. Some even more ambitious statutes cover all misappropriations except robbery, using the same logic that misappropriation is the core evil behind taking, converting, deceiving, receiving, forging, uttering, and extorting. Only robbery, a crime involving imminent physical harm, stands apart.

Although larceny, embezzlement, false pretenses, and receiving stolen property protect property almost exclusively, forgery, uttering, extortion, and robbery protect other interests as well. Forgery and uttering protect society in general from the disruptive effects created by impairing confidence in the authenticity of documents. They protect not only property but also society's interest in smoothly operating business in modern, complex society. Robbery and extortion are crimes against persons as well as property, because they involve violence or threatened violence. Sometimes called aggravated larceny, their laws punish violent property misappropriations. By punishing when victims suffer fear but sustain no property loss, they demonstrate a wider application than for misappropriated property offenses.

REVIEW QUESTIONS

1. What are the differences between larceny, embezzlement, and false pretenses? Should these offenses be grouped as one crime?

2. Why should receiving stolen property be a crime? Is it more serious than, as serious as, or less serious than theft?

3. What is the purpose of the law of forgery? Is forgery a more serious crime than theft? Why? Why not?

4. What interest does uttering protect?

5. Why are robbery and extortion aggravated misappropriations? Are they crimes against property or persons? What is the most important interest they protect?

KEY TERMS

asportation The carrying away of another's property.

claim of right The belief that property taken rightfully belongs to the taker.

conversion Illegal use of another's property.

extortion Misappropriation of another's property by means of threat to inflict bodily harm in the future.

forgery Making false writings or materially altering authentic writings.

intellectual property Information and services stored in and transmitted to and from electronic data banks; a rapidly developing area of property crimes.

misappropriation Gaining possession of another's property.

robbery Taking and carrying away another's property by force or threat of force with the intent to permanently deprive the owner of possession.

theft Consolidated crimes of larceny, embezzlement, and false pretenses.

trespassory taking Wrongful taking required in larceny *actus reus*.

uttering Knowing or conscious use or transfer of false documents.

Suggested Readings

1. Jerome Hall, *Theft, Law, and Society*, 2d ed. (Indianapolis, Ind.: Bobbs-Merrill, 1952). An excellent demonstration of the relationship between law and society in historical development. Hall convincingly shows that larceny and other misappropriation crimes grew out of English social history. This is an interesting and authoritative work written for the general reader as well as the specialist.

2. Rollin M. Perkins and Ronald N. Boyce, *Criminal Law*, 3d ed. (Mineola, N.Y.: Foundation Press, 1982), chap. 4. Surveys in detail all the property crimes, analyzes their development, discusses new developments, and presents arguments concerning most reforms.

3. Wayne R. LaFave and Austin W. Scott, Jr., *Handbook on Criminal Law*, 2d ed. (St. Paul, Minn.: West Publishing Co., 1986). This book has a useful chapter on property crimes.

4. American Law Institute, *Model Penal Code and Commentaries*, vol. 2 (Philadelphia: American Law Institute, 1980), pt. II. Deals with property crimes. This is the most comprehensive treatment of the history and content of property crimes. The commentary treats extensively its recommended consolidated theft provision, compares that provision with the consolidated theft statutes of various states, and discusses the influence of the *Model Penal Code* provision on those statutes.

Notes

1. Rollin M. Perkins and Ronald N. Boyce, *Criminal Law*, 3d ed. (Mineola, N.Y.: Foundation Press, 1982), chap. 4; Wayne R. LaFave and Austin W. Scott, Jr., *Handbook on Criminal Law*, 2d ed. (St. Paul, Minn.: West Publishing Co., 1986), chap. 8.

2. Perkins and Boyce, *Criminal Law*, p. 289.

3. Jerome Hall, *Theft, Law, and Society*, 2d ed. (Indianapolis, Ind.: Bobbs-Merrill, 1952).

4. V.T.C.A., Penal Code §§ 31.01, 31.02, 31.03. 7th ed. (St. Paul, Minn.: West Publishing Co., 1988).

5. I am grateful to David J. Cooper, Jr., Director of Research, South Carolina Legislative Council, for the reference to the South Carolina law, § 16-13-30, Code of Laws of South Carolina, 1976, as amended.

6. West's Ann.Cal. Penal Code, § 487. 1988 Compact Edition (St. Paul, Minn.: West Publishing Co., 1989).

7. American Law Institute, *Model Penal Code and Commentaries*, vol. 2 (Philadelphia: American Law Institute, 1980), pt. II, pp. 175–176.

8. Ibid., p. 151.

9. 30 Geo. II c. 24.

10. *Model Penal Code*, Arts. 223.0 to 223.9.

11. Quoted in *People v. Shirley*, 78 Cal.App.3d 424, 144 Cal.Rptr. 282, 289 (1978).

12. Ibid.

13. Quoted in Carl Benson, Andrew J. Jablon, Paul J. Kaplan, and Mara Elena Rosenthal, "Computer Crimes," *American Criminal Law Review*, 34 (1997):409, 431, n. 147.

14. West's Ann.Cal. Penal Code, tit. 13 (Added by Stats. 1979, c. 858; Amended by Stats. 1981, c. 837; Stats. 1983, c. 1092, eff. Sept. 27, 1983, operative Jan. 1, 1984; Stats. 1984, c. 949; Stats. 1985, c. 571.)

15. West's Ann.Cal. Penal Code (1970), enacted 1872, amended by Stats. 1905, c. 515, 673, 1; Stats. 1968, c. 713, 1414, 1.

16. American Law Institute, *Model Penal Code, tentative draft no. 11* (Philadelphia: American Law Institute, 1960).

17. Arkansas Crim.Code 41–2103 (1977); *Wilson v. State*, 262 Ark. 339, 556 S.W.2d 657 (1977).

18. New York Penal Code, §§ 160.00–160.15.

CHAPTER TWELVE

Crimes Against Public Order and Morals

CHAPTER MAIN POINTS

1. Balancing the community interest in order and the individual interest in liberty is a fundamental requirement of our constitutional system.

2. Ancient public order and morals offenses are altered to suit the social reality of life at the turn of the twenty-first century.

3. Quality of life crimes are intended to enforce minimum standards of decent behavior in public.

4. Controversy over the quality of life crimes stems from the belief that they are used to keep "undesirables" from bothering "respectable" people, and that they violate the right of free expression, the right of peaceable assembly, the right against cruel and unusual punishment, and the right not to be deprived or liberty without due process of law.

5. The "broken windows" theory posits that behavior that threatens the quality of life can lead not only to increased disorder but also to more serious crime.

6. National attention focuses on the serious crimes while local concerns center on the quality of life crimes.

7. Both the criminal law and the civil action of injunction to abate public nuisances are used to regulate behavior in public.

8. A number of state and municipal governments have enacted laws making gang-related behavior criminal.

9. For centuries, the ancient vagrancy and loitering laws have made the status of being poor a crime.

10. Modern laws affecting the poor are aimed at specific behavior, such as sleeping in public.

11. The regulation of panhandling represents another effort to improve the quality of life in cities by means of regulating begging in public.

12. Blanket prohibitions on panhandling probably are not constitutional; prohibitions against aggressive panhandling probably are constitutional.

Are They "Quality of Life" Criminals?

Rocksprings is an urban war zone. The four-square-block neighborhood, claimed as the turf of a gang variously known as Varrio Sureno Town, Varrio Sureno Treces (VST), or Varrio Sureno Locos (VSL), is an occupied territory. Gang members, all of whom live elsewhere, congregate on lawns, on sidewalks, and in front of apartment complexes at all hours of the day and night. They display a casual contempt for notions of law, order, and decency — openly drinking, smoking dope, sniffing toluene, and even snorting cocaine laid out in neat lines on the hoods of residents' cars. The people who live in Rocksprings are subjected to loud talk, loud music, vulgarity, profanity, brutality, fistfights, and the sound of gunfire echoing in the streets. Gang members take over sidewalks, driveways, carports, and apartment parking areas, and impede traffic on the public thoroughfares to conduct their drive-up drug bazaar. Murder, attempted murder, drive-by shootings, assault and battery, vandalism, arson, and theft are commonplace.

The community has become a staging area for gang-related violence and a dumping ground for the weapons and instrumentalities of crime once the deed is done. Area residents have had their garages used as urinals; their homes commandeered as escape routes; their walls, fences, garage doors, sidewalks, and even their vehicles turned into a sullen canvas of gang graffiti. The people of this community are prisoners in their own homes. Violence and the threat of violence are constant. Residents remain indoors, especially at night. They do not allow their children to play outside. Strangers wearing the wrong color clothing are at risk. Relatives and friends refuse to visit. The laundry rooms, the trash dumpsters, the residents' vehicles, and their parking spaces are used to deal and stash drugs. Verbal harassment, physical intimidation, threats of retaliation, and retaliation are the likely fate of anyone who complains of the gang's illegal activities or tells police where drugs may be hidden.

INTRODUCTION

The tension between order and liberty is timeless. The United States Supreme Court has recognized the importance of balancing the social interest in both by repeatedly holding that "ordered liberty" is a fundamental requirement of our constitutional system. In this chapter, **order** refers to behavior in public that comports with minimum community standards of civility. **Liberty** refers to the right of individuals to go about in public free of undue interference. This chapter examines the balance between order and liberty in the creation and enforcement of laws directed at behavior in public places, such as sidewalks, streets, and parks. Significant numbers of people across the spectrum of age, sex, race, ethnicity, and class consider breaches of minimum standards of decent behavior in public places as threats both to the quality of life and to the requirement of ordered liberty. Others view the use of the criminal law to enforce these standards as a threat to the individual liberty and privacy that our constitutional democracy guarantees.

Historically labeled crimes against public order and morals, these breaches of minimum standards of decent behavior in public are now increasingly referred to as **quality of life crimes.** Most of them have ancient roots, but from the 1930s onward they have aroused concern and controversy. The list of public order and morals offenses is long, and embraces a wide range of behavior. Among other offenses, it includes public drinking and drunkenness; begging and aggressive panhandlng; threatening behavior and harassment; obstruction of streets and public places; vandalism and graffiti; street prostitution; public urination and defecation; unlicensed vending; and even "squeegeeing"—washing the windshields of stopped cars and demanding money for the "service."

The controversy over quality of life crimes has generated heated debate since the early 1980s. Two prominent scholars sensed a deep public yearning for what seemed to be a lost sense of decency and order in national life, particularly in the nation's largest cities. Professors James Q. Wilson and George L. Kelling suggested that what were labeled "petty crimes" were not only upsetting law-abiding people, but Kelling and Wilson suggested that the offenses could also lead to a rise in serious crime. The article—and incidentally the name of the authors' theory as to a cause of crime—was entitled "Broken Windows."[1]

According to Kelling, research conducted since the article was written in 1982 has demonstrated "a direct link between disorder and crime . . ." Wilson described the **broken windows theory** in 1996 more cautiously. In the foreword to a book written by Kelling and Catherine M. Coles, entitled *Fixing Broken Windows*, Wilson wrote:

We used the image of broken windows to explain how neighborhoods might decay into disorder and even crime if no one attends faithfully to their maintenance. If a factory or office window is broken, passersby observing it will conclude that no one cares or no one is in charge. In time, a few will begin throwing rocks to break more windows. Soon all the windows will be broken, and now passersby will think that, not only is no one in charge of the building no one is in charge of the street on which it faces. Only the young, the criminal, or the foolhardy have any business on an unprotected avenue, and so more and more citizens will abandon the street to those they assume prowl it. Small disorders lead to larger and larger ones, and *perhaps even to crime.*[2] [emphasis added]

Professor Wesley G. Skogan, the author of some of the research on which Kelling relies, has also characterized his and others' research more cautiously than Kelling:

Our concern with common crime is limited to whether disorder is a cause of it. . . . [N]eighborhood levels of disorder are closely related to crime rates, to fear of crime, and the belief that serious crime is a neighborhood problem. This relationship *could reflect the fact that the link between crime and disorder is a causal one, or that both are dependent on some third set of factors (such as poverty or neighborhood instability).*[3] [emphasis added]

Skogan did, however, say that his data do "support the proposition that disorder needs to be taken seriously in research on neighborhood crime, and that both directly and through crime, it plays an important role in neighborhood decline."[4]

Whatever the relationship between crime and disorder, the attention given to quality of life crimes varies significantly. The serious crimes against persons, habitations, and property analyzed in chapters 8 through 11 receive most of the attention in the national debate against crime—and in this and other books on criminal law. However, surveys have revealed a disconnect between the national debate and local concern. Of course, mayors and the residents of local communities worry about murder, rape, burglary, and theft. But they also care a great deal about order on their streets and in their parks and other public places. Public drinking, followed closely by loitering youths, in fact, top the list of worries in a representative sample of residents in forty high- and low-crime neighborhoods scattered throughout the country's major cities. Survey participants also list begging (particularly aggressive panhandling), street harassment, noisy neighbors, vandalism, street prostitution, illegal vending, and, in New York City, "squeegeeing."[5]

Criminal law not only embodies the established principles and doctrines presented in chapters 3 through 5, and the definitions of the serious crimes against persons, habitations, and property analyzed in chapters 8 through 11. The criminal law in action in the late 1990s also reflects the social reality in the twilight of the twentieth century. That reality includes local concerns about the quality of life, particularly in the nation's cities. State statutes and city ordinances have reinvigorated and molded the old crimes against public order and morals to fit the public demand that criminal justice preserve, protect, and even restore the quality of life in their communities. The courts have assumed the burden of balancing the social interest in public order and decency against the social interest in individual liberty and privacy. The sections that follow provide a sample of the laws, court opinions, and debate about how to balance order and liberty, and thereby preserve the fundamental ordered liberty without which our society could not survive. We examine how states and localities have shaped some of the traditional public order and morals offenses in order to respond to the behavior in public of some groups believed to reduce the quality of life in contemporary cities, namely street gangs, the homeless, and panhandlers.[6]

STREET GANGS

"Bands of loitering youth" are considered by many city residents to be serious threats to the quality of life. These "gangs range from casual groupings engaging in a bit of drinking and social conversation to organized fighting squads," according to Wesley G. Skogan. The less threatening merely bother residents. According to one observer: "As far as I know they have no name. They are neighborhood kids and they sometimes make a nuisance of themselves. Actually they stand there because they have no place to go." Gangs composed of older, rowdier members are more threatening. According to a resident in a neighborhood with one of these gangs:

> Sometimes I walk out of my house and start to try to walk down the street, and a gang will cross the street and try to scare me and my mother. A gang used to sit and drink beer and smoke pot in front of our stairs. My mom used to come out and tell them to get off; they would, and then when she would go into the house they'd come back, sit down, and look at us. Actually we're afraid to walk around in the neighborhood after it gets dark. I stay right in front of the house where my mom can see me.[7]

A number of state and local governments have passed criminal laws related to gang behavior. In a number of states, it is a crime to participate in a gang. Some have stiffened the penalties for crimes committed by gang members. Others make it a crime to encourage minors to participate in gangs. Some have applied organized crime statutes to gangs. A few have punished parents for their children's gang activities. Cities have also passed ordinances banning gang members from certain public places, particularly city parks.[8]

In addition to criminal penalties, cities have also turned to civil remedies in order to control gang activity. The ancient civil remedy — the injunction to abate public nuisances — is available. In these actions, city attorneys ask courts to declare gang activities and gang members public nuisances, and to issue injunctions to abate the nuisance. **Public nuisances** are "offenses against, or interferences with, the exercise of rights common to the public." According to the California Supreme Court, in *People ex rel. Gallo v. Acuna*, excerpted below, a public nuisance may be any act

> which alternatively is injurious to health or is indecent, or offensive to the senses; the result of the act must interfere with the comfortable enjoyment of life or property; and those affected by the act may be an entire neighborhood or a considerable number of people.[9]

An **injunction** is a court order, commanding an individual or group to do — or to stop doing — something. In *People ex rel. Gallo v. Acuna*, excerpted below, the city attorney asked for an injunction ordering gang members to stop doing all of the following:

"(a) Standing, sitting, walking, driving, gathering or appearing anywhere in public view with any other defendant herein, or with any other known 'VST' (Varrio Sureno Town or Varrio Sureno Locos) member;

"(b) Drinking alcoholic beverages in public excepting consumption on properly licensed premises or using drugs;

"(c) Possessing any weapons including but not limited to knives, dirks, daggers, clubs, nunchukas [sic; nunchakus], BB guns, concealed or loaded firearms, and any other illegal weapons as defined in the California Penal Code, and any object capable of inflicting serious bodily injury including but not limited to the following: metal pipes or rods, glass bottles, rocks, bricks, chains, tire irons, screwdrivers, hammers, crowbars, bumper jacks, spikes, razor blades; razors, sling shots, marbles, ball bearings;

"(d) Engaging in fighting in the public streets, alleys, and/or public and private property;

"(e) Using or possessing marker pens, spray paint cans, nails, razor blades, screwdrivers, or other sharp objects capable of defacing private or public property;

"(f) Spray painting or otherwise applying graffiti on any public or private property, including but not limited to the street, alley, residences, block walls, vehicles and/or any other real or personal property;

"(g) Trespassing on or encouraging others to trespass on any private property;

"(h) Blocking free ingress and egress to the public sidewalks or street, or any driveways leading or appurtenant thereto in 'Rocksprings';

"(i) Approaching vehicles, engaging in conversation, or otherwise communicating with the occupants of any vehicle or doing anything to obstruct or delay the free flow of vehicular or pedestrian traffic;

"(j) Discharging any firearms;

"(k) In any manner confronting, intimidating, annoying, harassing, threatening, challenging, provoking, assaulting and/or battering any residents or patrons, or visitors to 'Rocksprings', or any other persons who are known to have complained about gang activities, including any persons who have provided information in support of this Complaint and requests for Temporary Restraining Order, Preliminary Injunction and Permanent Injunction;

"(l) Causing, encouraging, or participating in the use, possession and/or sale of narcotics;

"(m) Owning, possessing or driving a vehicle found to have any contraband, narcotics, or illegal or deadly weapons;

"(n) Using or possessing pagers or beepers in any public space;

"(o) Possessing channel lock pliers, picks, wire cutters, dent pullers, sling shots, marbles, steel shot, spark plugs, rocks, screwdrivers, 'slim jims' and other devices capable of being used to break into locked vehicles;

"(p) Demanding entry into another person's residence at any time of the day or night;

"(q) Sheltering, concealing or permitting another person to enter into a residence not their own when said person appears to be running, hiding, or otherwise evading a law enforcement officer;

"(r) Signaling to or acting as a lookout for other persons to warn of the approach of police officers and soliciting, encouraging, employing or offering payment to others to do the same;

"(s) Climbing any tree, wall, or fence, or passing through any wall or fence by using tunnels or other holes in such structures;

"(t) Littering in any public place or place open to public view;

"(u) Urinating or defecating in any public place or place open to public view;

"(v) Using words, phrases, physical gestures, or symbols commonly known as hand signs or engaging in other forms of communication which describe or refer to the gang known as 'VST' or 'VSL' as described in this Complaint or any of the accompanying pleadings or declarations;

"(w) Wearing clothing which bears the name or letters of the gang known as 'VST' or 'VSL';

"(x) Making, causing, or encouraging others to make loud noise of any kind, including but not limited to yelling and loud music at any time of the day or night."[10]

Injunctions, like laws against gang activities, call for balancing the rights of the community and those of the individual. The community interest in the quality of life requires peace, quiet, order, and a sense of security. At the same time, even members of street gangs have the right to associate, express themselves, travel freely, and be free from vague laws (see the section on the void-for-vagueness doctrine in chapter 2). In *People ex rel. Gallo v. Acuna*, the California Supreme Court attempted to balance the community interest in the quality of life and the rights of individual gang members.

C A S E

Were They Public Nuisances?

People ex rel. Gallo v. Acuna et al., 14 Cal.4th 1090, 929 P.2d 596, 60 Cal.Rptr.2d 277 (1997)

The city of San Jose sought injunctive relief against members of an alleged criminal street gang. After a temporary restraining order was granted, the Superior Court, Santa Clara County, entered a preliminary injunction prohibiting gang members from engaging in certain behavior in the neighborhood. Gang members appealed. The Court of Appeal modified the injunction and affirmed it as modified. At the request of the City Attorney of the City of San Jose, the California supreme court granted review to resolve an array of challenges to two provisions of the preliminary injunction. The underlying action was instituted under the California civil "public nuisance" statutes. The supreme court reversed the Court of Appeal.

BROWN, Justice.

FACTS

. . . Rocksprings is an urban war zone. The four-square-block neighborhood, claimed as the turf of a gang variously known as Varrio Sureno Town, Varrio Sureno Treces (VST), or Varrio Sureno Locos (VSL), is an occupied territory. Gang members, all of whom live elsewhere, congregate on lawns, on sidewalks, and in front of apartment complexes at all hours of the day and night. They display a casual contempt for notions of law, order, and decency—openly drinking, smoking dope, sniffing toluene, and even snorting cocaine laid out in neat lines on the hoods of residents' cars. The people who live in Rocksprings are subjected to loud talk, loud music, vulgarity, profanity, brutality, fistfights and the sound of gunfire echoing in the streets. Gang members take over sidewalks, driveways, carports, apartment parking areas, and impede traffic on the public thoroughfares to conduct their drive-up drug bazaar. Murder, attempted murder, drive-by shootings, assault and battery, vandalism, arson, and theft are commonplace.

The community has become a staging area for gang-related violence and a dumping ground for the weapons and instrumentalities of crime once the deed is done. Area residents have had their garages used as urinals; their homes commandeered as escape routes; their walls, fences, garage doors, sidewalks, and even their vehicles turned into a sullen canvas of gang graffiti. The people of this community are prisoners in their own homes. Violence and the threat of violence are constant. Residents remain indoors, especially at night. They do not allow their children to play outside. Strangers wearing the wrong color clothing are at risk. Relatives and friends refuse to visit. The laundry rooms, the trash dumpsters, the residents' vehicles, and their parking spaces are used to deal and stash drugs. Verbal harassment, physical intimidation, threats of retaliation, and retaliation are the likely fate of anyone who complains of the gang's illegal activities or tells police where drugs may be hidden.

Among other allegations, the City's complaint asserted that the named defendants and others

> [f]or more than 12 months precedent to the date of [the] complaint, continuing up to the present time . . . [have] occupied [and] used the area commonly known as 'Rocksprings' . . . in such a manner so as to constitute a public nuisance . . . injurious to the health, indecent or offensive to the senses, [and] an obstruction to the free use of property so as to interfere with the comfortable enjoyment of life or property by those persons living in the . . . neighborhood.

After alleging the usual requisites for equitable relief—the prospect of "great and irreparable injury" and the absence of "a plain, adequate and speedy remedy at law"—the complaint prayed for a broad and comprehensive injunction against defendants' al-

leged activities in Rocksprings. [**Equitable relief** means seeking an injunction according to justice and fairness when the strict rules of law cannot do so.] The superior court granted an ex parte temporary restraining order enjoining all 38 defendants named in the complaint and issued an order to show cause (OSC) why a preliminary injunction should not be entered.

Only five of the named defendants appeared in response to the OSC. Following a hearing, the superior court entered a preliminary injunction against the 33 defendants who had not appeared and continued the matter as to those 5 defendants who opposed entry of a preliminary injunction, leaving the temporary restraining order in force as to them. Eleven of the named defendants (the five who had originally appeared in opposition to the OSC, together with another six of the named defendants) moved to vacate the injunctions. After the matter was briefed and argued, the superior court entered a preliminary injunction. [A **preliminary injunction** is a temporary injunction, issued until the court can finally decide the merits of the case.] The multipart decree, consisting of some 24 paragraphs, was the subject of an interlocutory appeal by these 11 defendants. [An interlocutory appeal is a provisional or temporary appeal. In other words, it is not final. An interlocutory appeal usually decides some point in the case but is not the final resolution of the whole case.]

The Court of Appeal disagreed with the superior court, upholding only provisions of the preliminary injunction enjoining acts or conduct defined as crimes under specific provisions of the Penal Code. Although its premise is never clearly articulated, that ruling effectively limits the scope of permissible injunctive relief under California's public nuisance statutes to independently criminal conduct. The Court of Appeal also concluded many of the provisions of the preliminary injunction were void and unenforceable under either the First and Fifth Amendments to the federal Constitution as unconstitutionally vague or overbroad. Altogether, 15 of the 24 provisions of the trial court's preliminary injunction were partially or entirely invalidated. However, the City's petition only sought review of two provisions—paragraphs (a) and (k). We granted the City's petition and now reverse.

OPINION

. . .

I. Equitable Jurisdiction To Enjoin Public Nuisances
A. The Origin And Nature Of Actions To Enjoin Public Nuisances

Often the public interest in tranquillity, security, and protection is invoked only to be blithely dismissed, subordinated to the paramount right of the individual. In this case, however, the true nature of the trade-off becomes painfully obvious. Liberty unrestrained is an invitation to anarchy. Freedom and responsibility are joined at the hip. "Wise accommodation between liberty and order always has been, and ever will be, indispensable for a democratic society." There must be an irreducible minimum of reciprocity for civil society to function. "[T]he very concept of ordered liberty precludes allowing every person to make his own standards on matters of conduct in which society as a whole has important interests."

The state has not only a right to "maintain a decent society" but an obligation to do so. In the public nuisance context, the community's right to security and protection must be reconciled with the individual's right to expressive and associative freedom. Reconciliation begins with the acknowledgment that the interests of the community are not invariably less important than the freedom of individuals. Indeed, the security and protection of the community is the bedrock on which the superstructure of individual liberty rests. From Montesquieu to Locke to Madison, the description of the pivotal compact remains unchanged: by entering society, individuals give up the unrestrained right to act as they think fit; in return, each has a positive right to society's protection. . . . (Montesquieu, *The Spirit of the Laws* (U. Cambridge Press 1989) ch. 6, p. 157; and see Locke, *Two Treatises on Government* (U. Cambridge Press, student ed. 1988) §§ 122, 140, 211, 227; Madison, *The Federalist* No. 51 (Rossiter ed. 1961) pp. 324, 325.)

. . . [A] principal office of the centuries old doctrine of the "public nuisance" has been the maintenance of public order—tranquillity, security and protection—when the criminal law proves inadequate. There are few "forms of action" in the history of AngloAmerican law with a pedigree older than suits seeking to restrain nuisances, whether public or private. . . . The public nuisance doctrine is aimed at the protection and redress of community interests and, at least in theory, embodies a kind of collective ideal of civil life which the courts have vindicated by equitable remedies since the beginning of the 16th century.

. . .

Section 370 of the Penal Code . . . combin[es] . . . the characteristics of nuisances generally with a distinctly public quality: that a given activity "interfere with the comfortable enjoyment of life or property by an entire community or neighborhood, or by any considerable number of persons." (Pen.Code, § 370 . . . It is . . . [the] community aspect of the public nuisance, reflected in the civil and criminal counterparts of the California code, that . . . makes possible its use, by means of the equitable injunction, to protect the quality of organized social life. Of course, not every interference with collective social interests constitutes a public nuisance. To qualify, and thus be enjoinable, the interference must be both substantial and unreasonable. . . .

B. Expansion And Contraction Of "Criminal Equity"

With the legitimacy of equitable relief to control public nuisances well established, American courts began to enlarge the jurisdiction of what has been called by some "criminal equity" and, by others, "government by injunction." (See Mack, The Revival of Criminal Equity (1903) 16 Harv.L.Rev. 389, 397; Fiss, Injunctions (1972) p. 580.) The highwater mark of this trend may have been reached in *In re Debs* (1896) 158 U.S. 564, 15 S.Ct. 900, 39 L.Ed. 1092, where a strike by employees at the Pullman car works in Chicago paralyzed much of the nation's rail transportation and, with it, national commerce. The strike was broken by the entry of a public nuisance injunction—the controversial "Pullman injunction." . . .

. . . [O]ur opinion in *People v. Lim*, 18 Cal.2d 872, 118 P.2d 472, affirms the equal dignity, at least as far as the protection of equity is concerned, of private, property-based interests and those values that are in essence collective, arising out of a shared ideal of community life and the minimum conditions for a civilized society. "Courts have held that public and social interests, as well as the rights of property," Chief Justice Gibson wrote, "are entitled to the protection of equity." In a sense that cannot easily be dismissed, the availability of equitable relief to counter public nuisances is an expression of "the interest of the public in the quality of life and the total community environment."

C. The Relation Between Crimes And Public Nuisances

As Justice Brewer noted in the *Debs* case: "A chancellor has no criminal jurisdiction. Something more than the threatened commission of an offense against the laws of the land is necessary to call into exercise the injunctive powers of the court. There must be some interference, actual or threatened, with property or rights . . . but when such interferences appear the jurisdiction of a court of equity arises, and is not destroyed by the fact that they are accompanied by or are themselves violations of the criminal law. . . ."

The Court of Appeal was thus partly accurate in reasoning that "a public nuisance is always a criminal offense," for indeed it is. (See Pen.Code, § 372 [maintenance of a public nuisance is a misdemeanor].) It is the corollary to that proposition—that the superior court's injunction was valid only to the extent that it enjoined conduct that is independently proscribed by the Penal Code—that is flawed. Acts or conduct which qualify as public nuisances are enjoinable as civil wrongs or prosecutable as criminal misdemeanors, a characteristic that derives not from their status as independent crimes, but from their inherent tendency to injure or interfere with the community's exercise and enjoyment of rights common to the public. It is precisely this recognition of—and willingness to vindicate—the value of community and the collective interests it furthers rather than to punish criminal acts that lie at the heart of the public nuisance as an equitable doctrine. . . .

II. Defendants' Constitutional Challenges to Provisions (a) and (k) of the Preliminary Injunction

. . .

B. First Amendment Challenges

1. Associational Interests

The [U.S. Supreme Court] . . . has identified two kinds of associations entitled to First Amendment protection—those with an "intrinsic" or "intimate" value, and those that are "instrumental" to forms of religious and political expression and activity. Of the first, the court has said that it is "central to the concept of liberty" and is exemplified by personal affiliations that "attend the creation and sustenance of a family—marriage . . . the raising and education of children; and cohabitation with one's relatives." Such affiliations, the court has remarked, "involve deep attachments and commitments to the necessarily few other individuals with whom one shares not only a special community of thoughts, experiences, and beliefs but also distinctively personal aspects of one's life. Among other things . . . they are distinguished by such attributes as relative smallness, a high degree of selectivity in decisions to begin and maintain the affiliation, and seclusion from others in critical aspects of the relationship."

The second kind of association that merits First Amendment protection is composed of groups whose members join together for the purpose of pursuing "a wide variety of political, social, economic, educational, religious, and cultural ends." This instrumental right of protected association is directly related to the "individual's freedom to speak, to worship, and to petition the government for the redress of grievances" because, without it, these liberties themselves could scarcely exist, much less thrive.

It is evident that whatever else it may be in other contexts, the street gang's conduct in Rocksprings at issue in this case fails to qualify as either of the two protected forms of association. Manifestly, in its activities within the four-block area of Rocksprings, the gang is not an association of individuals formed "for the purpose of engaging in protected speech or religious activities." Without minimizing the value of the gang to its members as a loosely structured, elective form of social association, that characteristic is in itself insufficient to command constitutional protection, at least within the circumscribed area of Rocksprings. . . .

Freedom of association, in the sense protected by the First Amendment, "does not extend to joining with others for the purpose of depriving third parties of their lawful rights." We do not, in short, believe that the activities of the gang and its members in Rocksprings at issue here are either "private" or "intimate" as constitutionally defined; the fact that defendants may "exercise some discrimination in choosing associates [by] a selective process of inclusion and exclusion" does not mean that the association or its activities in Rocksprings is one that commands protection under the First Amendment.

. . .

C. Defendants' Fifth Amendment "Void-For-Vagueness" Challenge To Provisions (a) And (k)

We consider next the claim of defendants that provisions (a) and (k) of the interlocutory injunction are "void for vagueness." . . . [T]he claim that a law is unconstitutionally vague is not dependent on the interests of absent third parties. Instead, the underlying concern is the core due process requirement of adequate notice. "No one may be required at peril of life, liberty or property to speculate as to the meaning of penal statutes. All are entitled to be informed as to what the State commands or forbids." (Lanzetta v. New Jersey (1939) 306 U.S. 451, 453, 59 S.Ct. 618, 619, 83 L.Ed. 888) The operative corollary is that "a statute which either forbids or requires the doing of an act in terms so vague that men of common intelligence must necessarily guess at its meaning and differ as to its application, violates the first essential of due process of law."

In its more recent applications of the vagueness doctrine, the high court has also expressed a concern for the potential for arbitrary and discriminatory enforcement inherent in vague statutes. . . . The Court of Appeal found paragraph (k), enjoining defendants from "confronting, intimidating, annoying, harassing, threatening, challenging, provoking, assaulting and/or battering any residents or patrons, or visitors to 'Rocksprings' . . . known to have complained about gang activities [,]," impermissibly vague. . . . [A]ccording to the Court of Appeal, provision (k) fails to define sufficiently the words "confront," "annoy," "provoke," "challenge," or "harass"; it thus fails to provide a standard of conduct for those whose activities are proscribed. Yet similar words were upheld against claims of vagueness by the Supreme Court . . . [T]he high court affirmed injunctive relief prohibiting petitioners from engaging in similar—if not more broadly phrased—conduct: "intimidating, harassing, touching, pushing, shoving, crowding, or assaulting persons entering or leaving." We find nothing in the context of this case . . . constitutionally infirm. . . .

V. Conclusion

To hold that the liberty of the peaceful, industrious residents of Rocksprings must be forfeited to preserve the illusion of freedom for those whose ill conduct is deleterious to the community as a whole is to ignore half the political promise of the Constitution and the whole of its sense. The freedom to leave one's house and move about at will, and to have a measure of personal security is "implicit in the concept of ordered liberty" enshrined in the history and basic constitutional documents of English-speaking peoples. Preserving the peace is the first duty of government, and it is for the protection of the community from the predations of the idle, the contentious, and the brutal that government was invented.

Writing in 1834 of the events that shaped the American Revolution, Alexis De Tocqueville remarked how the American struggle for independence was uniquely shaped by "a love for law and order." In this case we consider whether, after the passage of more than two centuries, we remain free to reaffirm those fundamental values of ordered liberty. We do.

The judgment of the Court of Appeal is reversed. . . .

GEORGE, C.J., and BAXTER and WERDEGAR, JJ., concur.

DISSENT

MOSK, Justice, dissenting.

No doubt Montesquieu, Locke, and Madison will turn over in their graves when they learn they are cited in an opinion that does not enhance liberty but deprives a number of simple rights to a group of Latino youths who have not been convicted of a crime. Mindful of the admonition of another great 18th century political philosopher, Benjamin Franklin, that "[t]hey that can give up essential liberty to obtain a little temporary safety deserve neither liberty nor safety," I would, unlike the majority, in large part affirm the judgment of the Court of Appeal.

. . .

The majority would permit our cities to close off entire neighborhoods to Latino youths who have done nothing more than dress in blue or black clothing or associate with others who do so; they would authorize criminal penalties for ordinary, nondisruptive acts of walking or driving through a residential neighborhood with a relative or friend. In my view, such a blunderbuss approach amounts to both bad law and bad policy. Chief Justice Warren warned in *Jay v. Boyd* (1956) 351 U.S. 345, 367, 76 S.Ct. 919, 932, 100 L.Ed. 1242: "Unfortunately, there are some who think that the way to save freedom in this country is to adopt the techniques of tyranny." The majority here appear to embrace that misguided belief. Accordingly, I dissent.

QUESTIONS FOR DISCUSSION

1. List all of the gang activities affecting the quality of life in San Jose.

2. Why did the supreme court reverse the court of appeal?

3. Assume that you are the city attorney. Relying on the court's opinion and the facts of the case, defend the constitutionality and the wisdom of granting an injunction for some or all of the gang activities.

4. Assume that you are the attorney for the gang members. Relying on the facts and court opinion in the case, argue that some or all of the gang activities are protected by the Constitution.

5. Assume you had the power to issue an injunction. How would you word it in this case?

SLEEPING IN PUBLIC

For at least 600 years, vagrancy and loitering statutes have made crimes out of idleness and roaming about without visible means of support. Our first constitution — the Articles of Confederation — specifically denied paupers rights that other citizens enjoyed — the right to travel from state to state and to the equal protection of the laws. In 1837, the United States Supreme Court approved the efforts by the state of New York to exclude paupers arriving by ship. The Court noted that it is "as competent and as necessary for a state to provide precautionary measures against the moral pestilence of paupers, vagabonds, and possibly convicts as it is to guard against the physical pestilence, which may arise from unsound and infectious articles." Every state in the union had and enforced vagrancy and loitering statutes that reflected these views.[11]

Both the earlier social attitudes and public policies regarding the regulation of the conduct of poor people began to change during the Great Depression. By 1941, the Supreme Court had struck down a statute that prohibited the importation of paupers into the state of California. In response to the argument that the regulation of paupers enjoyed a long history, the Court dismissed the earlier decisions as out of date. According to the Court, "[W]e do not think that it will now be seriously contended that because a person is without employment and without funds he constitutes a 'moral pestilence.'" In a concurring opinion, Justice Robert Jackson encouraged the Court to "say now, in no uncertain terms, that a mere property status, without more, cannot be used by a state to test, qualify, or limit his rights as a citizen of the United States."[12]

During the 1960s and 1970s, courts began to strike down vagrancy laws because they unfairly discriminated against the poor. The following excerpt from an opinion written by Chief Justice Thompson of the Nevada Supreme Court reflects this trend.

> It is simply not a crime to be unemployed, without funds, and in a public place. To punish the unfortunate for this circumstance debases society. The comment of [U.S. Associate Supreme Court] Justice Douglas is relevant: "How can we hold our heads high and still confuse with crime the need for welfare or the need for work?"[13]

Finally, in 1972, in *Papichristou v. City of Jacksonville*, the United States Supreme Court struck down the Jacksonville, Florida, vagrancy ordinance, an ordinance nearly identical to virtually every other vagrancy law in the country. Writing for an unanimous Court, Justice Douglas wrote that the ordinance was void for vagueness because it both failed to give adequate notice to individuals and encouraged arbitrary law enforcement. The Court warned that criminal statutes aimed at the poor "teach that the scales of justice are so tipped that even-handed administration of the law is not possible. The rule of law, evenly applied to minorities as well as majorities, to the poor as well as the rich, is the great mucilage that holds society together."[14]

In the important 1983 decision, *Kolender v. Lawson*, the United States Supreme Court narrowed the scope of another kind of statute aimed at regulating the conduct of loitering. The Court struck down a California loitering statute that authorized the punishment of anyone wandering the streets who failed to produce credible identification when a police officer asked for it. As in *Papichristou*, the Court ruled that the statute was void for vagueness.[15]

According to Harry Simon, staff attorney, Legal Aid Society, Orange County, Santa Ana,

> With the Supreme Court's decisions in *Papichristou* and *Kolender*, loitering and vagrancy laws ceased to be effective tools to punish and control the displaced poor. While judicial attitudes on vagrancy and loitering laws had changed, local officials perceived the invalidation of these laws as a dangerous assault on their authority to enforce social order.[16]

Laudable as these decisions might be, according to Robert C. Ellickson, Professor of Property and Urban Law at the Yale Law School:

> Many judges at the time seemed blind to the fact that their constitutional rulings might adversely affect the quality of urban life and the viability of city centers. It is one thing to protect unpopular persons from wrongful confinement; it is another to imply that these persons have no duty to behave themselves in public places. In addition, federal constitutional rulings are one of the most centralized and inflexible forms of lawmaking. In a diverse and dynamic nation committed to separation of powers and federalism, there is much to be said for giving state and local legislative bodies substantial leeway to tailor street codes to city conditions, and for giving state judges ample scope to interpret the relevant provisions of state constitutions.[17]

The easing of social control over behavior in public fostered both by these decisions and a more tolerant attitude toward individual differences occurred at the same time that deinstitutionalization of the mentally ill, family breakdown, the increase in the use of crack cocaine, hard economic times, and tightening budgets for social programs were contributing to a rising—and to many, a frightening—underclass. By the late 1980s, this rising underclass and its public presence and behavior led many city dwellers to conclude that "things had gone too far." The liberal columnist Ellen Goodman, in a piece entitled "Swarms of Beggars Cause 'Compassion Fatigue,'" captured this "things have gone too far" attitude when she wrote, "Today at least, this tourist, walking from one block to another, one cup to another, one city to another wants to join in a citizens' chorus: 'Enough's enough.'" Municipal codes reflected this growing intolerance of the misbehavior of homeless people. According to Juliette Smith, by the late 1990s, "at least thirty-nine American cities had initiated or continued policies that criminalize activities associated with homelessness."[18]

Enforcing the laws regulating the behavior of homeless and other "street people" generates controversy because they seem to target the poorest and weakest residents in order to provide for the comfort and convenience of better-off residents. But James Q. Wilson defends laws that target the misbehavior of street people. He notes that the special competence of courts lies in defining and applying rights. Courts typically hear the cases of "an *individual* beggar, sleeper, or solicitor." Such an individual rarely poses a threat to anyone, "and so the claims of communal order often seem, in the particular case, to be suspect or overdrawn."

> But the effects on a community of *many* such individuals taking advantage of the rights granted to *an* individual (or often, as the court sees it, an abstract depersonalized individual) are qualitatively different from the effects of a single person. A public space—a bus stop, a market square, a subway entrance—is more than the sum of its parts; it is a complex pattern of interactions that can become dramatically more threatening as the scale and frequency of those interactions increase. As the number of unconventional individuals increases arithmetically, the number of worrisome behaviors increases geometrically.[19]

San Francisco was one of many cities whose officials enforced the "quality of life" laws against the public misbehavior of street people. It is also a city where a few individuals turned to the courts to vindicate the rights of the homeless. In *Joyce v. City of San Francisco*, Federal District Judge Jensen heard a motion to grant a **preliminary injunction**—a temporary court order issued following notice and a hearing—to stop the city of San Francisco from continuing its Matrix Program to preserve the quality of life on San Francisco streets and other public places.

C A S E

Did the Program Violate the Rights of Homeless People?

Joyce v. City and County of San Francisco, 846 F.Supp. 843 (N.D. Cal 1994)

Homeless persons brought an action against the city seeking a preliminary injunction against the Matrix Program which targeted violation of certain ordinances and thus allegedly penalized homeless persons for engaging in life sustaining activities. U.S. District Judge Jensen denied the plaintiffs' motion for a preliminary injunction.

ORDER

JENSEN, District Judge.

FACTS

Plaintiffs to this action seek preliminary injunctive relief on behalf of themselves and a class of homeless individuals alleged to be adversely affected by the City and County of San Francisco's (the "City's") "Matrix Program." While encompassing a wide range of services to the City's homeless, the Program simultaneously contemplates a rigorous law enforcement component aimed at those violations of state and municipal law which arguably are committed predominantly by the homeless. Plaintiffs endorse much of the Program, challenging it not in its entirety, but only insofar as it specifically penalizes certain "life sustaining activities" engaged in by the homeless.

Institution of the Matrix Program followed the issuance of a report in April of 1992 by the San Francisco Mayor's Office of Economic Planning and Development, which attributed to homelessness a $173 million drain on sales in the City. In August of 1993, the City announced commencement of the Matrix Program, and the San Francisco Police Department began stringently enforcing a number of criminal laws.

The City describes the Program as "initiated to address citizen complaints about a broad range of offenses occurring on the streets and in parks and neighborhoods.... [The Matrix Program is] a directed effort to end street crimes of all kinds." The program addresses offenses including public drinking and inebriation, obstruction of sidewalks, lodging, camping or sleeping in public parks, littering, public urination and defecation, aggressive panhandling, dumping of refuse, graffiti, vandalism, street prostitution, and street sales of narcotics, among others.

An illustration of the enforcement efforts characteristic of the Program can be found in a four-page intradepartmental memorandum addressed to the Police Department's Southern Station Personnel. That memorandum, dated August 10, 1993 and signed by acting Police Captain Barry Johnson, defines "Quality of Life" violations and establishes a concomitant enforcement policy. Condemning a "type of behavior [which] tends to make San Francisco a less desirable place in which to live, work or visit", the memorandum directs the vigorous enforcement of eighteen specified code sections, including prohibitions against trespassing, public inebriation, urinating or defecating in public, removal and possession of shopping carts, solicitation on or near a highway, erection of tents or structures in parks, obstruction and aggressive panhandling.

Pursuant to the memorandum,

All station personnel shall, when not otherwise engaged, pay special attention and enforce observed "Quality of Life" violations. . . . One Officer . . . shall, daily, be assigned specifically to enforce all "Quality of Life" violations. . . .

Officers are to stop and advise all individuals pushing shopping carts that said carts are the property of local stores (Grocery/Drug etc.) and that these carts are never sold: Therefore the carts will, in the near future, be confiscated for return to their rightful owner or otherwise disposed of by the police. . . . Note: This phase of the "Quality of Life" operation will be implemented when appropriate containers, for the contents of the shopping carts, are available. . . .

In a Police Department Bulletin entitled "Update on Matrix Quality of Life Program," dated September 17, 1993, Deputy Chief Thomas Petrini paraphrased General Order D6, the source of the intended nondiscriminatory policy of the Program's enforcement measures:

All persons have the right to use the public streets and places so long as they are not engaged in specific criminal activity. Factors such as race, sex, sexual preference, age, dress, unusual or disheveled or impoverished appearance do not alone justify enforcement action. Nor can generalized complaints by residents or merchants or others justify detention of any person absent such individualized suspicion.

The memorandum stated that the "[r]ights of the homeless must be preserved", and included as an attachment a Department Bulletin on "Rights of the Homeless", which stated that:

[All members of the Department] are obligated to treat all persons equally, regardless of their economic or living conditions. The homeless enjoy the same legal and individual rights afforded to others. Members shall at all times respect these rights. . . .

The Police Department has, during the pendency of the Matrix Program, conducted continuing education for officers regarding nondiscriminatory enforcement of the Program. When, in mid-August of 1993, concerns were raised by interests outside the Department about proper enforcement of the ordinances prohibiting lodging and sleeping in public parks, the Department issued a clarification of its policies. Again, in mid-November of 1993, inquiries were made of the Police Department concerning the confiscation of grocery store shopping carts. Police Chief Anthony Ribera responded with the issuance of a Department Bulletin establishing topical guidelines.

Since implementation of the Matrix Program, the City estimates that "[a]ccording to unverified statistics kept by the Department", approximately sixty percent of enforcement actions have involved public inebriation and public drinking, and that other "significant categories" include felony arrests for narcotics and other offenses, and arrests for street sales without a permit. Together, enforcement actions concerning camping in the park . . . , sleeping in the park during prohibited hours . . . , and lodging . . . have constituted only approximately 10% of the total.

Plaintiffs, pointing to the discretion inherent in policing the law enforcement measures of the Matrix Program, allege certain actions taken by police to be "calculated to punish the homeless." As a general practice, the Program is depicted by plaintiffs as "target[ing] hundreds of homeless persons who are guilty of nothing more than sitting on a park bench or on the ground with their possessions, or lying or sleeping on the ground covered by or on top of a blanket or cardboard carton." On one specific occasion, according to plaintiffs, police "cited and detained more than a dozen homeless people, and confiscated and destroyed their possessions, leaving them without medication, blankets or belongings to cope with the winter cold."

The City contests the depiction of Matrix as a singularly focused, punitive effort designed to move "an untidy problem out of sight and out of mind." Instead, the City characterizes the Matrix Program as

an interdepartmental effort . . . [utilizing] social workers and health workers . . . [and] offering shelter, medical care, information about services and general assistance. Many of those on the street refuse those services, as is their right; but Matrix makes the choice available. . . .

The City emphasizes its history as one of the largest public providers of assistance to the homeless in the State, asserting that "individuals on general assistance in San Francisco are eligible for larger monthly grants than are available almost anywhere else in California." Homeless persons within the City are entitled to a maximum general assistance of $345 per month — an amount exceeding the grant provided by any of the surrounding counties. General assistance recipients are also eligible for up to $109 per

month in food stamps. According to the City, some 15,000 City residents are on general assistance, of whom 3,000 claim to be homeless.

The City's Department of Social Services encourages participation in a Modified Payments Program offered by the Tenderloin Housing Clinic. Through this program, a recipient's general assistance check is paid to the Clinic, which in turn pays the recipient's rent and remits the balance to the recipient. The Clinic then negotiates with landlords of residential hotels to accept general assistance recipients at rents not exceeding $280 per month.

By its own estimate, the City will spend $46.4 million for services to the homeless for 1993–94. Of that amount, over $8 million is specifically earmarked to provide housing, and is spent primarily on emergency shelter beds for adults, families, battered women and youths. An additional $12 million in general assistance grants is provided to those describing themselves as homeless, and free health care is provided by the City to the homeless at a cost of approximately $3 million.

The City contends that "few of the Matrix-related offenses involve arrest." Those persons found publicly inebriated, according to the City, are taken to the City's detoxification center or district stations until sober. "Most of the other violations result in an admonishment or a citation."

Since its implementation, the Matrix Program has resulted in the issuance of over 3,000 citations to homeless persons. Plaintiffs contend these citations have resulted in a cost to the City of over $500,000. Citations issued for encampment and sleeping infractions are in the amount of $76, according to Alissa Riker, Director of the Supervised Citation Release Program ("SCRP") with the Center for Juvenile and Criminal Justice. Those cited must pay or contest the citation within twenty-one days; failure to do so results in a $180 warrant for the individual's arrest, which is issued approximately two months after citation of the infraction. Upon the accrual of $1,000 in warrants, which equates roughly to the receipt of six citations, an individual becomes ineligible for citation release and may be placed in custody. The typical practice, however, is that those arrested for Matrix-related offenses are released on their own recognizance or with "credit for time served" on the day following arrest. [Seventeen homeless persons were held in custody as a result of high bail amounts accruing from Matrix-identified infraction warrants.] In each instance, the individual was released after being sentenced to "credit for time served." Plaintiffs characterize the system as one in which "homeless people are cycled through the criminal justice system and released to continue their lives in the same manner, except now doing so as 'criminals'."

According to plaintiffs, the City has conceded the inadequacy of shelter for its homeless. Plaintiffs have cited as supporting evidence an application made to the State Department of Housing and Community Development in which the City's Director of Homeless Services described an "emergency situation" created by the closure of the Transbay Terminal, which had served as "the largest de facto shelter for homeless individuals."

Plaintiffs have proffered estimates as to the number of homeless individuals unable to find nightly housing. Plaintiffs cite a survey conducted by Independent Housing Services, a nonprofit agency which among its aims seeks the improvement of access to affordable housing for the homeless. Begun in July of 1990 and conducted most recently in August of 1993, the survey tracks the number of homeless individuals turned away each night from shelters in the San Francisco area due to a lack of available bed space. Based on the data of that survey, plaintiffs contend that from January to July of 1993, an average of 500 homeless persons was turned away nightly from homeless shelters. That number, according to plaintiffs, increased to 600 upon the closing of the Transbay Terminal.

. . .

OPINION

Plaintiffs have at this time moved the Court to preliminarily enjoin the City's enforcement of certain state and municipal criminal measures which partially define the Matrix Program. Given this posture of the litigation, the Court is called upon to decide whether to grant a preliminary injunction in the exercise of its equitable powers. Such relief constitutes an extraordinary use of the Court's powers, and is to be granted sparingly and with the ultimate aim of preserving the status quo pending trial on the merits.

As the Court is acting in equity, the decision whether to grant preliminary injunctive relief is largely left to its discretion. However, this discretion has been circumscribed by the presence or not of various factors, notably, the likelihood that the moving party will prevail on the merits and the likelihood of harm to the parties from granting or denying the injunctive relief. At the extremes, a party seeking injunctive relief must show either (1) a combination of probable success on the merits and the possibility of irreparable harm, or (2) that serious questions are raised and the balance of hardships tips sharply in the moving party's favor. . . .

The injunction sought by plaintiffs at this juncture of the litigation must be denied for each of two independent reasons. First, the proposed injunction lacks the necessary specificity to be enforceable, and would give rise to enforcement problems sufficiently inherent as to be incurable by modification of the proposal. Second, those legal theories upon which plaintiffs rely are not plainly applicable to the grievances sought to be vindicated, with the effect that the Court cannot find at this time that, upon conducting the required balance of harm and merit, plaintiffs have established a sufficient probability of success on the merits to warrant injunctive relief.

[Only the discussion of the second reason is included in this case excerpt.]

II. Under the Posited Legal Theories, Plaintiffs Have Not Demonstrated a Clear Probability of Success on the Merits

A. Whether the Eighth Amendment Prohibits Enforcement of Matrix as Punishing "Status"

Plaintiffs contend enforcement of the Matrix Program unconstitutionally punishes an asserted "status" of homelessness. The central thesis is that since plaintiffs are compelled to be on the street involuntarily, enforcement of laws which interfere with their ability to carry out life sustaining activities on the street must be prohibited. This argument, while arguably bolstered by decisions of courts in other jurisdictions, has not been adopted by any case within the Ninth Circuit. Moreover, it is the opinion of this Court that plaintiffs' position, if adopted, would represent an improper reach by this Court into matters appropriately governed by the State of California and the City of San Francisco.

. . .

[The court summarized the holdings of *Robinson v. California* and *Powell v. Texas. Robinson v. California* held that it was cruel and unusual punishment to make the disease of drug addiction a crime. *Powell v. Texas* held that it was not cruel and unusual punishment to make the act of drinking in public a crime, even though the person who was drunk in public is an alcoholic. These cases are discussed in chapter 3 in the section on status as a criminal act. You should review that discussion here.]

Plaintiffs argue, however, on the basis of Justice White's concurring opinion, that *Powell* was decided as it was solely because the convicted defendant had not been shown to be on the streets involuntarily. In casting the fifth vote to uphold the appellant's conviction in Powell, Justice White wrote,

> The fact remains that some chronic alcoholics must drink and hence must drink somewhere. Although many chronics have homes, many others do not. For all practical purposes the public streets may be home for these unfortunates, not because their disease compels them to be there, but because, drunk or sober, they have no place else to go and no place else to be when they are drinking. This is more a function of economic station than of disease, although the disease may lead to destitution and perpetuate that condition. For some of these alcoholics I would think a showing could be made that resisting drunkenness is impossible and that avoiding public places when intoxicated is also impossible. As applied to them this statute is in effect a law which bans a single act for which they may not be convicted under the Eighth Amendment—the act of getting drunk.

Plaintiffs contend on the basis of this concurring opinion that, had the appellant in *Powell* been homeless, five justices would have voted to reverse his conviction. "Powell effectively establishes that a person who is involuntarily in public may not be punished for doing an act or being in a condition that he or she is powerless to avoid."

. . .

This Court is unable to conclude at this time that the extension of the Eighth Amendment to the "acts" at issue here is warranted by governing authorities. Plaintiffs argue that the failure of the City to provide sufficient housing compels the conclusion that homelessness on the streets of San Francisco is cognizable as a status. This argument is unavailing at least for the fundamental reason that status cannot be defined as a function of the discretionary acts of others.

As an analytical matter, more fundamentally, homelessness is not readily classified as a "status." Rather, as expressed for the plurality in *Powell* by Justice Marshall, there is a "substantial definitional distinction between a 'status' . . . and a 'condition,' . . ." While the concept of status might elude perfect definition, certain factors assist in its determination, such as the involuntariness of the acquisition of that quality (including the presence or not of that characteristic at birth), and the degree to which an individual has control over that characteristic.

Examples of such "status" characteristics might include age, race, gender, national origin and illness. The reasoning of the Court in including drug addiction as status involved the analogy of drug addiction to a disease or an illness which might be contracted involuntarily. While homelessness can be thrust upon an unwitting recipient, and while a person may be largely incapable of changing that condition, the distinction between the ability to eliminate one's drug addiction as compared to one's homelessness is a distinction in kind as much as in degree. To argue that homelessness is a status and not a condition, moreover, is to deny the efficacy of acts of social intervention to change the condition of those currently homeless.

The Court must approach with hesitation any argument that science or statistics compels a conclusion that a certain condition be defined as a status. The Supreme Court has determined that drug addiction equals a status, and this Court is so bound. But the Supreme Court has not made such a determination with respect to homelessness, and because that situation is not directly analogous to drug addiction, it would be an untoward excursion by this Court into matters of social policy to accord to homelessness the protection of status.

. . .

B. Whether Matrix Violates the Equal Protection Clause

Predicate to an equal protection clause violation is a finding of governmental action undertaken with an intent to discriminate against a particular individual or class of individuals. Such intent may be evinced by statutory language, or in instances where an impact which cannot be explained on a neutral ground unmasks an invidious discrimination. Under the latter approach, a neutral law found to have a disproportionately adverse effect upon a minority classification will be deemed unconstitutional only if that impact can be traced to a discriminatory purpose.

In the present case, plaintiffs have not at this time demonstrated a likelihood of success on the merits of the equal protection claim, since the City's action has not been taken with an evinced intent to discriminate against an identifiable group. As discussed above, various directives issued within the Police Department mandate the nondiscriminatory enforcement of Matrix. See, e.g., "Update on Matrix Quality of Life Program," Petrini Decl., Exh. A at 12 (providing that "[r]ights of the homeless must be preserved"); Department Bulletin on "Rights of the Homeless", discussed in Petrini Decl. at ¶ 2 (stating that "[all members of the Department] are obligated to treat all persons equally, regardless of their economic or living conditions. The homeless enjoy the same legal and individual rights afforded to others. Members shall at all times respect these rights. . . ."). Further, the Police Department has, during the pendency of the Matrix Program, conducted continuing education for officers regarding nondiscriminatory enforcement of the Program.

It has not been proven at this time that Matrix was implemented with the aim of discriminating against the homeless. That enforcement of Matrix will, de facto, fall predominantly on the homeless does not in itself effect an equal protection clause violation. . . .

Even were plaintiffs able at this time to prove an intent to discriminate against the homeless, the challenged sections of the Program might nonetheless survive constitutional scrutiny. Only in cases where the challenged action is aimed at a suspect classification, such as race or gender, or premised upon the exercise of a fundamental right, will the governmental action be subjected to a heightened scrutiny.

Counsel for plaintiff proposed at the hearing that this Court should be the first to recognize as a fundamental right the "right to sleep." This is an invitation the Court, in its exercise of judicial restraint, must decline. Despite the seeming innocence of a right so defined, the natural corollary to recognition of a right is an obligation to enforce it. The discovery of a right to sleep concomitantly requires prohibition of the government's interference with that right. This endeavor, aside from creating a jurisprudential morass, would involve this unelected branch of government in a legislative role for which it is neither fit, nor easily divested once established. . . .

C. Whether the Matrix Program Impermissibly Burdens the Right to Travel

This argument proffered by plaintiffs is essentially a subset of equal protection analysis, in which the right to travel is deemed a fundamental right which a state government may not abridge unless necessary to achieve a compelling state interest. The right to travel has found its strongest expression in the context of attempts by states to discourage the immigration of indigents. The application of strict scrutiny to such laws, however, has been limited to those which are facially discriminatory (holding unconstitutional statutory provision requiring welfare assistance applicants to reside in state at least one year immediately preceding application for assistance); *Edwards v. California*, 314 U.S. 160, 62 S.Ct. 164, 86 L.Ed. 119 (1941) (curtailing immigration of new residents); *Memorial Hospital v. Maricopa County*, 415 U.S. 250, 94 S.Ct. 1076, 39 L.Ed.2d 306 (1974) (denying medical services to new residents).

The Matrix Program does not facially discriminate between those who are, and those who might be, the City's residents. Accordingly, the application of strict scrutiny to the Program would be unwarranted. . . .

Assuming the right to travel encompasses protection to intrastate travel, it is nevertheless doubtful that facially neutral laws impacting intrastate travel should be subjected to such strict scrutiny. "Both the United States Supreme Court and [the California Supreme Court] have refused to apply the strict construction test to legislation . . . which does not penalize travel and resettlement [through disparate treatment] but merely makes it more difficult for the outsider to establish his residence in the place of his choosing." . . .

D. Whether the Matrix Program Violates Plaintiffs' Rights to Due Process of Law

Plaintiffs contend the Matrix Program has been enforced in violation of the due process clause . . . of the United States . . . Constitution. . . . Plaintiffs specifically argue that due process has been violated by employing punitive policing measures against the homeless for sleeping in public parks; plaintiffs also argue that certain state codes are unconstitutionally vague.

1. Punishing the Homeless for Sitting or Sleeping in Parks

Plaintiffs claim that San Francisco Park Code section 3.12 has been applied by police in an unconstitutional manner. That section provides,

No person shall construct or maintain any building, structure, tent or any other thing in any park that may be used for housing accommodations or camping, except by permission from the Recreation and Park Commission.

Plaintiffs contend the Police Department has impermissibly construed this provision to justify citing, arresting, threatening and "moving along" those "persons guilty of nothing more than sitting on park benches with their personal possessions or lying on or under blankets on the ground." Plaintiffs have submitted declarations of various homeless persons supporting the asserted application of the San Francisco Park Code section. See, e.g., Homeless Decls. at 34 (lying down atop blankets eating lunch), 121 ("sleeping on bench"), 125 ("sleeping on boxes").

It appears, if plaintiffs have accurately depicted the manner in which the section is enforced, that the section may have been applied to conduct not covered by the section and may have been enforced unconstitutionally. . . .

2. . . . Vagueness Challenges to Enforcement Measures

Plaintiffs also contend that San Francisco Park Code section 3.12, discussed supra, and California Penal Code Section 647(i) [Every person who commits any of the following acts is guilty of disorderly conduct, a misdemeanor: . . . Who lodges in any building, structure, vehicle, or place, whether public or private, without the permission of the owner or person entitled to the possession or in control thereof. Cal. Penal Code § 647(i).] are unconstitutionally overbroad and vague."

. . .

The possible success of the vagueness challenge is also in doubt, as it seems readily apparent the measure is not "impermissibly vague in all of its applications. . . ." This likely failing follows from plaintiffs' inability to prove at this stage that police have been granted an excess of discretion pursuant to the statute. Plaintiffs assert vagueness in the San Francisco Park Code prohibition against maintaining "any other thing" that "may be used for . . . camping", and in enforcing the Penal Code prohibition against one "who lodges in . . . public," claiming "[t]he vagueness of these [Park Code] terms has apparently allowed San Francisco police officers to determine that blankets or possessions in carts are sufficiently connected to 'camping' to violate the ordinance." Plaintiffs have also submitted declarations of homeless persons supporting these assertions, and a concession by Assistant District Attorney Paul Cummins to the effect that the standards for enforcement are vague.

. . .

Similarly, the challenged Penal Code section cannot be concluded by the Court at this time to be unconstitutionally vague. Read in conjunction with supplemental memoranda, the challenged measures appear, as a constitutional matter, sufficiently specific. Police officers were specifically cautioned in a September 17, 1993 memorandum that "the mere lying or sleeping on or in a bedroll of and in itself does not constitute a violation." While plaintiffs argue the additional memoranda were circulated too late to save the enforcement measures from vagueness, see Reply at 23, and also that they do not eliminate the confusion, it is far from clear that plaintiffs could meet the requisite showing that the measure was impermissibly vague in all its applications. Accordingly, even if the limits of permissible enforcement of these sections have not been perfectly elucidated, preliminary injunctive relief is inappropriate at this stage of the litigation.

CONCLUSION

In common with many communities across the country, the City is faced with a homeless population of tragic dimension. Today, plaintiffs have brought that societal problem before the Court, seeking a legal judgment on the efforts adopted by the City in response to this problem.

The role of the Court is limited structurally by the fact that it may exercise only judicial power, and technically by the fact that plaintiffs seek extraordinary pretrial relief. The Court does not find that plaintiffs have made a showing at this time that constitutional barriers exist which preclude that effort. Accordingly, the Court's judgment at this stage of the litigation is to permit the City to continue enforcing those aspects of the Matrix Program now challenged by plaintiffs.

The Court therefore concludes that the injunction sought, both as it stands now and as plaintiffs have proposed to modify it, is not sufficiently specific to be enforceable. Further, upon conducting the required balance of harm and merit, the Court finds that plaintiffs have failed to establish a sufficient probability of success on the merits to warrant injunctive relief. Accordingly, plaintiffs' motion for a preliminary injunction is DENIED.

IT IS SO ORDERED.

QUESTIONS FOR DISCUSSION

1. Describe the main elements of the Matrix Program.
2. Why did San Francisco adopt the Matrix Program?
3. What are the plaintiffs' objections to the Matrix Program?
4. Why does the court grant injunctions rarely?
5. Do you agree with the reasons given for granting injunctions "sparingly"?
6. What requirements must the plaintiffs satisfy before they can obtain an injunction in this case?
7. Do you think the plaintiffs have satisfied the requirements? Defend your answer.
8. Assume you are the attorney for San Francisco. Argue why the court should deny the injunction.
9. Assume you are the attorney for the homeless people. Argue why the court should issue the injunction.
10. If you could, what terms would you include in an injunction in this case?

PANHANDLING

The regulation of public begging represents yet another example of the reaction during the 1990s to the so-called rights revolution of the 1970s. According to Robert Tier, General Counsel of the American Alliance for Rights and Responsibilities, "not all urbanites are giving up" on maintaining the quality of life in their cities.

> Many City Councils have been convinced to adopt new and innovative controls on anti-social behavior to maintain minimal standards of public conduct and to keep public spaces safe and attractive. These ordinances range from prohibitions on camping in parks to restrictions on lying down on sidewalks. One of the most common examples of these efforts are ordinances aimed at aggressive begging.[20]

Most of the ordinances specifically exclude organized charities from the reach of the anti-begging ordinances. Hence, it is a crime for a private beggar to panhandle, but not for the Salvation Army to ring their bells for contributions. Several arguments are advanced to support the anti-panhandling ordinances, and for excluding organized charities from their reach. However, the principal reason for enacting the ordinances is that the rights revolution had gone too far. It created a situation in which individual rights were allowed to trump the interest of the whole community in the quality of life. Associate Supreme Court Justice Clarence Thomas, commenting on "how judicial interpretations of the First Amendment and of 'unenumerated' constitutional rights have affected the ability of urban communities to deal with crime, disorder, and incivility on their public streets," told the Federalist Society in 1996:

> Vagrancy, loitering, and panhandling laws were challenged [during the rights revolution] because the poor and minorities could be victims of discrimination under the guise of broad discretion to ensure public safety. Moreover, as a consequence of the modern tendency to challenge society's authority to dictate social norms, the legal system began to prefer the ideal of self-expression without much attention to self-discipline or self control. What resulted was a culture that declined to curb the excesses of self-indulgence — vagrants and others who regularly roamed the streets had rights that could not be circumscribed by the community's sense of decency or decorum.[21]

"Hey, buddy, can you spare some change?" is clearly speech. The First Amendment guarantees individuals freedom of speech. However, free speech does not mean you can say anything you want anywhere at anytime. In the most classic example, no one is free to shout "Fire" in a crowded theater. And the United States Supreme Court has "rejected the notion that a city is powerless to protect its citizens from unwanted exposure to certain methods of expression which may legitimately be deemed a public nuisance." The Court has established a number of tests to determine whether limits on speech violate the First Amendment guarantee of free speech.[22]

The degree to which the government can limit speech depends on a number of factors. One is the forum for the speech. In **traditional public forums** — streets, sidewalks, and parks — where people have since ancient times expressed their views, the freedom to solicit is virtually unrestricted. In **designated public forums** — places the government chooses to make available to the public — the government has more leeway to regulate solicitation. In **nonpublic forums** — airports, bus terminals, railway stations, and subways, for example — the government has broad power to restrict or even prohibit solicitation.[23]

Second, the First Amendment free speech clause permits the placing of limits on aspects of speech, frequently referred to as "time, place, and manner" regulations. According to the Supreme Court, "restrictions of this kind are valid provided that

1. they are justified without reference to the content of the regulated speech,

2. they are narrowly tailored to serve a significant government interest, and

3. they leave open ample alternative channels for communication of the information."[24]

The first part of the test means that the regulation cannot be used for the purpose of suppressing any message about social conditions that panhandlers are trying to convey. Part 2 of the test is often hotly debated. Advocates for panhandlers argue that the regulation of panhandling is really a government policy of removing unsightly poor people from public view. Others maintain that the "purpose is to permit people to use the streets, sidewalks, and public transportation free from the borderline robbery and pervasive fraud which characterizes so much of today's panhandling." The third part of the test requires that the regulation allows panhandlers alternative methods of solicitation. Hence, a panhandling ordinance that prohibits only "aggressive panhandling" permits panhandlers to solicit peaceably. Prohibitions against fraudulent panhandling or panhandling in subways also permit alternative means of solicitation.[25]

In addition to forum and time, place, and manner restrictions, the First Amendment allows greater regulation of expressive conduct, such as approaching a person or blocking the sidewalk in order to solicit, or the act of receiving the money solicited. Government has considerable latitude to regulate expressive conduct.

Finally, the First Amendment grants commercial speech less protection than other types of speech. Since it relates almost exclusively to the use of speech to get a listener to transfer money, panhandling is probably commercial speech. The United States Court of Appeals for the Second Circuit decided whether a New York City ordinance barring all panhandling from all public places violated the free speech clause of the First Amendment in *Loper v. New York Police Department.*

C A S E

Do They Have a Constitutional Right to Panhandle?

Loper v. NYPD,
999 F.2d 699 (2d Circuit, 1993)

MINER, Circuit Judge:

The New York City Police Department and Lee F. Brown, Commissioner of the Department, ("City Police") appealed from a summary judgment entered in the United States District Court for the Southern District of New York (Sweet, J.) in favor of plaintiffs-appellees Jennifer Loper and William Kaye, on behalf of themselves and all others similarly situated ("Plaintiffs"). The judgment declared unconstitutional on First Amendment grounds the provision of the New York Penal Law that provided: "A person is guilty of loitering when he . . . loiters, remains or wanders about in a public place for the purpose of begging. . . ." The District Court also enjoined the City Police from enforcing the ordinance.

FACTS

. . . The City Police regard the challenged statute as an essential tool to address the evils associated with begging on the streets of New York City. They assert that beggars tend to congregate in certain areas and become more aggressive as they do so. Residents are intimidated and local businesses suffer accordingly. Panhandlers are said to station themselves in front of banks, bus stops, automated teller machines and parking lots and frequently engage in conduct described as "intimidating" and "coercive." Panhandlers have been known to block the sidewalk, follow people down the street and threaten those who do not give them money. It is said that they often make false and fraudulent representations to induce passers-by to part with their money. The City Police have begun to focus more attention on order maintenance activities in a program known as "community policing." They contend that it is vital to the program to have the statute available for the officers on the "beat" to deal with those who threaten and harass the citizenry through begging.

Although it is conceded that very few arrests are made and very few summonses are issued for begging alone, officers do make frequent use of the statute as authority to order beggars to "move on." The City Police advance the theory that panhandlers, unless stopped, tend to increase their aggressiveness and ultimately commit more serious crimes. According to this theory, what starts out as peaceful begging inevitably leads to the ruination of a neighborhood. It appears from the contentions of the City Police that only the challenged statute stands between safe streets and rampant crime in the city.

OPINION

It is ludicrous, of course, to say that a statute that prohibits only loitering for the purpose of begging provides the only authority that is available to prevent and punish all the socially undesirable conduct incident to begging described by the City Police. There are, in fact, a number of New York statutes that proscribe conduct of the type that may accompany individual solicitations for money in the city streets. For example, the crime of harassment in the first degree is committed by one who follows another person in or about a public place or places or repeatedly commits acts that place the other person in reasonable fear of physical injury. N.Y. Penal Law § 240.25 (McKinney Supp.1993). If a panhandler, with intent to cause public inconvenience, annoyance or alarm, uses obscene or abusive language or obstructs pedestrian or vehicular traffic, he or she is guilty of disorderly conduct. N.Y. Penal Law §§ 240.20(3), (5) (McKinney 1989). A beggar who accosts a person in a public place with intent to defraud that person of money is guilty of fraudulent accosting. § 165.30(1). The crime of menacing in the third degree is committed by a panhandler who, by physical menace, intentionally places or attempts to place another person in fear of physical injury. N.Y. Penal Law § 120.15 (McKinney Supp.1993).

The distinction between the statutes referred to in the preceding paragraph and the challenged statute is that the former prohibit conduct and the latter prohibits speech as well as conduct of a communicative nature. Whether the challenged statute is consonant with the First Amendment is the subject of our inquiry. We do not write upon a clean slate as regards this inquiry, since the Supreme Court as well as this Court has addressed restrictions on the solicitation of money in public places.

In *Young v. New York City Transit Authority*, 903 F.2d 146 (2d Cir.), cert. denied, 498 U.S. 984, 111 S.Ct. 516, 112 L.Ed.2d 528 (1990), there was at issue before us a regulation prohibiting begging and panhandling in the New York City Subway System. In that case we "wonder[ed]" whether the beggars' "conduct is not divested of any expressive element as a result of the special surrounding circumstances involved in" begging in the subway, but we did not rest our decision "on an ontological distinction between speech and conduct." We did find that the conduct element of begging, in the confined atmosphere of the subway, " 'disrupts' and 'startles' passengers, thus creating the potential for a serious accident in the fast-moving and crowded subway environment." This finding led to our conclusion that the New York City Transit Authority's "judgment that begging is alarmingly harmful conduct that simply cannot be accommodated in the subway system is not unreasonable."

In our First Amendment analysis in *Young*, we applied the "more lenient level of judicial scrutiny," prescribed in *United States v. O'Brien*, 391 U.S. 367, 88 S.Ct. 1673, 20 L.Ed.2d 672 (1968) (conviction for destruction of draft card in antiwar protest allowed to stand where speech and nonspeech elements combined in same course of conduct). In accordance with the test outlined in *O'Brien*, we determined: 1) that the subway regulation was within the constitutional power of government; 2) that the regulation advanced substantial and important governmental interests; 3) that the governmental interests were not related to the suppression of free expression; and 4) that, because "the exigencies created by begging and panhandling in the subway warrant the conduct's complete prohibition," the First Amendment freedom restrictions were no greater than were essential to further the government's interest. Citing *Ward v. Rock Against Racism*, 491 U.S. 781, 802, 109 S.Ct. 2746, 275960, 105 L.Ed.2d 661 (1989), we observed that ample alternative channels of communication were open. Most pertinent to our analysis in the case at bar, we stated:

> Under the regulation, begging is prohibited only in the subway, not throughout all of New York City. It is untenable to suggest, as do the plaintiffs, that absent the opportunity to beg and panhandle in the subway system, they are left with no means to communicate to the public about needy persons.

The case before us does prohibit begging throughout the City and does leave individual beggars without the means to communicate their individual wants and needs.

We also decided in *Young* that the district court erred in concluding that the subway is a public forum where begging and panhandling must be allowed. We indicated that the subway is at best a limited forum that could be, and was, properly restricted as to the types of speech and speakers permitted:

> [T]here can be no doubt that the [New York City Transit Authority] intended to continue its

long-standing prohibition of begging and panhandling even after revising the regulation to permit solicitation by organizations.

The special conditions of the subway system were said to require a limitation on expressive activity, and we referred in *Young* to our earlier holding in *Gannett Satellite Information Network, Inc. v. Metropolitan Transportation Authority*, 745 F.2d 767, 77273 (2d Cir.1984), that the subway is not an open forum for public communication either by tradition or designation. Despite government ownership, it is the nature of the forum that we must examine in order to determine the extent to which expressive activity may be regulated. It long has been settled that all forms of speech need not be permitted on property owned and controlled by a governmental entity.

In *International Society for Krishna Consciousness, Inc. v. Lee*, 505 U.S. 672, 112 S.Ct. 2701, 120 L.Ed.2d 541 (1992), the Supreme Court agreed with us that a regulation prohibiting solicitation of funds in airline terminals operated by a public authority did not violate the First Amendment. The plaintiff in that case was a religious sect whose members solicited funds in public places as part of a ritual. The Court "conclude[d] that the terminals are nonpublic fora and that the regulation reasonably limits solicitation." . . .

The forum-based approach for First Amendment analysis subjects to the highest scrutiny the regulation of speech on government property traditionally available for public expression. Such property includes streets and parks, which are said to "have immemorially been held in trust for the use of the public and, time out of mind, have been used for purposes of assembly, communicating thoughts between citizens, and discussing public questions." *Hague v. CIO*, 307 U.S. 496, 515, 59 S.Ct. 954, 964, 83 L.Ed. 1423 (1939).

In these quintessential public forums, the government may not prohibit all communicative activity. For the State to enforce a content-based exclusion it must show that its regulation is necessary to serve a compelling state interest and that it is narrowly drawn to achieve that end. . . . The State may also enforce regulations of the time, place, and manner of expression which are content-neutral, are narrowly tailored to serve a significant government interest,

and leave open ample alternative channels of communication. *Perry Educ. Ass'n v. Perry Local Educators' Ass'n*, 460 U.S. 37, 45, 103 S.Ct. 948, 955, 74 L.Ed.2d 794 (1983)

. . .

The sidewalks of the City of New York fall into the category of public property traditionally held open to the public for expressive activity. See *United States v. Grace*, 461 U.S. 171, 17980, 103 S.Ct. 1702, 1708, 75 L.Ed.2d 736 (1983) (sidewalks comprising the outer boundaries of the Supreme Court grounds are indistinguishable from other sidewalks in Washington, D.C. and constitute a proper public forum). Conduct of a communicative nature cannot be regulated in "these quintessential public forums" in the same manner as it can be regulated on the streets of a military reservation. See *Greer v. Spock*, 424 U.S. 828, 96 S.Ct. 1211, 47 L.Ed.2d 505 (1976).

It cannot be gainsaid that begging implicates expressive conduct or communicative activity. As agreed by the parties in *International Society*, begging is at least "a form of speech." In *Village of Schaumburg v. Citizens for a Better Environment*, 444 U.S. 620, 100 S.Ct. 826, 63 L.Ed.2d 73 (1980), the Supreme Court struck down an ordinance prohibiting solicitation by charitable organizations that did not use at least seventy-five percent of their revenues for charitable purposes. The Court held that

charitable appeals for funds, on the street or door to door, involve a variety of speech interests — communication of information, the dissemination and propagation of views and ideas, and the advocacy of causes — that are within the protection of the First Amendment. . . . [S]olicitation is characteristically intertwined with informative and perhaps persuasive speech seeking support for particular causes or for particular views on . . . social issues, and . . . without solicitation the flow of such information and advocacy would likely cease.

Inherent in all the charitable solicitation cases revolving around the First Amendment is the concept that "[c]anvassers in such contexts are necessarily more than solicitors for money." *Village of Schaumburg*, 444 U.S. at 632, 100 S.Ct. at 834. While we indicated in *Young* that begging does not always involve the transmission of a particularized social or political message, it seems certain that it usually involves some communication of that nature. Begging frequently is accompanied by speech indicating the need for food, shelter, clothing, medical care or transportation. Even without particularized speech, however, the presence of an unkempt and disheveled person holding out his or her hand or a cup to receive a donation itself conveys a message of need for support and assistance. We see little difference between those who solicit for organized charities and those who solicit for themselves in regard to the message conveyed. The former are communicating the needs of others while the latter are communicating their personal needs. Both solicit the charity of others. The distinction is not a significant one for First Amendment purposes.

Having established that begging constitutes communicative activity of some sort and that, as far as this case is concerned, it is conducted in a traditional public forum, we next examine whether the statute at issue: (1) is necessary to serve a compelling state interest and is narrowly tailored to achieve that end; or (2) can be characterized as a regulation of the time, place and manner of expression that is content neutral, is narrowly tailored to serve significant government interests and leaves open alternate channels.

First, it does not seem to us that any compelling state interest is served by excluding those who beg in a peaceful manner from communicating with their fellow citizens. Even if the state were considered to have a compelling interest in preventing the evils sometimes associated with begging, a statute that totally prohibits begging in all public places cannot be considered "narrowly tailored" to achieve that end. Because of the total prohibition, it is questionable whether the statute even can be said to "regulate" the time, place and manner of expression but even if it does, it is not content neutral because it prohibits all speech related to begging; it certainly is not narrowly tailored to serve any significant governmental interest, as previously noted, because of the total prohibition it commands; it does not leave open alternative channels of communication by which beggars can convey their messages of indigency. In regard to the "alternative channels" issue in *Young*, we observed that the prohibition on panhandling in the subway did not

foreclose begging "throughout all of New York City." Where, as here, a regulation is neither content neutral nor narrowly tailored, it cannot be justified as a proper time, place or manner restriction on protected speech, regardless of whether or not alternate channels are available.

Even if we were to apply the *O'Brien* analysis, as we did in *Young*, we would find that the New York statute does not pass First Amendment muster. According to *O'Brien*, it is permissible to establish "incidental limitations on First Amendment freedoms" in order to protect a "sufficiently important governmental interest" that is "unrelated to the suppression of free expression." Here, the total prohibition on begging in the city streets imposed by the statute cannot be characterized as a merely incidental limitation, because it serves to silence both speech and expressive conduct on the basis of the message. See Helen Hershkoff & Adam S. Cohen, Begging to Differ: The First Amendment and the Right to Beg, 104 Harv.L.Rev. 896, 909 (1991). Carrying out the *O'Brien* analysis, the statute in no way advances substantial and important governmental interests. If it did, the State would not allow, as it does, the solicitation of contributions on city streets by individuals who represent charitable organizations that have registered with the Secretary of the State of New York. Moreover, certain religious, educational and fraternal organizations are entitled to solicit contributions in New York through individual solicitors even without registration, due to a statutory exemption. If individuals may solicit for charitable and other organizations, no significant governmental interest is served by prohibiting others for soliciting for themselves. Certainly, a member of a charitable, religious or other organization who seeks alms for the organization and is also, as a member, a beneficiary of those alms should be treated no differently from one who begs for his or her own account. See Charles Feeney Knapp, Note, Statutory Restriction of Panhandling in Light of Young v. New York City Transit: Are States Begging Out of First Amendment Proscriptions?, 76 Iowa L.Rev. 405, 416 (1991).

Assuming that the statute at issue were to be classified as an incidental restriction on free expression, *O'Brien* requires that the restriction be "no greater than is essential to the furtherance" of the government's interest. According to the City Police, the interest of the government lies in preventing the fraud, intimidation, coercion, harassment and assaultive conduct that is said frequently to accompany begging by individual street solicitors who do not solicit on behalf of any organization. But, as has been demonstrated, there are a number of statutes that address this sort of conduct specifically. The statute that prohibits loitering for the purpose of begging must be considered as providing a restriction greater than is essential to further the government interests listed by the City Police, for it sweeps within its overbroad purview the expressive conduct and speech that the government should have no interest in stifling. A verbal request for money for sustenance or a gesture conveying that request carries no harms of the type enumerated by the City Police, if done in a peaceful manner. However, both the organizational solicitor and the individual solicitor are prosecutable for conduct that oversteps the bounds of peaceful begging.

. . . [T]he statute before us prohibits verbal speech as well as communicative conduct, not in the confined precincts of the subway system, or in the crowded environment of a state fair, but in the open forum of the streets of the City of New York. The New York statute does not square with the requirements of the First Amendment. The plaintiffs have demonstrated that they are entitled to the relief they seek.

The judgment appealed from is affirmed.

QUESTIONS FOR DISCUSSION

1. Why does the New York City Police Department regard the loitering statute as essential?

2. Do you agree that the loitering statute is essential? Defend your answer.

3. Do you agree or disagree with the court's conclusion that the loitering statute violates the First Amendment? Defend your answer.

SUMMARY

The ancient crimes against public order and decency were used for centuries to control public misbehavior. Although the list of public order and morals offenses is long, the most frequently used among them included public drunkenness, vagrancy, loitering, prostitution, nuisance, and begging. Some of these offenses, such as public drunkenness and nuisance, were aimed primarily at conduct. However, most of them were also used to control "undesirable" groups — the poor, particularly the unemployed wandering poor, prostitutes, drunks, and panhandlers. In other words, they were status offenses.

Until the twentieth century, these minor offenses aroused little attention and certainly no controversy. Beginning in the 1930s, the crimes against public order and morals were criticized as discriminatory weapons of the wealthy to keep the poor out of sight, or at least off the streets. Then, as a result of the Civil Rights movement of the 1960s and the so-called rights revolution that followed in its aftermath, the public order and morals offenses came under fire in the courts. State courts first struck down vagrancy and loitering statutes. Then the U.S. Supreme Court declared that both the typical vagrancy and loitering statutes were void for vagueness and denied equal protection of the laws to the poor and the weak. Furthermore, the high court ruled that status offenses denied members of the criminalized group life, liberty, or property without due process of law.

During the 1980s, a combination of developments turned the tide against the rights offensive. Economic hard times, court rulings that deinstitutionalized the mentally ill, lack of housing, and other factors not yet fully identified combined with the rights revolution to increase the numbers and visibility of people in public places, apparently

without anywhere else to go. The behavior of these "street people," and that of their highly vocal advocates created a backlash across a broad social spectrum of employed "respectable" people—men and women, minorities and whites, rich and poor. Academic support for the backlash came from the "broken windows" theory that suggested a link between these minor offenses against public order and morals and serious crimes against persons, their homes and property.

The backlash found legislative expression in a rash of new city ordinances and some state statutes. These new laws have tailored some of the old public order offenses to meet the social reality of the United States—particularly of city life—at the end of the twentieth century. And these new laws have called upon not only the traditional criminal law but also upon the civil remedy of injunctions to abate public nuisances to control public misbehavior. Both the criminal laws and the civil remedies are based on the idea that state and municipal governments are responsible for preserving the quality of life by enforcing a minimum level of decent conduct in public. The quality of life crimes and their enforcement challenge criminal law to preserve the fundamental requirement of our constitutional democracy—ordered liberty—by balancing individual rights and community order. In other words, individual rights cannot trump the community interest in preserving the quality of life. It remains to be seen whether the new laws and remedies can prevent the community interest in the quality of life from trumping the rights of unconventional but law-abiding individuals who "bother" "respectable" people.

REVIEW QUESTIONS

1. Identify and explain the fundamental requirement of our constitutional system in formulating its crimes against public order.

2. Explain how the ancient public order and morals offenses have been altered to suit the social reality of life at the turn of the twenty-first century.

3. Define, describe, and list the purposes of quality of life crimes.

4. Describe and explain the controversy over the quality of life crimes.

5. Describe the "broken windows" theory and the degree of empirical support for it.

6. Identify and explain the disconnect between national attention and local concerns regarding serious crimes and quality of life offenses.

7. Define injunctions and explain their role in regulating behavior in public.

8. Explain the purposes of and the differences between the ancient vagrancy and loitering laws and modern laws affecting the poor.

9. Describe modern panhandling laws and discuss which ones are probably constitutional and which types are probably not constitutional.

KEY TERMS

broken windows theory The theory that minor offenses can lead to a rise in serious crime.

designated public forums Places the government chooses to make available to the public.

equitable relief The seeking of an injunction according to justice and fairness when the strict rules of law cannot do so.

injunction A court order to do or to stop doing something.

liberty The right of individuals to go about in public free of undue interference.

nonpublic forums Places, such as airports, bus terminals, railway stations, and subways, where the government has broad power to restrict or even prohibit solicitation.

order Behavior in public that comports with minimum community standards of civility.

public nuisances Offenses against, or interferences with, the exercise of rights common to the public.

preliminary injunction A temporary order issued by a court after notice and hearing.

quality of life crimes Breaches of minimum standards of decent behavior in public.

traditional public forums Streets, sidewalks, parks, and other places where people have since ancient times expressed their views.

Notes

1. James Q. Wilson and George L. Kelling, "Broken Windows," *Atlantic Monthly,* March 1982.

2. James Q. Wilson, "Foreword," George L. Kelling and Catherine M. Coles, *Fixing Broken Windows* (New York: Free Press, 1996), p. xiv.

3. Wesley G. Skogan, *Disorder and Decline* (New York: Free Press, 1990), 10.

4. Ibid., p. 75.

5. Ibid., ch. 2.

6. Ibid., p. 21.

7. Ibid., pp. 23–24.

8. Christopher S. Yoo, "The Constitutionality of Enjoining Criminal Street Gangs as Public Nuisances," *Northwestern University Law Review,* 89 (1994):212, fns. 2, 4.

9. *People ex rel. Gallo v. Acuna,* 929 P.2d 596 (1997).

10. Ibid.

11. Harry Simon, "Towns Without Pity: A Constitutional and Historical Analysis of Official Efforts to Drive Homeless Persons from American Cities," *Tulane Law Review* 66 (1992): 631 (1992); *Mayor of New York v. Miln,* 36 U.S. (11 Pet.) 102 (1837).

12. *Edwards v. California,* 314 U.S. 162 (1941), 174, 184.

13. *Parker v. Municipal Judge,* 427 P.2d 642 (Nev. 1967).

14. 405 U.S. 156 (1972), quote from 169.

15. 461 U.S. 352 (1983).

16. Simon, "Towns without Pity," p. 645.

17. Robert C. Ellickson, "Controlling Chronic Misconduct in City Spaces: Of Panhandlers, Skid Rows, and Public-Space Zoning," *Yale Law Journal,* 105 (1996):1213–1214.

18. Goodman quote, ibid., p. 1218; Juliette Smith, "Arresting the Homeless for Sleeping in Public: A Paradigm for Expanding the *Robinson* Doctrine," *Columbia Journal of Law and Social Problems,* 29 (1996):293.

19. Kelling and Coles, p. xiv.

20. Robert Tier, "Maintaining Safety and Civility in Public Spaces: A Constitutional Approach to Aggressive Begging," *Lousiana Law Review,* 54 (1993):287.

21. Clarence Thomas, "Federalist Society Symposium: The Rights Revolution," *Michigan Law and Policy Review,* 1(1996):269.

22. Kent S. Scheidegger, *A Guide to Regulating Panhandling* (Sacramento, Calif.: Criminal Justice Legal Foundation, 1993), p. 7.

23. Ibid., pp. 7–9.

24. *R.A.V. v. St. Paul,* 112 S.Ct. 2538 (1992).

25. Scheidegger, *A Guide,* pp. 10–11.

Constitution of the United States

Preamble

We the People of the United States, in Order to form a more perfect Union, establish Justice, insure domestic Tranquility, provide for the common defence, promote the general Welfare, and secure the Blessings of Liberty to ourselves and our Posterity, do ordain and establish this Constitution for the United States of America.

Article I

Section 1 All legislative Powers herein granted shall be vested in a Congress of the United States, which shall consist of a Senate and House of Representatives.

Section 2 The House of Representatives shall be composed of Members chosen every second Year by the People of the several States, and the Electors in each State shall have the Qualifications requisite for Electors of the most numerous Branch of the State Legislature.

No Person shall be a Representative who shall not have attained to the Age of twenty five Years, and been seven Years a Citizen of the United States, and who shall not, when elected, be an Inhabitant of that State in which he shall be chosen.

Representatives and direct Taxes shall be apportioned among the several States which may be included within this Union, according to their respective Numbers, which shall be determined by adding to the whole Number of free Persons, including those bound to Service for a Term of Years, and excluding Indians not taxed, three fifths of all other Persons. The actual Enumeration shall be made within three Years after the first Meeting of the Congress of the United States, and within every subsequent Term of ten Years, in such Manner as they shall by Law direct. The Number of Representatives shall not exceed one for every thirty Thousand, but each State shall have at Least one Representative; and until such enumeration shall be made, the State of New

Hampshire shall be entitled to choose three, Massachusetts eight, Rhode Island and Providence Plantations one, Connecticut five, New York six, New Jersey four, Pennsylvania eight, Delaware one, Maryland six, Virginia ten, North Carolina five, South Carolina five, and Georgia three.

When vacancies happen in the Representation from any State, the Executive Authority thereof shall issue Writs of Election to fill such Vacancies.

The House of Representatives shall choose their Speaker and other Officers; and shall have the sole Power of Impeachment.

Section 3 The Senate of the United States shall be composed of two Senators from each State, chosen by the Legislature thereof, for six Years; and each Senator shall have one Vote.

Immediately after they shall be assembled in Consequence of the first Election, they shall be divided as equally as may be into three Classes. The Seats of the Senators of the first Class shall be vacated at the Expiration of the second Year, of the second Class at the Expiration of the fourth Year, and of the third Class at the Expiration of the sixth Year, so that one third may be chosen every second Year; and if Vacancies happen by Resignation, or otherwise, during the Recess of the Legislature of any State, the Executive thereof may make temporary Appointments until the next Meeting of the Legislature, which shall then fill such Vacancies.

No Person shall be a Senator who shall not have attained to the Age of thirty Years, and been nine Years a Citizen of the United States, and who shall not, when elected, be an Inhabitant of that State for which he shall be chosen.

The Vice President of the United States shall be President of the Senate, but shall have no Vote, unless they be equally divided.

The Senate shall choose their other Officers, and also a President pro tempore, in the Absence of the Vice President, or when he shall exercise the Office of President of the United States.

The Senate shall have the sole Power to try all Impeachments. When sitting for that Purpose, they shall be on Oath or Affirmation. When the President of the United States is tried, the Chief Justice shall preside: And no Person shall be convicted without the Concurrence of two thirds of the Members present.

Judgment in Cases of Impeachment shall not extend further than to removal from Office, and disqualification to hold and enjoy any Office of honor, Trust, or Profit under the United States: but the Party convicted shall nevertheless be liable and subject to Indictment, Trial, Judgment, and Punishment, according to Law.

Section 4 The Times, Places and Manner of holding Elections for Senators and Representatives, shall be prescribed in each State by the Legislature thereof; but the Congress may at any time by Law make or alter such Regulations, except as to the Places of choosing Senators.

The Congress shall assemble at least once in every Year, and such Meeting shall be on the first Monday in December, unless they shall by Law appoint a different Day.

Section 5 Each House shall be the Judge of the Elections, Returns, and Qualifications of its own Members, and a Majority of each shall constitute a Quorum to do Business;

but a smaller Number may adjourn from day to day, and may be authorized to compel the Attendance of absent Members, in such Manner, and under such Penalties as each House may provide.

Each House may determine the Rules of its Proceedings, punish its Members for disorderly Behavior, and, with the Concurrence of two thirds, expel a Member.

Each House shall keep a Journal of its Proceedings, and from time to time publish the same, excepting such Parts as may in their Judgment require Secrecy; and the Yeas and Nays of the Members of either House on any question shall, at the Desire of one fifth of those Present, be entered on the Journal.

Neither House, during the Session of Congress, shall, without the Consent of the other, adjourn for more than three days, nor to any other Place than that in which the two Houses shall be sitting.

Section 6 The Senators and Representatives shall receive a Compensation for their Services, to be ascertained by Law, and paid out of the Treasury of the United States. They shall in all Cases, except Treason, Felony and Breach of the Peace, be privileged from Arrest during their Attendance at the Session of their respective Houses, and in going to and returning from the same; and for any Speech or Debate in either House, they shall not be questioned in any other Place.

No Senator or Representative shall, during the Time for which he was elected, be appointed to any civil Office under the Authority of the United States, which shall have been created, or the Emoluments whereof shall have been increased during such time; and no Person holding any Office under the United States, shall be a Member of either House during his Continuance in Office.

Section 7 All Bills for raising Revenue shall originate in the House of Representatives; but the Senate may propose or concur with Amendments as on other Bills.

Every Bill which shall have passed the House of Representatives and the Senate, shall, before it become a Law, be presented to the President of the United States; If he approve he shall sign it, but if not he shall return it, with his Objections to the House in which it shall have originated, who shall enter the Objections at large on their Journal, and proceed to reconsider it. If after such Reconsideration two thirds of that House shall agree to pass the Bill, it shall be sent together with the Objections, to the other House, by which it shall likewise be reconsidered, and if approved by two thirds of that House, it shall become a Law. But in all such Cases the Votes of both Houses shall be determined by Yeas and Nays, and the Names of the Persons voting for and against the Bill shall be entered on the Journal of each House respectively. If any Bill shall not be returned by the President within ten Days (Sundays excepted) after it shall have been presented to him, the Same shall be a Law, in like Manner as if he had signed it, unless the Congress by their Adjournment prevent its Return in which Case it shall not be a Law.

Every Order, Resolution, or Vote, to which the Concurrence of the Senate and House of Representatives may be necessary (except on a question of Adjournment) shall be presented to the President of the United States; and before the Same shall take Effect, shall be approved by him, or being disapproved by him, shall be repassed by two thirds of the Senate and House of Representatives, according to the Rules and Limitations prescribed in the Case of a Bill.

Section 8 The Congress shall have Power To lay and collect Taxes, Duties, Imposts and Excises, to pay the Debts and provide for the common Defence and general Welfare of the United States; but all Duties, Imposts and Excises shall be uniform throughout the United States;

To borrow Money on the credit of the United States;

To regulate Commerce with foreign Nations, and among the several States, and with the Indian Tribes;

To establish an uniform Rule of Naturalization, and uniform Laws on the subject of Bankruptcies throughout the United States;

To coin Money, regulate the Value thereof, and of foreign Coin, and fix the Standard of Weights and Measures;

To provide for the Punishment of counterfeiting the Securities and current Coin of the United States;

To establish Post Offices and post Roads;

To promote the Progress of Science and useful Arts, by securing for limited Times to Authors and Inventors the exclusive Right to their respective Writings and Discoveries;

To constitute Tribunals inferior to the supreme Court;

To define and punish Piracies and Felonies committed on the high Seas, and Offenses against the Law of Nations;

To declare War, grant Letters of Marque and Reprisal, and make Rules concerning Captures on Land and Water;

To raise and support Armies, but no Appropriation of Money to that Use shall be for a longer Term than two Years;

To provide and maintain a Navy;

To make Rules for the Government and Regulation of the land and naval Forces;

To provide for calling forth the Militia to execute the Laws of the Union, suppress Insurrections and repel Invasions;

To provide for organizing, arming, and disciplining, the Militia, and for governing such Part of Them as may be employed in the Service of the United States, reserving to the States respectively, the Appointment of the Officers, and the Authority of training the Militia according to the discipline prescribed by Congress;

To exercise exclusive Legislation in all Cases whatsoever, over such District (not exceeding ten Miles square) as may, by Cession of particular States, and the Acceptance of Congress, become the Seat of the Government of the United States, and to exercise like Authority over all Places purchased by the Consent of the Legislature of the State in which the Same shall be, for the Erection of Forts, Magazines, Arsenals, dock-Yards, and other needful Buildings; — And

To make all Laws which shall be necessary and proper for carrying into Execution the foregoing Powers, and all other Powers vested by this Constitution in the Government of the United States, or in any Department or Officer thereof.

Section 9 The Migration or Importation of such Persons as any of the States now existing shall think proper to admit, shall not be prohibited by the Congress prior to the Year one thousand eight hundred and eight, but a Tax or duty may be imposed on such Importation, not exceeding ten dollars for each Person.

The privilege of the Writ of Habeas Corpus shall not be suspended, unless when in Cases of Rebellion or Invasion the public Safety may require it.

No Bill of Attainder or ex post facto Law shall be passed.

No Capitation, or other direct, Tax shall be laid, unless in Proportion to the Census or Enumeration herein before directed to be taken.

No Tax or Duty shall be laid on Articles exported from any State.

No Preference shall be given by any Regulation of Commerce or Revenue to the Ports of one State over those of another: nor shall Vessels bound to, or from, one State be obliged to enter, clear, or pay Duties in another.

No Money shall be drawn from the Treasury, but in Consequence of Appropriations made by Law; and a regular Statement and Account of the Receipts and Expenditures of all public Money shall be published from time to time.

No Title of Nobility shall be granted by the United States: And no Person holding any Office of Profit or Trust under them, shall, without the Consent of the Congress, accept of any present, Emolument, Office, or Title, of any kind whatever, from any King, Prince, or foreign State.

Section 10 No State shall enter into any Treaty, Alliance, or Confederation; grant Letters of Marque and Reprisal; coin Money; emit Bills of Credit; make any Thing but gold and silver Coin a Tender in Payment of Debts; pass any Bill of Attainder, ex post facto Law, or Law impairing the Obligation of Contracts, or grant any Title of Nobility.

No State shall, without the Consent of the Congress, lay any Imposts or Duties on Imports or Exports, except what may be absolutely necessary for executing it's inspection Laws: and the net Produce of all Duties and Imposts, laid by any State on Imports or Exports, shall be for the Use of the Treasury of the United States; and all such Laws shall be subject to the Revision and Control of the Congress.

No State shall, without the Consent of Congress, lay any Duty of Tonnage, keep Troops, or Ships of War in time of Peace, enter into any Agreement or Compact with another State, or with a foreign Power, or engage in War, unless actually invaded, or in such imminent Danger as will not admit of delay.

Article II

Section 1 The executive Power shall be vested in a President of the United States of America. He shall hold his Office during the Term of four Years, and, together with the Vice President, chosen for the same Term, be elected, as follows:

Each State shall appoint, in such Manner as the Legislature thereof may direct, a Number of Electors, equal to the whole Number of Senators and Representatives to which the State may be entitled in the Congress; but no Senator or Representative, or Person holding an Office of Trust or Profit under the United States, shall be appointed an Elector.

The Electors shall meet in their respective States, and vote by Ballot for two Persons, of whom one at least shall not be an Inhabitant of the same State with themselves. And they shall make a List of all the Persons voted for, and of the Number of Votes for each; which List they shall sign and certify, and transmit sealed to the Seat of the Government of the United States, directed to the President of the Senate. The President of the Senate shall, in the Presence of the Senate and House of Representatives, open all the Certificates, and the Votes shall then be counted. The Person having the greatest Number of Votes shall be the President, if such Number be a Majority of the whole Number of

Electors appointed; and if there be more than one who have such Majority, and have an equal Number of Votes, then the House of Representatives shall immediately choose by Ballot one of them for President; and if no Person have a Majority, then from the five highest on the List the said House shall in like Manner choose the President. But in choosing the President, the Votes shall be taken by States, the Representation from each State having one Vote; A quorum for this Purpose shall consist of a Member or Members from two thirds of the States, and a Majority of all the States shall be necessary to a Choice. In every Case, after the Choice of the President, the Person having the greater Number of Votes of the Electors shall be the Vice President. But if there should remain two or more who have equal Votes, the Senate shall choose from them by Ballot the Vice President.

The Congress may determine the Time of choosing the Electors, and the Day on which they shall give their Votes; which Day shall be the same throughout the United States.

No person except a natural born Citizen, or a Citizen of the United States, at the time of the Adoption of this Constitution, shall be eligible to the Office of President; neither shall any Person be eligible to that Office who shall not have attained to the Age of thirty five Years, and been fourteen Years a Resident within the United States.

In Case of the Removal of the President from Office, or of his Death, Resignation or Inability to discharge the Powers and Duties of the said Office, the same shall devolve on the Vice President, and the Congress may by Law provide for the Case of Removal, Death, Resignation or Inability, both of the President and Vice President, declaring what Officer shall then act as President, and such Officer shall act accordingly, until the Disability be removed, or a President shall be elected.

The President shall, at stated Times, receive for his Services, a Compensation, which shall neither be increased nor diminished during the Period for which he shall have been elected, and he shall not receive within that Period any other Emolument from the United States, or any of them.

Before he enter on the Execution of his Office, he shall take the following Oath or Affirmation: "I do solemnly swear (or affirm) that I will faithfully execute the Office of President of the United States, and will to the best of my Ability, preserve, protect and defend the Constitution of the United States."

Section 2 The President shall be Commander in Chief of the Army and Navy of the United States, and of the Militia of the several States, when called into the actual Service of the United States: he may require the Opinion, in writing, of the principal Officer in each of the executive Departments, upon any Subject relating to the Duties of their respective Offices, and he shall have Power to grant Reprieves and Pardons for Offenses against the United States, except in Cases of Impeachment.

He shall have Power, by and with the Advice and Consent of the Senate to make Treaties, provided two thirds of the Senators present concur; and he shall nominate, and by and with the Advice and Consent of the Senate, shall appoint Ambassadors, other public Ministers and Consuls, Judges of the supreme Court, and all other Officers of the United States, whose Appointments are not herein otherwise provided for, and which shall be established by Law; but the Congress may by Law vest the Appointment of such inferior Officers, as they think proper, in the President alone, in the Courts of Law, or in the Heads of Departments.

The President shall have Power to fill up all Vacancies that may happen during the Recess of the Senate, by granting Commissions which shall expire at the End of their next Session.

Section 3 He shall from time to time give to the Congress Information of the State of the Union, and recommend to their Consideration such Measures as he shall judge necessary and expedient; he may, on extraordinary Occasions, convene both Houses, or either of them, and in Case of Disagreement between them, with Respect to the Time of Adjournment, he may adjourn them to such Time as he shall think proper; he shall receive Ambassadors and other public Ministers; he shall take Care that the Laws be faithfully executed, and shall Commission all the Officers of the United States.

Section 4 The President, Vice President and all civil Officers of the United States, shall be removed from Office on Impeachment for, and Conviction of, Treason, Bribery, or other high Crimes and Misdemeanors.

Article III

Section 1 The judicial Power of the United States, shall be vested in one supreme Court, and in such inferior Courts as the Congress may from time to time ordain and establish. The Judges, both of the supreme and inferior Courts, shall hold their Offices during good Behavior, and shall, at stated Times, receive for their Services a Compensation, which shall not be diminished during their Continuance in Office.

Section 2 The judicial Power shall extend to all Cases, in Law and Equity, arising under this Constitution, the Laws of the United States, and Treaties made, or which shall be made, under their Authority;—to all Cases affecting Ambassadors, other public Ministers and Consuls;—to all Cases of admiralty and maritime Jurisdiction;—to Controversies to which the United States shall be a Party;—to Controversies between two or more States;—between a State and Citizens of another State;—between Citizens of different States;—between Citizens of the same State claiming Lands under Grants of different States, and between a State, or the Citizens thereof, and foreign States, Citizens or Subjects.

In all Cases affecting Ambassadors, other public Ministers and Consuls, and those in which a State shall be a Party, the supreme Court shall have original Jurisdiction. In all the other Cases before mentioned, the supreme Court shall have appellate Jurisdiction, both as to Law and Fact, with such Exceptions, and under such Regulations as the Congress shall make.

The Trial of all Crimes, except in Cases of Impeachment, shall be by Jury; and such Trial shall be held in the State where the said Crimes shall have been committed; but when not committed within any State, the Trial shall be at such Place or Places as the Congress may by Law have directed.

Section 3 Treason against the United States, shall consist only in levying War against them, or, in adhering to their Enemies, giving them Aid and Comfort. No Person shall be convicted of Treason unless on the Testimony of two Witnesses to the same overt Act, or on Confession in open Court.

The Congress shall have Power to declare the Punishment of Treason, but no Attainder of Treason shall work Corruption of Blood, or Forfeiture except during the Life of the Person attainted.

Article IV

Section 1 Full Faith and Credit shall be given in each State to the public Acts, Records, and judicial Proceedings of every other State. And the Congress may by general Laws prescribe the Manner in which such Acts, Records and Proceedings shall be proved, and the Effect thereof.

Section 2 The Citizens of each State shall be entitled to all Privileges and Immunities of Citizens in the several States.

A Person charged in any State with Treason, Felony, or other Crime, who shall flee from Justice, and be found in another State, shall on Demand of the executive Authority of the State from which he fled, be delivered up, to be removed to the State having Jurisdiction of the Crime.

No Person held to Service or Labour in one State, under the Laws thereof, escaping into another, shall, in Consequence of any Law or Regulation therein, be discharged from such Service or Labor, but shall be delivered up on Claim of the Party to whom such Service or Labor may be due.

Section 3 New States may be admitted by the Congress into this Union; but no new State shall be formed or erected within the Jurisdiction of any other State; nor any State be formed by the Junction of two or more States, or Parts of States, without the Consent of the Legislatures of the States concerned as well as of the Congress.

The Congress shall have Power to dispose of and make all needful Rules and Regulations respecting the Territory or other Property belonging to the United States; and nothing in this Constitution shall be so construed as to Prejudice any Claims of the United States, or of any particular State.

Section 4 The United States shall guarantee to every State in this Union a Republican Form of Government, and shall protect each of them against Invasion; and on Application of the Legislature, or of the Executive (when the Legislature cannot be convened) against domestic Violence.

Article V

The Congress, whenever two thirds of both Houses shall deem it necessary, shall propose Amendments to this Constitution, or, on the Application of the Legislatures of two thirds of the several States, shall call a Convention for proposing Amendments, which, in either Case, shall be valid to all Intents and Purposes, as part of this Constitution, when ratified by the Legislatures of three fourths of the several States, or by Conventions in three fourths thereof, as the one or the other Mode of Ratification may be proposed by the Congress; Provided that no Amendment which may be made prior to the Year One thousand eight hundred and eight shall in any Manner affect the first and fourth Clauses in the Ninth Section of the first Article; and that no State, without its Consent, shall be deprived of its equal Suffrage in the Senate.

Article VI

All Debts contracted and Engagements entered into, before the Adoption of this Constitution shall be as valid against the United States under this Constitution, as under the Confederation.

This Constitution, and the Laws of the United States which shall be made in Pursuance thereof; and all Treaties made, or which shall be made, under the Authority of the United States, shall be the supreme Law of the Land; and the Judges in every State shall be bound thereby, any Thing in the Constitution or Laws of any State to the Contrary notwithstanding.

The Senators and Representatives before mentioned, and the Members of the several State Legislatures, and all executive and judicial Officers, both of the United States and of the several States, shall be bound by Oath or Affirmation, to support this Constitution; but no religious Test shall ever be required as a Qualification to any Office or public Trust under the United States.

Article VII

The Ratification of the Conventions of nine States shall be sufficient for the Establishment of this Constitution between the States so ratifying the Same.

Amendment I [1791]

Congress shall make no law respecting an establishment of religion, or prohibiting the free exercise thereof; or abridging the freedom of speech, or of the press; or the right of the people peaceably to assemble, and to petition the Government for a redress of grievances.

Amendment II [1791]

A well regulated Militia, being necessary to the security of a free State, the right of the people to keep and bear Arms, shall not be infringed.

Amendment III [1791]

No Soldier shall, in time of peace be quartered in any house, without the consent of the Owner, nor in time of war, but in a manner to be prescribed by law.

Amendment IV [1791]

The right of the people to be secure in their persons, houses, papers, and effects, against unreasonable searches and seizures, shall not be violated, and no Warrants shall issue, but upon probable cause, supported by Oath or affirmation, and particularly describing the place to be searched, and the persons or things to be seized.

Amendment V [1791]

No person shall be held to answer for a capital, or otherwise infamous crime, unless on a presentment or indictment of a Grand Jury, except in cases arising in the land or naval forces, or in the Militia, when in actual service in time of War or public danger; nor shall any person be subject for the same offence to be twice put in jeopardy of life or limb; nor shall be compelled in any criminal case to be a witness against himself, nor be deprived of life, liberty, or property, without due process of law; nor shall private property be taken for public use, without just compensation.

Amendment VI [1791]

In all criminal prosecutions, the accused shall enjoy the right to a speedy and public trial, by an impartial jury of the State and district wherein the crime shall have been committed, which district shall have been previously ascertained by law, and to be informed of the nature and cause of the accusation; to be confronted with the witnesses against him; to have compulsory process for obtaining witnesses in his favor, and to have the Assistance of Counsel for his defence.

Amendment VII [1791]

In Suits at common law, where the value in controversy shall exceed twenty dollars, the right of trial by jury shall be preserved, and no fact tried by jury, shall be otherwise re-examined in any Court of the United States, than according to the rules of the common law.

Amendment VIII [1791]

Excessive bail shall not be required, nor excessive fines imposed, nor cruel and unusual punishments inflicted.

Amendment IX [1791]

The enumeration in the Constitution, of certain rights, shall not be construed to deny or disparage others retained by the people.

Amendment X [1791]

The powers not delegated to the United States by the Constitution, nor prohibited by it to the States, are reserved to the States respectively, or to the people.

Amendment XI [1798]

The Judicial power of the United States shall not be construed to extend to any suit in law or equity, commenced or prosecuted against one of the United States by Citizens of another State, or by Citizens or Subjects of any Foreign State.

Amendment XII [1804]

The Electors shall meet in their respective states, and vote by ballot for President and Vice-President, one of whom, at least, shall not be an inhabitant of the same state with themselves; they shall name in their ballots the person voted for as President, and in distinct ballots the person voted for as Vice-President, and they shall make distinct lists of all persons voted for as President, and of all persons voted for as Vice-President, and of the number of votes for each, which lists they shall sign and certify, and transmit sealed to the seat of the government of the United States, directed to the President of the Senate; — The President of the Senate shall, in the presence of the Senate and House of Representatives, open all the certificates and the votes shall then be counted; — The person having the greatest number of votes for President, shall be the President, if such number be a majority of the whole number of Electors appointed; and if no person have such majority, then from the persons having the highest numbers not exceeding three on the list of those voted for as President, the House of Representatives shall choose immediately, by ballot, the President. But in choosing the President, the votes shall be taken by states, the representation from each state having one vote; a quorum for this purpose shall consist of a member or members from two thirds of the states, and a majority of all states shall be necessary to a choice. And if the House of Representatives shall not choose a President whenever the right of choice shall devolve upon them, before the fourth day of March next following, then the Vice-President shall act as President, as in the case of the death or other constitutional disability of the President. — The person having the greatest number of votes as Vice-President, shall be the Vice-President, if such number be a majority of the whole number of Electors appointed, and if no person have a majority, then from the two highest numbers on the list, the Senate shall choose the Vice-President; a quorum for the purpose shall consist of two thirds of the whole number of Senators, and a majority of the whole number shall be necessary to a choice. But no person constitutionally ineligible to the office of President shall be eligible to that of Vice-President of the United States.

Amendment XIII [1865]

Section 1 Neither slavery nor involuntary servitude, except as a punishment for crime whereof the party shall have been duly convicted, shall exist within the United States, or any place subject to their jurisdiction.

Section 2 Congress shall have power to enforce this article by appropriate legislation.

Amendment XIV [1868]

Section 1 All persons born or naturalized in the United States, and subject to the jurisdiction thereof, are citizens of the United States and of the State wherein they reside. No State shall make or enforce any law which shall abridge the privileges or immunities of citizens of the United States; nor shall any State deprive any person of life, liberty, or property, without due process of law; nor deny to any person within its jurisdiction the equal protection of the laws.

Section 2 Representatives shall be apportioned among the several States according to their respective numbers, counting the whole number of persons in each State, excluding Indians not taxed. But when the right to vote at any election for the choice of electors for President and Vice President of the United States, Representatives in Congress, the Executive and Judicial officers of a State, or the members of the Legislature thereof, is denied to any of the male inhabitants of such State, being twenty-one years of age, and citizens of the United States, or in any way abridged, except for participation in rebellion, or other crime, the basis of representation therein shall be reduced in the proportion which the number of such male citizens shall bear to the whole number of male citizens twenty-one years of age in such State.

Section 3 No person shall be a Senator or Representative in Congress, or elector of President and Vice-President, or hold any office, civil or military, under the United States, or under any State, who having previously taken an oath, as a member of Congress, or as an officer of the United States, or as a member of any State legislature, or as an executive or judicial officer of any State, to support the Constitution of the United States, shall have engaged in insurrection or rebellion against the same, or given aid or comfort to the enemies thereof. But Congress may by a vote of two thirds of each House, remove such disability.

Section 4 The validity of the public debt of the United States, authorized by law, including debts incurred for payment of pensions and bounties for services in suppressing insurrection or rebellion, shall not be questioned. But neither the United States nor any State shall assume or pay any debt or obligation incurred in aid of insurrection or rebellion against the United States, or any claim for the loss or emancipation of any slave; but all such debts, obligations and claims shall be held illegal and void.

Section 5 The Congress shall have power to enforce, by appropriate legislation, the provisions of this article.

Amendment XV [1870]

Section 1 The right of citizens of the United States to vote shall not be denied or abridged by the United States or by any State on account of race, color, or previous condition of servitude.

Section 2 The Congress shall have power to enforce this article by appropriate legislation.

Amendment XVI [1913]

The Congress shall have power to lay and collect taxes on incomes, from whatever source derived, without apportionment among the several States, and without regard to any census or enumeration.

Amendment XVII [1913]

Section 1 The Senate of the United States shall be composed of two Senators from each State, elected by the people thereof, for six years; and each Senator shall have one vote. The electors in each State shall have the qualifications requisite for electors of the most numerous branch of the State legislatures.

Section 2 When vacancies happen in the representation of any State in the Senate, the executive authority of such State shall issue writs of election to fill such vacancies: Provided, That the legislature of any State may empower the executive thereof to make temporary appointments until the people fill the vacancies by election as the legislature may direct.

Section 3 This amendment shall not be so construed as to affect the election or term of any Senator chosen before it becomes valid as part of the Constitution.

Amendment XVIII [1919]

Section 1 After one year from the ratification of this article the manufacture, sale, or transportation of intoxicating liquors within, the importation thereof into, or the exportation thereof from the United States and all territory subject to the jurisdiction thereof for beverage purposes is hereby prohibited.

Section 2 The Congress and the several States shall have concurrent power to enforce this article by appropriate legislation.

Section 3 This article shall be inoperative unless it shall have been ratified as an amendment to the Constitution by the legislatures of the several States, as provided in the Constitution, within seven years from the date of the submission hereof to the States by the Congress.

Amendment XIX [1920]

Section 1 The right of citizens of the United States to vote shall not be denied or abridged by the United States or by any State on account of sex.

Section 2 Congress shall have power to enforce this article by appropriate legislation.

Amendment XX [1933]

Section 1 The terms of the President and Vice President shall end at noon on the 20th day of January, and the terms of Senators and Representatives at noon on the 3d day of January, of the years in which such terms would have ended if this article had not been ratified; and the terms of their successors shall then begin.

Section 2 The Congress shall assemble at least once in every year, and such meeting shall begin at noon on the 3d day of January, unless they shall by law appoint a different day.

Section 3 If, at the time fixed for the beginning of the term of the President, the President elect shall have died, the Vice President elect shall become President. If the President shall not have been chosen before the time fixed for the beginning of his term, or if the President elect shall have failed to qualify, then the Vice President elect shall act as President until a President shall have qualified; and the Congress may by law provide for the case wherein neither a President elect nor a Vice President elect shall have qualified, declaring who shall then act as President, or the manner in which one who is to act shall be selected, and such person shall act accordingly until a President or Vice-President shall have qualified.

Section 4 The Congress may by law provide for the case of the death of any of the persons from whom the House of Representatives may choose a President whenever the right of choice shall have devolved upon them, and for the case of the death of any of the persons from whom the Senate may choose a Vice-President whenever the right of choice shall have devolved upon them.

Section 5 Sections 1 and 2 shall take effect on the 15th day of October following the ratification of this article.

Section 6 This article shall be inoperative unless it shall have been ratified as an amendment to the Constitution by the legislatures of three-fourths of the several States within seven years from the date of its submission.

Amendment XXI [1933]

Section 1 The eighteenth article of amendment to the Constitution of the United States is hereby repealed.

Section 2 The transportation or importation into any State, Territory, or possession of the United States for delivery or use therein of intoxicating liquors, in violation of the laws thereof, is hereby prohibited.

Section 3 This article shall be inoperative unless it shall have been ratified as an amendment to the Constitution by conventions in the several States, as provided in the Constitution, within seven years from the date of the submission hereof to the States by the Congress.

Amendment XXII [1951]

Section 1 No person shall be elected to the office of the President more than twice, and no person who has held the office of President, or acted as President, for more than two years of a term to which some other person was elected President shall be elected to the office of President more than once. But this Article shall not apply to any person holding the office of President when this Article was proposed by the Congress, and shall not prevent any person who may be holding the office of President, or acting as President, during the term within which this Article becomes operative from holding the office of President or acting as President during the remainder of such term.

Section 2 This article shall be inoperative unless it shall have been ratified as an amendment to the Constitution by the legislatures of three-fourths of the several States within seven years from the date of its submission to the States by the Congress.

Amendment XXIII [1961]

Section 1 The District constituting the seat of Government of the United States shall appoint in such manner as the Congress may direct:
A number of electors of President and Vice President equal to the whole number of Senators and Representatives in Congress to which the District would be entitled if it were a State, but in no event more than the least populous state; they shall be in addition to those appointed by the states, but they shall be considered, for the purposes of the election of President and Vice President, to be electors appointed by a state; and they shall meet in the District and perform such duties as provided by the twelfth article of amendment.

Section 2 The Congress shall have power to enforce this article by appropriate legislation.

Amendment XXIV [1964]

Section 1 The right of citizens of the United States to vote in any primary or other election for President or Vice President, for electors for President or Vice-President, or for Senator or Representative in Congress, shall not be denied or abridged by the United States, or any State by reason of failure to pay any poll tax or other tax.

Section 2 The Congress shall have power to enforce this article by appropriate legislation.

Amendment XXV [1967]

Section 1 In case of the removal of the President from office or of his death or resignation, the Vice President shall become President.

Section 2 Whenever there is a vacancy in the office of the Vice President, the President shall nominate a Vice President who shall take office upon confirmation by a majority vote of both Houses of Congress.

Section 3 Whenever the President transmits to the President pro tempore of the Senate and the Speaker of the House of Representatives his written declaration that he is unable to discharge the powers and duties of his office, and until he transmits to them a written declaration to the contrary, such powers and duties shall be discharged by the Vice President as Acting President.

Section 4 Whenever the Vice President and a majority of either the principal officers of the executive departments or of such other body as Congress may by law provide, transmit to the President pro tempore of the Senate and the Speaker of the House of Representatives their written declaration that the President is unable to discharge the powers and duties of his office, the Vice President shall immediately assume the powers and duties of the office as Acting President.

Thereafter, when the President transmits to the President pro tempore of the Senate and the Speaker of the House of Representatives his written declaration that no inability exists, he shall resume the powers and duties of his office unless the Vice President and a majority of either the principal officers of the executive department or of such other body as Congress may by law provide, transmit within four days to the President pro tempore of the Senate and the Speaker of the House of Representatives their written declaration and the President is unable to discharge the powers and duties of his office. Thereupon Congress shall decide the issue, assembling within forty-eight hours for that purpose if not in session. If the Congress, within twenty-one days after receipt of the latter written declaration, or, if Congress is not in session, within twenty-one days after Congress is required to assemble, determines by two thirds vote of both Houses that the President is unable to discharge the powers and duties of his office, the Vice President shall continue to discharge the same as Acting President; otherwise, the President shall resume the powers and duties of his office.

Amendment XXVI [1971]

Section 1 The right of citizens of the United States, who are eighteen years of age or older, to vote shall not be denied or abridged by the United States or by any State on account of age.

Section 2 The Congress shall have power to enforce this article by appropriate legislation.

Amendment XXVII
[Proposed 1789; Ratified 1992]

No law, varying the compensation for the services of Senators and Representatives, shall take effect until an election of Representatives have intervened.

Glossary

accessory The party liable for separate, lesser offenses following a crime.

accomplices The parties liable as principals before and during a crime.

actual possession Physical possession; on the possessor's person.

actus reus The criminal act or the physical element in criminal liability.

adequate provocation rule The rule that only certain defined circumstances will reduce murder to voluntary manslaughter.

affirm To uphold a trial court's decision.

affirmative defense A defense in which the defendant bears the burden of production.

alter ego **doctrine** The principle that high corporate officers are the corporation's brain.

appellant A party who appeals a lower court decision.

appellate court A court that reviews decisions of trial courts.

appellee The party against whom an appeal is filed.

asportation Carrying away another's property.

assault An attempt to commit a battery, or intentionally putting another in fear.

attempted battery assault The crime of assault that focuses on *actus reus*.

battery Offensive bodily contact.

bias-motivated crimes Crimes committed because of race, gender, ethnic, or religious prejudice.

burden of persuasion The responsibility to convince the fact finder of the truth of the defense.

burden of production The responsibility to introduce initial evidence to support a defense.

burden of proof The responsibility to produce the evidence to persuade the fact finder.

"but for" or *sine qua non* **causation** The actor's conduct sets in motion a chain of events that, sooner or later, leads to a result.

capital murder First-degree murders for which the penalty is either death or life imprisonment.

carnal knowledge Sexual intercourse.

castle exception The principle stating that defenders have no need to retreat when attacked in their homes.

causation The substantial reason for the harm in crimes requiring a specific result.

citation A reference to the published report of a case.

civil law The law that deals with private rights and remedies.

claim of right The belief that property taken rightfully belongs to the taker.

collateral attack A proceeding asking an appellate court to rule against the trial court's jurisdiction to decide a question or case.

common law The body of law consisting of all the statutes and case law background of England and the colonies before the American Revolution, based on principles and rules that derive from usages and customs of antiquity.

common-law crimes Crimes originating in the English common law.

concurrence The requirement that *actus reus* must join with *mens rea* to produce criminal conduct or to cause a harmful result.

concurring opinion An opinion that supports the court's result but not its reasoning.

constructive force A substitute for actual force in rape cases.

constructive intent Intent in which the actors do not intend any harm but should have known that their behavior created a high risk of injury.

constructive possession Legal possession or custody of an item or substance.

conversion Illegal use of another's property.

criminal negligence homicides Deaths resulting from action actors should have known, but did not know, would cause death or serious bodily harm.

culpability Deserving of punishment because of individual responsibility for actions.

damages Money awarded in civil lawsuits for injuries.

defendant The person against whom a civil or criminal action is brought.

defenses Justifications and excuses to criminal liability.

deliberate The requirement in murder *mens rea* that killings must be committed with a cool, reflecting mind.

diminished capacity Mental capacity less than "normal" but more than "insane."

discretion The freedom of individuals to base decisions on factors other than written rules.

dissent The opinion of the minority of justices.

distinguish cases To find that facts differ enough from those in a prior case to release judges from the precedent of the decision in that case.

doctrine of complicity The principle regarding parties to crime that establishes the conditions under which more than one person incurs liability before, during, and after committing crimes.

due process Constitutional protection against vague and overbroad laws.

due process clauses Clauses within the U.S. Constitution stating that government cannot deny citizens life, liberty, or property without notice, hearing, and other established procedures.

Durham **rule,** or **product test** An insanity test to determine whether a crime was a product of mental disease or defect.

elements The parts of a crime that the prosecution must prove beyond a reasonable doubt, such as *actus reus*, *mens rea*, causation, and harmful result.

equivocality approach The theory that attempt *actus reus* requires an act that can have no other purpose than the commission of a crime.

ex post facto **laws** Laws passed after the occurrence of the conduct constituting the crime.

excuse A defense admitting wrongdoing without criminal responsibility.

extortion Misappropriation of another's property by means of threat to inflict bodily harm in the future.

extraneous factor A condition beyond the attempter's control.

factual causation Conduct that in fact leads to a harmful result.

factual impossibility The defense that some extraneous factor makes it impossible to complete a crime.

felonies Serious crimes generally punishable by one year or more in prison.

felony murder doctrine The rule that deaths occurring during the commission of felonies are murders.

fetal death statutes Laws defining when life begins for purposes of the law of criminal homicide.

fighting words Words that provoke or threaten to provoke immediate violence or disorder.

first-degree murder Premeditated, deliberate killings and other particularly heinous capital murders.

forgery Making false writings or materially altering authentic writings.

general deterrence or prevention Preventing crime by threatening potential lawbreakers.

general intent Intent to commit the *actus reus*—the act required in the definition of the crime.

general principles of criminal liability The theoretical foundation for the elements of *actus reus, mens rea,* causation, and harm.

gross criminal negligence Very great negligence; actions without even slight care but not amounting to intentional or conscious wrongdoing.

habeas corpus petition A request for a court to review an individual's detention by the government.

hate crimes Crimes motivated by race, gender, ethnic background, or religious prejudice.

holding The legal principle or rule that a case enunciates.

imperfect defense Defense reducing but not eliminating criminal liability.

incapacitation Punishment by imprisonment, mutilation, and even death.

inchoate crimes Offenses based on crimes not yet completed.

intervening cause or supervening cause The cause that either interrupts a chain of events or substantially contributes to a result.

involuntary manslaughter Criminal homicides caused either by recklessness or gross criminal negligence.

irresistible impulse Impairment of the will that makes it impossible to control the impulse to do wrong.

jurisdiction Territory or subject matter under the control of a government body.

justification A defense deeming acceptable under the circumstances otherwise criminal conduct.

knowing possession Awareness of the item possessed.

legal causation Cause recognized by law to impose criminal liability.

legal impossibility The defense that what the actor attempted was not a crime.

M'Naghten rule, or right-wrong test A defense pleading insanity due to mental disease or defect that impairs the capacity to distinguish right from wrong.

majority opinion The opinion of the majority of justices.

malice aforethought The common law designation for murder *mens rea* that covered a broad range of states of mind.

malum in se A crime inherently bad, or evil.

malum prohibitum A crime not inherently bad, or evil, but merely prohibited.

marital rape exception The rule that husbands cannot rape their wives.

mens rea The mental element in crime, of which there are four mental states: purpose, knowledge, recklessness, and negligence.

mere possession Possession of an item or substance without knowledge of what it is.

misappropriation Gaining possession of another's property.

misdemeanor A minor crime for which the penalty is usually less than one year in jail or a fine.

misdemeanor manslaughter rule The rule that deaths occurring during the commission of misdemeanors are manslaughter.

mitigating circumstances Facts that reduce but do not eliminate culpability.

Model Penal Code The code developed by the American Law Institute to guide reform in criminal law.

Model Penal Code **attempt standard** The precept that attempt *actus reus* requires substantial steps that strongly corroborate the actor's purpose.

motive The reason why a defendant commits a crime.

negligence The unconscious creation of risk, or the mental state in which actors create substantial and unjustifiable risks of harm but are not aware of creating them.

nulla poena sine lege An ancient rule stating that there can be no punishment without a specific law.

nullum crimen sine lege An ancient rule stating that there is no crime without a specific law.

objective test An external measure of reasonableness of belief; used to determine immediate or present danger of attack.

paramour rule The rule that a husband who witnesses his wife in the act of adultery is adequate provocation to reduce murder to manslaughter.

perfect defense A defense that leads to outright acquittal.

physical proximity doctrine The principle that the number of remaining acts in attempt determines attempt *actus reus.*

plaintiff The person who sues another party in a civil action.

plurality opinion An opinion that announces the result of the case but whose reasoning does not command a majority of the court.

precedent Prior court decision that guides judges in deciding future cases.

premeditated The requirement in first-degree murder *mens rea* that killings must be planned in advance.

principle of legality A principle stating that there can be no crime or punishment if there are no specific laws forewarning citizens that certain specific conduct will result in a particular punishment.

principle of proportionality A principle of law stating that the punishment must be proportionate to the crime committed.

probable desistance approach An approach that considers whether the act in attempt would naturally lead to the commission of the crime.

procedural due process An expression of the rule of law requiring the government to follow established practices in criminal law enforcement, trial, and punishment.

proximate cause The most common expression of legal causation, suggesting a nearness in time and place between the actor and the action.

reasonable resistance standard The requirement that women must use the amount of force required by the totality of the circumstances surrounding sexual assault.

reasoning The reasons a court gives to support its holding.

reckless or "depraved heart" murder Deaths resulting from purposely or consciously creating substantial and unjustifiable risks that someone will either die or suffer serious injury.

recklessness The conscious creation of substantial and unjustifiable risk; the state of mind in which actors know they are creating risks of harm.

rehabilitation Prevention of crime by treatment.

remand To send a case back to a trial court for further proceedings consistent with the reviewing court's decision.

respondeat superior The doctrine that employers are responsible for their employees' actions.

retribution Punishment based on just deserts.

reverse To set aside the decision of the trial court and substitute a different decision.

riot The crime of the unlawful act in which unlawful assemblies and routs culminate.

robbery Taking and carrying away another's property by force or threat of force with the intent to permanently deprive the owner of possession.

rout The crime of any movement toward completing the crime of unlawful assembly.

rule of law Decisions made on the basis of principles, not individual discretion.

second-degree murder A catchall offense including killings that are neither manslaughter nor first-degree murder.

special deterrence The threat of punishment aimed at individual offenders in the hope of deterring future criminal conduct.

specific intent The intent to do something beyond the *actus reus.*

stare decisis The principle that binds courts to stand by prior decisions and to leave undisturbed settled points of law.

statutes Rules or doctrines enacted by legislatures.

statutory rape Carnal knowledge of a person under the age of consent whether or not accomplished by force.

strict liability Liability without fault, or in the absence of *mens rea.*

subjective test An internal or "honest belief" test used to determine immediate or present danger of attack.

substantial capacity test Insanity due to mental disease or defect impairing the substantial capacity either to appreciate the wrongfulness of conduct or to conform behavior to the law.

substantive due process An expression of the rule of law limiting the power of the government to create crimes.

superior officer rule The precept that only the highest corporate officers can incur criminal liability for a corporation.

surreptitious remaining Entering a structure lawfully with the intent to commit a crime inside.

theft Consolidated crimes of larceny, embezzlement, and false pretenses.

threatened battery assault The crime of assault that focuses on the *mens rea.*

tort A legal wrong for which the injured party may sue the injuring party.

transferred intent Actor intends to harm one victim but instead harms another.

trespassory taking Wrongful taking required in larceny *actus reus.*

unlawful assembly The crime of three or more people gathered for an unlawful purpose.

unprivileged entry Entering a structure without right, license, or permission.

utmost resistance standard The requirement that rape victims must use all the physical strength they have to prevent penetration.

uttering Knowing or conscious use or transfer of false documents.

verbal acts Words.

vicarious liability The principle regarding liability for another based on relationship.

violation A minor legal infraction subject to a small fine.

void for overbreadth The principle that a statute is unconstitutional because it includes in its definition of undesirable behavior conduct that is protected under the U.S. Constitution.

void for vagueness The principle that a law violates due process if it does not clearly define crime and punishment in advance.

voluntary manslaughter Intentional killings committed in the sudden heat of passion upon adequate provocation.

Wharton rule The principle that more than two parties must conspire to commit crimes that naturally involve at least two parties.

writ of *certiorari* Discretionary Supreme Court order to review lower court decisions.

Index